NEW!

5th edition

Baby

BARGAINS

S E C R E T S

to saving 20% to 50% on
babyfurniture, equipment,
clothes, toys, maternity wear
and much, much more!

Denise & Alan Fields
Authors of the Best-seller.
Bridal Bargains

D0954064

Copyright Page, Credits and Zesty Lo-Cal Recipes

Saxophone, lead guitar and breast-feeding by Denise Fields
Drums, rhythm guitar and father stuff by Alan Fields
Congas on "Grandparents" by
Max & Helen Coopwood, Howard & Patti Fields
Cover/interior design and keyboard solo by Epicenter Creative
Screaming guitar solos on "(Let's Go) Perego" by
Charles & Arthur Troy
Additional guitar work on "Diaper Changing Blues"
by Todd Snider
Backing vocals on "(She's Got A) LATCH Car Seat" by Ric Ocasek
Band photography by Moses Street

*This book was written to the music of the Barenaked Ladies,
which probably explains a lot.*

Distribution to the book trade by Publisher's Group West, Berkeley, CA 1-800-788-3123. Thanks to the entire staff of PGW for their support.

To order this book, call 1-800-888-0385. Or send $16.95 plus $3 shipping (or, in Canada, $27 plus $4 shipping) to Windsor Peak Press, 436 Pine Street, Boulder, CO 80302. Questions or comments? Please call the authors at (303) 442-8792. Or fax them a note at (303) 442-3744. Or write to them at the above address in Boulder, Colorado. E-mail the authors at authors@babybargainsbook.com.

Updates to this book are on the web at www.BabyBargainsBook.com

Library Cataloging in Publication Data

Fields, Denise
Fields, Alan
    Baby Bargains: Secrets to saving 20% to 50% on baby furniture, equipment, clothes, toys maternity wear and much, much more/ Denise & Alan Fields
    544 pages.
    Includes index.
    ISBN 1-889392-14-6
    1. Child Care—Handbooks, manuals, etc. 2. Infants' supplies—Purchasing—United States, Canada, Directories. 3. Children's paraphernalia—Purchasing—Handbooks, manuals. 4. Product Safety—Handbooks, manuals. 5. Consumer education.
    649'.122'0296—dc20. 2003.

We miss you Dee Dee.

Version 5.0

CONTENTS

Chapter 3

BABY BEDDING & DECOR

Chapter 6

FEEDING: BREASTFEEDING, BOTTLES, HIGH CHAIRS

Chapter 7

AROUND THE HOUSE: BABY MONITORS, TOYS, BATH, & SWINGS

Chapter 8

CAR SEATS

Chapter 9

STROLLERS, DIAPER BAGS, CARRIERS AND OTHER TO GO GEAR

Chapter 10

AFFORDABLE BABY PROOFING

Chapter 11

ETC: ANNOUNCEMENTS, CATALOGS, CHILD CARE & MORE

Chapter 12

CONCLUSION: WHAT DOES IT ALL MEAN?

ICONS

 Getting
Started

 Money-
Saving
Secrets

 Sources

 Best Buys

 Parents In
Cyberspace

 The Name
Game

 What Are
You
Buying?

 Do it By
Mail

 Safe &
Sound

 Email from
the Real
World

 Smart
Shopper

 More Money
Buys You . . .

 Wastes of
Money

 Bottom
Line

CHAPTER 1

"It's Going to Change Your Life!"

Inside this chapter

That had to be the silliest comment we heard while we were pregnant with our first baby. Believe it or not, we even heard this refrain more often than "Do you want a boy or a girl?" and "I'm sorry. Your insurance doesn't cover that." For the friends and relatives of first-time parents out there, we'd like to point out that this is a pretty stupid thing to say. Of course, we knew that a baby was going to change our lives. What we didn't realize was how much a baby was going to change our pocketbook.

Oh sure, we knew that we'd have to buy triple our weight in diapers and be subjected to dangerously high levels of Thomas the Tank Engine. What we didn't expect was the endless pitches for cribs, gear, toys, clothing and other items parents are required to purchase by FEDERAL BABY LAW.

We quickly learned that having a baby is like popping on the Juvenile Amusement Park Ride from Consumer Hell. Once that egg is fertilized, you're whisked off to the Pirates of the Crib ride. Then it's on to marvel at the little elves in StrollerLand, imploring you to buy brands with names you can't pronounce. Finally, you take a trip to Magic Car Seat Mountain, where the salespeople are so real, it's scary.

Consider us your tour guides—the Yogi Bear to your Boo Boo Bear, the Fred to your Ethel, the . . . well, you get the idea. Before we enter BabyLand, let's take a look at the Four Truths That No One Tells You About Buying Stuff For Baby.

The Four Truths That No One Tells You About Buying Stuff for Baby

I **BABIES DON'T CARE IF THEY'RE WEARING DESIGNER CLOTHES OR SLEEPING ON DESIGNER SHEETS.** Let's be realistic. Babies just want to be comfortable. They can't even distinguish between the liberals and conservatives on "Meet the Press," so how would they ever be able to tell the difference between Baby Gucci crib bedding and another less famous brand that's just as comfortable, but 70% less expensive? Our focus is on making your baby happy—at a price that won't break the bank.

2 **YOUR BABY'S SAFETY IS MUCH MORE IMPORTANT THAN YOUR CONVENIENCE.** Here are the scary facts: 69,500 babies per year are injured (and 65 deaths are caused) by juvenile products, according to government estimates. Each chapter of this book has a section called "Safe & Sound," which arms you with in-depth advice on keeping your baby out of trouble. We'll tell you which products we think are dangerous and how to safely use other potentially hazardous products.

3 **MURPHY'S LAW OF BABY TOYS SAYS YOUR BABY'S HAPPINESS WITH A TOY IS INVERSELY RELATED TO THE TOY'S PRICE.** Buy a $200 shiny new wagon with anti-lock brakes, and odds are baby just wants to play with the box it came in. In recognition of this reality, we've included "wastes of money" in each chapter that will steer you away from frivolous items.

4 **IT'S GOING TO COST MORE THAN YOU THINK.** Whatever amount of money you budget for your baby, get ready to spend more. Here's a breakdown of the average costs of bringing a baby into the world today:

The Average Cost of Having a Baby

(based on industry estimates for a child from birth to age one)

Crib, mattress, dresser, rocker	*$1500*
Bedding / Decor	*$300*
Baby Clothes	*$500*
Disposable Diapers	*$600*
Maternity/Nursing Clothes	*$1200*
Nursery items, high chair, toys	*$400*
Baby Food / Formula	*$900*
Stroller, Car Seat, Carrier	*$300*
Miscellaneous	*$500*
TOTAL	**$6200**

The above figures are based on buying name brand products at regular retail prices. We surveyed over 1000 parents to arrive at these estimates.

Bedding/Decor includes not only bedding items but also items like lamps, wallpaper, and so on for your baby's nursery. Baby Food/Formula assumes you'd breastfeed for the first six months and then feed baby jarred baby food ($400) and formula ($500) until age one. If you plan to bottle-feed instead of breastfeed, add another $500 on to that figure.

Sure, you do get an automatic tax write-off for that bundle of joy, but that only amounts to about $3050 for 2003 (plus you also get an additional $500 child care tax credit, depending on your income—note, as we were going to press, Congress was debating whether to double the child care credit to $1000). But those tax goodies won't nearly offset the actual cost of raising a child. And as you probably realize, our cost chart is missing some expensive "extras" . . . like medical bills, childcare, saving for college and more. Here's an overview of what can add to the tab:

◆ *Medical/adoption bills.* Yes, for most couples, conceiving a child is free (although some may argue about that). But not everyone is that lucky—fertility treatments for the estimated 10% to 15% of couples who can't conceive naturally can run $10,000 to $15,000 a try (although there are less expensive treatments out there as well). Only a handful of states require health insurance policies to cover infertility—hence, the vast majority of couples who face this challenge do so without insurance and must pay those costs out of pocket. Or if their insurance covers infertility, it may just pay for the infertility *diagnosis* but not treatments. Bottom line: it is not uncommon couples spend upwards of $40,000 on infertility treatments (again, check with your doctor for less expensive alternatives).

Besides the normal prenatal visits to the doctor, the biggest medical bill is for the birth—about $7090 for a "normal" delivery at a hospital. The same study (Expenditures on Children by Families, 2001 annual report by the US Dept of Agriculture) pegs the cost of a Caesarian at $11,450. Medical bills for first year routine check-ups and immunizations can cost $700 or more. Yes, insurance typically picks up most of those costs, but there are many children (15% of the total births this year) that are born without any coverage. So, if you have insurance, count yourself among the lucky.

Couples who adopt a baby typically face fees and expenses that range from $15,000 to $25,000. There is a $10,000 federal tax credit that offsets some adoption expenses—check with your tax preparer for details (see IRS publication 968, "Tax Benefits for

Adoption"). One bargain for parents who are considering an over-
seas adoption: some airlines now offer adopting parents a break on
airfares. Several airlines offer 50% or more discounts off full coach
fares (the ones adopting parents have to use, as most adoptions are
done on short notice). The baby's one-way fare back home is also
discounted. Always ask the airline you want to use if they have an
adoption fare deal.

◆ **Child Care.** According to the Department of Agriculture, the
average cost of childcare for a 3 to 5 year old child is $1590 per
year. But those costs seemed low to us—our research on child care
costs (detailed in Chapter 11, Etcetera) revealed family daycare runs
$4000 to $10,000 and center care can cost up to $13,000 per
year. What about a nanny? Most run $10,000 to $20,000 in average cities, but that depends on whether they are live-in or not. In
high cost cities like New York or San Francisco, childcare costs for
families can top $30,000 a year.

◆ **Housing.** Those neighborhoods with the best schools aren't
cheap. The government estimates the average middle-class family
with one child will spend an *extra* $57,360 on shelter until the child
is 18. The average annual cost of housing one child is $2500 to
$5370, according to government estimates.

◆ **Transportation.** Yes, a brand new minivan today tops
$20,000 and some models approach $30,000. All those trips to
daycare (and later, the mall) add up—the government says average
parents will spend $24,500 to transport a child to all those required
activities until the age of 18.

◆ **And more.** Additional expenses that parents face include
health care (the government says even the average, healthy child
can rack up $12,180 in medical bills for the first 18 years), clothing (if
you think baby clothes are pricey, check out the $10,400 bill the
average kid racks up in clothes until age 18), and education (private
school, anyone?).

The bottom line. If you're still with us, let's see what the government says is the GRAND TOTAL of expenses to raise a baby to
age 18. Are you sitting down? Try $170,460. And that's for middle
class Americans. More affluent parents spend $249,180. Yes, there
are economies of scale if you add more children—but there's a limit
to the savings. On average, each additional child costs just 24% less
than a single child. (Source: 2001 Annual Report, Expenditures on
Children by Families, US Dept of Agriculture).

But wait! The government leaves two critical costs out of its equation: saving for college and lost wages from a parent who stays at home. Let's look at both:

◆ **College.** Price college tuition lately? Even if you forget about Harvard, the cost of attending a state school today is staggering—and rising rapidly in recent years. And with college costs expected to continue to rise in the future, you'll have to put away $375 each month for baby's college fund if you start at birth to pay for the average state school's four-year program. Wait longer to get started and the costs rise rapidly. T Rowe Price (www.troweprice.com) has an excellent free "college planner" feature on their web site that lets you compare savings plans for public versus private schools. Fidelity also has a college cost calculator that is easy to use.

◆ **Lost wages.** Having a baby is a financial double-whammy—not only are your expenses rising, but your income drops. Why? At least one parent will have to take off time to care for the baby. Yes, lost wages could be a short six-week maternity leave . . . or the next 18 years for a stay-at-home parent.

Hence, when you add in saving for college and lost wages for a stay-at-home parent for 18 years, the cost of raising an average middle class child to age 18 will run $1,455,581. Amazing, eh?

(Source: the above numbers are from the 2001 "Expenditures on Children by Families" by the US Dept of Agriculture and US News & World Report's "The Cost of Children", March 30, 1998).

Reality Check: Does it Really Cost that Much to Have a Baby?

Now that we've thoroughly scared you enough to inquire whether the stork accepts returns, we should point out that children do NOT have to cost that much. Even if we focus just on the first year, you don't have to spend $6200 on your baby. And that's what this book is all about: how to save money and still buy the best. Follow all the tips in this book, and we estimate the first year will cost you $3790. Yes, that's a savings of over $2400!

Now, at this point, you might be saying "That's impossible! I suppose you'll recommend buying all the cheap stuff, from polyester clothes to no-name cribs." On the contrary, we'll show you how to get *quality* name brands and safe products at discount prices. For example, we've got outlets and catalogs that sell all-cotton baby clothing at 20% to 40% off retail. You'll also learn about web sites that sell car seats and strollers for 40% off. And much more. Yes, we've got the maximum number of bargains allowed by federal law.

A word on bargain shopping: when interviewing hundreds of parents for this book, we realized bargain seekers fall into two frugal camps. There's the "do-it-yourself" crowd and the "quality at a discount" group. As the name implies, "do-it-yourselfers" are resourceful folks who like to take second-hand products and refurbish them. Others use creative tricks to make homemade versions of baby care items like baby wipes and diaper rash cream.

While that's all well and good, we fall more into the second camp of bargain hunters, the "quality at a discount" group. We love discovering a hidden factory outlet that sells goods at 50% off. Or finding a great web or mail-order source that discounts name-brand baby products at rock bottom prices. We also realize savvy parents save money by not *wasting* it on inferior goods or useless items.

While we hope that *Baby Bargains* pleases both groups of bargain hunters, the main focus of this book is not on do-it-yourself projects. Books like the *Tightwad Gazette* (check your local library for a copy) do a much better job on this subject. Our main emphasis will be on discount web sites, catalogs, outlet stores, brand reviews and identifying best buys for the dollar.

What? There's No Advertising in This Book?

Yes, it's true. This book contains zero percent advertising. We have never taken any money to recommend a product or company and never will. We make our sole living off the sales of this and other books. (So, when your friend asks to borrow this copy, have them buy their own book!) Our publisher, Windsor Peak Press, also derives its sole income from the sale of this book and our other publications. No company recommended in this book paid any consideration or was charged any fee to be mentioned. (In fact, some companies probably would offer us money to leave them *out* of the book, given our comments about their products or services).

As consumer advocates, we believe this "no ads" policy helps to ensure objectivity. The opinions in the book are just that—ours and those of the parents we interviewed.

We also are parents of two small children. As far as we know, we are the only authors of a consumer's guide to baby products that actually have young kids. We figure if we actually are recommending these products to you, we should have some real world experience with them. (That said, we should disclose that our sons have filed union grievances with our company over testing of certain jarred baby foods and that litigation is ongoing.)

Of course, given the sheer volume of baby stuff, there's no way we can test everything personally. To solve that dilemma, we rely on reader feedback to help us figure out which are the best products to recommend. We receive over 100 emails a day from parents; this helps us spot overall trends on which brands/products parents love. And which ones they want to destroy with a rocket launcher.

Finally, we have a panel of moms who also test new products for us, evaluating items on how they work in the real world. One bad review from one parent doesn't necessarily mean we won't recommend a product; but we'll then combine these tests with other parent feedback to get an overall picture.

What about prices of baby products? Trying to stay on top of this is often like attempting to nail Jell-O to a wall. Yet, we still try. As much as we can confirm, the prices quoted in this book were accurate as of the date of publication. Of course, prices and product features can change at any time. Inflation and other factors may affect the actual prices you discover in shopping for your baby. While the publisher makes every effort to ensure their accuracy, errors and omissions may exist. That's why we've established a web site where you can get the latest updates on this book for free (www.babybargainsbook.com). You can also talk directly to us: call (303) 442-8792 or e-mail us at authors@BabyBargainsBook.com to ask a question, report a mistake, or just give us your thoughts. Finally, you can write to us at "Baby Bargains," 436 Pine Street, Suite 700, Boulder, CO 80302.

What about the phone numbers listed in this book? We list contact numbers for manufacturers so you can find a local dealer near you that carries the product (or request a catalog, if available). Unless otherwise noted, these manufacturers do NOT sell directly to the public.

So, Who Are You Guys Anyway?

Why do a book on saving money on baby products? Don't new parents throw caution to the wind when buying for their baby, spending whatever it takes to ensure their baby's safety and comfort?

Ha! When our first son was born in 1993, we quickly realized how darn expensive this guy was. Sure, as a new parent, you know you've got to buy a car seat, crib, clothes and diapers . . . but have you walked into one of those baby "superstores" lately? It's a blizzard of baby stuff, with a bewildering array of "must have" gear, gadgets and gizmos, all claiming to be the best thing for parents since sliced bread.

Becoming a parent in this day and age is both a blessing and curse. The good news: parents today have many more choices for baby products than past generations. The *bad* news: parents today have many more choices for baby products than past generations.

What you need, when

Yes, buying for baby can seem overwhelming, but there is a silver lining: you don't need ALL this stuff immediately when baby is born. Let's look at what items you need quickly and what you can wait on. This chart indicates usage of certain items for the first 12 months of baby's life:

	MONTHS OF USE				
ITEM	BIRTH	3	6	9	12+
Nursery Necessities					
Cradle/bassinet	▬▬				
Crib/Mattress	▬▬▬▬▬▬▬▬▬				
Dresser	▬▬▬▬▬▬▬▬▬				
Glider Rocker	▬▬▬▬▬▬▬▬▬				
Bedding: Cradle	▬▬				
Bedding: Crib	▬▬▬▬▬▬▬▬▬				
Clothing					
Caps/Hats	▬▬▬▬▬▬▬				
Blanket Sleepers	▬▬▬▬▬▬▬				
Layette Gowns	▬▬▬▬				
Booties	▬▬▬				
All other layette	▬▬▬▬▬▬▬▬▬				
Around the House					
Baby Monitor	▬▬▬▬▬▬▬▬▬				
Baby Food (solid)			▬▬▬▬▬		
High Chairs			▬▬▬▬▬		
Places to Go					
Infant Car Seat	▬▬▬				
Convertible Car Seat*			▬▬▬▬▬		
Carriage Stroller	▬▬▬▬				
Umbrella Stroller			▬▬▬▬		
Front Carrier	▬▬▬▬				
Backpack Carrier			▬▬▬▬		
Safety items		▬▬▬▬▬▬▬			

You can use a convertible car seat starting immediately with that first ride home from the hospital. However, it is our recommendation that you use the infant car seat for the first six months or so, then, when baby grows out of it, buy the convertible car seat.

Our mission: make sense of this stuff, with an eye on cutting costs. As consumer advocates, we've been down this road before. We researched bargains and uncovered scams in the wedding business when we wrote *Bridal Bargains*. Then we penned an exposé on new homebuilders in *Your New House*.

Yet, we found the baby business to be perilous in different ways—instead of outright fraud or scam artists, we've instead discovered some highly questionable products that don't live up to their hype—and others that are outright dangerous. We were surprised to learn how most juvenile items face little (or no) government scrutiny, leaving parents to sort out conflicting safety claims. In addition, in recent years new "discount" baby product web sites have failed to live up to their own promises of prompt delivery and customer service.

So, we've gone on a quest to find the best baby products, at prices that won't send you to the poor house. Sure, we've sampled many of these items first hand. But this book is much more than our experiences—we interviewed over 1000 new parents to learn their experiences with products. We also attend juvenile product trade shows to quiz manufacturers and retailers on what's hot and what's not. The insights from retailers are especially helpful, since these folks are on the front lines, seeing which items unhappy parents return.

Our focus is on safety and durability: which items stand up to real world conditions and which don't. Interestingly, we found many products for baby are sold strictly on price . . . and sometimes a great "bargain" broke, fell apart or shrunk after a few uses. Hence, you'll note some of our top recommendations aren't always the lowest in price. To be sensitive to those on really tight budgets, we try to identify "good, better and best" bets in different price ranges.

First Time Parent 101

As a first-time parent, it's easy to get confused by all the jargon in the world of parenting books. But since you've never had a baby before, you may wonder how we define basic terms like "newborn," "infant," "toddler," "sleep deprivation" and so on. So, here's a quick primer:

◆ **Newborn.** As you'd expect, these are very young bambinos just recently born. Most folks define a newborn as a baby under 4 weeks or so in age.

◆ **Infant/baby.** We generally refer to children under age 2 to be babies or infants.

◆ **Toddler.** For purposes of our books (*Baby Bargains* and *Toddler Bargains*—see below for more detail), we define a toddler as a child who is age two to five. As the name implies, these are young children who are just learning to walk. Okay, obviously most babies do this before age 2. Some books define "toddler hood" as age 18 months to 3 years. "Toddler" clothes are typically for children age 1 to 3. Confused yet? Just realize there isn't one single definition of "toddler." Just realize we use "toddler" to describe the slew of products for older babies (booster car seats, potty seats, etc).

◆ **Sleep deprivation.** See "newborn."

We get questions: the Top 5 Questions & Answers

From the home office here in Boulder, CO, here are the top five questions we get asked here at *Baby Bargains*:

1 **DO YOU HAVE A BOOK FOR OLDER CHILDREN? WHY DOESN'T BABY BARGAINS COVER PRODUCTS FOR OLDER CHILDREN LIKE POTTIES, TOYS OR BICYCLES?** *Baby Bargains* focuses on products for babies age birth to 2. We did this to a) keep this book from becoming 800 pages long and b) to maintain our sanity. We realize there is a whole universe of products out there that parents buy for older kids. So, to help out those parents of toddlers, we have published a separate book called *Toddler Bargains* (www. ToddlerBargains.com). This book focuses on products for toddlers age 2 to 5. Check the back of this book for more details on *Toddler Bargains*.

2 **HOW DO I KNOW IF I HAVE THE CURRENT EDITION?** We strive to keep *Baby Bargains* as up-to-date as possible. As such, we update it periodically with new editions. But if you just borrowed this book from a friend, how do you know how old it is? First, look at the copyright page. There at the bottom you will see a version number (such as 5.0). The first number (the 5 in this case) means you have the 5th edition. The second number indicates the printing—every time we reprint the book, we make minor corrections, additions and changes. Version 5.0 is the initial printing of the 5th edition, version 5.1 is the first reprint of the fifth edition and so on.

So, how can you tell if your book is current or woefully out of date? Go to our web page at www.BabyBargainsBook.com and click on "Which version?" There we will list what the most current version is. (One clue: look at the book's cover. We note the edition number on each cover. And we change the color of the cover with each edition). We update this book every two years (roughly).

About 30% to 40% of the content will change with each edition. Bottom line: if you pick up a copy of this book that is one or two editions old, you will notice a significant number of changes.

3 **WHAT IF I SEE A NEW PRODUCT IN STORES? HOW CAN I FIND INFO ON THAT?** First, make sure you have the latest edition of *Baby Bargains* (see previous question). If you can't find that product in our latest book, go to our web page at www. BabyBargainsBook.com. There you will find a treasure trove of information. First, check out the "News" section with updates on industry trends and, yes, new products. Second, search the "Message Boards" section to see if other readers have tried out the product and reported to us on their experiences. If that doesn't work, post a query to the Message Boards for other parents to respond to. Of course, you can email us with a question as well (see the How to Contact Us page at the back of this book). Be sure to sign up for our "Free E-Newsletter" to get the latest news on our book, web page, product recalls and more. All this can be done from www.BabyBargainsBook.com. (A note on our privacy policy: we NEVER sell reader email addresses or other personal info).

Even though we have a treasure trove of FREE stuff on our web page, please note that we do not post the entire text of *Baby Bargains* online (hey, we have to make a living somehow). If a friend gives you a ten year-old edition of this book, you can't go online and just download all the changes/updates for free. Yes, someday soon, we will probably offer "e-book" versions of our book to download from our web page but there will still be a cost.

4 **I AM LOOKING FOR A SPECIFIC PRODUCT BUT I DON'T KNOW WHERE TO START! HELP!** Yep, this book is 400+ pages long and we realize it can be a bit intimidating. But you have a friend in the Index—flip to the back of the book to look up just about anything. You can look up items by category, brand name and more.

If that doesn't work, try the Table of Contents. We sort the book into major topic areas (strollers, car seats, etc). In some chapters, we have "also known as" boxes that help you decode brand names that might be associated with other companies (for example, Eddie Bauer car seats are made by Cosco).

Don't forget the handy Telephone/Web Site Directory in the back of the book as well. You can pop to any company's web page to find more details about a product we review in *Baby Bargains*. Finally, I f you still can't find contact info for a company, try a simple web search like Google.com (which is sort like 411 for the 'net).

5 **WHY DO YOU SOMETIMES RECOMMEND A MORE EXPENSIVE PRODUCT THAN A CHEAPER OPTION?** Yes, this is a book about bargains, but sometimes we will pick a slightly more expensive item in a category if we believe it is superior in quality or safety. Sometimes it makes sense to invest in better-quality products that will last through more than one child. And don't forget about the hassle of replacing a cheap product that breaks in six months.

To be sure, however, we recognize that many folks are on tight budgets. To help, we offer "Good, Better, Best" product suggestions that are typically sorted by price (good is most affordable, best is usually more expensive). Don't torture yourself if you can't afford the "best" in every category; a "good" product will be just as, well, good.

Another note: remember that our brand reviews cover many options in a category, not just the cheapest. Don't be dismayed if we give an expensive brand an "A" rating—such ratings are often based on quality, construction, innovation and more. Yes, we will try to identify the best values in a category as well.

Why does our advice sometimes conflict with other publications like *Consumer Reports*? See the box on the next page for more on this.

Let's Go Shopping!

Now that all the formal introductions are done, let's move on to the good stuff. As your tour guides to BabyLand, we'd like to remind you of a few park rules before you go:

1 **NO FEEDING THE SALESPEOPLE.** Remember, the juvenile products industry is a $5.75 BILLION DOLLAR business. While all those baby stores may want to help you, they are first and foremost in business to make a profit. As a consumer, you should arm yourself with the knowledge necessary to make smart decisions. If you do, you won't be taken for a ride.

2 **KEEP YOUR PERSPECTIVE INSIDE THE VEHICLE AT ALL TIMES.** With all the hormones coursing through the veins of the average pregnant woman, now is not the time to lose it. As you visit baby stores, don't get caught in the hype of the latest doo-dad that converts a car seat to a toaster.

3 **HAVE A GOOD TIME.** Oh sure, sifting through all those catalogs of crib bedding and convertible strollers will frazzle your mind. Just remember the goal is to have a healthy baby—so, take care of yourself first and foremost.

Baby Bargains versus Consumer Reports

First off, let us say right here and now that we are BIG fans of *Consumer Reports* (CR) magazine. The magazine (and now web site) are the gold standard of consumer journalism.

That said, we often get deluged with email from readers when CR reviews and rates a baby product category. Many folks ask us why we at *Baby Bargains* sometimes come to different conclusions than *Consumer Reports*.

First, understand that we have different research methods. *Consumer Reports* often lab tests products to make sure they are safe and durable. At *Baby Bargains*, we rely on parent/reader feedback to make our recommendations. Yes, we do hands-on inspections of products and meet with manufacturers at trade shows to demo the latest gear, but the reader feedback loop is our secret sauce.

Not surprisingly, most of the time we actually agree with *Consumer Reports*. In recent articles on strollers in CR and in our book, we both picked the same three of four brands as best. Yet, sometimes there are differences—we might pick a model as a "best bet" that CR thinks is only a second runner-up. And vice versa. We suppose you can chalk up the differences in rating to our research methods.

Another issue: out of date reports. We love CR, but sometimes they are WAY behind when it comes to reviewing baby products. Since they don't focus on baby products, it can be YEARS between reports for certain categories. Models and brands change very quickly in this industry. Trying to compare a five year old report in a CR back issue with a current edition of this book isn't very helpful.

Of course, we don't take everything *Consumer Reports* says as the gospel truth. They (like us) make mistakes; we always try to verify results if CR determines a product is unsafe. In cases where we differ with CR, we'll point that out in our book and on our web site.

What's New in This Edition?

As usual, we just couldn't leave well enough alone. With the fifth edition of *Baby Bargains*, you'll notice some additions and improvements. As always, we've updated the book to include the most current models, including the latest scoop on car seats and strollers. We'll talk in-depth about the new LATCH car seat standard, giving you new advice about which flavor of LATCH works best in our opinion.

First, however, check out our crib chapter ("Nursery Necessities"). You'll note over a dozen new crib maker reviews, including the latest brands from Europe to debut in North America. We also have new outlet stores for nursery furniture. Plus: we'll explore how to get discount rugs for your nursery and the latest sources for deals on glider-rockers.

Next, let's talk diapers—we've added more tips/advice from readers on cloth diapers (including a doubling of the web site sources for cloth diapers). There is also new info on so-called "eco-friendly" disposable diapers. Plus, we'll show you who has the cheapest prices for diapers, with an updated price survey. The same chapter (Reality Layette) also has new sources for baby's first pair of shoes.

You'll notice a brand new chapter called "Feeding" in this edition. This new chapter combines our advice on breast-feeding, bottle-feeding and solid foods into one easy-to-read primer. Speaking of feeding, we've got the scoop on the newest high chairs to debut, which are providing parents with new choices at lower prices. And let's talk nursing pads—we've got reader feedback on which ones work best in the real world.

Our car seat chapter includes the offerings from new players such as Baby Trend and Combi. You'll read about innovative new car seat models that can use a five-point harness far beyond the standard 40 lbs limit (including one model that goes up to 65 pounds).

All-terrain strollers are all the rage this year and we've got the latest info on such hot models from makers like Zooper and Mountain Buggy. Then we'll go over new lightweight stroller options from Chicco, Maclaren and Inglesina. New carriers are also on the market this year and we've got the latest scoop.

As always, you'll find lots of new web site resources in our book, including advice on how to buy nursery furniture on eBay.

Finally, we've tried to make *Baby Bargains* easier to use with new visual tabs on the sides of the book (so you can quickly find what you want when you are standing in the aisles of a baby store, wondering just where the heck our ratings of high chairs are). Plus, we've got pictures! We've tried to add more photos to the book to illustrate our points.

Of course, we've kept the features you love about *Baby Bargains*, including those handy comparison charts that sum up our picks and our ever-popular baby registry at-a-glance (Appendix B). Don't forget the handy phone/web directory (Appendix D) in the back of the book. We also have updates for our Canadian readers (Appendix A) and a section on recommendations for parents of twins (Appendix C).

So, buckle your seat belts and secure all loose items like sunglasses and your sanity. We're off to Baby Gear Land.

CHAPTER 2

Nursery Necessities:
Cribs, Dressers & More

Inside this chapter

How can you save 20% to 50% off cribs, dressers, and other furniture for your baby's room? In this chapter, you'll learn these secrets, plus discover smart shopper tips that help clarify all those confusing crib options and features. Then, you'll learn which juvenile furniture has safety problems and a toll-free number you can call to get the latest recall info. Next, we'll rate and review over 30 top brands of cribs, focusing on quality and value. Finally, you'll learn which crib mattress is best, how to get a deal on a dresser, and several more items to consider for your baby's room.

Getting Started:
When Do You Need This Stuff?

So, you want to buy a crib for Junior? And, what the heck, why not some other furniture, like a dresser to store all those baby gifts and a changing table for, well, you know. Just pop down to the store, pick out the colors, and set a delivery date, right?

Not so fast, o' new parental one. Once you get to that baby store, you'll discover that most don't have all those nice cribs and furniture *in stock.* No, that would be too easy, wouldn't it? You will quickly learn that you have to *special order* much of that booty.

To be fair, we should note that in-stock items vary from shop to shop. Some (especially the larger chain stores) may stock a fair number of cribs. Yet Murphy's Law says the last in-stock Futura Crib with that special chartreuse trim was just sold five minutes ago. And while stores may stock a good number of cribs, dressers are another story–these bulky items almost always must be special-ordered.

Most baby specialty stores told us it takes four to six weeks to order many furniture brands. And here's the shocker: some imported cribs can take 12 to 16 weeks. Or longer. Making matters worse is the practice by most Italian furniture makers of shutting down for two weeks in July and again at Christmas. It's hard to believe that it takes so long for companies to ship a simple crib or dresser—we're not talking space shuttle parts here. The way it's going, you'll soon have to order the crib *before* you conceive.

Obviously, this policy is more for the benefit of the retailer than the consumer. Most baby stores are small operations and they tell us that stocking up on cribs, dressers and the like means an expensive investment in inventory and storage space. Frankly, we could care less. Why you can't get a crib in a week or less is one of the mysteries of modern juvenile product retailing that will have to be left to future generations to solve. What if you don't have that much time? There are a couple of solutions: some stores sell floor models and others actually keep a limited number of styles in stock. Discounters also stock cribs—the only downside is that while the price is low, often so is the quality.

Here's an idea given to us by one new mother: don't buy the crib until *after* the baby is born. The infant can sleep in a bassinet or cradle for the first few weeks or even months, and you can get the furniture later. (This may also be an option for the superstitious that don't want to buy all this stuff until the baby is actually born.) The downside to waiting? The last thing you'll want to do with your newborn infant is go furniture shopping. There will be many other activities (such as sleep deprivation experiments) to occupy your time.

So, when should you make a decision on the crib and other furniture for the baby's room? We recommend you place your order in the sixth or seventh month of your pregnancy. By that time, you're pretty darned sure you're having a baby, and the order will arrive several weeks before the birth. (The exception: if your heart is set on an imported crib, you may have to order in your fourth or fifth month to ensure arrival before Junior is born).

First-time parent question: so, how long will baby use a crib? Answer: it depends (and you thought we always have the answer). Seriously, most babies can use a crib for two or three years. Yes, some babies are out of the crib by 18 months, while others may be pushing four. One key factor: when does baby learn they can climb out of the crib? Once that happens, the crib days are numbered, as you can understand. Of course, there may be other factors that push baby out of a crib—if you are planning to have a second child and want the crib for the new baby, it may be time to transition to a "big boy/girl" bed. We discuss more about the transition out of a crib (as well as reviewing toddler and twin beds) in our book *Toddler Bargains*. See the back of this book for more info on that title.

Cribs: Sources to Find

This year, more than 1.2 million households plan to buy infant/nursery furniture, according to a survey by Furniture Today. That translates into $4 billion in sales of infant and youth bedroom furniture—yes, this is big business. In their quest for the right nursery, parents have five basic sources for finding a crib, each with its own advantages and drawbacks:

1 **BABY SPECIALTY STORES**. Baby specialty stores are pretty self-explanatory—shops that specialize in the retailing of baby furniture, strollers, and accessories. Some also sell clothing, car seats, swings, and so on. Independents come in all sizes: some are small mom and pop stores; others are as large as a chain superstore. A good number of indie retailers have joined together in "buying groups" to get volume discounts on items from suppliers—these groups include Baby Furniture Plus (www.babyfurnitureplus.com), Baby News (www.BabyNewsStores.com, NINFRA (www.ninfra.com) and USA Baby (www.USAbaby.com). The web sites for those four groups have store locators so you can find a specialty store near you.

Like other independent stores, many baby specialty shops have been hard hit by the expansion of national chains like Babies R Us. Yet, those that have survived do so by emphasizing service and products you can't find at the chains. Of course, quality of service can vary widely from store to store . . . but just having a breathing human to ask a question of is a nice plus. The problems with specialty stores? Consumers complain the stores only carry expensive brand names. One parent told us the only baby specialty store in her town doesn't carry any cribs under $500. We understand the dilemma faced by mom and pop retailers—in order provide all that service, they have to make a certain profit margin on furniture and other products. And that margin is easier to get on high-end goods. That's all well and good, but failing to carry products in entry-level price points only drives parents to the chains.

Another gripe with some indie stores: some shops can be downright hostile to you if they think you are "price-shopping" them. A reader said she found this out when comparing Ragazzi and Morigeau furniture in her town. "When I asked to price cribs and dressers at two baby stores, I met with resistance and hostility. At one store, I was asked if I was a 'spy' for their competition! The store managers at both baby stores I visited said they didn't want people to comparison shop them on price, yet both advertise they will 'meet or beat' the competition's prices." Crazy as it sounds, the only way to write down prices at some stores is to have a friend distract the sales help (Hey, look over there! A naked basketball team crossing the street!).

The bottom line: despite the hassles, if you have a locally owned baby store in your town, give them a shot. Don't assume chains always have lower prices and better selection.

2 THE CHAINS. There are two types of chains that sell baby products: specialty chains like Babies R Us that focus on juvenile products and general discounters like Wal-Mart, Target, and K-Mart that have baby departments. We'll discuss each more in-depth later in this chapter. The selection at chains can vary widely—some carry more premium brands, but most concentrate on mass-market names to appeal to price-conscious shoppers. Service? Fuggedaboutit—often, you'll be lucky to find someone to help you check out, much less answer questions.

3 DEPARTMENT STORES. Traditional department stores like Sears still have baby departments that carry furniture, clothing and equipment. Prices aren't typically as low as the discounters, but occasional sales sometimes bring bargains.

4 THE WEB/MAIL-ORDER CATALOGS. You can mail order many items for baby, but furniture is somewhat tricky. Why? Shipping bulky items like cribs and dressers is prohibitively expensive. There's also the risk of damage from shipping. But that doesn't keep some companies and catalogs from trying: Forever Mine (see review later in this chapter) is a Canadian-based furniture maker that has had great success selling dressers and cribs online. JCPenney (800-222-6161) has a catalog with nursery items and, yes, you can even buy a crib or dresser via the mail. Baby product web sites like those reviewed in Chapter 11 and catalogs like Pottery Barn also sell a limited number of cribs. Be careful of exorbitant shipping charges for cribs; Pottery Barn adds a whopping $130 shipping charge onto a crib that is already $830. Other sites refuse to ship furniture items to Alaska, Hawaii, Canada or military (APO) addresses. As a result of shipping costs and challenges, most mail order catalogs and web sites concentrate more on selling nursery accessories—glider rockers, changing tables, decor, etc. And if you find a crib for sale online, it will usually be a more obscure brand (like Delta, Angel Line or Million Dollar Baby's DaVinci line—all of these are reviewed later in this chapter).

5 REGULAR FURNITURE STORES. You don't have to go to a "baby store" to buy juvenile furniture. Many regular furniture stores sell name-brand cribs, dressers and other nursery items. Since these stores have frequent sales, you may be able to get a better price than at a juvenile specialty store. On the other hand, the salespeople may not be as knowledgeable about brand and safety issues.

Parents in Cyberspace: What's on the Web?

There are an amazing number of sites out there where you can look at cribs and get safety information. Unfortunately, actually BUYING a crib or dresser online is another matter. As we discussed above, the sheer bulk and weight of furniture typically limits mail-order options to a few peripheral items like glider-rockers, bassinets and the like. Here are the best sites for both buying and info:

Danny Foundation

Web site: www.dannyfoundation.org
What it is: The best source for crib safety info.
What's cool: Founded in 1986, the Danny Foundation's mission is to educate parents about crib dangers and to warn the public about the millions of unsafe cribs still in use or storage. You can read the latest recalls with cribs and portable play yards (which often have a bassinet feature) on the site. Danny Foundation's excellent crib safety checklist is a must read. Sample: below is a sketch from the site that illustrates all the hazards that old cribs may include such as cut outs and corner posts (Figure 1).

♦ **Other sites.** The best selection of Dutailier rocker-gliders and

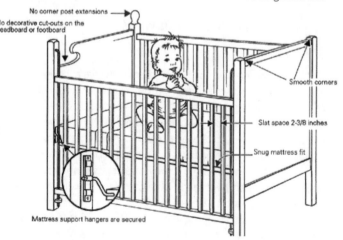

Figure 1. Crib safety points from the Danny Foundation's web site.

ottomans has to be on **Baby Catalog** (www.babycatalog.com), the online offshoot of a Connecticut store and catalog. We love the prices, but the site requires many clicks/scrolls to get pricing and ordering info on the gliders.

The smallish collection of cribs on **Baby Style** (www.babystyle. com) includes cribs from $158 to $400. On the plus side, we loved the "Nursery Collections" section on Baby Style. Here the site features cribs, bedding, lamps and other décor accessories for a complete look. Very cool . . .even if you don't buy anything the ideas are interesting.

Burlington Coat Factory's **Baby Depot** (www.coat.com) has over a dozen different styles of cribs available on their site, mostly by Delta (see review later). Prices are affordable ($150 to $360) and shipping is reasonable (about $30, depending on the style). But we have been put off by the site's nutty organization that requires you to sift through several menus and sub-menus to actually see products. The selection of other nursery items (dressers, glider-rockers, etc.) is also a bit thin.

The **Pottery Barn Kids** catalog is online at PotteryBarnKids.com. While cribs are available from PBK, we found them very overpriced. And the added shipping charge can make them even more outrageous. PBK's cribs are typically made by regular manufacturers like Simmons and Status so you will be able to find similar styles at much better prices if you buy from bricks and mortar baby stores.

Looking for a comprehensive listing of web sites that sell baby products? Check out Chapter 11 (Etcetera), which has reviews of the biggest baby sites.

What Are You Buying?

While you'll see all kinds of fancy juvenile furniture at baby stores, focus on the items that you really need. First and foremost is a crib, of course. Mattresses are typically sold separately, as you might expect, so you'll need one of those. Another nice item is a dresser or chest to hold clothes, bibs, washcloths, etc. A changing table is an optional accessory; some parents just use the crib for this (although that can get messy) or buy a combination dresser and changing table. Some dressers have a removable changing table on top, while others have a "flip top": a hinged shelf that folds up when not in use.

So, how much is this going to cost you? Crib prices start at $100 for an inexpensive metal crib at a discounter like Wal-Mart. A hardwood crib by such domestic manufacturers as Simmons or Child Craft (see reviews later in this chapter) starts at about $200 and go up to $500. Import brands (Pali, Ragazzi, Status) can range from $250 to $700. At the top end, designer cribs from posh stores like Bellini and catalogs like Pottery Barn can soar to $700, $800 and more. And we'd be remiss not to mention the wrought iron cribs by Corsican, which top $1000 to $1500.

Fortunately, mattresses for cribs aren't that expensive. Basic mattresses start at about $50 and goes up to $200 for fancy varieties. Later in this chapter, we'll have a special section on mattresses that includes tips on what to buy and how to save money.

Dressers and changing tables (known in the baby business as case pieces) have prices that are all over the board. At the low end are the "ready to assemble" dressers from Sauder (reviewed later in this chapter) that sell for just $120 to $200. Name brand, already-assembled dressers run $400 to $700 in most styles, while top-of-the-line designer cases pieces can push $1000.

Where to change baby? If you have room for a separate changing table, these run $70 to $200. A better solution may be the "combo" (also called hi-lo) dressers/changers pioneered by Rumble Tuff (see review later in this chapter). Such styles run $500 to $700.

So, you can see that a quest for a crib, mattress, dresser, and/or changing table could cost you as little as $300 or more than $1000.

More Money Buys You . . .

Here's a little secret most baby stores don't want you to hear: ALL new cribs (no matter what price) sold in the U.S. or Canada must meet federal safety standards. Yes, the governments of both the U.S. and Canada strictly regulate crib safety and features—that's one reason why most cribs have the same basic design, no matter the brand or price. So, whether you buy a $100 crib special at K-Mart or a $700 Italian design at a posh specialty boutique, you are getting a crib that is equally safe.

Now, that said, when you spend more money, you do get some perks. First: double-drop sides (cheaper cribs have only a single drop side). Spend a bit more and you also get an under-crib storage drawer. But the biggest thing you get for more money: styling and a quieter rail release. The more money you spend, the fancier the crib's design (thicker corner posts, fancy colors, etc.) And more expensive cribs tend to have quieter drop-sides (cheap cribs can be noisy when you raise or lower the side rail). Another perk when you spend more: pricey cribs are likely to convert into a twin or double bed. Lower-price cribs are just, well, cribs.

Safe & Sound

Here's a fact to keep you up at night: cribs are the third-biggest cause of injuries and deaths among all nursery products. In the latest year for which statistics are available, over 11,000 injuries and 26 deaths were blamed on cribs alone. Altogether, nursery equipment and furniture account for over 65,000 injuries serious enough to require emergency room treatment each year.

Now, before you get all excited, let's point out that old cribs cause the vast majority of injuries related to cribs. Surprisingly, these old cribs may not be as old as you think—some models from the 1970s and early 1980s have caused many injuries and deaths. (Safety standards for cribs were first enacted in 1973 then again in 1976; these rules were revised in 1982). Nearly all *new* cribs sold in the United States meet the current safety standards designed to prevent injuries. In fact, the annual death rate for cribs (26) is dramatically below that in the 1970's, when nearly 200 children died each year from crib hazards.

These facts bring us to our biggest safety tip on cribs:

◆ ***Don't buy a used or old crib.*** Let's put that into bold caps: **DON'T BUY A USED OR OLD CRIB.** And don't take a hand-me-down from a well-meaning friend or relative. Why? Because old cribs can be death traps—spindles that are too far apart, cutouts in the headboard, and other hazards that could entrap your baby. Decorative trim (like turned posts) that look great on adult beds are a major no-no for cribs—they present a strangulation hazard. Other old cribs have lead paint, a dangerous peril for a teething baby.

Another hazard to hand-me-down cribs (regardless of age): missing parts and directions. It only takes one missing screw or bolt to make an otherwise safe crib into a death trap. Without directions, you can assemble the crib wrong and create additional safety hazards. So, even if your friend wants to give/sell you a recent model crib, you could still have problems if parts or directions are missing.

It may seem somewhat ironic that a book on baby bargains would advise you to go out and spend your hard-earned money on a new crib. True, we find great bargains at consignment and second-hand stores. However, you have to draw the line at your baby's safety. Certain items are great deals at these stores—toys and clothes come to mind. However, cribs (and, as you'll read later, car seats) are no-no's, no matter how tempting the bargains. And second hand stores have a spotty record when it comes to selling safe products. A recent report from the CPSC said that a whopping two-thirds of all US thrift/second-hand stores sell baby products that have been recalled, banned or do not meet current safety standards (specifically 12% of stores stocked old cribs). Amazingly, federal law does not prohibit the sale of cribs (or other dangerous products like jackets with drawstring hoods, recalled playpens or car seats) at second hand stores.

Readers of the first edition of this book wondered why we did not put in tips for evaluating old or hand-me-down cribs. The reason is simple: it's hard to tell whether an old crib is dangerous just by looking at it. Cribs don't always have "freshness dates"—some manufacturers don't stamp the date of manufacture on their cribs. Was the crib made before or after the current safety standards went into effect in 1982? Often, you can't tell.

Today's safety regulations are so specific (like the allowable width for spindles) that you just can't judge a crib's safety with a cursory examination. Cribs made before the 1970's might contain lead paint, which is difficult to detect unless you get the crib tested. Another problem: if the brand name is rubbed off, it will be hard to tell if the crib has been involved in a recall. Obtaining replacement parts is also difficult for a no-name crib.

What if a relative insists you should use the "family heirloom" crib? We've spoken to dozens of parents who felt pressured into using an old crib by a well-meaning relative. There's a simple answer: don't do it. As a parent, you sometimes have to make unpopular decisions that are best for your child's safety. This is just the beginning.

◆ **Cribs with fold-down railings or attached dressers are a major safety hazard.** Most cribs have a side rail that drops to give you access to an infant. However, a few models have fold-down railings—to gain access to the crib, the upper one-third of the railing is hinged and folds down. These are also called swing gate cribs (see picture above).

What's the problem? Actually, there are two problems. First, the folding rail can be a pinch point (see Baby's Dream review later in this chapter for details on a recall that addressed this very issue).

The second problem: toddlers can get a foothold on the hinged rail to climb out of the crib, injuring themselves as they fall to the floor. Attached dressers pose a similar problem. Children can climb onto the dresser and then out of the crib. One mother we interviewed was horrified to find her ten month-old infant sitting on top of a four-foot-high dresser one night. (Kindercraft still makes one of these models, although they've been de-emphasizing this product line in recent years).

So what's the appeal of these cribs? Well, manufacturers like Baby's Dream (whose Crib 4 Life has a fold-down rail) say the design lets you easily convert the crib into a youth bed (a small size bed that uses the crib mattress). We say big deal—most children can go directly from a crib to a twin bed, making the "youth" bed an unnecessary item. Another point to remember: if you plan to have subsequent children, you can't use the crib again (because the older child is using its frame for his bed).

♦ **Metal beds.** Metal cribs are cheap (under $100 retail), but we have safety concerns with these products. First, sloppy welding between parts of the crib can leave sharp edges. Clothing can snag and fingers can get cut. Remember that when your baby starts to stand, she will be all over the crib—chewing on the railing, handling the spindles, and more. We've also noticed that inexpensive metal cribs tend to have inadequate mattress support. In many models, the mattress is held up with cheap vinyl straps.

♦ **Forget about no-name cribs.** In the past, a few less-than-reputable baby stores imported cheap no-name cribs from foreign countries whose standards for baby safety are light years behind the U.S. Why would stores do this? Bigger profits—cheap imports can be marked up big-time and still be sold to unsuspecting parents at prices below name-brand cribs. Take the Baby Furniture Outlet of Marathon, Florida. These scam artists imported cribs and playpens that grossly failed to meet federal safety standards. From the construction to the hardware, the cribs were a disaster waiting to happen. As a result, 19 babies were injured, and the Consumer Products Safety Commission permanently banned the items in 1987. Sold under the "Small Wonders" brand name at the Baby Furniture Outlet (and other outlets nationwide), parents were undoubtedly suckered in by the "outlet" savings of these cheap cribs. Instead of recalling the cribs, the company declared bankruptcy and claimed it couldn't pay to fix the problem. (By the way, this company is not related to Baby Furniture Outlet of Canada, which is mentioned later in this chapter).

There is one exception to our advice to avoid no-name cribs—JCPenney's catalog sells several "private label" cribs that are made exclusively for Penney's and sold under names like Domusindo and Bright Future. Penney's has strict standards that make these cribs a decent buy, despite their lack of a brand name.

♦ **Watch out for sharp edges.** It amazes us that any company today would market a baby furniture item with sharp edges. Yet, there are still some on the market. We've seen changing tables with sharp edges and dressers with dangerous corners. A word to the wise: be sure to check out any nursery item carefully before buying—look in less-than-obvious places, like the bottom edges of a dresser or the under-crib drawer.

◆ **Be aware of the hazards of putting a baby in an adult bed.** Co-sleeping (where a baby sleeps in an adult bed) has been linked to 122 deaths of babies from 1999 to 2001, says the Consumer Products Safety Commission. Of those deaths, many were caused when a child's head became entrapped between the bed and another object (a headboard, footboard, wall, etc). Other deaths were caused by falls or suffocation in bedding. We are alarmed by these statistics and urge any parent who is considering co-sleeping to consult with a pediatrician before going forward. (For the record, we should note that a product we recommend later in this book, the Arm's Reach Co-sleeper, is safe since a baby doesn't actually sleep in the adult bed when using this product.)

◆ **Some Italian cribs can make bumper tying a challenge.** Those thick corner posts on Italian cribs sure look pretty, but they can create problems—using a bumper pad (a bedding item discussed in the next chapter) on these cribs can be darn near impossible. Why? Many bumper pads have short ties that simply don't fit around thick corner posts. And some Italian cribs (particularly Pali, Sorelle/C&T, and Bonavita) have side rails that preclude use of many bumper pads. Why? The side rail release mechanism is designed in such a way that you can't move the rail down with a bumper tied to the corner post. So, what's the solution? First, we should note that other cribs with thick corner posts don't have this problem with the side rail—domestic makers like Child Craft/Legacy and Canadian maker Morigeau have bumper-friendly crib designs. Second, there is a bedding company (Luv Stuff, reviewed in the next chapter) that has designed bumpers to overcome the Italian problem. Finally, we should note that some Italian crib makers (particularly Pali) have redesigned their cribs to fix the problem. (Check with a retailer before you buy to get an update on this). And some folks think bumper pads themselves aren't really necessary, as we'll discuss in the next chapter.

◆ **When assembling a crib, make sure ALL the bolts and screws are tightened**. A recent report on *Good Morning America* pointed out how dangerous it can be to put your baby in a miss-assembled crib—a child died in a Child Craft crib when he became trapped in a side rail that wasn't properly attached to the crib. How did that happen? The parent didn't tighten the screws that held the side rail to the crib. All cribs (including the Child Craft one here in question) are safe when assembled correctly; just be sure to tighten those screws! A smart safety tip: check your crib once a month to make sure all screws and bolts are firmly attached.

◆ **What about the finish?** Some crib makers are now touting "non-toxic water-based finishes" for their cribs. One (Natart) even charges an extra $30 for this option. Another example: the web site EcoBaby.com sells a $720 crib that is "hand rubbed with pure beeswax and tung oil." The implication: older oil-based finishes for baby furniture are somehow dangerous. Rubbish! We've seen no evidence that a baby that sleeps in a crib finished/painted with an oil-based product is somehow at risk for health problems. In 1978, the federal government required ALL cribs to be finished with non-toxic materials. Of course, there is no requirement that the finish be water-based or oil-based—each is equally safe in our opinion. While we realize some eco-sensitive parents might shell out extra for the water-based finish, we don't see a problem or a reason to spend more.

◆ **Recalls: where to find information**. The U.S. Consumer Product Safety Commission has a toll-free hotline at (800) 638-2772 and web site (www.cpsc.gov) for the latest recall information on cribs and other juvenile items. Both are easy to use—the hotline is a series of recorded voice mail messages that you access by following the prompts. You can also report any potential hazard you've discovered or an injury to your child caused by a product. Write to the U.S. Consumer Products Safety Commission, Washington, D.C. 20207.

Also: consider subscribing to our free e-newsletter. We send out updates on product recalls and other matters to our readers on a periodic basis. Go to www.BabyBargainsBook.com and click on "E-Newsletter" to subscribe.

 Smart Shopper Tips

Smart Shopper Tip #1
Beware of "Baby Buying Frenzy."

"I went shopping with my friend at a baby store last week, and she just about lost it. She started buying all kinds of fancy accessories and items that didn't seem that necessary. First there was a $50 womb sound generator and finally the $200 Star Trek Diaper Changing Docking Station. There was no stopping her. The salespeople were egging her on—it was quite a sight. Should we have just taken her out back and hosed her down?"

Yes, you probably should have. Your friend has come down with a severe case of what we call Baby Buying Frenzy—that overwhelming emotional tug to buy all kinds of stuff for Junior—especially when Junior is the first child. Baby stores know all about this disease and do their darnedest to capitalize on it. Check out this quote from *Juvenile Merchandising* (October 1993) advising salespeople on how to sell to expectant parents: "It's surprising how someone who is making a purchase (for baby) sometimes can be led into a buying frenzy." No kidding. Some stores encourage their staff by giving them bonuses for every additional item sold to a customer. Be wary of stores that try to do this, referred to in the trade as "building the ticket." Remember what you came to buy and don't get caught up in the hype.

Smart Shopper Tip #2
The Art and Science of Selecting the Right Crib.

"How do you evaluate a crib? They all look the same to me. What really makes one different from another?"

Selecting a good crib is more than just picking out the style and finish. You should look under the hood, so to speak. Here are our eight key points to look for when shopping for a crib:

◆ ***Mattress support.*** Look underneath that mattress and see what is holding it up. You might be surprised. Some lower-end cribs use cheap vinyl straps. Others use metal bars. One crib we saw actually had a cardboard deck holding up the mattress—boy, that looked real comfortable for baby. The best option: a set of springs that provide both mattress support and a springy surface to stand on when Junior gets older. Remember, your infant won't just lie there for long. Soon, she will be standing up in the crib, jumping up and down, and causing general mayhem.

◆ ***Ease of release.*** At least one side of the crib has a railing that lowers down so you can pick up your baby. There are five types of crib rail releases:

1 **FOOT-BAR.** You release the crib drop side by lifting up the side rail while depressing a foot bar. This used to be the most common rail release type, especially on American-made cribs. But domestic makers Child Craft and Simmons have abandoned the foot-bar in recent years for alternatives like the knee-push (see below). The negatives to the foot-bar seemed to spell its doom—some parents find the foot-bar release awkward, requiring them to balance on one foot while lowering the rail with one hand.

Another negative: the foot-bar release requires exposed hardware (rods, springs, etc.) that can be noisy and look unattractive. While we think there is no safety concerns with the foot-bar release or exposed hardware, Canada has banned the use of the foot bar release. As a result, you'll see less and less of the foot-bar in the market in coming years. Million Dollar Baby and Angel Line (see reviews later) are two of the few holdouts still using the foot-bar release.

2 KNEE-PUSH. By lifting the side rail and pushing against it with your knee, the drop side releases. We first saw this release on more expensive cribs imported from Europe or Canada, but in recent years nearly all crib makers (both domestic and imported) have turned to this type of release. This is probably the quietest release, although that can vary from maker to maker. Another plus: the hardware is often hidden inside the crib posts, so there are no rods and springs like the foot-bar release. We should note that one version of the knee-push rail (most notably used by Ragazzi) has exposed plastic brackets on the crib posts. The Italian crib makers are more likely to have the completely hidden hardware.

3 DOUBLE TRIGGER. This release is used on low-price cribs from makers like Stork Craft and Delta. The drop side is released by simultaneously pulling on two plastic triggers on either side of the rail. Crib makers that use this type of release tout its safety (only an adult can release the rail) and the lack of exposed hardware like that used on foot-bar releases. However, we see two major drawbacks: first, you need *two* hands to operate the release, not really possible if you have a baby in your arms (unless you can grow extras!). Also, the double trigger release uses plastic hardware that can be a problem if you live in a dry climate. Why? The wood posts can shrink, causing the plastic hardware to crack.

4 FOLD DOWN/SWING-GATE. Rarely used in the market today, the fold-down rail release does what it sounds like—instead of lowering, the rail has a hinge that allows the top portion to fold down. The biggest user of the fold-down release is Baby's Dream. As we'll mentioned earlier, we're not big fans of fold-down rails—we believe the hinge can be a pinch point, as well as an opportunity for larger toddlers to gain a foothold to climb out of the crib.

5 STATIONARY. This is the latest rage with crib design—side rails that don't move at all! Child Craft started this trend with their Millennium crib (also called the Crib and Double Bed), which was such a hot seller that other crib makers quickly copied it. The advantage to this design: there are no moving parts to break and these cribs seem much more stable/solid than other models. The downside: for shorter parents, it can be a long reach to put a sleeping infant down on the mattress when set in its lowest position. Our advice: try these cribs out in the store before committing.

◆ *Hardware: hidden or exposed?* In order to make that side rail slide up or down, cribs need hardware that enables that motion. Less expensive cribs have exposed hardware—either a rod/cane that the side rail slides up and down on or plastic brackets. More expensive cribs have "hidden" hardware, which is hidden inside the headboard and footboards. Is there a difference in safety or durability? No, it often boils down to an aesthetic decision—some parents like hidden hardware because it gives the crib a cleaner, sleeker look. Hidden hardware does have another benefit over exposed hardware: it tends to be quieter. The trend over the last few years has been a move toward hidden hardware. Now you can find hidden hardware on cribs from as little $200 at Baby Depot to $800 expensive Italian designs at a specialty store. And don't forget about the trend toward stationary drop sides—these cribs have no hardware at all!

One safety note: some crib headboards have a exposed plastic track where the slide rail slides up and down in—even if they have hidden hardware. This is a safety hazard in our opinion, as little fingers can get caught in the track. The safest option is a hidden track.

◆ *Mattress height adjustment.* Most cribs have several height levels for the mattress—you use the highest setting when the baby is a newborn. Once she starts pulling up, you adjust the mattress to the lowest level so she won't be able to punt herself over the railing. You have two choices when it comes to this topic: bolt/screws or a hooked bracket. The first system requires you to loosen a bolt or screw that connects a strap to each of the four posts. Then you lower the mattress and screw the bolt back to the post. The only problem with the bolt/screw method: cheap cribs use uncoated bolts that over time can strip the holes on the post, weakening the support system. The bolt/screw is used on cribs with knee-push or double trigger rail releases. The alternative is the hooked brackets—the mattress lies on top of springs, anchored to the crib frame by hooked brackets. Some makers use this system on their cribs with foot-bar releases. Yet, as we mentioned, those makers are phasing out the foot-bar release and, with it, the hooked bracket hardware.

◆ *How stable is the crib?* Go ahead and abuse that crib set up in the baby store. Knock it around. The best cribs are very stable. Unfortunately, cheap models are often the lightest in weight (and hence, tend to wobble). Cribs with a drawer under the mattress are probably the most stable, as are those with stationary side rails. Unfortunately, all this extra stability comes at a price—models with these features start at $400 and can go up to $500 or $600. Keep in mind that some cribs may be wobbly because the store set them up incorrectly. Check out the same model at a couple of different stores if you have stability concerns.

◆ *Check those casters.* Metal casters are much better than plastic. We also prefer wide casters to those thin, disk-shaped wheels. You'll be wheeling this crib around more than you think—to change the sheets, to move it away from a drafty part of the room, etc. One solution: if you find a good buy on a crib that has cheap casters, you can easily replace them. Hardware stores sell heavy-duty metal casters for $10 to $20—or less.

◆ *How easy is it to assemble?* Ask to see those instructions—most stores should have a copy lying around. Make sure they are not in Greek. The worst offenders in the "lousy assembly directions department" are the importers (from Asia and Europe). Poorly translated directions and incomprehensible illustrations can frustrate even the most diligent parent. Even worse: instructions that are OMITTED altogether. This occasionally happens with furniture that is imported from Europe. Yes, this problem would be solved if manufacturers put their instructions online as a back up . . . but few do.

◆ *Compare the overall safety features of the crib.* In a section earlier in this book, we discuss crib safety in more detail.

◆ *Which wood is best?* Traditionally, cribs were made of hardwoods like maple, oak, ash and cherry. Crib makers considered these woods superior since they were more durable and easier for them to stain/paint. In the last couple of years, however, the latest craze is pine furniture—and pine has also come to baby cribs. The problem? Pine is a softwood that tends to nick, scratch and damage. Of course, not all pine is the same. North American pine is the softest, but pine grown in cold climates (Northern Europe, for example) is harder. Hence, the pine you're most likely to see used in baby furniture is hardwood pine.

So, which wood is best? To be honest, it doesn't really matter much. The traditional hardwoods like oak and maple are fine, as is ramin (a hardwood grown in Asia). Italian crib makers use beech wood (a European hardwood), while Canadian makers often use birch. Again, each is fine. Based on feedback from parents, we haven't heard any complaints about one wood being inferior to another when it comes to cribs.

Of course, dressers are another subject that we'll cover later in this chapter. Wood choices (including man-made substitutes like MDF) are more of a factor in that decision than with cribs. And if you want your furniture to match, you may want to read the section on dressers before making a crib decision.

Another note: some stores and web sites tout "cherry" cribs when they are actually referring to the finish, not the actual wood. It may be a "cherry" stain, but the wood is probably not.

◆ **Consider other special needs.** As we noted above, noisy crib railing release mechanisms can be a hassle—and this seems especially so for short people (or, in politically correct terms, the vertically challenged). Why? Taller folks (above 5' 8") may be able to place the baby into a crib *without* lowering the side rail (when the mattress is in the highest position). Shorter parents can't reach over the side rail as easily, forcing them to use the release mechanism more often than not. Hence, a quieter release on a more expensive brand might be worth the extra investment.

Disabled parents also may find the foot bar difficult or impossible to operate. In that case, we recommend a crib that has a knee-push rail release, described earlier.

Smart Shopper Tip #3
Cyber-Nursery: Ordering furniture online

"We don't have any good baby stores nearby, so I want to order furniture online. How do you buy items sight unseen and make sure they arrive in one piece?"

As we've mentioned, ordering furniture via the web/mail can be tricky. Damage from shipping and exorbitant costs have convinced many retailers to not offer this service. Yet, other web sites, mail-order catalogs and even eBay sellers have figured out how to ship nursery furniture across the country without breaking the bank—or the furniture itself.

First, deal with an established seller that has a good customer service track record. We review several companies in this chapter that sell online—stick with the ones with the best reputations when buying furniture via the mail. You want a company that *specializes* in selling furniture online, not a general baby products web site that also sells a few dressers among their car seats, strollers and baby monitors. If you buy from an eBay seller, make sure they have a good track record based on their online feedback. Do a search of the message boards on our web site to make sure other parents have been happy.

In general, readers who bought direct from a manufacturer or from an established catalog like Pottery Barn or JCPenney seemed happier with their experiences. Why? These sources know how to pack a dresser or crib for shipment cross-country. Problems some-time happen when a manufacturer "drop-ships" items for a web site reseller—then you can get in a situation where one blames the other for faulty packaging that leads to a damage claim. And nothing gets resolved. See the following email from the real world for an example of how a dresser purchase went wrong for one reader.

Consider spending extra for insurance. And make sure you get all shipping costs and delivery details in writing. Will the items be delivered to your door if you live on the third floor of an apartment building? Does delivery include set-up? Confirm the details.

 Wastes of Money

1 **SURPRISE COSTS WITH "CONVERTIBLE" CRIBS.** Convertible to what, you might ask? Manufacturers pitch these more expensive cribs as a money-saver since they are convertible to "youth beds," which are smaller and narrower than a twin bed. But, guess

E-MAIL FROM THE REAL WORLD
Spending $385 for a $50 dresser.

A reader in Ohio shared this bad experience with shopping for a dresser online:

"I ordered a three drawer combo dresser from BabyUniverse. com. It had all of the things suggested in your book and was $385 (the Rumble Tuff line around here was $700 for the same thing). The manufacturer is Angel Line. The item arrived with split wood on the corner, a knob missing, a missing wall strap and one of the drawers didn't shut completely and was crooked. I called Baby Universe and they said I had to contact the manufacturer directly to get the problem resolved. It took four calls and the best I could get was another knob sent to me and another drawer sent to me with corners that did not fit together. So, I essentially paid $400 for something that looks like it was $50 at a garage sale.

what? Most kids can go straight from a crib to a regular twin bed with no problem whatsoever. So, the youth bed business is really a joke. Another rip-off: some manufacturers sell cribs that convert to adult-size beds. The catch? You have to pay for a "conversion kit," which will set you back another $30 to $200. And that's on top of the hefty prices ($400 to $600) that many of these models cost initially. (There is good news to report on the price front, though. In the past year or so, several crib makers have rolled out new, lower-price convertible cribs. We'll discuss such models later in this chapter in the manufacturer reviews). Another negative to convertible cribs: if you have more than one child, you'll have to buy another crib, because the older child is using the "convertible" crib frame for their bed.

2 **CRADLE.** Do you really need one? A newborn infant can sleep in a regular crib just as easily as a cradle. And you'll save a bundle on that bundle of joy—cradles run $100 to $400. Of course, the advantage of having the baby in a cradle is you can keep it in your room for the baby's first few weeks, making midnight (and 2 am and 4 am) feedings more convenient. If you want to go this way, consider a bassinet instead of a cradle (bassinets are baskets set on top of a stand, while cradles are miniature versions of cribs that rock). We priced bassinets at only $40 to $180, much less than cradles. Is it worth the extra money? It's up to you, but our baby slept in his crib from day one, and it worked out just fine. If the distance between your room and the baby's is too far and you'd like to give a bassinet a try, see if you can find one at a consignment or second-hand store. We'll discuss good buys on bassinets later in this chapter.

3 **CRIBS WITH "SPECIAL FEATURES."** It may be tempting to buy a special crib (like the round cribs from Little Miss Liberty, reviewed later in this chapter), but watch out. A special crib may require additional expenses, such as custom-designed mattresses or bedding. While Little Miss Liberty includes a round foam mattress with every crib it sells, the round bedding is extra . . . prepare to spend as much as $800. And since few companies make bedding for round cribs, your choices are limited. The best advice: make sure you price out the total investment (crib, mattress, bedding) before falling in love with an unusual brand.

4 **CHANGING TABLES.** Separate changing tables are a big waste of money. Don't spend $70 to $200 on a piece of furniture you won't use again after your baby gives up diapers. A better bet: buy a dresser that can do double duty as a changing table. A good example is the hi-low or combo dressers (pioneered by Rumble Tuff, reviewed later in this chapter), which start at $500 (not much more than a regular dresser). Best of all, a hi-low dresser doesn't look like a changing table and can be used as a real piece of furniture as your child grows older. Other parents we interviewed did away with the changing area altogether—they used a crib, couch or countertop to do diaper changes.

Money Saving Secrets

1 **GO FOR A SINGLE INSTEAD OF A DOUBLE.** Cribs that have a single-drop side are usually less expensive ($50 to $100 cheaper) than those with double-drop sides. Sure, double-drop side cribs are theoretically more versatile (you can take the baby out from either side), but ask yourself if your baby's room is big enough to

---

E-MAIL FROM THE REAL WORLD
Get all the details on delivery before you mail-order furniture

A mom-to-be in Chicago discovered Sears was a much better deal than JCPenney for her nursery furniture. Here's her story:

"While I was searching for baby furniture, I thought JCPenney's would be a good choice. The catalog gave me a large selection to choose from and it would be less time consuming than hitting all the little shops. So, I put in an order for a crib and mattress and a four-drawer dresser. The prices on the furniture were pretty good (about $150 less than in other stores). However, the furniture has to be shipped directly from the warehouse to your home. Shipping and handling would have been $110 and the shipping company would only drop off the material at the front door—not into the home (or, in our case, a second floor apartment!) I could hardly believe it! If I had to spend over a hundred dollars extra on shipping, I would rather spend it on a higher quality crib and dresser than on shipping and handling. Hence, the search continued.

"Next I went to Sears where they had a 'Sculptured' series Child Craft crib and matching flip-top dresser. The prices were reasonable, you could pick the delivery day (including Saturdays) and they would deliver for just $25! They had these items in stock, so we got it in two days. Even if it did have to be shipped from the main warehouse, however, we would still only be charged the $25 fee and would have to wait at most four weeks. Needless to say, we bought the crib and dresser at Sears!"

---

take advantage of this feature. Most small rooms necessitate that the crib be placed against a wall—a double-drop side crib would then be a tad useless, wouldn't it?

2 FORGET THE DESIGNER BRANDS. What do you get for $600 when you buy a fancy crib brand like Bellini or Ragazzi? Safety features that rival the M-1 tank? Exotic wood from Bora Bora? Would it surprise you to learn that these cribs are no different than those that cost $180 to $300? Oh sure, "Italian-designed" Bellini throws in an under-crib drawer for storage and Canadian-import Ragazzi has designer colors. But take a good look at these cribs—except for fancy styling, they are no better than cribs that cost half as much.

3 CONSIDER MAIL ORDER. Say you live in a town that has one baby shop. One baby shop that has sky-high prices. What's the antidote? Try mail order. JCPenney and Sears sell such famous (and quality) name brands as Child Craft and Bassett. Granted, they don't sell them at deep discount prices (you'll find them at regular retail). But this may be more preferable than the price-gouging local store that thinks it has a license from God to overcharge everyone on cribs and juvenile furniture. You can also check the web sites mentioned in this chapter for quotes on cribs and other nursery items. One note of caution: be sure to compare delivery costs and policies. See the box "E-Mail from the Real World" about a story on this subject earlier in this chapter. (One important note: Sears does NOT have a catalog; some Sears' stores carry juvenile furniture. You can also buy nursery furniture from Sears.com).

4 SHOP AROUND. We found the same crib priced for $100 less at one store than at a competitor down the street. Use the manufacturers' phone numbers and web sites (printed later in this chapter) to find other dealers in your area for price comparisons. Take the time to visit the competition, and you might be pleasantly surprised to find that the effort will be rewarded.

5 GO NAKED. Naked furniture, that is. We see an increasing number of stores that sell unfinished (or naked) furniture at great prices. Such places even sell the finishing supplies and give you directions (make sure to use a non-toxic finish). The prices are hard to beat. At a local unfinished furniture store, we found a three-drawer pine dresser (23" wide) for $100, while a four-drawer dresser (38" wide) was $175. Compare that to baby store prices, which can top $300 to $600 for a similar size dresser. A reader in California e-mailed us with a great bargain find in the Bay Area: "Hoot

Judkins" has three locations (Redwood City, Fremont, Millbrae; www.hootjudkins.com) that sell unfinished furniture. She found a five-drawer dresser in solid pine for just $239 and other good deals on nursery accessories. Another idea: Million Dollar Baby (see review later in this chapter) is one of the few crib makers to offer unfinished crib models (the Alpha and a Jenny Lind, M0301). While unfinished cribs are somewhat rare, naked furniture stores at least offer afford-able alternatives for dressers, bookcases, and more.

6 **HEAD TO CANADA.** A weak Canadian dollar has created some incredible cross-border bargains. Thanks to NAFTA, it's now even easier to shop in Canada—there are no duties or taxes. The best deals are on juvenile furniture actually made in Canada (as opposed to imported from Asia). If you want to explore this tip, first start by calling a Canadian manufacturer to find the names of both U.S. and Canadian dealers (the numbers/web sites are in our man-ufacturer review section later in this chapter). Then compare prices over the phone or email.

What if you don't live near Canada? Can you just call up a Canadian baby shop and have a crib shipped to the U.S.? Well, you *used* to be able to do this about a year ago. Since then, Canadian crib makers have cracked down on this practice, fearing that cross-border shipping was cutting into their lucrative sales to U.S. baby retailers. As a result, only a few brands (such as Morigeau/Lepine) permit their Canadian retailers to ship across the border. Also, we should note Dutailier (the glider/rocker company reviewed later in this chapter) does permit cross-border shipping; sites such as *Baby Furniture Outlet* in Canada (800-613-9280, 519-649-2590, www.babyfurnitureoutlet.com), *BabyCatalog.com*, *CribNCarriage.com* and *Good Night Ben* (www.goodnight-ben.com) sell their rocker-gliders online at great prices. Shipping for a glider-rocker is usually in the $30 to $40 range; the savings typi-cally far outweighs that fee. Who's got the best prices and service on rocker gliders among those discounters? We'd have to give that award to *Good Night Ben* (www.goodnightben.com) and *RockingChairOutlet.com*—the feedback on these Canada-based discounters is excellent, according to posts on our message boards.

7 **CHECK OUT REGULAR FURNITURE STORES FOR ROCKERS, DRESSERS, ETC.** Think about it—most juvenile furniture looks very similar to regular adult furniture. Rockers, dressers, and book-cases are, well, just rockers, dressers, and bookcases. And don't you wonder if companies slap the word "baby" on an item just to raise the price 20%? To test this theory, we visited a local discount furni-ture store. The prices were incredibly low. A basic three-drawer dresser was $56. Even pine or oak three-drawer dressers were just $129 to $189. The same quality dresser at a baby store by a "juvenile furniture" manufacturer would set you back at least $400, if not twice that. We even saw cribs by such mainstream names as Bassett at decent prices in regular furniture stores. What's the disadvantage to shopping there? Well, if you have to buy the crib and dresser at different places, the colors might not match exactly. But, considering the savings, it might be worth it.

8 SKIP THE SLEIGH CRIB. Lots of folks fall in love with the look of a sleigh-style crib, which looks like, well, a sleigh. The only problem? Most sleigh cribs have solid foot and headboards. All that extra wood means higher prices, as much as $100 to $300 more than non-sleigh crib styles. If you have your heart set on a sleigh style, look for one that doesn't have solid wood on the ends. Such models sold in the JCPenney's catalog and web site aren't much more than non-sleigh styles.

9 CONSIDER AN AFFORDABLE CONVERTIBLE CRIB. Now, the key word here is "affordable." Earlier in this chapter, we derided most "convertible" cribs for their high prices and expensive conversion kits. And then there is whole issue of whether you really want a crib to morph into a twin bed. But we realize that many parents like the convertible concept, so let's talk about how to get a deal. Good news: several companies have rolled out affordable convertible cribs. Take Child Craft's Crib and Double Bed (36101), for example. For $550, you get a decent crib that converts to a toddler bed and then to a real-size double bed with the addition of simple bed rails. There are no conversion kits to buy; and the

"Exclusive" cribs hard to shop

When you visit a local baby store and see a particular crib style, you might think you can price shop this furniture online, or at least, at another store across town. But sometimes it isn't that easy. That's because juvenile furniture makers sometimes make "exclusive" cribs and dresser styles for certain groups of baby stores like NINFRA's Baby Express group or the USA Baby stores. These exclusive models aren't sold to other stores or online. In fact, you can't even look them up on a manufacturer's web site. The reason is clear: baby stores know you can't price shop the crib and that means fatter profits for them.

design has a true headboard and shorter footboard (many low-end convertible cribs cheat on this point by having the same size head and foot boards). The only quirk to this model–there is no under crib drawer and the side rail is fixed (it doesn't move up or down). We should also note that Child Craft makes several convertible crib styles, including one in pine that starts at just $400. Again, these convert to true double beds. And, of course, other crib makers also have jumped on this bandwagon as well. We'll review other options later in this chapter for convertible cribs.

10 CHECK FOR REBATES. Some of the companies we review later in this chapter have rebates on products. Check the web directory at the back of this book to find the web addresses of major baby product makers. Another idea: stores like Toys R Us and Babies R Us have rebate bulletin boards where they post deals.

Baby Superstores: The Good, Bad & Ugly

What a long strange trip it's been.

When we wrote the first edition of this book back in 1993, a new breed of baby stores was emerging: the superstore. With 30,000 or more square feet, these big box stores promised to stock everything a new parent needed, at prices that were below that of specialty stores. Instead of visiting multiple stores and shops to buy for baby, superstores promised one-stop convenience.

There was no shortage of competitors in this category. Baby Superstore was first in the market in 1991 and held sway in the Southeast, with rapid expansion planned nationwide. Lil' Things was launched in Texas in 1993 and quickly spread to California, Arizona and Colorado. KidsSource launched superstores in Florida. Even the big boys got into the act: Toys R Us rolled out "Babies R Us" stores and the Burlington Coat Factory put "Baby Depot" departments in its stores, as well as launching free-standing Totally for Kids stores.

Experts predicted these big box baby stores would steam roll the competition (namely, independent juvenile retailers), blanketing the country with locations selling discount furniture and equipment.

Fast forward to the present day. As it turns out, only one superstore chain survived: Babies R Us. Baby Superstore was bought out by Toys R Us in 1996 and absorbed into their Babies R Us operation. Lil' Things went bankrupt and eventually closed all its stores in 1998. KidsSource failed, closing all locations. Burlington Coat Factory scrapped plans to roll out more Totally for Kids stores (though they have increased Baby Depot departments in its regular stores).

What happened? Well, the giants found the baby business

tougher than they anticipated. While each failure had its own peculiarities, there was one common thread: not enough profit. You might think selling baby products in the booming 90's economy would be a no-brainer, but the chains discovered a truth about big box retailing—it doesn't help to have a narrow market. Unlike other superstores that sell one product (office supplies, say) to a wide market (small business, big business and everything in between), baby superstores had the opposite strategy—sell a wide range of goods to a narrow market. In the end, there wasn't enough room in the market for more than one superstore concept.

While superstore competition has dwindled, there is another wild card player in the baby product biz: the 'net. Despite the dot-com bust, the business of selling baby products online is still going strong. From the big boys like Amazon's BabiesRUs.com and Target.com to the small independent site that discounts glider-rockers from Canada, the web has filled the competition gap left by bankrupt superstore chains.

And entrepreneurs haven't given up on the baby superstore concept. One of the most promising new entrants into the field is Buy Buy Baby, which is run by the sons of the family that founded the Bed, Bath & Beyond chain. Yes, they only have seven locations in New York, New Jersey and Maryland (check www.BuyBuyBaby.com for locations), but they are expanding. Readers rave about Buy Buy Baby's selection, service and prices, so if there's one near you, check it out. And BuyBuyBaby.com's web site carries a small selection of the store's offerings for online shoppers.

Here's a look at the key players that are left in the field:

Babies R Us

To find a store near you, call 888-BABYRUS. Over 165 locations.
What's Cool: We love the selection in this chain, which includes everything from diapers to car seats, cribs to clothes. Unlike Toys R Us' puny baby departments, Babies R Us actually carries good-to-better brand names like Peg Perego strollers, Britax car seats and Child Craft cribs. Some of the best buys are their in-house brands for diapers and wipes. What about the rest of the prices? Yes, you can find better deals on the web or at Wal-Mart, but Babies R Us is generally competitive. Overall, the baby registry gets good marks from parents we've interviewed. Their return policy is more customer-friendly than that of Target or Baby Depot. New at Babies R Us: more private-label goods, such as their Koala Baby line of bedding (made for them by Crown Crafts). We'll review that bedding in the next chapter.

Needs work: Did someone say service? Unfortunately, that's not

Babies R Us' strong suit. Our reader email is filled with stories of inconsistent service at Babies R Us, and our own personal experiences echo that sentiment. Sometimes we find helpful, friendly salespersons who can give you basic facts about products. On other visits, however, we're lucky to find someone to check us out, much less answer questions.

Now, in a past edition of this book, we compared the IQ of *some* Babies R Us sales associates to that of a rutabaga. As a result, we received angry letters from rutabagas nationwide, including one pointed missive from the Rutabaga Anti-Discrimination League (RADL). But seriously, Babies R Us has told us they are trying to improve service. One area of improvement could be to stop the mis-information that some BRU sales associates give out to parents. Example: when a product is dropped by Babies R Us, some sales associates erroneously tell customers "the manufacturer has discontinued it." Yes, that sometimes is true—but more often than not, you can still find that product somewhere else . . . just not at BRU. Other complaints about Babies R Us center on snafus with special order items, especially furniture and glider-rockers. Some of this is a lack of communication between corporate and the stores; other times, it is an error at the store level.

Yes, mistakes can happen at any store, chain or not. The key is how the store deals with/fixes the problem. Most of the time, Babies R Us does the right thing and takes care of the customer
.

Web: www.babiesrus.com Babies R Us' web site is actually run by Amazon. Hence the selection of products (and the prices) you see online may not exactly correspond to what is in BRU's stores. Like all Amazon sites, BabiesRUs.com is well organized and easy to use. Recent improvements to the site include the ability to return online purchases to Babies R Us stores, a nice plus. Prices are good, although you can often find items for less elsewhere. You can create a baby registry online—either by picking individual items you like or selecting from list of best sellers that BRU recommends.

Baby Depot (Totally for Kids)
To find a store near you, call 800-444-COAT. 220 locations.
What's Cool: The Burlington Coat Factory has 330 locations, but only 250 have "Baby Depot" departments. The company also operates two freestanding baby stores (one is called Totally For Kids; the other Baby Depot—check their web site at www.coat.com for a store locator, which also tells you which location has what). Baby Depot's strength is its low prices, often lower than competitors like Babies R Us and even Wal-Mart. Yes, a Baby Depot department is smaller than a Babies R Us store, but we're always amazed at the

top-quality brands they sell, including Combi, Peg Perego and Chicco. Baby Depot's furniture selection is also impressive—crib brands include Simmons, Child Craft, Basset, Delta, C&T/Sorelle and Babi Italia. Baby Depot also has added a maternity section and carries a small but decent layette selection. Also at Baby Depot: a national gift registry that offers a 5% rebate of purchases made for you. And look for Burlington's in-store magazine with coupons for select items. Some Entertainment coupon books will have a $10 off deal when you purchase $50 worth of stuff at Baby Depot.

Needs work: "Inconsistent" would be a charitable way to describe the Baby Depot experience. Some Baby Depots have the ambience

E-MAIL FROM THE REAL WORLD
The world's worst return policy?

Baby Depot's draconian no-cash refund policy draws harsh criticism from our readers:

"Add yet another dissatisfied Baby Depot customer to your list. I was aware of their awful return policy, but somehow, I lost my mind, and we ordered a Simmons crib from them anyway. Four weeks after we ordered, we get a message saying that our order was in at Baby Depot. But when we went to the store to pick it up not only could they not find the crib we had ordered, our order had been listed as "combo unit", not a crib, and had been marked as "picked up" on the same day that we ordered it. So not only did we have to wait for 30 minutes while the lone salesperson in that department searched for our item, we have to find some way to spend $50 of store credit at a store we never want to set foot in again."

"We bought a Century car seat at Baby Depot, got it home, and opened the box only to discover that the wrong car seat was in the box! We took it back to Baby Depot, and were told that we could be issued a store credit, but that's it. They don't give refunds. We were also told the model we wanted had been discontinued. After the rude treatment we received at the store, I am not inclined to purchase anything else there."

A word to the wise: make sure you REALLY want an item before buying it at Baby Depot. And check carefully for any damage (open boxes, confirm the right thing is in the box, etc.) before giving them your money.

of a decrepit warehouse, while others are bright and cheerful. Obviously, much of the blame on this can be pinned on parent Burlington Coat Factory, which doesn't seem to have a clue about marketing strategy and hence operates in widely disparate locations (outlet malls, power centers, free standing stores, etc). Our last visit to Baby Depot was disappointing—the drone of the harsh florescent lights was only matched by the apathetic sales help and disorganized aisles. And watch out for Baby Depot's return policy, which is among the worst in North America. Basically, there are no cash refunds—if you buy something that doesn't work or breaks, that's tough. All you get is store credit. And, generally, there are no returns after 14 days. As a result of that return policy, quite a few of our readers boycott Baby Depot. At a bare minimum, we would recommend passing on Baby Depot's gift registry. As a side note, we did have an employee of Baby Depot email us with some "inside" info on the return policy. She told us if you have a miscarriage or stillbirth, Baby Depot will give you a cash refund on returned purchases—but only if you go through their corporate headquarters. Wow, how considerate! (See the previous page email from the real world for more on Baby Depot's return policy.)

Web: www.coat.com. Burlington's web site has come along way in the last year or so. Besides the standard store locator, you can shop from several "baby" categories, like Nursery, Baby Travel, Maternity and more. But we still found the site very hard to use—you have to click through numerous menus just to get to something to buy.

The Discounters: Target, Wal-Mart, K-Mart

What's Cool: Any discussion of national stores that sell baby items wouldn't be complete without a mention of the discounters: Target, Wal-Mart, K-Mart and their ilk. In recent years, the discounters have realized one sure-fire way to drive traffic—discount toys and baby stuff in order to get parents to buy other higher-margin items. As a result, you'll often see formula, diapers and other baby essentials at rock-bottom prices. And there are even better deals on "in-house" brands.

Of all the discounters, we think Target is best (with one big caveat—their new draconian return policy, see below for a discussion). Target's baby department is just a notch above Wal-Mart and K-Mart when it comes to brand names and selection. Yes, sometimes Wal-Mart has lower prices—but usually that's on lower-quality brands. Target, by contrast, carries Perego high chairs and a wider selection of products like baby monitors. The best bet: Super Targets, which have expanded baby products sections.

Needs work: If you're looking for premium brand names, forget it.

Most discounters only stock the so-called mass-market brands: Graco strollers, Cosco car seats, Gerber sheets, etc. And the baby departments always seem to be in chaos when we visit, with items strewn about hither and yon. K-Mart is probably the worst when it comes to organization; Wal-Mart the best. We like Target's selection (especially of feeding items and baby monitors), but their prices are somewhat higher than Wal-Mart. What about service? Forget it—you are typically on your own.

While we do recommend Target, we should warn readers about their return policy. Once among the most generous, Target's return policy was changed significantly in 2001. Once, you could return just about anything for up to 90 days, no questions asked; now, you *must* have a receipt. A raft of new rules and restrictions greet customers (sample: exchanges now must be in made for items within the same department). This has understandably ticked off a fair number of our readers, especially those who have unfortunately chosen to register at Target for their baby gifts. Among the biggest roadblocks: Target won't let you exchange duplicate baby gifts if you don't have a gift receipt (and there are numerous other rules/restrictions as well). Yes, you'd think Target would have a record of this since YOUR baby registry resides on THEIR computers, but no. Our email box has been stuffed with complaints about this and angry consumers have even started a web site devoted to this topic (www.target-sucks.com).

Bottom line: DO NOT register for baby products at Target. Instead, we'd suggest Babies R Us—their registry is much more customer (and return) friendly. One smart move: be sure to read the fine print for ANY baby registry before registering at any store. Ask about returns and exchange policies, including specifically what happens if you have to return/exchange a duplicate item without a gift receipt.

Web: Each of the major discounters sells baby products online. Here's an overview of each site:

◆ *WalMart.com:* This redesigned site is easy to use, complete with a "baby" tab at the entry page. Moving into the Nursery category, we noticed the site had a smattering of furniture, bedding and other products for sale. We like the detailed info for each product, including weight, dimensions, shipping info and more. Yet, in some cases, the brand names for items were omitted. And the selection was quite small—just one infant car seat? Four baby monitors? We thought WalMart.com could do better than this, although prices were very competitive.

◆ *Kmart.com*: K-Mart's online outpost is a winner—we liked the bright graphics and easy navigation. Kmart has fixed some of the problems with this site that we noted in our last edition . . . navigation is easier and categories are logically organized. The selection of items (notably strollers, carriers and car seats) was better than WalMart.com.

◆ **_Target.com_** has probably the coolest looking web site of all the discounters—click on the "baby" section and then select from sections like furniture, safety or strollers. Like the store, Target.com focuses on more stylish and better-quality goods than their discount competition. Sample: the $299 rocker-glider deal from Shermag, which we'll discuss more in depth later. A handy drop-down menu on most pages lets you sort items by price, brand and more. Most cool feature: Target lets consumers rate and review products, a la Amazon. Often, you'll find out more about a product in the user reviews than is provided in Target's own descriptions.

Specialty Chains: Pottery Barn, Room And Board, CargoKids, Land of Nod

Inspired by the success of Pottery Barn Kids, several chains have ventured into the nursery business. An example: Room & Board (web: www.RoomandBoard.com), an 11-store chain with locations in California, Colorado, Illinois and Minnesota. Their well-designed web site has a nursery section with a couple of cribs ($400 to $450), dressers and accessories. Quality is good and prices are reasonable, say our readers who've ordered from them.

Baby gift registries disappoint

The Internet age was supposed to make this so easy—just register for gifts at a baby stores and the computers do the rest. Need to change something? Stores promised you could create/change your registry via the web. Sounds so easy? Not so fast. Baby gift registries generate a big number of complaints, judging from our reader email. The gripes: duplicate gifts, out of stock items, backorders and other frustrations. And it doesn't seem to matter the size of the registry—we hear complaints about small retailers' registries and those of the big chains and web sites. (The exception: Buy Buy Baby, mentioned earlier in this section, seems to have figured out how to do it right). We don't know what the problem is here. Perhaps retailers should take their web programmers out back, give them 30 lashes and withhold the Starbucks for a week. Until they can figure out how to work their computer systems, we urge caution with all baby gift registries.

cribs

And that's just the beginning. Bombay Co of Ft. Worth, Texas opened their first Bombay Kids store in 2002 and plans to open another 130 by 2005. Pier 1 Imports, also of Ft. Worth, acquired the CargoKids chain in 2001 and plans to roll out 300 more stores in the next decade. Finally, Crate & Barrel plans to launch Land of Nod stores in the next few years that feature their funky nursery furniture and bedding.

What's driving this is a boom in babies, especially to older moms and dads. Tired of the cutesy baby stuff in chains stores, many parents are looking for something more sophisticated and hip. Of course, what this means for bargain shoppers remains to be seen. On one hand, more competition is always good—having a wide diversity of places to buy nursery furniture and accessories is always a plus. On the downside, most of these chains are chasing that "upscale" customer with outrageously priced cribs and bedding. "As much as parents love the furniture at Pottery Barn Kids, some wince at the prices," said the *Wall Street Journal* in a recent article on this trend. And we agree—you gotta love the PBK look, our goal in life is to try to find that same look . . . at half the price!

Outlets

There are be dozens of outlets that sell kids' clothing, but when it comes to furniture the pickings are slim. In fact, we found just two major manufacturers (Child Craft and Cosco) and two catalogs that have outlets.

One of the biggest outlets is **Cosco's** in Indiana. Located in the Prime Outlet Mall in Edinburgh, IN, (812) 526-0860 about 30 minutes south of Indianapolis, the Cosco outlet sells cribs, high chairs, play pens and more. In fact, the store carries nearly every product with the Cosco name on it. Cosco's metal cribs are $79 and up. In general, prices are up to 50% off retail; all the products are new and first quality. As we mentioned in the Name Game, we're not really wild about their cribs, but their other products are good buys.

Child Craft has a strange arrangement for their outlet stores. First, there is the "official" (and only) Child Craft factory outlet. Then there are two semi-official outlets (blessed by Child Craft) that are operated by CC dealers in Kentucky and Massachusetts.

First, the official outlet: Child Craft quietly opened this location in Indiana in 1999 to sell their discontinued and overstock furniture. Located 90 minutes south of Indianapolis in Uniontown off I-65 (exit 41, 812-524-1999), the outlet sells only first-quality merchandise including discontinued pieces. While there is little damaged merchandise, some of the pieces are "off color." Prices are discounted

30% to 70%—cribs start at $179 and most are $200 to $400 or so.

A reader who scoped out the outlet for us said she was a little disappointed with the selection (none of the fancier models were in the outlet at the time she visited) but the "prices were terrific." She also pointed out that a nearby Child Craft dealer in Louisville, KY (Kiddie Kastle) was so miffed at the official outlet that they convinced the manufacturer to let them open their own Child Craft Outlet. The **Kiddie Kastle Warehouse Outlet** is at a different location than the main store (502-499-9667) and is only open limited hours (mainly Fridays, Saturdays and Sundays—call first). But the deals are great— "the selection is small but there are some very desirable models." She found a cherry sleigh crib (original $600) for just $350. And the same outlet also carries bedding at very good prices.

Live in the Northeast? Check out **Baby Boudoir,** a baby store in New Bedford, MA. (800-272-2293, 508-998-2166) that is also authorized by Child Craft to sell their discontinued furniture at wholesale prices or below. Baby Boudoir has 60-75 cribs in stock at any one time at prices that start at $139 and up. The store also carries glider rockers, bedding and other baby products at 30% to 70% off retail. FYI: There is both a Baby Boudoir store and a warehouse outlet—you want to visit the outlet for the best deals. The outlet is around the corner from the main store. Of course, Baby Boudoir sells more than just Child Craft—they also sell discontinued Childesigns cribs (30% to 70% off) and certain discontinued Ragazzi styles (25% off), as well as factory seconds from such bedding lines as Kids Line, Lambs & Ivy and more.

Along the same lines, **Baby Furniture Warehouse**, with stores in Reading and Braintree, MA (781-942-7978 or 781-843-5353; web: www.BabyFurnitureWarehouse.com), is a Ragazzi outlet that specializes in selling overstock and discontinued cribs. You can save up to 40% off Ragazzi's regular retail prices here—cribs run $299 to $599 and case pieces are also available. One special we noticed was a $569 Ragazzi crib with under crib drawer marked down to $329. FYI: The Reading location is twice the size as their Braintree store.

Pottery Barn Kids has two outlets for their kids catalog in Memphis, TN (901-763-1500) and Dawsonville, GA (706-216-6456). A reader found some good deals there, including a changing table for $99 (regularly $199) and a rocker for $199 (down from $700). The outlet also carries the PBK bedding line at good discounts. A reader in Georgia said the PBK outlet there features 75% off deals on furniture and you can get a coupon book at the foot court for an additional 10% discount. "The best time to shop is during the week—they run more specials then," she said. "And bring a truck—they don't deliver."

Simmons is one of the few crib makers that has factory overstocks for sale right from their web site (www.simmonsjp.com/closeout). On a recent visit, we saw a crib for as little as $139 (although other styles did go up to $230). There were also dressers ($179 for a combo hi-lo!), hutches, changing tables and more. Shipping costs range from $40 to $100 per item, although Simmons offers savings if you buy three or more items. Shipping takes two to three weeks or you can pick up the items from their New London, WI warehouse if you are nearby. One reader scored an entire nursery full of furniture (crib, combo dresser and regular chest) for just $1000 with shipping!

Finally, don't forget that *JCPenney* has 15 outlet stores nationwide. The stores carry a wide variety of items, including children's and baby products (always call before you go to confirm selection). Check out the web site Outlet Bound (www.outletbound.com) for a current listing of locations.

The Name Game: Reviews of Selected Manufacturers

Here is a look at some of the best-known brand names for cribs sold in the U.S. and Canada. There are over 100 companies in the U.S. that manufacture and/or import cribs, but, because of space limitations, we can't review each one. We decided to concentrate on the best and most common brand names. If you've discovered a brand that we didn't review, feel free to share your discovery by calling or emailing us (see our contact info at the end of the book).

How did we evaluate the brands? First, we inspected samples of cribs at stores and juvenile product trade shows. With the help of veteran juvenile furniture retailers, we checked construction, release mechanisms, mattress supports, and overall fit and finish. Yes, we did compare styling among the brands but this was only a minor factor in our ratings (we figure you can decide what looks best for your nursery).

Readers of previous editions have asked us how we assign ratings to these manufacturers—what makes one an "A" vs. "B"? The bottom line is quality *and* value. Sure, anyone can make a high-quality crib for $500 or $800. The trick is getting that price down to $300 or less while maintaining high quality standards. Hence, we gave our highest ratings to manufacturers that make high-quality cribs at prices that don't break the bank.

What about the crib makers who got the lowest ratings? Are their cribs unsafe? No, of course not. ALL new cribs sold in the U.S. and Canada must meet minimum federal safety standards. As we mentioned earlier in this chapter, a $100 crib sold at Wal-Mart today is just as safe as a $700 designer brand sold at a posh boutique. The only difference is styling, features and durability—more expensive cribs have thick wood posts, fancy finishes, features like "hidden hardware" on the rail release, under-crib storage drawers and durability to last through two or more kids.

Brands that got our lowest rating typically have had a problem with recalls in previous years. Some were fined by the CPSC for failing to report injuries or problems with their products. That doesn't mean that their current production cribs are unsafe; but we were troubled enough by their past track record or behavior to assign that lower rating.

Ratings here *only apply to cribs*; many of these manufacturers also make dressers and other furniture pieces. Later in this chapter, we'll discuss our brand recommendations for these items.

Please note: we've included phone numbers and web addresses in this section so you can find a local dealer. These manufacturers do NOT sell directly to the public, unless otherwise noted. Some (but not all) may have catalogs or brochures to send out; others have web sites that feature a selection of their cribs.

The Ratings

A **EXCELLENT**—*our top pick!*
B **GOOD**— *above average quality, prices, and creativity.*
C **FAIR**—*could stand some improvement.*
D **POOR**—*yuck! could stand some major improvement.*

Alta Baby 180 Vreeland Rd., West Milford, NJ 07480. Call (888) 891-1489 for a dealer near you. Web: www.altababyweb.com. Alta is the latest Italian crib maker to debut in the U.S., launching nationwide in 2002. Like other Italian cribs, Alta's styles feature solid beechwood construction, hidden hardware, knee-push rail releases and under crib drawers. The cribs look much like those of Pali, Sorelle and Bonavita—basic styling with just a handful of finish options. Yes, there are a few accessories (Alta has a line of crib bedding as well as changing tables) but there are no matching dressers. And the prices are rather high: $600 for the cribs, for example. Yes, we did hear from one reader who found an Alta Baby crib for half off (just $300, which was a steal) but we'd be hard-pressed to recommend this line at full retail prices. And Alta Baby is a bit hard to find—the company just has a handful of dealers, mostly in the East. On the upside, we liked the fact that their cribs are JPMA certified (something you don't see with most Italian cribs). *Rating: B-*

Angel Line *17 Peak Place, Sewell, NJ 08080, Call (800) 889-8158 or (856) 863-8009 for a dealer near you. Web: www. angelline.com* This low priced line offers good quality even though the styling is rather boring. Their entry-level Jenny Lind-style crib sells for $150, but other more contemporary styles are in the $200 to $400 range. Typical of the plain vanilla styling is the Angel II crib with curved headboard and single drop side (all Angel Line models have single drop sides). Available finishes are natural, white, maple, white wash, oak and cherry. As for the quality, we liked the overall construction (they use a spring mattress platform, for example) and large casters. One negative: most of Angel Line's cribs featured exposed rail hardware and a foot-bar rail release mechanism, which most of their competition has abandoned in recent years. On the plus side, Angel Line is one of the few crib brands you can buy online (see the Cyberspace section earlier in this chapter for a list of sites that sell cribs). In the past year, Angel Line has rolled out new styles including an Italian-style line of cribs with hidden hardware on the rail releases and under-crib storage drawers for $350. Angel Line (whose parent is Longwood Forest Products) also makes canopy cribs, changing tables, cradles, rockers and high chairs, all made in Taiwan. The company's detailed web site features extensive info on their cribs (even size and weight), as well as thumbnail pictures of each model (which can be enlarged for viewing). Angel Line is one of the few crib makers that puts their assembly instructions online. **Rating: B-**

Hotel cribs: hazardous at $200 a night?

Sure, your nursery at home is a monument to safety, but what happens when you take that act on the road? Sadly, many hotels are still in the dark ages when it comes to crib safety. A 2000 survey by the CPSC found unsafe cribs in a whopping 80% of hotels and motels checked by inspectors. Even worse: when the CPSC invited hotel chains to join a new safety effort to fix the problem, only the Bass Hotel chain (Inter-Continental, Holiday Inn, Crowne Plaza) agreed to join. That chain pledged to have their staffs inspect all cribs, making sure they meet current safety standards. We urge other hotels to join this effort, as research shows children under age two spend more than seven MILLION nights per year in hotels and motels. And if you find yourself in a hotel with your baby, don't assume the crib you request is safe—check carefully for loose hardware, inadequate size sheets and other problems.

A.P. Industries *346 St. Joseph Blvd., Laurier Station, Quebec, Canada, Call (800) 463-0145 or (418) 728-2145. Web site: www. apindustries.com* Quebec-based crib maker A.P. Industries (also known as Generations) offers stylish cribs and case pieces, which are available in nine different collections. All the items are made in Quebec of solid birch (except one, made of beech). Sample price: $500 to $600 for a crib with hidden hardware and a knee-push rail release. We thought A.P had the best look of all the Canadian cribs we reviewed (the 20 finish options provide more choice than most crib makers), although the rail release does make a rather loud "click" when it is locked into position, at least on one model we tested. Another plus: A.P. makes some very affordable dressers; a reader spied an A.P. hi-low dresser for just $309 at Baby Depot. Despite all the positives, we should note a few problems with A.P. Last year, A.P. ran behind production, irking both retailers and consumers who faced delivery delays. While that problem has been now fixed, it shook our confidence in the brand. Even more serious: we received several complaints from readers about A.P.'s customer service. As we've often stated before, EVERY crib and furniture maker has problems (delivery snafus, damage from shipping, etc). The key is how well (or poorly) they take of the problems. On that score, A.P. needs some work—more than one parent commented that their customer service "stinks." When problems happened, A.P.'s response was either rude or indifferent, often referring the customer back to the store. The assembly instructions on the cribs are also quite confusing. As a result of these complaints, we decided to lower A.P.'s rating this year. Bottom line: A.P. still does quality furniture, but their customer service needs help. **Rating: B**

Baby's Dream *PO Box 579, Buena Vista, GA 31803, Call (800) TEL-CRIB or (912) 649-4404 for a dealer near you. Web: www. babysdream.com* Baby's Dream's claim to fame is their "Crib 4 Life," a design that converts from a crib to a youth bed to a twin bed to an adult bed to, finally, a thermonuclear weapon. Just kidding on that last one. But seriously . . . some parents are fans of these cribs, citing their functionality and stability. Well, they should be stable—weighing in at a whopping 135 pounds, these monsters can't be lifted by mere mortals. And that functionality comes at a price: Baby's Dream cribs can run $700 (depending on the finish). Not bad for all those uses, you think? Hold it—in order to morph the crib into a twin or adult bed, you have to buy a separate "conversion kit." This could set you back another $130. In the end, you've probably spent just as much as, or more than, the cost of a simple crib and twin bed.

Of course, Baby's Dream does make some less expensive models (all of which are made in Georgia). Many styles are in the $300 to $500 range; one reader reported seeing a simpler crib model for $250, with the conversion kit running just $70. But, that crib was in pine, wood that easily nicks and scratches. Hence, we recommend sticking with Baby's Dream's other woods (oak, sycamore, beech).

Safety is another concern with these cribs. While Baby's Dream likes to tout its safety reputation (they're JPMA certified), we have serious concerns about their rail release. Unlike other crib brands that use a rail that drops down, the majority of Baby's Dream cribs use a folding design, where the rail folds down to give you access to the baby. We find this dangerous for two reasons: the risk of finger entrapment and the possibility that an older baby might be able to climb out of the crib. As your baby starts standing up, she can use this extra ledge (the rail's hinge) to get a foothold to climb out. And our fears of finger entrapment were unfortunately verified by the CPSC: in February 1998, the government ordered the recall of 13,000 Generation cribs for this very reason. Baby's Dream received eight reports of babies' fingers being trapped in the rail release's "drop gate," including seven reports of severe lacerations. To correct the problem, Baby's Dream replaced the crib's four small hinges with a piano-style hinge that runs the entire length of the drop gate.

Making matters worse, the CPSC charged that Baby's Dream failed to "timely report defects" with the suspect cribs. There's no excuse for that kind of behavior. To settle those charges, Baby's Dream agreed to pay a $200,000 fine.

So, it's hard for us to recommend this company's cribs. If you go for this style of crib, we suggest the model that doesn't have the fold-down rail (the Eternity, made of beech wood). While we realize many parents will consider this brand because of its convertibility, the hefty initial investment and later "conversion" kit expenses makes this crib no bargain. Finally, we should note the new design with Baby's Dream Generation cribs (which have a 5" panel in front) makes it difficult to secure a crib bumper in place. **Rating: C+**

Babi Italia This is a special brand made by Bonavita for chain stores. See the Bonavita review later in this section for more info.

Babies Love by Delta See the review of Delta later in this section.

Bassett *3525 Fairystone Park Hwy, Bassett, VA 24055. Call (540) 629-6000 for a dealer near you. Web: www.bassettfurniture.com* Bassett cribs are sold to chain stores like Babies R Us and JCPenney, which features the cribs in their baby catalog. A Bassett crib with solid head and footboards with wainscot detailing in pine with a single drop side is $350, not a bad value. Other readers have scored Bassett cribs for as little as $242 on sale at Baby Depot. As for quality, we'd say it is above average—most are made of wood from New Zealand and Australia, although other parts are made in such diverse places as Indonesia and Slovenia. Final assembly is in the U.S. at Bassett's factory in Virginia. As for rail releases, it's all over the board—some Bassett cribs have the old-style foot bar releases with exposed hardware, while newer models have hidden hardware and knee-push releases. Among Bassett's better new models is the Urban Loft 4-in-1 crib for $400 at Babies R Us. This knee-push crib converts to a double bed and has exposed hardware. There's even a Bassett crib with stationary side rail, which is the current rage. We also like the new Bassett Chris Madden sleigh-style cribs. We'll raise Bassett's rating this time out—their quality has improved in recent years, as has their styling and pricing. **Rating: B+**

Bellini *Call (805) 520-0974, (800) 332-BABY or (516) 234-7716 for a store location near you. Web: www.bellini.com* When Italian cribs were hard to find prior to the mid 1990's, Bellini had the market to themselves. With 50+ locations (mostly on the East and West coasts), Bellini made a killing selling expensive cribs, furniture and other products to the monied crowds in California and New York. Cribs at Bellini are $500 to $1000. Yet today you can find Italian cribs with similar styling and features in Babies R Us for a fraction of the Bellini price. Heck, even offerings from Pali and Bonavita look affordable next to Bellini. So, what's the appeal of Bellini today? Fans cite the customer service, but detractors of Bellini say it can be inconsistent (each Bellini is independently owned). Whether the service makes it worth the high prices is up to you, but we find the snob appeal of the chain a turn-off. Another major negative: Bellini uses the outdated double-trigger method for some of its rail releases. Most crib makers (and especially the Italian crib competition) have long moved to the knee-push rail release. **Rating: C+**

Who Is Jenny Lind?

You can't shop for cribs and not hear the name "Jenny Lind." Here's an important point to remember: Jenny Lind isn't a brand name; it refers to a particular style of crib. But how did it get this name? Jenny Lind was a popular Swedish soprano living in the 19th century. During her triumphal U.S. tour, it was said that Lind slept in a "spool bed." Hence, cribs that featured turned spindles (which look like stacked spools of thread) became known as Jenny Lind cribs. All this begs the question—what if today we still named juvenile furniture after famous singers? Could we have Britney Spears cribs and Shania Twain dressers? Nah, bad idea.

Berg *(908) 354-5252. Web: www.bergfurniture.com.* In business since 1984, Berg recently branched out into juvenile furniture. The company offers several different crib models. Solid pine cribs (made in Russia) run $349 to $449, while convertible cribs (that convert to twin beds; made in the U.S.) run $649 to $849. That is pricey, but the convertible models do include the conversion kit. Quality is good, although this brand is so new to the juvenile market we don't have much feedback on them yet. We liked the hidden hardware on the knee-push rail releases, but the attached dressers on their "Crib N Beds" were a turn-off (for safety reasons, as we discussed earlier). Perhaps the biggest criticism with this line is a lack of choice—there are just four furniture collections; only two that don't have cribs with attached dressers. ***Rating: B***

Bonavita *125 Jackson Ave., Edison, NJ 08837. Call (888) 266-2848 or (732) 346-5150 for a dealer near you. Web site: www. bonavita-cribs.com, www.issi-gallery.com.* Italian importer Bonavita has been the most prolific promoter of Italian cribs in the past decade. Their success in bringing down the prices of Italian cribs—and expanding their distribution into chain stores—has helped expand the popularity of Italian cribs that were once relegated to pricey specialty stores. Bonavita divides their line into three areas: the upper-end "Issi" line debuted in 1999 with high-price "architectural" style cribs and is sold in specialty stores for $500 to $1000. The middle-of-the-road Bonavita cribs are simpler in style and sell for $350 to $600, again mostly in specialty stores. The basic Babi Italia cribs run $299 to $399 and are sold in chains stores like Babies R Us. All the cribs (no matter what the price point) feature hidden hardware rail releases, solid beechwood construction and (in most models) under crib storage drawers. While the cribs are imported from Italy, the case pieces are made in Bonavita's own plant in Virginia. Sample price: $600 for a matching hi-lo dresser at Babies R Us. So, how's the quality? The cribs are good, as are most of the case pieces.

So why did we lower Bonavita's rating this year by an entire letter grade? Well, let's talk about Bonavita's customer service. Houston, we have a problem. In the past year, Bonavita took the crown for generating the most complaints among all crib makers. Problems ranged from the merely frustrating (unreturned phone calls, unhelpful phone reps, delivery delays) to the really annoying (shipping damage, warped wood on some cribs and drawers and a crib rail that separated from the headboard). As we've stated before, shipping damage and order snafus happen to all crib makers—the difference is how you handle it. Bonavita fumbled the ball more often than not in the past year. A good number of the complaints focused on the case goods, including situations where stain on the dressers didn't match the cribs. Why? Bonavita makes its case goods in Virginia and apparently had some kinks in starting up that operation last year (though they've pledged they've fixed the problems now). Adding insult to injury was a recall in December 2001 that focused on a small number of cribs that Bonavita imported with dangerous cutouts that could have been an entrapment hazard. Okay, it just affected 400 cribs and thankfully there were no reported injuries, but Bonavita should have known better.

Bottom line: Bonavita needs to improve its customer service. If you decide to buy a Bonavita or Babi Italia crib, be sure to check the box BEFORE leaving the store to make sure nothing is damaged. And buy it from a store with a good return policy as well as a reputation for helping out consumers in case something is wrong when you get home. ***Rating: B-***

Bridgeport Cosco makes wood cribs under this name and Jardine. See Jardine for a full review. (See Cosco's review for contact information and web site).

Bright Future *See the JCPenney catalog (800) 222-6161, web: www.jcpenney.com.* This is a private label brand made for JCPenney and imported from Asia. A recent Penney's catalog featured a single drop side crib for $250. The cribs are similar to other low-end brands in quality; on the plus side, the newer models have knee-push release rails and spring mattress supports. The styling is rather plain; don't look for any fancy features like under-crib drawers or cutting-edge looks from Bright Future. On the upside, Penney's cribs have a good reputation for safety and durability. The company dispatches its own representative to suppliers to make sure quality is up to snuff. Yet, you get what you pay for here—a low-end crib at a decent price. You sacrifice things like a spring mattress platform on the older models (a reader who bought a Penney's sleigh crib reported the mattress platform was made of plywood). Nonetheless, this might make a good secondary crib for grandma's house. ***Rating: B-***

Bratt Décor *PO Box 20808, Baltimore, MD 21209. Call (888)-24-BRATT or (410) 327-4600 for a dealer near you. Web: www. brattdecor.com.* Well, at least you have to give this company bonus points for creativity—they made their name with cribs like the "Casablanca Plume" crib that was topped with (and we're not making this up) ostrich feathers. That (and the $1050 price tag) enabled Bratt Décor to earn a distinguished place on our list of the most ridiculous baby products in a previous edition for this book. In the past year, Bratt has expanded their line to include a series of wood cribs in various "vintage" and whimsical looks. Their Heritage Four Poster Crib with Stars is a take-off of a 1940's design with four finials that can be changed from stars to bunnies, flowers, planes or balls. Price: $700. All in all, we've noticed Bratt Décor's prices have drifted downward in recent years—gone are most of the $1000+ options, replaced by cribs that now sell for $600 to $900. However, we're a bit surprised these pricey cribs still have exposed hardware (rod/cane) and drop sides with foot bar releases (most of the industry has moved to hidden hardware and knee-push releases). What parents seem to like here is the style and colors of the cribs (Bratt Décor is one of the few crib makers out there today that does a navy blue or bright red finish). New this year, Bratt Décor plans to roll out a line of matching accessories such as nightstands, mirrors, bookcases and other decorative options. All in all, we'll give Bratt Décor thumbs up for style—but you're going to pay for it. **Rating: B**

C&T International This importer now sells their cribs under the name Sorelle. See their review later in this section.

Rug Burn: How to save on nursery rug prices

Yes, it's always exciting to get that new Pottery Barn Kids catalog in the mail here at the home office in Boulder, CO. Among our favorites are those oh-so-cute rugs Pottery Barn finds to match their collections. But the prices? Whoa! $300 for a puny 5′ 8′ rug! $600 for an 8′ by 10′ design! Time to take out a second mortgage on the house. We figured there had to be a much less expensive alternative out there to the PBK options. To the rescue, we found *Fun Rugs* by General Industries (www.funrugs.com; 800-557-7060). This giant kids' rug maker has literally hundreds of options to choose from in a variety of sizes. Fun Rugs makes matching rugs for such well-known bedding lines as California Kids and Olive Kids. Now, their web site lets you see their entire collection, but you can't order direct from Fun Rugs. Instead, go to one of their dealers like *American Blind & Wallpaper* (www.DecorateToday.com), *RugsUSA* (www.RugsUSA.com) and *NetKidsWear* (www.netkidswear.com—click on rugs then "Fun Time"). All of those web sites sell Fun Rugs at prices that are significantly below similar rugs at PBK. Example: a 5′ by 8′ log cabin quilt design rug is $179 on DecorateToday.com; PBK's price is $300 for a similar size rug. We found most of those web sites sell rugs for 40% less than PBK or posh specialty stores.

Certifications:
Do they really matter?

As you shop for cribs and other products for your baby, you'll no doubt run into "JPMA-Certified" products sporting a special seal. But who is the JPMA and what does its certification mean?

The Juvenile Products Manufacturers Association (JPMA) is a group of over 400 companies that make juvenile products, both in the United States and Canada. Twenty years ago, the group started a testing program to help weed out unsafe products. Instead of turning this into a propaganda effort, they actually enlisted the support of the Consumer Products Safety Commission and the American Society of Testing and Materials to develop standards for products in several categories: carriages/strollers, cribs, play yards, high chairs, safety gates, portable hook-on chairs, and walkers (which we think are dangerous, but more on this later).

Manufacturers must have their product tested in an independent testing lab and, if it passes, they can use the JPMA seal. To the group's credit, the program has been so successful that the JPMA seal carries a good deal of credibility with many parents we interviewed. But does it really mean a product is safe? Well, yes and no.

First, as with any product, you must carefully follow instructions for assembly and use. Second, realize the testing program and standards are voluntary. Since certification can cost $10,000 or more, some smaller manufacturers claim they can't afford to test their products.

Furthermore, many Canadian and European manufacturers do not certify their products through the JPMA. They claim that safety standards in Canada and Europe are already more strict than the U.S. or JPMA's rules, so they believe the certification process is unnecessary. Hence, you're more likely to see the JPMA seal on domestically made cribs from brands like Simmons.

One important point to remember: ALL cribs sold in the U.S. must meet government safety standards. Yes, the JPMA certification rules for cribs are slightly stricter than the government's rules, but the difference is negligible. And most of the JPMA's standards for other products (like high chairs, strollers, etc.) are merely labeling requirements. For more info on the JPMA program or to get a list of certified products, you can call (856) 439-0500 or check out their web site at www.jpma.org. A safety brochure (in both English and Spanish) is available online.

cribs

Canalli *PO BOX 197, Pine Brook, NJ 07058, Call (973) 247-7222 for a dealer near you. Web: www.canallifurniture.com* This small imported line is sold in just a handful of stores in New Jersey and New York, most notably the Crib & Teen City chain (www.crib-teencity.com). And that's not by accident—Canalli's owner (Ed Kloss) is the son of the owner of Crib & Teen City. Canalli was started in 1993 to give Crib & Teen City the ability to import top quality Italian cribs direct from Italy, bypassing the mark-up they'd have to pay to Sorelle or Bonavita. All Canalli cribs are made by Golden Baby in Italy, the same manufacturer that sells to Sorelle. As a result, the quality is excellent—these cribs are double bolted for stability, under crib drawers are reinforced and drop sides feature the same hidden hardware/knee push rail releases you find in Child Craft's Legacy line. Prices are fantastic—$299 to $479, about 30% less than you'd pay for similar styles from other comparable brands. A sample: Bellini sells the "Annie" crib with its unique curved headboard for $700. The same style imported by Canalli goes for $450. While Canalli imports all their cribs from Italy, their case goods are made in New Jersey. Canalli has patterned itself after Rumble Tuff (reviewed later in this chapter) for their case goods—they use solid wood construction (no MDF or particle board), dovetail joints and European glide tracks. Again, prices for case goods are excellent—$399 to $549 for combo units. So, what's the downside to Canalli? Well, you have to live in or near New York to find any Canalli dealers. Yes, they have a handful of dealers in places like Florida, but you can't find Canalli west of the Mississippi as of this writing. Their web site is a joke, with little info and poor pictures of their product. If a crib is not in stock at their NJ warehouse, you'll have to cool your heals for 12 weeks while it ships from Italy. Canalli's selection is also limited—just four convertible cribs and five regular models. Finally, we are a bit nervous about Canalli's customer service. While they offer a lifetime warranty, the message on Canalli's voice mail says their corporate mailbox is only checked once every 15 *days*! Wow, that's quick customer service. One reader tip on this line: be sure to check Canalli prices at other dealers besides Crib & Teen City; one parent found other stores can be more aggressive on prices for Canalli during sales. Bottom line: the quality for their cribs and case goods is excellent and the prices are a great value—if you can find them! ***Rating: A***

Cara Mia *146 Needham St #6, Lindsay, Ontario Canada K9V 4Z6 Call (877) 728-0342 or (705) 328-0342 for a dealer near you. Web: www.CaraMiaFurniture.com.* These affordable cribs (most are $249 to $450, although one entry-level style is only $150) are sold in specialty stores and touted as "European crafted." This apparently has a better ring than "Made in Slovenia in the former Yugoslavia." Nonetheless, we were impressed with the quality and features of these cribs. No, there are not many styles to choose from (nine at last glance), but there is a nice mix of both convertible cribs and styles with under crib drawers. Among their best models is "Tammy," a knock-off of Child Craft's Millennium convertible crib with stationary side rail. Cara Mia's price: $450, about a $100 less than Child Craft. Other Cara Mia cribs feature hidden hardware and knee push rail releases (although a few styles on their web site still had the exposed hardware). Delivery is 6-8 weeks on average, which is rather zippy in this industry. As for the wood, most styles are solid beech with a selection of nice finishes such as cognac, pecan and cherry. Optional under crib drawers add another $50 or so to most styles (although Cara Mia's newer styles now include the drawer). How about the quality? The cribs are excellent; the case goods are another story—Cara Mia's dressers are made with particleboard and feature very plain styling at too-high prices. Stick with the cribs and get a matching dresser from another vendor. FYI: Cara Mia also makes cribs sold under the names Mother Hubbard's Cupboard and Nini Scott. These are the same as Cara Mia's offerings, just a different brand name. ***Rating: B+***

E-Mail from The Real World
Layaway Pitfalls

A mom in Kentucky writes:
"I put a crib and dresser on layaway at a baby store, only to discover the items were later discontinued! The store forced me to buy used floor samples; if not, I would have lost my deposit!"

Layaway sounds like a great idea—you can freeze the price of an item and make small payments each month until it's paid off. Yet, there are many ways that layaway can turn into a consumer nightmare: products can be discontinued, items disappear out of stock rooms and more. Worse yet, some dishonest shop owners (realizing they have a big chunk of your money) may coerce you into completing the deal. If you don't take this substitute product or trashed sample, you can kiss your money good bye. As a result, we do not recommend using layaway. Besides, there's been so little inflation in recent years that "holding a price" doesn't mean much these days. If you feel compelled to use layaway, only do it for a short term (no more than 30 or 60 days). And check refund policies—some stores let you back out of a layaway for a minimal fee (say $5).

Child Craft *PO Box 444, Salem, IN 47167. Call (812) 883-3111 for a dealer near you. Web: www.childcraftind.com* Founded in Salem, Indiana in 1910, Child Craft is one of the largest domestic producers of cribs in the U.S. As such, you'll see them everywhere: from chain stores like Babies R Us and Baby Depot to catalogs like JCPenney. For specialty stores, Child Craft markets a separate line of cribs and juvenile furniture called "Legacy" (reviewed separately later in this section). Styling at Child Craft runs the gamut, from traditional low-price models to elaborate canopy and convertible cribs. Child Craft's web site gives you a good overview of several collections. A best buy: style 10171, a simple maple crib with a single-drop side that sells for $200 to $250 or so. Other cribs from this company sell for $250 to $500, depending on the finish. All Child Craft's cribs are made of hard woods like maple and oak and the company has been aggressive in rolling out convertible models recently. The quality is also very good; in recent years, Child Craft has abandoned the noisy foot bar rail release for much quieter knee-push releases with hidden hardware. That eliminated one of our biggest beefs with Child Craft. Among the hottest-selling models at Child Craft is their Crib N' Double bed (36101, which also goes under the name Millennium and is available in several styles/finishes). This crib is a winner at $550—it features a stationary side rail and converts to an attractive double bed without any expensive conversion kits (you just buy standard bed rails). This is probably the best looking convertible crib on the market today; a pine version of the crib runs just $400 at Babies R Us! A couple final notes on Child Craft: don't forget about Child Craft's outlet stores in Indiana, Kentucky and Massachusetts (see the outlet section earlier in this chapter for details). And kudos to Child Craft for their commitment to safety—CC now tests all their case goods with 50-pound weights hanging from a top drawer. That would prevent a climbing toddler from tipping a dresser over. Child Craft even adds weight to the bottom of their case goods to make sure they pass this 50 pounds test. And all CC dressers include drawer glides that have safety bumps to prevent them from coming all the way out plus a tip restraint that attaches to the wall to prevent tipping. ***Rating: A***

Childesigns *Made by Generation 2 Worldwide 113 Anderson Court Suite 1, Dothan, AL 36301. For a dealer near you, call (800) 736-1140 or (334) 792-1144. Web: www.childesigns.com* This company used to be known as Nelson, a low-end crib maker that was always an also-ran in the crib market. Generation 2 (the parent company) has been trying to jump-start their sales in recent years with a combination of fresher styling and hardware improvements. Until recently, the company had two different brand names: Childesigns and Next Generation (each is assembled in Alabama from parts made in Asia). In the last year, the company decided to stick with one brand name (Childesigns—although sometimes you see these cribs marketed as Generation 2) and expand its offerings. In addition to their basic designs, which sell for $150 to $250, Childesigns is debuting a $300 crib with a more sculptured design. The company even has a $200 model with an under crib drawer in solid wood, which is a good deal. All Childesigns cribs have knee-push rail release systems (although you might still see double trigger rail releases on a few older models—confirm the type of release before you buy this brand). The rail release rides in exposed plastic tracks. The company calls this system "Quiet-Glide" and claims the crib rail can be raised or lowered without any squeaks or clanks. Well, we tried it out and though it was quieter than other competitors, it's still not whisper-quiet. On a positive note, all the cribs feature dual-wheeled casters and metal spring mattress supports. The more expensive models have a few more doo-dads (teething rail guards on both sides, a three versus two position mattress height adjustment, etc.). We also like the fact the cribs come pre-assembled. And Childesigns has greatly expanded its case good offerings in the past year, adding solid pine and ramin dressers sold at Wal-Mart and Target.

Want an even bigger bargain on a Childesigns crib? Check out their online factory discount outlet (http://search.childesigns.com/garage/). Readers have found great deals on these factory seconds, including cribs for just $100 to $125 including shipping! Hello! Here's the perfect crib bargain for twins or grandma's house—yes, these cribs meet all the safety standards, they just have some minor cosmetic damage. Even if you pay full-price for a Childesigns model (they are just $130 at Wal-Mart), they are still deals.

So, we'll give Childesign/Generation 2 a thumbs-up: this furniture won't win any awards for cutting-edge design, but they are well constructed and represent a decent value. ***Rating: B+***

Concord *For a dealer in Canada, call (905) 738-0084.* This Canadian crib maker is on our short list of not recommended manufacturers. Why? A local Pittsburgh TV station reported in 2002 that a mother there discovered the slats on her Concord crib fell apart. "As she was pulling the gate to the crib up, it fell apart with all the slats coming completely out of the side rails," the report said. This points up a problem with some cribs that the CPSC has moved to correct—in the last eleven years, there have been 138 instances of crib slat disengagements that have resulted in the deaths of 12 children. To fix the problem, the U.S. government enacted new standards in the late 1990's to make sure the slats don't come out. The Pittsburgh mom bought her crib in 2000 (after the new rules were in effect), yet she still had a problem crib. Making matters worse, when contacted by the parent, Concord refused to help. Instead, they referred her back to the USA Baby store she bought the crib from. Fortunately, USA baby offered to repair the crib and—after the TV station got involved—refund the consumer the price she paid for the crib. Shame on Concord for telling the consumer, in effect, "tough luck." We contacted Concord about this situation and, while they didn't deny the basic facts involved in the case, they claimed the crib was much older than the consumer claimed. FYI: Concord is no longer sold in the US, just Canada—but their cribs still pop up on eBay from time to time. Yes, they are cheap ($169 to $229), but we say pass. ***Rating: D***

Why do all Italian cribs look alike?

Walk into a baby store to look at Italian cribs and you'll be hard pressed to tell any difference between the Italian brands. Heck, there is rarely any difference, except for the finish color. Why is that? First, understand that most Italian cribs are made by just a handful of manufacturers. All these crib makers are located in the same region of Italy; in fact, they are clustered right across the street from one another. (Memo to any IRS auditor reading this book: at some point, we will have to take a business trip to Italy to confirm this fact.) Second, while manufacturers like Pali and Bonavita assemble their own cribs, they buy many component pieces (like side rails) from the same supplier. That's why the rail releases on Italian cribs are nearly identical. Finally, consider the wood used to make the cribs—nearly all the manufacturers use 100% Italian beech. (No wonder things look so alike!).

Where this gets confusing is the brand names. Most Italian manufacturers (with the exception of Pali) do not directly export to the U.S. and Canada. They sell their wares to importers like Bellini, Sorelle, Mondi and Bonavita. Then those importers sometimes slap different model names on cribs sold in discount stores or specialty stores (Bonavita's cribs in Babies R Us go under the name Babi Italia; in specialty stores, the same importer has a high-price line called Issi).

That's not to say there are no differences between the Italian crib brands. Often, the importers have different track records for delivery and customer service (we'll note who is better in this chapter). And some importers have been more aggressive than others to target the entry-level price points at stores like Babies R Us. But if you wonder why all the Italian cribs look alike, there's your answer.

Corsican Kids *2417 E. 24th St, Los Angeles, CA 90058. Call (800) 421-6247 or (323) 587-3101 for a dealer near you. Web: www. Corsican.com.* Looking for a wrought iron crib? California-based Corsican Kids specializes in iron cribs that have a vintage feel, with detailed headboard and footboard decoration. Before you fall in love with the look, however, be sure to turn over the price tag. Most Corsican Kids iron cribs sell for a whopping $1000 to $2000! Yes, you can choose from a variety of cool finishes like pewter and antique bronze but these prices are hard to swallow. And there are some downsides to wrought iron cribs: first, they are darn noisy when raising or lowering the side rail. And Corsican's drop-sides are those exposed (rod/cane) hardware foot bar releases that most of the market long abandoned (most parents find knee push easier to use). And forget about looking at Corsican's offerings on their web site—it's for dealers only. So, it's a mixed review for these guys. Yes, they are cool to look at but the practical drawbacks of wrought iron cribs (as well as the stratospheric prices) make us give this brand only an average rating. **Rating: C+**

E-MAIL FROM THE REAL WORLD
Leg got stuck in crib slats

"Yesterday, my nine month old somehow wedged his leg between two slats of the crib. I heard him scream shortly after I put him to bed for his afternoon nap and found his leg entrapped up to the thigh. I couldn't pull the slats apart and get his leg out myself, so I called 911. A police officer was able to pull the slats apart just enough so I could gently guide by son's leg back through. I took him to the doctor and he's fine, other than a bruise on his leg. Any tips on how we can avoid this in the future?"

Crib slats are required by federal law to be a certain maximum distance apart (2 5/8"). This is done to prevent babies from getting their heads trapped by the crib spindles or slats, a common problem with cribs made before 1973 when the rule was enacted. Of course, just because baby can't get a head stuck in there doesn't mean an arm or leg can't be wedged between the slats. Unfortunately, we don't have any solution for this problem. Most babies who do this are mobile and, hence, parents can't put bumpers in their cribs (not that that would solve the problem, however, as some babies can just push their legs through the slats, bumper or no). Fortunately, this type of problem is quite rare. And even though it is scary for both parent and child, the greater good is served by the slat rule that prevents head entrapments.

Cosco *2525 State St., Columbus, IN 47201. Call (800) 544-1108 or (812) 372-0141 for a dealer near you. Web: www.coscoinc.com.* Cosco's claim to fame is their very inexpensive metal cribs (one in four cribs sold in the U.S. is a metal crib). Cosco is probably the biggest crib maker in North America, shipping 250,000 cribs each year. One big reason: price. Most Cosco metal cribs sell for $100 to $150, among the lowest prices for a full size crib on the market. But what do you get for that money? Not much, as it turns out. Like most metal cribs, the mattress doesn't rest on a set of springs but instead sits on a series of straps or metal bars, which is inadequate in our opinion. The welding of the joints looks sloppy, and the mattress height adjustment mechanism consists of a metal bar that screws into the side post. The problem? Those screws can strip and the mattress could conceivably disconnect from the frame. Although unrelated to that potential problem, Cosco has suffered three major recalls in recent years. In 1995, the company recalled 190,000 metal cribs when it discovered the spindles of the side rails could loosen and separate from the side rail, creating an entrapment hazard. Then in 1997, Cosco warned consumers to check more than 390,000 cribs manufactured since 1995 that "may have been miss assembled with the mattress platform being used as a side rail." The CPSC reported "Cosco has received more than 47 reports of cribs being miss-assembled with the mattress platform being used as a side rail, including 27 reports of babies becoming entrapped, resulting in one death." Apparently, the crib's confusing assembly instructions led to the mistake. Yet another child death prompted a third recall by Cosco in 1997—this time, the CPSC found that mattresses Cosco sold with their metal cribs could compress and be pushed between the bars on the crib's platform. Cosco received 12 complaints of mattress compression (where babies slipped between the crib's platform and became entrapped) including one 11-month-old baby boy who died after becoming entrapped. As a result of all these safety problems, we cannot recommend Cosco's metal cribs. (We should note Cosco also makes wood cribs under the names Bridgeport, Dorel and Jardine; see Jardine's review later in this section for details). **Rating: D**

DaVinci *See Million Dollar Baby later in this chapter for contact info.* Da Vinci is the online name for Million Dollar Baby (MDB), reviewed later in this section. We guess Million Dollar Baby uses the different name for its cribs sold online so as to not offend its regular retail stores. Basically, Da Vinci cribs are just a re-packaged version of MDB's cribs—same styles, same finishes. Hence, like MDB, you'll see two price groups of Da Vinci. The lower price ones (under $200) are imported from Asia and feature foot bar releases, and simple styling. The upper-end Da Vinci cribs are similar to MDB's "Reflections" line. Styles like the Leonardo are $400 to $500 and feature knee push rail releases. And despite the Italian sounding name, most of these cribs are NOT made in Italy (a few models are made of Italian parts, but final assembly is in the U.S.). As for quality, we give Da Vinci the same rating as MDB since they are basically the same thing. You can find Da Vinci cribs online at BabyUniverse.com. *Rating: B*

Delta 175 Liberty Ave., Brooklyn, NY 11212. Call (718) 385-1000 for a dealer near you. Web: www.deltaenterprise.com. Imported from Indonesia, Delta (also known as Delta Luv and Babies Love by Delta) is one of the few cribs you can find sold online. We saw Delta cribs on several sites, including Baby Age and Burlington Coat Factory (see Chapter 11 for review of these sites). The prices are sure hard to beat—most Delta cribs sell for $130 to $240. Among the hottest sellers is their convertible crib, the 4-in-1 Crib Bed ($270 at Sears.com and Burlington's coat.com). This single-drop side crib converts to a full size bed with headboard and footboard. No, it is not as nice looking as Child Craft's convertible crib, but, hey, it is half the price. So, what is Delta's quality like? Well, our biggest beef with Delta is the wood platform that form's the crib's base. Delta claims its wood platform is better for baby's back than the more common spring platform you see in other brands, but we remain unconvinced. On the plus side, Delta has eliminated the double trigger rail releases on some of its models; now all cribs will have knee push releases (although the hardware is still exposed). Also good: all Delta cribs feature hardwood construction, heavy-duty furniture-style casters and easy assembly (all models ship pre-assembled from the factory and require no tools to set up). Yes, the styling of Delta is very plain (especially the dressers) but they have introduced a few models with carved headboards that add a bit more pizzazz to the line. Also new: a Baby Snoopy line of furniture (cribs, bassinets) and strollers. Basically, the Snoopy line is the same as the Delta furniture, just with a picture of, well, Snoopy on the headboard. If you decide to go with a Delta crib, leave plenty of time however. The president of one major baby product web site told us Delta is perennially back-ordered, as the company struggles to keep up with production. *Rating: B-*

Domusindo Web: www.domusindo.com Imported from Indonesia exclusively for JCPenney's catalog, Domusindo cribs are affordably priced ($200 to $300) and feature decent quality, features and styling. The downside? Most Domusindo cribs have wood mattress platforms (not springs) and exposed hardware. Don't expect any extras like under crib drawers, either. That's a bit behind similarly priced competitors at Babies R Us. As for safety, we are impressed with Penney's track record and quality assurance programs. Penney's actually sends inspectors into their supplier's plants to make sure things are being assembled correctly and rigorously makes sure its cribs meet safety standards. Hence, while we probably would be a bit nervous about other cribs imported from Indonesia, Penney's Domusindo's cribs are worthy of recommendation. *Rating: A-*

Dorel Cosco's wood cribs are sold under this name, Bridgeport and Jardine; see the Jardine review later in this chapter for details.

EA Kids. See Ethan Allen below

EG Furniture *381 Principale, La Perade, Quebec, Canada G0X 2J) Call 418-325-2050 or (888) 422-5534. Web: www.egfurniture.com.* EG is part of the Canadian invasion into juvenile that started in the late 1990's. In fact, until 1999, EG didn't even make cribs (although they've been doing youth furniture since 1988). Despite the late start, we have been impressed with this Quebec-based furniture maker's quality—their 13 collections feature solid birch wood construction and an impressive list of customizations. You can choose from more than 30 colors and finishes and each of their eight collections includes a wide variety of accessories like matching toy boxes, twin beds, armoires and more. For the cribs, all the hardware is hidden and EG has one of the quietest releases on the

E-MAIL FROM THE REAL WORLD
Tricks from the sale floor

Reader Jennifer Gottlieb shared an interesting story about a trick some baby stores use to convince parents to buy more expensive cribs:

"Here's an interesting tidbit we heard recently and wanted to pass along: A guy in our childbirth education class works at a baby furniture store, and let us in on a marketing ploy. Evidently, some stores purposely loosen the screws on the floor models of less expensive cribs so that when you're checking them out they seem more rickety than their pricey counterparts. This makes most nervous parents naturally turn to the cribs that appear to be more solid—not to mention expensive!"

market. Delivery is 4-8 weeks, which is quite a bit quicker than other Canadian furniture makers. What's the quality like? A reader who ordered five pieces of furniture from EG said it was good, although she was disappointed that the backing of some items was MDF. Yet, she felt it was still a good deal for the price—$2200 was much less than she would have paid Ragazzi for similar, made-in-Canada furniture. FYI: Several readers told us they saved big on EG Furniture by ordering from a Winnipeg-based web site, E-ChildrenOnline.com (www.e-childrenonline.com)—over $800 in savings in one case. Customer service and delivery from that web site are excellent. **Rating: B+**

Ethan Allen (888) EAHELP1; web: ethanallen.com. You gotta love the EA Kids catalog, which is available in any of Ethan Allen's 300 stores nationwide, but the prices! Whoa! A basic crib, $700 to $800. An armoire, $1350. A three-drawer dresser, $780. Even when EA puts this stuff on "sale," the prices are hard to swallow if you haven't won the lottery recently. That said, readers who've bought Ethan Allen furniture for their nursery sing their praises for quality and durability. "We found their furniture isn't much more expensive than Morigeau or Ragazzi, but is much better quality. I'm confident the EA furniture we purchased will last for a very long time." Point well taken. So we'll give this line a "B" rating—great quality, style and features—if you can afford it. **Rating: B**

Evenflo For a dealer near you, call (800) 233-5921. Web: www.evenflo.com. Evenflo just sells a few crib models, which they inherited from their merger with Gerry a few years back. A basic Jenny Lind style crib is available in white or oak and runs about $120 to $140 at places like Sears (you can see them online at Sears.com). We weren't impressed with the quality of the crib, which had a foot bar release with exposed hardware. In the last year, Evenflo has introduced a couple of Jenny Lind models with double-trigger releases—again, not very impressive. Finally, we should note that Evenflo has withdrawn from the foldaway mini-crib market after recalling 364,000 cribs in 2003 for a safety defect. We recommended these fold-away cribs in a previous edition of our book, so if you have one sitting in your home or grandma's house, you need to call (800) 582-9359 (web: www.portable-woodcrib.com) for an upgrade kit that will fix the problem. **Rating: C**

Fisher Price This line of cribs is made by Stork Craft, reviewed later in this chapter.

cribs

Co-sleepers

If you can't borrow a bassinet or cradle from a friend, there is an alternative: the *Arm's Reach Bedside Co-Sleeper* (call 800-954-9353 for a dealer near you; web: www.armsreach.com). This innovative product is essentially a bassinet that attaches to your bed under the mattress and is secured in place. The three-sided co-sleeper is open on the bed side. The result: you can easily reach the baby for feedings without ever leaving your bed, a boon for all mothers but especially those recuperating from Caesarean births. Best of all, the unit converts to a regular playpen when baby gets older (and goes into a regular crib). You can also use the co-sleeper as a diaper changing station. The cost for the basic model? $160 to $190, which is a bit pricey, considering a plain playpen with bassinet feature is about $100 to $120. But the unique design and safety aspect of the Arm's Reach product may make it worth the extra cash layout.

In recent years, Arm's Reach has rolled out several variations on its co-sleeper. The "Universal" model ($190 to $225) is re-designed to fit futons, platform and European beds. The removable sidebar and new liner can also be positioned at the top level of the play yard to create a four-sided freestanding bassinet. New in the past year is the "Mini-Bassinet Co-Sleeper," which does not convert to a playpen and sells for around $140 to $160.

If you like the functionality of a co-sleeper but not the look, there is good news. Arm's Reach web site (see above; click on accessories) now sells seven floor-length liners in various colors. Another cool idea: the company also sells a "Catch All" cover that converts a co-sleeper into a toy storage bin and playground. Finally, there is a wood version of the Arm's Reach we still see sold online for $280 or so.

Of course, Arm's Reach isn't the only co-sleeper on the market. The *Baby Bunk* (www.BabyBunk.com) is a wood co-sleeper than either be purchased for $200 to $300 or rented by the month. That's right, you can rent one for just $30 a month (with a $50 refundable deposit) in case you want to see if this is for you. That might be the best bargain of all when it comes to co-sleepers! Baby Bunk also sells a series of accessories for their co-sleepers, including sheets, mattresses, bumpers and more.

While we like the co-sleeper, let us point out that we are not endorsing the concept of co-sleeping in general. Co-sleeping (where baby sleeps with you in your bed) is a controversial topic that's beyond the scope of this book. Consult your doctor and other parenting books for more pros/cons on co-sleeping.

Forever Mine *Web: www.ForeverMine.com.* Canadian furniture manufacturers have invaded the U.S. in recent years, taking advantage of the favorable exchange rate to compete against other import competition. While most crib makers have gone the retail route, one (Forever Mine) decided to go direct, using the Internet. Since you are buying "factory direct," there is big savings. How big? How about a convertible crib (the All American) that converts into a double bed for just $249. Yes, you typically see these styles for $400 to $500 in stores. Forever Mine also sells three and four drawer chests ($249), nightstands, bookcases and other accessories. So, how's the quality? Readers—who had to take a big leap ordering these items sight unseen—say they are generally very happy with Forever Mine. "Beautiful finish," said one reader and others said their crib was "very sturdy and excellent quality." Delivery takes 5-6 weeks and the company is reliable with their shipments. The downsides? Well, first there aren't many colors/finishes to choose from. Some cribs have exposed hardware and one style even has a fold-down/swing-date rail, which as you know we do not recommend for safety reasons. Stick with the standard drop sides like on the All American crib. Finally, the assembly instructions could be clearer, based on feedback from parents who've actually assembled their cribs. Forever Mine has an excellent web site with detailed information, including a shipping cost chart (a crib runs $60 to $75 to ship; add another $50 to $100 for a dresser). Best of all, the customer service at Forever Mine is excellent—they answer questions over the phone and nail their delivery dates on the nose. We've been impressed with the feedback on Forever Mine and recommend them. *Rating: A-*

Generation 2 This is the parent company of Childesigns, reviewed earlier in this section.

Golden Baby This crib is imported from Italy by C&T International. This company is reviewed under their main trade name, Sorelle, later in this section. Golden Baby cribs are sold at Babies R Us. Basically, there are very few differences between Golden Baby and Sorelle cribs.

Graco *Rt. 23, Main St., Elverson, PA 19520. For a dealer near you, call (800) 345-4109, (610) 286-5951. Web: www.gracobaby.com.* Graco has entered the metal crib market in recent years with the "4-in-one sleep system" for $199. This single-drop side crib (made in China) has a knee push release and converts first into a toddler bed, day bed and finally a twin bed. While there is no conversion kit, the twin bed version only has a headboard (no foot board like other competing models). Although we promised to keep our opinions on crib styling to a minimum in this book, we do have to comment on how Graco's cribs look. They are god awful ugly. The wood trim accent on these crib's head and footboards gives these models all the panache of the Brady Bunch's wood paneled station wagon. We realize this is Graco's first stab at this market, but we expected a bit more from such a major player as Graco. While we give Graco bonus points for value, the styling of these cribs leaves much to be desired. ***Rating: D+***

Issi This is Bonavita's upper-end line, reviewed earlier in this chapter.

Jardine (*See Cosco's review for contact information and web site*). Jardine is Cosco's latest attempt to crack the wood crib market. After a false start with the Bridgeport line, Cosco has had more success with Jardine. This line of cribs is sold only in Babies R Us and is made in China. A typical offering: a $240 cherry-stained crib with knee-push rail release (but exposed hardware) and spring mattress support. Other Jardine cribs ranged from $200 to $320, all good values. Some styles have under-crib drawers but we noted that others lacked casters. While we liked the Jardine cribs, we will give a lower rating for their matching dressers and changing tables. We've received several complaints about Jardine's case goods, including poor construction, sloppy finish work and more. Jardine's glider-rockers are great deals ($140 to $240) but again, inferior in quality to Dutailier and Shermag. As for their safety record, Jardine has been fine but parent Cosco has suffered a black eye from safety recalls for their metal cribs. No wonder the "Cosco" name isn't anywhere to be found on Jardine's cribs. ***Rating (cribs): B+. Rating (dressers, glider rockers): C-.***

Jenny Lind This is a generic crib style, not a brand name. We explain what a Jenny Lind crib is in the box below.

Kinderkraft *Web: www.Kinderkraft.com* Manufactured in their own plant in Central America, Kindercraft sells 2000 cribs a month through Babies R Us (the only chain where they are available). A typical offering: a $200 Vermont Crib'n Toddler crib. These are no-frills cribs—the Vermont has no under crib drawer and is a single-drop side. Yes, they do have knee-push rail releases but the hardware is exposed and the mattress support is wood slats (we prefer springs). That said, we think they are a pretty good deal for $200— no, the Central American pine isn't as fancy as the maple, birch or beech you see with other brands . . . but you're paying half the price of those cribs. Assembly is easy and quick. We also think Kinderkraft has a good safety track record—all their styles are JPMA certified. They have not had a recall in their 20-year history, all their drop rails are steel pinned and glued for strength and durability and their dressers are counterweighted in the rear to avoid tipping. So, we'll raise Kinderkraft's rating this year to a B. Why not higher? Well, Kinderkraft still sells a crib model with attached dresser (Crib'n Youth or Crib'n Junior, $400), which as you know we are not big fans of (see earlier discussion). And we still think Kinderkraft's dressers pale in comparison to competitor's options, quality and style-wise. Stick with the cribs. *Rating: B*

La Jobi This is the parent company for Babi Italia and Bonavita. See their review earlier in this section.

Legacy *See Child Craft for contact and web info.* How do you serve two masters? That's the dilemma faced by crib makers today, who have to keep both independent specialty stores and the giant chains happy. Small baby shops don't want to carry the same crib brands as the chains, who can often under-cut them on price. The solution? Come out with a separate "high end" label that's just sold to specialty stores (no chains allowed). That was the idea behind Legacy, launched by mass-market crib maker Child Craft in 1997. Yet it would be nice if these high-end cribs were actually better (or at least) different from the more pedestrian Child Craft cribs. Perhaps it's just the cynics in us, but these cribs didn't look much different from the stuff Child Craft sells to Babies R Us. Oh, yeah, there are some fancier finishes (cognac or pear wood, anyone?) and a few items that sport that hip Shaker look. But that doesn't justify higher prices Legacy charges ($500 to $750). Yes, there are a few small differences between Legacy and Child Craft. Most Legacy cribs are made in the U.S., although a few models are imported from Croatia (Child Craft cribs are made from parts made in Asia and assembled in the U.S.). Unlike Child Craft, most Legacy models have an under crib drawer . . . but this is made of MDF, not solid wood. (Some of Legacy's upper-end competitors have solid wood drawers). As for the rail releases, both Legacy and Child Craft now use knee-push mechanisms with hidden hardware. So, bottom line, the big difference is between Legacy and Child Craft is styling. Whether you think Legacy is worth the 30% price premium over Child Craft is up to you. Yet, if you don't need the designer colors or look, save your money and buy a Child Craft. It's basically the same thing. *Rating: B*

Li'l Angels. *Web: www.lilangelsstore.com* This eBay seller (id: lababy2) of cribs also has a web page at www.lilangelsstore.com. They describe themselves as a "Canadian-based manufacturer and distributor" of baby furniture. When pressed about who manufac-

Bait and Switch with Floor Samples

Readers of our first book, *Bridal Bargains*, may remember all the amazing scams and rip-offs when it came to buying a wedding gown. As you read this book, you'll notice many of the shenanigans that happen in the wedding biz are thankfully absent in the world of baby products.

Of course, that doesn't mean there aren't ANY scams or rip-offs to be concerned about. One problem that does crop up from time to time is the old "bait and switch scheme," this time as it applies to floor samples of baby furniture. A reader in New York sent us this story about a bait and switch they encountered at a local store:

"We ordered our baby furniture in August for November delivery. When it all arrived, the crib was damaged and both the side rails were missing paint. We were suspicious they were trying to pass off floor samples on us—when we opened the drawer on a dresser, we found a tag from the store. The armoire's top was damaged and loose and the entire piece was dirty. There was even a sticky substance on the door front where a price tag once was placed. Another sign: both the changing table and ottoman were not in their original boxes when they were delivered."

The store's manager was adamant that the items were new, not floor samples. Then the consumer noticed the specific pieces they ordered were no longer on the sales floor. After some more haggling, the store agreed to re-order the furniture from the factory.

Why would a store do this? In a down economy, a store's inventory may balloon as sales stall. The temptation among some baby store owners may be to try to pass off used floor samples as new goods, in order to clear out a backlog at the warehouse. Of course, you'd expect them to be smarter about this than the above story—the least they could have done was clean/repair items and make sure the price tags were removed! But some merchants' dishonesty is only matched by their stupidity.

Obviously, when you buy brand new, special-order furniture that is exactly what you deserve to get. While this is not an everyday occurrence in the baby biz, you should take steps to protect yourself. First, pay for any deposits on furniture with a credit card—if the merchant fails to deliver what they promise, you can dispute the charge. Second, carefully inspect any order when it arrives. Items should arrive in their original boxes and be free of dirt/damage or other telltale signs of age. If you suspect a special-order item is really a used sample, don't accept delivery and immediately contact the store.

tures their cribs, a reader said a representative of Li'l Angels told her their cribs are made by Concord (reviewed earlier). We asked that question directly to Li'l Angels via email and the phone and we got a different answer—they told us they make their own cribs and dressers. Yet Concord later did confirm to us over the phone that Li'l Angels is a dealer for their cribs. So, we're not sure what to believe with these guys. Yes, the prices are low ($199 to $249 for cribs; $149 to $259) and their feedback on eBay is mostly positive . . . but we can't give them a recommendation until we get some straight answers. **Rating: C**

Little Miss Liberty *3040 N. Avon St., Burbank, CA 91504. Call (800) RND-CRIB or (310) 281-5400 for a dealer near you. Web: www.crib.com.* Little Miss Liberty has two claims to fame. First, they are one of the very few companies that make round cribs. Second, they are the only crib maker owned by the wife of the cartoon voice of Shaggy (of Scooby Doo fame). Yes, actress Jean Kasem (who played Loretta Tortelli on "Cheers" and is the wife of Casey "America's Top 40" Kasem) is the driving force behind this company, which took over the country's largest round crib maker a few years ago. The company plays up its Hollywood connection to the hilt, with Jean dropping celebrity client names (Melanie Griffith, Roseanne) on her many talk show appearances to plug the cribs.

So, what's so special about a round crib, except for its price tag? The company points out that the first cribs commissioned for European royalty were round or oval. In press materials, Jean says "those who want the best cribs favor the rounded shape because they don't restrict the child's view. They can focus on the whole world and they are the center of it." Uh huh.

Well, we can say one thing about Little Miss Liberty—that unrestricted worldview ain't cheap. A Little Miss Liberty wood round crib will set you back a cool $1000—and that doesn't include the bedding. Matching bedding sets can add another $500 to $1500 to the price.

Not expensive enough for you? How about a brass or chrome round crib? The "Biker Baby Crib" in chrome is just $2400. Brass will set you back $4400. New this year is the "Crystal Crib" with sterling silver mylar rope spindles for $4800. Of course, you should buy your baby a cradle for those first few weeks. To help with this, Little Miss Liberty offers a "Swan Cradle," a hand carved replica of a 16th century design, finished in cherry and gold leaf. Your bargain price today, just $3800.

It's apparent the company realized those prices were a wee bit high for those of us non-Hollywood types and has since introduced a low-price crib model (and bedding). The "Dura Crib" is made from molded "poly-plastic" components (the regular round cribs are made of wood) and features a canopy. The original price: $570, but we've seen it recently on close-out on Little Miss Liberty's web site for $200.

So, is it worth it? Well, we don't buy Little Miss Liberty's argument that round cribs are safer than rectangular ones. We monitor the federal government's reports on injuries caused by juvenile products and see no evidence that rectangular cribs are a problem. So, if you're going to go for a round crib, do it because you like the crib's aesthetics. And save up those pennies—when you add in the bedding, this investment can soar above $1000 quickly. ***Rating: B***

MIBB This Italian crib maker withdrew from the US market in 2002.

Million Dollar Baby *855 Washington Blvd., Montebello, CA 90640. Call (877) 600-6688 or (323) 728-9988 for a dealer near you. Web: www.milliondollarbaby.com* Hong Kong entrepreneur Daniel Fong started Million Dollar Baby (MDB) in 1990 and quickly established it as a successful maker of low-price cribs. The Los Angeles-based company is mostly known for its $99 "Jenny Lind" cribs sold in discount stores. These cribs never really impressed us quality-wise; we spoke with one baby store manager who claimed they've received returns on low-end Million Dollar Baby cribs who's spindles have broken. In recent years, Million Dollar Baby has greatly expanded their offerings to include more upper-end cribs. To compete on the 'net, they launched the "Da Vinci" line (see review earlier in this section) that is sold online. Da Vinci is just a version of Million Dollar Baby cribs that are re-packaged to be sold online—same styles, just a different brand name so as not to offend MDB's retailers. It's quite hard to assign a rating for this brand—their offerings are all over the board. On one hand are older style cribs like the Notre Dame that still feature foot-bar rail releases and exposed hardware. Newer models feature knee-push releases, although the hardware is still exposed. And in the past year, MDB has released their knock-off of the Child Craft Millennium crib with stationary side rail called the "Emily." This crib converts to a full size bed. While we're glad MDB finally offers a convertible crib option (since many parents look for that, despite our opinion on the subject!), we still think this line is more of a follower than a leader in terms of features. On the plus side, Million Dollar Baby does offer crib styles (the Alpha and Jenny Lind) in an unfinished option, which is a boon for parents who want to paint/finish a crib themselves for a small savings. And it's nice that you can actually buy one of MDB's cribs online, which is a rarity. ***Rating: B***

E-MAIL FROM THE REAL WORLD
IKEA fans love ready-to-assemble furniture

A European furniture superstore with stylish furniture at down-to-earth prices, IKEA has 15 stores in the U.S., most of which are on the East and West Coast (plus Chicago and Houston). For a location near you, call 610-834-0180 or web: www.ikea.com. IKEA has a special baby/kids area called "Children's IKEA", a 5000 square foot area that showcases IKEA's nursery and kids' furniture as well as accessories. While our readers applaud IKEA's prices, they are mixed on the quality. Here's a sampling:

"We outfitted our entire nursery for just $300 at IKEA. The crib was $79, a basic dresser was $110, while the changing tabletop was $50. The beauty of Ikea is that many of the furnishings come flat-packed, ready to take home and assemble yourself—don't fret, though, each piece comes with easy-to-follow, logical instructions. Only drawback: IKEA furniture isn't for traditionalists. Most items are made of beech, wood veneer or laminate and particleboard. Despite this, they are very durable and of high quality."

"IKEA is a great place for changing tables—the model we purchased (Narvik) was $200 and very sturdy. It can be screwed into the wall so it won't tip over if baby decides to climb up the drawers. Another great feature: it has a flip-top shelf."

"We love Ikea but their $79 crib has no drop sides and the mattress height can not be adjusted, so it is a bit of a problem for short parents. Ikea does have a lovely crib with a drop side (double trigger mechanism) and adjustable height but it's priced at around $229. They have a nice selection of inexpensive dressers, though."

Another reader wasn't impressed with IKEA's quality:
"We looked at the Ikea crib, as one of your readers did, and found it substandard—plastic hardware, shaky and thin particle board construction. Hard to imagine it even lasting through one baby."

Our advice: before you make a special trip to IKEA, first pre-shop their catalog. This 39-page publication has a special section on kids' items. IKEA's web site also features children's furniture and accessories. If you browse the catalog or web site before you visit the store, you'll have a better idea of the offerings, prices and styles.

Morigeau/Lepine *3025 Washington Rd., McMurray, PA 15317. Call (800) 326-2121 or (724) 941-7475 or (970) 845-7795 for a dealer near you Web: www.morigeau.com* Based in Quebec, Canada, this family-run juvenile furniture company has been in business for over 50 years. Like other Canadian manufacturers, Morigeau/Lepine's specialty is stylish cribs and dressers that look like adult furniture. The quality is impeccable, but you're going to pay for it—cribs run $500 to $700 and a simple dresser can run $600 to $900. What do you get for those bucks? Solid wood construction (Morigeau even runs its own sawmill to process the maple and birch it uses in the furniture), drawers with dove-tailed joints and cribs with completely hidden hardware and self-lubricating nylon tracks, which makes Morigeau cribs some of the quietest on the market. Safety-wise, Morigeau's dressers have side-mounted glides with safety stops. We also liked the fact that most of Morigeau's dressers are oversized with 21" deep drawers to give you extra storage. The styling of the line is quite sophisticated—in fact, this is probably the most "adult" looking baby furniture on the market today. In the past year, Morigeau has introduced a new "value" line called the 8000 series with more affordable price points (a crib for $399; a combo hi-low dresser for $499). We should also note that Morigeau's sister line is "Lepine," a smaller collection of cribs at slightly lower prices (cribs are $450 to $660). All in all, we liked Morigeau—the prices are high, but so is the quality. Perhaps the biggest beef we've heard about Morigeau is their slow delivery; some retailers complain it can take forever to get in special order items. ***Rating: A-***

Mother Hubbard's Cupboard *Call (416) 661-8201 for a dealer near you. Web: www.mhcfurniture.com* This Canadian-based maker of dressers and case goods also sells Cara Mia cribs under their own label. See Cara Mia for a review of that brand. As for their dressers, readers praise their high-quality yet affordable prices. They feature solid wood, dove-tailed drawers with side rolling casters. A five-drawer chest is $399 to $499 while a combo hi-lo design is $599. Their finishes match most major brands of cribs and we were impressed with the company's slick web site, complete with detailed info on all their collections. ***Rating: A***

Natart *240 Rue Pratte, Princeville, Quebec, Canada G6L 4T8. Call (819) 364-2052 for a dealer near you. Web: www.natartfurniture. com* Natart—a company in desperate need of a catchier name—is one of a number of Quebec-based nursery furniture makers to come to the US market in recent years. The emphasis is on a stylish look with high quality (and often, high prices). Sample: like the look for

Pottery Barn's sleigh crib but not the $800 price tag? Natart makes a similar style called the Logan that is $700. Not much of a deal, eh? Yes, but we noticed that price included the conversion kit at a USA Baby store, while PBK wanted another $80 bucks for their conversion kit. All in all, you get the PBK look at 20% less. Other Natart cribs are less expensive, including some models that retail for $550 (a reader even spied them on sale for as little as $300 at one store). Matching dressers are pricey, most in the $700 range. Natart is a newcomer to the juvenile market in the US, having debuted in 2001 but we've heard good reports on their quality from readers. Sadly, their web site is quite lacking, with little info and grainy pictures. Another bummer: despite the hefty prices, most Natart cribs have exposed hardware for their knee push rail releases. For this price, we'd expect completely hidden hardware. If that isn't important, however, this might be a brand to consider. ***Rating: A-***

Pali *For a dealer near you, call (877) 725-4772. Web: www.pali-italy. com* Pali's had its ups and downs over the last few years, but the company still makes great cribs. Readers of previous editions may recall our tales of how Pali dropped the ball when it re-shuffled its distribution in 2000, causing delivery delays, customer service disruptions, and worse. So what's the status now? Pali is back on track, even though it can still get behind in production (requiring customers to cool their heels for up to 12 weeks for certain crib styles). The cribs, of course, are still great—all cribs feature knee push rail releases with hidden hardware and solid beech wood construction. Most Pali cribs are in the $400 to $600 range, although one model even tops $800. You won't find Pali sold online or in discount stores; it's only at specialty stores, which means there is only a limited opportunity to price shop this brand. If we had one gripe about Pali's release, it would have to be the visible track inside the rail—other Italian-made cribs have completely hidden tracks. And Pali's release isn't as quiet as other Italian crib makers or even Canadian makers Ragazzi and Morigeau. While we like the quality, someone at Pali has got to fix its terrible assembly instructions, apparently written in 16th century Latin. ***Rating: A-***

Pottery Barn *(800) 430-7373 or www.potterybarnkids.com.* We'll review Pottery Barn in depth later in this chapter in the Do It By Mail section. We should mention that Pottery Barn's cribs are made by Status and Simmons, both brands we review later in this section. Unfortunately, Pottery Barn doesn't say which cribs are made by which manufacturers—a cardinal sin in our view. Why? As a consumer, you should know the brand name of the crib you are purchasing BEFORE you buy it so you can compare safety track records, rail release methods, etc. And watch out for the exorbitant shipping charges Pottery Barn slaps on their cribs—as much as $100 or more, on top of the already high prices. Bottom line: use this catalog for décor items like bedding or lamps and skip the furniture.

Ragazzi *8965 Pascal Gagnon, St. Leonard, Quebec H1P 1Z4. Call (514) 324-7886 for a dealer near you. Web: www.ragazzi. com* Readers of past editions of this book may remember that Ragazzi wasn't our favorite crib brand (to put it charitably). Our biggest beef with Ragazzi was their high prices—many of their cribs sell for $500, $600 or more (although some of our sharp-eyed readers have seen them on sale for $400 or so). And that's still true today. You can find the same look/features/quality from Italian crib importers for HALF the Ragazzi price. Parents who've bought Ragazzi acknowledge the high prices, but say the quality is worth it—they like the construction and hip styling. Like Morigeau and other Canadian-based crib makers, Ragazzi's styling emphasis is on fancy adult-like looks. Founded by the son of an Italian carpenter, Ragazzi started out in 1972 making TV consoles (of all things), then segued into cribs and juvenile furniture in 1991. The company's "3 child or 15-year warranty" is unique in the industry and we have to admit their new "Colors of the Rainbow" collection with seven mix-and-match colors is cool. Also new this year: Ragazzi has joined the rest of the upper-end crib competition by adopting hidden hardware on their rail releases. Yet, we still can't get past the prices of this brand. Bottom line: nice furniture, too high a price. *Rating: B*

Relics Furniture *607 Washington Ave N, Minneapolis, MN 55401. For a dealer near you, call 612-374-0861. Web: www.relics-furniure.com.* Minneapolis furniture maker Relics specializes in antique looking furniture that has been "distressed" for a retro feel. Relics cribs are actually made by another company that specializes in commercial cribs; Relics finishes and distresses the cribs to fit their collection. While styles are limited, Relics does offer ten color options, including a "fire truck" red and an ivory "French cream." Matching case goods, including a changer are also available. Quality is good. While we loved the look, the prices are going to limit Relic's appeal—a crib with hidden hardware and knee-push drop side is $789. A spindle crib with exposed hardware and foot bar release is $649. The changer with three drawers is $1325. If you're going to drop that much money, we'd go for one of their funky finishes. You can find a white or ivory crib for much less elsewhere. *Rating: B*

eBay for cribs: 3 smart shopper tips

Yep, you can buy just about anything on eBay these days, so why not a crib? At last glance, we noticed over 200 cribs for sale including some steals starting at just $100. So should you buy your crib this way? Before you start bidding, consider these caveats:

◆ *What exactly are you buying?* eBay lets just about any crib be listed online—even those that are clearly "antiques" that don't meet current safety standards. Most of the time, however, the cribs sold are imported from Canada (eBay sellers are taking advantage of the currency exchange rate to give you a deal). The best eBay sellers like IEP Visions identify the brand names in the listings (although even that seller occasionally lists no-name cribs imported from China). Other eBay sellers aren't so honest—they list a crib as an "exclusive" with no brand name. If you email them, they might reveal their source . . . odds are it is a Canadian crib that isn't sold here in the U.S. Or a crib imported from Asia. A key question: is the crib JPMA certified? At least then you know the crib will meet a certain level of safety. While all cribs sold in the U.S. must by law meet federal safety standards, eBay is like the Wild West of Baby Products . . . it's hard to say whether some of those obscure cribs really meet the standards or not.

◆ *Beware shipping charges—and damage!* As we have discussed earlier in this chapter, very few retailers attempt to sell cribs online or via catalogs. The expense of shipping a crib that can weigh 100 pounds or more is simply prohibitive. Of course, that doesn't keep eBay sellers from trying—you will have to pay a hefty shipping charge ($50 to $100) on top of some sales and that can turn a bargain into a bad deal. And let's not forget about damage. Shipping anything this heavy is risky—if not packed correctly, a crib can be easily damaged in transport. Make sure the item is insured. And check the seller's track record to see if others have complained about shipping damage.

◆ *Is the crib new?* Some eBay items are returned stock, discontinued items or worse. Most honest sellers will report damage—but if a crib has been sitting in a hot warehouse somewhere for the last five years, we'd pass.

So, let's review. If you find a crib on eBay, consider bidding IF: the crib is a name brand that is JPMA certified or reviewed in this book, has no damage, reasonable shipping and the seller has a good standing on eBay for taking care of problems like shipping damage. As always, compare prices in a local store and factor in shipping/insurance before bidding.

Sauder *Web: www.sauder.com.* We mentioned this brand of RTA (ready-to-assemble) furniture in our *Toddler Bargains* book as an inexpensive option for dressers and wanted to include a quick mention here. Some readers were surprised that we'd recommend Sauder, given their past reputation for cheap, particle board/laminate offerings that were poor quality and prone to damage. But they've improved the line lately and we do recommend you consider it as an option, especially if you are a do-it-yourselfer who wants to finish the furniture (Sauder offers both finished and unfinished options). Yes, you do have to assemble the furniture and that can be a hassle. But the prices are amazing—you'll see Sauder at Wal-Mart, Lowe's and other stores. We're talking (at Wal-Mart) a hi-low combo dresser for $198, five-drawer chest for $169 and armoire for $165. For unfinished options, Lowe's offers a four-drawer chest for just $122. If you go this route, be sure to get the ALL-WOOD Sauder furniture (the Sand Castle for Kids collection at Wal-Mart is an example). And see it before you buy to make sure it is what you expect. ***Rating: A-***

Simmons *613 E. Beacon Ave., New London, WI 54961. Call (920) 982-2140 for a dealer near you. Web: www.simmonsjp.com.* Simmons (which also goes under the name Little Folks in some specialty stores and Canada) is one of the largest domestic producers of cribs and juvenile furniture. The Wisconsin-based company was started in 1917 by Thomas Alva Edison to provide wooden cabinets for one of his recent inventions (the phonograph). The company launched infant furniture in 1927. Like their domestic competitor Child Craft, Simmons produces cribs with conservative styling (some would say it's a tad boring). Quality is very good—Simmons uses hardwoods like maple and ash for its products. Like Child Craft, Simmons has abandoned the foot-bar release with exposed hardware in favor of a system it calls "Easy Glide." Now, nearly all Simmons cribs have this knee-push rail release (one big exception: the "exclusive" cribs Simmons sells at Sears—some of these still have the old style exposed hardware with foot bar releases). As far as prices go, we think Simmons is a very good value. We saw Simmons cribs in Baby Depot that started at $240. Other models were $300 to $350. At the top of the line is Simmons Crib N More, a convertible crib that converts into a full bed for $550. That's about what Child Craft charges for their convertible model, although we give the edge to Child Craft on styling. One caveat: Pottery Barn sells Simmons cribs at a major mark-up. One Simmons model we saw was $399 plus $100 shipping in the Pottery Barn Kids catalog—we'd rather buy this crib for just $219, the price we saw it at other stores! A sleigh-style Simmons crib in PBK's catalog is $800! Another caution on Simmons: while readers love the cribs, some have complained about the quality of their optional under-crib drawers, which are made entirely of laminate (no wood). Bottom line: this company won't win any styling awards, but they offer a good quality crib at a great price. Simmons has a one-year warranty on their cribs. ***Rating: A***

Sorelle *170 Roosevelt Place, Palisades Park, NJ 07650. Call (888) 470-1260 or (201) 461-9444. Web: www.sorellefurniture.com for a dealer near you.* Sorelle is the new name for C&T, an Italian importer that has been on the market since 1977. In previous editions of this book, we knocked C&T for their high prices and a 1997 recall for defective side rails. Well, there is some good news. The company has addressed those quality problems and has become much more competitive on price. Now, most models are $250 to $400 retail, which makes them very competitive with other entry-level Italian cribs like Babi Italia. (FYI: Sorelle cribs are sold under the name Golden Baby at Babies R Us). Quality is above average; all the cribs are made from 100% Italian beech wood, feature knee push rail releases and many have under crib drawers. While the cribs are made in Italy, the cradles are manufactured in Russia and Sorelle's case pieces are made in New York. The only negative we can criticize Sorelle for is their lack of models in the hot convertible crib category. We wish they had more offerings that converted into full size beds. And be prepared to wait for Sorelle furniture if it isn't in stock: our readers report waiting 10 to 16 weeks for special orders. Nevertheless, as a result of the new lower prices and improved quality, we've decided to up the rating for this company. ***Rating: A-***

Status *571 Lepine Ave., Dorval, Quebec, Canada, H9P 2R2 . For a dealer near you, call (514) 631-0788. Web: www.statusfurniture. com* Yet another Canadian juvenile furniture maker that's recently come to the U.S., Status offers several coordinating sets of cribs and dressers. We liked the neo-shaker looks, as well as the French Country motifs. The oversized dressers with bun feet echo similar looks in the adult furniture market. The quality of Status is very good—the cribs use a knee-push rail release and are made from hardwoods like maple and birch. Prices for a crib are $400 to $700. And there is good news on Status' rail release: as of 2003, Status cribs now have all hidden hardware. Also new: a pine crib model available in two finishes for just $299. In fact, Status now has a couple of affordable collections with convertible cribs (that convert to full size beds) for just $340. Dressers in that collection sell for $399 to $499. The company offers 21 colors, from natural finishes to pastel painted colors. The only caveat to this line: some of Status' case pieces are made of painted MDF (medium density fiberboard) instead of wood. While we liked the styling of this group, we'd rather get solid maple or birch wood instead of MDF at these prices. On the upside, all their cribs are now JPMA-certified for safety. So, we'll raise the rating for this brand this time out—those new lower prices and all hidden hardware rail releases are a nice improvement. *Rating: A-*

Stork Craft 11511 No. 5 Road, Richmond, British Columbia, Canada, V7A4E8. For a dealer near you, call (604) 274-5121. Web: www.storkcraft.com Unlike other Canadian crib makers that concentrate on the upper-end markets, Stork Craft's cribs are priced for the rest of us. Most are in the $150 to $250 range (although a few reach $400) and are sold in such places as Babies R Us and other chain stores. Manufactured in Mississauga, Ontario (just outside Toronto), Stork Craft has three collections. The entry-level "Fisher Price" brand cribs sell for $129 to $299 and feature very simple styling, painted MDF construction (not solid wood) and wood mattress platforms (no springs). The middle-level cribs (Signature or Traditional) feature mixed species of wood and a bit more fancy styling (as well as spring mattress platforms). The top-end "Diamond" cribs are solid maple. All Storkcraft cribs now feature knee-push rail release (gone are the foot-bar rail releases with exposed hardware). The hardware on Storkcraft is exposed, which is a bit behind the times. FYI: These cribs are sold at Wal-Mart. *Rating: B*

Tracers 39 Westmoreland Ave., White Plains, NY 10606. Call (914) 686-5725 for a dealer near you. Tracers cribs are made in Israel and Macedonia (in the former Yugoslavia). The styling mimics that of Italian cribs, but we think the quality isn't quite there. Yes, all Tracers cribs feature knee-push rail releases with hidden hardware (a change from previous years when the hardware was exposed) but we found the rail releases to be quite noisy. Second, the warranty on these cribs (90 days) is among the shortest in the business. We also didn't like the metal straps that hold up the mattress and the side rails that lack teething guards. The prices are also somewhat high: the average Tracers crib sells for $400. Simple models without under-crib drawers are $340, while top-of-the-line styles run $600+. On the plus side, we liked the stability of their cribs. And Tracers dressers (made in Canada) feature solid wood drawers and sides made from 100% beech wood. So, it's a mixed review for this brand. And when will Tracers join the rest of the modern world with a web site? *Rating: C+*

Vermont Precision *249 Professional Dr., Morrisville, VT 05454. For a dealer near you, call (802) 888-7974. Web: www.vtprecision.com* This children's furniture veteran launched a crib line in 1998, winning kudos from our readers. Their handcrafted cribs boast solid wood (maple) construction that exceeds Pali and Ragazzi in quality and stability, according to recent customers we've interviewed. The cribs use the knee-push rail release and all the hardware is concealed. But the prices are steep: a crib from Vermont Precision will set you back $500 to $750. A combo maple and cherry crib this year nears $800. That's a bit disappointing, especially since you don't get an under-crib drawer for storage. And all the cribs are only single-drop sides. But this is really an heirloom-quality piece of furniture, so some readers have felt the high price was worth it. Vermont Precision has limited distribution (about 30 stores nationwide), so it may take searching if you want to check them out. Finally, we should note that Vermont Precision had a recall in 2002 for about 1000 cribs for defective side rail slats. Vermont Precision said they made changes to their production process to fix this problem, but we were a bit disappointed that a $700 crib would have this problem. ***Rating: B-***

Other crib brands. Besides the major brand names reviewed above, there are a small number of other crib brands out there. Here's a quick overview:

Mondi (630-953-9519; web: www.mondibaby.com; rating: B) is the latest Italian import to reach the U.S. Made in Italy by the same factory that turns out Bellini's cribs, Mondi cribs are similar to other Italian models you see on the market (solid beech wood, hidden hardware, under crib storage drawers). Mondi's differences: heavier side rails and more ornate carved headboards. Prices are about $300 to $550. FYI: Mondi also imports cribs from Poland under the Vox label; these stationary-side cribs sell for about $300.

Readers have emailed us their kudos for Maine-based *Moosehead* (207) 997-3621 (web: www.mooseheadfurniture.com, rating: B+) cribs and other juvenile furniture. The company has been in business since 1947, but just started making cribs and other infant items a few years ago. Moosehead has two lines: a Shaker look made of maple and a Mission-style in ash. Prices for a crib are $349 to $499. Moosehead is sold in 200+ stores in the US, but their distribution is somewhat spotty (they are not sold in Canada).

Stephanie Anne's "Room to Grow" (888-885-6700;www.stephanieanne.com; rating C) offers whimsical cribs with pencil post designs and interesting finishes. The company (with two locations in Dallas and Houston) sells its cribs through a catalog for about $785 to $1075, depending on the finish. That's very pricey, considering the cribs have exposed hardware (rod and cane) rail releases. And we did receive a complaint about Stephanie Anne's customer service from a reader who bought over $4000 of the designer's furniture for her daughter's nursery. The reader complained that her furniture was damaged upon delivery and despite the company's pledge to promptly fix the problem, it took nine months and numerous calls to finally get in replacement items.

Brand Recommendations: Our Picks

Good. On a tight budget? A decent single-drop side crib from domestic makers Child Craft or Simmons is a safe bet. Prices run $200 to $300 for a wood, single-drop side crib with a knee-push release. You can find these cribs in stores like Babies R Us and Baby Depot. A good model: Child Craft's 10171 (see picture) is sold on Target.com for $199.

Better. Want to step up a bit in style? Consider the Italian crib lines Sorelle or Pali. Each features all beech wood construction and hidden hardware rail releases that are a bit quieter than domestic makers. A basic Sorelle crib (also sold under the name Golden Baby or C&T) is about $250 to $400 and is sold at chain stores like Babies R Us. Pictured is the Sorelle Nina crib. A slight step up in price is Pali ($400 to $500 for an entry-level model), which is only sold at specialty stores.

Best. How about a convertible crib? Yes, they are more expensive to start with but you are actually getting two products—a crib that later converts into a full-size bed. The best bets here are Child Craft's Crib N' Double (style #36101, also called the Millennium—see picture at left as a crib and then converted to a full-size bed) for $400 to $550 (depending on the wood). Simmons offers a similar style (the Crib 'N More, $550). If you don't want a convertible crib, consider something from Canadian makers Morigeau or Status. Both make very stylish cribs with under crib drawers and hidden hardware. These will set you back $300 to $500 or so.

Grandma's house. If you need a secondary crib for Grandma's house, consider a simple crib from Delta, which start at $170 in chain stores. These cribs can be assembled quickly with no tools.

NURSERY NECESSITIES

CRIB RATINGS

NAME	RATING	COST	WHERE MADE?
ANGEL LINE	B-	$ TO $$	TAIWAN
A.P. INDUSTRIES	B	$$$	CANADA
BABY'S DREAM	C+	$$ TO $$$	USA
BASSETT	B+	$$	ASIA/USA
BELLINI	C+	$$$	ITALY
BERG	B	$$ TO $$$	RUSSIA/USA
BONAVITA/BABI ITALIA	B-	$$ TO $$$	ITALY
BRATT DECOR	B	$$$	ASIA
CANALLI	A	$$ TO $$$	ITALY
CHILD CRAFT	A	$$ TO $$$	ASIA/USA
CHILDESIGNS	B+	$ TO $$	ASIA/USA
COSCO	D	$	ASIA
DAVINCI	B	$ TO $$$	ASIA/USA
DELTA	B-	$ TO $$	ASIA
DOMUSINDO	A-	$$	ASIA
E.G.	B+	$$$	CANADA
FOREVER MINE	A-	$$ TO $$$	CANADA
GRACO	D+	$	ASIA
JARDINE	B+ (CRIBS)	$$	ASIA
KINDERKRAFT	B	$$	CENTRAL AMERICA
LEGACY	B	$$$	CROATIA/USA
LITTLE MISS LIBERTY	B	$$ TO $$$	USA
MILLION $ BABY	B	$ TO $$$	ASIA/USA
MORIGEAU/LEPINE	A-	$$$	CANADA
NATART	A-	$$$	CANADA
PALI	A-	$$$	ITALY
RAGAZZI	B	$$$	CANADA
SIMMONS	A	$$ TO $$$	USA
SORELLE	A-	$$	ITALY
STATUS	A-	$$ TO $$$	CANADA
STORK CRAFT	B	$ TO $$	CANADA
TRACERS	C+	$$ TO $$$	ISRAEL/MACEDONIA
VERMONT PRECISION	B-	$$$	USA

KEY

RATING: Our opinion of the manufacturer's quality and value.

COST: $=under $200, $$=$200-400, $$$=over $400.

WHERE MADE? Where the cribs parts are made; in many cases, final assembly may be in the US. In those cases, we note the country of origin as "Asia/USA."

RELEASE: How does the crib drop-side release? For a discussion of the different releases, see the section earlier in this chapter. Note that the release type may vary by model within the same manufacturer's line.

HARDWARE: This refers to the hardware that operates the crib drop-side, whether it is concealed or exposed.

cribs

A quick look at some top crib brands:

RELEASE	HARDWARE	STABILITY	WARRANTY
FOOT-BAR**	EXPOSED	AVERAGE	6 MONTHS
KNEE-PUSH	HIDDEN	EXCELLENT	1 YEAR
FOLD-DOWN*	HIDDEN	EXCELLENT	1 YEAR
FOOT-BAR/KNEE PUSH**	EXPOSED	AVERAGE	1 YEAR
DOUBLE TRIGGER	HIDDEN	EXCELLENT	NONE
KNEE-PUSH	HIDDEN	GOOD	1 YEAR
KNEE-PUSH	HIDDEN	EXCELLENT	1 YEAR
FOOT-BAR	EXPOSED	GOOD	2 YEARS
KNEE-PUSH	HIDDEN	EXCELLENT	LIFETIME
KNEE-PUSH	HIDDEN	EXCELLENT	2 YEARS
KNEE-PUSH	HIDDEN	AVERAGE	2 YEARS
KNEE-PUSH	EXPOSED	AVERAGE	1 YEAR
FOOT-BAR/KNEE-PUSH**	VARIES	AVERAGE	15 YEARS
KNEE-PUSH	EXPOSED	AVERAGE	1 YEAR
KNEE-PUSH	EXPOSED	AVERAGE	1 YEAR
KNEE-PUSH	HIDDEN	EXCELLENT	N/A
KNEE-PUSH/SWING GATE	VARIES	EXCELLENT	LIFETIME
KNEE-PUSH	EXPOSED	AVERAGE	1 YEAR
KNEE-PUSH	EXPOSED	GOOD	N/A
KNEE-PUSH	EXPOSED	AVERAGE	7 YEARS
KNEE-PUSH	HIDDEN	EXCELLENT	NONE
DOUBLE-TRIGGER	EXPOSED	GOOD	30 DAYS
FOOT-BAR/KNEE-PUSH**	VARIES	AVERAGE	15 YEARS
KNEE-PUSH	HIDDEN	EXCELLENT	1 YEAR
KNEE-PUSH	EXPOSED	EXCELLENT	1 YEAR
KNEE-PUSH	HIDDEN	EXCELLENT	6 MONTHS
KNEE-PUSH	HIDDEN	EXCELLENT	15 YEARS
KNEE-PUSH	HIDDEN	GOOD	1 YEAR
KNEE-PUSH	HIDDEN	EXCELLENT	NONE
KNEE-PUSH	HIDDEN	EXCELLENT	LIFETIME
KNEE-PUSH	HIDDEN	AVERAGE	1 YEAR
KNEE-PUSH	HIDDEN	AVERAGE	90 DAYS
KNEE-PUSH	HIDDEN	EXCELLENT	1 YEAR

STABILITY: Our opinion of a crib's stability based on hands-on inspection. "Average" is the lowest rating; "good" is better and "excellent" is tops.

WARRANTY: Some companies don't have written warranties. Several crib makers (Simmons, Vermont Precision and Bellini) told us they "stand behind their cribs and will replace parts if they break," but that's not in writing and there are no time guidelines. Our position: if it isn't in writing, there is no warranty.

*While most of Baby's Dream models have a fold-down rail release, a few have the knee-push drop-sides.

** These lines have cribs with foot-bar rail release/exposed hardware; a few models also feature knee-push releases and concealed hardware.

Do it by Mail: The Best Mail-Order Sources for Cribs and Baby Furniture

JCPENNEY

To order call: (800) 430-7373.
Web: www.potterybarnkids.com

JCPenney has been selling baby clothes, furniture, and more for over 90 years. Their popular mail-order catalog has two free "mini-catalogs" that should be of particular interest to parents-to-be.

"The Baby Book" is Penney's main juvenile furniture catalog, with over 50 pages of cribs, bedding, mattresses, safety items, car seats, strollers, swings, and even a few pages of baby clothes. The crib section features such famous brand names as Child Craft, Simmons, Bassett and more. Basic wood cribs from name brands start at about $160, although convertible models can top $340.

We should also note that Penney's sells it's own private label cribs under the name Bright Future and Domusindo. (Sometimes, Penney's catalog doesn't delineate a brand name for their in-house cribs. One clue that you are dealing with a private label: the catalog will just say the crib is imported from Indonesia). Many readers have asked us about these cribs. Here's our take: Penney's has an excellent safety track record for their in-house cribs. While the cribs are made in Asia and imported to the U.S., Penney's strict safety standards make them comparable to cribs made in the U.S. and Canada.

All of Penney's catalog is also available online at Penney's web site. We found the site easy to use, but you did have to click several times to get to their baby/children's section. And the descriptions of the products could be beefed up a bit. But, overall, the web site functions just fine.

While Penney's catalog is a good place to start researching juvenile furniture, actually ordering from the catalog can be an exercise in frustration. First, consider Penney's customer service. Don't ask any detailed questions of the reps—all the info they have is the same that is in the catalog or web site. For additional details, Penney's customer service reps must email their warehouse and then they'll call you back . . . within three weeks! Whoa, that's fast.

Then, let's talk about ordering. Talk with three different reps and you'll get three different shipping quotes. Once you place the order, Penney's may change the shipping fee; if so, they'll call you. Finally, consider how long it takes to get most items—Penney's can take six weeks or more to ship some items.

Prices in the Penney's catalog aren't discounted—but since most of the brands Penney's carries are affordable to begin with, we find the catalog to be a decent value. If you live in a remote area of the U.S. or Canada with few or no baby stores, however, this catalog might be a savior, despite the ordering hassles.

POTTERY BARN KIDS

To order call: (800) 430-7373.
Web: www.potterybarnkids.com

You've got to give Pottery Barn credit for their excellent kid's catalog—it's rare that one catalog can actually influence an entire industry. But that's exactly what happened when this smartly designed book landed in parents' mailboxes in 1998—the "Pottery Barn" look suddenly spread from mail order to baby stores and beyond. Even Penney's has been trying to make their baby catalog more hip in response to PBK.

So, what's all the fuss about? PBK smartly mixes stylish looks (patchwork quilts; denim accents) with upscale furniture and accessories to create contemporary layouts that don't scream "baby."

The best bets: those cute rugs, lamps and other accessories. And we generally found the bedding to be high quality (see review in the next chapter). But what about the furniture? Grossly overpriced, we're sad to say. As we mentioned earlier in this chapter, the cribs Pottery Barn sells are good brands (Status, Simmons, etc.). But the prices! What are these guys thinking? A sleigh crib for $800? Plus $100 shipping? The huge mark-ups on these items are obscene. Our advice: go buy a Status or Simmons crib in a regular baby store, pay retail and still save 30% over this catalog.

One little trick to getting a deal at Pottery Barn: their regular stores sometimes sell the same stuff you see at Pottery Barn Kids stores, but at lower prices. A reader who fell in love with a $50 laundry hamper in the kid's catalog was surprised to see the same hamper in a natural finish in Pottery Barn's regular store. Price? $27.49 on sale. Sometimes we wonder if you slap the word "baby" on an item, the price doubles.

So, it's a mixed review for PBK—love the look, but the furniture is a no go. Use this catalog as design inspiration for your nursery, even if you decided to buy items elsewhere. And we wish PBK didn't have to be so secretive as to who makes their cribs—we noticed the catalog omits any details on this and operators refuse to say when asked.

Bassinets/Cradles

A newborn infant can immediately sleep in a full size crib, but some parents like the convenience of bassinets or cradles to use for the first few weeks. Why? These smaller baby beds can be kept in the parents' bedroom, making for convenient midnight feedings.

What's the difference between a bassinet and a cradle? Although most stores use the terms interchangeably, we think of bassinets as small baskets that are typically put onto a stationery stand (pictured at top right). Cradles, on the other hand, are usually made of wood and rock back and forth.

A third option in this category is "Moses baskets," basically woven baskets (bottom right) with handles that you can use to carry a newborn from room to room. (A web site with a good selection of Moses baskets is Babies Boutique, www.babiesboutique.com).

As for prices, we noticed a Badger Basket bassinet (a rather common brand, www.badgerbasket.com) runs about $40 at Babies R Us, but that price doesn't include the "soft goods" (sheets, liners, skirts and hoods). Models that include soft goods typically run closer to $90 and up to $180. Cradles, on the other hand, run about $100 to $400 but don't need that many soft goods (just a mattress, which is usually included, and a sheet, which is not). Moses baskets run $100 to $250.

So, which should you buy? We say none of the above. As we mentioned at the beginning of this section, a newborn will do just fine in a full-size crib. If you need the convenience of a bassinet, we'd suggest skipping the ones you see in chain stores. Why? Most are very poorly made (stapled together cardboard sheets, etc) and won't last for more than one child. One reader said the sheets with her chain store-bought bassinet "were falling apart at the seams even before it went into the wash" for the first time. And the function of these products is somewhat questionable. For example, the functionality of a Moses basket, while pretty to look at, can be easily duplicated by an infant car seat carrier, which most folks buy anyway.

Instead, we suggest you borrow a bassinet or cradle from a friend. . . or buy a portable playpen with a bassinet feature. We'll review specific models of playpens in Chapter 7, but basic choices like the Graco Pak 'N Play run $80 to $130 in most stores. The bassinet feature in most playpens (basically, a small insert that creates a small bed area at the top of the playpen) can be used up to 15 pounds, which is about all most folks would need. Then, you simply remove the bassinet attachment and voila! You have a standard size playpen. Since many parents get a playpen anyway, going for a model that has a bassinet attachment doesn't add much to the cost and eliminates the separate $100 to $200 expense. (See the next chapter for a discussion of bassinet sheets).

Another way to save: check out second-hand stores and garage sales. Just make sure the bassinet or cradle is in good repair and not missing any pieces. Most parents use these items for such a short period of time that there is little wear and tear.

Of course, you can also go for the Arm's Reach Co-Sleeper (reviewed earlier) as an alternative to the bassinet as well.

Mattresses

Now that you've just spent several hundred dollars on a crib, you're done, right? Wrong. Despite their hefty price tags, most cribs don't come with mattresses. So, here's our guide to buying the best quality mattress for the lowest price.

Safe & Sound

Babies don't have the muscle strength to lift their heads up when put face down into soft or fluffy bedding—some have suffocated as a result. The best defense: buy a firm mattress (foam or coil) and DO NOT place your baby face down in soft, thick quilts, wool blankets, pillows, or toys. (Futon mattresses are also a no-no). Never put the baby down on a vinyl mattress without a cover or sheet since vinyl can also contribute to suffocation. In addition, you should know that several studies into the causes of Sudden Infant Death Syndrome (SIDS) have found that a too-soft sleep surface (such as the items listed above) and environmental factors (a too-hot room, cigarette smoke) are related to crib death, though exactly how has yet to be determined. Experts therefore advise against letting infants sleep on a too-soft surface. Another important tip: make sure you put your baby to sleep on her back. Studies suggest that babies who are put to sleep on their stomachs have an increased risk of SIDS.

Another point to remember: while mattresses come in a standard size for a full-size crib, the depth can vary from maker to maker. Some mattresses are just four inches deep; others are six. Some crib sheets won't fit the six-inch thick mattresses; it's unsafe to use a sheet that doesn't snugly fit OVER the corner of a mattress and tuck beneath it.

Mattresses should fit your crib snugly with no more than a finger's width between the mattress and all sides of the crib. Since most cribs and mattresses are made to a standard size, this is usually not a major problem. However, we occasionally hear about imported, obscure-brand cribs that are too large or too small for a standard American size crib mattress. In that case, you may need to either return the crib or get a specialized mattress from the manufacturer that fits the crib correctly.

Smart Shopper Tips

Smart Shopper Tip #1
Foam or Coil?

"It seems the choice for a crib mattress comes down to foam or coil? Which is better? Does it matter?"

Yes, it does matter. After researching this issue, we've come down on the foam side of the debate. Why? Foam mattresses are lighter than those with coils, making it easier to change the sheets in the middle of the night when Junior reenacts the Great Flood in his crib. Foam mattresses typically weigh less than eight pounds, while coil mattresses can top 20 or 30 pounds! Another plus: foam mattresses are less expensive, usually less than $100. Coil mattresses can top out at $150.

We get quite a few calls from readers on this issue. Many baby stores only sell coil mattresses, claiming that coil is superior to foam. One salesperson even told a parent that foam mattresses aren't safe for babies older than six months! Another salesperson actually told a parent they should expect to replace a foam mattress two to three times during the two years a baby uses a crib. Please! We've consulted with pediatricians and industry experts on this issue and have come to the conclusion that the best course is to choose a *firm* mattress for baby—it doesn't matter whether it's a firm coil mattress or a firm foam one. What about the claim that foam mattresses need to be replaced constantly? In the ten years we've been researching this topic, we've never heard from one parent whose foam mattress had to be replaced!

What's going on here? Many baby stores try to make up for the thin profit margins they make on cribs by pitching parents to buy an ultra-expensive mattress. The latest rage are so-called "2 in 1" mattresses that combine foam *and* coil (foam on one side; coil on the other). These can run $200 or more! While these mattresses are nice, they are totally unnecessary. A $100 foam mattress will do just as well.

So why all the pressure to get the fancy-shmancy double dip mattress? Such mattresses cost stores just $40 at wholesale, yet they sell for $200 or more!

Bottom line: foam mattresses are the best deal, but can be hard to find. As a result, we'll recommend mattresses in both the coil and foam categories just in case the baby stores near you only stock coil.

Smart Shopper Tip #2
Coil Overkill and Cheap Foam Mattresses
"How do you tell a cheap-quality coil mattress from a better one? How about foam mattresses—what makes one better than the next?"

Evaluating different crib mattresses isn't easy. Even the cheap ones claim they are "firm" and comparing apples to apples is difficult. When it comes to coil mattresses, the number of coils seems like a good way to compare them, but even that can be deceiving. For example, is a 150-coil mattress better than an 80-coil mattress?

Well, yes and no. While an 80-coil mattress probably won't be as firm as one with 150 coils, it's important to remember that a large number of coils do not necessarily mean the mattress is superior. Factors such as the wire gauge, number of turns per coil and the temper of the wire contribute to the firmness, durability and strength of the mattress. Unfortunately, most mattresses only note the coil count (and no other details). Hence, the best bet would be to buy a good brand that has a solid quality reputation (we'll recommend specific choices after this section).

What about foam mattresses? The cheapest foam mattresses are made of low-density foam (about .9 pounds per cubic foot). The better foam mattresses are high-density with 1.5 pounds per cubic foot. Easy for us to say, right? Once again, foam mattresses don't list density on their packaging, leaving consumers to wonder whether they're getting high or low density. As with coil mattresses, you have to rely on a reputable brand name to get a good foam mattress (see the next section for more details).

One good, basic test for crib mattress firmness: take the mattress between your two hands and push your hands together. Okay, that sounds silly but you'll notice some differences in firmness right off the bat.

Smart Shopper Tip #3
Flatulent foam mattresses?
"I read on the 'net that some foam mattresses have an out-gassing problem. Is this true?"

We've noticed that several eco-catalogs and web sites have raised concerns that standard crib mattresses are a possible health hazard. One even went on to say that such mattresses are "unhealthy combinations of artificial foams, fluorocarbons, synthetic

Sleep positioners and special mattresses: Helpful products or SIDS scare tactic?

The baby products industry is good at churning out products that pray on parents' fears. Most parents have heard the warnings about Sudden Infant Death Syndrome (SIDS), which claims about 2100 lives a year. SIDS is a real danger and safety advocates have done a good job explaining to parents how to lessen its occurrence; yet the baby products industry sometimes can't stop itself from creating "helpful" products that are, at the least, a waste of money and at worst, dangerous frauds.

On the waste of money end are the "sleep positioners." SIDS advocates recommend putting babies to sleep on their backs as a proven way to reduce SIDS. Between 1992 and 1998, the number of babies placed on their backs to sleep increased from 21% to 70%. This corresponded with a reduction in the death rate from SIDS by 38% in the same years—and another 20% decline was registered from 1999 to 2000. To "help" parents put babies to sleep on their backs, the baby product industry has come out with "sleep positioners," basically foam blocks that sell for $10 to $15.

Do babies really need sleep positioners? No, most babies that are put on their backs to sleep will stay there throughout the night. Most infants simply don't have the muscle strength to roll over yet. And if baby does start rolling over, you can use a low-tech solution to keep them on their backs: rolled up towels. Two small rolled up towels (placed below the waist) will do the trick at no cost.

In 2000, a host of "SIDS prevention" products were recalled by the CPSC. Turns out many of these "breathable mattresses" and other contraptions simply didn't work. Worse still, parents who used such devices might have been lulled into a false sense of security about SIDS, perhaps even putting babies to sleep on their stomachs.

The only SIDS product tested that actually worked was the Halo Crib Mattress (218-525-5158; web: www.halosleep.com). This mattress has a small built-in fan that quietly re-circulates air around a baby. Cost: about $200.Readers who bought the Halo Mattress praise it overall, although with some caveats. One reader pointed out that you should be certain your crib is large enough for the mattress, since it is not as flexible as regular mattresses (apparently the first crib she bought didn't work). "The mattress is much quieter than we though it would be," she said, but the bumper pad that comes with the mattress should be avoided (it makes the sheets harder to put on). And be aware that the mattress is very heavy, which makes changing sheets quite a challenge. A couple of readers complained that the company didn't promptly answer its emails. That aside, the product is a winner overall.

For more information about SIDS check out the excellent web site for the SIDS Alliance (www.SidsAlliance.org).

fibers and formaldehyde, all materials that give off toxic fumes." The solution? Buy *their* organic cotton crib mattress for a whopping $650 and your baby won't have to breathe that nasty stuff.

Hold it. We checked with pediatricians and industry experts and found no evidence that such a problem exists. While it is possible that a foam or coil mattress might give off a few vapors when you first take it out of the packaging, there's no ongoing fume problem in our opinion. There are also no medical studies linking, say, lower SAT scores to kids who slept on foam mattresses as babies. While it is possible that a few children who have extreme chemical sensitivities might do better on "organic" mattresses, it's doubtful such products will make any difference to the vast majority of infants. We think it's irresponsible of such eco-crusaders to raise bogus issues intended to scare parents without providing corresponding proof of their claims.

What about mattresses that are hypo-allergenic with special anti-microbial covers? These all-natural, organic mattresses are again pitched to parents as the ultimate safe place for baby to sleep. Even regular "conventional" crib mattress makers are jumping on the bacteria hysteria wagon by coating their mattress covers with Microban and other additives. Yet there are no studies showing these mattresses give babies a better night sleep, stop sicknesses or prevent allergies. If your baby develops severe allergies (which is rare for infants), then we can see a reason for attempting to outfit a nursery with such pricey special products. But for the vast majority of parents, these mattresses are a waste of money.

Here are a few more shopping tips/myths about crib mattresses:

◆ *What's the best way to test a crib mattresses' firmness?* Test the center of the mattress (not the sides or corners)—place the palm of one hand flat on one side of the mattress and then put your other hand on the opposite side. The greater the pressure needed to press your hands together, the more firm the mattress.

◆ *Are all crib mattresses the same size?* No, they can vary a small amount—both in length/width and thickness. Most foam mattresses come in thicknesses of 4", 5" and 6". Most coil mattresses are 5" to 6" in depth. What's the best thickness? It doesn't matter, but 5" should be fine. Remember the safest crib mattress is the one that snugly fits your crib—you shouldn't be able to fit more than two fingers between the headboard/side rails and the mattress.

◆ *All foam mattresses look alike—what separates the better ones from the cheaper options?* Test for firmness (see above). The more firm, the better. Another clue: weight. A slightly heavier foam mattress usually means they used a better-quality foam to make the product. Finally, look at the cover: three layers of laminated/reinforced vinyl are better than a single or double layer. Anti-bacterial covers are also a worthwhile feature. What about quilted covers? They are a waste of money, in our opinion.

Top Picks: Brand Recommendations

When it comes to mattresses, it's best not to scrimp. Go for the best mattress you can afford. Besides, the price differences between the cheap products and the better quality ones are often small, about $50 or less.

◆ **Foam Mattresses.** Our top brand recommendation for foam mattresses is **Colgate** (call 404-681-2121 for a dealer near you; web: www.colgatekids.com). This Georgia-based company makes a full line of foam mattresses which range from $50 to $125. Among the best of Colgate's offerings is the "Classica," a group of five-inch foam mattresses with varying firmness. The Classica I was top-rated

Is SIDS linked to second-hand mattresses?

We're big fans of second-hand and hand-me-down products for baby as a money-saver—except when it comes to old cribs and car seats. And based on a new study from Scotland, we're going to add crib mattresses to that list.

According to a study published in the *British Medical Journal* (November 2, 2002), Scottish researchers said "babies who sleep on a second-hand mattress seem to be at a higher risk of sudden infant death syndrome (SIDS)" than those that don't. The lead author of the study, Dr. David Tappin, compared 131 children who died of SIDS between 1996 and 2000 with 278 healthy infants. The babies that died of SIDS were "roughly three times as likely as other children to have regularly slept on a mattress that was previously used by another child," according to a Reuters article on the study. The association was stronger if the mattress was from another home.

So, why might this be the case? Researchers don't know if it is really the mattress that is causing the problem, but some speculate that "toxic bacteria might grow in the mattress after it becomes repeatedly soaked with milk, urine or saliva. Such bacteria might contribute to illness or death of the second child," the article stated.

While more research needs to be done on this issue, we'll come down on the side of safety—use a NEW mattress for your child, not a hand-me-down. And even though the problem seems to be worse with second-hand mattresses from another home, we'd recommend a new mattress for your baby's future siblings as well.

by *Consumer Reports* and is available in discount stores and mail order catalogs like Baby Catalog of America (1-800-PLAYPEN; web: www.babycatalog.com) for $80. Of course, just about any Colgate foam mattress will do the trick; the company has several different lines but we found little difference among them. One caution to Colgate mattresses: they can be harder to find than other brands. Colgate isn't sold in chain stores; instead, the company concentrates on independent juvenile retailers–check their web site for the current list of dealers.

Another great deal on mattresses: the Kolcraft "Deluxe Extra Heavy Density Foam Mattress" at Target for $30. Readers who've bought this mattress think it is just as firm as the Colgate Classica.

♦ **Coil Mattresses.** We liked the **Sealy** (by Kolcraft) "Ultra Soft" 150 coil mattress for $60 at Babies R Us as a best buy for the dollar. Also good: **Simmons** "Baby Beauty" 104 coil mattress for $70 and Simmons Super Maxipedic 160 coils for $90 (again at Babies R Us). We also liked the Evenflo's "Serta" line, sold at Baby Depot and other stores for $60 to $110.

If you can find the Colgate brand, they too make a decent coil mattress–a 150-coil model is about $100. Another Colgate best buy in the coil mattress category: the Little Aristrocrat I for $69.

In the past year, **Child Craft** and **Pali** have rolled out their own mattress lines. Child Craft offers both a foam and coil mattress under the Legacy and Child Craft names at $50 to $150. Pali has teamed with Canadian mattress maker Jupiter Industries

E-Mail from The Real World
Colic remedy turns mattress into magic fingers.

Colic, that incessant crying by young infants at night, can drive parents to distraction. A mom in Tennessee writes about one solution she found:

"After several relatively sleepless nights with our two-week old infant, I found a product called the Sleep Tight Infant Soother. This product basically makes sleeping in the crib similar to riding in the car. A vibration device attaches underneath the mattress and you can either get a sound box for the crib, which plays white noise, or get a 90-minute cassette tape. If you opt for the sound box, the price is $129; it is $89 if you go for the cassette tape. The product has a 15-day trial period and can be ordered online at www. colic.com or by calling 1-800-NO COLIC. The FDA has approved it as a medical device so insurance may reimburse the cost."

(www.BoPeepNurseryProducts.com) for their new line. Among the unique features for Pali's mattresses: antibacterial covers and a combo foam/coil mattress. Prices are high, however (about $190).

What about those fancy vibrating mattresses? Kolcraft makes a "Tender Vibes" mattress for $130 to $170 that features 150 coils, a vibrating feature and an automatic timer that turns off the vibration after 15 minutes. Is this necessary? Unless you have a history of colic (that never-ending crying that afflicts some babies) in your family, it's overkill. Nothing wrong with it, but save your money and get a regular non-vibrating mattress.

Bottom line: there isn't much difference between coil mattress brands—each does a good job. Stick with the ones at 150 coils (80 is too little; 250 is overkill).

Still can't decide between foam or coil? Well, Colgate has a solution—a "2 in 1" mattress that is half foam and half coil. The company suggests the extra-firm foam side for infants. When your baby reaches toddler hood, you flip the mattress over to the coil side. The price: $120 to $130. As we pointed out earlier, the "2 in 1" mattress isn't something we'd recommend (it really isn't necessary), but we realize some parents will consider it.

Dressers & Changing Tables

The juvenile trade refers to dressers, changing tables, and the like as "case pieces" since they are essentially furniture made out of a large case (pretty inventive, huh?). Now that you've got a place for the baby to sleep (and a mattress for her to sleep on), where are you going to put all those cute outfits that you'll get as gifts from Aunt Bertha?

And let's not forget that all too important activity that will occupy so many of your hours after the baby is born: changing diapers. The other day we calculated that by our baby's first birthday, we had changed over 2400 diapers! Wow! To first-time parents, that may seem like an unreal number, but babies actually do go through 70 to 100 diapers a week for the first six months or so. That translates into ten to 15 changes a day.

What are You Buying

DRESSERS. As you shop for baby furniture, you'll note a wide variety of dressers—three drawer, four drawer, armoires, combination dresser/changing tables, and more. No matter which type you choose, we do have two general tips for getting the most for your money. First, choose a dresser whose drawers roll out on roller bearings (located on the drawer sides). Cheap dressers have drawers that simply sit on a track at the bottom center of the drawer. As a result, they don't roll out as smoothly and are prone to coming off the track. Our second piece of advice: make sure the dresser top is laminated. If you're in a rush and put something wet on top, you want to make sure you don't damage the finish. Also, non-laminated tops are more prone to scratches and dings. Finally, look at the drawer sides—the best furniture makers use "dove-tailed" drawer joints (they look like interlocking fingers) where the side panel meets the front of the drawer.

What about wood substitutes like medium density fiberboard (MDF)? MDF by itself isn't necessarily good or bad. It really depends on the overall construction (drawer glides, joints, etc.), not so much the wood content. Yes, some high-price furniture makers tout their "all wood" construction (where even the sides and backs of the dressers are wood), but that might be overkill. How often will you be looking at the back of your child's dresser anyway? While you should avoid dressers made of cheap laminate, we've seen several good MDF dressers by makers like Status that were impressive.

2 CHANGING AREA. Basically, you have two options here. You can buy a separate changing table or a combination dresser/changing table. As mentioned earlier, we think a separate changing table is a waste of money (as well as a waste of space).

A better option is the combo package, a dresser and changing table all rolled into one. These come in two varieties: hi-low (also called combo units; see picture at right) and regular chests with add-on changing areas. Hi-low dressers are a popular option. These dressers (also called "combo" or "castle" units) were pioneered by Rumble Tuff, reviewed later in this section. The two-tier design of these dressers provides a convenient space to change diapers while not looking like a diaper-changing table. Most parents keep diaper-changing supplies in the upper drawer, while the lower dresser functions as clothing storage, etc. Hi-low dressers start at $500 and range up to $700. As an option, some manufactures offer a hutch that attaches to a hi-low dresser to give you shelf space.

Let's say you're on a really tight budget. What should you do? Forget the diaper changing station altogether! Some mothers we interviewed just change their baby in the crib or on a countertop. Of course, there are a couple of disadvantages to this alternative. First, there's not a convenient place for diapers and supplies. A rolling storage cart could solve this (cost: about $25 in many catalogs and stores; we saw one for $18 at the Container Store 800-733-3532; web: www.containerstore.com; Sam's Club has a plastic "six drawer mini chest" for $24). Another disadvantage: if you have a boy, he could spray the crib sheets, bumper pads, and just about anything else in the crib with his little "water pistol." Hence, you might find yourself doing more laundry.

One mom sent us an e-mail with a solution to the changing table dilemma—she bought a "Rail Rider," changing table that fits across a crib and can be removed when the baby is sleeping. For $32, it did the trick. Made by Burlington Basket Company (for a dealer near you, call 800-553-2300 or 319-754-6508) and sold online at BabyCenter.com. The Rail Rider does have a few drawbacks: it doesn't fit all cribs and shorter folks find it more difficult to use.

Safe & Sound

Safety doesn't stop at the crib—also consider the nursery's other furniture items when baby-proofing.

◆ *Anchor those shelves.* A nice bookcase (whether on the floor or on top of the dresser) can become a tip-over hazard as the baby begins pulling up on objects. The best advice is to attach any shelves to a wall to provide stability.

◆ *Baby proof the diaper station.* If your diaper changing area has open shelves, you may have to baby proof the bottom shelves. As the baby begins to climb, you must remove any dangerous medicines or supplies from easily accessible shelves.

◆ *Choose a dresser that doesn't have drawer pulls.* Those little knobs can make it easy for baby to open the drawers—and it's those open drawers that can be used as a step stool to scale the dresser. A good tip is to buy a dresser without drawer pulls; quite a few styles have drawers with grooves that let you open them from below. While this isn't totally baby proof, it reduces the attraction for baby. Another good tip: anchor the dresser to the wall. In case baby does find a way to climb it, at least the unit won't tip over.

◆ *Air out all that new nursery paint, furniture and decor.* A University of Maryland School of Medicine study suggests new parents should air out freshly painted or wallpapered rooms before baby arrives. New furniture and mattresses also "out-gas" fumes, so consider ventilating the nursery when they arrive as well. How much ventilation? The study suggested four to eight weeks of open window ventilation, which seems a bit excessive to us. But it makes sense to do some air-out of the nursery before baby arrives. Another idea: look for environmentally friendly paints that have lower out-gas emissions. If you install new carpet in the house, leave during the installation and open the windows (and turn on fans) for two days.

Our Picks: Brand Recommendations

As previously noted in this chapter, many of the crib makers also manufacture "case pieces" (dressers, armoires, etc). For contact information on these brands, refer to the reviews earlier in this chapter. Here's a round up:

Good. The dressers from domestic manufacturers *Simmons*, *Bassett* and *Child Craft* are good entry-level options. A simple four-drawer dresser from Bassett is $290; the same item from Child Craft is $350 (both available at Babies R Us). Hi-low combo dressers are a bit more ($540 to $600 from Simmons and Child Craft) but do offer more flexibility. As for quality, we noted Simmons uses solid wood drawer sides, while Child Craft's drawer sides are pressed wood. The only bummer: most drawers in this price range lack dovetail joints and feature plain styling.

Better. If you're looking for better quality and more style, check out the offerings from Canadian manufacturers. *Morigeau*, *Ragazzi* and *Status* make dressers with hip adult looks like bun feet and shaker styling. Quality is better, but you're going to pay for it: most dressers start at $500 and go up to $700 or more.

Morigeau has a hi-low combo dresser for $500, while a simple four-drawer dresser runs $600 to $900. Status' basic three-drawer dresser with changer top is $500. In this "better" category, we'd also put the brands like Pali and Sorelle/C&T. Most of these dressers are made in Canada; quality is excellent but you will pay for it with a 30% premium over domestic makers you'd see at Babies R Us.

Best. Our top pick for juvenile furniture is an obscure Utah-based company that doesn't even make cribs—they concentrate solely on case pieces (dressers, bookshelves and more). *Rumble Tuff* (for a dealer near you, call 800-524-9607 or 801-226-2648; web: www.rumbletuff.com) is also a best buy—their prices are often 10% to 25% less than the competition. Their strategy is to knock-off the big guys, making similar furniture styles in the exact same finishes as the crib makers so everything will match. (Well, to be fair, they don't match EVERY last finish offered by crib makers, but darn close).

Rumble Tuff's claim to fame is their popular combo dresser. This unit combines a three-drawer dresser/changing table and a taller base cabinet and drawer. Price: $500 to $600, depending on the finish. These combo units have proven so popular that other furniture makers have knocked them off. In fact, Simmons and Child Craft have tried to match Rumble Tuff on price for their combo units, but you'll note that the competition is still much higher when you look at accessories like book shelves, desks and so on.

All in all, Rumble Tuff makes 30 different pieces, in both contemporary and traditional finishes. The quality is excellent: all of Rumble Tuff's drawers feature roller bearings. Every dresser is made of solid wood like maple and oak (except for the sides and tops, which are veneers). Best of all, the furniture comes in 20 different colors; you can mix and match color accents for knobs or tops to your heart's content.

While the drawer sides are not solid wood, we found the overall construction to be good. We bought a Rumble Tuff dresser and bookshelf unit and have been very happy—it matched our Child Craft crib exactly and we saved over $100.

One caveat to Rumble Tuff: the brand can be difficult to find, as their distribution is spotty in places like New England. Go to their web site to find a list of dealers.

Another brand to consider: Readers write to us to say **Camelot Furniture** of Anaheim, Calif. (714-283-4194) has some great deals on dressers and other case pieces. "The infant and case pieces by Camelot gave me the most bang for the buck, not to mention a perfect match in color for my Pali crib," says a reader. Yes, it's made of laminate but the drawer glides have a lifetime warranty and the

---

E-MAIL FROM THE REAL WORLD
Antique bargains

A reader reminds us that antique stores can be great sources for baby furniture.

"You might remind readers not to overlook the local antique store when shopping for nursery furniture. We found a great English dresser from the 1930s with ample drawer and cupboard space for $325 that has a lot more character than anything we've seen in baby stores, plus it can be easily moved to another room/use when our baby outgrows it."

prices are great—$479 for an armoire, $198 for a bookshelf.

Finally, a reader recommended a source for dressers from Canada: *Mother Hubbard's Cupboard* (416) 661-8201. This Toronto-based furniture maker offers a four-drawer dresser for $399 to $499 and an armoire for $599; quality is very good. The reader was especially pleased that the Mother Hubbard dresser she was considering matched her crib's finish.

Even More Stuff To Spend Money On

Just because to this point you have spent an amount equivalent to the gross national product of Peru on baby furniture doesn't mean you're done, of course. Nope, we've got four more items to consider for your baby's room:

1 **ROCKER-GLIDER.** We're not talking about the rocking chair you've seen at grandma's house. No, we're referring to the high-tech modern-day rockers that are so fancy they aren't mere rockers—they're "glider-rockers." Thanks to a fancy ball-bearing system, these rockers "glide" with little or no effort.

Quebec-based *Dutailier* (call 800-363-9817 or 450-772-2403; web: www.dutailier.com), is to glider-rockers what Microsoft is to software—basically, they own the market. Thanks to superior quality and quick delivery, Dutailier probably sells one out of every two glider rockers purchased in the U.S. and Canada each year.

Dutailier has an incredible selection of 45 models, seven finishes, and 80 different fabrics. The result: over 37,000 possible combinations. All wood is solid maple or oak and features non-toxic finishes. You have to try real hard to avoid seeing Dutailier—the company has 3500 retail dealers, from small specialty stores to major retail chains.

Prices for Dutailier start at about $350 for a basic model at Babies R Us (although you can find them for less online). Of course, the price can soar quickly from there—add a swivel base, plush cushions or leather fabric and you can spend $500. Or $1000.

If we had to criticize Dutailier on something, it would have to be their cushions. Most are not machine washable (the covers can't be zipped off and put into the washing machine). As a result, you'll have to take them to a dry cleaner and pay big bucks to get them looking like new. A few of our readers have solved this problem by sewing slipcovers for their glider-rockers (most fabric stores carry pattern books for such items). Of course, if the cushions are shot, you can always order different ones when you move the glider-rocker into a family room.

It can take 10-12 weeks to order a custom Dutailier rocker, but the company does offer a "Quick Ship" program—a selection of 17 chair styles in two or three different fabric choices that are in stock for shipment in two weeks. We have received occasional complaints about how long it takes to order a Dutailier—one reader special-ordered a Dutailier from Babies R Us, only to find out some weeks later that the fabric they wanted was discontinued (Dutailier "forgot" to tell Babies R Us, who, to their credit, tried to fix the problem immediately). Other readers complain about fabric backorders, which cause more delays in delivery. Our advice: make sure the store double checks the order to make sure Dutailier doesn't drop the ball.

While Dutailier's web site lacks a product catalog, Dutailier is one of those products that is easy to research (and buy) online. Several sites carry the brand at a discount, including BabyCatalog.com. Two sites that have a great selection of Dutailier are CribNCarriage (www.cribncarriage.com) and Rocking Chairs 100% (www.rocking-chairs.com; 800-4-ROCKER), a web site off-shoot of the Corte Madera, CA store of the same name. The latter site is easy to navigate, with thumbnails of different models and little color chips for available colors. A reader also recommended American Health &Comfort's site (www.ForYourBaby.com; 800-327-4382) for deals on Dutailiers.

So, who's got the very best deals on Dutailier? Readers lately have emailed their kudos for RockingChairOutlet.com—excellent service and great prices. One reader saved $100 on her Dutailier from RockingChairOutlet.com, compared the seven other discounters/stores she got quotes from for the chair. Similar raves go to Good Night Ben (www.GoodNightBen.com), where readers found prices much less than stores.

An optional accessory for glider rockers is the ottoman that glides too. These start at $99 without a cushion, but most cost $125 to $150 with cushion. We suggest forgetting the ottoman and ordering an inexpensive "nursing" footstool (about $30 to $40 in catalogs like Motherwear 800-950-2500 or on line). Why? Some moms claim the ottoman's height puts additional strain on their backs while breast-feeding. While the nursing footstool doesn't rock, it's lower height puts less strain on your back. (That said, we should note that some ottoman fans point out that once their mom/baby get the hang of nursing, that gliding ottoman is a nice luxury).

Is a glider-rocker a waste of money? Some parents have written to us with that question, assuming you'd just use the item for the baby's first couple of years. Actually, a glider-rocker can have a much longer life. You can swap the cushions after a couple of years (most makers let you order these items separately) and move the glider-rocker to a family room.

Of course, there are several other companies that make glider-rockers for nurseries. Here are some alternatives to Dutailier:

◆ **Brooks** *Call 800-427-6657 or 423-626-1111 for a dealer near you.* Tennessee-based Brooks has been around for 40 years, but only entered the glider-rocker business in 1988. Their glider-rockers retail for $169 to $399, while the ottomans are $100-$150. Unlike Dutailier, all their fabrics are available on any style chair. Brooks chairs feature solid base panels (Dutailier has an open base), which the company touts as more safe. While we liked Brooks' styles and fabrics, one baby storeowner told us he found the company very disorganized with poor customer service.

◆ **Jardine** (see review earlier in this chapter). This line, manufactured in China by Cosco, sells bargain basement glider rockers at Babies R Us. We've seen Jardine glider rockers for as little as $100 on sale, but most run $140 to $240. The quality is disappointing—these chairs don't rock as easily as a Dutailier or Shermag. We say pass on this one.

◆ **Shermag/Conant Ball** *In the U.S., call 800-363-2635 for dealer near you or 800-556-1515 Canada. Web: www.shermag.com.* We saw this brand at chain stores and the prices can't be beat. Sample: Target.com sells a Shermag glider AND ottoman for just $199 to $299 total. Yes, you read that right—prices

start at $199. A similar Shermag (see picture above) available from BabiesRUs.com is $199—again, including ottoman! Okay, what's the catch? First, these styles are a bit smaller in size than other glider-rockers—they fit most moms fine, but those six-foot dads may be uncomfortable. The color choices are also limited (just one or two, in most cases). And you should try to sit in these first to make sure you like the cushions (no, they aren't as super comfy as more expensive options but most parents think they're just fine).

Of course, Shermag offers many more styles and options than just those rock-bottom deals at Target and elsewhere. We noticed other Shermag gliders were $300 to $350 while ottomans were an extra $150 or so. What's Shermag's quality like compared to Dutailier? Frankly, we couldn't tell much of a difference—both are excellent.

◆ **Relax-R** *Call 800-850-2909 for a dealer near you.* Relax-R is a Vermont company that makes leather glider rockers that swivel,

 CHAPTER 2: NURSERY NECESSITIES **103**

glide and recline. New to the market, Relax-R also offers another unique feature: heated massage. We tried out a Relax-R rocker recently and were impressed—they were very comfortable, require no assembly and feature several leather choices. The downside? First, they're pricey: $500 for a basic model (add $100 for the massage option). Second, they're kind of ugly. The overstuffed cushions and armrests win points for comfort but not style.

◆ **Towne Square** *Call 800-356-1663 for a dealer near you; web: www.gliderrocker.com.* Hillsboro, Texas-based Towne Square has a lifetime warranty for all its glider-rockers. They feature a "long-glide" rocking system that has no ball bearings that can wear out. Towne Square's gliders sell for $300 to $500. Their "nursing ottoman" is low to the ground at a height that the manufacturer claims is "ideal for nursing" and gives you control over the chair's rocking motion. Like Brooks, Towne Square gliders feature solid sides as a safety measure (to keep little hands out of the rocking mechanism). As for looks, we'd put Towne Square in the "traditional" category—if you want a contemporary look, this probably isn't for you.

◆ **And more ideas.** What about plain rocking chairs (without cushions)? Almost all the glider-rockers we recommend above can be ordered without cushions. Of course, just about any furniture store also sells plain rocking chairs. We don't have any preference on these items—to be honest, if you think you want a rocker, we'd go for the glider-rocker with cushions. Considering the time you'll spend in it, that would be much more comfortable than a plain rocking chair with no padding.

2   **CLOSET ORGANIZERS.** Most closets are a terrible waste of space. While a simple rod and shelf might be fine for adults, the basic closet doesn't work for babies. Wouldn't it be better to have small shelves to store accessories, equipment and shoes? Or wire baskets for blankets and t-shirts? What about three more additional rods at varying heights to allow for more storage? The solution is closet organizers and you can go one of two routes. For the do-it-yourself crowd, consider a storage kit from such brands as Closet Maid (call 800-874-0008 for a store near you; web: www.closetmaid.com), Storage Pride (800) 441-0337 or Lee Rowan (800) 325-6150 web: www.leerowan.com. Closet Maid's web site (closetmaid.com) is particularly helpful, with a useful "Design Selector" and how-to guide. Two catalogs that sell storage items include Hold Everything (800) 421-2264 web: www.holdeverything.com and the Container Store (800) 733-3532 web: www.containerstore.com. A basic storage kit made of laminated particleboard ranges from $50

to $120 (that will do an average size closet). Kits made of coated wire run $30 to $60.

What if you'd rather leave it to the professionals? For those parents who don't have the time or inclination to install a closet organizer themselves, consider calling Closet Factory (call 800-692-5673 for a dealer near you; web: www.closetfactory.com) or California Closets (call 800-274-6754 for a dealer near you; web: www.californiaclosets.com). You can also check your local phone book under "Closets" for local companies that install closet organizers. Professionals charge about $400 to $500 for a typical closet.

While a closet organizer works well for most folks, it may be especially helpful in cases where baby's room is small. Instead of buying a separate dresser or bookshelves, you can build-in drawer stacks and shelves in a closet to squeeze out every possible inch of storage. Another idea: a deep shelf added to a closet can double as a changing area.

We invested in a closet organizer for our youngest child's room and were more than pleased with the results.

3 STEREO. During those sleep deprivation experiments, it's sure nice to have some soothing music to make those hours just whiz by. Sure, you could put a cheap clock radio in the baby's room, but that assumes you have decent radio stations. And even the best radio station will be somewhat tiring to listen to for the many nights ahead. Our advice: buy (or register as a gift) one of those CD/cassette boom box radios that run $100 to $300 in most electronics stores.

4 DIAPER PAIL. Well, those diapers have to go somewhere. We'll review our top picks for diaper pails in Chapter 7, Around the House. A safety note on this subject: many basic diaper pails come with "deodorizers," little cakes that are supposed to take the stink out of stinky diapers. The only problem: many contain toxic chemicals that can be poisonous if toddlers get their hands on them. A new solution to this problem comes from Sassy (616) 243-0767 web: www.sassybaby.com. This Michigan-based company makes a "no touch" diaper pail deodorizer that is completely non-toxic.

5 A CUTE LAMP. What nursery would be complete without a cute lamp for junior's dresser? A good web site for this is BabyCenter.com, which has a decent selection of lamps and nightlights.

The Bottom Line:
A Wrap-Up of Our Best Buy Picks

For cribs, you've got two basic choices: a simple model that is, well, just a crib or a "convertible" model that eventually morphs into a twin or full size bed. In the simple category for best buys, Child Craft's 10171 is a simple maple crib with single-drop side for just $200 (see picture earlier in this chapter) at Target.com or Babies R Us. In a similar vein, a basic Simmons model at Baby Depot ran $240.

Other features that are nice (but not necessary) for cribs include a quiet rail release and hidden hardware. If you fancy an imported crib, there are few bargains but we found Sorelle/C&T has reasonable prices ($250 to start) for above average quality.

The best mattress? We like the foam mattresses from Colgate ($90 for the Classica I). Or, for coil, go for a Sealy (Kolcraft) 150 coil mattress for $60 at Babies R Us.

Where to buy a crib and other nursery furniture? Our readers say chains like Babies R Us and Baby Depot have the lowest prices, but the web can be a great source for discounts on non-bulky items like rocker gliders. Good ol' JCPenney has the best mail order catalog for nursery deals. For design inspiration, consider the Pottery Barn Kids catalog for ideas (but few deals).

Dressers and other case pieces by Rumble Tuff were great deals—they exactly match the finishes of Child Craft and Simmons, but at prices 10% to 25% less than the competition. We liked their three-drawer combo unit that combines a changing table and a dresser for $450 to $600. Finally, we recommend the Dutailier and Shermag brands of glider-rockers. At $200 to $300, their basic models are well made and stylish. A matching ottoman runs $110 to $180.

So, let's sum up some of our recommendations:

Child Craft single drop-side crib	$200
Sealy 150 coil mattress	$60
Rumble Tuff Hi-Lo dresser	$500
Shermag glider-rocker	$200
Miscellaneous	$200
TOTAL	$1160

By contrast, if you bought a Bellini crib ($600), a 200-coil mattress ($160), a Ragazzi dresser ($750), a fancy glider-rocker ($500), separate changing table ($200) and miscellaneous items ($200) at full retail, you'd be out $2410 by this point. Of course, you don't have any sheets for your baby's crib yet. Nor any clothes for Junior to wear. So, next we'll explore those topics and save more of your money.

CHAPTER 3

Baby Bedding & Decor

Inside this chapter

How can you find brand new, designer-label bedding for as much as 50% off the retail price? We've got the answer in this chapter, plus you'll find nine smart shopper tips to help get the most for your money. We'll share the best web sites and mail-order catalogs for baby linens. Then, we'll reveal nine important tips that will keep your baby safe and sound. Finally, we've got reviews of the best bedding designers and an interesting list of seven top money-wasters.

Getting Started: When Do You Need This Stuff?

Begin shopping for your baby's linen pattern in the sixth month of your pregnancy, if not earlier. Why? If you're purchasing these items from a baby specialty store, they usually must be special-ordered—allow at least four to eight weeks for delivery. If you leave a few weeks for shopping, you can order the bedding in your seventh month to be assured it arrives before the baby does.

If you're buying bedding from a store or catalog that has the desired pattern in stock, you can wait until your eighth month. It still takes time to comparison shop, and some stores may only have certain pieces you need in stock, while other accessories (like wall hangings, etc.) may need to be special ordered.

Sources

There are six basic sources for baby bedding:

1 **BABY SPECIALTY STORES.** These stores tend to have a limited selection of bedding in stock. Typically, you're expected to choose the bedding by seeing what you like on sample cribs or by looking through manufacturers' catalogs. Then you have to special-order your choices and wait four to eight weeks for arrival. And that's the main disadvantage to buying linens at a specialty store: THE WAIT. On the upside, most specialty stores do carry high-quality brand names you can't find at discounters or baby superstores. But you'll pay for it—most specialty stores mark such items at full retail.

2 **DISCOUNTERS.** The sheer variety of discount stores that carry baby bedding is amazing—you can find it everywhere from Wal-Mart to Target, Marshall's to TJ Maxx. Even Toys R Us sells baby bedding and accessories. As you'd expect, everything is cash and carry at these stores—most carry a decent selection of items in stock. You pick out what you like and that's it; there are no special orders. The downside? Prices are cheap, but so is the quality. Most discounters only carry low-end brands whose synthetic fabrics and cheap construction may not withstand repeated washings. There are exceptions to this rule, which we'll review later in this chapter.

3 **DEPARTMENT STORES.** The selection of baby bedding at department stores is all over the board. Some chains have great baby departments and others need help. For example, JCPenney carries linen sets by such companies as NoJo and Cotton Tale (see the reviews of these brands later in this chapter), while Foley's (part of the May Department Store chain) seems to only have a few blankets and sheets. Prices at department stores vary as widely as selection; however, you can guarantee that department stores will hold occasional sales, making them a better deal.

4 **BABY SUPERSTORES.** The superstores reviewed in the last chapter (Babies R Us, Baby Depot, etc.) combine the best of both worlds: discount prices AND quality brands. Best of all, most items are in stock. Unlike Wal-Mart or Target, you're more likely to see 100% cotton bedding and better construction. Yet, the superstores aren't perfect: they are often beaten on price by online sources (reviewed later in this chapter). And superstores are more likely to sell bedding in sets (rather than a la carte), forcing you to buy frivolous items.

5 **THE WEB.** If there were a perfect baby product to be sold on-line, it would have to be crib bedding and linens. The web's full-color graphics let you see exactly what you'll get. And bedding is lightweight, which minimizes shipping costs. The only bummer: you can't feel the fabric or inspect the stitching. As a result, we recommend sticking to well-known brand names when ordering online.

6 **MAIL-ORDER CATALOGS.** In the last few years, there's been a marked increase in the number of catalog sellers who offer baby linens, and that's great news for parents. Catalogs like Pottery Barn Kids, Land's End and Company Kids offer high quality bedding (100% cotton, high thread counts) at reasonable prices. Best of all, you can buy the pieces a la carte (eliminating unnecessary items found in sets) while at the same time, mixing and matching to your heart's content. If you want "traditional" bedding sets, JCPenney's catalog won't disappoint. We'll review these and more catalogs later in this chapter.

Parents in Cyberspace: What's on the Web?

Burlington Coat Factory Direct (Baby Depot)
Web site: www.bcfdirect.com
What it is: The online version of discounter Burlington Coat Factory's Baby Depot.
What's Cool: This site offers good discounts (about 20% to 30%) on bedding from such famous names as Lambs & Ivy, Cotton Tale, CoCaLo and more. Best of all, you can order a la carte if you don't want a complete set—each page lists a plethora of matching accessories for each grouping plus you can click on thumbnail swatches for a closer look. Finally, Baby Depot lets you know how long each item takes to ship and the shipping costs are reasonable.
Needs work: We were a bit disappointed with the navigation on this site in our last edition and it hasn't improved. It takes a tremendous number of clicks to see all the bedding offerings. We had to navigate through four menus to get to the bedding list (go first to Baby, then Nursery). Even more confusing: the site mixed in general categories like "boy" and "girl" or "florals" and "bears" with specific manufacturers like Glenna Jean. Once you do choose a brand name, all you get is a list of collections without any thumbnails. This means you either have to know which collection you want or you have to go through all the patterns to see what's up, a very time consuming process.

Baby Bedding Online
Web site: www.babybeddingonline.com
What it is: The online outpost for bedding manufacturer Carousel.
What's cool: Carousel used to sell its line of bedding exclusively

through retail stores at about $250 to $300 per set. A couple years ago, however, they decided to sell directly to the public via their web site, Baby Bedding Online. The prices have taken a huge drop as a result. For example, their four-piece Blue and Yellow plaid used to sell for $268. Online it's a modest $179. Can't beat those prices for an all cotton bedding line. And best of all, Carousel doesn't do this half way: the web site offers free fabric swatches other goodies. Looking for quality portacrib sheets or matching cradle sheets? How about rocking chair pads and high chair pads? They've got them. Lastly, Baby Bedding Online has an outlet store as well. Check the web site to find out when the outlet store is open.

Needs work: The main page for each collection just includes a photo of the item and the price of a four-piece set. You have to click again to get details and prices. And this site isn't going to win any awards for design innovation either. It's basically a text driven site with very simple graphics, however it still gets the job done.

Babies Best Buy

Web: www.babiesbestbuy.com
What it is: A discount site for baby basics.
What's cool: If you're looking for basic sheets, bumpers and blankets here's an excellent source. Babies Best Buy offers percale, flannel and knit sheets in a variety of solids as well as stripes and checks. You can buy them in packs ($78 for percale sheet, bumper and dust ruffle) or a la carte. Cotton knit sheets and flannel sheets start at $7.50. They also carry sheet savers, mattress pads and changing pad covers.
Needs work: Forget finding out who makes this stuff. No manufacturer info is available. And colors are certainly limited. The only patterns are stripes, stars and checks. But if you want to follow our advice to get basics, this is a very affordable place to do it.

◆ **Other web sites to check out:** Don't forget manufacturers' web sites—one of the best is **Brandee Danielle's** (www.brandeedanielle. com). Their entire catalog is online so you can surf to your heart's content. Since most baby stores only carry a few patterns from any one manufacturer, it's informative to see the *entire* collection.

For parents looking for accessories and bedding with a Beatrix Potter theme, check out **Country Lane** (www.countrylane.com). This site sells 750 different accessories and bedding pieces available in the Beatrix Potter line. They also have Pooh themed merchandise and Precious Moments. The discounts are up to 40% off.

Finally, one of the better sites for upper end bedding is **Baby Style** (www.babystyle.com). With designers like Amy Coe, Wendy Bellissimo and CoCaLo the prices are a bit on the higher side, although they do a limited discount. The selection is smaller, but they offer free shipping for sales over $100 and various coupons for new customers. They also have a sale area with items 20% to 30% off retail.

What Are You Buying?

Walk into any baby store, announce you're having a baby, and stand back: the eager salespeople will probably pitch you on all types of bedding items that you MUST buy. We call this the "Diaper Stacker Syndrome," named in honor of that useless (but expensive) linen item that allegedly provides a convenient place to store diapers. Most parents aren't about to spend the equivalent of the Federal Deficit on diaper stackers. So, here's our list of the absolute necessities for your baby's linen layette:

◆ **Fitted sheets**—at least three to four. When it comes to crib sheets, you have three choices: woven, knit and flannel. Woven (also called percale) sheets are available in all cotton or cotton blend fabrics, while knit and flannel sheets are almost always all cotton. As to which is best, it's up to you. Some folks like flannel sheets, especially in colder climates. Others find woven or knit sheets work fine. One tip: look for sheets that have elastic all-around the edges (cheaper ones just have elastic on the corners). See the "Safe & Sound" section for more info on crib sheet safety issues.

If you plan to use a bassinet/cradle, you'll need a few of these special-size sheets as well . . . but your choices here are pretty limited. This type of sheets are often found together in the same section, so be sure to get the right size for your mattress. You'll usually find solid color pastels or white. Some linen manufacturers do sell bassinet sheets, but they can get rather pricey. And you may find complete bassinet sets that come with all the linens for your baby. Just be sure to check the fabric content (all cotton is best) and washing instructions. By the way, one mom improvised bassinet sheets by putting the bassinet mattress inside a king size pillowcase. You may want to secure the excess fabric under the mattress so it doesn't un-tuck.

◆ **Mattress Pads/Sheet Protector.** While most baby mattresses have waterproof vinyl covers, many parents use either a mattress pad or sheet protector to protect the mattress or sheet from leaky diapers. A mattress pad is the traditional way of dealing with this problem and is placed between the mattress and the crib sheet. A more recent invention, the sheet protector, goes on top of the crib sheet.

A sheet protector has a waterproof vinyl backing to protect against leaking. And here's the cool part: it Velcro's to the crib's posts, making for easy removal. If the baby's diaper leaks, simply pop off the sheet protector and throw it in the wash (instead of the fitted crib sheets). You can buy sheet protectors in most baby stores or catalogs. See an "Email from the Real World" on the next page for information on one brand of sheet saver, the Ultimate Crib Sheet.

◆ **A Good Blanket.** Baby stores love to pitch expensive quilts to parents and many bedding sets include them as part of the package. Yet, all babies need is a simple cotton blanket. Not only are thick quilts overkill for most climates, they can also be dangerous. The latest report from the Consumer Product Safety Commission on Sudden Infant Death Syndrome (SIDS) concluded that putting babies face down on such soft bedding may contribute to as many as 30% of SIDS deaths (that's 900 babies) each year in the U.S. (As a side note, there is no explanation for the other 70% of SIDS cases, although environmental factors like smoking near the baby and a too-hot room are suspected). Some baby bedding companies have responded to these concerns by rolling out decorative flannel-backed blankets (instead of quilts) in their collections.

But what if you live in a cold climate and think a cotton blanket won't cut it? Consider crib blankets made from Polartec (a lightweight 100% polyester fabric brushed to a soft fleece finish) available in most stores and catalogs. For example, Lands End sells a polar fleece crib blanket $24.50. Of course, polar fleece blankets are also available from mainstream bedding companies like California Kids (reviewed later in this chapter). Or how about a "coverlet," which is lighter than a quilt but more substantial than a blanket? Lightweight quilts (instead of the traditional thick and fluffy version) are another option for as little as $70 in mail order catalogs.

Finally, we found a great product to keep baby warm and avoid a blanket altogether. Halo Sleep Systems (www.halosleep.com), the manufacturer of Halo crib mattresses, also makes a product called the Sleep Sack. This "wearable blanket" helps baby avoid creeping under a blanket and suffocating. Available in three sizes and fabrics, the Sleep Sack is $25 to $30. A portion of the sale price goes to the SIDS Alliance. Kiddopotamus also has a version called the BeddieBye Zip-Around Safety Blanket for $14 to $16.

◆ **Bumper Pads.** In a previous edition of this book, we called bumper pads "an important safety item." We've since changed our mind and now consider them to be an optional accessory that we don't necessarily recommend. Why the change of heart? All the warnings about SIDS and soft bedding (see previous section) that

E-Mail from The Real World
Sheet savers make for easy changes

Baby bedding sure looks cute, but the real work is changing all those sheets. Karen Naide found a solution:

"One of our best buys was 'The Ultimate Crib Sheet.' I bought one regular crib sheet that matched the bedding set, and two Ultimate Crib Sheets. This product is waterproof (vinyl on the bottom, and soft white cotton on the top) and lies on top of your regular crib sheet. It has six elastic straps that snap around the bars of your crib. When it gets dirty or the baby soils it, all you have to do is unsnap the straps, lift it off, put a clean one on, and that's it! No taking the entire crib sheet off (which usually entails wrestling with the mattress and bumper pads)... it's really quick and easy! While the white sheet may not exactly match your pattern, it can only be seen from inside the crib, and as you have so often stated, it's not like the baby cares about what it looks like. From the outside of the crib, you can still see the crib sheet that matches your bedding. Anyway, I think it's a wonderful product, and really a must."

*The **Ultimate Crib Sheet** is made by Basic Comfort (call 800-456-8687 for a store near you; web: www.basiccomfort.com). It sells for $16 to $19 and is available at Babies R Us or we've seen it for as little as $13 on web sites like www.BabyAbby.com. Older versions of the Ultimate Crib Sheet have become a problem with older babies. Some of our readers report that their children were able to get under the Ultimate Crib Sheet as they got a bit older. This scary scenario can be avoided by using their new, improved version with snaps on the ends, not just the sides.*

*Of course, there are several other companies that sell similar sheets; we've seen them in general catalogs like One Step Ahead and Baby Catalog of America. Another sheet saver is made by **Kiddopotamus** (800) 772-8339 (web: www.kiddopotamus.com).*

*One of the coolest new products we found was the **Quick Zip** crib sheet from Clouds and Stars (www.cloudsandstars.com). Here's how it works: the sheet base covers the bottom of the mattress and stays in place. The top of the sheet is secured via a plastic zipper. Baby's diaper leaks at two in the morning, you zip off the top of the sheet and zip on a spare. No lifting of the mattress (except when you first set it up) and no untying bumpers. The white or ecru sheet sets are $32 and additional top sheets are $14. They even make a version for portacribs. Hand painted and custom sheets are available for a bit more.*

no soft bedding should be in a crib, even if bumpers are designed as a "safety item." The CPSC "recommend that infants under 12 months be put to sleep in a crib with no soft bedding of any kind under or on top of the baby." Note the CPSC doesn't specifically say anything about banning bumpers but some safety experts have extrapolated their warning to include crib bumpers. As we went to press on this edition, the issue was still up in the air.

After having two babies of our own, we also question the usefulness of bumpers, since you're suppose to remove them after baby begins pulling himself up (so he doesn't use them as a step-stool to get out of the crib). That means, in most cases, you are removing the bumpers when baby is six months old or less. Besides, most parents have heeded SIDS warnings and now put babies to sleep on their backs, making it tougher for them to do much moving around in the crib. On the other side of the debate are parents who think bumpers keep antsy babies from knocking into the side rails (some babies move around the crib more than others). Bumpers can also keep little arms and legs inside a crib, so they don't get lodged in the space between spindles.

If you choose to purchase bumpers, don't buy the ultra-thick or pillow-like bumpers. Instead choose firm bumpers that are made to properly and securely fit the crib (that means no overlapping sections or wide gaps between the ends at the corner sections). Check to see if you can machine-wash them—thinner bumpers can be popped into a washing machine, while ultra-thick bumpers may have to be dry-cleaned. Some parents are concerned that the chemical residue from dry-cleaning might be harmful to their baby. (As a side note, federal law requires the fill in bumpers be 100% polyester).

We'll have more comments on the safety aspects of bumpers in the Safe & Sounds section later in this chapter.

More Money Buys You . . .

Baby bedding sets vary from as little as $40 in discount stores up to nearly $1000 in specialty stores. The basic difference: fabric quality and construction. The cheapest bedding is typically made of 50/50 cotton-poly blends with low thread counts (120 threads per inch). To mask the low quality, many bedding companies splash cutesy licensed cartoon characters on such low-end bedding. So what does more money buy you? First, better fabric. Usually, you'll find 100% cotton with 200 thread counts or more. Better quality bedding sets include more substantial bumpers with more ties.

Some may even have slipcovers removable for easy cleaning. Cheap quality crib sheets often lack elastic all the way around and some shrink dangerously when washed (see Safe and Sound next for details). Beyond the $300 price point, you're most likely paying for a designer name and frilly accessories (coordinating lamp shade, anyone?).

As a side note, we've noticed many of the manufacturers who made only all-cotton bedding sets are adding some blends to keep prices down. Patch Kraft and Cotton Tale are a couple brands we've noticed who are adding a bit of cotton-poly to their designs. Sheets and most bumpers are still typically all cotton, but you may find accent fabrics on quilts and bumpers that are blends. We still recommend these manufacturers as long as the sheets are all cotton.

 ## Safe & Sound

While you might think to cover your outlets and hide that can of Raid, you might not automatically consider safety when selecting crib sheets, comforters, and bumpers. Yet, your baby will be spending more time with these products than any others. Here are several safety points to remember:

◆ **Make sure the crib sheets snugly fit the mattress.** One quality sign: check to make sure the sheet's elastic extends around the entire sheet (cheaper quality crib sheets only have elastic on the ends, making a good fit more difficult to achieve). Another problem: shrinkage. Never use a sheet that has shrunk so much it no longer can be pulled over the corners of the mattress. Unfortunately, some sheets shrink more than others. Which ones shrink least? In a past edition of this book, we printed the results of a Good Housekeeping (GH) test of various crib sheets as a guide. But we've omitted it from this edition. Why? First, the last test was three years ago and we think the results may be of date. Second, we found GH's last test produced results that were inconsistent with their first test back in 1998. The results was something that was more confusing than helpful. You can read the results of the tests on our web site (BabyBargainsBook.com, click on "Bonus Material") for the curious. So, what do we recommend now? First, for any crib sheet you buy, be sure to wash it several times according to the directions and see if it correctly fits your crib. If not, return it to the store. Second, consider a special crib sheet that is designed NOT to come off the crib. Example: The Stay Put safety sheet (www.babysheets.com). Another web site to check out is Baby-Be-

Safe (www.baby-be-safe.com). These "pocket" sheets wrap around the mattress and close with Velcro. Finally, Baby Sleep Safe (www.babysleepsafe.com) makes a crib sheet anchor that helps keep a crib sheet snug to the mattress. A six-point harness attaches to the sheet from the underside of the mattress.

◆ **Recent studies of Sudden Infant Death Syndrome** (SIDS, also known as crib death) have reported that there is an increased incidence of crib death when infants sleep on fluffy bedding, lambskins, or pillows. A pocket can form around the baby's face if she is placed face down in fluffy bedding, and she can slowly suffocate while breathing in her own carbon dioxide. The best advice: put your infant on her back when he or she sleeps. And don't put pillows, comforters or other soft bedding or toys inside a crib.

In 1999, the Consumer Product Safety Commission issued new guidelines regarding SIDS and soft bed linens. The CPSC now recommends that parents not use ANY soft bedding around, on top of, or under baby. If parents want to use a blanket, tuck a very thin blanket under the mattress at one end of the crib to keep it from moving around. The blanket should then only come up to baby's chest. Safest of all: avoid using any blankets in a crib and put baby in a blanket sleeper (basically, a thick set of pajamas) and t-shirt for warmth. (More on blanket sleepers in the next chapter). See the above picture for an example of the correct way to use a blanket.

Finally, one mom wrote to tell us about a scary incident in her nursery. She had left a blanket hanging over the side of the crib when she put her son down for a nap. He managed to pull the blanket down and get wrapped up in it, nearly suffocating. Stories like that convince us that putting any soft bedding in or near a crib is risky.

◆ **Beware of ribbons, long fringe and chenille.** These are possible choking hazards if they are not attached properly. Remove any questionable decoration.

◆ **If you decide to buy bumper pads,** go for ones with well-sewn ties at the top *and* bottom (at least 12 to 16 total). Ties should be between seven and nine inches in length. That's the industry's voluntary standard for safety—ties that are too short can't be tied correctly around a crib post. If ties exceed nine inches, they can be a strangulation hazard. We should note that while that's the standard, our investigation of baby bedding found many manufacturers exceed the limit—one even had ties that were 14" in length! As a defense, expensive bedding makers claim their customers put their bedding on high-price Italian cribs, whose thick corner posts require longer ties. We think that's a weak excuse—14" is too long, even for cribs with the thickest posts. If you buy bumpers with ties that exceed 9", we recommend cutting off any excess length after you install them on the crib. (See the previous chapter's Safe & Sound section for a discussion of Italian cribs and bumper pads).

A related issue to the length of the ties is their location: some companies have just have ties on the top of bumpers. In this case, we've had many reports of babies scooting under the bumper and getting trapped (see our Email from the Real World earlier in this chapter). If you fall in love with bedding that has ties only on the top, consider adding additional ties yourself. Just be sure to sew them on securely. A chart later in this chapter will compare the tie length and location among different brands.

As we noted earlier, make sure the bumpers fit well with no overlapping and no gaps at the ends. And avoid bumpers that are two thick and fluffy. They pose the same kind of risk as pillows. Look for firm, flat bumpers.

E-MAIL FROM THE REAL WORLD
Lack of Bumper Ties Cause a Scare for Parents

Nicole Morely of Chicago wrote to tell us of a frightening incident with borrowed bedding that did not have ties on the bottom of the bumper. (Keep in mind, there is no requirement for bumpers to have ties top and bottom. We recommend it highly, however.)

"We were spending the holidays with grandparents who bought a crib and borrowed bedding so that our five-month-old would sleep comfortably. We failed to check the crib bumpers for ties at the top and bottom and woke up in the middle of the night to shrieking—we found our baby's head and arms trapped under the crib bumper! Scary and unbelievable! Fortunately, we got there in time. I can't believe that so many manufacturers still make them that way. We've called nearby stores and all the bumpers they sell only tie at the top. The one our daughter was trapped under is Classic Pooh made by Red Calliope. I can't imagine that it doesn't happen more often!

◆ *Remove bumper pads immediately when your child starts to pull up or stand.* Why? Bumpers make a great step stool that lets baby launch herself out of the crib! Also: as we discussed previously, make sure bumpers are firm (not pillow-like) and snugly fit your crib with no gaps or overlapping sections.

◆ *Never use an electric blanket/heating pad.* Babies can dangerously overheat, plus any moisture, such as urine, can cause electric shock.

◆ *Avoid blankets that use nylon thread.* Nylon thread melts in the dryer and then breaks. These loose threads can wrap around your baby's neck, fingers or toes or break off and become a choking hazard. Cotton thread is best.

◆ *Look out for chenille.* It's the hip new thing and sort of like the shag carpeting of fabric—chenille is all over the market (sweaters, blankets, etc.) and now it has come to baby products. At a recent trade show, we saw many bedding manufacturers who had chenille groupings. Some use chenille as an accent on bumpers, while others have chenille blankets. Yet, some safety advocates wonder if chenille is safe for baby's bedding—with some chenille, you can actually pull out fibers from the fabric backing with little effort. And that might be a choking hazard for baby.

◆ *Travel.* Now that you've created a safe nursery at home, what about when you travel? Parents who frequently travel are often frustrated by hotels, which not only have unsafe cribs (see previous chapter) but also questionable sheets. At one hotel, we've been given queen size bed sheets to use in a crib! A solution: one reader recommended bringing a crib sheet from home. That way you know your baby will be safe and sound. (When you reserve a crib find out if it is a portable crib or a standard crib so you know what size sheet to bring.) Check with some of our recommended safety sheet manufacturers listed above and consider buying their port-a-crib versions for travel.

◆ *All linens should have a tag* indicating the manufacturer's name and address. That's the only way you would know if the linens were recalled. You can also contact the manufacturer if you have a problem or question. While this is the law, some stores may sell discounted or imported linens that do not have tags. Our advice: DON'T buy them.

 **Smart Shopper Tips**

bedding

Smart Shopper Tip
Pillow Talk: Looking for Mr. Good Bedding

"Pooh and more Pooh—that seemed to be the basic choice in crib bedding at our local baby store. Since it all looks alike, is the pattern the only difference?"

There's more to it than that. And buying baby bedding isn't the same as purchasing linens for your own bed—you'll be washing these pieces much more frequently, so they must be made to withstand the extra abuse. Since baby bedding is more than just another set of sheets, here are nine quality points to look for:

1 **RUFFLES SHOULD BE FOLDED OVER FOR DOUBLE THICKNESS— INSTEAD OF A SINGLE THICKNESS RUFFLE WITH HEMMED EDGE.** Double ruffles hold up better in the wash.

2 **COLORED DESIGNS ON THE BEDDING SHOULD BE PRINTED OR WOVEN INTO THE FABRIC, NOT STAMPED** (like you'd see on a screen-printed t-shirt). Stamped designs on sheets can fade with only a few washings. The problem: the pieces you wash less frequently (like dust ruffles and bumpers) will fade at different rates, spoiling the coordinated look you paid big money for. In case you're wondering how to determine whether the design is printed rather than stamped, printed fabrics have color that goes through the fabric to the other side. Stamped patterns are merely applied onto the top of the fabric.

3 **MAKE SURE THE PIECES ARE SEWN WITH COTTON/POLY THREAD, NOT NYLON.** Nylon threads will melt and break in the dryer, becoming a choking hazard. Once the thread is gone, the filling in bumpers and quilts can bunch up.

4 **CHECK FOR TIGHT, SMOOTH STITCHING ON APPLIQUÉS.** If you can see the edge of the fabric through the appliqué thread, the appliqué work is too skimpy. Poor quality appliqué will probably unravel after only a few washings. We've seen some appliqués that were actually fraying in the store—check before you buy.

5 **HIGH THREAD-COUNT SHEETS.** Unlike adult linens, most packages of baby bedding do not list the thread count. But, if you can count the individual threads when you hold a sheet up to the light, you know the thread count is too low. High thread-count sheets (200 threads per inch or more) are preferred since they are softer and smoother against baby's skin, last longer and wear better. Unfortunately, most affordable baby bedding has low thread counts (80 to 120 thread counts are common)—traditionally, it's the design (not the quality) that sells bedding in this business. But there is good news on this front: there are several upstart brands (reviewed later) that are actually touting high thread counts for their sheets.

Another telltale sign of a quality sheet is the elastic. The best sheets will have elastic that encircles the entire sheet.

6 **FEEL THE FILLING IN THE BUMPER PADS.** If the filling feels gritty, it's not the best quality. Look for bumpers that are firm when you squeeze them (Dacron-brand filling is a good bet).

7 **THE TIES THAT ATTACH THE BUMPER TO THE CRIB SHOULD BE BETWEEN SEVEN AND NINE INCHES IN LENGTH.** Another tip: make sure the bumper has ties on both the top and bottom and are securely sewn. For more discussion on this issue, see "Safe & Sound" earlier in this chapter.

8 **THE DUST RUFFLE PLATFORM SHOULD BE OF GOOD QUALITY FABRIC**—or else it will tear. Longer, full ruffles are more preferable to shorter ones. As a side note, the dust ruffle is sometimes referred to as a crib skirt.

9 **REMEMBER THAT CRIB SHEETS COME IN DIFFERENT SIZES**— bassinet/cradle, portable crib, and full-size crib. Always use the correct size sheet.

 Wastes of Money/Worthless Items

"I have a very limited budget for bedding, and I want to avoid spending money on stuff that I won't need. What are some items I should stay away from?"

It may be tempting to buy every new fad and matching accessory. And you'll get a lot of sales pressure at some stores to go for the entire "coordinated" look. Yet many bedding items are a complete waste of money—here's our list of the worst offenders:

1 **DIAPER STACKER.** This is basically a bag (in coordinating fabric, of course) used to store diapers—you hang it on the side of your crib or changing table. Apparently, bedding makers must think stacking diapers on the shelf of your changing table or storing them in a drawer is a major etiquette breach. Take my word for it: babies are not worried if their diapers are out in plain sight. Save the $30 to $50 that bedding makers charge for diaper stackers and stack your own.

2 **PILLOWS.** We are constantly amazed at the number of bedding sets that include pillows or pillowcases. Are the bedding designers nuts, or what? Haven't they heard that it's dangerous to put your baby to sleep on a pillow? What a terrible safety hazard, not to mention a waste of your money. We don't even think a decorative pillow is a good idea. Forget the pillow and save $20 to $30.

3 **SETS OF LINENS.** Sets may include useless or under-used items like those listed above as well as dust ruffles and window valances. Another problem: sets are often a mixed bag when it comes to quality. Some items are good, while others are lacking. Many baby stores or even chains will sell bedding items a la carte. That way you can pick and choose just the items you need—at a substantial savings over the all-inclusive sets.

4 **CANOPIES.** Parents-to-be of girls are often pressured to buy frilly accessories like canopies. The emphasis is on giving her "everything" and achieving a "feminine" look for your nursery. Don't buy into it. The whole set-up for a canopy is going to be more expensive (you'll need a special crib, etc.)—it'll set you back $75 to $175 for the linens alone. And enclosing your baby's crib in a canopy won't do much for her visual stimulation or health (canopies are dust collectors).

5 **ALL-WHITE LINENS**. If you think of babies as pristine and unspoiled, you've never had to change a poopy diaper or clean spit-up from the front of an outfit. I'm amazed that anyone would consider all-white bedding, since keeping it clean will probably be a full-time job. Stick with colors, preferably bright ones. If you buy all-white linens and then have to go back to buy colored ones, you'll be out another $100 to $200. (Yes, some folks argue that white linens are easier to bleach clean, but extensive bleaching over time can yellow fabric.)

6 **TEETHING PADS FOR CRIB RAILS.** Most new, name brand cribs will already have plastic teething guards on the side rails, so adding pads (cost: $20 extra) is redundant. One storeowner pointed out that if your baby has nothing better to teeth on than the crib railing, he is spending too much time in the crib anyway.

7 **HEADBOARD BUMPERS.** Whatever side you come down on in the bumper debate (some parents think they're a good safety item; others worry about the suffocation risk), there is a certain bumper that definitely is a waste of money—the headboard bumper. This bumper is designed to cover the entire headboard of the crib. Regular bumpers are just a six to nine-inch tall strip of padding that goes around the crib . . . and that's all you need if you want bumpers. Headboard bumpers are more expensive than regular bumpers, running another $25 to $75, depending on the maker. Skip them and save the money.

Money Saving Secrets

1 **IF YOU'RE ON A TIGHT BUDGET, GO FOR A GOOD BLANKET AND A NICE SET OF HIGH THREAD-COUNT SHEETS.** What does that cost? A good cotton blanket runs $10 (even fancy Polartec ones are only $20), while a fitted sheet runs $15 to $20. Forget all the fancy items like embroidered comforters, duvet covers, window valances, diaper stackers and dust ruffles. After all, your baby won't care if she doesn't have perfectly coordinated accessories.

2 **DON'T BUY A QUILT.** Sure, they look pretty, but do you really need one? Go for a nice cotton blanket, instead—and save the $50 to $200. Better yet, hint to your friends that you'd like receiving blankets as shower gifts.

3 **SKIP EXPENSIVE WALL HANGINGS—DO DECOR ON THE CHEAP.** One of the best new products we've discovered for this is Wall Nutz (www.wallnutz.com). These innovative iron-on transfers let you create paint-by-number masterpieces in your baby's room. Paint a six-by-eight foot mural or just add some decorative borders. Cost: $30 (plus the cost of paints).

Of course, crafts stores are another great source for do-it-yourself inspiration. Michaels Arts & Crafts (800-MICHAELS; web: www.michaels.com) sells stencils and supplies for nursery decor.

4 **MAKE YOUR OWN SHEETS, DUST RUFFLES AND OTHER LINEN ITEMS.** Think that's too complicated? A mom in Georgia called in this great tip on curtain valances—she bought an extra dust ruffle, sewed a curtain valance from the material and saved $70. All you need to do is remove the ruffle from the fabric platform and sew a pocket along one edge. I managed to do this simple procedure on my sewing machine without killing myself, so it's quite possible you could do it too. A good place for inspiration is your local fabric store—

Cyber bedding deals: Overstock.com

What happens when those high-flying dot-coms crash down to earth? Liquidators move in to sell their warehouses stuffed with unsold goods. Since they pay pennies on the dollar, these liquidators can turn around and sell you the goods at substantial discounts and still make a buck. (And how do liquidators sell distressed inventory from dot-coms? The Internet, of course). Case in point: Overstock.com, the premier liquidator of dot-coms. This company has an excellent web site that sells brand-new merchandise at 50% off and more. At times we've seen designer four-piece set of all-cotton crib bedding that retails for $235, you pay just $99 and $2.48 shipping? We also saw crib mobiles for $34 (originally $56), toys, baby clothes, shoes and more. To see what's available for babies at Overstock.com, go to the "Gifts & Seasonal" section, then to General Gifts and finally Baby Gifts. Bedding is also listed in "Home & Garden" (go to Bed, Bath & Linens and then Infant Bedding). Selection does vary from time to time.

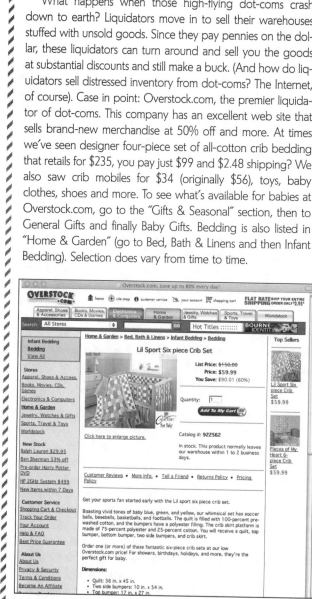

Figure 2: Why pay $150 for this six-piece crib set when you can snag it on OverStock.com for just $59? The deals on bedding make this site a great bargain find.

most carry pattern books like Butterick, Simplicity and McCalls, all of which have baby bedding patterns that are under $10. There are other pattern books you can purchase that specialize in baby quilts—some of these books also have patterns for other linen items like bumpers. Even if you buy good quality fabric at $10 per yard, your total savings will be 75% or more compared to "pre-made" items.

5 **SHOP AT OUTLETS.** Scattered across the country, we found a few outlets that discount linens. Among the better ones were House of Hatten and Carousel (also known as www.babybedding-online.com)—see their reviews in this chapter. Another reader praised the Pottery Barn Outlet. They have three locations: Jeffersonville, OH (740) 948-2004, Dawsonville, GA (706) 216-5211 or (706) 216-6465, Memphis, TN (901) 763-1500. The discounts start at 50% and only get better from there. They have cribs, bedding and other furniture on sale.

6 **DON'T PICK AN OBSCURE BEDDING THEME.** Sure, that "Exploding Kiwi Fruit" bedding is cute, but where will you find any matching accessories to decorate your baby's room? Chances are they'll only be available "exclusively" from the bedding's manu-facturer—at exclusively high prices. A better bet is to choose a more common theme with lots of accessories (wall decor, lamps, rugs, etc.). The more plentiful the options, the lower the prices. Winnie the Pooh is a good example (see the box on "Pooh at a discount" later in this chapter), although you'll find quite a few accessories for other common themes like Noah's Ark, teddy bears, rocking horses, etc.

7 **GO FOR SOLID COLOR SHEETS AND USE THEMED ACCESSORIES.** Just because you want to have a Beatrix Potter-themed nurs-ery doesn't mean you have to buy Beatrix Potter *bedding*. A great money-saving strategy: use low-cost solid color sheets, blankets and other linen items in the crib. Get these in colors that match/compliment theme accessories like a lamp, clock, poster, wallpaper, rugs, etc. (Hint: register for these items, which make nice shower gifts). You still have the Beatrix Potter look, but without the hefty tag for Beatrix Potter bedding. Many of the mail-order cata-logs we review later in this chapter are excellent sources for afford-able, solid-color bedding. Another bonus: solid color sheets/linens from the catalogs we recommend are often much higher quality (yet at a lower price) than theme bedding.

8 **SURF THE WEB.** Earlier in this chapter, we discussed the best web sites for baby bedding deals. Later in this chapter you'll find additional mail-order sources for bedding on a budget. The savings can be as much as 50% off retail prices. Even simple items like crib sheets can be affordably mail ordered. Next up: the best outlets for saving on baby bedding.

Outlets

Garnet Hill

Location: Historic Manchester Outlet Center, Manchester, Vermont. (802) 362-6198.

Love the look of the Garnet Hill bedding catalog but think the prices are hard to swallow? Then check out this outlet in Vermont, which features first-quality overstock items from the current catalog like flannel sheets, quilts, blankets, children's clothing and more. The savings is 30% to 50% and the outlet welcomes phone inquires and ships nationwide.

House of Hatten

Location: 3939 IH-35, Suite 725, San Marcos, TX. (512) 392-8161.

Perhaps the only thing more beautiful than a great quilt is a great quilt on sale. That's why we love House of Hatten's fantastic outlet store in San Marcos, Texas—the only one like it in the country. You can find their quilts, as well as mobiles, bumper pads, dust ruffles, and sheets at 50% off retail. The store also sells their clothing line, which features smocked outfits for girls and boys (starting at 3-6 month sizes). You can find a nice selection of gift items like rattles, bibs, pillows and more. Look for their sales near holidays for additional savings. The outlet offers mail-order service and ships nationwide. All items are discontinued, and some are imperfect or flawed.

The Interior Alternative

Locations: 9 locations, most of which are in the East, Midwest and South. Call (413) 743-1986 for a location near you.

Looking for fabric to decorate your baby's room or do-it-yourself bedding projects, but shocked at retail fabric prices? Then seek out the Interior Alternative, a fantastic fabric outlet. We visited their Dallas location and were amazed at the deals—literally THOUSANDS of bolts of fabric in just every imaginable pattern. If you like Waverly patterns, you'll find them here for just $8 a yard (half of retail). There's also wallpaper, borders, upholstery, pre-made curtain valances (for just $20) and more. Everything here is factory seconds, but we couldn't see any flaws. If you buy the entire bolt, take another 10% off.

The Name Game: Reviews of Selected Manufacturers

Here are reviews of some of the brand names you'll encounter on your shopping adventures for baby bedding. Note: we include the phone numbers, web sites and addresses of each manufacturer—this is so you can find a local dealer near you (most do not sell directly to the public, nor send catalogs to consumers). We rated the companies on overall quality, price, and creativity, based on an evaluation of sample items we viewed at retail stores. We'd love to hear from you— tell us what you think about different brands and how they held up in the real world by emailing authors@BabyBargainsBook.com.

The Ratings

A **EXCELLENT**—*our top pick!*
B **GOOD**— *above average quality, prices, and creativity.*
C **FAIR**—*could stand some improvement.*
D **POOR**—*yuck! could stand some major improvement.*

Amy Coe *For a dealer near you, call (203) 221-3050. Web: www. amycoe.com.* Designer Amy Coe turned her hobby of collecting vintage fabrics into a business when she launched her eponymous baby bedding line in 1993. The result is a linen collection with a flair for nostalgia: Coe takes fabrics that replicate patterns from the 1930's to 1950's and crafts a full line of bedding items. We previewed the collection recently and were impressed: we liked the flannel ticking stripes, gingham checks and cotton chambrays. New, Amy has added chenille throws ($104-$116), flannel blankets ($39), and waffle weave blankets ($56). Quality is high (everything is all-cotton), but so too are the prices—a single sheet is $32 to $48 and a set including only the bumper and bed skirt and was a whopping $326 to $345 on BabyStyle.com (unfortunately, those prices are about 20% higher than the last time we looked. Despite the cost, we still like Coe. While the rest of the market has knocked off the vintage prints idea, Amy Coe still has some interesting designs that might be worth a look.

New this year, Amy Coe debuted a lower priced collection (amy coe) at Target stores. The vintage circus themed bedding includes all-cotton sheets for only $8.99, a duvet and bumpers ($40 each), and blankets for $10 to $17. There is also a series of accessories like wall borders and lampshades. By the time you read this, there will be diaper bags ($18 to $23) as well. Thanks to this new, affordable line, we'll raise Coe's rating this time out. ***Rating: A-***

Baby Guess *Manufactured by Crown Crafts. For a dealer near you, call (714) 895-2250. Web: www.crowncraftsinfantproducts. com.* Baby Guess has sure made the rounds since their baby bedding first came on the market. The license has been sold to a series of manufacturers over the years, most recently by bedding giant Crown Crafts who bought the brand along with NoJo bedding (see their review later in this section). After a few real design duds, Baby Guess finally seems back on the fashion track with simple designs in muted colors plus 100% cotton fabrics (knits and weaves). Baby Guess is available widely at discounters like Baby Depot and Babies R Us at prices ranging from $180 to $240 for a four-piece set. *Rating: B*

Baby Martex This brand is distributed by CoCaLo. See their review later in this section.

BananaFish *For a dealer near you, call (800) 899-8689 or (818) 727-1645.* "Sophisticated" and "tailored" is how we'd describe this California-based bedding maker. BananaFish's emphasis is on all-cotton fabric with adult-like finishes (such as pique) and muted color palettes. It's not cheap—prices range from $240 to $400 at retail for a four-piece set. We weren't really wild about the styling (a bit too dull for our tastes) but the quality is high. Finally, we can't believe these guys still don't have a web site! What are they waiting for? *Rating: B*

Beatrix Potter This brand is licensed by Crown Crafts. See their review later in this section.

Affordable Artwork

Framed artwork for baby's room has to be very expensive, right? Nope, not if you buy a framed print from Creative Images (call 800-784-5415 or 904-825-6700 for a store near you; web: www.crimages.com). This Florida-based company sells prints, growth charts, wall hangings and more at very affordable prices—just $20 to $80. Each print is mounted on wood and laminated (no glass frame) so baby can enjoy it at eye-level (just sponge it off if it gets dirty). Best of all, there are hundreds of images in any theme to choose from: Pooh, Beatrix Potter, Noah's Ark, plus other collections of animals, sports and pastels. Check out their web site for samples.

Beautiful Baby *For a dealer near you, call (903) 295-2229. Web: www.bbaby.com.* Next to Nava's (reviewed later), this is probably the most over-the-top bedding in the market today. There's nothing subtle about Beautiful Baby's linens, which feature satin, lace and tulle. The bumpers are so huge they're like king-size pillows sewn together (okay, that's an exaggeration, but trust us, they are BIG) but they do have the most bumper ties of any manufacturer (26). Good news, though, you can custom choose the thickness. As we noted earlier, thinner bumpers are safer, in our opinion. In fact, you can custom change just about anything in this line. Another plus: their sheets all have safety straps, an added feature we applaud. With over 1300 fabrics to choose from, Beautiful Baby says it takes four to six weeks to ship most orders. Prices are high: expect to shell out $400 to $800 for a four-piece set, although all the pieces are priced individually. Most but not all fabrics are 100% cotton. Bottom line: this line isn't cheap, but if you're looking for bedding you can customize with an over-the-top style, this is the brand for you. **Rating: B**

Bedtime Originals This brand is made by Lambs & Ivy. See their review later in this section.

Blueberry Lane *Call (413) 528-9633 for a dealer near you. Web: www.blueberrylanehome.com.* Designer Diane Sorrell uses textured blends to give Blueberry Lane's baby bedding a unique look. Quality is good; the bedding is sewn in North Carolina and Massachusetts. Blueberry Lane offers "total room concepts" that pair bedding with coordinating hand-painted furniture pieces and window treatments. Prices for the bedding run $350 to $520 for a four piece set. One bummer: their web site is for retailers only so consumers can't look at their offerings online. **Rating: B+**

Blue Moon Baby *For a dealer near you, call (626) 455-0014. Web: www.bluemoonbaby.com.* In business for seven years, California-based Blue Moon Baby specializes in chenille bedding. Their four collections feature chenille in a variety of patterns and designs for both boys and girls. One of the best bets: The Cowboy Collection with its red bandanna trim and denim accents, along with a chenille cowboy. For girls, the Cotton Tail collection featured cute pink bunnies that are sure to draws ooh's and aah's from grandparents. Blue Moon Baby also sells coordinating furniture, stuffed animals and other decorative accents. Prices are about $400 for a three-piece set which includes bumper, skirt and quilt (Blue Moon Baby doesn't sell sheets). The fabric is all cotton. We thought the quality was very good and we really like the unique designs—

bedding

LICENSE TRANSLATOR

Who makes what brand of bedding

One of the hottest trends in crib bedding is licensed characters—just about every cartoon character imaginable has been licensed to one of the big bedding makers for use in juvenile bedding. But how can tell you tell who makes what? Here is a list of popular licensed characters and their bedding makers:

LICENSE	SEE BEDDING MAKER
BABY GUESS	CROWN CRAFTS
BABY GUND	LAMBS & IVY
BABY LOONEY TUNES	GERBER
BABY MARTEX	COCALO
BEATRIX POTTER	NOJO
BLUES CLUES	CROWN CRAFTS
HELLO KITTY	QUILTEX
LENNON BABY FOR CARTER'S	RIEGEL/MT. VERNON MILLS
LAURA ASHLEY	SUMERSAULT
MY FIRST THOMAS	QUILTEX
OSH KOSH B'GOSH	COCALO
PRECIOUS MOMENTS	CROWN CRAFTS
RAGGEDY ANN & ANDY	LAMBS & IVY
RAINBOWFISH	KIDSLINE
SAVE THE CHILDREN	QUILTEX
SESAME STREET	MT. VERNON MILLS
SNOOPY	LAMBS & IVY
SUZY'S ZOO	GERBER
TODD PARR	QUILTEX
WINNIE THE POOH	CROWN CRAFTS

no one else is doing sculptured chenille designs. The use of chenille in baby bedding is quite controversial. See the Safe and Sound section earlier in this chapter. Another downside: the price is rather high for what is just a three-piece set of bedding. Blue Moon Baby also makes bassinet bedding in four designs. Because of the controversy over chenille, we're going to give this line a lower rating this year. ***Rating: C***

Brandee Danielle For a dealer near you, call (800) 720-5656, (714) 957-1240. Web: www.brandeedanielle.com. Despite its feminine-sounding name, Brandee Danielle is one of the few makers that designs bedding with strongly "boyish" themes. One pattern, "Sports Fan," even featured a series of vintage sport equipment illustrations for the sport fan. In recent years they've added some new feminine patterns like "Baby Lilac" to round out their selection. Brandee Danielle is one of the few companies that sews all its bedding in-house (most use outside contractors). The bedding is widely available at specialty shops. Prices are $200 to $400 for a four-piece set. Even at that price level, it's a pretty good buy; most of the fabrics are 100% cotton. One negative: Brandee's only has top ties for their bumpers (hence the lower rating this year). **Rating: B+**

The Marketing of Baby Linens: Dangerous Impressions?

Flip through any bedding catalog or web site and you'll see decked-out cribs, stuffed with sumptuous linens. Some linen companies like Baby Martex even use long ago recalled cribs (with dangerous corner posts) to market "antique" looking patterns. Yet, in their haste to market their products, baby linen makers may be sending a wrong (and dangerous) message to parents—that it's OK to put soft bedding items like pillows, comforters and the like in cribs. Safety advocates clearly warns against this, but it still amazes us to see bedding brochures with many offending items loaded into cribs, some of which are missing a drop-side (in order to show the merchandise more clearly, of course). The reason why this happens is clear: linen manufacturers make fat profits off of such "decorative" accessories. And what better way to sell such items for baby than to deck out cribs? But we wonder if this sends the wrong message to parents—some folks may think that's how their crib *should* look. Yeah, many bedding makers include warning labels (in six-point type) that says you shouldn't put such items in a crib—but that's usually in the fine print if it exists at all. All bedding makers should eliminate this practice at once.

By the way, in March 2000, retailers including JCPenney, Sears, Babies R Us, Target, IKEA and Lands End promised the CPSC they would discontinue marketing soft bedding in cribs including quilts and pillows. In a spot check of Sears' and JCPenney's online catalogs, we continued to see quilts draped over crib railings as we went to press. On a recent visit to our local Babies R Us, we also noted they are continuing to drape crib rails with quilts. So much for promises.

California Kids *For a dealer near you, call (800) 548-5214, (650) 637-9054.* One of our favorite bedding lines, California Kids specializes in bright and upbeat looks. In the past few years, they've added more girl-oriented themes as well as a line of coordinating drawer pulls. Look for their Waverly prints and matching rugs plus new sports-themed groupings. The quality is excellent; everything is 100% cotton and made in California. Prices run $250 to $350 for a five-piece set (the average is about $300). With an amazing array of options (60+ patterns were available at last count), California Kids is available in specialty stores and upper-end department stores. Available accessories include wall hangings, lamp shades and fabric by the yard. ***Rating: A***

Carousel. Now available on line at www.babybeddingonline.com. This line is reviewed in the Cyberspace section.

Carter's *Made by Riegel. Call (800) 845-3251 or (803) 275-2541 for a dealer near you. Web: www.carters.com or www.parentinformation.com.* Carter's is one of the biggest names in baby products—you'll find clothes, high chairs, strollers and even bedding sporting the name. One big reason: clever design, like the runaway success of the John Lennon Real Baby collection. The collection (which also includes coordinating clothing and accessories) is based on a series of drawings Lennon made for his youngest son, Sean. We were impressed with the quality of this whimsical bedding—100% cotton, 200-thread count with sewn appliqués. That's not what we expect from a brand known for its affordable sleepers. And, amazingly enough, the price isn't that high—a four-piece set of Lennon baby is $140-$160.

If you don't like the Lennon look, Carter's has two other bedding lines: Baby Basics, a mix and match coordinates line in 100%, 200-thread count cotton and the Emu line, designed by Emu Namae, a blind Japanese artist famous for his children's illustrations. The Baby Basics line runs about $60 for a four-piece set while Emu is similar in price to the Lennon line.

We are impressed with the improvements to the Carter's line. We think the Baby Basics are an amazing value (although the bumpers are a bit skimpy) and the flexibility of buying just what you need is terrific. The line is also available just about everywhere including at their outlet stores. ***Rating B+***

Celebrations *Call (310) 532-2499 for a dealer near you. Web: www.baby-celebrations.com.* This bedding maker offers a couple dozen styles with feminine, sophisticated looks—we saw patchwork motifs, eyelet laces, chenille trim and layered dust ruffles. The all-cotton linens range from $300 to $590. Quality is excellent; we noticed the bumpers sported ties on the top and bottom (16 total). *Rating: B+*

CoCaLo *Call (714) 434-7200 for a dealer near you. Web: www.cocalo.com.* You could say baby bedding runs in the family at CoCaLo. Owner Renee Pepys Lowe's mother (Shirley) founded Nojo in 1970 and Renee worked at the family business before it was sold to Crown Crafts a few of years ago. Since then, Renee has branched out on her own, launching the CoCaLo line in 1999 (the name comes from the first two letters of Renee's daughters, Courtenay and Catherine Lowe). CoCaLo is made up of four lines: Osh Kosh, Baby Martex, an eponymous collection and Kimberly Grant, which CoCaLo acquired in 2002 and is reviewed separately later in this section. The lowest priced (and largest) group is Osh Kosh, ranging from $180 to $250 for a four-piece set. Unfortunately, not all of this collection is all-cotton (some sets are blends). CoCaLo has their own line of bedding that features extra long ruffles for $200 to $300 per set and featured a pastel patchwork motif (although we noticed CoCaLo has de-emphasized their own brand in recent years). Design-wise, the Osh Kosh line features their trademark denim look in most groupings, while CoCaLo is more whimsical, in brighter hues. Baby Martex (priced around $200 at Babies R Us and up to $300 at specialty stores) is simpler with checks, plaids and seersucker looks, although one grouping also showcased vintage floral prints. Quality-wise, we were impressed with Baby Martex and Kimberly Grant (which are all cotton), although some Osh Kosh sets are cotton-poly blends. We'd stick with the 100% cotton selections. *Rating: B+*

Company Kids This bedding is sold via mail order in the Company Store catalog. See the "Do it By Mail" section later in this chapter for details. *Rating: A*

Cotton Tale *Call (800) 628-2621 or (714) 435-9558 for a dealer near you. Web: www.cottontaledesigns.com.* What most impresses us about Cotton Tale is their originality. There are no licensed cartoon characters or trendy fabrics like chenille here. Instead, you'll see hand-painted looks in beautiful soft pastels, all made in the U.S. We loved the whimsical animal prints and the feminine touches. Best of all, Cotton Tale's prices are affordable—most range from $200 to $350 with an average of $275 for a four piece set. Most of the fabrics are 100% cotton, although a few patterns have satin trim that is a blended fabric. The biggest news at Cotton Tale in the past year was their roll out of a "Safe & Sound" bedding system, a revolutionary and somewhat controversial solution to the concern over bumpers. The system includes a "safety bumper" that eliminates the gap between bumper and mattress and a safety crib sheet with more elastic and deeper corner pockets for a snug fit. Best of all, the Safe & Sound bedding is affordable—$120 for an all-cotton three piece set (bumper, sheet, dust ruffle). Sheets sell separately for $16 (there are six different patterns available in the Safe & Sound line. Cotton Tale also sells a "safety sleep sack" that eliminates the need for a blanket for $28. Now, we said earlier this new product line is controversial—we point this out because some baby stores have balked at carrying it, worrying that the name implies all other bedding (especially those with regular bumpers) is not safe. As we discussed previously, there is no clear consensus on the safety of bumpers in cribs. But we're proud of Cotton Tale for coming up with a solution that enables parents to still have bumpers without the worry of entrapment. So, we'll give this line a big thumbs up for their innovative designs and beautiful patterns. FYI: Cotton Tale bedding is available just about everywhere. . . even in the JCPenney catalog and Babies R Us. ***Rating: A***

Crown Crafts *Call (800) 421-0526 or (714) 895-9200 for a dealer near you. Web: www.CrownCraftsInfantProducts.com.* Baby bedding behemoth Crown Crafts seems to have snapped up every possible character license you can imagine. For example, Crown Crafts now makes Eddie Bauer, Beatrix Potter, Precious Moments, Baby Guess, Winnie-the-Pooh, and Blues Clues crib bedding and more. The offerings range from the low-price Fisher Price bedding sold in discount stores to the upper-end Waverly bedding sold in Babies R Us. Crown Crafts also owns sub-lines NoJo, Little Bedding and Red Calliope (see later reviews for details on some of these lines). The word that best sums up Crown Crafts is CHEAP. Cheap prices—but also cheap fabric and quality. Yes, the Waverly line is the exception with all cotton, high thread count fabrics, but most of the licensed character bedding is cotton/poly blends with low thread counts. And the prices correspond. For example, a four-piece screen printed Disney Baby's Simba's Circle of Life set in cotton/poly is a mere $87. On the high end, Baby Guess four piece sets are as much as $240, a bit pricey compared to similar brands. Bottom line, you get what you pay for with this manufacturer. Stick with the Waverly or all cotton sets and avoid the cheap-o licensed sets. ***Rating: C+***

Eddie Bauer. Once only available in their catalog, this bedding now is sold exclusively at Babies R Us and is made by Crown Craft (see above). Prices are high for the quality, which is average.

Fisher Price. This is made by Crown Crafts; see review above.

Gerber *For a dealer near you, call (800) 4GERBER Web:* www.gerber.com. While Gerber offers some cute patterns in their bedding line and they're available almost everywhere. The bedding's quality leaves much to be desired. One reader emailed us this typical story: "I bought several of the Gerber Everyday Basics knit sheets. They fit my 5" thick Sealy mattress well when I bought them, they were super soft, and had elastic all the way around for safety. BUT THEN...I washed them on the delicate cycle in cold water and dried them on low/delicate as instructed in the package, and they shrunk so much I couldn't even get them on the mattress anymore!" Other parents complained about colors that faded after just a couple washes and bumpers that loss their form after a couple washes. Gerber's biggest licenses are Suzy's Zoo and Baby Looney Tunes. And yes, the prices are cheap—a three-piece set of Baby Looney Tunes from Babies R Us is a mere $40. But the designs are screen printed on low quality cotton/poly fabrics. We can't recommend this brand. ***Rating: D***

Glenna Jean *For a dealer near you, call (800) 446-6018 or (804) 561-0687.* We liked Glenna Jean's designs—as long as you stick with non-appliquéd patterns. The quality and sewing construction of the appliqués just wasn't very impressive. Glenna Jean is big on teddy bear designs and accessories, although most of the colors tend toward the darker side. A four-piece set starts at $150 to and averages $280 per set. We like their pretty, textured fabrics and denim patchwork design. Overall, the best bets in the Glenna Jean line are the 100% cotton patchwork and floral print designs (only certain groupings are all-cotton; the rest are blends). FYI: this bedding is sold and often discounted deeply all over the Internet. Be sure to do a search to see what deals are available. ***Rating: B-***

Hoohobbers *For a dealer near you, call (773) 890-1466. Web:* www.hoohobbers.com. The quality of this brand was impressive—all of the comforters are made duvet-style with Velcro enclosures. The result: it's easy to remove the cover for washing. Even the bumpers feature zippered covers. Hoohobbers' dozen designs tend to have interesting color combinations in both brights and pastels. Prices for all their four-piece collections are $375; that's expensive, but everything is 100% cotton and well constructed (the sheets feature all-around elastic, for example). The good news is you can see and buy any of their patterns on their web site. All bedding is made at Hoohobbers' Chicago factory. Finally, we should mention Hoohobbers' bassinets and Moses baskets come in coordinating fabrics as well. In fact, the company makes a wide range of accessories including furniture, bouncer seat covers and more. ***Rating: B+***

House of Hatten *For a dealer near you, call (800) 5-HATTEN (542-8836) or (512) 819-9600. Web: www.houseofhatten.com.* House of Hatten's specialty is beautiful appliquéd and embroidered quilts. When we first reviewed this manufacturer, we saw mostly pastel and white designs. While they still have a few of those designs they've added a number of bolder looks. Accessories for each collection are extensive—you'll see matching clocks, picture frames, light switch plates, knobs and toys among others. Quilts are $80 to $150; a four-piece set that adds a sheet, dust ruffle and bumper runs about $210 to $400. All of the fabrics are 100% cotton. As a side note, House of Hatten has a discount outlet in Texas as well as online; for more info, see the Outlet section earlier in this chapter. **Rating: B+**

Infantino *Call (800) 365-8182 or (858) 689-1221 for a dealer near you. Web: www.Infantino.com.* Infantino announced in 2002 that it was getting out of the bedding market. Earlier, Infantino had marketed bedding under the names Judi's Originals and Studio Spot. We still see some of their sets available on line. Quality was OK and if you can get a deal on it on line it's a good option. Last we looked, four-piece sets were selling online for $100 to $190. **Rating: B**

Koala Baby *Available exclusively at Babies R Us.* Koala Baby is Babies R Us' attempt at establishing an in house brand of bedding and it seems pretty promising. Made for them by NoJo/Red Calliope, six piece sets sell for $150 to $170 and include the quilt, bumper, sheet, dust ruffle, diaper stacker and valance. They also offer four piece sets for about $100. The designs are all made in China and come in three designs. So what's the downside? As one reader put it "This brand is TERRIBLE!!!! I washed the fitted sheet before putting it on my crib mattress and it shrunk about 6" in length! I wouldn't recommend these sheets to anyone." While the idea is a great one, it seems that Babies R Us has missed with their Koala Baby line. **Rating: C**

KidsLine *151 W. 135th St., Los Angeles, CA 90061. Call (310) 660-0110 for a dealer near you. Web: www. Kidslineinc.com.* We continue to find plenty to impress us about KidsLine bedding. Not least of which is that it is all over Babies R Us so it's easy to find. They continue to carry some licensed good like Rainbow Fish. The line ranges from cutesy babyish designs to more sophisticated patchwork patterns. And prices are a bit more reasonable ranging from $140 to $200 for a six-piece set (four piece sets are also available). how's the quality? We noticed that most of KidsLine patterns are poly-cotton blends. And even many of the all-cotton options featured low thread (below 200) counts. So what you're paying for with KidsLine is the design, not so much the fabric. But those designs are colorful and playful. Bottom line: we think they're a good mid-priced brand. *Rating: B*

Kimberly Grant *Call (714) 546-4411 for a dealer near you. Web: www.kimberlygrant.com.* If you're looking for bedding designs that are a bit more low key and not too cutesy, Kimberly Grant is a great option. They were purchased recently by CoCaLo (see review above), but the styling seems to continue along in the same vein as when West Coast designer Kimberly Grant started her business. We liked the sophisticated look (floral prints, plaids) and fabrics (velvets, satins, cotton), all in a warm palette. Prices run $389 to $529 for a four-piece set. Pricey but good quality. *Rating: A-*

Lambs & Ivy *For a dealer near you, call (800) 345-2627 or (310) 839-5155. Web: www.lambsivy.com* Barbara Lainken and Cathy Ravdin founded this LA-based bedding company in 1979. Their specialty: fashionable baby bedding that is sold in discount and mass market stores (you'll also see them sold in JCPenney's catalog and on many web sites). This year they've added some whimsical looks along with vintage prints and licensed characters. In fact, they've expanded their Snoopy license to include three options now. They've really improved their stamped designs by using a photo quality heat transfer technology. This is a clever way of achieving a nicer look without big cost (you have to see the bedding in person to note the difference). Prices are still reasonable at $120 to $250 for a four-piece set. Bedtime Originals, a sub-line of Lambs & Ivy, is lower in price (around $50 for a three piece set) and quality. We'd rank the overall quality of Lambs & Ivy a bit ahead of other mass-market bedding brands. Yes, most of the fabrics are blends (50-50 cotton/poly), but the stitching and construction is a cut above. *Rating: B+*

Little Bedding This is a sub-line of Crown Crafts. See their review earlier in this section.

Lands End This bedding is sold via mail order in the Lands End catalog. See the "Do it By Mail" section later in this chapter for details. *Rating: A*

Laura Ashley This is a licensed line of Sumersault. See their review later in this section.

Luv Stuff *Call (800) 825-BABY or (972) 278-BABY for a dealer near you. Web: www.luvstuffbedding.com.* Texas-based Luv Stuff's claim to fame is their unique, hand-trimmed wall hangings, which match their custom bedding. You can mix and match to your heart's content (all items are sold a la carte). The quality is high: the company's exclusive fabrics are mostly 100% cotton and high thread count plus all their collections are made in house in Texas. As you might expect, however, all this quality isn't free—a four-piece ensemble (sheet, comforter, bumper, dust ruffle) runs $400 to $500. And Luv Stuff's bumpers aren't very consumer friendly—they are surface clean (with a mild detergent) or dry-clean only. And they continue to be rather overstuffed. Despite this, we liked the brand's unique and bold styles. This bedding is a tour de force of color and contrast. And new this year: closeouts on their web site. We saw prices as low as $129 for a set. They don't offer online ordering; you have to call (800) 835-BABY. **Rating: B**

Martha Stewart *Kmart's version is made by Riegel (see comments at the end of this section) Web: www.kmart.com.* Martha used to sell two different bedding sets, one in Kmart for the very budget conscious and one in her eponymous catalog that threatened to give some folks a coronary. Interestingly, she has discontinued the overpriced, high-end bedding. Now the Kmart version is the only option. It's 100% cotton, 200 thread count, but overall the quality is disappointing: the appliqué and stitching are only average, the bumper has only six ties on the top and the elastic does not go all the way around the sheet. Okay, the prices are a great deal ($40 for a three-piece set), but it's obvious Martha (and Kmart) cut some corners to bring the bedding in at that price. The colors are generally muted with patchworks and ginghams. You'll even find coordinating chenille blankets, diaper stackers, receiving blankets and more. These sheets ($8 to $10) have to be cold water washed which makes us wonder if they are shrinkage prone. On the plus side, the design and styling of Martha's bedding is a cut above what you usually expect to find at Kmart. But nagging quality issues lead us to give this brand only an average rating. **Rating: C**

Nava's Designs *For a dealer near you, call (818) 988-9050. Web: www.navasdesigns.com.* Speaking of over the top, you can't talk about super-expensive bedding without mentioning Nava's Designs. But unlike other high-end manufacturers, we found the designs less innovative and more over-priced. A typical example: a patchwork pattern of yellow, blue and white plaid with touches of chambray. The price? Are you sitting down? How about a whopping $780 to $940 for a set? A major negative (besides the price): some designs don't wash well and may even have to be dry-cleaned (check the washing instructions carefully). On the upside, the fabrics are very heavy, high-quality cottons, and the stitching is excellent. Among the stand outs in Nava's line are her floral prints, lushly rendered with large cabbage roses, delicate lace and shimmering rope piping. This might be the bedding in Bill Gates' baby's nursery (we're only guessing, but he's the only one who could afford it), but Nava's just doesn't impress us. **Rating: C+**

NoJo *Noel Joanna Inc. For a dealer near you, call (800) 854-8760 or (310) 763-8100. Web: www.nojo.com* NoJo was founded in 1970 and made just one product—a quilted infant car seat cover. Since then, NoJo has expanded into a wide range of bedding and nursery products (the company was acquired in 1997 by textile giant Crown Crafts, which also owns Red Calliope). Nojo is sold everywhere, from discounters like Wal-Mart to specialty stores and chains like Babies R Us. In the past year, Crown Crafts has repositioned NoJo as more of a 100% cotton "better" bedding line. Prices for a four-piece, all-cotton set are about $180 to $240. We did notice Nojo bedding online at sites like www.babyparadise.com that sold for as little as $140 including a Pottery Barn knockoff called Flower Patch. Design-wise, the line is moving away from the licensed characters like Babar, Paddington Bear and Spot. Instead you see more simple patchwork and gingham designs and subtle colors like violet. In the past we've criticized NoJo's cheaper bedding for poor quality, but with the repositioning of the brand, we've decided to raise the rating a bit. **Rating: B**

OshKosh B'Gosh This brand is licensed by CoCaLo. See their review earlier in this section.

Patchkraft *Call (800) 866-2229 or (973) 340-3300 for a dealer near you. Web: www.patchkraft.com* Patchkraft has one of the best web sites of any bedding manufacturer. They have done a terrific job of showcasing their extensive bedding line with clear thumbnails and enlargements that even include a swatch of fabric in many cases. While there is no substitute for feeling the fabric first-hand, the site helps you picture how these well made, mostly 100% cotton bedding collections look in real life. Besides the web site, we were also impressed with Patchkraft owner Paula Markowitz's commitment to safety. All the bumpers feature ties on the top and bottom and the company provides detailed safety and care instructions to its customers. We also liked the fact that Patchkraft has eliminated the comforter from some of its sets (instead, they substitute a flannel blanket; the quilt is now an optional accessory). You do have to pay for all that quality at prices ranging from $300 up to $500 for a four-piece set, but it is a good brand if you want to splurge.

Most designs are in the $380 to $400 range. New this year you'll see some lightweight velour fabrics and flannels among the patchwork designs. They've also added a wallpaper line in addition to borders. Our only gripe: we wish Patchkraft had more entry-level options below $300 (they have two as of this writing). We've seen some designs on www.Dmart2000.com at about $200. Despite the criticism, we'll give them our highest rating based on safety, quality and design. **Rating: A**

Pine Creek *Call (503) 266-6275 for a dealer near you. Web: www.pinecreekbedding.com* Oregon-based Pine Creek Bedding has come back to their signature look with more flannel options, while offering sets with a new vintage feel. Look for old-fashioned graphics and soft colors. All the fabrics are 100% cotton. Considering the quality, we thought Pine Creek's prices were reasonable at $280 to $360 for a four-piece set. Pine Creek also sells accessories like lampshades and curtain valances, plus fabric is available by the yard. Another related web site, www.comfortlines.com carries the entire Pine Creek line. So if you don't have a retailer near you, you'll find even accessories like wallpaper here. **Rating: A-**

Pooh Classic Pooh and Disney Pooh bedding are made by Crown Crafts subsidiary Red Calliope; see review below.

Pottery Barn See review later in this chapter. **Rating: B+**

Quiltex *For a dealer near you, call (800) 237-3636 or (212) 594-2205. Web: www.quiltex.com* Quiltex is famous for their licensed bedding items, including Hello Kitty, Precious Moments and our son's favorite, Thomas the Tank Engine. Style-wise, we'd put Quiltex into the "cutesy, baby-ish" category—the groupings are heavy on the pastel colors and frilly ruffles. Unfortunately, most of the line is blends (50/50 cotton-poly fabric). The quality of the Quiltex designs is middle-of-the-road: some appliqué work leaves a bit to be desired, while other designs are merely stamped on the fabric. Their prices ($140 to $190 for a four-piece set) are a bit more reasonable. **Rating: B-**

Red Calliope *For a dealer near you, call (800) 421-0526 or (310) 763-8100. Web: www.redcalliope.com* Red Calliope is a division of Crown Crafts, the billion dollar bedding behemoth that also owns Nojo. And like Nojo, Red Calliope is sold just about everywhere. The bread and butter designs at Calliope are Pooh—that's Winnie the Pooh. For years this runaway best seller inspired all kinds of spin offs: Disney Pooh, Classic Pooh, Son of Pooh (oops! not that one!). Alas,

Pooh's popularity is waning. Yes, you can still find some Pooh in stores like Babies R Us although they are sometimes marketed under the Disney Baby moniker. A sample four piece set runs $180 to $250. The bottom line: while it's understandable why Pooh is so popular, the quality of most of Calliope's Pooh bedding is just not worth the price. And Red Calliope's other designs aren't much to write home about either. **Rating: C+**

Sumersault *Call (800) 232-3006 or (201) 768-7890 for a dealer near you. Web: www.sumersault.com* Owner Patti Sumergrade imports beautiful fabrics from Portugal and other European countries to create this top-shelf bedding line. We loved the plaids and whimsical character fabrics, which featured off beat colors that match the richer wood tones popular for cribs in New England and the Northeast. Sumersault does few appliqués and leaves most of the cutesy touches to optional wall hangings. A four piece set retails for $325 to $400. We should note that Sumersault also makes the Laura Ashley Mother and Child bedding collection, which sells for $250 to $400 for four pieces. As for the designs, Sumersault continues to roll out more muted pastel themes. Look for coordinating hand painted lamps and other accessories. Overall, we like the quality of Sumersault. **Rating: A**

Sweet Pea *Call (626) 578-0866 for a dealer near you.* You gotta like Sweet Pea . . . their fun and funky fabrics are imported from places like the Vatican (which we didn't realize exported anything other than Popes). Sweet Pea's 100% cotton bedding features a variety of very-adult finishes including jacquards, satins and even crushed velvets. If you don't like the damask-woven fabric, consider a floral chintz that looks like Laura Ashley on acid. One impossibly over-the-top design featured mix-and-match cabbage roses, corded piping trim and ribbon accents. Unfortunately, the prices are also over-the-top: five piece sets *start* at $400 and can top $1000. Ouch. While the quality is high, the prices are way out of the ballpark. **Rating: B**

Waverly See Crown Crafts review earlier in this section.

Wendy Bellissimo Baby N Kids *Call (818) 348-3682 for a dealer near you. Web: www.wendybellissimo.com.* Wendy Bellissimo is a hot young designer from California whose bedding is often seen at upper-end baby stores like Bellini. The look: beautiful, sophisticated patterns made with 100% cotton fabrics. Accents include velour, appliqués and lace touches. All Bellissimo's bumpers are slip-covered so you can wash them separately. So what does all this quality and cache cost you? We saw prices at BabyStyle.com ranging from $360 to $660 for a four to five piece set (some sets include a second dust ruffle for a layered effect). Whoa! And if you don't have a pricey baby boutique nearby, you can buy all these designs online from her web site (which is a bit of a surprise). The web site also lets you see large swatch samples of the fabrics and tells you if the designs are in stock. One unique feature to this line: boutiques that carry Bellissimo also may participate in her computer-assisted custom design options. Finally, you'll find accessories including diaper covers and swaddling blankets as well as Moses baskets ($230 to $280) and bassinets. While the prices are no bargain, the designs are interesting and the quality is exceptional.

New this year, Wendy has created a second, lower priced line

Winnie the Pooh at a Discount

Who's the hottest bear in baby bedding? Why, it's Pooh, Winnie the Pooh to be exact. Sales of Pooh bedding have been off the charts for the past several years and it seems like there's no stopping that silly old bear. But with the price for a basic four-piece set running close to $200 (or more), how can you get Pooh at a discount?

Unfortunately, there's only one company that makes Pooh crib bedding (Crown Crafts' Little Bedding, reviewed earlier in this chapter), so you can't choose among several suppliers to get a better deal. On the upside, the bedding is widely available, so you can get it on sale (at places like JCPenney) or regularly discounted from mail-order sources or web sites (see later in this chapter for possibilities).

While many parents like Pooh, some told us they are less than thrilled with the quality of the Pooh bedding. In the past, much of this bedding was poly/cotton blends with low thread counts. But there is good news: recently, Red Calliope has added several 100% cotton collections, albeit at rather stiff prices ($300+).

So what can you do? Here's an idea: who says you have to have Pooh bedding to do a Pooh-themed nursery? Our advice: buy solid color matching sheets and linens and then accessorize with Pooh items. Fortunately, a myriad of companies make Pooh licensed accessories. And you'll find virtually every accessory available at *Country Lane* (www.country-lane.com). As we mentioned earlier, they specialize in items from many well-known collections including Pooh.

called Wendy Bee. Prices for a four-piece set are only $219 while a Moses basket is only $99. The styles are definitely simpler, but the quality of the fabric is still excellent. **Rating: B+**

◆ *Other brands to consider: Simmons* (the crib maker) also makes bedding ranging from $130 to $280. The designs are simple with patchwork accents in some cases. They have quite a wide range of accessories to go with each collection and they are discounted heavily on the web and in chain stores.

For folks living in those ice cold climates who want to add a bit of island chic to their baby's room, check out Uhula.com. Their Hawaiian themed bedding (also very popular in Hawaii as you can imagine) will have you imagining warm beaches and cool island breezes in no time. We love this site's laid back style and the patterns are like nothing you'll find anywhere else.

Riegel (800) 845-3251 or (803) 275-2541 (web: www.parentinformation.com) made by Mt. Vermont Mills is a big player in the bedding market—but you might not recognize the name. Riegel is the company behind the in-store bedding brands at discounters like Target and Wal-Mart. The company also sells two collections under their own name, makes the Carter's Lennon Baby (reviewed earlier, ($150 for a four-piece 100% cotton 200 thread count set) and the Carter's Coordinates ($60 for four pieces in 100% cotton). Finally, Riegel manufacturers Sesame Street crib bedding for $40 for a four-piece set. While the Carter's line is good quality, the Sesame Street and Riegel collections are poly/cotton blends intended for mass-market discount stores. Just to confuse you more, Riegel is also the manufacturer of Kmart's Martha Stewart brand (see review above).

Springs (call 212-556-6300 for a dealer near you; web: www.springs.com) has three patterns available in their collection. Wamsutta Baby is a standout with 100% cotton sheets and matte lasse finish on the coverlet and bumpers. Entry-level bedding sets sell in Wal-Mart for $40 and go up to $100 for a four-piece set.

New on the upper-end bedding scene is *Bebe Chic* (201) 941-5414 (www.bebechic.com), a New Jersey-based designer who says their bedding combines "old world charm (with) soft textures, jacquards and quilted solids." Their prices: $200 to $300 for a comforter, $40 to $60 for a single sheet. Available in Bellini stores.

 ## Do It By Mail

Here's an overview of several catalogs that offer baby bedding. In most cases, the catalogs carry private label merchandise (with the exception of JCPenney and Baby Catalog, which sell name brands). In general, we find that the bedding from most mail-order catalogs is very high quality and unique in design. Another big plus: you can find affordable basic items like solid color sheets and blankets.

BABY CATALOG OF AMERICA

Call (800) PLAYPEN or (203) 931-7760; Fax (203) 933-1147.
Internet: www.babycatalog.com
Accept: all major credit cards
Order by mail or visit the Baby Club of America Warehouse Outlet, 719 Campbell Ave., West Haven, CT 06516.

How can you get name-brand bedding at a big discount? Unfortunately, most catalogs sell bedding at full retail and baby stores are loath to discount fancy brands.

Well, here's the good news: Baby Catalog of America is a one-stop source for brand new bedding, linen, decor and other accessories at prices 20% to 50% off retail. And we're not talking about just the low quality bedding brands either. Baby Catalog of America sells a wide variety of premium brands, including Sumersault and Pine Creek.

What about accessories? You can find lamps, wall decor, and other nursery items at good prices too. There's a big selection of Pooh items as well as basics like solid color sheets and blankets.

If those prices weren't low enough, Baby Catalog will give you another 10% off each purchase if you buy an annual membership ($25). And that's just the beginning: the catalog also sells strollers, car seats, accessories and more. The only caveat to using this catalog and web site is we don't recommend using their baby registry. We've received many complaints from past readers about this service.

COMPANY KIDS

To Order Call: (800) 323-8000
Web: www.companykids.com
Shopping Hours: 24 hours a day, seven days a week.
Or write to: 500 Company Store Rd., La Crosse, WI 54601.
Credit Cards Accepted: MC, VISA, AMEX, Discover.

A subsidiary of the Company Store, Company Kids now offers a complete catalog catering to the bedding whims of parents and little ones alike. Basically, Company Kids offers a selection of quilts for infants, which can then be paired with sheets in solids or checks. There are also some bedding sets (sold a la carte with matching

Continued on page 146

BEDDING RATINGS

Name	Rating	Cost
Amy Coe	A-	$ TO $$$
Baby Guess	B	$$
Banana Fish	B	$$ TO $$$
Beautiful Baby	B	$$$
Brandee Danielle	A-	$$
California Kids	A	$$
Carters	B+	$
Celebrations	B+	$$ TO $$$
CoCaLo	B+	$$
Company Kids	A	$
Cotton Tale	A	$$
Crown Crafts	C+	$ TO $$
Gerber	D	$
Glenna Jean	B-	$ TO $$$
Hoohobbers	B+	$$
House of Hatten	B+	$$ TO $$$
Infantino	B	$ TO $$
Koala Baby	C	$
KidsLine	B	$ TO $$
Kimberly Grant	A-	$$ TO $$$
Lambs & Ivy	B+	$ TO $$
Lands End	A	$
Luv Stuff	B	$$$
Martha Stewart	C	$
Nava's Designs	C+	$$$
Nojo	B	$ TO $$
Patchkraft	A	$$ TO $$$
Pine Creek	A-	$$
Pottery Barn	B+	$$
Quiltex	B-	$ TO $$
Red Calliope	C+	$ TO $$
Sumersault	A	$$ TO $$$
Sweet Pea	B	$$$
Wendy Bellissimo	B+	$$ TO $$$

Key

* **N/A.** In some cases, we didn't have this information by press time.
Cost: Cost of a four-piece set (comforter, sheet, dust ruffle/bed skirt, bumpers) $=under $200; $$=$200 to $400; $$$=over $400
Fiber Content: Some lines have both all-cotton and poly/cotton blends—these are noted with the word "Mix."

FIBER CONTENT	BUMPER TIES	TIE LENGTH
100% COTTON	TOP/BOTTOM	10″
100% COTTON	TOP	8″
100% COTTON	TOP	6″
MIX	TOP/BOTTOM	8″
MIX	TOP	7″
100% COTTON	TOP/BOTTOM	10″
100% COTTON	*	*
100% COTTON	TOP/BOTTOM	9″
MIX	*	*
100% COTTON	*	*
100% COTTON	TOP	7.5″
MIX	TOP	8″
POLY/COTTON	*	*
MIX	TOP	10″
100% COTTON	TOP	6″
100% COTTON	TOP/BOTTOM	8.5″
MIX	*	*
100% COTTON	TOP	*
MIX	TOP/BOTTOM	7″ TO 9″
100% COTTON	*	*
POLY/COTTON	TOP	10″
100% COTTON	TOP/BOTTOM	*
MIX	TOP	11″
100% COTTON	TOP	*
100% COTTON	TOP/BOTTOM	14″
MIX	TOP	7″
100% COTTON	TOP/BOTTOM	9″
100% COTTON	TOP/BOTTOM	8″
100% COTTON	*	*
POLY/COTTON	TOP	7″
MIX	*	*
100% COTTON	TOP	7″-9″
100% COTTON	TOP/BOTTOM	10″
100% COTTON	TOP/BOTTOM	*

BUMPER TIES: refers to the location of bumper ties, top and bottom or top only.
TIE LENGTHS: the length of the bumper ties; these are approximate estimates and may vary from style to style.

bumpers, sheets and dust ruffles) as well. Duvets are also available.

Sheets run $12 to 19 each while comforters range from $50 to $88 each. Not a bad deal at all for 100% cotton percale, flannel or knit bedding fabrics.

Bottom line: we think Company Kids sells high quality baby bedding at great prices. We also liked their web site, which is easy-to-navigate and features clearance items for even bigger savings. If you're in the vicinity of The Company Store's outlet store, don't miss it. One reader found the prices amazing including sheets at only $5.

GARNET HILL

To Order Call: (800) 622-6216; In Canada, call (603) 823-5545.
Shopping Hours: 24 hours a day, seven days a week.
Or write to: Garnet Hill, 231 Main St., Franconia, NH 03580.
Credit Cards Accepted: MC, VISA, AMEX, Discover.
Outlet: Historic Manchester Outlet Center, Manchester VT (802) 362-6198.

If you want to spend the big bucks on bedding, check out Garnet Hill. This catalog makes a big deal out of its "natural fabric" offerings, and they do sell products we haven't seen elsewhere. But you'll pay for the privilege.

Garnet Hill sells woven, knit and flannel crib bedding. Fitted sheets range from $20 to $28 each and the designs are attractive—we especially like the "Ballerina" and "Dragons and Wizards" patterns. The quality is high: all sheets are 200 thread count and some are made of Egyptian cotton. One reader emailed her thoughts on Garnet Hill's flannel sheets: "A big thumbs up," she said, adding "even though the price was high, the sheets were very high quality, soft and didn't pill." She wasn't as thrilled with their bumper pads, which only have ties at the top and the filling "got a bit munched in the washing machine." By the way, when we went online to review their options, no bumper pads appeared for any of the crib bedding. After calling customer service, we were told that all their crib sets have bumpers available, they just didn't "have enough room to list them" online. How dumb is that?

The catalog's patchwork quilts are quite beautiful and cost $78 to $98. Another kudos for Garnet Hill: the *Wall St. Journal's* "Catalog Critic" rated a Garnet Hill crib quilt as Best Overall. High praise indeed.

GRAHAM KRACKER

To Order Call: (800) 489-2820; Fax: (915) 697-1776
Web: www.grahamkracker.com; Credit Cards Accepted: MC, VISA.

This mail order company specializes in custom bedding. You can mix and match your own selections from 17 styles or choose from five ready-made collections. Or you can provide your own fabric. The price? A whopping $450 for a five-piece set, which includes a headboard bumper and baby pillow (don't use this in the crib, please!). But, everything is 100% cotton and there are all sorts of matching accessories. Most of the choices are bright, cheerful colors, but not too cutesy. Shipping time is two to three weeks.

JCPENNEY

To Order Call: (800) 222-6161.
Web: www.JCPenney.com/shopping
Shopping Hours: 24 hours a day, seven days a week.
Credit Cards Accepted: MC, VISA, JCPenney, AMEX, Discover.

JCPenney have carried quite a wide range of name brand baby bedding from manufacturers like Simmons, Carter's (Lennon Baby), Baby Loony Tunes, Nojo, Lambs & Ivy, Glenna Jean, KidsLine and Red Calliope (Disney Pooh). Their brands often vary and they add new manufacturers frequently. While Penney's prices aren't always affordable (we compared some designs to other mail-order sources and found Penney's to be a few dollars higher), they do offer quite a few matching accessories. For example, they carry every accessory available for the "Stargazer Snoopy" by Bedtime Originals—valances, wallpaper borders, mobiles, and wall hangings for these and other bedding designs. If you want a "complete look," give Penney's a call. Good news this year: they appear to have fixed some of their problems with incorrect links. Searching for bedding is a bit easier, although using the search function is still the fastest method.

THE LAND OF NOD

To Order Call: (800) 933-9904. Web: www.landofnod.com
Shopping Hours: Mon-Fri 7:30am to 9:00pm, Weekends 9am to 5pm
Or Write to: PO Box 1404, Wheeling, IL 60090
Credit Cards: MC, VISA, AMEX, Discover.

This stunning catalog (now owned by Crate & Barrel) features sumptuous layouts of baby's and kid's rooms, replete with expensive linens and accessories. Even if you don't buy anything, the Land of Nod is a great place to get decorating ideas.

Crib bedding is sold a la carte and some designs only have the quilt, bed skirt and bumpers available. A four-piece set runs $218 to $270, while a single sheet can cost $24. The prices have definitely come down in recent years. We loved the color palette, which ranged from patchwork denim to bright pastels. Check out the whimsical lamps and other accessories, even a Moses basket with a farmyard print. Finally, you can order on line from these guys instead of only from an 800 number—a welcome change.

LANDS' END

To Order Call: (800) 345-3696; Web: www.landsend.com
Shopping Hours: 24 hours a day, seven days a week.
Or write to: Lands' End Inc., 1 Lands' End Lane, Dodgeville, WI 53595.
Credit Cards Accepted: MC, VISA, AMEX, Discover.
Retail Outlets: Lands' End has 20 outlet stores, mostly in the Midwest and Northeast—call the number above for the nearest location to you.

Lands' End calls them Crib Sheets that fit. They come in prints and solids, 220-count cotton percale and have elastic all the way around. The best part? The price. They sell two sheets for $36. Not bad for all that quality. Flannel sheets are also available as are cotton knit. We love Lands' End's "coverlets" (which are more substantial than a blanket but not as thick as a quilt/comforter) instead of those huge quilts sold by other manufacturers. The Polartec blankets ($18) are also a good option for parents in cold climates.

While the offerings change each season, Land's End designs have tended toward the simple, with no cartoons or appliqués to clutter up the basic look. Another bonus: Lands' End web site has fantastic overstock deals, posted twice weekly.

POTTERY BARN KIDS

To Order Call: (800) 430-7373. Web: www.potterybarnkids.com
Shopping Hours: 24 hours a day, seven days a week.
Or write to: P.O. Box 379909, Las Vegas, NV, 89137.
Credit Cards Accepted: MC, VISA, AMEX.
Outlet Stores: Jeffersonville, OH (740) 948-2004, Dawsonville, GA (706) 216-5211 or (706) 216-6465, Memphis, TN (901) 763-1500.

No catalog has shaken up the baby bedding and décor business in recent years like the Pottery Barn Kids (PBK) catalog. Their cheerful baby bedding, whimsical accessories and furniture have overrun the rest of the industry. PBK isn't cutesy-babyish or overly adult. It's playful, fun and bright. And hot. We get more questions about this catalog than any other.

So let's answer a few of those questions. PBK's bedding is 100% cotton, 200-thread count. The sheets have 10" corner pockets and they *used* to have elastic that went all the way around the edge. We're disappointed to say that they now only make their crib sheets with elastic on the ends. While the fabric they use is good, the lack of elastic leads us to recommend parents shop for sheets elsewhere.

Several readers have also complained about the bumpers, which are knocked as "thin and insubstantial." One reader wrote saying "they are very thin and my child can get his arms and legs out of the slats of the crib because the bumpers smush down so easily!" Another reader complained that the ties kept pulling off her bumper.

Prices for quilts range from $59 to $79, bumper sets are $59 to $69, sheets are $18 to $25 and dust ruffles are $59. Not bad for the quality. Compared to other bedding manufacturers, Pottery Barn is a pretty good deal. Frequent sales make more expensive items like lamps and rugs even more affordable. The best deal: PBK's outlet stores. One reader saw sheets on sale for $8, duvet covers for $15 and even a crib for $175 at the outlet (see above for locations).

What really seems to be PBK's strong suit is accessories. The catalog is stuffed with so many rugs, lamps, storage options and toys, you can shop one place for a complete look. For example, how about a nursery theme with flowers and butterflies? You can find the bedding ($148 for the bumper and quilt) plus a coordinating butterfly lamp ($49), rug ($79-$200) butterfly stamps and paint to match ($35 and $16, respectively) and more.

Overall, we like PBK. One caveat: their success has led to some growing pains. You may find some items back-ordered. Our advice: order early to be sure you get what you want on time. And if you have to go back for something later, you may find it unavailable.

◆ *Other Catalogs to Consider*. Here are several other catalogs that carry basic linens and supplies:

The Right Start (800) 548-8531, web: www.rightstart.com
One Step Ahead (800) 274-8440, web: www.onestepahead.com
Baby Universe Web: www.babyuniverse.com

The Bottom Line: A Wrap-Up of Our Best Buy Picks

For bedding, we think Cotton Tale and Lambs & Ivy combine good quality at a low price. If you can afford to spend more, check out the offerings from Patchkraft, Sumersault, and California Kids. And if money is no object, try Wendy Bellissimo. Of course, there's no law that says you have to buy an entire bedding set for your nursery—we found that all baby really needs is a set of sheets and a good cotton blanket. Catalogs like Lands' End and Company Store sell affordable (yet high-quality) basics like sheets and blankets. Instead of spending $300 to $500 on a bedding set with ridiculous items like pillows and diaper stackers, use your creativity to decorate the nursery affordably and leave the crib simple.

And if you fall in love with Pooh, don't shell out $300 on a fancy bedding set. Instead, we recommend buying solid color sheets and accessorizing with affordable Pooh items like lamps, posters, rugs, etc.

Who's got the best deals on bedding? If it's a set you desire, check out web sites like Baby Depot (www.coat.com) for discounts of 20% to 40%. If you're lucky to be near a manufacturer's outlet, search these stores for discontinued patterns.

Let's take a look at the savings:

Lands' End 100% cotton fitted sheets (three)	$36
Cotton coverlet blanket from Lands' End	$40
Miscellaneous (Transfer-Mations, lamp, other decor)	$100
TOTAL	$176

If you live in a cold climate, you might want to get a Polar fleece blanket from a catalog like the Company Store for $20.

In contrast, if you go for a designer brand and buy all those silly extras like diaper stackers, you could be out as much as $800 on bedding alone—add in wall paper, accessories like wall hangings, matching lamps and you'll be out $1100 or more. So, the total savings from following the tips in this chapter could be as much as $800 to $900.

Now that your baby's room is outfitted, what about the baby? Flip to the next chapter to get the lowdown on those little clothes.

REALITY LAYETTE

CHAPTER 4

The Reality Layette:
Little Clothes for Little Prices

Inside this chapter

What the heck is a "onesie"? How many clothes does your baby need? How come such little clothes have such big price tags? These and other mysteries are unraveled in this chapter as we take you on a guided tour of baby clothes land. We'll reveal our secret sources for finding name brand clothes at one-half to one-third off department store prices. Which brands are best? Check out our picks for the best clothing brands for your baby and our nine tips from smart shoppers on getting the best deals. Next, read about the many outlets for children's apparel that have been popping up all over the country. At the end of this chapter, we'll even show you how to save big bucks on diapers.

Getting Started:
When Do You Need This Stuff?

◆ **Baby Clothing.** You'll need basic baby clothing like t-shirts and sleepers as soon as you're ready to leave the hospital. Depending on the weather, you may need a bunting (a snug-fitting, hooded sleeping bag of heavy material for infants) at that time as well.

You'll probably want to start stocking up on baby clothing around the seventh month of your pregnancy. It's important to have some basic items on hand (like sleepers or stretchies) in case you deliver early; however, you may want to wait to do major shopping until after any baby showers to see what clothing your friends and family give as gifts.

Be sure to keep a running list of your acquisitions so you won't buy too much of one item. Thanks to gifts and our own buying, we had about two thousand teeny, side-snap shirts by the time our baby was born. In the end, our son didn't wear the shirts much (he grew out of the newborn sizes quickly and wasn't really wild about them anyway), and we ended up wasting the money we spent.

◆ **Diapers.** How many diapers do you need for starters? Are you sitting down? If you're going with disposables, we recommend 600 diapers for the first six weeks (about 14 diapers a day). Yes, that's six packages of 100 diapers each (purchase them in your eighth month of pregnancy, just in case Junior arrives early). You may think this is a lot, but believe us, we bought that much and we still had to do another diaper run by the time our son was a month old. Newborns go through many more diapers than older infants. Also, remember that as a new parent, you'll find yourself taking off diapers that turn out to be dry. Or worse, you may change a diaper three times in a row because Junior wasn't really finished.

Now that you know how many diapers, what sizes should you buy? We recommend 100 newborn-size diapers and 500 "size one" (or Step 1) diapers. This assumes an average-size baby (about seven pounds at birth). But remember to keep the receipts—if your baby is larger, you might have to exchange the newborns for size one's (and some of the one's for two's). Note for parents-to-be of multiples: your babies tend to be smaller at birth, so buy all newborn diapers to start. And double or triple our recommended quantity!

If you plan to use a diaper service to supply cloth diapers, sign up in your eighth month. Some diaper services will give you an initial batch of diapers (so you're ready when baby arrives) and then await your call to start up regular service. If you plan to wash your own cloth diapers, buy two to five dozen diapers about two months before your due date. You'll also probably want to buy diaper covers (6 to 10) at that time. We'll discuss cloth diapers in depth later in this chapter.

Even if you plan to use disposable diaper, you should pick up one package of high-quality cloth diapers. Why? You'll need them as spit-up rags, spot cleaners and other assorted uses you'd never imagined before becoming a parent.

 **Sources**

There are ten basic sources for baby clothing and diapers:

I **BABY SPECIALTY STORES.** Specialty stores typically carry 100% cotton, high-quality clothes, but you won't usually find them affordably priced. While you may find attractive dressy clothes, play clothes are typically a better deal elsewhere. Because the stores themselves are frequently small, selection is limited. On the upside, you can still find old-fashioned service at specialty stores—and that's helpful when buying items like shoes. In that case, the extra help with sizing may be worth the higher price.

As for diapers, you can forget about it—most specialty baby stores long ago ceded the diaper market to discounters and grocery stores (who sell disposables), as well as mail-order companies (who dominate the cloth diaper and supply business). Occasionally, we see specialty stores carry an offbeat product like Tushies, an eco-friendly disposable diaper. And some may have diaper covers, but the selection is typically limited.

2 DEPARTMENT STORES. Clothing is a department store's bread and butter, so it's not surprising to see many of these stores excel at merchandising baby clothes. Everyone from Sears to Nordstrom does baby clothes and frequent sales often make the selection more affordable.

3 SPECIALTY CHAINS. Our readers love Old Navy (see money-saving tips section) and Gap Kids. Both sell 100% cotton, high-quality clothes that are stylish and durable. Not to mention their price adjustment policies. On reader told us that they if you buy an item and it gets marked down within seven days, you get the new price. Old Navy's (798 stores nationwide; 13 in Canada) selection of baby clothes is somewhat limited compared to Gap Kids. Other chains to check out include Gymboree, and Talbots for Kids. All are reviewed later in this chapter.

4 DISCOUNTERS. Wal-Mart, Target and K-Mart have moved aggressively into baby clothes in the last decade. Instead of cheap, polyester outfits that were common a decade ago at these stores, most discounters now emphasize 100% cotton clothing in fashionable styles. Even places like Toys R Us now stock basic layette items like t-shirts, sleepers and booties.

Target has vastly expanded their baby clothes with their in-store brand, Cherokee, and others like B.U.M. Not only have they expanded, but also the quality is terrific in most cases. We shop Target for all cotton play clothes and day care clothes. They seem to last pretty well with the active play our kids indulge in.

Diapers are another discounter strong suit—you'll find both name brand and generic disposables at most stores; some even carry a selection of cloth diaper supplies like diaper covers (although they are the cheaper brands; see the diaper section later in this book for more details). Discounters seem to be locked into an endless price battle with warehouse clubs on baby care items, so you can usually find the prices to be rock bottom.

5 **BABY SUPERSTORES.** Both Babies R Us and Baby Depot carry a decent selection of name-brand clothing at low prices. Most of the selection focuses on basics, however. You'll see more Carter's and Little Me than the fancy brands common at department stores. We've noticed in recent years that places like Babies R Us have "dumbed-down" their clothing section, trading fancy dress clothes and brands for more staples at everyday low prices. In that respect, Babies R Us has ceded the hip, stylish market to specialty chains like Gap Kids.

Diapers are a mixed bag at superstores. Babies R Us carries them, but Baby Depot doesn't. When you find them, though, the prices are comparable to discounters. We've seen diapers priced 20% to 30% lower at Babies R Us than grocery stores.

6 **WAREHOUSE CLUBS.** Members-only warehouse clubs like Sam's, Price/Costco and BJ's sell diapers at rock-bottom prices. The selection is often hit-or-miss—sometimes you'll see brand names like Huggies and Pampers; other times it may be off-brands. While you won't find the range of sizes that you'd see in grocery stores, the prices will be hard to beat. The downside? You have to buy them in "bulk," huge cases of multiple diaper packs that might require a forklift to get home.

As a side note, we've even seen some baby clothes at warehouse clubs from time to time. We found very good quality blanket sleepers at Sam's for $8 each during one visit. Costco has also greatly improved their kid's clothing offerings in recent years. We love Costco's 100% cotton pajamas for toddlers at $10 a pair (compare at $32 a pair in catalogs). Costco also has infant-size play clothes and sleepers at bargain prices.

7 **MAIL-ORDER.** There are a zillion catalogs that offer clothing for infants. The choices can be quite overwhelming, and the prices can range from reasonable to ridiculous. It's undeniably a great way to shop when you have a newborn and just don't want to drag your baby out to the mall. Another mail order strength: cloth diapers and related supplies. Chains and specialty stores have abandoned these items, so mail order suppliers have picked up the slack. Check out "Do it By Mail" later in this chapter for the complete low-down on catalogs that sell clothing and diapers.

8 **THE WEB.** Baby clothing sales on the 'net have been somewhat slow to take off. We suspect this might have to do with the glut of mail order catalogs that vie for parents' attention, as well as the fact that clothing's relative low prices make the discounts less dramatic. As for diapers, several web sites have popped up in recent years to offer discount disposables. And the web is a great source for cloth diapers and supplies. We'll discuss the best web sites for all these items later in the chapter.

9 **CONSIGNMENT OR THRIFT STORES.** You might think of these stores as dingy shops with musty smells—purveyors of old, used clothes that aren't in great shape. Think again—many consignment stores today are bright and attractive, with name brand clothes at a fraction of the retail price. Yes, the clothes have been worn before, but most stores only stock high-quality brands that are in excellent condition. And stores that specialize in children's apparel are popping up everywhere, from coast to coast. Later in this chapter, we'll tell you how to find a consignment store near you.

10 **GARAGE/YARD SALES.** Check out the box on the next page for tips on how to shop garage sales like the pros.

Baby Clothing

So you thought all the big-ticket items were taken care of when you bought the crib and other furniture? Ha! It's time to prepare for your baby's "layette," a French word that translated literally means "spending large sums of cash on baby clothes and other such items, as required by Federal Baby Law." But, of course, there are some creative (dare we say, sneaky?) ways of keeping your layette bills down.

CPSC Issues Thrift Shop Warning

Do second-hand stores sell dangerous goods? To answer that question, the Consumer Product Safety Commission surveyed 301 random thrift stores in 2000, looking for recalled or banned products like clothing with drawstrings (an entanglement and strangulation hazard). The results: 51% of stores were selling clothing (mostly outerwear) with drawstrings at the waist or neck. This is particularly disturbing since 22 deaths and 48 non-fatal accidents since 1985 are attributed to drawstrings. If you buy clothing at a consignment or thrift store or from a garage sale, be sure to avoid clothes with drawstrings. Another disturbing finding: about two-thirds of the stores surveyed had at least one recalled or banned product on the shelves.

At this point, you may be wondering just what does your baby need? Sure you've seen those cute ruffled dresses and sailor suits in department stores—but what does your baby *really* wear everyday?

Meet the layette, a collection of clothes and accessories that your baby will use daily. While your baby's birthday suit was free, outfitting him in something more "traditional" will cost some bucks. In fact, a recent study estimated that parents spend $12,000 on clothes for a child by the time he or she hits 18 years old—and that sounds like a conservative estimate to us. That translates into a 20 *billion* (yes, that's billion with a B) dollar business for children's clothing retailers. Follow our tips, and we estimate that you'll save 20% or more on your baby's wardrobe.

Garage & Yard Sales
Eight Tips to Get The Best Bargains

It's an American institution—the garage sale.

Sure you can save money on baby clothes and products at an outlet store or get a deal at a department store sale. But there's no comparing to the steals you can get at your neighbor's garage sale.

We love getting e-mail from readers who've found great deals at garage sales. How about 25¢ stretchies, a snowsuit for $1, barely used high chairs for $5? But getting the most out of garage sales requires some pre-planning. We interviewed a dozen parents who call themselves "garage sale experts" for their tips:

1 CHECK THE NEWSPAPER FIRST. Many folks advertise their garage sales a few days before the event—zero in on the ads that mention kids/baby items to keep from wasting time on sales that won't be fruitful.

2 GET A GOOD MAP OF THE AREA. You've got to find obscure cul-de-sacs and hidden side streets.

3 START EARLY. The professional bargain hunters get going at the crack of dawn. If you wait until mid-day, all the good stuff will be gone. An even better bet: if you know the family, ask if you can drop by the day *before* the sale. That way you have a first shot before the competition arrives. One trick: if it's a neighbor, offer to help set-up for the sale. That's a great way to get those "early bird" deals.

4 DO THE "BOX DIVE." Many garage sale hosts will just dump kid's clothes into a big box, all jumbled together in different sizes, styles, etc. Figuring out how to get the best picks while three

Parents in Cyberspace: What's on the Web?

Bella Kids

Web: www.bellakids.com

What it is: Site with domestic and European baby clothing.

What's cool: Organized by season, boy/girl and age, this site is easy to navigate. They carry brands from Zutano, Baybotte, Cakewalk and more. Although prices are quite high, the clothes are excellent quality and they offer up to 50% off sale items. Free shipping is another plus.

other moms are digging through the same box is a challenge. The best advice: familiarize yourself with the better name brands in this chapter and then pluck out the best bets as fast as possible. Then evaluate the clothes away from the melee.

5 **CONCENTRATE ON "FAMILY AREAS."** A mom here in Colorado told us she found garage sales in Boulder (a college town) were mostly students getting rid of stereos, clothes and other junk. A better bet was nearby Louisville, a suburban bedroom community with lots of growing families.

6 **HAGGLE.** Prices on big-ticket items (that is, anything over $5) are usually negotiable. Another great tip we read in the newsletter *Cheapskate Monthly*—to test out products, carry a few "C" and "D" batteries with you to garage sales. Most swings and bouncing seats use those type batteries, so you want to make sure they're working before buying.

7 **DON'T BUY A USED CRIB OR CAR SEAT.** Old cribs may not meet current safety standards. It's also difficult to get replacement parts for obscure brands. Car seats are also a second-hand no-no— you can't be sure it wasn't in an accident, weakening its safety and effectiveness. And watch out for clothing with drawstrings, loose buttons or other safety hazards.

8 **BE CREATIVE.** See a great stroller but the fabric is dirty? And non-removable so you can't through it in the washing machine? Take a cue from one dad we interviewed. He takes dirty second-hand strollers or high chairs to a car wash and blasts them with a high-pressure hose! Voila! Clean and useable items are the result. For a small investment, you can rehabilitate a stroller into a showpiece.

Needs work: Well, they're darned expensive. But if you're looking for items you saw in magazines like Baby Talk, check them out. They often list where an outfit was advertised or promoted.

Patsy Aiken

Web: www.patsyaiken.com or www.chezami.com
What it is: The only source now for this well-liked brand.
What's cool: We've always loved Patsy Aiken's clothes, but their distribution used to be limited to fancy baby boutiques. The good news: their site now sells the entire collection online. The US-made clothes are all 100% cotton with amazing embroidery, appliqué and smocking. You'll find adorable lambs, sailboats, and more in pale pastels. They also offer beautiful holiday outfits for those family portraits. Prices average around $25 to $30 for a typical bubble, dress or pantsuit. Not cheap but the quality is terrific. This is a great site for grandmas looking for that perfect shower gift.

Since they've decided to discontinue selling their line in stores, they've added a new method of buying their designs. Called Chez Ami it's a take off on the old Tupperware parties. You get a group of your friends together and have a Patsy Aiken clothing party. Check out the web site for more details.
Needs work: Now on the site, you have to download a PDF of their catalog. Its better than the old thumbnails, but we'd recommend signing up for their mailed catalog. It'll be easier to use.

One of a Kind Kid

Web: www.oneofakindkid.com, see Figure 1 on the next page.
What it is: Discount outlet offering deals on high-quality kids clothes.
What's cool: This site specializes in the upper-end clothes you see in Nordstrom and Neiman Marcus. We saw brands like Flapdoodles, Sweet Potatoes and Mulberribush among others. One of a Kind Kids sells all their clothes at 70% off, a great deal only topped by the flat $6 shipping fee. New items appear weekly so checking back frequently is a good idea.
Needs work: Unfortunately, the site notes that many of the items on their site are "one of a kind." This means if you see something you like, you may have to order it on the spot. While the thumbnails of the clothes are expandable, their tiny size makes it hard to get a quick read on what's available.

◆ *Other great sites. Preemie.com* (www.preemie.com) is a wonderful oasis for parents of preemies. You'll find items like hospital shirts, basics, sleepwear, caps and booties. Not to mention, they have a selection of diaries and books as well as preemie announcements. If you've got a preemie, this is the site for you.

Figure 1: Great prices, high-quality brands and flat fee shipping make OneOfAKindKid.com a winner.

While **SuddenlyMommies** (www.suddenlymommies.com) does not have a huge selection of baby wear, it sure is cute stuff. All white with colorful ribbon borders, the outfits are generally all cotton and include booties, pants sets, diaper covers, dresses and more. Prices are a bit high. For example, a short sleeve cotton knit dress is $33.

Kid Surplus (www.kidsurplus.com) is another discounter/closeout store. They seem to carry mostly Carters brand in their layette section but we also saw Halo Sleep Sacks and Goldbug socks and slippers.

We'd be remiss if we didn't also mention **eBay** (web: www. ebay.com) in this section. Their baby area is often stuffed with great deals on baby clothes. One tip: look for listings that say NWT— that's eBay-speak for "New With Tags." Obviously, these items are worth the most, yet often still sell for 50% off retail. EBay has just about everything it comes to baby clothes, from basic items to luxury goods. When we recently appeared on the NBC Today Show, we showed off several eBay deals on high-end baby apparel. A producer for the show snagged a Geisswein jacket made from Austrian felted wool. The jacket retails for a whopping $225 in boutiques. We bought it on eBay for $122, a savings of over $100. (Of course, we'd never spend $100+ on a winter jacket for our child, but if you have to that Geisswein look, eBay is da bomb).

Of course, remember our mantra: never pay retail. You don't have to pay full retail for these clothes online. A great way to save is to use web coupons. See the box in the next chapter ("Coupon deals cut the cost of online shopping") for a list of sites that catalog the best web deals.

What Are You Buying?

Figuring out what your baby should wear is hardly intuitive to first-time parents. We had no earthly idea what types of (and how many) clothes a newborn needed, so we did what we normally do—we went to the bookstore to do research. We found three-dozen books on "childcare and parenting"—with three-dozen different lists of items that you *must* have for your baby and without which you're a very bad parent. Speaking of guilt, we also heard from relatives, who had their own opinions as to what was best for baby.

All of this begs the question: what do you *really* need? And how much? We learned that the answer to that last, age-old question was the age-old answer, "It depends." That's right, nobody really knows. In fact, we surveyed several department stores, interviewed dozens of parents, and consulted several "experts," only to find no consensus whatsoever. So, in order to better serve humanity, we have developed THE OFFICIAL FIELDS' LIST OF ALMOST EVERY ITEM YOU NEED FOR YOUR BABY IF YOU LIVE ON PLANET EARTH. We hope this clears up the confusion. (For those living on another planet, please consult our *Baby Bargains* edition for Mars and beyond).

Feel free to now ignore those lists of "suggested layette items" provided by retail stores. Many of the "suggestions" are self-serving, to say the least.

Of course, even when you decide what and how much to buy for your baby, you still need to know what *sizes* to buy. Fortunately, we have this covered, too. First, recognize that most baby clothes come in a range of sizes rather than one specific size ("newborn to 3 months" or "3-6 months"). *We recommend you buy "3-6 month" sizes (instead of newborn) so your child won't grow out of his clothes too quickly.* Stay away from newborn to three-month sizes unless you are having multiples. If you have a premature baby or an infant who is on the small side (parents of multiples, take note), we have identified a couple of catalogs that specialize in preemie wear. And, if on the other hand, you deliver a 10-pounder, make sure you keep all receipts and labels so you can exchange the clothes for larger sizes—you may find you're into six-month sizes by the time your baby hits one month old! (Along the same lines, don't wash *all* those new baby clothes immediately. Wash just a few items for the initial few weeks. Keep all the other items in their original packaging to make returns easier).

Ever wonder how fast your baby will grow? Babies double their birth weight by five months . . . and triple it by one year! On average, babies grow 10 inches in their first year of life. Given those stats, you can understand why we don't recommend stocking up on "newborn" size clothes.

Also: remember, you can always buy more later if you need it. In fact, this is a good way to make use of those close friends and relatives who stop by and offer to "help" right after you've suffered through 36 hours of hard labor—send them to the store!

We should point out that this layette list is just to get you started. This supply should last for the first month or two of your baby's life. Also along these lines, we received a question from a mom-to-be who wondered, given these quantities, how often do we assume you'll do laundry. The answer is in the next box.

The "Baby Bargains" Layette

♦ **T-Shirts.** Oh sure, a t-shirt is a t-shirt, right? Not when it comes to baby t-shirts. These t-shirts could have side snaps, snaps at the crotch (also known as onesies or creepers) or over-the-head openings. If you have a child who is allergic to metal snaps (they leave a red ring on their skin), you might want to consider over-the-head t-shirts. As a side note, you have to wait until your baby's umbilical stump falls off (don't ask; this usually happens in a week or two) until you can use the snap-at-the-crotch t-shirts.

E-MAIL FROM THE REAL WORLD
How Much Laundry Will I Do?

Anna Balayn of Brooklyn, NY had a good question about baby's layette and laundry:

"You have a list of clothes a new baby needs, but you don't say how often I would need to do laundry if I go with the list. I work full time and would like to have enough for a week. Is the list too short for me?"

Our answer: there is no answer. Factors such as whether you use cloth or disposable diapers (cloth leaks more; hence more laundry) and how much your baby spits up will greatly determine the laundry load. Another factor: breast versus bottle feeding. Bottle-fed babies have fewer poops (and hence, less laundry from possible leaks). An "average" laundry cycle with our layette list would be every two to three days, assuming breast feeding, disposable diapers and an average amount of spit-up.

By the way, is a onesie t-shirt an outfit or an undergarment? Answer: it's both. In the summer, you'll find onesies with printed patterns that are intended as outfits. In the winter, most stores just sell white onesies, intended as undergarments.

HOW MANY? T-shirts usually come in packs of three. Our recommendation is to buy two packages of three (or a total of six shirts) of the side-snap variety. We also suggest buying two packs of over-the-head t-shirts. This way, if your baby does have an allergy to the snaps, you have a backup. Later you'll find the snap-at-the-crouch t-shirts to be most convenient since they don't ride up under clothes.

◆ **Gowns**. These are one-piece gowns with elastic at the bottom. They are used as sleeping garments in most cases. (We'll discuss more pros/cons of gowns later in this chapter.)

HOW MANY? This is a toss-up. If you want to experiment, go for one or two of these items. If they work well, you can always go back and get more later.

◆ **Sleepers**. This is the real workhorse of your infant's wardrobe, since babies usually sleep most of the day in the first months. Also known as stretchies, sleepers are most commonly used as pajamas for infants. They have feet, are often made of flame-retardant cloth and snap up the front. While most are made of polyester, we've seen an increase in the numbers of cotton sleepers in recent years. Another related item: cotton long johns for baby. These are similar to sleepers, but don't have feet (and hence, may necessitate the use of socks in winter months).

One parent emailed us asking if she was supposed to dress her baby in pants, shirts, etc. or if it was OK to keep her daughter in sleepers all day long. She noted the baby was quite comfortable and happy. Of course, you can use sleepers exclusively for the first few months. We certainly did. As we've said all along, a comfortable baby is a happy parent!

HOW MANY? Because of their heavy use, we recommend parents buy at least four to six sleepers.

◆ **Blanket Sleepers.** These are heavyweight, footed one-piece garments made of polyester. Used often in winter, blanket sleepers usually have a zipper down the front. In recent years, we've also seen quite a few "Polartec" blanket sleepers, their key advantage being a softer fleece fabric and a resistance to pilling.

HOW MANY? If you live in a cold climate or your baby is born in the winter, you may want to purchase two to four of these items. As an alternative to buying blanket sleepers, you could put a t-shirt on underneath a sleeper or stretchie for extra warmth. (Note: we've upped the recommended quantity of blanket sleepers from past editions of this book. Why? Safety advocates are increasingly worried about any soft bedding/blankets in a crib. So, using a blanket sleeper to keep baby warm in the winter and not using a blanket is a more preferred alternative).

Another option is a new product: the sleep sack. A couple manufacturers, Halo (www.halosleep.com) and Kiddopatomus (www.kiddopatomus.com) have these new wearable blankets. Typically make of lightweight fleece, they are worn over t-shirts or light sleepers (see picture of the Halo at right).

 ◆ **Coveralls**. One-piece play outfits, coveralls (also known as rompers) are usually cotton or cotton/poly blends. Small sizes (under 6 months) may have feet, while larger sizes don't.
HOW MANY? Since these are really play clothes and small infants don't do a lot of playing, we recommend you only buy two to four coveralls for babies less than four months of age. However, if your child will be going into daycare at an early age, you may need to start with four to six coveralls.

 ◆ **Booties/socks**. These are necessary for outfits that don't have feet (like gowns and coveralls). As your child gets older (at about six months), look for the kind of socks that have rubber skids on the bottom (they keep baby from slipping when learning to walk).
HOW MANY? Three to four pairs are all you'll need at first, since baby will probably be dressed in footed sleepers most of the time.

◆ **Sweaters**. HOW MANY? Most parents will find one sweater is plenty (they're nice for holiday picture sessions). Avoid all-white sweaters, since they show dirt much faster.

 ◆ **Hats**. Believe it or not, you'll still want a light cap for your baby in the early months of life, even if you live in a hot climate. Babies lose a large amount of heat from their heads, so protecting them with a cap or bonnet is a good idea. And don't expect to go out for a walk in the park without the baby's sun hat either.
HOW MANY? A couple of hats would be a good idea—sun hats in summer, warmer caps for winter. We like the safari-style hats best (they have flaps to protect the ears and neck).

♦ **Snowsuit/bunting.** Similar to the type of fabric used for blanket sleepers, buntings also have hoods and covers for the hands. Most buntings are like a sack and don't have leg openings, while snowsuits do. Both versions usually have zippered fronts. FYI: Snowsuits and buntings should NOT be warn by infants when they ride in a car seat. Why? Thick fabric on these items can compress in an accident, compromising the infant's safety in the seat. So how can you keep your baby warm in an infant car seat? Check out Chapter 7 (Car Seats)—we'll discuss several car seat cover-ups/warmers that keep baby toasty without compromising the safety of the seat.

HOW MANY? Only buy one of these if you live in a climate where you need it. Even with the Colorado winter, we got away with layering clothes on our baby, then wrapping him in a blanket for the walk out to a warmed-up car. If you live in an urban city without a car, you might need two or three snowsuits for those stroller rides to the market.

♦ **Kimonos**. Just like the adult version. Some are zippered sacks with a hood and terry-cloth lining. You use them after a bath.

HOW MANY? Are you kidding? What a joke! These items are one of our "wastes of money." We recommend you pass on the kimonos and instead invest in good quality towels.

♦ **Saque Sets**. Two-piece outfits with a shirt and diaper cover.

HOW MANY? Forget buying these as well. We'll discuss later why saque sets are a waste of money.

♦ **Bibs**. These come in two versions, believe it or not. The little, tiny bibs are for the baby that drools the volume of Lake Michigan. The larger versions are used when you begin feeding her solid foods (at about six months). Don't expect to be able to use the drool bibs later for feedings, unless you plan to change her carrot-stained outfit frequently.

HOW MANY? Skip the drool bibs (we'll discuss why later in this chapter under Wastes of Money). When baby starts eating solid foods, you'll need at least three or four large bibs. One option: plastic bibs for feeding so you can just sponge them off after a meal.

♦ **Washcloths and Hooded Towels**. OK, so these aren't actually clothes, but baby washcloths and hooded towels are a necessity. Why? Because they are small and easier to use, plus they're softer than adult towels and washcloths.

HOW MANY? At first, you'll probably need only three sets of towels and washcloths (you get one of each per set). But as baby gets older and dirtier, invest in a few more washcloths to spot clean during the day.

 ◆ **Receiving Blankets**. You'll need these small, cotton blankets for all kinds of uses: to swaddle the baby, as a play quilt, or even for an extra layer of warmth on a cold day.

HOW MANY? We believe you can never have too many of these blankets, but since you'll probably get a few as gifts, you'll only need to buy three or four yourself. A total of seven to eight is probably optimal.

What about the future? While our layette list only addresses clothes to buy for a newborn, you will want to plan for your child's future wardrobe as well. For the modern baby, it seems clothes come in two categories: play clothes (to be used in daycare situations) and dress-up clothes. Later in this chapter, we'll discuss more money-saving tips and review several brands of play and dress-up clothes.

 ## More Money Buys You . . .

Even the biggest discounters now offer good quality clothing. But with more money you tend to get heavier weight cottons, nicer fasteners, better quality embellishments and more generous sizing. At some point, however, considering how fast your little one is growing, you'll be wasting money on the most expensive clothes out there.

 ## Safe & Sound

Should your baby's sleepwear (that is, the items he'll wear almost non-stop for the first several months of life) be flame retardant? What the heck does "flame retardant" mean anyway?

According to the Consumer Product Safety Commission (CPSC), items made of flame retardant fabric will not burn under a direct flame. Huh? Doesn't "flame retardant" mean it won't burn at all? No—that's a common myth among parents who think such clothes are a Superman-style second skin that will protect baby against any and all fire hazards.

Prior to 1996, the CPSC mandated that an item labeled as sleepwear be made of "flame retardant fabric." More often than not, that meant polyester because the alternative (untreated cotton fabric) DOES burn under direct flame. While there are a few companies that make cotton sleepwear that is chemically treated to be fire retardant, the prices of such items were so high that the de facto standard for children's sleepwear for many years was polyester.

Then the government changed its mind. The CPSC noticed that many parents were rebelling against the rules and putting their babies in all-cotton items at bedtime. After an investigation, the CPSC revised the rules to more closely fit reality.

First, pajamas for babies nine months and under were totally exempt from the flame-retardancy rules. Why? Since these babies aren't mobile, the odds they'll come in contact with a fire hazard that would catch their clothes on fire is slim. What if the whole house catches fire? Well, the smoke is much more dangerous than the flames—hence, a good smoke detector in the nursery and every other major room of your house is a much better investment than fire retardant clothes.

What about sleepwear for older babies? Well, the government admits that "close-fitting" all-cotton items don't pose a risk either. Only flowing nightgowns or pajamas that are loose fitting must meet the flame retardancy rules today.

If you still want to go with "flame retardant" baby items, there are a couple of options beyond plain polyester. The Land's End catalog now sells "Polar Fleece" pajamas for babies and young children ($24.50). The fabric, while polyester, is specially woven to breathe and be more comfortable. Another option: some catalogs listed later in this chapter sell cotton clothes treated to be flame retardant.

Finally, one final myth to dispel on this topic: does washing flame-retardant clothing reduce its ability to retard flames? Nope—fabrics like polyester are naturally flame retardant (that is, there is no magic chemical they've been doused with that can wash out in the laundry). What about those expensive treated all-cotton clothes? We don't think that's a problem either. While we haven't seen any evidence to the contrary, we think those companies that sell these pricey items would be drummed out of business in a heartbeat if the flame-retardancy of their clothes suddenly disappeared after a few spins in the rinse cycle.

There is one exception to the laundry rule: if you do choose to buy flame-retardant clothing, be sure to avoid washing such clothing in soap flakes like Dreft. Soap flakes actually add a flammable chemical residue to clothes. And so do dryer sheets and liquid softeners. We recommend you use regular powder or liquid laundry detergent and avoid sheets and softeners. What about other safety hazards with children's clothing? Here are a few more to consider:

◆ *Check for loose threads.* These could become a choking hazard, or the threads could wrap around fingers or toes, cutting off circulation. Be careful about appliqués as well. "Heat-welded" plastic appliqués on clothes can come off and cause choking. Poorly sewn appliqués can also be a hazard.

◆ *Avoid outfits with easy-to-detach, decorative buttons or bows—these may also be a choking hazard.* If you have any doubts, cut the decorations off.

◆ *Watch out for drawstrings.* In recent years, most manufacturers have voluntarily eliminated such drawstrings. But if you get hand-me-downs or buy second-hand clothes, be sure to remove any strings.

 Smart Shopper Tips

Smart Shopper Tip

Tips and Tricks to Get the Best Quality

"I've received several outfits from friends for my daughter, but I'm not sure she'll like all the scratchy lace and the poly/cotton blends. What should she wear, and what can I buy that will last through dozens of washings?"

Generally, we recommend dressing your child for comfort. At the same time, you need clothes that can withstand frequent washings. With this in mind, here are our suggestions for baby clothing:

1 SEE WHAT YOUR BABY LIKES BEFORE INVESTING IN MANY GARMENTS. Don't invest $90 in fancy sweaters, only to find baby prefers cotton onesies.

2 WE GENERALLY RECOMMEND 100% COTTON CLOTHING. Babies are most comfortable in clothing that breathes.

3 IF YOU DISCOVER YOUR CHILD HAS AN ALLERGY TO METAL SNAPS (you'll see red rings on his skin), consider alternatives such as shirts that have ties. Another option is a t-shirt that pulls on over the head. Unfortunately, many babies don't like having anything pulled over their heads. Another alternative for allergic babies: clothes with plastic snaps or zippers.

4 IN GENERAL, BETTER-MADE CLOTHES WILL HAVE THEIR SNAPS ON A REINFORCED FABRIC BAND. Snaps attached directly to the

One Size Does Not Fit All

A six month-size t-shirt is a six-month-size t-shirt, right? Wrong. For some reason, baby clothing companies have yet to synchronize their watches when it comes to sizes. Hence, a clothing item that says "six-month size" from one manufacturer can be just the same dimensions as a "twelve-month size" from another. All this begs the question: how can you avoid widespread confusion? First, open packages to check out actual dimensions. Take your baby along and hold up items to her to gauge whether they'd fit. Second, note whether items are pre-shrunk—you'll probably have to ask the salesperson or catalog representative (if not, allow for shrinkage). Third, don't key on length from head to foot. Instead, focus on the length from neck to crotch—a common problem is items that seem roomy but are too tight in the crotch. Finally, forget age ranges and pay more attention to labels that specify an infant's size in weight and height, which are much more accurate. To show how widely sizing can vary, check out the following chart. *Parenting Magazine* compared "six-month" t-shirts from six major clothing makers (we've added dimensions from three popular catalogs, Hanna Anderssen, Land's End and Talbot's Kids). Here's what these six-month t-shirts really translated to in terms of a baby's weight and height:

What a six month t-shirt really means

MAKER	WEIGHT	HEIGHT
Baby Gap	17-22 lbs.	27-29"
Carter's Layette	19-21 lbs.	27"
Gymboree	17-22 lbs.	24-28"
Hanna Anderson	14-21 lbs.	26-30"
Health-Tex	13-17 lbs.	25-28"
Land's End	14-18 lbs.	25-27"
Little Me	12-16 lbs.	24-27"
Oshkosh	16.5-18 lbs.	27-28.5"
Talbot's Kids	13-17 lbs.	24-27"

Here's another secret from the baby clothing trade: the more expensive the brand, the more roomy the clothes. Conversely, cheap items usually have the skimpiest sizing. What about the old wives' tale that you should just double your baby's age to find the right size (that is, buying twelve-month clothes for a six-month old?). That's bogus—as you can see, sizing is so all over the board that this rule just doesn't work.

body of the fabric may tear the garment or rip off when changing.

5 **IF YOU'RE BUYING 100% COTTON CLOTHES, MAKE SURE THEY'RE PRE-SHRUNK.** Some stores, like Gymboree (see review later in this chapter), guarantee that their clothes won't shrink. In other cases, you're on your own. Our advice: read the label. If it says "wash in cold water" or " tumble dry low," assume the garment will shrink (and hence buy a larger size). On the other hand, care instructions that advise washing in warm water usually indicate that the garment is already preshrunk.

6 **GO FOR OUTFITS WITH SNAPS AND ZIPPERS ON BOTH LEGS, NOT JUST ONE.** Dual-leg snaps or zippers make it much easier to change a diaper. Always check a garment for diaper accessibility—some brands actually have no snaps or zippers, meaning you would have to completely undress your baby for a diaper change! Another pet peeve: garments that have snaps up the back also make diaper changes a big hassle.

7 **BE AWARE THAT EACH COMPANY HAS ITS OWN WARPED IDEA ABOUT HOW TO SIZE BABY CLOTHES.** See the box on the next page for more details.

8 **BEWARE OF APPLIQUÉS.** Some appliqué work can be quite scratchy on the inside of the outfit (it rubs against baby's skin). Also, poor-quality appliqué may unravel or fray after washing.

9 **KEEP THE TAGS AND RECEIPTS.** A reader emailed us her strategy for dealing with baby clothes that shrink: until she has a chance to wash the item, she keeps all packaging, tags and receipts. If it shrinks, she returns it immediately.

 Wastes of Money

Waste of Money #1
Clothing that Leads to Diaper Changing Gymnastics

"My aunt sent me an adorable outfit for my little girl. The only problem: it snaps up the back making diaper changes a real pain. In fact, I don't dress her in it often because it's so inconvenient. Shouldn't clothing like this be outlawed?"

It's pretty obvious that some designers of baby clothing have never had children of their own. What else could explain outfits that snap up the back, have super tiny head, leg and arm openings, and snaps in inconvenient places (or worse, no snaps at all)? One mother we spoke with was furious about outfits that have snaps only down one leg, requiring her baby to be a contortionist to get into and out of the outfit.

Our advice: stay away from outfits that don't have easy access to the diaper. Look instead for snaps or zippers down the front of the outfit or on the crotch. If your baby doesn't like having things pulled over his head, look for shirts with wide, stretchie necklines.

Waste of Money #2
The Fuzz Factor

"My friend's daughter has several outfits that aren't very old but are already pilling and fuzzing. They look awful and my friend is thinking of throwing them out. What causes this?"

Your friend has managed to have a close encounter with that miracle fabric known as polyester. Synthetics such as polyester will often pill or fuzz after washing, making your baby look a little rag-tag. Of course, this is less of a concern with sleepwear—some parents believe the flame retardancy of the fabric outweighs the garment's appearance.

However, when you're talking about a play outfit, we recommend sticking to all-cotton clothes. They wash better, usually last longer, and generally look nicer—not to mention they feel better to your baby. Cotton allergies are rare, unlike sensitivities to the chemicals used to make synthetic fabrics. You will pay more for all-cotton clothing, but in this case, the extra expense is worth it. Remember, just because you find the cheapest price on a polyester outfit doesn't mean you're getting a bargain. The best deal is not wasting money on outfits that you have to throw away after two washings.

If you get polyester outfits as gifts, here's a laundry tip: wash the items inside out. That helps lessen pilling/fuzzing. And some polyester items are better than others—polar fleece sweatshirts and pajamas are still made of polyester, but are softer and more durable.

Waste of Money #3
Do I Really Need These?

"My mother bought me a zillion gowns before my baby was born, and I haven't used a single one. What the heck are they for?"
"The list of layette items recommended by my local department store includes something called a saque set. I've never seen one, and no one seems to know what they are. Do I really need one?"

"A kimono with matching towel and washcloth seems like a neat

baby gift for my pregnant friend. But another friend told me it probably wouldn't get used. What do you think?"

All of these items come under the heading "Do I Really Need These?" Heck, we didn't even know what some of these were when we were shopping for our baby's layette. For example, what in the world is a saque set? Well, it turns out it's just a two-piece outfit with a shirt and diaper cover. Although they sound rather benign, saque sets are a waste of money. Whenever you pick up a baby under the arms, it's a sure bet her clothes will ride up. In order to avoid having to constantly pull down the baby's shirt, most parents find they use one-piece garments much more often than two-piece ones.

As for gowns, the jury is still out on whether these items are useful. We thought they were a waste of money, but a parent we interviewed did mention that she used the gowns when her baby had colic. She believed that the extra room in the gown made her baby more comfortable. Other parents like how gowns make diaper changes easy, especially in the middle of the night. Finally, parents in hot climates say gowns keep their infants more comfortable. So, you can see there's a wide range of opinions on this item.

There is no question in our minds about the usefulness of a baby kimono, however. Don't buy it. For a baby who will only wear it for a few minutes after a bath, it seems like the quintessential waste of your money (we saw one Ralph Lauren baby kimono for $39. And that was on sale). Instead, invest in some good quality towels and washcloths and forget those cute (but useless) kimonos.

Waste of Money #4
Covering Up Those Little Piggies

"I was looking at shoes for my baby the other day, and I saw a $43 pair Merrell JungleMoc Juniors at the store! This must be highway robbery! I can't believe babies' shoes are so expensive. Are they worth it?"

Developmentally, babies don't need shoes until after they become quite proficient at walking. In fact, it's better for their muscle development to go barefoot or wear socks. While those expensive Baby Air Jordans might look cute, they're really a waste of time and money. Of course, at some point, your baby will need some shoes. See the following box for our tips on how to buy babies' first shoes.

Baby Needs a New Pair of Shoes

As your baby gets older, you may find she's kicking off her socks every five minutes. And at some point she's going to start standing, crawling and even walking. So what's a parent to do? You need something that will stay on and protect her feet as she moves through these milestones. Here are some suggestions:

First, look for shoes that have the most flexible soles. You'll also want fabrics that breath and stretch, like canvas and leather—stay away from vinyl shoes. The best brands we found were recommended by experienced parents. Reader Teri Dunsworth wrote us about Canadian-made **Robeez** (800) 929-2623 or (604) 435-9074; web: www.robeez.com. (See picture at right). "They are the most AWESOME shoes—I highly recommend them," she said in an email. And Teri wasn't the only one who loves them. Our email has been blitzed by fans. Robeez are made of leather, have soft, skid-resistant soles and are machine washable. They start at $22 for a basic pair. Another reader recommended New Zealand-made **Bobux** shoes ($25 at www.bobuxsa. com). These cute leather soft soles "do the trick by staying on extremely well," according to a reader. Finally, another reader recommended **Scootees** (www. scootees.com). These slippers "really stay on babies' feet!"

By the way, one of our readers, Priscilla Wallace, pointed out a cool deal she found on shoes: "I wanted to tell you about how you can get your baby's 1st pair of shoes free. Go to a Payless Shoe Source and fill out a registration card and you get to pick a free pair of shoes (choices pink, blue or white). I believe it is the softer shoe that is to be worn before he is walking."

What about shoes for one or two year olds? We've found great deals at Target, whose wide selection of sizes and offerings were impressive. Another good source: Gap Kids/Baby Gap. Their affordable line of sneakers are very good quality. Parents have also told us they've had success with Babies R Us' in-house brand; others like Stride Rite shoes, which are often on sale at department stores. If none of these stores are convenient, consider the web or mail order—see the Do It By Mail section later in this chapter for possibilities. We discuss how to get more deals on shoes for toddlers in our *Toddler Bargains* book. See back of this book for details.

Waste of Money #5
To Drool or Not to Drool

"I received a few bibs from my mother-in-law as gifts. I know my baby won't need them until she's at least four to six months old when I start feeding her solids. Plus, they seem so small!"

What you actually got as a gift from your mother-in-law was a supply of drool bibs. Drool bibs are tiny bibs intended for small infants who drool all over everything. Or infants who spit-up frequently. Our opinion: they're pretty useless—they're too small to catch much drool or spit-up.

When you do buy bibs, stay away from the ones that tie. Bibs that snap or have Velcro are much easier to get on and off. Another good bet: bibs that go on over the head (and have no snaps or Velcro). Why? Older babies can't pull them off by themselves.

Stay away from the super-size vinyl bibs that cover the arms, since babies who wear them can get too hot. However, we do recommend you buy a few regular-style vinyl bibs for travel. You can wash them off much more easily than the standard terry-cloth bibs. As for sources of bibs, many of the catalogs we review in this book carry such items.

As a side note, many readers wrote to us to disagree with this tip. They claim that their babies are like water faucets stuck in the "on" position and a bib was a necessity. If you have a leaker, consider using larger bids that can also be used later when you begin solid foods. We still think the tiny drool bibs are a waste of money even in these cases.

Waste of Money #6
The Dreft Syndrome
"I see ads in parenting magazines that say an infant's clothes should be washed in special laundry detergent. Is this true?"

No, not in our opinion. We call it the "Dreft Syndrome" (after the laundry soap that claims it's better for infant clothes)—parents, typically first-timers, think if they don't wash Junior's clothes separately with expensive special soap, something bad will happen to their baby. Hogwash. Unless you have the rare child who suffers from skin allergies (and chances are, you don't), just throw baby's clothes in with the rest of the wash. And use regular laundry soap. If you're worried about perfumes or dyes, use one of the "clear" detergents free of such additives. Another idea: do a second rinse cycle to make sure all soap is removed from clothing on a first washing.

Other laundry tips: use the delicate cycle when washing baby items, since this lessens the wear and tear. Turn the clothes inside out to protect against pilling/fuzzing. And put the clothes through an extra rinse cycle if you are using bleach or other additives. In fact, one reader recommended adding a 1/2 cup of white vinegar to your whites during the fabric softener stage. She said this will stop "the corrosiveness of the bleach, preserve the elastic and eliminate the bleach smell."

The bottom line: Washing your baby's clothes separately in special soap is not only expensive, but you'll have to do much more laundry, since you can't throw the items in with your regular laundry.

Money Saving Secrets

Two words: Old Navy. The hip, discount offshoot of the Gap (www.gap.com) was launched in 1994 and now has 700+ stores nationwide. Readers rave about the buys they find at Old Navy (sample: "adorable" 100% cotton onesies for just $4; gripper socks, 3 for $4.50), although most admit the selection is limited. The options change rapidly and Old Navy's sales and clearance racks are "bargain heaven," say our spies. An insider tip to Old Navy and Gap Kids: the stores change out their merchandise every six weeks, moving the "old" stuff to the clearance racks rather quickly. Ask your local Old Navy or Gap Kids which day they do their markdowns (typically it is mid-week).

Here's another tip for folks who shop Old Navy or the Gap regularly: check to see if your recent purchases have been marked

E-Mail from The Real World
Second-hand bargains easy to find

Shelley Bayer of Connecticut raved about Once Upon A Child, a nationwide chain of resale stores with 100+ locations (call 614-791-0000 for locations; web: www.OnceUponAChild.com).

"We have two locations of Once Upon A Child in Connecticut and I love them! The clothes and toys are of great quality and very affordable. The good thing about these stores is that when you take something in to be sold, they pay you cash. You do not have wait for something to be sold and keep checking your account like a traditional consignment shop."

One caution about second-hand stores—if you buy an item like a stroller or high chair at a resale shop, you may not be able to get replacement parts. One mom told us she got a great deal on a stroller that was missing a front bar . . . that is, it was a great deal until she discovered the model was discontinued and she couldn't get a replacement part from the manufacturer.

down. You may be able to get a refund if items you've bought are marked down even more. One reader emailed us her great deal: "Last month I found a hooded sweatshirt for baby on clearance. It was originally $15 marked down to $10.50. The next week, I went back and the same sweatshirt had been marked down from $10.50 to $1.99. So they refunded me $8.60!" Old Navy only refunds money on markdowns if they occur within seven days of original purchase. However, the Gap gives you up to 14 days to return them. And you don't even have to bring in the item—just the receipt.

2 **WAIT UNTIL AFTER SHOWERS AND PARTIES TO PURCHASE CLOTHES.** Clothing is a popular gift item—you may not need to buy much yourself.

3 **STICK WITH BASICS—T-SHIRTS, SLEEPERS, CAPS, SOCKS AND BLANKETS.** For the first month or more, that's all you need since you won't be taking Junior to the opera.

4 **TAKE ADVANTAGE OF BABY REGISTRIES.** Many baby stores offer this service, which helps avoid duplicate shower gifts or too many of one item. This saves you time (and money) in exchanging gifts.

5 **GO FOR THE SALES!** The baby area in most department stores is definitely SALE LAND. At one chain we researched, the baby section has at least some items that are on sale every week! Big baby sales occur throughout the year, but especially in January. You can often snag bargains at up to 50% off the retail price. Another tip: consider buying for the future during end-of-season sales. If you're pregnant during the fall, for example, shop the end-of-summer sales for next summer's baby clothes. Hint: our research shows the sale prices at department stores are often better deals than the "discounted" prices you see at outlets.

6 **CHOOSE QUALITY OVER LOW PRICE FOR PLAYCLOTHES AND BASICS.** Sure that polyester outfit is 20% cheaper than the cotton alternative. HOWEVER, beware of the revenge of the washing machine! You don't realize how many times you'll be doing laundry—that play outfit may get washed every couple of days. Cheap polyester clothes pill or fuzz up after just a few washings—making you more likely to chuck them. Quality clothes have longer lives, making them less expensive over time. The key to quality is thicker or more heavyweight 100% cotton fabric, well-sewn seams and appliqués, and snaps on reinforced fabric bands.

7 **FOR SLEEPWEAR, TRY THE AFFORDABLE BRANDS.** Let's get real here: babies pee and poop in their sleepers. Hence, fancy designer brands are a money-waster. A friend of ours who lives in Texas uses affordable all-cotton onesies as sleepwear in the hot summer months. For the winter here in Colorado, we use thermal underwear, which we've found for as little as $10.50 in Target.

8 **CAN'T RETURN IT?** Did you get gifts of clothing you don't want but can't return? Consign it at a local thrift store. We took a basketful of clothes that we couldn't use or didn't like and placed them on consignment. We made $40 in store credit or cash to buy what we really needed.

9 **SPEAKING OF CONSIGNMENT STORES, HERE IS A WONDERFUL WAY TO SAVE MONEY:** Buy barely used, consigned clothing for your baby. We found outfits ranging from $5 to $7 from high quality designers like Alexis. How can you find a consignment or thrift shop in your area specializing in high-quality children's clothes? Besides looking in the phone book, check out web sites like the National Association of Resale & Thrift Shops (www.narts.org, click on the shopping icon). Here are two tips for getting the biggest bargains at second-hand stores. First, shop the resale stores in the richest part of town. Why? They are most likely to stock the best brands with steep discounts off retail prices. Such stores also have clothes with the least wear (we guess rich kids have so many clothes they don't have time to wear them all out)! Second: ask the consignment store which day is best to shop. Some stores accept new consignments on certain days; others tell us that days like Tuesday and Wednesday offer the best selection of newly consigned items.

10 **CHECK OUT DISCOUNTERS.** In the past, discount stores like Target, Wal-Mart and Marshall's typically carried cheap baby clothes that were mostly polyester. Well, there's good news for bargain shoppers: in recent years, these chains have beefed up their offerings, adding more all-cotton clothes and even some brand names. We've been especially impressed with Target's recent offerings. For basic items like t-shirts and play clothes that will be trashed at day care, these stores are good bets. Wal-Mart sure impressed one of our readers: "I spent $25 for a baby bathing suit in a specialty store, and for a little over twice that (about $60) I go my daughter's entire summer wardrobe at Wal-mart—shorts, t-shirts, leggings, Capri pants, overalls and matching socks. Some of the pieces were as low as $2.88." And don't forget other discounters like Marshalls, TJ Maxx and Ross Dress for Less. Bargain tip: ask the manager when they get in new shipments—that's when selection is best.

11 **CHECK OUT WAREHOUSE CLUBS.** Warehouse clubs like Sam's and Costco carry baby clothes at prices far below retail. On our latest visit we saw Carter's fleece sleepers for only $7 and lightweight sleepers for $5. All cotton play clothes were a mere $10 as were all-cotton pajamas. Even baby Halloween costumes and kids outerwear (raincoats, fleece jackets) are terrific seasonal deals.

12 **DON'T FORGET ABOUT CHARITY SALES.** Readers tell us they've found great deals on baby clothes and equipment at church-sponsored charity sales. Essentially, these sales are like large garage/yard sales where multiple families donate kids' items as a fund-raiser for a church or other charity.

Outlets

There's been a huge explosion in the number of outlet stores over the last few years—and children's clothing stores haven't been left out of the boom. Indeed, as we were doing research for this section, we heard from many manufacturers that they had even more outlets on the drawing board. Therefore, if you don't see your town listed below, call the numbers provided to see if they've opened any new outlets. Also, outlet locations open and close frequently—always call before you go.

CARTER'S

Locations: Over 130 outlets.
Call (888) 782-9548 or (770) 961-8722 for the location nearest you.

It shows you how widespread the outlet craze is when you realize that Carter's has over 140 outlets in the U.S. That's right, 140. If you don't have one near you, you probably live in Bolivia.

We visited a Carter's outlet and found a huge selection of infant clothes, bedding, and accessories. Sleepers, originally $12, were available for $7, gowns were $5 (regularly $12) and side snap t-shirts were $10 for three (regularly $20).

As for baby bedding, we noted the outlet sells quilts (including the popular Lennon Baby—$65, regularly $115), bumpers, and pillows as well as fitted bassinet sheets and towels at low prices. All Carter's bedding is made by Riegal (see previous chapter for a review of their bedding line).

If you think those deals are great, check out the outlet's yearly clearance sale in January when they knock an additional 25% to 30% off their already discounted prices. A store manager at the Carter's outlet we visited said that they also have two other sales: back-to-school and a "pajama sale." In the past, we noted that all the goods in their outlet stores were first quality. However, they have recently added a couple "seconds" racks (called "Oops" racks) in most of their stores with flawed merchandise. Our readers report that most seconds have only minor problems and the savings are worth it.

Esprit

Locations: 11 outlets. Call (415) 648-6900 for the location nearest you.

Not all of the Esprit outlets carry infant and toddler clothing, but those that do have sizes from 12 months through youth sizes (girls' designs only). The options include dresses, pants and shorts. The prices are 30% to 70% off, and they sell only first quality overruns—no seconds. Call the outlet nearest you to see if it carries baby clothes

Flapdoodles

Location: Dillon, CO (970) 262-9351

The all-cotton designs from Flapdoodles are a great value even at retail, but you can actually find the clothes at 20% to 40% off retail in their outlet stores. With first quality merchandise and sizes from six months up to youth size 14, Flapdoodles outlet is worth a peek for long-lasting, high-quality play clothes.

Seconds are sold usually at the first of every month at their Newark, DE factory. Call (302) 731-9793 for the latest sale schedule.

Hanna Andersson

Locations: Outlets Stores: Lake Oswego, OR (503) 697-1953 ; Michigan City, IN (219) 872-3183; Portsmouth, NH (603) 433-6642; Bloomington, MN (612)884-9390; Kittery, ME (207) 439-1992; Lakewood, CO (303) 384-0937.

If you like Hanna Anderson's catalog, you'll love their outlet stores, which feature overstocks, returned items and factory seconds. For more information on Hanna Anderson, see "Do It By Mail" later in this chapter.

Hartstrings

Locations: 22 outlets, mostly in the eastern U.S. Call (610) 687-6900 for the location near you.

Hartstrings' outlet stores specialize in first-quality apparel for infants, boys, and girls and even have some mother/child outfits. Infant sizes start at three months and go up to 24 months. The savings range from 30% to 50%.

HEALTH-TEX

Locations: 61 outlets. Call (800) 772-8336 for the location near you.

Health-Tex children's clothing is owned by Vanity Fair Corporation, which also produces such famous brands as Lee jeans, Wrangler, and Jantzen. The company operates over four-dozen outlets under the name VF Factory Outlet. They sell first-quality merchandise; most are discontinued items. Most of the VF outlets carry the Health-Tex brand at discounts up to 70% off retail.

JCPENNEY

Locations: 15 outlets; call (800) 222-6161, Web: www.JCPenney.com

A reader in Columbus, Ohio emailed her high praise for the Penney's outlet there. She snagged one-piece rompers for $5 (regularly $25) and hand-loomed coveralls for $2.99 (compared to $28 in stores). She also found satin christening outfits for both boys and girls for just $5 that regularly sell for as much as $70! The outlet carries everything from layette to play clothes, at discounts of 50% or more. (Hint: the outlet stores also have maternity clothes).

OSHKOSH

Locations: 133 outlets. Call (920) 231-8800 for the nearest location.

OshKosh, the maker of all those cute little overalls worn by just about every kid, sells their clothes direct at over 125 outlet stores. With prices that are 30% to 70% off retail, buying these play clothes staples is even easier on the pocketbook. For example, footed sleepers were $7.70 (regularly $11), and receiving blankets were $18.20 (regularly $24).

We visited our local OshKosh store and found outfits from infant sizes up to children's size 7. They split the store up by gender, as well as by size. Infant and toddler clothes are usually in the back of the store.

The outlet also carries OshKosh shoes, socks, hats, and even stuffed bears dressed in overalls and engineer hats. Seasonal ensembles are available, including shorts outfits in the summer and snowsuits ($42) in the winter. Some clothes are irregulars, so inspect the garments carefully before you buy.

TALBOT'S KIDS

Location: 9 stores, most of which are in the Eastern U.S. Call (800) 543-7123 or (781) 740-8888. Web: www.talbots.com

A reader who calls herself a "devoted Talbot's shopper" emailed in her compliments for Talbot's outlet stores, which carry a nice selection of baby and children's clothes that didn't sell in their stores or catalog. "The deals can be fantastic, especially given the quality," she said, adding that you can get on the outlet's mailing list to get notices about additional markdowns. She estimated she saved 40% to 60% on items for her baby. Hint: Talbot's regular stores hold major sales twice a year (after Christmas and the end of June). What doesn't get sold then is shipped to the outlets.

◆ **Other outlets.** A great source for outlet info is **Outlet Bound** magazine, which is published by Outlet Marketing Group ($9 plus $4 shipping, 1-888-688-5382; web: www.outletbound.com). The magazine contains detailed maps noting outlet centers for all areas of the U.S. and Canada, as well as store listings for each outlet center. We liked the index that lists all the manufacturers, and they even have a few coupons in the back.

Outlet Bound also has an excellent web site with the most up-to-date info on outlets in the U.S. and Canada. We did a search on children's clothing outlets (you can search by location, store, brand or product category) and found several additional interesting outlets. These included outlets for Little Me (12 outlets), the Disney catalog outlet (4 locations) and the Oilily catalog (four outlets).

If you can't get enough of the **Gap**, check out their outlet stores (650) 952-4400 (web: www.gaponline.com). With 5 locations nationwide, most Gap outlets have a baby/kid's clothing section and great deals (50% off and more).

Yet another outlet: **Pingorama** offers periodic factory sales from their Novato and Redwood, CA locations. Check their web site, (www.pingorama.com, click on the the where to buy link) for dates and directions.

Did you discover an outlet that you'd like to share with our readers? Call us at our office at 303-442-8792 or e-mail authors@ BabyBargainsBook.com.

The Name Game: Our Picks for the Best Brands

Walk into any department store and you'll see a blizzard of brand names for baby clothes. Which ones stand up to frequent washings? Which ones have snaps that stay snapped? Which are a good value for the dollar? We've got the answers, based on extensive parent feedback.

We've broken our recommendations into three areas: best bets, good but not great and skip it. As always, remember most of these manufacturers do not sell directly to consumers (those that do sell online are identified by an asterisk*). The phone numbers and web sites are included so you can locate a retailer near you who carries that brand. Here we go:

Best Bets

ALEXIS	(800) 253-9476	ALEXISUSA.COM
BABY GAP*	(800) GAP-STYLE	BABYGAP.COM
COTTON TALE ORIG.	(800) 628-2621	COTTONTALEDESIGNS.COM
EARTHLINGS*	(888) GOBABYO	EARTHLINGS.NET
FLAP HAPPY	(800) 234-3527	FLAPHAPPY.COM
FLAPDOODLES	(302) 731-9793	FLAPDOODLES.COM
FLORENCE EISMAN	(414) 272-3222	FLORENCEEISEMAN.COM
GYMBOREE*	(800) 990-5060	GYMBOREE.COM
HARTSTRINGS	(610)687-6900	HARTSTRINGS.COM
JAKE AND ME*	(970) 352-8802	JAKEANDME.COM
LITTLE ME		LITTLEME.COM
MINI CLASSICS	(201) 569-7357	
MOTHER-MAID	(770) 479-7558	MOTHERMAID.COM
MULBERRI BUSH (TUMBLEWEED TOO)		MULBERRIBUSH.COM
OSHKOSH B'GOSH*		OSHKOSHBGOSH.COM
PATSY AIKEN*	(919) 872-8789	PATSYAIKEN.COM
PINGARAMA		PINGARAMA.COM
SARAH'S PRINTS*	(888) 4-PRINTS	SARASPRINTS.COM
SKIVVYDOODLES	(212) 967-2918	SKIVVYDOODLES.COM
SWEET POTATOES/SPUDZ	(510) 527-7633	SWEETPOTATOESINC.COM
WES & WILLY		WESANDWILLY.COM

Good But Not Great

CARTER'S	(770) 961-8722	CARTERS.COM
GOOD LAD OF PHILA.*	(215) 739-0200	GOODLAD.COM
LE TOP	(800) 333-2257	
TARGET*		TARGET.COM
(CHEROKEE BABY, B.U.M., BRAMBLY HEDGE, LULLABY CLUB, NATURAL BASICS)		

Skip It: HEALTH TEX**, GERBER, HANES.

**After we said to skip Health Tex in our last edition, Health Tex contacted us and pointed out they are trying to improve the brand. Let us know what you think. If you have any recent experiences with Health Tex, email us at authors@BabyBargainsBook.com!

Do it by Mail

CHILDREN'S WEAR DIGEST (CWD)

To Order Call: (800) 242-5437; Fax (800) 863-3395.
Shopping Hours: 24 hours a day, seven days a week.
Or write to: 3607 Mayland Ct., Richmond, VA 23233.
Web: www.cwdkids.com
Outlet: "CWD Outlet," Gayton Crossing Shopping Center, Richmond, VA.
Also two company stores in Virginia. Call or visit the web site for more info.

If you're looking for name brands, check out Children's Wear Digest (CWD), a catalog that features clothes in sizes 12 months to 14 years for both boys and girls. In a recent catalog, we saw clothes by Sweet Potatoes, Mulberribush, S.P.U.D.Z., Flapdoodles, and Sarah's Prints. Unlike other catalogs that de-emphasize brand names, CWD prominently displays manufacturer info.

Children's Wear Digest doesn't offer much of a discount off regular retail, but it does have a selection of sale clothes from time to time with savings of 15% to 25%. A best buy: CWD's web site (www.cwdkids.com) has online bargains, with savings of up to 50% on quite a few items and the latest news on their outlet store.

HANNA ANDERSSON

To Order Call: (800) 222-0544; Fax (503) 321-5289.
Shopping Hours: 5 am to 9 pm Pacific Time, seven days a week.
Or write to: 1010 NW Flanders, Portland, OR, 97209.
Web: www.hannaandersson.com
Retail Stores: 125 Westchester Ave., Suite 3370, White Plains, NY 10601; (914) 684-2410; 327 NW Tenth Ave., Portland, OR 97209; (503) 321-5275.
Outlets Stores: Lake Oswego, OR (503) 697-1953 ; Michigan City, IN (219) 827-3183; Portsmouth, NH (603) 433-6642; Lakewood, CO (303) 384-0937.

Hanna Andersson says it offers "Swedish quality" 100% cotton clothes. Unfortunately, Swedish quality is going to set you back some big American bucks. For example, a simple coverall with zippered front was a whopping $34. While Andersson's clothing features cute patterns and attractive colors, it's hard to imagine buying a complete wardrobe at those prices.

These aren't clothes you'd have your baby trash at daycare— Hanna Andersson's outfits are more suitable for weekend wear or going to Grandma's house. One note of caution: while the quality is very high, some items have difficult diaper access (or none at all).

Another negative: Hanna Andersson uses "European sizing," which can be confusing. (Yes, there is an explanation of this in the catalog, but we still found it difficult to follow). Furthermore, some items (like dresses) are cut in a boxy, unstructured way.

On the plus side, we liked their web site (www.hannaandersson.com), which features an online store, sizing info and more. The site has a sale page that offers 20% to 40% off on overstock items; you can quickly glance at the specials by category, size and price.

LANDS' END

To Order Call: (800) 963-4816,; Fax (800) 332-0103.
Web: www.landsend.com
Shopping Hours: 24 hours a day, seven days a week.
Or write to: 1 Lands' End Ln., Dodgeville, WI 53595.
Discount Outlets: They also have a dozen or so outlet stores in Iowa, Illinois and Wisconsin—call the number above for the nearest location.

Lands' End children's catalog features a complete layette line— and it's darn cute. The clothes feature 100% cotton "interlock knit," which the catalog claims gets softer with every washing and doesn't pill. Choose from playsuits, cardigans, onesies, pants, even cashmere sweaters—all in sizes three to 12 months. Most items were $10 to $26. For older babies, Lands' End all-cotton play clothes range from size 6 months to 4T. Don't look for fancy dress clothes from this catalog; instead Lands' End specializes in casual playwear basics like sweat pants, overalls and hiking shoes (for toddlers no doubt).

Land's End web site is a continuation of the catalog's easy-to-use layout—you can buy items online, find an outlet store and more. Best bet for deals: check the great overstock deals, posted twice weekly.

LL KIDS

To Order Call: (800) 552-5437; Fax (207) 552-3080
Shopping Hours: 24 hours a day; seven days a week.
Or write to: LL Bean, Freeport, ME 04033; Web: www.llbean.com
Retail store: Freeport, ME

The baby version of big brother LL Bean, LL Kids originally emphasized outdoor gear: coats, snowsuits, hats, gloves, etc. Then the options expanded to include pants and leggings, sleepwear, jumpers and more. Recently, though we only found sleepers available in infant sizes. Their regular kids clothes start at size 4. We're disappointed that there isn't more for infants and toddlers since their quality is terrific. Maybe they'll bring infant/toddler clothes back in the future.

PATAGONIA KIDS

To Order Call: (800) 638-6464; Fax (800) 543-5522.
Shopping Hours: Monday-Friday 6 am to 6 pm Pacific; Saturday and
Sunday 8 am- 4 pm Pacific Time.; Web: www.patagonia.com
Or write to: 8550 White Fir St., PO Box 32050, Reno, NV 89533.

Outdoor enthusiasts all over the country swear by Patagonia's scientifically engineered clothes and outerwear. They make clothing for skiing, mountain climbing, and kayaking—and for kids. That's right, Patagonia has a just-for-kids catalog of outdoor wear. In their recent kids' section on line, we found a few pages of clothes for babies and toddlers. They offer synchilla (Patagonia's version of polar fleece) clothes like cardigans ($44-47), coveralls ($36), and baby buntings ($64). We bought our baby a bunting from Patagonia and found that it had some cool features. For example, with a flick of its zipper, it converts from a sack to an outfit with two leg openings, making it more convenient for use with a car seat. It also has a neck to knee zipper (speeding up diaper changes), flip-per hands, and a hood. When your baby's bundled up in this, you can bet she won't get cold.

Other gear for tots includes sets of capilene long underwear ($36), coverall ($48) and interesting accessories like "Baby Pita Pocket" mittens ($18) and assorted hats and booties. The on line store also has a section called "Enviro Action," a series of essays and info on Patagonia's environmental efforts.

The bottom line: this is great stuff. It ain't cheap, but their cold weather gear is unlike that from any other manufacturer in terms of quality and durability.

TALBOT'S KIDS

To Order Call: (800) 543-7123.
Shopping Hours: 24 hours a day, 7 days a week.
Or write to: Talbot's Kids, 1 Talbots Dr. Hingham, MA 02043.
Web: www.talbots.com
Retail stores: 600 stores in the U.S., Canada and the United Kingdom.
Talbot's also has 18 outlets—call the above number for the nearest location.

Talbot's splashes its bright colors on both layette items for infants (three months to 12 months) and toddlers (up to 4T sizes). For baby, the catalog features a good selection of t-shirts, sleepwear, and overalls. Prices, as you might expect, are moderate to expensive. We saw a cotton cardigans for $48, cotton t-shirts with crotch snaps for $20. Nearly all of Talbot's Kids offerings are 100% cotton. The web site is easy to use.

WOODEN SOLDIER

To Order Call: (800) 375-6002; Fax (603) 356-3530.
Shopping Hours: Monday-Friday 8:30 am to midnight, Saturday and
Sunday 8:30 am to 9 pm Eastern Time.
Or write to: The Wooden Soldier, PO Box 800, North Conway, NH 03860.

If you really need a formal outfit for your child, Wooden Soldier has the most expansive selection of children's formalwear we've ever seen. Unfortunately, the prices are quite expensive—a girls' plaid dress with embroidered collar is $54; a boy's suspendered knicker set with shirt is $68. And those are for infant sized clothes!

On the plus side, the *Wall Street Journal* lauded this catalog for its high quality in a recent comparison of girl's holiday dresses from major catalogs. Wooden Soldier continues to expand their casual offerings, which now include overalls, jumpsuits and cotton sweaters.

◆ **Other catalogs.** Looking for Disney cartoon clothing and accessories? *Disney's* Catalog (800) 237-5751 (web: www.disneystore. com) has a few infant options. We liked the too-cute Halloween costumes as well as the winter gear. We found the quality from the Disney catalog to be quite good; most items wash and wear well.

Fitigues (www.fitigues.com) sells casual baby clothes at outrageous prices. Yes, the items are made of thermal knit or French terry with velvet trim, but we couldn't see ourselves spending $60 for a girl's crew neck tee in thermal knit. One plus: the kid's outfits do coordinate with the pricey adult clothes Fitigues offers.

If you need outdoor gear, check out **Campmor** (800) 226-7667 (web: www.campmor.com) or **Sierra Trading Post** (800) 713-4534 (web: www.sierratradingpost.com). Both heavily discount infant and children's outerwear, including snowsuits. They also have backpacks. Since these items are closeouts, the selection varies from issue to issue.

Our Picks: Brand Recommendations

What clothing brands/catalogs are best? Well, there is no one correct answer. An outfit that's perfect for day care (that is, to be trashed in Junior's first painting experiment) is different from an outfit for a weekend outing with friends. And dress-up occasions may require an entirely different set of clothing criteria. Hence, we've divided our clothing brand recommendations into three areas: good (day care), better (weekend wear) and best (special occasions). While some brands make items in two or even three categories, here's how we see it:

Good. For everyday comfort (and day-care situations), basic brands like Carter's, Little Me, and OshKosh are your best bets. We also like the basics (when on sale) at Baby Gap (Gap Kids) for day-care wardrobes. For great price to value, take a look at Old Navy and Target. As for catalogs, most tend to specialize in fancier clothes. However, Lands' End has a nice selection of everyday clothing.

Better. What if you have a miniature golf outing planned with friends? Or a visit to Grandma's house? The brands of better-made casual wear we like best include Alexis, Baby Gap, Flapdoodles, and Gymboree. Also recommended: Jake and Me, MulberriBush, and Sweet Potatoes. For catalogs, we like the clothes in Hanna Anderson and Talbot's Kids as good brands.

Best. Holidays and other special occasions call for special outfits. We like the brands of Patsy Aiken, Florence Eisman, and the fancier items at Baby Gap. Of course, department stores are great sources for these outfits, as are consignment shops. As for catalogs, check out Wooden Soldier.

Note: For more on finding these brands, check out the Name Game earlier in this chapter. See "Do it By Mail" for more information on the catalogs mentioned above.

Diapers

The great diaper debate still rages on: should you use cloth or disposable? On one side are environmentalists, who argue cloth is better for the planet. On the other hand, those disposable diapers are darn convenient.

Considering the average baby will go through 2300 diaper changes in the first year of life, this isn't a moot issue—you'll be dealing with diapers until your baby is three or four years old (the average girl potty trains at 35 months; a boy at 39 months). Yes, you read that last sentence right . . . you will be diapering for the next 35 to 39 MONTHS.

Now, in this section, we've decided to NOT rehash all the environmental arguments pro or con for cloth versus disposable. Fire up your web browser and you'll find plenty of debate on parenting sites like BabyCenter.com or ParentsPlace.com. Instead, we'll focus here on the FINANCIAL and PRACTICAL impacts of your decision. Let's look at each option:

Cloth. Prior to the 1960's, this was the only diaper option available to parents. Fans of cloth diapering point to babies that have less diaper rash and toilet train faster. From a practical point of view, cloth diapers have improved in the design over the years, offering more absorbency and fewer leaks. They aren't perfect, but the advent of diaper covers (no more plastic pants) has helped as well.

Another practical point: laundry. You've got to decide if you will use a cloth diaper service or launder at home. Obviously, the latter requires more effort on your part. We'll have laundry tips for cloth diapers later in this chapter. Meanwhile, we'll discuss the financial costs of cloth in general at the end of this section.

Final practical point about cloth: most day care centers don't allow them. This may be a sanitation requirement governed by state day care regulators and not a negotiating point. Check with local day care centers or your state board.

Disposables. Disposable diapers were first introduced in 1961 and now hold an overwhelming lead over cloth—about 95% of all households that have kids in diapers use disposables. Today's diapers have super-absorbent gels that lower the number of needed diaper changes, especially at night (which helps baby sleep through the night sooner). Even many parents who swear cloth diapers are best still use disposables at night. The downside? All that super-absorbency means babies are in no rush to potty train—they simply don't feel as wet or uncomfortable as babies in cloth diapers.

The jury on diaper rash is still out—disposable diaper users tell us they don't experience any more diaper rash than cloth diaper users.

Besides the eco-arguments about disposables, there is one other disadvantage—higher trash costs. In some communities, the more trash you put out, the higher the bill. Hence, using disposable diapers may result in higher garbage expenses.

The financial bottom line: Surprisingly, there is no clear winner when you factor financial costs into this equation.

Cloth diapers may seem cheap at first, but consider the hidden costs. Besides the diapers themselves ($100 for the basic varieties; $200 to $300 for the fancy ones), you also have to buy diaper covers. Like everything you buy with baby, there is a wide cost variation with diaper covers. The cheap stuff (like Dappi covers at Target) will set you back $4 to $6 each. And you've got to buy several in different sizes as your child grows so the total investment could be $100+. If you're lucky, you can find diaper covers second-hand for $1 to $3. Of course, some parents find low-cost covers leak and quickly wear out. As a result, they turn to the more expensive covers—a single Mother-Ease (see later for more info on this brand) is $9.75. Invest in a half dozen of those covers (in various sizes, of course) and you've spent another $200 to $400 (if you buy them new).

What about laundry? Well, washing your own cloth diapers at home may be the most economical way to go, but often folks don't have the time or energy. Instead, many parents use a cloth diaper service. In a recent cost survey of such services across the U.S., we discovered that most cost $500 to $725 a year. While each service does supply you with diapers (relieving you of that expense), you're still on the hook for the diaper covers.

Proponents of cloth diapers argue that if you plan to have more than one child, you can reuse those covers spreading out (and lowering) the cost. You may also not need as many sizes depending on the brands you use and the way your child grows.

So, what's the bottom line cost for cloth diapers? We estimate the total financial damage for cloth diapers (using a cloth diaper service and buying diaper covers) for just the first year is $600 to $800.

By contrast, let's take a look at disposables. If you buy disposable diapers from the most expensive source in town (typically, a

E-MAIL FROM THE REAL WORLD
Cloth diaper laundry tips

Once you make the decision to use cloth diapers, you'll want to research the "art" of cleaning them. Too many harsh chemicals can damage and fade cloth diapers and covers, not enough will leave diapers looking less than pristine. So what's a parent to do? Here's some advice from readers who've experienced lots of diaper cleaning.

Rowan Cerrelli writes:

"I do not like to use chlorine bleach to wash out diapers since they are expensive and the chlorine ruins them. There are some products out there that use natural enzymes to predigest 'stuff' out of the diapers, therefore eliminating he need for bleach. Companies that have these products include Seventh Generation and Ecover. They are also available in natural food grocery stores."

Catherine Advocate-Ross recommends:

"I use Bi-O-Kleen laundry powder on the diapers. Works great and you need very little."

Bi-O-Kleen has a web site at www.biokleen.com that explains their products and directs consumers to stores or web sites that carry them. They have an extensive line including liquid as well as powder detergent and stain and odor eliminator. The main ingredient in the line is grapefruit seed and pulp extract.

Kelly Small, from Wallingford, CT emailed us to say:

"I highly recommend OxyClean— it is great on the poop stains!!!"

grocery store), you'd spend about $600 to $650 for the first year. Yet, we've found discount sources (mentioned later in this chapter) that sell disposables in bulk at a discount. By shopping at these sources, we figure you'd spend $300 to $375 per year (the lowest figure is for private label diapers, the highest is for brand names).

The bottom line: the cheapest way to go is cloth diapers laundered at home. The next best bet is disposables. Finally, cloth diapers from a diaper service are the most expensive.

Parents in Cyberspace: What's on the Web?

All Together Diaper Company

Web: www.clothdiaper.com
What it is: Home of the all-in-one cloth diaper made in house by

---

Finally, Rebecca Parish has some practical advice on cloth diapers:

"We (my friends and I) have run across a shortcut that I had not heard about before we attempted cloth diapering. Mainly, we have found it entirely unnecessary to rinse diapers out at all before laundering them. We own a four-day supply of pre-fold diapers and wraps. When our baby poops, we take an extra diaper wipe with us to the toilet, and use it to scrape what easily comes off into the toilet. Then we throw the dirty diaper into our diaper pail, right along with all the other dirty diapers. There's no liquid in the pail for soaking— they just sit in there dry. About every three or four days we throw the entire contents of the diaper pail into the laundry machine, add regular detergent (we use Cheer) and two capfuls of bleach (about 4 teaspoons), and run the machine. The diapers and wraps all come out clean. Just two extra loads of laundry a week (which is nothing compared to the extra loads of clothes we now wash), and no dipping our hands into toilet water. I generally use about five diaper wipes every time I change a messy diaper as it is, so using one extra one for scraping poop into the toilet seems like no big deal.

I think washer technology has improved significantly enough in recent years to allow for this much easier diaper cleaning. We own a fairly new front-loader washer. I don't think the brand name is important; we have a friend who owns a different brand of front-loader, and gets equally good results. However, one of our friends with an older top-loader uses our same system but ends up with stains; she doesn't care but I would. "

Bottom line: new technologies (detergents, additives and washers) have led to great improvements in the cleaning of cloth diapers.

the All Together Diaper Company.

What's cool: We loved the simplicity of this site. In business since 1990, the All Together Diaper Company sells its own cloth diaper system in various packages. The accompanying FAQ, washing instructions and analysis of diaper costs are really helpful. While some of their price comparisons between cloth and disposable are a bit inaccurate (slanted toward cloth, of course), the information on the cost of home washing was helpful.

What about the diapers? We were impressed with the cool design—the all-in-one system has cotton inside against baby's skin, a waterproof outer shell, adjustable snaps and elastic leg openings. These diapers (the Deluxe) are $8 to $12 each or $84 to $132 per dozen. Less expensive are the Fitted Diapers, which do not have the waterproof shell. Price: $7 to $8.50 each or $72 to $90 per dozen. Packages of diapers do offer some savings: the Deluxe package which includes 30 small diapers, and 24 medium, large and toddler sizes plus 24 diaper doublers runs $699 ($6.68 per diaper).

Needs work: Prices have definitely gone up in recent years. When we first wrote about All Together diapers a newborn size deluxe was $5. That's an increase of 38% over two years. Considering inflation was relatively flat in that time period, we're a bit shocked at the increase.

The Baby Lane

Web: www.thebabylane.com

What it is: A comprehensive baby product and information site with a selection of cloth diapers and accessories.

What's cool: This is really the Mother of All Cloth Diaper sites. You'll find offerings from Under the Nile, Bumkins, Kushies, Aristocrats, Plushies, Imse Vimse, Alexis, Bummis and Green Earth. Kushies Ultras were $8.95 for size small (discounts available for five packs).

Needs work: Unfortunately, this site could use a little more organization. The topics list (in varying type sizes) was rather annoying.

Diapers 4 Less

Web: www.diapers4less.com, see figure 2 on the next page.

What it is: The web site for Diaper Factory Plus, a manufacturer of generic disposable diapers.

What's cool: Rock bottom prices. Even with shipping costs, this site's diapers are about 20% less than any other discount diaper sites. Rock-a-bye "premiums" have a cloth-like backing, elastic leg openings and tape closures. The price for a case of 256 small size diapers is $50 and includes shipping. The per diaper cost is 20¢, slightly more than in years past. In the chart following this section, you'll see this price compares well with grocery stores (and of

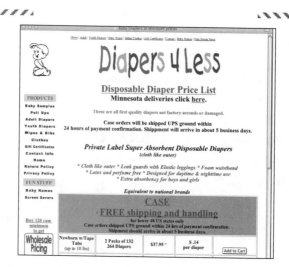

Figure 2: Even when you factor in shipping costs,
Diapers4Less.com often beats grocery store prices.

course, these diapers are delivered to your home). Sample packs
are available if you want to check out the quality.

Needs work: One reader complained that after she ordered a
quantity of diapers from Diapers4Less.com, she was notified that
they had run out of that size. Apparently, the company knew they
did not have stock, yet still charged her credit card. They did not
update the site until later to reflect the stock. Hopefully, Diapers4Less
has figured out their inventory since then, but we'd suggest con-
firming they have what you want before you place an order.

◆ Other sites to consider:

Disposables: We found several more sites that sell disposable diapers on line. Among the best: **Drug Emporium** (www.drugempo-
rium.com), **CVS Pharmacy** (www.cvspharmacy.com), **Baby's
Heaven** (www.babysheaven.com), and **Diaper Site** (www.diaper-
site.com). And don't forget about the online companions to bricks
and mortar stores like **Costco**. On www.costco.com you can purchase the same diapers at the same price (plus shipping) as you
find in their warehouses.

Cloth: Several readers have recommended **WeeBees.com**. One
reader noted, "WeeBees.com has the most wonderful quilty,
absorbent, affordable diapers that I've seen!" Also check out **Baby
J** (www.babyj.com). You'll find all-in-ones, folded diapers, wraps,

Who's got the cheapest diapers?

What's the best place to buy disposable diapers? We did a price comparison among several major sources, listed here from least to most expensive:

WEB SITE OR STORE	DIAPER TYPE	COUNT	PRICE	PER DIAPER
COSTCO	HUGGIES #1	228	$29	13¢
WALMART	HUGGIES #1	136	$19.47	14¢
SAM'S CLUB	HUGGIES #1	228	$32	14¢
BJ'S	HUGGIES #1	228	$32	14¢
TARGET	HUGGIES #1	68	$11.19	16¢
BABIES R US	HUGGIES #1	84	$15	18¢
COSTCO.COM	HUGGIES #1	228	$43.57¥	19¢
DIAPERS4LESS.COM	HOUSE BRAND	256	$50	20¢
GROCERY STORE*	HUGGIES #1	84	$17	20¢
BABYSHEAVEN.COM	HUGGIES #1	175	$48	27¢
DIAPERSITE.COM	HOUSE BRAND	100	$27.95**	28¢

Price: Includes shipping.
Per Diaper: The cost per diaper.

¥ Includes shipping and tax to Colorado. If you have a Costco in your state, you will be charged sales tax.
* Checked at Safeway.
** Flat shipping fee regardless how many you order.
† Free shipping over $35 purchase.

Prices checked as of 2003.

liners and more with such brands as Kushies, Cotton Kids, and Bummis. **Barefoot Baby** (www.barefootbaby.com) is another site recommended by readers. Besides their own brand of diapers, they carry Bumkins, Bummis, Cot'n Wrap and Fuzzi Bunz. Check out any of the following web sites as well: **www.kellyscloset.com, www. jardinediapers.com** and **www.babybunz.com**. Reader Sherri Wormstead noted that all three of these sites are competitively priced and have a nice wide variety of supplies. Finally, check out **Organic Bebe** (www.organicbebe.com). They carry a huge assortment of folded diapers, all-in-one systems and diaper covers. Samples are available as well as diaper bags and accessories.

Our Picks: Brand Recommendations

Disposables. The evolution of disposable diapers is rather amazing. They started out in the 1960's as bulky and ineffective at stopping leaks. In 40 years, disposables morphed into ultra-thin, super-absorbent miracle workers that command 95% of the market.

And writing about disposable diaper brands is like trying to nail Jell-O to a wall—every five minutes, the diaper makers come out with new features and new gimmicks as they jostle for a piece of the $3.6 billion diaper market. In the ten years since the first edition of this book came out, we're amazed at the constant innovation in the category. Before we get to our brand recommendations, consider the three basic types of disposables:

◆ *Basic.* These are the cheapest diapers and also the most bulky.
◆ *Ultrathin.* Even though they are thinner than basic diapers, they are more absorbent, thanks to high-tech absorbent jells. Most of the diapers sold today are ultrathins.
◆ *Premium/Supreme.* As the name implies, these are the most expensive diapers on the market. What do you get for that 25% higher price? Well, some premium diapers have cloth-like outer covers and fancier closures like Velcro. You may also find additives like aloe to prevent diaper rash.

No matter what brand you try, remember that sizing of diapers is all over the board. The size 2 diaper in one brand may be cut totally different than the "medium" of another, even though the weight guidelines on the package are similar. Finding a diaper that fits is critical to you and your baby's happiness.

Now, let's answer some common questions about disposables:

Q. What makes one brand different from another?
A. Surprisingly, the absorbency of diapers varies little from brand to brand. A *Consumer Reports* test (August 1998) of 8000 diaper changes on 80 babies at a day care center found that of 13 diaper types tested, eight were judged excellent. And three more were "very good." Translation: no matter what brand you choose, you'll probably have a diaper that fits well and doesn't leak. Yes, the premium/supreme diapers scored highest in CR's tests, but the difference between them and the cheaper options was minimal (except for the price, of course).

Besides absorbency, gimmicks and marketing ploys are the only differences between brands. This market goes through fads faster than Madison Avenue. Remember gender-specific diapers? That was more hype than real benefit and now they're gone (we're back to unisex versions). Another fad that came and went: "Pampers Rash Care," a premium diaper which "contains the same active ingredients as many diaper rash creams" to prevent diaper rash. Next week we expect Huggies to come out with a brand that promises higher college entrance test scores (call it Huggies "SAT Boost Supreme").

The latest rage: making diapers that fit babies' development stages. For example, Pampers Cruisers are for active older babies.

Q. What about store brands like Babies R Us and others? Is there much difference?

A. Although store diapers used to be less impressive than name brands, in the last few years they've caught up in terms of cloth like covers, Velcro fasteners and ultra absorbency. And they cost as much as 30% less too.

Q. Do certain brands work better for boys or girls?

A. We used to hear anecdotal evidence from our readers that Huggies were better with boys and Pampers better with girls. In recent years, however, parents tell us there doesn't seem to be a gender difference at all.

Q. How many diapers of each size is a good starting point?

A. Most babies go through 12 to 14 diapers *per day* for the first few months. That translates into about 500 to 600 diapers for the first six weeks. As you read at the beginning of the chapter we recommend buying 100 "newborn" size diapers and 400 to 500 "size one" diapers before baby is born. Caveat: some families have large babies, so keep the receipts just in case you have to exchange some of those newborns for size 1.

So how many do you need of the larger sizes? Starting with a case of each size as you transition to larger diapers is a good idea. There are typically a 100 diapers or more in a case. As you near a transition to a larger size, you'll want to scale back the amount of smaller size diapers you buy so you don't have any half opened packs lying around.

Finally, remember that as your baby grows, she will require fewer diaper changes. One you add solid foods to her feeding schedule you may only be doing eight to ten changes a day. Plus you'll be much more experienced about when a diaper really is wet.

Let's break down the diaper choices:

◆ **Huggies.** Huggies is an excellent brand. However, in the last few years, Huggies hasn't added much to their line of diapers. They continue to carry the Ultratrims with the new "Leak-Lock System". This is supposed to avoid leaks once baby becomes for active.

Huggies Supremes are their top of the line diapers with a fabric-like cover and Velcro closures. They've added a new stretchiness to the Supremes supposedly to allow for better fit. Newborn diapers have a fold down waistband for umbilical cord care and the same Leak-Lock system. Overnights are made to be even more absorbent so babies can actually sleep through the night (and parents too!). A couple specialty diapers round out the options: Preemies and Little Swimmers diapers.

Huggies web site (www.huggies.com) is easy to use with buttons for deals and explanations of each diapering product. A plus: you can use their "Product Chooser" feature to help decide which diapers will work best for your baby. Kimberly Clark, the company that makes Huggies has set up a separate web site called Parentstages (www.parentstages.com). Intended to be more informative and less commercial, the site allows parents to search for advice on health, family, entertainment and more. They even have a section for dads. Ads are kept to a minimum and the emphasis is on information not products.

◆ *Pampers.* Scored highest in *Consumer Reports* tests (specifically, the Pampers Premium) and we agree—these are great diapers. New this year, Pampers has expanded their line to add Swaddlers, Cruisers and the Baby Dry line. Swaddlers are intended for newborns to size two. Claiming to "swaddle your baby in comfort" these diapers are for very young, inactive babies. For the next stage when babies begin to kick, roll over, crawl and stand, Pampers has introduced their Cruisers. These are supposed to have more elasticity and give for active babies. The go from size three to six. Baby Dry diapers are yet another line of diapers in sizes from newborn to toddler. They've added a new closure system as well as cloth like cover to these. Finally, they still make the Premium diapers and have added a new Premium Custom Fit diaper.

Pampers' easy to use web site (www.pampers.com) explains the new offerings pretty well, and there is an easy-to use chart that helps you figure out what's available for you baby at any particular stage. Coupons and deals were not available on the site when we visited.

◆ *Luvs.* Made by the same company that makes Pampers, Luvs are marketed as a lower-price brand. Once again, we didn't see much difference between Luvs and Pampers . . . or Huggies.

Luvs' web site (www.luvs.com) is heavy on Barney, the purple dinosaur. You can read about their "Barney Rewards" program, which lets you earn points toward free toys and other prizes. Whoopee. After you wade through all the Barney plugs, you'll note Luvs has recently added swim diapers to their line up and ultra

Eco Friendly Disposables

Is there a diaper that combines the convenience of disposables with the ecological benefits of cloth diapers? Yes—here's an overview of the so-called eco-friendly disposables:

Tushies, first invented by a Denver pediatrician in the late 1980's, bills its diapers as a gel-free, latex-free, perfume-free alternative to name brand disposables. Made with non-chlorine bleached wood pulp surrounding an absorbent cotton core, they also offer a new "cloth-like" cover. Tushies mentions that without the gel, their diapers won't "explode" in the swimming pool. The disadvantages to Tushies? They are considerably thicker than regular diapers and one of our readers complained that the old version of Tushies were stiff and uncomfortable. And like most "all-natural" versions of consumer goods, Tushies ain't cheap. They sell a case of 160 size small diapers for $48. That's 30¢ per diaper. Compare that to grocery store prices of 20¢ per diaper and warehouse clubs of 14¢ per diaper. By the way, you'll also see a brand of diapers on Tushies site called ***Tender Care***. One reader mentioned they were thinner than Tushies; Tushie's site isn't very helpful in comparing the two brands. Tushies are available in 6000 stores (although not at Sam's, Costco or BJs) or on line at www.tushies.com.

Nature Boy and Girl is another option in the eco-friendly disposable diaper market. Based on a Swedish design, these diapers are almost completely organic. In fact, their goal is to ultimately make a diaper that can be completely composted at recycling centers rather than buried at landfills. While Nature Boy does use a small amount of super absorbent polymer, they claim to use much less than regular disposables. The pulp is chlorine free, and the outer film cover is made of a GMO-free cornstarch base. How PC can you get? Nature Boy's web site (www.natureboyandgirl.com) includes references to studies claiming to show comparable absorbency with Pampers. They also claim their diapers are soft and flexible compared to their competitors. Even their packaging is biodegradable. Price per diaper if you buy on line? 25¢. A 192-diaper case of size small costs $48.

Ultimately, while these products are promising options for parents looking for a natural alternative to mainstream disposables, the price is certainly going to be a factor in getting parents to use them. And there is still an issue of where these diapers will go. Until recycling centers with composting options become available more widely, there's a question as to whether these diapers won't still end up buried under tons of earth and trash waiting to decompose.

thick wipes. Ultra Leakguards seem to be the big thing at Luvs, similar to the no leak features from Pampers and Huggies.

◆ **Store brands**. We've received numerous emails from parents who love store-brand diapers at Target, Wal-Mart, K-Mart and Toys R Us. Even grocery stores are getting into the game with private label diapers at prices to rival the discounters. Generally, these diapers are 20% to 30% cheaper than name brands. In the past, they were inferior in terms of features and quality but no more—most have the same ultrathin design, cloth-like covers and Velcro-closures. Toys R Us and Target's in-house brands received the highest marks from our readers; we noticed *Consumer Reports* liked Walgreens generic brand as well. Yes, there are several other obscure brands of diapers out there (among them, Drypers, Dri-Bottoms, and Fitti), but we didn't receive enough feedback from parents to form an opinion on them.

Cloth Diapers. Ask 100 parents for their recommendations on cloth diapers and you're likely to get 100 different opinions—it seems everyone has their special system or favorite. We did see one common thread amongst cloth diaper devotees: most used a variety of brands/types to make it through the day. Like a well-armed soldier going into battle, the cloth-diapering parent typically has an arsenal of various products, schemes and tactics.

It seems that cloth diaper advocates all have their own favorite brands (see Email from the Real World for some comment). And there are so many brands of diapers, all-in-one systems and covers that we can't review all of them here. For additional tips on this subject, check out the web site BornToLove (www.BornToLove.com). Their "World Wide Cloth Diapering Resources" is a massive index of 214 U.S. cloth diaper companies and 41 Canadian manufacturers plus links to cloth diaper books, magazine articles, associations, discussion lists, and message boards. A good book on using cloth diapers is *Diaper Changes* by Theresa Rodriquez (Homekeepers Publishing, 1997, 800-572-1826, web: www.homekeepers.com). Finally, check out our online message boards on our web site at www.babybargainsbook.com. They have extensive commentary from cloth diaper parents with tips and recommendations.

There are six categories of cloth diapers (plus covers):
◆ **Flat fold diapers.** Sold in stores like Target and Wal-Mart, these are nice for clean-up rags but rather useless for diapers.

◆ **Standard pre-fold diapers.** Two common brands: Dundee and Curity. Our verdict: not much more useful than flat-fold diapers. Skip 'em.

◆ **Diaper service diapers.** Yes, you can buy the diapers used by cloth diaper services via mail order or specialty stores. Used with pins or covers, these diapers come in three sizes (newborn, standard and toddler) and run $25 per dozen. Sometimes these are referred to as Chinese fold. The only bummer: these diapers can be bulky when used on infants under 15 pounds. Hence, most parents use these after a baby is six months old or so.

◆ **Fitted diapers.** The Mercedes of this category is Canada-made "Mother-Ease" (www.mother-ease.com), a brand that has a fanatical following among cloth diaper devotees. Suffice it to say, they ain't cheap but the quality is excellent. Mother-Ease sells both fitted diapers and covers; the diapers run $9 to $10 a pop, while the covers are about $9.75. Before you invest $73 to $375 in one of Mother-Ease's special package deals, consider trying their "introductory offer" (see details below in our money-saving tips section).

Other parents like Kushies (800) 841-5330 (web: www.kushies.com), another Canadian import. (For some reason, Kushies are known as "Kooshies" in the rest of the world). This brand offers several models, which sell for $5 to $7 each.

One note: both Kushies and Mother-Ease are sold via mail order only. Yes, you can sometimes find these diapers at second-hand or thrift stores, but most parents buy them from a catalog or on the 'net. Kushies are trying to branch out into retail stores—check your local baby specialty shop.

◆ **Terry flannel diapers.** These are marketed to parents as the ultimate "eco-friendly" choice—terry flannel diapers are typically made of 100% organic cotton. Cost: $42 to $120 per dozen depending on the brand (these diapers are sold via web sites like www.diaperdance.com or www.daisydiapers.com). Terry flannel diapers can take quite a while to dry and may be overkill for most parents. On the upside, they are contoured and less bulky, which means they fit newborn infants well.

◆ **All-in-one diapers.** As the name implies, these diapers combine a diaper and cover. And they aren't cheap: $6.25 to $15, depending on the brand. Most moms we interviewed say these diapers are too expensive for everyday use, but their convenience makes them handy for long trips. Once again, Mother-Ease and Kushies are two of the better brands to consider in this category. Other good all-in-one-diapers are made by All Together (801-566-7579, web: www. clothdiaper.com; $6.25 to $8.50) and Bumkins (800-338-7581 web: www. bumkins.com; $14 each). We've also received parental kudos for Indisposables (800-663-1730; sold at the

BabyTown web site (www.eskimo.com/~babytown). Indisposables are cotton diapers. They will accommodate a paper insert that can then be flushed down the toilet. Cost: $75 to $84 for a dozen. The inserts are $5.25 per roll (one roll lasts about a week).

◆ *Inserts and liners.* One of the criticisms of cloth diapers (fairly or not) is that they leak, especially at night. To help your baby sleep through the night and avoid those 3 am crib changes, consider

E-Mail from The Real World
Which cloth diapers work best

Cloth diapering (know as CDing to those hip mammas out there) can be a bit overwhelming when you first decide to take the plunge. Since most parents choose to use disposables, you may not have a network of moms to look to for advice on this subject. So one of our long time readers, Tamara, has a few comments on what worked for her:

"We are currently using a diaper service. I researched and purchased several types of wraps and here is my feedback.

Bummis. These are Canadian and, according to my husband, breathe the most. He is an engineer and actually conducted some weird little test sucking and blowing on the various wraps to determine the ones that breathe the best. My complaint is that their Velcro is too narrow. Our baby is a wiggler and has actually wiggled out of the Bummis a couple of times. They lack leg gussets, which make side leaks and blowouts more frequent. Though size wise they last longer. I ordered these from Born To Love. They cost $7+ dollars depending on the site.

Dappi's. These have a cloth outside and plastic lining material with mesh over it plus a big Velcro band and tabs. These leak less, but poop tends to get caught in the mesh, which is messy. They cost $6.00 a pop at Target.

Diaperaps. Love 'em! My doula told me about them. They have colorful cloth outside and a plastic interior as well as a big Velcro band and tabs, and leg gussets. They are great! Fred Meyer sells them for roughly $11.00 for a 2 pack. They are hard to get hold of here in Seattle area, since they are very popular and sell out quickly. To my delight I discovered you can order these on the web, direct from Diaper Wraps (www.diaperaps.com). They cost $6.25 each plus shipping. The website offers discounts on large orders and package deals. They also sell cloth diapers, training pants, and swim diapers."

adding liners or inserts to your cloth diapers. Inserts are additional absorbent pads placed in the strategic crotch area of a regular cloth diaper to soak up any extra wetness. We've seen them for between $2 and $4 per insert on cloth diaper web sites.

◆ *Covers.* With the exception of all-in-one cloth diapers, all other cloth diapers typically need covers, which help prevent leaks. The best diaper covers (also called wraps) not only must withstand leaks but also the washing machine—durability is a key factor.

Earlier in this chapter, we cited the wide variability in diaper cover costs, from the cheapest (Dappi covers at Target or Wal-Mart for $4 to $6) to the most expensive (wool Biobottoms at $20 each). Obviously, the cheap diaper covers wear out much quicker than the expensive ones. Realizing that fact, some parents use the cheaper covers when baby is younger and growing rapidly (the faster the growth, the less each cover is used) and switch to more pricey covers when baby is older (say over a year, when growth slows and covers are used for a longer period of time).

As for specific brands, one mom we interviewed didn't like Cottonwraps ("they leaked like crazy"), Ecology Kids (the Velcro wears out too quickly) or Snappiwraps (the elastic also wears out too fast). Bumkins covers got better marks, but they have a vent panel in the back that makes it hard to use. Once again, Mother-Ease received raves for their covers ($9.75 a pop), as did Kushies wraps ($6 each at the www.thebabylane.com). We also heard positive comments about Diaperwraps, although feedback was mixed on Nikki's (some loved them, others said they were overpriced). Once again, the Born to Love web page (web: www.born-tolove.com) has contact info for these cover makers, as well as mail-order catalogs like Baby Bunz (800) 676-4559.

Special thanks to readers Sheila Pierson and J. Russel in Baltimore, MD for their insightful emails on this topic.

Wipes. Like diapers, you have a basic choice with wipes: name brand or generic. Our advice: stick to the name brands. We found the cheap generic wipes to be inferior. With less water and thinner construction, store brand wipes we sampled were losers.

Money Saving Secrets

Here are some tips for saving on disposable diapers (cloth diaper bargain advice is at the end of this section):

1 **BUY IN BULK.** Don't buy those little packs of 20 diapers—look for the 80 or 100 count packs instead. You'll find the price per diaper goes down when you buy larger packs.

2 **GO FOR WAREHOUSE CLUBS.** Both Sam's (www.samsclub.com) and Costco (www.costco.com) wholesale clubs sell diapers at incredibly low prices. For example, Costco sells a 228-count package of Huggies Step 1-2 for just $29 or less than 13¢ per diaper. We also found great deals on wipes at the wholesale clubs. Another warehouse club is BJ's (www.bjswholesale.com), which has over 100 locations in 15 states, most in the Eastern U.S. By the way, one reader noted that the size 1-2 diapers she's seeing in warehouse clubs are really size 1. She's been frustrated with this sizing issue since the size 3 diapers are too big but there isn't anything in between the 1-2 and the 3 sizes.

3 **BUY STORE BRANDS.** As mentioned earlier in this chapter in brand reviews, many parents find store brand diapers to be equal to the name brands. And the prices can't be beat—many are 20% to 30% cheaper. Chains like Target, Wal-Mart, K-Mart and Toys R Us/Babies R Us carry in-house diaper brands, as do many grocery stores. Heck, even Sam's wholesale club stocked a generic brand of diapers that was 26% cheaper than name brands.

4 **CONSIDER TOYS R US.** You may not have a wholesale club nearby, but you're bound to be close to a Toys R Us (or their sister division, Babies R Us). And we found them to be a great source for affordable name-brand diapers. The best bet: buy in bulk. You can often buy diapers (both name brand and generic) by the case at Toys R Us, saving you about 20% or more over grocery store prices. As you might have noted in the earlier diaper cost comparison, Babies R Us was one of the lowest-priced sources for diapers we found.

Don't forget to check the front of the store for copies of Toys R Us' latest catalog. Occasionally, they offer in-store coupons for additional diaper savings—you can even combine these with manufacturer's coupons for double savings.

5 **WHEN YOUR BABY IS NEARING A TRANSITION POINT, DON'T STOCK UP.** Quick growing babies may move into another size faster than you think, leaving you with an excess supply of too-small diapers.

6 **DON'T BUY DIAPERS IN GROCERY STORES.** We compared prices at grocery stores and usually found them to be sky-high. Most were selling diapers in packages that worked out to 18¢ to 24¢ per diaper. We should note there are exceptions to this rule, however: some grocery chains (especially in the South) use diapers as a "loss-leader." They'll sell diapers at attractive prices in order to entice shoppers into the store. Also, store brands can be more competitively priced.

7 **USE COUPONS.** You'll be amazed at how many coupons you receive in the mail, usually for 75 cents off diapers and 50 cents off wipes. One tip: to keep those "introductory" packages of coupons coming, continue signing up to be on the mailing lists of the maternity chain stores (apparently, these chains sell your name to diaper manufacturers, formula companies, etc.) or online at diaper manufacturers' web sites.

8 **ASK FOR GIFT CERTIFICATES.** When friends ask you what you'd like as a shower gift, you can drop hints for gift certificates/cards from stores that sell a wide variety of baby items—including diapers and wipes. That way you can get what you really need, instead of cute accessories of marginal value. You'd be surprised at how many stores offer gift certificate programs.

9 **FOR CLOTH DIAPER USERS, GO FOR "INTRODUCTORY PACKAGES."** Many suppliers have special introductory deals (Mother-Ease offers one diaper, liner and cover for $17 US; $20 Canadian, which includes shipping). Before you invest hundreds of dollars in one brand, give it a test drive first.

 Do it By Mail

There are several catalogs that sell cloth diapers and diaper covers by mail. Here are some of the best:

BABY WORKS

To Order Call: (800) 422-2910.
Shopping Hours: Monday through Friday 9:00 am to 4:00 pm Pacific time.
Or write to: Baby Works, 11725 N. W. West Rd., Portland, OR, 97229.
Web: www.babyworks.com.
Credit Cards Accepted: VISA, MC, Discover.

Looking for baby products that are "gentle to the earth?" Then check out Baby Works. You'll find diaper covers like Nikkys, all-in-one diaper systems, cotton diapers, laundry products, and accessories. We saw the Bumkins all-in-one system for $12.50 per diaper. We liked all the washing instructions included on each page for the different items. Another nice feature: Baby Works has a recommended layette for cloth diapers. They even offer clothing and nursing items as well. Prices aren't anything to shout about, but the selection is good.

BORN TO LOVE

To Order Call: (905) 725-2559; Fax: (905-725-3297.
Shopping Hours: Monday to Saturday, 9am to 9pm (Eastern).
Or write to: 445 Centre Street S. Oshawa, ON Canada L1H 4C1.
Web: www. Borntolove.com.
Credit Cards Accepted: MC, VISA, AMEX.

This Canadian catalog and web site is the mother of all cloth diaper sources. You'll see page after page of cloth diaper systems (including such name brands as Bummis and Babykins). Heck, there are even 14 pages of accessories, plus selections of nursing bras, breast pumps, toys, safety products and more. Yes, the web site is a jumbled mess, but there's lots of useful info, articles and links when you sift through it all.

◆ *More sources for diaper covers. TC Kidco* (888) 825-4326 is a Canadian catalog that sells "Indisposables" all-in-one cloth diapers and diaper covers (mentioned earlier). You can buy from the catalog or from their direct representative. The catalog also has nursing bras, blankets, bibs and more.

As mentioned earlier, *Weebees* web site (www.weebees.com) sells a wide variety of cloth diapers, covers, and accessories. We even saw Australian Nappies, which they claim, are the most absorbent diapers they've ever seen. Another cool item: Little Squirt. This device is a power sprayer that hooks up to your toilet plumbing. It allows you to spray off baby's bottom and the waste goes directly into the toilet. It even has a toddler proof handle for $50.

 ## The Bottom Line:
A Wrap-Up of Our Best Buy Picks

In summary, we recommend you buy the following layette items for your baby (see chart on next page):

Quantity	Item	Cost
6	T-shirts/onesies (over the head)	$22
6	T-shirts (side snap)	$25
4-6	Sleepers	$64-$96
1	Blanket Sleeper*	$10
2-4	Coveralls	$40-$80
3-4	Booties/socks	$12-$16
1	Sweater	$16
2	Hats (safari and caps)	$30
1	Snowsuit/bunting*	$20
4	Large bibs (for feeding)	$24
3 sets	Wash cloths and towels	$30
7-8	Receiving blankets	$42-$48
TOTAL		$335 to $417

If you live in a cold climate.

These prices are from discounters, outlet stores, or sale prices at department stores. What would all these clothes cost at full retail? $500 to $600, at least. The bottom line: follow our tips and you'll save $100 to $300 on your baby's layette alone. (Of course, you may receive some of these items as gifts, so your actual outlay may be less.)

Which brands are best? See "Our Picks: Brand Recommendations" earlier in this chapter. In general, we found that 100% cotton clothes are best. Yes, you'll pay a little more for cotton, but it lasts longer and looks better than clothes made of polyester blends (the exception: fleece outerwear and sleepwear). Other wastes of money for infants include kimonos, saque sets, and shoes.

What about diapers? We found little financial difference between cloth and disposable, especially when you use a cloth diaper service. Cloth does have several hidden costs, however—diaper covers can add hundreds of dollars to the expense of this option although the cost can be spread out among additional children.

For disposables, we found that brand choice was more of a personal preference—all the majors did a good job at stopping leaks. The best way to save money on disposable diapers is to skip the grocery store and buy in bulk (100-diaper packages) from a warehouse club or Babies R Us. Diapers from discount sources run about $300 to $375. The same diapers from grocery stores could be $600 or more. Another great money-saver: generic, store-brand diapers from Wal-Mart, Target, K-Mart and like. These diapers performed just as well as the name brands at a 20% to 30% discount.

CHAPTER 5

Maternity & Nursing

Inside this chapter

*L*ove 'em or hate 'em, every mother-to-be needs maternity clothes at some point in her pregnancy. Still, you don't have to break the bank to get comfortable, and, yes, fashionable maternity items. In this chapter, we tell you which sources sell all-cotton, casual clothes at unbelievably low prices. Then, we'll review the top maternity chains and reveal our list of top wastes of money. You'll learn which nursing clothes moms prefer most.

Maternity & Nursing Clothes

Getting Started: When Do You Need This Stuff?

It may seem obvious that you'll need to buy maternity clothes when you get pregnant, but the truth is you don't actually need all of them immediately. The first thing you'll notice is the need for a new bra. At least, that was my first clue that my body was changing. Breast changes occur as early as the first month and you may find yourself going through several different bra sizes along the way.

Next, your belly will begin to "swell." Yes, the baby is making its presence known by making you feel a bit bigger around the middle. Not only may you find that you need to buy larger panties, but you may also find that skirts and pants feel tight as early as your third month. Maternity clothes at this point may seem like overkill, but some women do begin to "show" enough that they find it necessary to head out to the maternity shop.

If you have decided to breastfeed, you'll need to consider what type of nursing bras you'll want. Buy two or three in your eighth month so you'll be prepared. You may find it necessary to buy more nursing bras after the baby is born, but this will get you started. As for other nursing clothes, you may or may not find these worth the money. Don't go out and buy a whole new wardrobe right off the bat. Some women find nursing shirts and tops to be helpful while others manage quite well with regular clothes. More on this topic later in the book.

Sources

1 **MATERNITY WEAR CHAINS.** Not surprisingly, there are quite a few nationwide maternity clothing chains. Visit any mall and you'll likely see the names Pea in the Pod, Motherswork, Mimi Maternity, and Motherhood, to mention a few. More on these chains later in the chapter.

2 **MOM AND POP MATERNITY SHOPS.** These small, independent stores sell a wide variety of maternity clothes, from affordable weekend wear to high-priced career wear. Some baby specialty stores carry maternity clothes as well. The chief advantage to the smaller stores is personalized service—we usually found salespeople who were knowledgeable about the different brands. In addition, these stores may offer other services. For example, some rent formal wear for special occasions, saving you big bucks. Of course, you may pay for the extra service with higher prices.

3 **CONSIGNMENT STORES.** Many consignment or thrift stores that specialize in children's clothing may also have a rack of maternity clothes. In visits to several such stores, we found some incredible bargains (at least 50% off retail) on maternity clothes that were in good to excellent condition. Of course, the selection varies widely, but we strongly advise you to check out any second-hand stores.

4 **DISCOUNTERS.** When we talk about discounters, we're referring to chains like Target, Wal-Mart and K-Mart. Now, let's be honest here—these discounters probably aren't the first place you'd think of to outfit your maternity wardrobe. Yet, each has a surprisingly nice selection of maternity clothes, especially casual wear. Later, we'll tell you about the incredible prices on these all-cotton clothes.

5 **DEPARTMENT STORES.** As you might guess, most department stores carry some maternity fashions. The big disadvantage:

the selection is usually rather small. This means you'll often find unattractive jumpers in abundance and very little in the way of fashionable clothing. Department stores like Penney's and Sears often have end-of-the-season sales with decent maternity bargains.

6 **WEB/MAIL-ORDER.** Even if you don't have any big-time maternity chains nearby, you can still buy the clothes they sell. Many chains offer a mail-order service, either from printed catalogs or online stores. We also found several mail-order catalogs that have a selection of maternity clothes. In the "Do It By Mail" section of this chapter, we'll give you the run-down on these options.

7 **NON-MATERNITY STORES.** Maternity stores don't have a monopoly on large-size clothes—and you can save big bucks by shopping at stores that don't have the word "maternity" in their name. Later in this chapter, we'll give you some specific examples.

8 **YOUR HUSBAND'S CLOSET.** What's a good source for oversized shirts and baggy sweaters? Look no further than the other side of your closet, where your husband's clothes can often double as maternity wear.

9 **OUTLETS.** Yes, there are several outlets that sell maternity clothes and the prices can be a steal. We'll discuss some alternatives later in this chapter.

10 **YOUR FRIENDS.** It's a time-honored tradition—handing down "old" maternity clothes to the newly pregnant. Of course, maternity styles don't change that much from year to year and since outfits aren't worn for a long time, they are usually in great shape. Just be sure to pass on the favor when you are through with your pregnancy.

Parents in Cyberspace: What's on the Web?

Expressiva

Web: www.expressiva.com

What it is: Terrific source for *stylish* nursing clothes.

What's cool: Wow! That's all we could say when we took a look at Expressiva's designs. You really never would know they were nursing clothes. And they don't make you look like a sack of potatoes. Tops, dresses, casual clothes, workout gear, bras and even maternity clothes are available here. Sizes range from extra small to 3X and the site includes hints about sizing for specific outfits. Three styles of nursing openings are available: vertical, crop top and concealed with zippers or snaps underneath a top layer. Prices are reasonable for the quality. If you want to look good and still offer the best first food for your baby, this is a site to check out.

Motherwear

Web: www.motherwear.com
What it is: The online version of the nursing clothes catalog.
What's cool: "This catalog makes the best clothes for nursing!" gushed one mom in an email to us and we have to agree—this is a great catalog and web site. Prices aren't cheap (a long sleeve nightshirt is $38), but the quality is excellent. And they have a clearance section with additional bargains—that aforementioned nightshirt was last seen marked down to $29 (a 20% savings). Don't forget to check their weekly specials as well. A cool feature: want to see what the nursing openings look like on each garment? Just click on the little icon and a window pops open with clear photos of each opening. And Motherwear has a satisfaction guarantee and easy return policy.

eStyle

Web: www.estyle.com
What it is: A "lifestyle" retailer targeting pregnant women and new moms with fashions, tips and information.
What's cool: A fast-loading, color-saturated site with easy navigation, it's easy to see why eStyle is a favorite among new and expecting parents. Not only can you shop for maternity fashions, you'll also find tips, calendars, sizing and style suggestions and more. The brands they feature include Belly Basics, Diane Von Furstenburg, Belly Beautiful, Michael Stars and more. They even have their own in-house brand, BabyStyle as well as Majamas, a terrific line of nursing clothes. All the items we saw were quite stylish.
Needs work: But don't expect cut-rate prices for all that fashion. How 'bout a pair of stretch pants for $72? If you really want to buy something here, check for their specials and deals. And their BabyStyle in house brand is a bit less expensive than the name brand items.

◆ **Other sites:** While most towns only have a handful of maternity stores, the web is teeming with possibilities. **Anna Cris Maternity** (www.annacris.com) sells their own brand among others.

While most folks know **Gap** as a great place for kids clothes, few realize that Gap also does maternity. While most moms will only be able to find Gap Maternity online (www.gap.com), some BabyGap

Figure 1: Gap Maternity's web site lets you return items bought online to Gap stores.

maternity

bricks and mortar stores will begin to offer maternity instore as well. You'll find classics like cardigans and jeans as well as stretch silk shirts, capri pants and more. Check frequently for sale items—they seem to offer more sales than most maternity retailers. Readers have been impressed with the quality of Gap maternity, according to our email. Old Navy, Gap's low price sister chain is also selling maternity on line (www.oldnavy.com). As with other Old Navy clothes, the quality is a bit less but the so are the prices.

Recommended by a reader, **Little Koala** (www.littlekoala.com) sells a decent selection of maternity clothes including undergarments, plus infant clothes, diaper bags and carries/slings.

Maternity 4 Less (www.maternity4less.com) received yet another reader recommendation, this time for speedy delivery. Our reader reported that they exchanged a pair of maternity pants for her in only a matter of days, not the usual weeks other mail order sources take. They carry the gamut of maternity and nursing clothes and accessories. They also have a section of the site for plus sizes.

For a wide range of styles and sizes (up to 3X plus talls and petites), check out **Mom Shop** (www.momshop.com). With great full size photos and an easy to use site, we think MomShop.com is a top site.

Nursing clothes are where **One Hot Mama** (www.onehotmama.com) got their start, but they have expanded into maternity clothes as well. Either way, they attempt to showcase hip styles from manufacturers like Japanese Weekend. Just don't read the long-winded sermons on nursing from the site's owners.

For our Canadian readers, check out **Thyme Maternity** (www.thymematernity.com), recommended by a reader in Ontario. She thought the styles were more "real world," the sizing was great and prices were reasonable. They no longer offer mail order, but their web site has a directory of stores in Canada.

We could go on and on with all these maternity/nursing web sites, but let's condense it a bit for you. The following are yet more options to check out for maternity and nursing clothing:

Birth and Baby	birthandbaby.com
Mommy Gear	mommygear.com
Fit Maternity	fitmaternity.com
Just Babies	justbabies.com
Lattesa	attesa.com
Liz Lange Maternity	lizlange.com
Mothers In Motion	mothers-in-motion.com
Naissance Maternity	naissancematernity.com
Pumpkin Maternity	pumpkinmaternity.com
Style Maternity	stylematernity.com
Twinkle Little Star	twinklelittlestar.com

What Are You Buying?

What will you need when you get pregnant? There is no shortage of advice on this topic, especially from the folks trying to sell you stuff. But here's what real moms advise you to buy (divided into two topic areas, maternity clothes and then nursing clothes):

Maternity Clothes

◆ **Maternity Bras.** Maternity bras are available just about everywhere, from specialty maternity shops to department stores, mail order catalogs and discount chains. More on this topic later in this chapter, under our recommendations for maternity underwear.

HOW MANY? Two in each size as your bust line expands. I found that I went through three different sizes during my pregnancy, and buying two in each size allowed me to wear one while the other was washed.

◆ **Sleep Bras.** What do you need a bra to sleep in for, you ask? Well, some women find it more comfortable to have a little support at night as their breasts change. Toward the end of pregnancy, some women also start to leak breast milk (to be technical, this is actually colostrum). And once the baby arrives, a sleeping bra (cost, about $10) will keep those breast pads in place at night (to keep you from leaking when you inadvertently roll onto your stomach—yes, there will come a day when you can do that again). Some women just need light support, while others find a full-featured bra a necessity.

HOW MANY? Two sleep bras—one to wear while one is in the wash.

♦ **Underpants.** There are two schools of thought when it comes to underpants. Traditional maternity underwear goes over your tummy, while bikini-style briefs are worn under the belly. Some women like the traditional maternity briefs, while others find bikini-style underwear more comfortable. Whichever style you choose, be sure to look for all-cotton fabric, wide waistbands and good construction—repeated washings take their toll on cheap undies. See "Our Picks: Brand Recommendations" later in this section for the best bets.

HOW MANY? I don't like to do lots of laundry, so I bought eight pairs. Since you may be wearing them even after your baby is born for a few weeks, get some that will last.

♦ **Maternity belts and support items.** Pregnancy support belts can be critical for some moms. For example, Pam Anderson, one of our readers sent the following email when she was 7 1/2 months along:

"Last week I got the worst pain/cramp that I have ever had in my life. It kept coming and going while I was walking, but it was so bad that I doubled over in pain when it hit. I went to my doctor and she said that the baby was pushing on a ligament that goes between the abdomen and the leg. She recommended that I get

Plus-size Maternity Clothing

What's the number one frustration with maternity wear? Finding decent plus-size maternity clothes, say our readers. Some maternity clothing manufacturers think only women with bodies like Cindy Crawford get pregnant. But what to do if you want to look attractive and your dress size starts at 16 or above? Our readers have recommended the following sites:

Baby Becoming	babybecoming.com
JCPenney	jcpenney.com
Maternal Instinct	maternal-instinct.com
MomShop	momshop.com
Motherhood	maternitymall.com
One Hot Mama	onehotmama.com
Plus Maternity	plusmaternity.com

a "Prenatal Cradle" from www.aboutbabiesinc.com. I'll tell you what it is the most wonderful purchase I have ever made in my life. It was about $50, but it works wonders. It does not totally eliminate the pain, but it gives enough support that it drastically reduces the pain and even gives me time to change positions so that it does not get worse. I have even found that wearing it at night helps to elevate the pain at night rolling over in bed."

Your best bet, if you find you need some support, is to check with your doctor as Pam did. Many of these belts are available on general web sites like www.OneStepAhead.com and www.BabyCatalog.com.

HOW MANY? Kind of obvious, but one should be enough. And most likely you'll need this late in your pregnancy unless you are carrying multiples.

◆ **Career Clothing.** Our best advice about career clothing for the pregnant mom is to stick with basics. Buy yourself a coordinat-

---

News from Down Under: Maternity Bras for the Real World

What makes a great maternity bra? Consider the following points while shopping:

◆ *Support—part I.* How much support do you need? Some women we interviewed liked the heavy-duty construction of some maternity bras. For others, that was overkill.

◆ *Support—part II* Once you decide how much support you need, consider the *type* of support you like. The basic choices: under wire bras versus those that use fabric bands and panels. Some moms-to-be liked stretchy knit fabric while others preferred stiffer, woven fabric.

◆ *Appearance*. Let's be honest: some maternity bras can be darn ugly. And what about the bras that claim they'll grow with you during your pregnancy? Forget it—expect to go through several sizes as the months roll along.

◆ *Price*. Yes, the best maternity bras can be pricey. But I've found it doesn't pay to scrimp on underwear like bras and panties. Save money on other items in your maternity wardrobe and invest in comfortable undergarments.

---

ing outfit with a skirt, jacket, and pair of pants and then accessorize.

Now, we know what you're saying. You'd love to follow this advice, but you don't want to wear the same old thing several times a week—even if it is beautifully accessorized. I don't blame you. So, go for a couple dresses and sweaters too. The good news is you don't have to pay full price. We've got several money-saving tips and even an outlet or two coming up later in this chapter.

At some point, you'll notice that regular clothes just don't fit well, and the maternity buying will begin. When this occurs is different for every woman. Some moms-to-be begin to show as early as three months, while others can wait it out until as late as six months. But don't wait until you begin to look like a sausage to shop around. It's always best to scope out the bargains early, so you won't be tempted to buy outfits (out of desperation) at the convenient—and high-priced—specialty store.

By the way, thanks to the casual trend of office wear, pregnant woman can spend hundreds of dollars LESS than they might have had to five or ten years ago. Today, you can pair a knit skirt with a sweater set for the office. Gone are the days of the power suit, thank goodness.

♦ **Casual Clothes.** Your best bet here is to stick with knit leggings or sweat pants and big tops. You don't necessarily have to buy these from maternity stores. In fact, later in this chapter, we'll talk about less-expensive alternatives. If you're pregnant in the summer, dresses can be a cooler alternative to pants and shorts.

♦ **Dress or Formal Clothes.** Forget them unless you have a full social calendar or have many social engagements associated with your job. Sometimes, you can find a local store that rents maternity formalwear for the one or two occasions when you might need it.

Nursing Clothes

♦ **Nursing Bras.** The one piece of advice every nursing mom gives is: buy a well-made, high quality nursing bra *that fits you*. Easier said than done you say? Maybe. But here are some tips we gleaned from a reader poll we took.

First, what's the difference between a nursing bra and a maternity bra? Nursing bras have special flaps that fold down to give baby easy access to the breast. Access is usually with a hook or snaps either in the middle or on top of the bra near the straps. Readers insist new moms look for the easiest access they can find. You'll need to be able to open your nursing bra quickly with only one hand in most cases.

Next, avoid under wire bras at all cost. They can cause plugged ducts, a very painful condition. If you sport a large cup size, you'll need a bra that is ultra supportive. Check out Motherhood Maternity bras. Some of our readers told us they have a good selection of large cup sizes. And in most cases, nursing moms require a sleep bra too—some for support, some just to hold nursing pads.

Mothers who had a locally owned maternity shop or specialized lingerie store recommended going in and having a nursing bra fitted to you. One reader reported that "I was wearing a bra at least three cup sizes too small. The consultant fitted me properly and I couldn't believe how comfortable I was!" If you don't have the luxury of a shop full of specialists, the folks at Bravado (www.bravado-designs.com), Motherwear (www.motherwear.com) and Breast is Best (www.breastisbest.com) have terrific online consultants.

If you plan to nurse, you should probably buy at least two bras during your eighth month (they cost about $35 to $40 each). Why then? Theoretically, your breast size won't change much once your baby is born and your milk comes in. I'd suggest buying one with a little larger cup size (than your eighth month size) so you can compensate for the engorgement phase. You can always buy more later and, if your size changes once the baby is born, you won't have invested too much in the wrong size. If you want more advice on nursing bras, you can call **Playtex** (800-537-9955) for a free guide or check out their cool web site at www. playtex.com. Click on the apparel section, then "Products," and finally "Expectant Moment." You'll find info on bras and you can go to the "Fit" section for advice on sizing.

HOW MANY? Buy two to three bras in your eighth month. After the baby is born, you may want to buy a couple more.

◆ **Nursing Pads.** Readers in our last edition complained that we gave nursing pads short shrift. After all, just about every nursing mom will need some at least at the beginning. So here we are to make up for our past omission! There are two options with nursing pads: disposable and reusable. Common sense tells you that reusable breast pads make the most economical sense, particularly if you plan to have more children. Still, if you aren't a big leaker, don't plan to breast feed for long or just need something quick and easy when you're on the go, disposables are also a consideration.

When we polled our readers, we were surprised to learn that the majority preferred disposables. Those by Lansinoh (www.lansinoh.com; $9 for 60 at www.drugstore.com) were by far the favorite followed by Johnson and Johnson ($4 per 60), Gerber and Curity. What's the secret to these disposables? The same type of super absorbent polymer that makes your baby's diapers so absorbent. That makes them super thin too so you aren't embarrassed by tell tale "bulls-eyes" in your bra. Moms also love the individually wrapped pads because they can just grab a couple and throw them in the diaper bag on the way out of the house. Interestingly, moms were divided on whether they like contoured or flat pads or those with adhesive strips or without.

While there wasn't one discount source mentioned for disposable breast pads, moms told us when they saw their favorite brands on sale at Wal-Mart, Target or Babies R Us, they snapped up multiple boxes.

For the minority who preferred reusable, washable pads, Medela ($20 for four pair), Avent ($7 for three pair) and Gerber made the top of the list. Some moms recommend Bravado's (bravadodesigns.com) Cool Max pads ($16 for five pair) for superior absorption. Finally, a few parents have raved about Danish Wool pads (danishwool.com). These soft, felted pads contain natural lanolin, a godsend for moms with sore, cracked nipples. They aren't cheap ($12.50 to $22.50 per pair) but we thought them worth the mention.

◆ **Nursing Clothes.** You may not think so (especially at 8 1/2 months), but there will come a day when you won't need to wear those maternity clothes. But what if you want to nurse in public after baby is born? Many women swear by nursing clothes as the best way to be discreet, but others do just fine with loose knit tops and button front shirts. Bottom line: one obvious way to save money with nursing clothes is not to buy any. If you want to experiment, buy one or two nursing tops and see how they work for you. By the way, parents of twins found it difficult if not impossible to use a nursing top when nursing both babies at the same time. See the following box for more reader feedback on nursing clothes.

◆ **Nursing Pajamas.** Looking for something comfortable to sleep in that allows you to nurse easily? Check out *Majamas* (www.majamas.com). One of our product testers tried out their cotton/lycra t-shirt with her newborn and thought it was great, worthy of a recommendation. It allowed her to sleep without wearing a nursing bra since it had pockets for holding breast pads and had easy nursing access. Most moms, however, hated nursing gowns and found it much simpler to sleep in pajamas with tops they could pull up or unbutton quickly.

 More Money Buys You . . .

Like any clothing, the more you spend, the better quality fabric

MATERNITY NURSING

Reader Poll: Nursing clothes brands

When we polled our readers about nursing clothes we were immediately chastised by at least half the respondents for even considering recommending them. "A waste of money," "ugly!" and "useless" were a few of the more charitable comments from these readers. As many as one third had never even used a single nursing top. They preferred to wear button up shirts or t-shirts and loose tops that they just pulled up. One mom told us "I got pretty good at being discreet in public with my regular clothes and no one was the wiser."

But other moms loved nursing clothes. And their favorites were those from *Motherwear*, the catalog and Internet site we reviewed earlier in this chapter. In our poll over 100 respondents mentioned Motherwear as the best source for well-made, comfortable nursing clothes. The next closest company was *One Hot Mama* (www.onehotmama.com) with only 17 votes. The biggest complaint about Motherwear was that their clothes are expensive. Readers suggested checking out the clearance section, visiting their outlet (in Massachusetts), and buying them used from ebay.com. The site offers a discount for parents of multiples too.

Other sites recommended by parents included *Expressiva* (www.expressiva.com), *Birth and Baby* (www.birthandbaby.com) and *Breast Feeding Styles* (www.breastfeedingstyles.com). Breast Feeding Styles received special mention for their easy to use zippered openings.

Regardless of where nursing clothes were purchased, moms were universal in thinking that the best tops have two vertical openings over the breasts. Forget the single center opening! And no buttons either. Too hard, our moms said, to open with one hand while baby is screaming in your ear. Twin sets and cardigan sweaters were the preferred styles. Readers thought they looked least like nursing clothes. And lots of moms thought just having a few nursing camisoles and t-shirts to wear under a regular shirt was the way to go. Finally, several parents recommended the Super Secret Nursing Shirt from One Hot Mama. Maybe the one shirt you might want to invest in according those moms.

Want to make your own nursing clothes? Creative sewers will find great patterns on *Elizabeth Lee's* web site (www.elizabethlee.com) as well as *Mother Nurture* (www.mothernuture.com).

and construction you get. Of course, do you really need a cashmere maternity outfit you'll wear for only a few months? Besides fabric, you'll note more designer names as prices go up. For example, Lilly Pulitzer, Nicole Miller and Vivian Tam are making maternity clothes now. You can even buy maternity clothes from Laura Sara M, the designer for Hollywood stars.

 Smart Shopper Tips

Smart Shopper Tip #1
Battling your wacky thermostat

"It's early in my pregnancy, and I'm finding that the polyester-blend blouses that I wear to work have become very uncomfortable. I'm starting to shop for maternity clothes—what should I look for that will be more comfortable?"

It's a fact of life for us pregnant folks—your body's thermostat has gone berserk. Thanks to those pregnancy hormones, it may be hard to regulate your body's temperature. And those polyester-blend clothes may not be so comfortable anymore.

Our advice: stick with natural fabrics as much as possible, especially cotton. Unfortunately, a lot of lower-priced maternity clothing is made of polyester/cotton blend fabrics. To make matters worse, you may also find that your feet swell and are uncomfortable as your pregnancy progresses. As a result, wear comfortable shoes that have low heels for maximum comfort.

Smart Shopper Tip #2
Seasons change

"Help! My baby is due in October, but I still need maternity clothes for the hot summer months! How can I buy my maternity wardrobe without investing a fortune?"

Unless you live in a place with endless summer, most women have to buy maternity clothes that will span both warm and cold seasons. The best bets are items that work in BOTH winter or summer—for example, lightweight long-sleeve shirts can be rolled up in the summer. Leggings can work in both spring and fall. Another tip: layer clothes to ward off cold. Of course, there's another obvious way to save: borrow items from friends. If you just need a few items to bridge the seasons (a coat, heavy sweater, etc), try to borrow before buying.

Our Picks: Brand Recommendations for Maternity Undergarments

Thank goodness for e-mail. Here at the home office in Boulder, CO our e-mail (authors@BabyBargainsBook.com) has overflowed with great suggestions from readers on maternity undergarments.

God bless Canada—those Maple Leaf-heads make one of the best maternity bras in the world. Toronto-based *Bravado Designs* (for a brochure, call 800-590-7802 or 416-466-8652; web: www. bravadodesigns.com) makes a maternity/nursing bra of the same name that's just incredible. "A godsend!" raved one reader. "It's built like a sports bra with no under wire and supports better than any other bra I've tried . . . and this is my third pregnancy!" raved another. The Bravado bra comes in three support levels, sizes up to 42-46 with an F-G cup and a couple of wonderful colors/patterns (you can also call them for custom sizing information). Available via mail order, the bra costs $32 U.S. (or $33.50 Canadian). Another plus: the Bravado salespeople are knowledgeable and quite helpful with sizing questions. Some of our readers have criticized the Bravado for not providing enough support, especially in the largest sizes. If you have doubts, just try one at first and see if it works for you before investing in several. Our readers have noticed great prices on Bravado Bras at www.sierrablue.com ($28.80 including shipping and free breast pads) as well as on www.WearstheBaby.com ($29 including shipping).

Playtex Expectant Moments was mentioned by our readers as a good choice as well. And they offer sizing advice on their web site at www.playtex.com. You'll find these bras at stores like JCPenney. Medela, as you'd imagine, also has a good following for their bras. Available in a couple styles with a choice of thin or thick straps, they cost about $32.

Finally, one reader recommended a nursing bra she found on line at *iMaternity.com* for those with larger bra sizes:

"As a 36 H the Bravado Bra just didn't do much to stop inertia from taking over! I have to recommend instead a bra found at ima-ternity.com. On the site it is called the Cotton Under wire Nursing Bra, but the label reads Leading Lady Style #488. It comes in sizes up to or past H and does wonders for me! Just wanted to try to spare someone else the hassle of ordering so many bras at 30$ each in order to find one that gets the job done. " Leading Lady bras are available in many department stores at maternity outlets. Their web site is www.leadinglady.com and they manufacturer quite a wide assortment of bras is a huge range of sizes.

No Nonsense's web site (www.nonnonsense.com) is a great source for affordable maternity hose. For hose, five colors are offered and they cost $15 for a three pair pack. The website offers a frequent buyer club as well: when you buy six packs on line you get the seventh free and if you spend more than $20, the shipping is free as well. The only pain: you have to use the search function to find maternity. They are called out in any the lists under size, style, occasion or color.

Looking for maternity shorts/tights for working out? One of the best is *Fit Maternity* (www.fitmaternity.com; 530-938-4530). They offer an unbelievable assortment of workout clothes including uni-tards, tights, swimsuits and more. Also check out their books and work out tapes. On the same subject, the catalog *Title Nine Sports* (510) 655-5999 offers a few items. Pants are $58 and have a belly-band for extra support. The catalog also carries shorts and sports bras, which some women find is a more comfortable alternative to maternity bras. Another site, Raising a Racquet (www.raisingarac-quet.com) has active ware for pregnant moms as well.

What about underpants? The best I wore were *Japanese Weekend* (800) 808-0555 (web: www.japaneseweekend.com), a brand available in stores and via mail order (see review later in this chapter). Their "OK" bikini-style underwear boasts 100% thick cotton fabric and an extra-wide waistband that cradles your belly. Although they aren't cheap (three for $30), I found them incredibly comfortable *and* durable, standing up to repeated washings better than other brands. The company also carries tights and nursing bras. Other moms swear by their regular panties and don't see a need to get anything special or new for maternity. You'll find that it's easy to wear bikini underpants below your belly. Other moms have recommended brands from Target, Wal-Mart and Kmart. Since you're only wearing these for a rather short period of time, it might not make sense to spend loads of money on special maternity panties.

Our Picks: Brand Recommendations for Nursing Bras, Pads and Clothes

Nursing pads are a passionate topic for many of our readers with disposables beating out reusables as moms' favorites. They loved both *Lansinoh* and *Johnson & Johnson* disposable by an overwhelming number. *Medela*, *Advent* and *Bravado* make great reusable nursing pads.

Bravado is also quite popular as a nursing bra for all but the largest of cup sizes as are *Playtex* and *Medela*. If you need a size larger than DD, consider *Motherhood Maternity's* brand as well as *Leading Lady*. The web is the best place to find bras on deal including *Boe Baby Biz* (www.boebabybiz.com), *Decent Exposures* (www.decentexposures.com) and *Birth and Baby* (www.birthandbaby.com).

Most moms found that specialized nursing clothes weren't a necessity, but for those who want to try them, nearly everyone recommended *Motherwear* (www.motherwear.com). **One Hot Mama** (www.onehotmama.com) and *Expressiva* (www.expressiva.com) were other stylish sites to consider. Look for discounts on clearance pages or eBay.com.

Wastes of Money

Waste of Money #1
Maternity Bra Blues

"My old bras are getting very tight. I recently went to my local department store to check out larger sizes. The salesperson suggested I purchase a maternity bra because it would offer more comfort and support. Should I buy a regular bra in a larger size or plunk down the extra money for a maternity bra?

We've heard from quite a few readers who've complained that expensive maternity bras they've bought were very uncomfortable and/or fell apart after just a few washings. Our best advice: try on the bra before purchase and stick to the better brands. Compared to regular bras, the best maternity bras have thicker straps, more give on the sides and more hook and eye closures in back (so the bra can grow with you). Most of all, the bra should be comfortable and have no scratchy lace or detailing. I've had luck with the Bravado bra, mentioned earlier in this chapter. Readers tell us that a good sports bra can also be a fine alternative.

Waste of Money #2
Orange You Going to Wear Hose?

"Have you seen the horrendous colors available in maternity hose? I can't wear those orange things to work!"

Don't. You don't have to buy ugly maternity hose—those thick, itchy horrors only sold in four shades of orange (Ugly, Sheer Ugly, Super-Duper Ugly, and Son of Ugly). Maternity hose must have been invented by a third world country looking for a new torture device; they take their rightful place next to the bridesmaid's dress as one of the most dreaded apparel items for women.

No Nonsense (www. nononsense.com) sells a pack of three maternity hose (in five colors) for $15. They have a frequent buyer club and offer free shipping if you spend more than $10. If you'd prefer a fancier brand, we found Hue (made by Leslie Fay Co.; call 212-947-3666 for a store near you) comes in several attractive colors and retails for about $10 a pair.

What about large-size panty hose? A mother-to-be in Georgia e-mailed us a recommendation for *"Just My Size."* This special line for larger-size woman is manufactured by L'eggs and sold for half the price of "official preggo" pantyhose, she said.

Of course, there is another solution to the maternity hose dilemma: don't buy them. With a few modifications, you may be able to wear regular hose during *most* your pregnancy. Try rolling the waistband down under your tummy. It works, believe me. When I was six months pregnant and invited to a formal occasion, I wore regular hose in that manner and had no problem. Or you may find that cutting the waistband of your hose gives you some breathing room for a few months. If you wear only long skirts and dresses, knee-hi hose are an option; no one will know you're not wearing full hose. Some women swear by self-supporting thigh-high stockings, the kind with rubber-like grippers around the bands. While a few pregnant moms find them uncomfortable (check with your doctor if you have concerns about blood circulation in your legs), this tip worked for others we interviewed.

Waste of Money #3
Over the Shoulder Tummy Holder

"I keep seeing those 'belly bras' advertised as the best option for a pregnant mom. What are they for and are they worth buying?"

Belly bras provide additional support for your back during your pregnancy. One style envelopes your whole torso and looks like a tight-fitting tank top. No one can argue that, in many cases, the strain of carrying a baby (and the additional weight) is tough even on women in great physical shape. So, if you find your back, hips, and/or legs are giving you trouble, consider buying a belly bra.

However, in our research, we noticed most moms don't seem to need or want a belly bra. The price for one of these puppies can range from $35 to an incredible $55. The bottom line: hold off buying a belly bra or support panty until you see how your body reacts to your pregnancy. Also, check with your doctor to see if she has any suggestions for back, hip, and leg problems.

Waste of Money #4
Overexposed Nursing Gowns/Tops

"I refuse to buy those awful nursing tops! Not only are they ugly, but those weird looking panels are like wearing a neon sign that says 'BREASTFEEDING MOM AHEAD'!"

"I plan to nurse my baby and all my friends say I should buy nursing gowns for night feedings. Problem is, I've tried on a few and even though the slits are hidden, I still feel exposed. Not to mention they're the ugliest things I've ever seen. Can't I just wear a regular gown that buttons down the front?"

Of course you can. And considering how expensive some nursing gowns can be ($35 to $50 each), buying a regular button-up nightshirt or gown will certainly save you a few bucks. Every mother we interviewed about nursing gowns had the same complaint. There isn't a delicate way to put this: it's not easy to get a breast out of one of those teenie-weenie slits. Did the person who designed these ever breastfeed a baby? I always felt uncovered whenever I wore a nursing gown, like one gust of wind would have turned me into a centerfold for a nudist magazine.

And can we talk about nursing shirts with those "convenient button flaps for discreet breastfeeding"? Convenient, my fanny. There's so much work involved in lifting the flap up, unbuttoning it, and getting your baby positioned that you might as well forget it. My advice: stick with shirts you can pull up or unbutton down the front. These are just as discreet, easier to work with, and (best of all) you don't have to add some expensive nursing shirts (at $30 to $50 each) to your wardrobe. See box earlier for more feedback from real moms.

Another tip: if possible, try on any nursing clothing BEFORE you buy. See how easy they are to use. You might be surprised how easy (or difficult) an item can be. Imagine as you are doing this that you have an infant that is screaming his head off wanting to eat NOW, not five seconds from now. You can see why buying any nursing clothes sight unseen is a risk.

Money-Saving Secrets

1 CONSIDER BUYING "PLUS" SIZES FROM A REGULAR STORE.
Thankfully, fashion styles of late include stretch pants and oversized tops and sweaters. This makes pregnancy a lot easier since you can buy the same styles in larger ladies' sizes to cover your belly without compromising your fashion sense or investing in expensive and often shoddily made maternity clothes. We found the same fashions in plus-size stores for 20% to 35% less than maternity shops (and even more during sales).

One drawback to this strategy: by the end of your pregnancy, your hemlines may start to look a little "high-low"—your expanding belly will raise the hemline in front. This may be especially pronounced with skirts and dresses. Of course, that's the advantage of buying maternity clothes: the designers compensate with more fabric in front to balance the hemline. Nonetheless, we found that many moms we interviewed were able to get away with plus-size fashions for much (if not all) of their pregnancy. And how much can you save? We priced a pair of leggings from Mimi Maternity at $58. Meanwhile, we found that Eddie Bauer carries cotton/spandex leggings for only $28—and we'd hardly call Eddie Bauer a discount store. And Eddie Bauer sells leggings through their catalog in petites, talls, extra large, and extra, extra large sizes (see box below). In response, no doubt to the Eddie Bauer option, Mimi Maternity is selling a stripped down version of their leggings also for $28. But we still think the Eddie Bauer brand is better quality. And returns can't be any simpler with Eddie Bauer.

2 Don't over-buy bras. As your pregnancy progresses, your bra size is going to change at least a couple times. Running out to buy five new bras when you hit a new cup size is probably foolish—in another month, all those bras may not fit. The best advice: buy the bare minimum (two or three).

3 But don't skimp on quality when it comes maternity bras and underwear. Take some of the money you save from other parts of this book and invest in good maternity underwear. Yes, you can find cheap underwear for $3 a pair at discount stores, but don't be penny-wise and pound-foolish. We found the cheap stuff is very uncomfortable and falls apart, forcing you to go back and buy more. Investing in better-quality bras and underwear also makes sense if you plan to have more than one child—you can actually wear it again for subsequent pregnancies. Another obvious tip: if you like bikini style underwear, you may not need to buy special "maternity" style undies—just use your regular underwear.

4 Consider Discounters for casual clothes. Okay, I admit that I don't normally shop at K-Mart or Target for my clothes. But I was surprised to discover these chains (and even department stores like Sears) carry casual maternity clothes in 100% cotton at very affordable prices. Let's repeat that—they have 100% cotton t-shirts, shorts, pants, and more at prices you won't believe. Most of these clothes are in basic solid colors—sorry, no fancy prints. At Target, for example, I found a 100% cotton white maternity t-shirt (long sleeves) for $18. Jersey pull-on pants were only $18; jeans were $23. Even a knit skirt was a mere $17. If you buy from one of these discounters, just be sure that you check the fabric and try everything on before you buy. You don't want to have to lug the stuff back to the store. And new this year Target has added apparel from designers like Liz Lange. Our readers say the quality is a bit less than the regular, specialty store version, but the style is good and the prices can't be beat. Don't forget to check Target's sale rack too. One reader found items for as little as $4 on sale.

While the discounters don't carry much in the way of career wear, you'll save so much on casual/weekend clothes that you'll be ecstatic anyway. Witness this example. At A Pea in the Pod, we found a white, cotton-knit top and stretch twill shorts. The price for the two pieces: a heart-stopping $150. A similar all-cotton tank top/shorts outfit from Target was $30. Whip out a calculator, and you'll note the savings is an amazing 80%. Need we say more? Not to mention that nice casual clothes are acceptable for office wear these days anyway.

By the way, don't forget to check out stores like Kohls, Marshall's, Ross and TJ MAXX. One reader told us she found maternity clothes at 60% off from TJMAXX. Old Navy has added maternity to their on line stores and many readers how found great, comfortable clothes at good prices. Corrie, a reader from Chicago, did all her maternity shopping on line at Old Navy. She spent a total of $365 for eight pairs of pants, one pair of jeans, eleven sweaters, eight long sleeve tops, three button-down shirts, five sleeveless tops and two cardigans. She notes that works out to less than $10 per piece!

E-MAIL FROM THE REAL WORLD
Two thumbs up for Eddie Bauer

Annie M. of Brooklyn, NY found great deals at Eddie Bauer on clothes that can work as maternity fashions:

"Eddie Bauer is my salvation. I'd marry the man if I weren't so damn fond of my husband. The XL and XXL leggings are $28 and they last and last. The shirts are all available in petite through XXL sizes, the lengths are good for short or tall people, and they have many styles that are suitable for late in pregnancy without looking 'smocky.' I also know that I'll be able to wear most of the stuff again and again after I have the baby. Eddie Bauer's generously cut sundresses wear wonderfully and are accommodating me beautifully into my sixth month (with lots of room to grow). And another plus: they also have great sales!"

5 **RENT EVENING WEAR—DON'T BUY.** We found that some indie maternity stores rent evening wear. For example, a local shop we visited had an entire rack of rental formalwear. An off-white lace dress (perfect for attending a wedding) rented for just $50. Compare that with the purchase price of $175. Since you most likely would need the dress for a one-time wearing, the savings of renting versus buying would be $125.

6 **CHECK OUT CONSIGNMENT STORES.** You can find "gently worn" career and casual maternity clothes for 40% to 70% off the original retail! Many consignment or second-hand stores carry only designer-label clothing in good to excellent condition. If you don't want to buy used garments, consider recouping some of your investment in maternity clothes by consigning them after the baby is born. You can usually find listings for these stores in the phone book. (Don't forget to look under children's clothes as well. Some consignment stores that carry baby furniture and clothes also have a significant stock of maternity wear.) One web source to find consignment shops is www.narts.org.

7 **FIND AN OUTLET.** Check out the next section of this chapter for the low-down on maternity clothes outlets.

8 **BE CREATIVE.** Raid your husband's closet for over-sized shirts and pants. One mom we interviewed found a creative use for her pre-pregnancy leggings. She simply wore them backwards! The roomier backside gave her space for her expanding tummy.

9 **SEW IT YOURSELF.** A reader in California emailed in this recommendation: she loved the patterns for nursing clothes by Elizabeth Lee Designs (435-454-3350; web: www.elizabethlee. com). "I would think anyone with a bit of sewing experience could handle any of the patterns, which don't LOOK like nursing dresses or tops." Elizabeth Lee has both a catalog and web site; in addition to patterns, they also sell already-made dresses and tops. Another bonus: the company has one of the largest selections of nursing bras we've seen, including Bravado Bras.

10 **BEG AND BORROW.** Unless you're the first of your friends to get pregnant you know someone who's already been through this. Check around to see if you can borrow old maternity clothes from other moms. In fact, we loaned out a big box after our second baby was born and it has made the rounds of the whole neighborhood. And don't forget to be generous after your baby making days are over too.

11 CHECK OUT CLEARANCE AREAS IN CATALOGS AND ON WEB SITES. Many of our most devoted discount shopping readers have scored big deals on their favorite web sites' clearance pages. For example, on Motherwear.com we noticed a "Flyaway Cardigan Dress," regularly marked at $80 but on sale for only $39. Old Navy had some knit Capris marked down $17.50 and the Gap had a stretch hoodie, regularly $48 for only $30.

Outlets

MOTHERHOOD MATERNITY OUTLETS

Locations: 82 outlets (16 are called Maternity Works). For location info, call (800) 466-6223.

The offspring of the catalog and retail stores of maternity giant Motherhood Maternity (see review later in this chapter), Maternity Works outlets have started springing up in outlet malls across the country. On a recent visit, the outlet featured markdowns from 20% to 75% on the same top-quality designs you see in their catalog or retail stores.

MOTHERWEAR

Location: Northampton, MA (413) 586-2175.

The Motherwear catalog has a factory outlet that is open just Wednesday through Saturday. They sell returned merchandise, seconds, overstock and discontinued items. "Great bargains—worth the trip," says a reader who visited the outlet.

The Name Game: Reviews of Selected Maternity Stores

Usually this section is intended to acquaint you with the clothing name brands you'll see in local stores. But now there is only one giant chain of maternity wear in North America. Mothers Work Inc., which operates stores under three brand names and the Internet, is the 800 pound gorilla of maternity clothes with 900 stores in the US, Canada and Puerto Rico. Mothers Work has an almost 40% share of the $1.2 billion maternity clothing market in the US. So let's take a look at these three divisions and their Internet site.

◆ ***Motherhood.*** With 616 stores, Motherhood is the biggest sister in the chain. While most stores are located in malls and power centers, 132 are also leased departments within department stores like Macy's, Rich's, Lazarus and Babies R Us stores. Motherhood carries maternity clothes in the lowest price points. As an example, dresses at Motherhood range from $17 to $69. The also have 92 outlets.

◆ *Mimi Maternity.* Mimi is intended to be the middle price point of the three divisions. This division is supposed to be a more hip, youthful take on maternity. Here you'll find a more fashion forward look with dresses in the $40 to $168 price range.

◆ *A Pea in the Pod.* Finally, A Pea in the Pod (APIP) is Mothers Works' most expensive division. With dress prices ranging from $150 to $450, you can see what we mean. APIP has only 43 stores and is positioned to be more of a designer boutique. Hence you'll find them in locations like Beverly Hills and Madison Ave.

◆ *MaternityMall.com.* This is Mothers Works portal which includes sites for all three chains as well as advice and information for pregnant parents.

All three stores carry mostly merchandise designed in house, exclusively for the different divisions.

Now that you know the basics, what do real moms think of Mothers Works' stores? First and foremost, moms dislike, no, hate their return policy. The policy is pretty basic, once you've bought an item, it is non-refundable, non-returnable. What if it falls apart in the wash? Too bad for you.

As for individual chains, most moms agreed that the quality at Motherhood is poor. Although some readers have praised their maternity and nursing bras, in general, most agree with the following: "I have found the quality to be inconsistent. I've bought shirts that have unraveled within a few months. . . trashy!" The consensus seems to be that if you buy at Motherhood, you should stick to the sale rack and don't expect high quality except for their bras.

Mimi Maternity received better marks from our readers for their clothes. Prices are higher than at Motherhood, but so is the quality. We've received fewer complaints about this division. And many moms liked the more stylish clothing. They sell the Olga line of bras, which many readers liked as well.

A Pea in the Pod is just way too expensive. That's the general feeling among our readers about this store. Most moms don't feel the style of clothing at this chain is anything special. Certainly not to spend $90 for a cotton t-shirt. Considering how short a time a pregnancy is, it's a huge waste of money to spend over $150 on a

Pea in the Pod shorts outfit. And what about their "legendary" service, as Pea in the Pod likes to tout? It's a joke, say our readers. One mom summed it up best by saying: "For the price that one is paying, one expects a certain degree of customer service and satisfaction, both of which are lacking in this over-priced store. What a complete and utter disappointment!"

Do it By Mail

HANNAH ANDERSSON

To Order Call: (800) 222-0544; Fax (503) 321-5289.
Shopping Hours: 5 am to 9 pm Pacific Time, seven days a week.
Or write to: 1010 NW Flanders, Portland, OR, 97209.
Web: www.hannaandersson.com
Credit Cards Accepted: MC, VISA, AMEX, Discover.
Retail Stores: 125 Westchester Ave., Suite 3370, White Plains, NY 10601;
(914) 684-2410; 327 NW Tenth Ave., Portland, OR 97209; (503) 321-5275.
Outlets Stores: Lake Oswego, OR (503) 697-1953 ; Michigan City, IN (219)
827-3183; Portsmouth, NH (603) 433-6642; Lakewood, CO (303) 384-0937.

Watch out for return policies!

Have you bought a maternity dress you don't like or that doesn't fit? Too bad—most maternity stores have draconian return policies that essentially say "tough!" Most don't accept returns and others will only offer store credit. A word to the wise: make sure you REALLY like that item (and it fits) before you give any maternity store your money. A reader in Brisbane, California emailed us with the most horrific story we've ever heard about maternity stores' return policies.

"I recently visited a Dan Howard (now owned by Mothers Work) maternity store in San Francisco and was shocked to find their return policy stands even when you haven't left their store yet! They overcharged me for a sale item that was miss marked and then said all they could give me was store credit for the difference! I hadn't stepped one foot outside the store! They refused to credit my charge card, so now I'm stuck with a $65 store credit for a place I despise!"

But has it changed now that Mothers Work has taken over? Our readers say absolutely not! Now all three divisions of the chain share their appalling return/refund policies.

Hanna Andersson has always made comfortable knit clothes for women along with her famous kids designs, but now she's added maternity to the mix. All they're offering at this time are "basics" basically in black. A couple pants options, a dress, two tops and a cardigan round out the line. All cotton t-shirts, for example, run $28. The casual look is appealing, but the lack of color and limited options may send pregnant moms to other catalogs and sites.

JCPenney

To Order Call: (800) 222-6161. Ask for "Maternity Collection" catalog.
Web: www.JCPenney.com/shopping
Shopping Hours: 24 hours a day, seven days a week.
Credit Cards Accepted: MC, VISA, JCPenney, AMEX, Discover.

Perhaps the best aspect of Penney's maternity offerings is their wide range of sizes—you can find petites, talls, ultra-talls and women's sizes. It's darn near impossible to find women's sizes in maternity wear today, but Penney's carries sizes up to 32W.

What most impressed us about Penney's maternity catalog was

Japanese Weekend: Comfort, at a price

Japanese Weekend (JW) is a line of maternity clothing that emphasizes comfort. They are best known for their unusual "OK" belly-banded pants, which have a waistband that circles *under* your expanding tummy for support (rather than cutting across it). In recent years, JW has expanded its line beyond pants to include jumpers, tops, cat suits, nightgowns, and skirts. We really like the simple, comfortable style of the clothes and highly recommend them. For once, a company has created all-cotton clothing for moms-to-be, avoiding the all too common polyester blends. One nice plus: JW will send you a list of stores that carry their clothes (call the above number for more information). In addition, the designer has a company store in San Francisco (415-989-6667). As for JW's web site, they don't seem very committed to making it work. We've received complaints from readers about their customer service. The good news is you can find their clothes at quite a few outlets including on the 'Net. Prices are expensive, but we've seen them discounted occasionally. *To find a store near you that carries this brand of clothing, call (800) 808-0555, (415) 621-0555, or write to 22 Isis St., San Francisco, CA 94103. You can also ask for a catalog. Web: www.japaneseweekend.com*

their career clothes. For example, we saw a "three-piece wardrobe" suit (v-neck top with gold accents, matching skirt and pants) for just $50 to $60. This polyester outfit was available in every conceivable size. Another standout: Penney's "5-piece Wardrobe Set," a complete wardrobe of five pieces (shorts, long sleeve shirt, skirt, t-shirt

E-MAIL FROM THE REAL WORLD
Stay fit with pregnancy workout videos

Margaret Griffin e-mailed us with her opinions of several popular workout videos tailored for the pregnant woman. Here are her thoughts:

"As a former certified aerobics instructor, I have been trying out the video workouts for pregnancy. I have only found three videos available in my local stores, but I wanted to rate them for your readers.

"Buns of Steel 8 Pregnancy Workout with Madeleine Lewis ($20) gets my top rating. Madeleine Lewis has excellent cueing, so the workout is easy to follow. Your heart rate and perceived exertion are both used to monitor your exertion. There is an informative introduction. And I really like the fact that the toning segment utilizes a chair to help you keep your balance, which can be off a little during pregnancy. Most of the toning segment is done standing. This is a safe, effective work-

out led by a very capable instructor and I highly recommend it." The average customer review on Amazon.com: 4 1/2 stars out of 5.

"A middle rating goes to Denise Austin's Pregnancy Plus Workout ($15). Denise has a good information segment during which she actually interviews a physician. She also provides heart rate checks during the workout. However, there are a couple of things about this workout that I don't particularly like. First, during the workout, there are times when safety information is provided regarding a particular move. This is fine and good, but instead of telling you to continue the movement and/or providing a picture-in-a-picture format, they actually change the screen to show the safety information and then cut back into the workout in progress. Surprise! You were supposed to keep doing the movement. Second, Denise Austin is a popular instructor, but I personally find that her cueing is not as sharp as I prefer and sometimes she seems to be a little offbeat with the music. My suggestion is get this video to use in addition to other videos if you are the type who gets easily bored with one workout."

"The video I recommend that you skip altogether is the Redbook and leggings) in cotton/lycra spandex for $70 to $80.

While most of the career wear is blends of rayon and polyester, Penney's casual maternity clothes feature more all-cotton fabrics. We saw a wide array of affordably priced cotton maternity shirts and jeans, as well as denim dresses and jumpers. A selection of

Pregnancy Workout led by Diane Gausepohl. I have nothing positive to say regarding this workout. I did the workout once and immediately retired the tape. The instructor has poor cueing skills and does not keep time with the music well at all. This makes the workout hard to follow. My husband was actually laughing at the instruction, it was so poor. I also don't like the fact that it includes toning exercises that can be done (and are demonstrated) lying on your back. We all know that by the fifth month of pregnancy, the weight of the uterus can restrict the blood flow in the inferior vena cava, so you should not lie flat on your back. Even though these exercises can be modified I think it is better to avoid the temptation altogether. There are plenty of other toning exercises that are effective that do not require you to lie on your back at all. My advice is to skip this video altogether." The average customer review on Amazon.com: 1 1/2 stars.

Yoga is a terrific low impact exercise that does a wonderful job of stretching muscles you'll use while carrying and delivering your child, it's a terrific option for pregnant moms. And it's definitely become one of the most popular exercise options in North America. So it was only a matter of time before our readers began reviewing yoga tapes. Here are some of their comments:

Sheri Gomez, recommended Yoga Zone's video Postures for Pregnancy ($20), calling it "wonderful for stretching and preventing back problems. It's beginner friendly and not too out there with the yoga thing." Her only complaint: there is no accompanying music, so she played her own CDs along with the tape.

Eufemia Camapagna recommended Yoga Journal's Prenatal Yoga with Shiva Rea $20). She noted that each segment of the tape is done using three women different stages of pregnancy. "The segments are all accompanied by lovely, relaxing music and the instructor's directions are so clear that you don't even have to look at the TV to know what you need to do!" Another reader, Carolyn Oliner, also complimented this tape: "It's not so much of a traditional yoga workout but a great  series of poses and stretches that work for pregnant women and leave you feeling warm and stretched and (more gently) exercised."

Note: Amazon.com is a great source to find these videos.

nightgowns, swimsuits, nursing shirts and lingerie round out the offerings.

One bargain hint: Penney's has quite a few unadvertised sales and discounts on maternity wear. When placing your order, inquire about any current deals.

LANDS' END

To Order Call: (800) 963-4816,; Fax (800) 332-0103.
Web: www.landsend.com
Shopping Hours: 24 hours a day, seven days a week.
Or write to: 1 Lands' End Ln., Dodgeville, WI 53595.
Credit Cards Accepted: MC, VISA, AMEX, Discover.
Discount Outlets: They also have a dozen or so outlet stores in Iowa, Illinois and Wisconsin—call the number above for the nearest location.

Lands' End purveyor of clothing for middle America, has now made a foray into maternity clothing. With over 40 items in a recent catalog, we think they're making quite an impressive jump into this niche. From pants to tops and sweaters the line is very comprehensive. They've even added swimwear and exercise gear. And don't forget their terrific diaper bags. While the styles aren't exactly cutting edge, you'll find nice, quality basics to fill out your wardrobe. Prices aren't ultra cheap, but they aren't over priced either. And you can always return clothes to your local Sears store instead of having to send them through the mail (Sears bought the company a couple years ago).

Nursing fashions in Canada: The Toronto-based Breast is Best catalog sells a wide variety of nursing tops, blouses and dresses as well as maternity wear. For a free catalog and fabric swatches, call (877) 837-5439 toll free or check out their web site online at www. breastisbest.com.

The Bottom Line:
A Wrap-Up of Our Best Buy Picks

For career and casual maternity clothes, we thought the best deals were from the JCPenney catalog and Motherhood stores (not the other chains like A Pea in a Pod). Compared to retail maternity chains (where one suit can run $200 to $300), you can buy your entire wardrobe from these two places for a song.

If your place of work allows more casual dress, check out the prices at plus size stores. A simple pair of leggings that could cost $45 to $50 at a maternity shop are only $30 or less at "regular" stores. Another good idea: borrow from your husband's closet—shirts, sweat pants and sweatshirts are all items that can do double-duty as maternity clothes.

For weekend wear, we couldn't find a better deal than the 100% cotton shirts and shorts at discounters like Target, Wal-Mart and K-Mart. Prices are as little as $8.98 per shirt—compare that to the $80 price tag at maternity chain stores for a simple cotton shirt.

Invited to a wedding? Rent that dress from a maternity store and save $100 or more. Don't forget to borrow all you can from friends who've already had babies. In fact, if you follow all our tips on maternity wear, bras, and underwear, you'll save $700 or more. Here's the breakdown:

1. Career Wear: $240

JCPenney's maternity catalog features a three-piece "maternity suit" (jacket, skirt and pants) for just $60 to $70. Buy two of these in different colors, add a couple nice dresses (another $120) and you're set.

2. Casual Clothes: $100

Five outfits of 100% cotton t-shirts and shorts/pants from Target or K-Mart run $100. Again, JCPenney's sells a five-piece wardrobe set for only $70 to $80. And they offer a huge range of sizes. Don't forget sale items on Gap Maternity as well as Old Navy's maternity line.

3. Underwear: $200 to $300

We strongly suggest investing in top-quality underwear for comfort and sanity purposes. For example, a Bravado bra is $31 and Japanese Weekend "OK" bikini maternity underwear are three for $26. Some readers have found good deals on affordable underwear at Target or online. Either way, you need eight pairs of maternity underwear, plus six bras, including regular/nursing and sleep bras.

Total damage: $540 to $640. If you think that's too much money for clothes you'll only wear for a few months, consider the cost if you outfit yourself at full-price maternity shops. The same selection of outfits would run $1200 to $1400.

CHAPTER 6
Feeding

Inside this chapter

How much money can you save by breastfeeding? What are the best options for pumps? Which bottles are best? We'll discuss these topics as well as ways to get discount formula, including details on which places have the best deals. And of course, we'll have tips and reviews on the next step in feeding: solid food. Finally, let's talk about high chairs—who's got the best value? Durability? Looks?

Breastfeeding

As readers of past editions of this book know, we are big proponents of breastfeeding. The medical benefits of breast milk are well documented, but we realize the decision to breast or bottle-feed is a personal call for each new mom. In the past, we spent time in this chapter encouraging breast feeding . . . but we realize now we are preaching to the choir on this one. Our time is better spent discussing how to save on feeding your baby, no matter which way you go. So, we'll leave the discussion of breast versus bottle to other books (as well your doctor and family). Let's talk about the monetary impact of the decision, however.

Breastfeed Your Baby and Save $500

Since this is a book on bargains, we'd be remiss in not mentioning the tremendous amount of money you can save if you breastfeed. Just think about it: no bottles, no expensive formula to prepare, no special insulated carriers to keep bottles warm/cold, etc.

So, how much money would you save? Obviously, the biggest money-saver would be not having to buy formula. Even if you were to use the less expensive powder, you would still have to spend nearly $23 per 28.5 ounce can of powdered formula. Since each can makes 209 ounces of formula, the cost per ounce of formula is about 10¢.

That doesn't sound too bad, does it? Unless you factor in that a baby will down 32 ounces of formula per day by 12 weeks of age. Your cost per day would be $3.25. Assuming you breastfeed for the first six months, you would save a grand total of $546 *just on formula alone*. That doesn't include the expense for bottles, nipples and accessories!

To be fair, there are some optional expenses that might go along with breastfeeding. The biggest dollar item: you might decide to buy a breast pump. Costs for this item range from $60 for a manual pump to $300 for a piston electric breast pump. Or you can rent a pump for $50 a month (plus a kit—one time cost of about $40).

If $546 doesn't sound like a lot of money, consider the savings if you had to buy formula in the concentrated liquid form instead of the cheaper powder. A 32-ounce can of Similac ready-to-eat liquid costs about $4.99 at a grocery store and makes up only 4 bottles. The bottom line: you could spend over $700 on formula for your baby in the first six months alone!

Of course, we realize that some moms will decide to use formula because of a personal, medical or work situation—to help out, we have a section later in this chapter on how to save on formula, bottle systems and other necessary accessories.

Sources: Where to Find Breast Feeding Help

The basis of breastfeeding is attachment. Getting your new little one to latch onto your breast properly is not a matter of instinct. Some babies have no trouble figuring it out, while many others need your help and guidance. In fact, problems with attachment can lead to sore nipples and painful engorgement. Of course, you should be able to turn to your pediatrician or the nurses at the hospital for breastfeeding advice. However, if you find that they do not offer you the support you need, consider the following sources for breastfeeding help:

LA LECHE LEAGUE (800) LA LECHE or web: www.laleche-league.org. Started over 35 years ago by a group of moms in Chicago, La Leche League has traditionally been the most vocal supporter of breastfeeding in this country. You've got to imagine the amount of chutzpah these women had to have to buck the bottle trend and promote breastfeeding at a time when it wasn't fashionable (to say the least).

In recent years, La Leche has established branches in many communities, providing support groups for new moms interested in trying to nurse their children. They also offer a catalog full of books and videotapes on nursing, as well as other child care topics. Their famous book *The Womanly Art of Breastfeeding* is the bible for huge numbers of breastfeeding advocates. All in all, La Leche provides an important service and, coupled with their support groups and catalog of publications, is a valuable resource.

2 NURSING MOTHERS' COUNCIL (408) 272-1448, (web: www.nursingmothers.org). Similar in mission to La Leche League, the Nursing Mothers' Council differs on one point: the group emphasizes working moms and their unique needs and problems.

3 LACTATION CONSULTANTS. Lactation consultants are usually nurses who specialize in breastfeeding education and problem solving. You can find them through your pediatrician, hospital, or the International Lactation Consultants Association (703) 560-7330 web: www.iblce.org. Members of this group must pass a written exam, complete 2500 hours of clinical practice and 30 hours of continuing education before they can be certified. At our local hospital, resident lactation consultants are available to answer questions by phone at no charge. If a problem persists, you can set up an in-person consultation for a minimal fee (about $40 to $90 per hour, although your health insurance provider may pick up the tab).

Unfortunately, the availability of lactation consultants seems to vary from region to region. Our research shows that, in general, hospitals in the Western U.S. are more likely to offer support services, such as on-staff lactation consultants. Back East, however, the effort to support breastfeeding seems spotty. Our advice: call area hospitals before you give birth to determine the availability of breastfeeding support.

4 HOSPITALS. Look for a hospital in your area that has breastfeeding-friendly policies. These include 24-hour rooming in (where your baby can stay with you instead of in a nursery) and breastfeeding on demand. Pro-nursing hospitals do not supplement babies with a bottle and don't push free formula samples. Their nurses will also respect your wishes concerning pacifier usage, which is important if you are concerned about nipple confusion.

5 BOOKS. Although they aren't a substitute for support from your doctor, hospital, and family, many books provide plenty of information and encouragement. Check the La Leche League catalog for titles.

6 **THE WEB.** We found several great sites with breastfeeding information and tips. Our favorite was *Medela* (www.medela. com), which is a leading manufacturer of breast pumps. Medela's site features extensive information resources and articles on breast-feeding, as well as advice on how to choose the right breast pump. Of course, you can also get info on Medela's breast pumps and other products, find a dealer near you and more.

The catalog *Bosom Buddies* (www.bosombuddies.com or call 888-860-0041) has a web site with a good selection of breast-feeding articles, product information and links to other breastfeed-ing sites on the web.

Of course, the general parenting sites like BabyCenter.com have numerous message boards dedicated to issues like breast-feeding. Readers also tell us they find the boards on ParentsPlace.com help-ful as well.

7 **YOUR HEALTHCARE PROVIDER.** Contact your healthcare provider as soon as you become pregnant. They often have a variety of services available to policy holders, but you have to ask.

Parents in Cyberspace: What's on the Web?

Medela

Web: www.medela.com

What it is: A treasure trove of info on breastfeeding.

What's cool. Medela's web site is a great example of what makes the 'net so helpful—instead of just a thinly veiled pitch for their products, Medela stuffs their site with reams of useful info, tips and advice. Yeah, you can read about their different breast pumps, but the site is full of general breastfeeding tips, links to other sites and more. "Problems and Solutions" is an excellent FAQ for nursing moms. You'll also find instructions for all their products on line in case you misplace them!

Needs work: Although they've improved the site, you'll find it takes a lot of clicks to get where you want to go. And we'd still like to see approximate retail prices for Medela's products on the site.

MedRino

Web site: www.breastpumps-breastfeeding.com

What it is: A medical supply company with a selection of breast pumps and accessories.

What's cool: What's not? Here's a site with a huge selection of breast pumps from Medela at discount prices. For example, MedRino claims the Pump In Style Professional sells for $309 retail, but they sell it for $238. And when you order the Pump In Style, they give you free 2nd Day Air delivery (free UPS ground for all the other models) plus a free battery pack. Wow! When you pull up a product you're interested in, the site has clear photos, details on the product and a price grid with retail and sale prices. You'll also find breast shells, pads, storage products and more on the site.

Needs work: The site should sell more brands than just Medela. How about Avent and Ameda Egnell as well?

Nursing Mother Supplies

Web: www.nursingmothersupplies.com

What it is: An extensive nursing supply resource.

What's cool: Not only does this site carry breast pumps and supplies from Medela, Avent and Ameda Egnell (among others), they offer support to customers after they buy. Nursing Mothers Supplies has an excellent online FAQ as well as the opportunity to contact a counselor for one-on-one help. Prices are discounted a bit (the Purely Yours was $199, regular retail $249), and they offer free shipping for all orders over $75. A portion of sales goes to UNICEF (nice touch). Nursing pillows, storage options (the Mothers Milk Mate is $25), slings, Avent bottles and pads are also available.

Needs work: Not much to complain about here. The site is a bit primitive in design, but it does the job—loads fast, has a shopping cart feature, clear photos, etc. We also like the gentle approach to encouraging breast feeding. These guys aren't too preachy.

◆ *Other web sites:* Here are a couple sites with names that speak for themselves: *Affordable-medela-pumps.com*, *Affordable-breast-pumps.com* and *Affordablebreastpumps.com*. Readers have mentioned all three as great sites for pumps from Medela, Ameda, Nurture III and Whittlestone to name a few. *Mother's Milk Breastfeeding Supplies* (Mothersmilkbreastfeeding.com) is owned by a neonatal nurse who's been helping moms for over eight years. And a reader, Cherie Kannarr, thought that *BreastFeeding.com* "is a wonderful site, filled with facts, stories, humor, and support for nursing mothers."

What Are You Buying?

For moms interested in breast feeding, most eventually approach the issue of what to do when they can't be available to feed their baby. After all, you might want to go out to dinner. Maybe you'll have an overnight trip for your job or just need to get back to work full or part time. Your spouse might even be interested in relieving you of a night feeding (in your dreams; anything's possible). Whether you want to pump occasionally or every day, you have a wide range of options. Here's our take on them:

◆ **Manual Expression:** OK, technically, this isn't a breast pump in the sense we're talking about. But it is an option. There are several good breastfeeding books that describe how to express milk manually. Most women find that the amount of milk expressed, compared to the time and trouble involved, hardly makes it worth using this method. A few women (we think they are modern miracle workers) can manage to express enough for an occasional bottle; for the majority of women, however, using a breast pump is a more practical alternative.

◆ **Manual Pumps:** Non-electric, hand-held pumps create suction by squeezing on a handle. While they're cheap, manual pumps are generally also the least efficient—you simply can't duplicate your baby's sucking action by hand. Therefore, these pumps are best for moms who only need an occasional bottle or who need to relieve engorgement.

◆ **Mini-Electrics:** I bought one of these, and it was a waste of money. I thought these battery-operated breast pumps would be good for expressing an occasional bottle. Unfortunately, the sucking action is so weak that I quickly discovered it took twenty minutes *per side* to express a significant amount of milk. And doing so was not very comfortable, to say the least. Why is it so slow? Most models only cycle nine to fifteen times per minute—compare that to a baby who sucks the equivalent of 50 cycles per minute!

◆ **Piston Electric Pumps:** The Mercedes of breast pumps—we can't sing the praises of the piston electric pumps enough. In just ten to twenty minutes, you can pump *both* breasts. And piston electric pumps are much more comfortable than mini-electrics. In fact, at first I didn't think the piston electric pump I rented was working well because it was *so* comfortable. The bottom line: there is no better option for a working woman who wants to provide her

	Manual	Mini-Elec.	Piston Elec.	Rental*
BREAST PUMPS — *Which pump works best in which situation?*				
Do you need a pump for:				
A missed feeding?	■	◆		
Evening out from baby?	■	◆		
Working part-time.	■	◆		
Occasional use, a few times a week.	■	◆		
Working full-time.			●	●
Premature or hospitalized baby?			●	●
Low milk supply?			●	●
Sore nipples/engorgement?	■		●	●
Latch-on problems or breast infection?			■	●
Drawing out flat or inverted nipples?	■	◆	●	●

Key: ■ = Good ◆ = Better ● = Best

Rental refers to renting a hospital-grade pump. These can usually be rented on a monthly basis.

Source: Medela.

baby with breast milk.

Today, you have two options when it comes to these pumps: rent a hospital-grade pump or buy a high-end double-pump. As for rental, a wide variety of sources rent breast pumps on a daily, weekly or monthly basis. We called a lactation consultant at a local hospital who gave us a list that included maternity stores, small private companies, and home-care outfits. Another possibility is to call La Leche League (800-LALECHE; web: www.lalecheleague.org) or other lactation support groups for a referral to a company that rents piston electric pumps.

What does it cost to rent a hospital-grade pump? One company we surveyed rented pumps for $60 for one month or $45 per month if you rent for two or more months. In general, we found rental charges ranged from $1 to $3 per day, with the lower rates for longer rentals. You'll also have to buy a kit of the collection bottles, shields, and tubes (this runs about $50 to $60). Prices will vary according to where you live. Medela's Lactina Select (800) 435-8316, White River Concepts Model 9050 (800) 824-6351 and Egnell Elite

(800) 323-8750 are all hospital grade pumps available for rental.

What about buying? Yes, you can buy a piston-electric pump. The two best choices are Medela's "Pump In Style" ($280) and the Ameda Egnell "Purely Yours" ($200, available from the company at 800-323-4060 or from web sites mentioned earlier; web: www.ameda.com). I used the Pump In Style for my second child and was impressed—it's a fully automatic double pump that uses diaphragm action to best simulate a baby's sucking motion. Best of all, it's portable (about seven pounds) and is hidden in an attractive black leather bag for discretion.

Other moms we interviewed complimented the Ameda model, which comes with six storage bottles and carrying case. A reader said she could pump four ounces of milk in about 20 minutes. Fans of the Ameda like its lower price and weight (two pounds vs. the Medela at seven pounds). Another plus for Ameda: it can run on AA batteries; the Medela has that option . . . if you pay another $160 for a rechargeable battery pack!

One reader recommended the Nurture III breast pump available on line at www.baileymed.com. Manufactured by Bailey Medical Engineering, it looks a lot like the Purely Yours. But the price is amazing at $115. Quite a deal for a piston pump. Whittlestone also makes a breast pump, but we've had little to no feedback about this brand at this point.

As we went to press, we noticed Medela had just debuted a new piston electric pump called the Symphony. This new model is supposed to simulate baby's two-phase feeding process and can switch between single and double pumping. Best of all, the Symphony is very quiet and comes with rechargeable batteries. The price? Are you sitting down? It runs $1250 to $1450. We haven't heard any feedback from our readers on this new unit yet; check our message boards (BabyBargainsBook.com) for reader comments.

Introduce the Bottle Early

If you plan to introduce a bottle to your baby so you can go out on the town or back to work, do it around the sixth week of age. Most parenting books tell you about this, but they don't stress how important it is to keep giving a bottle regularly—perhaps two or three feedings per week. In our case, we didn't give a bottle consistently, and by the time our son was about four months old, he absolutely refused to take a bottle at all. Oops! That made going out alone to dinner and a movie a lot tougher. A word to the wise: keep up the occasional bottle.

Safe and Sound

Pop onto eBay (www.eBay.com) and you'll notice quite a few used breast pumps for sale, often for half the original retail—a bargain considering their hefty prices. Yet, major pump makers like Medela warn against using used pumps like the Pump N Style claiming they are a "single owner item" (unlike their rental pumps). So is it kosher to buy a used pump? Of course. Many readers say they've used second-hand pumps without any problem whatsoever. All of the recommended pumps in this chapter can last through more than one mom, if not several moms. Of course, you buy a new collection kit (the tubes and bottles) but a used pump itself is fine, in our opinion.

Some readers of our last edition took issue with us regarding used pumps. Dr. Jane Conley, a board certified pediatrician, had this to say in response: "As you may be aware, breast milk can transmit infections, most notably HIV (AIDS). Mothers who are infected with HIV are advised not to breastfeed their infants for that reason. My lactation consultant tells me that the hospital grade pumps (which she says cost around $1200) are safe for rental because they contain a barrier or filter unit that keeps that pump itself from contacting the actual breast milk. The next user buys her own personal tubing and supplies (as you stated), so there is no infection risk. However, the personal pumps, such

Nursing Extras

The wonder about nursing baby is how simple it can be—the milk is always ready, at the right temperature, etc. Yet, breastfeeding can be made even easier (and more comfortable) with one accessory: the nursing pillow. Our readers have emailed compliments for *My Brest Friend* by Zenoff Products (800-555-5522; web: www. zenoffproducts.com). Okay, it probably qualifies as the Most Stupid Name for a Baby Product Ever award, but it really works—it wraps around your waist and is secured with Velcro. It retails for about $40. Got twins? Check out *EZ-2-NURSE's* pillow (800-584-TWIN; we saw it on www.everythingmom.com). A mom told us this was the "absolute best" for her twins, adding "I could not successfully nurse my girls together without this pillow. It was wonderful." Cost: $56.

Another idea: Wal-Mart has a breastfeeding collection with *Lansinoh* products (including their amazing nipple cream and breast pads). Check the special displays in the store or on their web site at walmart.com.

The best milk storage bags

Once you've decided to express breast milk for your child, you'll need to consider how to store it. Freezer bags are the most common method and most major pump manufactures and bottle makers sell bags. Interestingly, our readers have been very disappointed with Avent disposable bags. One reader called them "crummy." She and other readers recommend the **Gerber Seal N Go** bags, which will fit most bottles including the Avent. A completely different alternative is **Mothers Milk Mate** (www.mothersmilkmate.com) a $30, ten-bottle storage system with rack.

as the Pump In Style from Medela DO NOT have such a barrier device. If you buy one from eBay, you could potentially be exposing yourself to any pathogens the previous user (or users) may have had, *even if you change the tubing*. So the issue is not the ability of the pump to withstand the wear and tear of multiple users. The issue is the potentially very serious question of transmitting infections such as HIV."

Here's our question, however. If you shouldn't buy a used pump, why is it OK to reuse your own Pump In Style for a second or third child? Wouldn't the newly expressed breast milk be contaminated by bacteria left in the pump? The lack of logic in that analysis is what leads us to think it is OK to use a second hand pump. Bottom line: this is your call but we need to see more evidence this is a problem before issuing a warning to our readers.

 **Smart Shopper Tip**

Smart Shopper Tip #1
When to buy that pump.
"I don't know how long I want to breastfeed. And I'll be going back to work pretty soon after my baby is born. When should I get a breast pump?"

We'd suggest waiting a bit before you invest in a breast pump or even nursing clothes. Many moms start with breast feeding, but can't or don't want to continue it after a few weeks. For them investing in a pump would be a waste of money. If you aren't sure how long you want to breast feed, but you'd like to pump some extra bottles of milk anyway, consider renting a hospital grade pump first and try it out before you invest a couple hundred dollars.

Breastfeeding in public:
Exposing yourself for onlookers' fun
and your baby's health

Here's a controversial topic to discuss around the office water cooler: breastfeeding in public. Since our society tends to see a woman's breasts as sexual objects rather than as utilitarian milk delivery systems, we often run into disapproval of public breastfeeding. Ironically, this is one of the chief advantages of breastfeeding—it's very portable. No hauling and cleaning bottles, mixing and warming formula, and your child gets nourishment exactly when he needs it.

Amazingly, some parts of this country still manage to equate breastfeeding in public with indecent exposure. Florida just recently repealed a law forbidding public breastfeeding after several woman were cited by the "breast" police for whipping it out at a local mall. It's hard to believe that until just recently laws in this country branded one of life's most basic needs—eating—as illegal. You can call your local La Leche League or other breastfeeding sources to find out if your city or state still has laws like these. If they do, consider getting involved in trying to get them repealed.

The irony is that breastfeeding in public involves very little flashing of flesh. As an admitted public breastfeeder, I can attest to the fact that it can be done discreetly. Here are some suggestions:

1 **IF THE THOUGHT OF BREASTFEEDING IN PUBLIC IS NOT YOUR CUP OF TEA, CONSIDER BRINGING A BOTTLE OF EXPRESSED MILK WITH YOU.** We know one couple who did this and never seemed to have a problem.

Waste of Money

Even Cows Opt for the Electric Kind

"I'm going back to work a couple of months after my baby is born. My co-worker who breastfeeds her baby thinks manual and mini-electrics pumps are a waste of money. What do you think?"

While they may be useful to relieve engorgement, manual pumps aren't very practical for long-term pumping when you're at

2 **Use the shawl method.** Many women breastfeed in public with a shawl or blanket covering the baby and breasts. While this works well, you must start practicing this early and often with your baby. Otherwise, you'll find that as she gets more alert and interested in her surroundings, she won't stay under the shawl.

3 **Find all the convenient rest room lounges in your town.** Whenever we visit the local mall, I nurse in one of the big department store's lounge areas. This is a great way to meet other breastfeeding moms as well. Of course, not every public rest room features a lounge with couches or comfy chairs, but it's worth seeking out the ones that do. We applaud stores like Babies R Us for having "breastfeeding rooms" with glider-rockers and changing tables for easy nursing.

Another creative alternative: stores will usually let you use a dressing room to breastfeed. Of course, some stores are not as "breastfeeding friendly" as others. New York City, for example, has 10 million people and about seven public rest rooms. In such places, I've even breastfed in a chair strategically placed facing a wall or corner in the back of a store. Not the best view, but it gets the job done.

4 **Try your car.** My son knows the back of both of our cars extremely well now. I found it easier and more comfortable to feed him there, especially when he started to become distracted in restaurants and stores. The car holds no fascination for him, so he tends to concentrate on eating instead of checking out the scenery. I suggest you keep some magazines in the car since you may get bored.

work. They are very slow, which makes it hard to get much milk. Mini-electric breast pumps are better but are really best only for occasional use—for example, expressing a small amount of milk to mix with cereal for a baby who's learning to eat solids. Mini-electrics, however, may be painful and are still too slow.

Your best bet if you plan to do some serious pumping is to rent a piston electric pump. These monsters maintain a high rate of extraction with amazing comfort. A lactation consultant we interviewed said piston electric pumps can empty both breasts in about 10 to 15 minutes—contrast that with 20 to 30 minutes for mini-electrics and 45 minutes to an hour for manual pumps.

As mentioned earlier, the only manual pump to receive high marks from our readers is the Avent Isis—and even though it is a vast improvement over previous options, it still is a MANUAL pump. It may not work well for moms who plan to work part or full-time and still nurse their baby. That said, one solution is to use two pumps— a mom we interviewed uses a Pump In Style when she's tired (during the evening or night-time) and the Avent Isis at work (it's much quieter; doesn't need electricity, etc).

Money Saving Tips

1 **CONTACT YOUR HEALTH INSURANCE PROVIDER.** One reader noted that her insurance provider will pay $50 toward the purchase of a breast pump. You'll have to ask; insurance companies aren't always forthcoming with such info. And other insurance providers will only pay for a pump if there is a medical reason. You may have to get a "note from your doctor" to qualify.

2 **CONSIDER EBAY.** Many readers have noted that breast pumps, including Medela's Pump In Style (PIS), are available for sale on eBay.com at huge discounts. We saw one, new in the box, for only $182. Some of them are older models or even used, so you'll need to educate yourself on what you're buying.

3 **DON'T FEEL LIKE YOU HAVE TO BUY THE "TOP BRAND."** There are several manufacturers of breast pumps besides Medela. And our readers say their products work just as great for a lot less money (we discuss these alternative brands later in this chapter). For example, the Ameda Purely Yours pump sells for only $250 retail, while the Medela PIS is a whopping $329 retail. The Nurture III pump is only $115! We recommend sticking with manufacturers who specialize in breastfeeding. The First Years, for example, makes a ton of other products from spoons to bath tubs as well as breast pumps. We aren't as impressed with the quality of their pumps compared to other brands, however.

Our Picks: Brand Recommendations

◆ **Manual Pump:** The best manual pump is the Avent "Isis" ($45, for a store near you, call 800-542-8368; web: www.aventamerica. com). Our readers love this pump, which Avent claims is as efficient as a mini-electric (it takes about

eight to ten minutes to empty a breast). You can buy the Isis by itself, or as part of a kit that includes extra bottles, cooler packs and more ($60 to $75).Yes, there are other manual pumps (Medela's "Manual-Ease" $50 with adjustable vacuum control is a good second bet), but we think the Isis is tops. (One caveat to the Isis, however: a reader recommends going for the model with the reusable bottle, instead of the disposable one. Why? The reader says Avent's bottle liners for the disposable bottles are terrible—you have to double bag to freeze them or they leak).

◆ **Mini Pump:** The Medela Mini Electric ($105, call 800-435-8316 for a store near you; web: www.medela.com) is one of the few battery operated breast pumps that actually operates at 34 to 36 cycles per minute. Medela also has the "Double Ease" double mini-electric pump (pictured) for $150. As for all the other models, once again you can find cheaper mini-electrics for, say, $30 to $50, but we wouldn't recommend them.

◆ **Piston Electric Pump:** Before you invest in a retail high-end pump like the Medela Pump In Style ($329; pictured right) or Ameda Purely Yours ($250; bottom right), *rent* a hospital-grade pump first for a week or two (or a month). After you decide you're serious about pumping and you're comfortable with the double-pumping action, *then* consider buying one of your own. Given the hefty retail prices, it makes sense to buy only if you plan to pump for several months or have a second child.

There are a couple disadvantages to these retail pumps. Some woman find the sucking action weaker than hospital-grade pumps—hence, it may take *longer* to pump. I've used both the Medela hospital-grade pump and the Pump In Style and while I definitely like the Pump In Style, the hospital-grade rental pump was more comfortable to use. On the other hand, the portability of the retail pumps may outweigh any of their disadvantages. Hospital grade pumps are bulky and are not very portable (they weigh over 20 lbs.).

Formula

Is there any nutritional difference between brands of formula? According to our research, the answer is no. The federal government regulates the ingredients in baby formula. Hence almost all the commercially available baby formula sold in the U.S. and Canada contains the *same* basic ingredients . . . usually the only difference is the color of the label on the outside of the can. That's right—the "generic" formula sold at Wal-Mart and Target is no different than pricey Similac.

What does formula cost these days? First realize that formula comes in three different versions: powder, liquid concentrate and ready-to drink. Powder is least expensive, followed by liquid concentrate. Ready-to-drink is the most pricey. A recent check of grocery stores revealed a 30 ounce can of powdered Similac with Iron was running about $22. This can makes 209 fluid ounces of formula, so the cost per ounce of formula is 10¢.

Of course, formula makers have tricks to make it difficult to compare prices. Each brand of formula comes in a different size can—Enfamil costs the same as Similac ($22), but comes in a can that holds only 28.5 oz. As a result, Enfamil works out to a price of 11¢ per ounce. Adding to the confusion: each brand has a different size scoop, which also frustrates apples to apples comparisons.

What Are You Buying?

In the past, formula was just formula. You basically had the regular version (with or without iron) and soy (also iron fortified or plain). Today, just as with other consumer products, there are increasing numbers of choices including organic formula, toddler versions, formula with or ARA additives and more. Here is our overview of some of the newer options:

◆ **Toddler formula.** First created by Carnation ("Follow Up" formula), then copied by other formula manufacturers, "toddler" formulas are intended to be used for older children (typically nine months old and up) instead of regular cows milk or soy milk. Typically, most parents move to whole milk or soy milk when their child reaches one year of age, leaving formula behind forever. In order to hang on to consumers longer, formula manufacturers have developed these toddler formulas. So what's the big difference between baby formula and toddler formula? Carnation adds extra calcium to their formula while Enfamil (Next Step) and Similac (Similac 2) have upped the amount of vitamins C and E as well as iron. We'll comment on the usefulness of these formulas later in this chapter.

◆ **DHA/ARA additives.** Scientists have been researching breast milk for years to find out what makes it the perfect food for our babies. The media has widely reported that the presence of two fatty acids in breast milk (DHA and ARA—also called lipids) may be responsible for the purported difference in IQ levels in breast-fed babies versus those that are formula-fed. As a result, formula companies have added DHA and ARA to their formulas as some kind of a "brain-boost." But the jury is still out on whether these additives really provide any benefit to formula. A 2002 report from the American Council on Science and Health stated that "experts disagree about whether it is necessary to include DHA and ARA in infant formulas to promote optimal brain and visual development."

◆ *Organic formula.* We are aware of only one organic baby formula available to consumers at this time. *Baby's Only Organic* baby formula (www.babyorganic.com) is manufactured by Nature's One, (www.naturesone.com). The product is made with no genetically engineered organisms, no bovine growth hormones, no antibiotics or steroids, and no insecticides or chemical fertilizers. That's the standard for any organically labeled food. Available only in a powder, they do offer both a regular (cow's milk) formula and a soy option as well, both with iron added.

 ## Safe and Sound

Formula is one of the most closely regulated food items in the US. The Food and Drug Administration has strict guidelines about what can and what cannot go into baby formula. They require expiration dates, warning labels and so on to protect our children from anything that might go wrong with the actual formula. So what are the safety hazards you might run up against? Here are a couple:

1 CONFUSING CANS CONFRONT SOY FORMULA USERS. Soy formula now accounts for 15% of the infant formula market. Yet, a case of mistaken identity has led some parents to nearly starve their infants. Apparently, some parents mistakenly thought they were feeding their babies soy formula, when in fact they were using soy milk. The problem: soy milk is missing important nutrients and vitamins found in soy formula. As a result, babies fed soy milk were malnourished and some required hospitalization. Adding to the confusion, soy milk is often sold in cans that look very similar to soy formula. The government has asked soy milk makers to put warning labels on their products, but some have still not complied. If you use soy formula, be careful to choose the right can at the grocery store.

Another concern: low-iron formula. A myth among some parents is that the iron in standard formula causes constipation—it does not, says a pediatrician we interviewed. Yes, constipation can be a problem with ALL formulas (although some parents tell us Similac is the least constipating since it was reformulated a couple of years ago). But, babies should NEVER be on low-iron formula unless instructed by a pediatrician.

2 EXPIRED FORMULA. Now we realize those cans of formula look like they could survive a nuclear attack (they remind us of the "bomb-proof" cans of Hawaiian Punch our moms used to buy in the '70's), but they do have expiration dates on them. And many of our readers have written to tell us that stores don't always remove expired formula from the shelves in a timely manner. That includes grocery stores, discounters and even warehouse clubs. So read the label carefully and check your own stores of formula before you open a can. Also, some formula sold on auction sites has been expired as well. Be sure to ask.

Money Saving Tips

1 STAY AWAY FROM PRE-MIXED FORMULA. Liquid concentrate formula and ready-to-drink formula are 50% to 200% more expensive than powdered formula. Yes, it is more convenient but you pay big time for that. We priced name-brand, ready to drink formula at a whopping 25¢ per ounce.

Guess what type of formula is given out as freebies in doctors' offices and hospitals? Yes, it's often the ready-to-drink liquid formula. These companies know babies get hooked on the particular texture of the expensive stuff, making it hard (if not impossible) to switch to the powdered formula later. Sneaky, eh?

2 CONSIDER GENERIC FORMULA. Most grocery stores and discounters sell "private" label formula at considerable savings, at least 30% to 40%. At one grocery store chain, their generic powdered formula worked out to just 7¢ per fluid ounce of formula, a 30% savings. One great brand of generic formula: BabyMil (800-344-1358; web: www.StoreBrandFormulas.com), whose formulas are 40% less expensive than national brands. BabyMil sells for $6 to $7 a 16 oz can, versus $10 plus for 16 oz of Enfamil. BabyMil comes both in regular and soy versions (BabySoy). Hint: BabyMil is sold under a variety of different names, depending on the retailer. Go to the web site www.StoreBrandFormulas.com and click on

"Available Across America." Find a grocery store/pharmacy/discounter near you. From there you'll find what BabyMil is called in your area. For example, Wal-Mart sells BabyMil formula as "Parents Choice," while K-Mart calls it "Little Ones" formula.

We should note that some pediatricians are concerned about recommending generic formula–doctors fret that such low-cost formula might discourage breastfeeding. Ironic when so many pediatricians hand out all those free samples of formula. We'd love to see them stop accepting samples from Similac, Enfamil and Carnation and start discouraging hospitals from doling them out to moms in the maternity wards.

3 Buy it online. Yep, you can buy formula online from eBay. You can save big but watch out–some unscrupulous sellers try to pawn off expired formula on unsuspecting buyers. Be sure to confirm the expiration date before buying formula online. And watch out for shipping charges–formula is heavy and shipping can outweigh any deal, depending on the price you pay. We saw one case of formula go for $53 on eBay. But the $6 shipping charge made the deal less sweet, considering a case would retail in stores for $65!

4 Buy in bulk. We found wholesale clubs had the best prices on name brand formula. For example, Sam's Club (www.samsclub.com) sells a 2.5 pound (40 oz) can of Enfamil for $24. That was 20% less than grocery stores. And generic formula at wholesale clubs is even a bigger bargain. Costco's Kirkland brand formula was $15 for a 36 ounce can making it only 6¢ an ounce.

5 Ask your pediatrician for free samples. Just make sure you get the powdered formula (not the liquid concentrate or ready to pour). One reader in Arizona said she got several free cases from her doctor, who simply requested more from the formula makers. OK, we know this sounds hypocritical since we just said we think doctors should take a stand against all the formula giveaways in their offices and hospitals. However, as long as doctors' offices are stuffed with such freebies, you might as well ask for them.

6 Shop around. Yes, powdered formula at a grocery store can run $22 to $25 for a 28-ounce can–but there's no federal law that says you must buy it at full retail. Readers of our first edition noticed that formula prices varied widely, sometimes even at different locations of the same chain. In Chicago, a reader said they found one Toys R Us charged $1.20 less per can for the same Similac with Iron ready-to-feed formula than another Toys R Us across town. "They actually have a price check book at the registers with the codes for each store in the Chicagoland area," the reader said. "At our last visit, we saved $13.20 for two cases (about 30% of the cost), just by mentioning we wanted to pay the lower price."

Another reader noticed a similar price discrepancy at Wal-Mart stores in Florida. When she priced Carnation Good Start powdered formula, she found one Wal-Mart that marked it at $6.61 per can. Another Wal-Mart (about 20 miles from the first location) sells the same can for $3.68! When the reader inquired about the price discrepancy, a customer service clerk admitted that each store independently sets the price for such items, based on nearby competition. That's a good lesson—many chains in more rural or poorer locations (with no nearby competition) often mark prices higher than suburban stores.

7 **JUST BUY REGULAR VERSIONS OF FORMULA.** When we say regular formula, we mean the basic formula you've seen on the shelves for years. We think those the new lipids enhanced formulas (with DHA and ARA) are a waste of money. Similac's Advance and Enfamil's Lipil are the top brands with DHA/ARA. These can cost as much as 20% more than basic formula. And as we discussed above,

---

Baby Formula Manufacturers: Out of control

In the past few editions of this book, we issued a long rant about the marketing tactics of the formula manufacturers. And we still feel that way today. When you check into the hospital to give birth, you start the long promotional parade of formula freebies—most new parents emerge after birth with formula samples, diaper bags emblazoned with formula logos and more. Is this good for parents? For the country?

Considering the fact that breast-feeding rates still trail national goals, we say no. We realize formula makers have the right to market their wares as they see fit . . . but we argue that hospitals and doctors' offices should be no-pitch zones. The subtle and not-so-subtle effect of all the endless formula freebies is to undermine moms who choose to breastfeed. While we realize most moms and dads are intelligent enough to realize the formula hype is just that, we are concerned that less-educated parents are led to believe that hospitals and doctors are endorsing formula over breast-feeding. And statistics bear that out—moms who are from lower socioeconomic groups are most likely to turn to formula instead of trying breastfeeding.

As a country, we have to ask ourselves—shouldn't hospitals and doctor's offices be a pitch-free area for formula?

---

there is no scientific proof that these lipids actually improve brain or eye function. Until we see serious and long-term studies that verify those claims we vote that parents forget these products.

And the same goes for toddler formulas. When your child is ready for whole milk (usually at one year of age, according most pediatricians), you can switch from formula (about 10¢ per ounce) to milk (about 2¢ per ounce) at a savings of 80%! What about the claim that toddler formulas have extra calcium, iron and vitamins? Nutritionists point out that toddlers should be getting most of their nutrition from solid foods, not formula. That extra calcium can be found in foods as diverse as yogurt and broccoli; iron in red meat and spinach; vitamins in a wide variety of foods. But what if you don't think your child is getting enough of those nutrients? Adding a vitamin and mineral supplement to your child's diet would *still* be less expensive than blowing your money on toddler formulas.

Bottles/Nipples

What's the best bottle for baby? Actually, it's not the bottle that's so important but the nipple—how the milk is delivered to baby is more important than the container.

When it comes to nipples, there are a myriad of choices. At the low end, **Playtex** and **Gerber** are available in just about every grocery store in the U.S. and Canada. Mid-price options like **Evenflo** and **Munchkin's** Healthflow (formerly made by Johnson & Johnson) are also widely available, as are the high-end **Avent** and **Dr. Brown** bottle systems.

So, which nipple (and bottle) system is best? This is like asking a baseball fan to name their favorite team. For many parents, the bottle/nipple system they start with is the one they stick by. And the low-end options can work just as well as the premium brands.

That isn't to say premium, reusable bottle brands like Avent don't have their advantages. The company claims its nipples are clinically proven to reduce colic, the endless crying that some infants develop around one month of age. Avent says its nipples are better since their shape mimics the breast—and many readers of this book tell us Avent is  superior to the competition. Avent bottles have wide-mouth openings that are easier to fill (for formula) and easier to clean than competing bottles. The thicker plastic Avent uses feels more substantial that that used by other brands; you can definitely re-use these bottles for later children (although the nipples should be replaced after six months of use).

Unfortunately, Avent isn't cheap. Their products can cost twice as much as other less-expensive bottles and nipples. A 9oz Avent bottle with nipple runs about $5 at Babies R Us, compared to $3.30 for a Playtex bottle, $2.50 for a Munchkin Health Flow and $5 for a an Evenflo bottle (all prices are for a bottle with nipple).

Until a couple of years ago, Avent only made reusable bottles, missing out on the one-third of the market that prefers the convenience of disposable nursers. Well, there's good news to report: Avent now sells a disposable bottle that includes their famous nipple and storage bags that clip on the bottle.

A couple of caveats about Avent: first, you can't use the disposable nipple on the reusable bottle (and vice versa)—you have to buy two separate sets of bottles and nipples. Another bummer: Avent's bottles only come with the newborn nipple, which has a very LOW flow rate. Why the company sells a giant NINE oz. bottle intended for a toddler with a nipple that's for an infant is beyond us—and a rip-off, since then you've got to buy separate nipples.

Remember that many bottles use "proprietary" nipples—hence, an Avent nipple won't work on someone else's bottle. Yes, some manufacturers let you mix and match, but you should check first before assuming compatibility.

One last gripe for Avent: If you screw the reusable bottle cap on too tight, it will leak. Many readers complained about this problem, but Avent's web site (www.avent.com) offers tips on how to tighten just enough. And they of course, if you put a disposable bottle nipple on a reusable bottle or visa versa, the bottle will also leak. Make sure you're using the right nipple on the right bottle!

Another high-end bottle recommended by our readers is Dr. Brown's Natural Flow. Their web site (www.handi-craft.com) claims these bottles will eliminate colic and reduce middle ear infections. How? A patented vent system eliminates bubbles and nipple collapse. Invented by a physician from Illinois (yes, Dr. Brown), our readers universally praise his unique bottle system. It isn't cheap, however. A four-ounce bottle will cost you $6 although we've seen it on line for about $4.

Among the more hip products on the bottle front are the "angled nursers." Munchkin's Health Flow (starting at $2.50 for a 4 ounce bottle) started the trend, which purportedly keeps baby from gulping too much air. The bottle makes it easier for parents to monitor the amount of liquid baby has consumed. Evenflo has introduced a similar product ($4.79) and several other companies have knocked-off the Health Flow in recent years.

Looking for a glass baby bottle? These have become scarce in recent years, although they seem to be making a comeback. Evenflo makes a glass bottle that sells for $2 for a four-ounce version.

Of course, there are other bottles out there besides the big brands. A reader recommended a new bottle from a company with the scary name of BreastBottle (www.breastbottle.com). Shaped like, well, a breast, this pricey bottle ($13) is made of soft plastic and is dishwasher safe.

Where can you find bottles at a discount? Readers say Avent bottles at Target are $4, about a $1 less than other stores. The web is another source: DrugStore (www.drugstore.com) has great prices on many Avent items. And many of the general baby product sites carry Avent at a discount as well. Kid Surplus (www.kidsurplus.com) has great prices on Dr. Brown's bottles. You'll find the four-ounce bottle for $4 a savings of about 30% of retail.

Smart Shopper Tip

Smart Shopper Tip #1
Nipple confusion?

"When I check the catalogs and look in baby stores, I see bottles with all different shaped nipples. Which one is best for my baby? How do I avoid nipple confusion?"

Nipple confusion occurs when a baby learns to suck one way at the breast and another way from a bottle. This happens because the "human breast milk delivery system" (i.e., the breast and nipple) forces babies to keep their sucking action forward in their mouth. The result: they have to work harder to get milk from a breast than from a conventional baby bottle.

So if you want to give an occasional bottle, what bottle is least likely to cause nipple confusion? Unfortunately, the answer is not clear—some parents swear that Avent's nipple is best. Fans of Dr. Brown's bottle say it is best. Others find less expensive options like the Playtex Nurser work just as well.

Are there really that many differences between nipples, besides shape? Not really. All major brands are dishwasher-safe, made of latex and have very similar flow rates. The bottom line: you may have to experiment with different nipples/bottles to find one your baby likes.

What about pacifiers? Some experts say early use of pacifiers may interfere with breastfeeding. The best advice: try to wait until lactation is firmly established before introducing a pacifier. Which type of pacifier is best? There are two types—regular pacifiers have round nipples, while "orthodontic" pacifiers have flat nipples. There's no consensus as to which type is best—consult with your pediatrician for more advice on this topic.

Bottle Warmers & Sterilizers

New moms never really know for sure if they have to have something or not. Take bottle sterilizers and warmers. Will their child die from some bacterial agent if they don't sterilize their baby bottles? Will Junior scream bloody murder if his bottle isn't a perfect 85 degrees Fahrenheit? The answer to both questions is: probably not. In most cases washing baby bottles in the dishwasher cleans them just fine and a room temperature bottle will make a hungry baby just as happy as a warmed bottle of formula or milk. But what if you want one of these items anyway? Here are our recommendations:

Like the competition in bottles, Avent also seems to win the sterilizer war: the "Sterilizer Express," a new model that is even zippier than their previous sterilizers. The Express comes in an electric ($65) that can sterilize six bottles in just four to six minutes (the lower figure is for the microwave; the higher one for the electric version).

What about bottle warmers? Avent's old bottle warmer ($40) got mixed reviews from our readers. It only worked with Avent bottles and took about six minutes to warm a bottle—"that's too long when your baby is screaming at the top of his lungs," says one mom. On the upside, it could warm baby food in addition to bottles. To address these complaints, Avent debuted the new "Express Bottle and Baby Food Warmer" ($40)—this new model can heat a bottle in four minutes. It also fits baby food and all types of baby bottles (not just Avent).

Baby Food

At the tender age of four to six months, you and your baby will depart on a magical journey to a new place filled with exciting adventures and never-before-seen wonders. Yes, you've entered the SOLID FOOD ZONE.

Fasten your seat belts and get ready for a fun ride. As your tour guide, we would like to give a few pointers to make your stay a bit more enjoyable. Let's take stock:

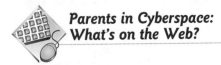

Parents in Cyberspace: What's on the Web?

Looking for a schedule of what foods to introduce when? Earth's

Best's web site has a comprehensive chart with suggestions (www.earthsbest.com, click on "baby nutrition"). Gerber's slick web site (www.gerber.com) also has baby development info (including when to start different stage foods). We also liked Beechnut's site (www.beechnut.com), which includes "suggested menus," "feeding FAQ's" and "mealtime pointers." Although it is designed for Canadian parents, Heinz's baby food web site, www.heinzbaby.com contains extensive nutritional advice and other helpful info. Canadians can take advantage of rebate offers and other deals on this site (hopefully, they'll add the rest of North America to the coupon deals soon).

Safe & Sound

1 **FEED FROM A BOWL, NOT FROM THE JAR.** Why? If you feed from a jar, bacterium from the baby's mouth can find their way back to the jar, spoiling the food much more quickly. Also, saliva enzymes begin to break down the food's nutrients. The best strategy: pour the amount of baby food you need into a bowl and feed from there (unless it's the last serving from the jar). And be sure to refrigerate any unused portions.

2 **DON'T STORE FOOD IN PLASTIC BAGS.** If you leave plastic bags on the baby's high chair, they can be a suffocation hazard. A better solution: store left-over food in small, Tupperware-type containers.

3 **DO A TASTE TEST.** Make sure it isn't too hot, too cold, or spoiled. We know you aren't dying to taste the Creamed Ham Surprise from Gerber, but it is a necessary task.

4 **CHECK FOR EXPIRATION DATES.** Gerber's jarred food looks like it would last through the next Ice Age, but check that expiration date. Most unopened baby food is only good for a year or two. Use opened jars within two to three days.

5 **A FINAL WORD OF ADVICE ON FEEDING BABY:** don't introduce nuts (like peanuts or peanut butter) until your child is at least three years old. This advice comes from a nationally known allergist we interviewed who's a specialist in nut allergies. He points out that nut allergies are potentially fatal and lifelong. So the longer you wait to introduce nuts, the better chance you have of avoiding these deadly allergies.

FEEDING

E-MAIL FROM THE REAL WORLD
Allergies and Baby Food:
Watch those labels!

If you've noticed you're hearing more and more about food allergies these days, you're not alone. In fact, there has been a distinct rise in the number of food allergies among children according to allergists we've interviewed. But can food allergies be avoided? Maybe. One strategy is to put off feeding the most allergenic of foods to your child. Specifically avoid nuts. But what about other foods? Here's a comment from one of our readers:

"You're the first people, other than myself it seems, to be bothered by the fact that baby food manufacturers put corn in their foods. I've been reading the labels (since I have a few food allergies and want to prevent my daughter from the same fate), and I've been noticing that all manufacturers add corn, milk products, strawberries, and other things that babies are advised to avoid during the first year to their foods intended for children under one year old. I was also bothered by the fact that companies have limited choices for 'stage one' foods, then offer stage two foods containing multiple ingredients not available at stage one, such as 'banana, mango, kiwi' blends."

 Smart Shopper Tips

Smart Shopper Tip #1
Tracking Down UFFOs (Unidentifiable Flying Food Objects)
"We fed our baby rice cereal for the first time. It was really cute, except for the part when the baby picked up the bowl and flung it across the kitchen! Should we have bought some special stuff for this occasion?"

Well, unless you want your kitchen to be redecorated in Early Baby Food, we do have a few suggestions. First, a bowl with a bottom that suctions to the table is a great way to avoid flying saucers. Plastic spoons that have a round handle are nice, especially since baby can't stick the spoon handle in her eye (yes, that does happen—babies do try to feed themselves even at a young age). Spoons with rubber coatings are also nice; they don't transfer the heat or cold of the food to the baby's mouth and are easier on the gums. One of our favorite spoons is Munchkin's "White Hot Infant Spoon" (call 800-344-2229 or 818-893-5000 to find a dealer near you; web: www.munchkininc.com). This spoon uses a special coating that changes color when baby's food is too hot (105 degrees or warmer). Now they offer three versions including one with airplane wings for the reluctant eater.

Smart Shopper Tip #2
Avoiding Mealtime Baths

"Our baby loves to drink from a cup, except for one small problem. Most of the liquid ends up on her, instead of in her. Any tips?"

Cups with weighted bottoms (about $5) help young infants to get the hang of this drinking thing. A sipping spout provides an interim learning step between bottle and regular cup. When your baby's older, we've found clear plastic cups to be helpful. Why? Your baby can see out the bottom and not feel like someone has turned out the lights.

No-spill cups are a godsend—Playtex (203) 341-4000 pioneered this category with a cup that doesn't leak when tipped over. Despite the fact that many other companies have jumped into the no-spill cup market in recent years, Playtex's cups are still the gold standard. Also check out Gerber's version—readers praise this no-spill cup as well.

You don't have to go to a baby store to find these items—we've seen many baby feeding accessories in grocery stores.

Smart Shopper Tip #3
Finger Foods

"When can we start giving our baby finger foods? What should we give her that she won't choke on?"

After stage one, the pureed versions of real food, you'll be ready to move on to stage two. And you can do this simultaneously, taking into account your child's maturity. Usually, around ten to twelve months your baby will be ready to try some finger foods like well cooked diced carrots. Make sure whatever you feed your baby at this stage it is soft and cut up rather small. You can include baby in your meals by cutting up cooked chicken as well as soft veggies and small bits of bread. Parents may still want to feed babies some pureed food, but waiting to long to introduce foods with more texture and flavor can be a mistake. If you're not sure what your baby can handle in the way of chunkier foods, check with your doctor.

Money-Saving Tips

1 **MAKE YOUR OWN.** Let's be honest: baby foods such as mashed bananas are really just . . . mashed bananas. You can easily whip up this stuff with that common kitchen helper, the food processor. Many parents skip baby food altogether and make their own. One tip: make up a big batch at one time and freeze the left-overs in ice cube trays. Check the library for cookbooks that provide tips on making baby food at home. A reader suggestion: the "Super Baby Food" book ($19.95, published by F. J. Roberts Publishing, web: www.superbabyfood.com). This 590-page book is about as comprehensive of a book as you can find on the subject.

2 **BELIEVE IT OR NOT, TOYS R US AND BABIES R US SELL BABY FOOD.** If you think your grocery store is gouging you on the price of baby food, you might want to check out the prices at Toys R Us or their sister store, Babies R Us. We found Gerber 1st Foods in a four-pack of 2.5 ounce jars for $1.99—that works out to about 50¢ per jar or about 37% less than grocery store prices. Toys R Us also sells four-packs of assorted dinners from Gerber's 2nd and 3rd Food collections.

3 **COUPONS! COUPONS! COUPONS!** Yes, we've seen quite a few cents-off and buy-one-get-one-free coupons on baby

---

E-MAIL FROM THE REAL WORLD
Making your own baby food isn't time consuming

A mom in New Mexico told us she found making her own baby food isn't as difficult as it sounds:

"My husband and I watch what we eat, so we definitely watch what our baby eats. One of the things I do is buy organic carrots, quick boil them, throw them in a blender and then freeze them in an ice cube tray. Once they are frozen, I separate the cubes into freezer baggies (they would get freezer burn if left in the ice tray). When mealtime arrives, I just throw them in the microwave. Organic carrots taste great! This whole process might sound complicated, but it only takes me about 20 minutes to do, and then another five to ten minutes to put the cubes in baggies."

food and formula—not just in the Sunday paper but also through the mail. Our advice: don't toss that junk mail until you've made sure you're not trashing valuable baby food coupons. Another coupon trick: look for "bounce-back" coupons. Those are the coupons put in the packages of baby food to encourage you to bounce back to the store and buy more.

4 Buy Heinz. As noted later in this section, Heinz baby food is often priced 10% to 20% below the competition. The only drawback: it isn't available everywhere. Another problem: Heinz also has more starches and fillers (like sugar) than other brands. Hence, you're saving money, but giving your baby less protein, minerals and vitamins with each spoonful. Hint: look for single food jars from Heinz without the fillers.

5 Substitute comparable adult foods. What's the difference between adult applesauce and baby applesauce? Not much, except for the fact that applesauce in a jar with a cute baby on it costs several times more than the adult version. While the adult applesauce isn't fortified with extra vitamins, it probably doesn't matter. Baby will get these nutrients from other foods. Another rip-off: the "next step" foods for older babies. Gerber loves to tout its special toddler meals in its "Graduates" line. What's the point? When baby is ready to eat pasta, just serve him small bites of the adult stuff.

6 Go for the better quality. That's a strange money-saving tip, isn't it? Doesn't better quality baby food cost more? Yes, but look at it this way—the average baby eats 600 jars of baby food until they "graduate" to adult foods. Sounds like a lot of money, eh? Well, that only works out to $300 or so in total expenditures (using an average price of 48¢ to 75¢ per jar). Hence, if you go for the better-quality food and spend, say, 20% more, you're only out another $60. Therefore it might be better to spend the small additional dollars to give baby better-quality food. And feeding baby food that tastes more like the real thing makes transitions to adult foods easier.

The Name Game: Reviews of Selected Manufacturers

Here's a round-up of some of the best known names in baby food. We should note that while we actually tried out each of the foods on our baby, you may reach different conclusions than we did. Unlike our brand name ratings for clothing or other baby products, food is a much trickier rating proposition. We rated the following brand names based on how healthy they are and how much they approximate real food (aroma, appearance, and, yes, taste). Our subjective opinions reflect our experience—always consult with your pediatrician or family doctor if you have any questions about feeding your baby. (Special thanks to Ben and Jack for their help in researching this topic.)

The Ratings

- **A** **EXCELLENT**—*our top pick!*
- **B** **GOOD**— *above average quality, prices, and creativity.*
- **C** **FAIR**—*could stand some improvement.*
- **D** **POOR**—*yuck! could stand some major improvement.*

Beech-Nut *(800) BEECHNUT; Web: www.beechnut.com* Beech-Nut was one of the first baby food companies to eliminate fillers (starches, sugar, salt) or artificial colors/flavors in its 120 flavors. While Beech-Nut is not organic, the company claims to have "stringent pesticide standards." Our readers generally give Beech-Nut good marks (some like it better than Gerber). The only bummer: it can be hard to find (not every state has stores that carry it). You can search their web page or call their 800-number to check availability. One bonus: Beech-Nut's web site includes on-line coupons and a rebate offer. (A last bit of good news on Beech-Nut: the company's plan to merge with Heinz was scuttled by anti-trust regulators, which is good news for consumers who want more choice.) ***Rating: B+***

Earth's Best *(800) 442-4221. Web: www.earthsbest.com* Organic food has gone mainstream in the last few years, so there's no surprise you can now buy organic baby food. One of our favorite brands: Earth's Best. Started in Vermont, Earth's Best was sold in 1996 to Heinz, one of the baby food giants. Heinz couldn't figure out what to do with the company and decided to sell it to natural foods conglomerate Hain Celestial (parent of Celestial Tea). Despite all the changes in ownership, Earth's Best still has the largest line of "natural" baby foods on the market—all vegetables and grains are certified to be organically grown (no pesticides are used), and meats are raised without antibiotics or steroids. Another advantage: Earth's Best never adds any salt, sugar or modified starches to its food. And the foods are only made from whole grains, fruits and vegetables (instead of concentrates). Surprisingly, Earth's Best costs about the same as Gerber (around 45¢ to 49¢ for a 2.5 ounce jar).

We tried Earth's Best and were generally pleased. Our only complaint: some of the dinners have corn, a highly allergenic food that is not supposed to be introduced until your baby is 12 months old. Another bummer: Earth's Best can be hard to find (it's more likely in health food stores like Whole Foods, but we've seen it in some "regular" grocery stores too). All in all, Earth's Best is a much-needed natural alternative to the standard fare that babies have been fed for far too many years. **Rating: A**

Gerber Web: www.gerber.com Dominating the baby food business with a whopping 70% market share (that's right, three out of every four baby food jars sold sport that familiar label), Gerber sure has come a long way from its humble beginnings. Back in 1907, Joseph Gerber (whose trade was canning) mashed up peas for his daughter, following the suggestion of a family doctor. We imagine those peas looked quite different from Gerber's peas today. Now,

"Toddler" foods a waste of money

When the number of births leveled off in recent years, the baby food companies began looking around for ways to grow their sales. One idea: make foods for older babies and toddlers who have abandoned the jarred mushy stuff! One company warns parents not to feed "adult" foods to babies too early, saying they won't provide "all the nutrition they need." To boost sales in the $1 billion baby food market, Gerber rolled out "Gerber Graduates" while Heinz debuted "Toddler Cuisine," microwaveable meals for kids as old as 36 months. Heck, even Enfamil rolled out the "EnfaGrow" line of fortified snacks. So, what do nutritionists and doctors think of these foods? Most say they are completely unnecessary. Yes, they are a convenience for parents but, besides that, so-called "toddler foods" offer no additional nutritional benefit. In their defense, the baby food companies argue that their toddler meals are meant to replace the junk food and unhealthy snacks parents give their babies. We guess we can see that point, but overall we think that toddler foods are a complete waste of money. Once your baby finishes with baby food, they can go straight to "adult food" without any problem—of course, that should be HEALTHY adult food. What's best: a mix of dairy products, fruits, vegetables, meat and eggs. And, no, McDonald's French fries don't count as a vegetable.

thanks to scientific progress, Gerber's peas are put through such a rigorous canning process that they don't even look like peas . . . instead more like green slime. And it's not just the look, have you actually smelled or tasted any of Gerber's offerings? Yuck. Sure it's cheap (about 49¢ for a 2 1/2 ounce jar of Gerber 1st Foods), but we just can't feed our baby this stuff with a clear conscience. On the upside, Gerber offers parents one key advantage: choice. The line boasts an amazing 200 different flavors. Gerber is sold in just about every grocery store on Earth. And we have to give Gerber credit: a few years ago, the company announced it would respond to parents' concerns and reformulate its baby food to eliminate starches, sugars and other fillers. Gerber also rolled out "Tender Harvest," a line of organic baby food to compete with Earth's Best. The new line is made with "whole grains and certified organic fruits and vegetables" (note that Gerber's regular line still uses fruit and vegetable concentrates). While we like the changes Gerber has made, we still have problems with the brand. First, we think their "Graduates" line of "toddler" foods is a waste of money. And their juice line is overpriced compared to others on the market. **Rating: C**

Heinz Web: www.heinzbaby.com Heinz is probably the best bargain amongst the national baby food brands. A recent price survey revealed Heinz's baby food is typically 10% to 20% cheaper than Gerber. The company has more success selling baby food abroad than here in the U.S.—it's not available in every state. One bummer: while Heinz has removed fillers like sugar or starch from 100 of its foods, there are still another 60 with those extra ingredients. We were also puzzled with Heinz's internet strategy—there isn't a baby food web site for US parents (but we did find one for Canadians). From that Canadian web site, we discovered in 1997 Heinz launched Earth's Best (reviewed earlier) in Canada as well as "Congee," an ethnic line of baby food for Chinese parents that incorporates traditional rice dishes. **Rating: B+**

High Chairs

As soon as Junior starts to eat solid food, you'll need this quintessential piece of baby furniture—the high chair. Surprisingly, this seemingly innocuous product generates 7430 injuries each year. So, what are the safest high chairs? And how do you use them properly? We'll share these insights, as well as some money-saving tips and brand reviews in this section.

Safe and Sound

1 MOST INJURIES OCCUR WHEN BABIES ARE NOT STRAPPED INTO THEIR CHAIRS. Sadly, four to five deaths occur each year when babies "submarine" under the tray. The safest high chairs now feature a "passive restraint" (a plastic post) under the tray to prevent this. Note: some trays attach this submarine protection to the tray; others have it on the seat. We prefer the seat. Why? If it is on the tray and the tray is removed, there is a risk a child might be able to squirm out of the safety belts (which is all that would hold them in the chair). We'll note which high chairs feature submarine guards on the seat versus tray later in the reviews section of this chapter.

FYI: Even if the high chair has a passive restraint, you STILL must strap in baby with the safety harness with EACH use. This prevents them from climbing out or otherwise hurting themselves. Finally, never put the high chair near a wall—babies have been injured in the past when they push off a wall or object, tipping over the chair. This problem is rare with the newest high chairs (as they have wide, stable bases), but you still can tip over older, hand-me-down models.

2 THE SAFETY STANDARDS FOR HIGH CHAIRS ARE VOLUNTARY. In a recent report, *Consumer Reports* claimed that not all high chairs meet these voluntary standards. Perhaps the safest bet: look for JPMA-certified high chairs. The JPMA requires a battery of safety tests, including checks for stability, a locking device to prevent folding, a secure restraining system, no sharp edges, and so on.

3 INSPECT THE SEAT—IS IT WELL UPHOLSTERED? Make sure it won't tear or puncture easily.

4 LOOK FOR STABILITY. It's basic physics: the wider the base, the more stable the chair.

5 CAREFULLY INSPECT THE RESTRAINING SYSTEM. Straps around the hips and between the legs do the trick. The cheapest high chairs have only a single strap around the waist. Expensive models have "safety harnesses" with multiple straps.

6 SOME HIGH CHAIRS OFFER DIFFERENT HEIGHT POSITIONS, INCLUDING A RECLINING POSITION THAT SUPPOSEDLY MAKES IT EASIER TO FEED A YOUNG INFANT. The problem? Feeding a baby solid foods in a reclining position is a choking hazard. If you want to use the reclining feature, it should be exclusively for bottle feeding.

More Money Buys You

Whether you spend $30 or $200, most high chairs do one simple thing—provide you with a place to safely ensconce your baby while he eats. The more money you spend, however, the more comforts there are for both you and baby. As you go up in price, you find chairs with various height positions, reclining seats, larger trays, more padding, casters for mobility and more. From a safety point of view, some of the more expensive high chairs feature five-point restraint harnesses (instead of just a waist belt). Nearly all high chairs feature the under-tray passive restraint mentioned earlier. As for usability, some high chairs are easier to clean than others, but that doesn't necessary correspond to price. Look for removable vinyl covers that are machine-washable (cloth covers on cheaper chairs are harder to clean). Nearly all high chairs sold today are made of plastic and metal, replacing the wooden high chairs that previous generations of babies used.

Smart Shopper Tips for High Chairs

Smart Shopper Tip #1
High Chair Basics 101
"I was looking at those fancy Italian high chairs and trying to figure out why they are so expensive. And does it matter what color you get? I like the white model best."

The high chair market is basically divided into two camps: the low-end chairs from companies like Graco and Cosco and the Italian imports from Peg Perego and Chicco. The key differences: styling (the Italian chairs admittedly look better) and quality/durability (the imports are generally better than the domestic brands, but you pay for it).

Peg Perego's Prima Pappa, for example, is a runaway success, thanks to its stylish looks and compact fold for storage. At $160 to $180, however, the Pappa is TWICE the price of Graco's top-of-the-line high chair. And, as you'll read later, some readers gripe that the Pappa is a nightmare to clean.

There finally is good news to report on the high chair front, however. In the past year, several new competitors have debuted in the market in the "mid" price range (that is, between the $50 Graco chairs and the $160 Peregos) with decent looks AND good features. Examples include Baby Trend, Fisher-Price, Zooper and Combi. We'll discuss each later in this section. Here are some basic features and new trends to keep an eye out for:

◆ **Tray release.** Nearly all high chairs now have a "one hand" tray release that enables you to easily remove the tray with a quick motion. The problem: not all releases are the same. The more expensive chairs generally have a release that's easier to operate. Warning: some models have a one-handed "pull" release that is under the tray. Some kids learn they can kick the release and send the tray flying across the kitchen. We'll review which models have this problem later; check under the tray to make sure the release can't be kicked off! (Note: to address this problem, some manufacturers are adding a "kick-guard" to the release). Other trays have a "push" release button that eliminates the kick issue.

◆ **Snack trays.** Some new high chairs have two trays—a big one for meals and a tiny one for snacks. Why? We have no idea.

◆ **Tray wars.** High chair makers like to battle their competitors by touting the newest gimmick on their trays. Hence, you'll now see trays with cup holders, compartmentalized snack areas and so on. Do you really need a cup holder? Don't worry—your baby will spill their juice, cup holder or not. The latest trend is dishwasher-safe tray liners or double trays (where one can go in the dishwasher). This is a cool feature that helps with clean-up.

◆ **Tray height.** Some parents complain the tray height of Italian high chairs is too high—making it hard for smaller babies to use. A smart tip: take your baby with you when you go high chair shopping and actually sit them in the different options. You can evaluate the tray heights in person to make sure the chair will work for both you and baby. We'll note which chairs have the best/worst tray heights later in our reviews. Generally, a chair with a tray height of under 8" should work for most babies. A few models have tray heights over 8'—those can be a major problem since a child can't reach the food on the tray.

◆ **Seat depth.** Most chairs have multiple tray positions and reclining seats. But what is the distance between the seat back when it is upright and the tray in its closest position? A distance of 5" to 7" is acceptable. Over 7" and you run the risk that there will be a large gap between your baby and the tray—and all their food will end up in their lap/chair. Again, take your baby with you when shopping for a chair, as smaller babies may be harder to fit. For larger babies,

high chairs

you may able to adjust the tray out a bit to create more room.

◆ *Less convertibility.* Here's an ironic twist: while the rest of the baby products market is awash in "convertible" products, high chairs are moving the other way. Gone are the high chairs that converted into a table and chair set, or some other future use. Parents seem to like high chairs that are, well, high chairs.

◆ *Washability.* Here's an obvious tip some first-time parents seem to miss: make sure the high chair you buy has a removable washable seat cover OR a seat that easily sponges clean. In the latter category, chairs with VINYL covers trump those made of cloth–vinyl can be wiped clean, while cloth typically has to be washed. This might be one of those first-time parent traps–seats with cloth covers sure look nicer than those made of vinyl. But cloth can't be wiped clean and requires washing–some cloth covers can't be thrown in the dryer either! That means waiting a day or more for a cover to line dry. Nojo does make a high chair cover ($20) that may be a handy option for parents who choose a high chair with a fabric seat pad. You could use the Nojo cover while you're washing and drying the original pad.

Of course, the cloth/vinyl issue becomes somewhat confusing when you consider some vinyl seats have cloth edging/piping. And one seat (the Fisher-Price Cozy Fit) has a "vinyl-coated fabric seat" which supposedly makes it easier to clean up than just plain cloth. Our advice: be careful of any seat with cloth edging/piping, as it might be very hard to clean. (Make sure the seat is washable and machine dryable).

What color cover should you get? Answer: anything but white. Sure, that fancy white "leatherette" high chair looks all shiny and new at the baby store, but it will forever be a cleaning nightmare once you start using it. Darker colors and patterns are better. Another tip: avoid high chairs that have lots of cracks and crevices near the tray and seat, which makes cleaning a nightmare. (This seems to be the Peg Perego Prima Pappa's biggest sin).

Smart Shopper Tip #2
Tray Chic and Other Restaurant Tips

"*We have a great high chair at home, but we're always appalled at the lack of safe high chairs at restaurants. Our favorite cafe has a high chair that must date back to 1952—no straps, a metal tray with sharp edges, and a hard seat with no cushion. Have restaurateurs lost their minds?*

We think so. People who run eating places must search obscure

South American countries to find the world's most hazardous high chairs. The biggest problem? No straps, enabling babies to slide out of the chair, submarine-style. The solution? When the baby is young, keep her in her infant car seat; the safe harness keeps baby secure. When your baby is older (and if you eat out a lot), you may want to invest in a portable booster seat. Because these products are designed for kids two and up, we review them in our book *Toddler Bargains*. You'll find all these "next-step" products reviews and rated in a separate chapter in that book.

The Name Game: Reviews of Selected Manufacturers

Many high-tech high chairs feature height adjustments and extra-large feeding trays. While most are made of plastic and metal, there are still fans out there who like traditional wood chairs. If you want a wood chair, consider offerings from Simmons and Child Craft (yes, they're the same names you saw in Chapter 2 in the crib reviews). Since wood high chairs lack fancy features (you can't adjust the height, they don't fold up, etc.), the majority of high chairs sold in the U.S. and Canada are those reviewed in this section:

The Ratings

A **EXCELLENT**–*our top pick!*
B **GOOD**– *above average quality, prices, and creativity.*
C **FAIR**–*could stand some improvement.*
D **POOR**–*yuck! could stand some major improvement.*

Baby Trend *For a dealer near you, call (800) 328-7363, (909) 902-5568, Web: www. babytrend.com.* We were so excited about this high chair when it debuted last year that we featured it on our appearance on NBC's Today Show as a good bargain. Why? The "Trend High Chair" (Baby Trend apparently hasn't figured out a catchy name for it; it is also called the Maitre D) is a good knock-off of the Perego and Chicco imports, yet it sells for 40% less. Yes, you get all the standard features you'd expect–five-point harness, four-position reclining seat, three-position tray with one hand release, six height positions, compact fold and casters. But the Baby Trend high chair has a lower tray than the Perego or Chicco models and is generally easier to use. Now, that said, the chair does (or did) have two faults.

Parents who used the first version of this chair found their babies could kick off the tray—Baby Trend has now fixed that with a kick guard. Second, it has a cloth seat that CANNOT be machine dried (you have to line dry it). Realizing this mistake, Baby Trend now offers a white vinyl pad that fits over the cloth pad for $21.75 (including shipping; mail order only). That's nice, but why not include it in the first place? And why all-white? Despite that criticism, most parents we interviewed gave this high chair excellent marks. So, we'll give it our second-highest rating. (FYI: This chair is also called the Breckenridge, after one of the available colors for the padding). *Rating: A-*

Carter's. This high chair is made by Kolcraft, see review later.

Chicco *4E Easy Street, Bound Brook, NJ 08805. For a dealer near you, call (877) 4CHICCO or (732) 805-9200.. Web: www. chiccousa.com* Considering the phenomenal success of Peg Perego's Prima Pappa high chair (reviewed later in this section), we figured it wouldn't take long for Italy's other major baby product maker (Chicco) to come up with their  version. And we weren't wrong. Chicco's version, the "Chicco Mamma" (cute, eh?) is a virtual clone of the Prima Pappa although it runs a bit less at retail ($130 to $150). You get a six-position height chair with three-position recline and the whole thing folds up for easy storage. But Chicco has gone one step further than Perego by adding some useful features: the chair is 7% wider and 20% taller than the Pappa. The Mamma's pad is easier to remove and clean than the Pappa's; and the tray features a built-in cup holder. Even better: the Chicco Mamma can fold at any height (the Pappa must be in the top position) and the unit is fully assembled in the box (the Perego requires some assembly). And the Chicco chair avoids some of the cleaning problems that dog the Perego model. So, what's not to like? Plenty, say our readers and for that reason we've knocked this chair off our list of top recommendations this time out (and low-ered its rating). The deal killer: like the Perego chair, the Chicco Mamma's tray is simply too high for most infants. Chicco has tried to address this problem by adding an "infant insert" to the Mamma, which raises the seat by an inch or so. That's nice, but we wonder if a baby squishes down the insert, negating the benefit. More tray problems: it's too heavy and hard to operate if you are left-handed plus the tray can be kicked off by an infant. Other parents complain the Mamma's vinyl chair pad rips too easily and their babies can get their arms stuck in the space between the chair and legs (a problem Perego corrected after having a safety recall a few years ago). Even more stupid: Chicco has made some strange modifications to the Mamma in recent years. First, inexplicably, Chicco eliminated the pegs off the back of the chair that held the tray when not in use. Realizing that was a mistake, Chicco said they'd add them back soon. Then, let's talk about the tray puzzle. In a variation on the chair called the Chicco Mamma Toy, the company added a strange tray puzzle and clear plastic tray that covers the puzzle. Nice concept, bad execution. The "toy activity tray" is really just a bizarre abstract puzzle that isn't attached to the tray—hence it takes about 37 milliseconds for a baby to toss it on the floor with a loud CLACK! As one parent noted, the "top tray is clear plastic, which makes feeding time somewhat of a battle since baby can see the tantalizing colors underneath and frantically wants to chuck something when it's time to eat." Basically, this thing must have been designed by someone who didn't have a baby. In past years, we gave this chair a good rating, but this year we'll pass. Thanks to new, competing chairs from Baby Trend and Fisher-Price this expensive chair has become passé. ***Rating: C***

Living the High Life

Hook-on chairs and booster seats are close relatives to the familiar high chair. Depending on your needs, each can serve a purpose. Hook-on chairs do exactly what they say—hook onto a table. While some have trays, most do not, and that is probably their biggest disadvantage: baby eats (or spills and throws food) on your table instead of hers. At least they're cheap: about $25 to $40 at most stores. Best use: if your favorite restaurants don't have high chairs (or don't have safe ones) or if you plan to do some road trips with Junior. One caveat: hook-on chairs are only safe when used with tables that have four legs (not pedestals).

Booster seats are more useful. With or without an attached tray, most strap to a chair or can be used on the floor. We use ours at Grandma's house, which spares us the chore of dragging along a high chair or hook-on chair. It's also convenient to do evening feedings in a booster seat in the baby's room, instead of dragging everyone to the kitchen. And you can't beat the price: $18 to $30 at most stores.

Both of these products are reviewed in depth in our *Toddler Bargains* book, as they are most useful for two to four year olds. See the back of this book for details on our other book.

FEEDING

Combi *199 Easy St., Carol Stream, IL 60188. For a dealer near you, call (800) 752-6624, (800) 992-6624, (630) 871-0404; Web: www.combi-intl.com.*  Best known for its strollers, Combi has been trying to expand its brand franchise into other categories in recent years. Example: the Easy Glide high chair, Combi's first effort to do something innovative in the high chair category. As the name implies, the Easy Glide is the first high chair that rocks back and forth to soothe baby. Like its competitors, it features a five-point harness, four-position height adjustment, one-had tray release, casters, adjustable footrest and more. What's unique about the Easy Glide? Well, its five-position reclining seat has a FULL recline, so we guess baby can take a nap before dinner. Combi has added their acoustic canopy to the high chair (in a "deluxe" version) so your baby can rock out with the latest Barenaked Ladies CD at dinner. We're not sure why a high chair needs a canopy, but hey—the music part is cool. FYI: This chair has a rather funky fold—it folds flat (horizontally), rather than up (vertically) as most chairs do. This could be an issue if you planned to store the chair out of sight in your kitchen pantry. Finally, consider the price: this chair runs $150 to $180, depending on where you find it (Babies R Us, online, etc). That's a bit much, despite the fact it looks cool (the metallic grey vinyl seat is very Upper East Side) and includes extras like an infant body pillow, storage basket, splat mat and more. It's large size (relative to other chairs), however, could be a deal killer for many parents. **Rating: B**

Cosco *2525 State St., Columbus, IN 47201. Call (812) 372-0141 for a dealer near you (or 514-323-5701 for a dealer in Canada). Web: www.coscoinc.com*  Like most things Cosco makes, their high chairs define the entry-level price point in this market. Simple Cosco high chairs (model 03-330) are bare bones models that sell for $30 to $40 in discount stores like K-Mart. These might make good choices for grandma's house, where occasional use is all that would be required. We should also note that Cosco makes high chairs under the Safety 1st brand, including a $50 model sold at Babies R Us (pictured at right). Cosco's main offering in the full feature high chair category was the Options 5 High Chair ($40 to $50)—a model that had a seven-position recline, four-position tray, removable pad and more. The chair is discontinued, but we still notice it sold online. Once again, safety concerns continue to dog Cosco—in late 2000, Cosco recalled one MILLION of the Options 5 High Chairs after they received reports that the seats could separate from the frame and fall to the ground. Cosco and the CPSC received 168 reports of such incidents, including 57 injury reports. We are still haunted by the sight of one Cosco high chair collapsing (with child inside), captured on home video and played on the local news. As a result, we can't recommend this brand. *Rating: F*

Evenflo *1801 Commerce Dr., Piqua, OH 45356. For a dealer near you, call (800) 233-5921 or (937) 415-3300. Web: www.evenflo.com* Evenflo has always been an also-ran in the high chair market. Lackluster models are one reason. Take the Evenflo "Easy Comfort" chair–parents we interviewed hated the tray  and the overall design. There was a monster 11" gap between the tray and the back of the seat, which meant all of baby's food quickly went into their lap. This chair was last seen in the markdown bin for about $70 (we say it isn't worth $7). So, Evenflo has gone back to the drawing board and now has two new models. The "Envision" is a much better effort–for $50, you get seven height adjustments, three recline positions, four-position tray with one-hand release and some extras (a towel rack, vinyl pad and easy fold). Evenflo also makes an upgraded version of this chair called the Envision Plus (pictured above, in Osh Kosh colors) for $70 that features a snack track and casters for mobility. Our only concern about this chair: the one-hand tray release doesn't have a kick-guard, meaning some enterprising toddlers may figure out how to remove the tray by foot. Besides the Envision, Evenflo has another model called the Simplicity Plus. This upgraded chair features eight

License mania

One thing that always confuses parents is all the licensed baby products out there. For example, Kolcraft licenses the names "Carter's" and "Lennon Baby" to put on their high chairs. Cosco does the same with Eddie Bauer and NASCAR for their car seats and Evenflo with Osh Kosh for strollers and more. Here's a little secret of the baby product biz: licensed products are often IDENTICAL to the same ones made under the manufacturer's own name. At most, there are just different fabric colors or patterns. BUT, you pay for that name–most licensed products are 10% to 30% more expensive them the plain vanilla versions. Whether that premium for a certain color or pattern is worth it is up to you.

height adjustments, four recline positions, snack tray, casters, three-position tray and a dishwasher-safe tray liner. Not a bad deal for $80, right? Hold it—check out the pad. It's cloth. And while it can be machine washed, it can only be tumbled dry on low for "10 to 15 minutes." That means you'll have to line dry it after that—a major negative in our opinion. While we like the extra padding in this chair and the tray that sits just 5 1/2" inches from the back of the seat, that cloth pad is a deal killer for us. **Rating: C**

Fisher-Price *636 Grand Ave., East Aurora, NY 14052. For a dealer near you, call (800) 828-4000 or (716) 687-3000. Web: www.fisher-price.com.* Folks, we have a winner! After years of fumbling around in this category, Fisher-Price finally hit a home run with the Healthy Care high chair last year. It features a three-position
seat recline, five-point restraint, one-hand tray removal and seven height adjustments. Best of all: the snap-off tray is dishwasher safe. And price? An affordable $70. The Healthy Care comes in two versions: the regular and Deluxe, which adds casters, infant headrest and three food trays for $85-90. Which one should you get? The basic version is fine if you don't need casters for mobility. But the Deluxe (pictured) has one additional advantage: it omits the fabric ruffle on the vinyl seat edge, which we worry might be a cleaning headache. Parents we interviewed praise the Healthy Care's ease of use and cleanability. As a result, it is our top recommendation. (FYI: as of press time, Babies R Us just carried the regular version of the Healthy Care, while Target and other retailers had the Deluxe). In other news, Fisher-Price also has released a low-price chair called the Cozy Fit for $50. It's basically a stripped down Healthy Care, omitting the snap-off dishwasher tray and casters. One cool feature: this chair has cushioned "wings" that adjust for smaller children. At $50, it's a bit much for Grandma's house but might not be a bad choice if you don't want a high chair with extra frills. Finally, we should mention Fisher-Price's other high chair, the Swing 'N' Meals ($99). This chair, now discontinued but still sold online, combined a high chair and swing. We found it innovative and well-designed, but perhaps a bit ahead of its time. Nonetheless, for the Healthy Care chairs, we'll give this brand our highest rating. **Rating: A**

Graco *Rt. 23, Main St., Elverson, PA 19520. For a dealer near you, call (800) 345-4109, (610) 286-5951. Web: www.gracobaby.com* Graco is probably the biggest player in the under $75 high chair market. The company offers everything from bare-bones models for $29 to top-of-the-line units with all the bells and whistles for $69. On the low-end, the "Easy Chair" ($30) is a very simple unit—basically a chair and tray. It might make a good back-up chair for grandma's house if you're on a budget. The "Easy Seat" ($30) has a five-position height adjustment and larger seat, while the "Neat Seat" comes in several different versions that range from $40 to $70. The top-

of-the-line Double Tray ($90; pictured) features, well, a double tray (a large, compartmentalized tray with cup holder and a small snack tray), five-point harness, removable, washable pad and footrest. Unfortunately, this chair has a cloth cover that must be lined dried, which is a deal killer for us. Another negative: while all Graco chairs have passive under-tray restraints to prevent submarining, often this guard is attached to the tray, NOT the seat. That's not our preference either, as an infant can possibly squirm out of the seat when the tray is off. And what about the quality of these chairs? Readers gripe about low quality seat cushions that rip and tear with only a few weeks of use, as well as tray releases that are harder to work than other competing models. Don't expect this chair to last beyond one child. If you get a Graco, plan on having a large kitchen or dining room—most models don't fold compactly for storage. *Rating: C+*

John Lennon. These chairs are made by Kolcraft, see below for review.

Kolcraft *3455 West 31st Pl., Chicago, IL 60623. For a dealer near you, call (773) 247-4494. Web: www.kolcraft.com.* Kolcraft's main emphasis in the high chair market is their licensed brands—this company makes both a Carter's high chair and a "collectible" Lennon Baby high chair. Of course, no matter what name is on the

chair, it's just a Kolcraft high chair with different fabrics. Prices are $49 for a Kolcraft model, $59 for the Carter's and $69 for the Lennon Baby. Whatever you pay, you basically get the same seat: three-position recline, six-position height adjustment and four-position adjustable tray with one-hand release. While we like the safety T-bar under the tray, we were disappointed this guard is attached to the tray (not the seat as we prefer). Another concern: the tray is too high—8.5" above the seat. And what about quality? Parents we interviewed knock Kolcraft high chairs for being hard to use (adjusting the straps is a pain), seat pads that rip too easily and other quality woes. And you gotta love the cloth pad that comes with this seat—it has to be HAND washed and lined dry. Skip this brand. *Rating: F*

Lennon Baby. This high chair is made by Kolcraft, see above.

Martinelli. Peg Perego markets their products in some specialty stores under the name Martinelli. Yet, the Martinelli high chairs are EXACTLY the same as the Perego models, just different colors. See Perego's review below for more details.

Peg Perego 3625 Independence Dr., Ft. Wayne, IN 46808. For a dealer near you, call (219) 482-8191. Web: www.perego.com Yes, this seat has been a best-seller but its day has come and gone. Sure, it looks stylish and features a four-position reclining seat, seven height adjustments, a dishwasher-safe dinner tray, five-point restraint and compact fold. But let's look  at the chair's key flaws: the tray. It sits a whopping 9" above the seat, making it too tall except perhaps for Shaq's kids. Another problem: the tray sits 9.5" from the back seat, creating a gap the size of the Grand Canyon between your baby and her food. Then let's talk about this chair's cleanability—it's notorious for collecting food in every little nook and cranny. All this for $160 to $170! Wow, what a deal. Perego hasn't really changed this seat much in recent years, besides introducing a spin-off called the "Roller." This chair features a bar that helps you roll it about the kitchen and a new storage basket. It's rather striking with a seat covered in black "leatherette" fabric, but beware: "The Roller" does NOT fold up like the Pappa, which is a major negative in our opinion. And it features the same tray and cleanability problems as the original model. If you like the looks of the Perego, save yourself $70 and get the Baby Trend knock-off. Same basic features but a much better tray and cleanability, 40% lower in price. **Rating: C+**

Safety 1st. These high chairs are made by Cosco, reviewed earlier in this chapter.

Zooper For a dealer near you, call 503-248-9469; web: www.zooperstrollers.com. Following Combi from the stroller world to the planet of high chairs, Zooper recently introduced their own spin on this category with the cutesy name "Peas & Carrots." Its ultra-cool look (black leatherette vinyl cover and brushed aluminum frame) has had  a few of our readers buzzing. It features four height positions, mesh basket, five point harness and locking wheels. Unfortunately, it is quite pricey ($160 retail, although readers have spied it on sale for as little as $130). All that and you don't get a snap-off tray for the dishwasher, as you'd see in chairs that cost $50 less. Another bummer: the chair doesn't fold as flat as the Italian chairs and, when folded, the basket sticks out a good four inches from the chair. The result: when folded, the Peas & Carrots doesn't stand because it isn't balanced. And we aren't wild about the tray height (too tall at 9") nor the seat depth (8.5" from the back of the seat to the tray). The passive restraint is on the tray instead of the seat, which is another negative. That said, parents who've used this chair say it functions well and is easy to clean. The seat is vinyl "leatherette," which is washable (but not machine dryable). Yes, it is hard to find (no chain stores carry it as of this writing), but it might be worth a look if you see it at a specialty store. The only thing holding back our rating of this chair is its high price. **Rating: B-**

◆ **Other Brands**. *Playskool* used to be a big player in the high chair market with their affordable 1-2-3 high chair, but the company has withdrawn from the baby products market amid slumping sales. The 1-2-3 was plagued by many recalls, so we'd skip it if you find one second-hand.

Our Picks: Brand Recommendations

Here is our round-up of the best high chair bets.

Good. The Fisher-Price Cozy Fit is a no-frills chair with cushioned "wings" that adjust in for smaller babies. This chair doesn't have any fancy features, but hey, it's only $50.

Better. Baby Trend's "Trend High Chair" (also referred to as the Breckenridge, one of its patterns) copies all the features/looks of the Italian imports, but for 40% less cash. We like the compact fold and casters, plus you also get a five-point harness and six height positions. And it looks pretty decent too. The only caveat: that cloth pad that requires line drying. Yes, you can buy a vinyl pad to cover the cloth for $21.75, but that makes this $90 chair somewhat less of a deal. On the other hand, even with the extra pad, you're still spending less than a $170 Peg Perego Prima Pappa . . . and you're getting a much better high chair with Baby Trend.

Best. The Fisher-Price "Healthy Care" has got it all—great safety features, easy of use, cleanability and more. We like the snap-off dishwasher-safe tray, good design and easy-to-clean vinyl pad. The only decision here is whether you want to get the basic version ($70 at Babies R Us) or the deluxe version for $85 to $90 (Target

HIGH CHAIRS

High chairs, compared

	PEREGO Prima Pappa	COMBI Easy Glider	CHICCO Mamma	BABY TREND Breckenridge
PRICE	$160	$150	$130	$90
TRAY HEIGHT (INCHES)	9"	8.5	9/8*	8
DEPTH (TRAY TO SEAT)	9.5"	7	9/7.5*	7.5
KICKABLE TRAY?	YES	NO	YES	NO
SUBMARINE?	SEAT	SEAT	TRAY	SEAT
SEAT	VINYL	VINYL	VINYL**	CLOTH

KEY

TRAY HEIGHT: Distance from the seat to the top of the tray. Any measurement under 8" is acceptable. Above 8" is too tall.

DEPTH (tray to seat): Distance from the back of the seat to the tray. 5" to 7" is acceptable.

KICKABLE TRAY? Can the tray be kicked off by a child? Thanks to poorly-designed one-hand tray releases, trays with pull releases and without kick guards can be trouble. If this is "yes," we judge that the tray can be kicked off by a toddler. Note: this isn't a safety hazard; more like a hassle for parents, as you might guess.

SUBMARINE: Most high chairs have a special guard to prevent a child from submarining under the tray. Some chairs attach this to the chair; others to tray. A better bet: those that attach to the seat. See discussion earlier in this chapter.

and other stores), which adds casters and three food trays. We liked the fact the Deluxe omits the fabric piping/edging you see on the basic version, which we worry about for cleaning reasons. Whether you go for the basic or Deluxe, this one's the best in the class.

Grandma's house. For grandma's house, a simple Graco Easy Chair ($30) should do the trick. It has a five-position height adjustment and large seat area. No, it doesn't have casters or other fancy features, but Grandma doesn't need all that.

The Bottom Line: A Wrap-Up of Our Best Buy Picks

What's the more affordable way to feed baby? Breastfeeding, by a mile. We estimate you can save $500 or in just the first six months

GRACO DOUBLE TRAY	CARTERS	EVENFLO ENVISION	EVENFLO SIMPLICITY PL.	FISHER PRICE HEALTHY CARE	ZOOPER PEAS/CARROTS
$90	$70	$70	$80	$70	$160
8	8.5	6.5	7.5	8	9
6.5	6	5	5.5	5	8.5
No	No	No	Yes	No	No
Tray	Tray	Seat	Seat	Seat	Tray
Cloth	Cloth	Vinyl	Cloth	Vinyl**	Vinyl

SEAT: Is the seat made of cloth or vinyl? We prefer vinyl for easier clean up. Cloth seats must be laundered and some can't be thrown in the drier (requiring a long wait for it to line dry). Of course, this feature isn't black and white—some vinyl seats have cloth edging/piping.

The Chicco Mamma comes with an infant insert to make it better fit smaller babies. The first figure the measurement without the insert; the second figure is with it.

** These seats have a vinyl seat with cloth piping. One version of the Fisher-Price chair has this piping; the Deluxe version does not.

high chairs

alone by choosing to breast instead of bottle feed.

Of course, that's easy for us to say—breastfeeding takes some practice, for both you and baby. One product that can help: a breast pump, to relieve engorgement or provide a long-term solution to baby's feeding if you go back to work. Which pumps are best? For manual pumps, we like the Avent Isis ($45) for that occasional bottle. If you plan to pump so you can go back to work, a piston electric pump works best. Tip: rent one first before you buy. If you like it and decide you are serious about pumping, we liked the Medela Pump In Style ($329) or Ameda Purely Yours for $250.

If you decide to bottle fee or need to wean your baby off breast milk, the most affordable formula are the generic brands like BabyMil sold in discount stores under various private-label names. You'll save up to 40% by choosing generic over name brands, but your baby gets the exact same nutrition.

Who makes the best bottles? Our readers save Avent is tops, but others find cheaper options like Playtex and Munchkin Health Flow work just was well at half the price. A dark horse brand: Dr. Brown's bottles, which help eliminate colic.

Let's talk baby food—besides the ubiquitous Gerber, there are several other brands that are good alternatives. One of the best is Earth's Best, although it is more pricey than affordable brands like Heinz and Beechnut. How can you save? Make your own baby food for pennies or buy jarred baby food in bulk at discount stores. And skip the toddler meals, which are a waste of money.

Finally, consider that quintessential piece of baby gear—the high chair. We felt the best bets were those that were easiest to clean (go for a vinyl, not cloth pad) and had snap-off dishwasher-safe trays. Our top pick is the Fisher Price Healthy Care ($70 to $90, depending on the version), although the Baby Trend "Trend High Chair" ($90) has all the looks of Italian high chairs for 40% less cash.

Now that you've got the food and kitchen covered, what about the rest of your house? We'll explore all the other baby gear you might need for your home next.

CHAPTER 7

Around the House: Monitors, Diaper Pails, Toys & More

Inside this chapter

What's a "Flatobearius"? Which baby monitor can save you $40 a year in batteries? What's the best—and least stinky—diaper pail? In this chapter, we explore everything for baby that's around the house. From a basic list of toys to the best baby monitors, we'll give you tricks and tips to saving money. You'll learn nine safety tips for toys as well as advice on humidifiers, playpens and swings—and even tips for making sure pet and baby get along.

Getting Started: When Do You Need This Stuff?

The good news is you don't need all this stuff right away. While you'll probably purchase a monitor before the baby is born, other items like high chairs, activity seats, and even bath-time products aren't necessary immediately (you'll give the baby sponge baths for the first few weeks, until the belly button area heals). Of course, you still might want to register for these items before baby is born. In each section of this chapter, we'll be more specific about when you need certain items.

What Are You Buying?

Here is a selection of items that you can use when your baby is three to six months of age. Of course, these ideas are merely suggestions—none of these items are "mandatory." We've divided them into three categories: bath-time, the baby's room and toys.

Bath

1 TOYS/BOOKS. What fun is it taking a bath without toys? Many stores sell inexpensive plastic tub toys, but you can use other items like stacking cups in the tub as well. And don't forget about tub safety items, which can also double as toys. For example, Safety 1st (800) 739-7233 (www.safety1st.com) makes a ***Bath Pal Thermometer***, a yellow duck or tugboat with attached thermometer (to make sure the water isn't too hot) for $3. ***Tubbly Bubbly*** by Kel-Gar (972) 250-3838 (web: www.kelgar.com) is a $10 elephant or hippo spout cover that protects against scalding, bumps and bruises. In fact, Kel-Gar makes an entire line of innovative bath toys and accessories.

2 TOILETRIES. Basic baby shampoo like the famous brand made by Johnson & Johnson works just fine, and you'll probably need some lotion as well. The best tip: first try lotion that is unscented in case your baby has any allergies. Also, never use talcum powder on your baby—it's a health hazard. If you need to use an absorbent powder, good old cornstarch will do the trick.

What about those natural baby products that are all the rage, like Mustela or Calidou? We got a gift basket of an expensive boutique's natural baby potions and didn't see what the big deal was. Worse yet, the $20-a-bottle shampoo dried out our baby's scalp so much he had scratching fits. We suppose the biggest advantage of these products is that they don't contain extraneous chemicals or petroleum by-products. Also, most don't have perfumes, but then, many regular products now come in unscented versions. The bottom line: it's your comfort level. If you want to try them out without making a big investment, register for them as a shower gift.

3 BABY BATHTUB. While not a necessity, a baby bathtub is a nice convenience (especially if you are bathing baby solo). See the section below for more info on bathtubs.

4 POTTY SEAT. Since this book focuses on products for babies age birth to 2, we have put this topic in our new book ***Toddler Bargains***, now in bookstores. You'll find an entire chapter devoted to reviews and ratings of the best potty seats!

Baby Bathtubs

Sometimes, it is the simplest products that are the best. Take baby bathtubs—if you take a look at the offerings in this category, you'll note tubs that have "4 in 1" uses, fold up and convert to small compact car. Okay, just kidding on the car, but this product is a good example of brand manager overkill—companies think the way to success with baby bath tubs is to make them work from birth to college.

So, it is a bit of a surprise that our top pick for a baby bathtub is, well, just a bathtub. The **EuroBath by Primo** ($25; web: www.primoba-by. com) is a sturdy tub for babies age birth to two. It weighs under 2 pounds and is easy to use—just add baby, water and poof! Clean baby.

The EuroBath is well designed, although it is big—almost three feet from end to end. That may be a tight fit if you have a small bathroom. In that case, you might want to consider the Fold-Up Tub by Safety 1st ($13). Nothing fancy, but it does have a foam liner and (as the name implies) folds up for compact storage. This might be a good choice for Grandma's house.

A baby bathtub is a great item to pick up second-hand or at a garage sale. Or borrow from a friend. Readers say they've snagged baby bath tubs for $2 or so at garage sales—with a little cleaning, they are just fine. What if you want to give baby a bath in a regular tub or kitchen sink? One reader writes with kudos for the **EZ Bather Deluxe** by Dex Products ($6, 800-546-1996; www.dexproducts.com), an L-shaped vinyl frame that keeps babies head above water in the bathtub or kitchen sink.

Baby's Room

1 **A Diaper Pail.** Yes, there are dozens of diaper pails on the market. We'll review and rate the offerings in the next section.

2 **Baby Monitor.** Later in this chapter, we have a special section devoted to monitors, including some creative money-saving tips. Of course, if you have a small house or apartment, you may not even need a baby monitor.

3 **The Changing Area.** The well-stocked changing area features much more than just diapers. Nope, you need wipes and lots of them. We discussed our recommendations for wipe brands in Chapter 4, the Reality Layette. We should note that we've heard from some thrifty parents who've made their own diaper wipes—they use old washcloths or cut-up cloth diapers and warm water.

What about wipe warmers? In previous editions of this book, we've recommended these $20 devices, which keep wipes at 99 degrees (and lessen the cold shock on baby's bottom at three in the morning). However, we've been concerned with safety issues about wipe warmers that have arisen in recent years.

First, Dex recalled a half million of their wipe warmers in 1997 after one alleged fire was caused by the unit (there were six additional instances "involving melting of the product," says the CPSC). While Dex fixed the problem in January 1997, we were so miffed about how the company handled the recall, we won't recommend them again. (See the box on the next page).

Then, we started getting complaints from readers about another brand of wipe warmers (Prince Lionheart) that damaged dresser tops. Prince Lionheart blamed the problem on the little feet under the warmer, which were apparently leaving marks on the dresser tops when the unit warmed up. The company claims it has now fixed the problem (and denies that wipe warmers "burn" wipes—they say the heat discolors the chemicals in the wipes), but we're still leery of these products in general.

If you still want a wipe warmer, we'd go for the ones that warm wipes from the top down (Prince Lionheart has one such model). These seem to be more trouble free than the older, bottom-up warmers.

Other products to consider for the diaper changing station include diaper rash ointment (A & D, Desitin, etc.), lotion or cream, cotton swabs, petroleum jelly (for rectal thermometers) and rubbing alcohol to care for the belly button area (immediately remove this item from the changing area once you finish belly button care—it's poisonous!). If you have a Container Store nearby (800) 733-3532 (www.containerstore. com), we noticed they sell simple plastic storage containers for all those diaper changing station items at $3 to $7.

4 **PORTABLE CRIBS/PLAYPENS.** While this item doesn't necessarily go in your baby's room, many folks have found portable cribs/playpens to be indispensable in other parts of the house (or when visiting grandma). Later in this chapter, we have a special section devoted to this topic.

5 **WHITE NOISE.** Some parents swear they'd never survive without the ceiling fan in their baby's room—the "white noise" made by a whirling fan soothed their fussy baby (and quieted sounds from the rest of the house). Just about anything can generate white noise—a humidifier, whole house fan, etc. Some parents play nature CDs or tapes on a boom box. One web site, Pure White Noise (www. purewhitenoise.com) sells white noise CDs for $16. A selection of white noise generators is available on line at Ear Plug Store (www.earplugstore.com) for $48 to $200. Fisher Price also makes a couple monitors with the option to turn on soothing sounds or music when baby needs calming. See reviews in the

How NOT to Run a Recall

If we had to give an award for the Worst Recall of a Baby Product, the winner would have to be Dex, the California-based maker of wipe warmers and other baby products. In 1997, Dex recalled a popular wipe warmer, instructing parents to call a toll-free number. First, it took FOREVER to get through to Dex's hotline after the recall was announced. Then, after reaching a human, we were instructed to call Halcyon, Dex's supplier in Canada (who actually manufactured the wipe warmer). At Halcyon, a not-too-helpful person who answered the phone told us we had to send our request for a replacement wipe warmer to Canada. The piece de resistance: the Halcyon folks didn't tell us to keep the warmer COVER, which we sent back with the recalled unit. So, the heating element they sent back *sans cover* was useless. The result: we curse Dex. Having your customers call your supplier in another country to fix a defective product you sold is NOT good customer service.

monitors section for more information.

6 HUMIDIFIER. See the section later in this chapter for tips on buying the best humidifier.

Diaper Pails

Pop quiz! Remember our discussion of how many diapers you will change in your baby's first year? What was the amount?

Pencils down—yes, it was 2300 diapers! A staggering figure . . . only made more staggering by figuring out what do with the dirty ones once you've changed baby. Yes, we can hear first-time parents raising their hands right now and saying "Duh! They go in the trash!" Oh, not so fast, new parental one. Stick a dirty diaper in a regular trashcan and you will quickly perfume your home—not to mention draw a curious pet and we won't even go there.

So, most parents use a diaper pail, that specialized trash can designed by trained scientists to limit stink and keep out babies, pets and stray relatives. But which diaper pail? Here's a Diaper Pail 411:

Diaper pails fall into two camps: those that use cartridges to wrap diapers in deodorized plastic and pails that use regular kitchen trash bags. As you'd guess, those plastic refill canisters are most expensive to use (they cost $4 to $8, depending on the size) and wrap about 140 or so diapers. The pail can hold 20-25 diapers at a time, which is about 3-5 days worth of diapers.

So, should you just get a diaper pail that uses regular kitchen trash bags? Yes, they are less expensive to use—but there is sometimes a major trade-off. Stink. Yes, these pails tend to stink more and hence, have to be emptied more frequently than the diaper pails that use special deodorized plastic—perhaps daily or every other day.

Obviously, the decision on which diaper pail is right for you and your baby's nursery depends on several factors. What is the distance to the trash? If you live in a house with easy access to an outside trashcan, it might be easier to go with the lower-cost alternatives and just take out the diapers more frequently. If you live in an apartment where the nearest dumpster is down three flights of stairs and a long walk across a parking lot, well, it might make sense to go with an option that requires less work. Another factor: how sensitive are you to the smell? Some folks don't have a major problem with this, while moms who are pregnant again with a second child may need an industrial strength diaper pail to keep from losing it when walking into baby's nursery.

Whatever your decision, remember you'll live with this diaper pail for three or more YEARS (that's how long before most children potty train). And it's a fact of life: diapers get stinkier as your baby gets older . . . so the diaper removal strategy that works for a newborn may have to be chucked for a toddler. Yes, you may be able to use a plain trashcan with liner when your newborn is breastfeeding . . . but after you start solid foods, it will be time to buy a diaper pail.

Given those caveats, here is overview of what's out there:

Diaper Champ by Baby Trend

Type: Kitchen trash bag.

Price: $30. Web: www.BabyTrend.com.

Pros: Did we mention no expensive refills? The Diaper Champ uses regular ol' kitchen bags, yet the contraption works to seal out odor by using a flip handle design. Very easy to use. Taller design means it holds more diapers than the Genie.

Cons: Not as stink-free as the Genie or Dekor, but close. Enterprising toddlers can learn how to put their toys into the diaper slot.

Comments: And in this corner. . . let's crown a new champ for diaper pails—the Diaper Champ by Baby Trend. It's simple design and ease of use wins fans, although a few detractors note it isn't as stink-free as the Genie or Dekor. And you do have to empty it every few days (more often than the Genie or Dekor), despite the large capacity. That could be a hassle for apartment dwellers or those without handy access to an outside trashcan. We should also mention that one mom emailed us with a Diaper Champ tale of woe—her toddler figured out how to put toys into the top slot (which is uncovered), plopping them into the pail. Not pretty. We realize a cover might defeat the advantage of the one-hand feature, but perhaps Baby Trend could offer this as an accessory in the future. Despite the drawbacks, the vast majority of parents we interviewed felt this was the best diaper pail on the market and we agree.

Bottom line: Best pick if you want to go the kitchen trash bag route.

Rating: A

DIAPER DEKOR BY BABY BJORN

Type: Refill canister

Price: $30 to $40. Refill packs are $17 and wrap 480 newborn diapers. Web: www.regallager.com

Pros: Hands free operation—you hit the foot petal and drop in a diaper. Large size can hold 5+ days worth of diapers. Converts to a regular trashcan after baby is done with diapers. Parents say it is much easier to use than the Genie. And refills cost half as much as the Genie, on a per diaper basis. More attractive design than the Genie.

Cons: Still have to buy those expensive refill canisters.

Comments: The Diaper Dekor (imported to the U.S. by Baby Bjorn) debuted in 2002 and is giving the Diaper Genie a good run for its money. It comes in two versions: a regular model and a "plus" version that is a few inches bigger/taller and holds more diapers. As for the stink factor, the jury is still out on this one—some parents say it is just as good as the Genie at odor control, while others think it isn't quite as effective. Overall, the Dekor does seem to get better marks for ease of use (love the foot petal idea) so we'll give it a slightly higher rating than the Genie. Plus we like the fact it can convert to a regular trashcan later after the diaper days are over.

Bottom line: A worthy alternative to the Genie.

Rating: A-

DIAPER GENIE BY PLATYEX

Type: Refill canister

Price: $25 to $30. Refill cartridges are $4 to $8 and wrap about 140 diapers (although this varies by size). Web: www.playtexbaby.com

Pros: Tops at stink control. Wraps each diaper in plastic; dirty diapers plop out the bottom like a chain of sausages. That makes it easier to carry them to the trash. Used properly, there is very little odor from the Genie. Newer Genies feature a wider-mouth opening, making it easier to use. Playtex also offers special refills for toddlers (they have a green top) with more odor control.

Cons: Expensive, since you have to keep buying those refills. Some parents complain it is difficult to use—you have to twist the top to seal the diaper, etc. Since the Genie can hold several days' worth of diapers, parents complain when they OPEN it to remove the diapers, the smell is overwhelming.

Comments: Yes, the Diaper Genie is the #1 best-selling diaper pail in the country and we did recommend it in the past several editions of this book. But, the competition has caught up the Genie and now there are several credible alternatives. When you talk to parents about the Diaper Genie, you get strong love/hate reactions. Fans think it is the best thing since sliced bread. Detractors complain bitterly about the extra cost of those refill cartridges and some parents find it hard to use (yes, it does have detailed instructions with pictures, but it still confounds some folks). And we've been disappointed that Playtex hasn't made any improvements to this product in the last few years—it could stand a re-design to keep up with the competition.

Bottom line: A favorite that is showing its age. We still recommend the Diaper Genie, although we will give the Diaper Dekor and Diaper Champ slightly higher ratings for their ease of use and lower cost.

Rating: B+

DIAPER NANNY BY COSCO

Type: Refill canister.

Price: $30 to $40, refills about $5 to $6.

Comments: This was Cosco's knock-off of the Genie, but it never caught on and was recently discontinued. You might see a few online or in the close-out bin of a local store. This pail never worked well; we say skip it.

Rating: D

ODOR-LESS DIAPER BY SAFETY 1ST

Type: Kitchen trash bag.

Price: $17. Web: www.safety1st.com

Pros: It's cheap. No refills required—uses kitchen trash bags. Child-resistant lock on top keeps out curious toddlers. Compartment inside is deodorized.

Cons: Does not seal out the stink. Low-quality pail breaks too easily.

Comments: This one's a loser—basically an over-priced trash can as one parent put it. The "odor-less" part of this pail is a joke. Safety 1st should be ashamed of this product.

Bottom line: Skip it.

Rating: D

◆ **Other brands.** *Fisher Price* made an "Odor Free" diaper pail that was anything but—fortunately, it is now discontinued. If you see one online or in a discount store, we'd suggest skipping it.

Humidifiers

Even if you don't live in a dry climate, you might consider a humidifier for baby's room during the winter months. Why? Forced-air heat or air conditioning can dry out a house quickly. When it comes to humidifiers, you have two choices:

◆ ***Cool mist.*** These models work either by evaporation (a filter traps minerals and impurities and then a fan sends the cool mist into the air) or ultrasonic (which uses an electronic transducer to create cool mist). Some folks like ultrasonic models since they are quieter; on the other hand, the fan in evaporative humidifiers generates white noise that can comfort a fussy baby.

◆ ***Warm mist.*** These humidifiers have a heating system to release warm mist into the air. Some warm mist humidifiers have a "vaporizer" feature that allows you to vaporize prescribed medicine into the baby's room (although doctors rarely prescribe that today). These models make a bit of noise when they heat up the water (usually, it's a gurgling sound), but they are quieter than cool mist evaporative models with fans.

So, should you get a warm or cool mist model? It's a toss-up. Warm mist models can raise the temperature in baby's room—that could be a plus (if your house is somewhat drafty) or a minus (if baby's room gets too warm). Each model requires regular cleaning every week and replacement of filters every four to eight weeks.

The disadvantages of humidifiers: evaporative coolers have filters that trap mineral deposits. Over time deposits can reduce the effectiveness of the wick. For ultrasonic humidifiers, mineral deposits can be dispersed through the air as "white dust" which is a cleaning hassle (and some believe a health hazard.) Yes, you can use distilled water in ultrasonic humidifiers, but that's expensive. Finally, what about warm mist humidifiers? Some doctors don't recommend these because they believe a warm, moist environment can lead to bacteria growth.

One feature we recommend: a built-in humidistat. This feature works much the same way a thermostat controls your heat or air conditioning. When the humidity in a room reaches a preset level, the humidistat shuts off the humidifier. If the humidity drops, the unit turns back on. Some cheaper humidifiers lack humidistats; we suggest skipping those models.

What are the best brands? We like the Holmes brand (800-5-HOLMES; www.holmesproducts.com) as well as models by Duracraft/Honeywell. Holmes makes both warm and cool mist models as well as ultrasonic units. They're sold at reasonable prices at discounters like Wal-Mart and Target (among many other stores).

One reader, Valerie Graham, recommended the Slant/Fin ultra-violet warm mist germ-free humidifier (pictured). "We live in a rural, arid mountainous environment and I suffer from many allergies. I purchased one for the nursery and found it at Babies R Us for $79. I did a lot of research, and this humidifier has a dual germicidal process—both ultraviolet light and boiling (vaporization). There is no white dust. There are no replacement filters, wicks, or cartridges. It operates very quietly. I have seen it in other catalogs—Brookstone, Hard to Find Tools, Harmony—for over $100. It kills 99.9% of bacteria and molds and spores. I think it is a wonderful product."

What about humidifiers by juvenile product makers? We find them to be overpriced and underpowered. For example, Evenflo sells both warm and cool-mist 2.5-gallon models for $40 at Babies R Us. That's nice, but we've seen the same size humidifiers at discounters for $30 or less. Another benefit for Holmes: all their humidifiers are treated with "Microban" antibacterial protection in the plastic (and in the cool mist wick filters).

A buying note: we suggest buying a humidifier from a store with a good return policy. Like any electronic device, you may have to return a defective one if you find it doesn't work properly. One reader who bought a humidifier online direct from the manufacturer found this out the hard way—she discovered the manufacturer wouldn't take back the defective model, even though it was just a week old!

What's the right size humidifier? For most standard size bedrooms, a 1.5 to 2.0-gallon humidifier should do. For larger rooms, check out these guidelines:

AREA HUMIDIFIED (IN SQ. FT.)	ROOM SIZE	NEEDED OUTPUT (GALLONS PER DAY)
500 OR LOWER	VERY SMALL	1.5 TO 2.0
530-600	SMALL TO MEDIUM	2.2 TO 2.5
700-800	MEDIUM	3.0 TO 3.5
900-1000	MEDIUM TO LARGE	4.0 TO 5.0
1000-2000	LARGE TO WHOLE HOUSE	7.0 TO 9.0
OVER 2000	WHOLE HOUSE	10.0 OR HIGHER

Source: www.holmesproducts.com

Toys

1 STACKING CUPS. Once your baby starts to reach for objects, a nice set of stacking cups can supply endless hours of fun— although we had second thoughts about whether we'd later regret teaching our son to knock over objects. Sage insight or the ramblings of a first-time parent? Anyway, you can find a set of stacking cups at grocery stores, toy stores and chains like Toys R Us. Cost: about $5. Speaking of affordable toys, we also liked the *Lamaze* line of baby toys by Learning Curve (800) 704-8697 (web: www. learningcurvetoys.com). These fun developmental toys (categorized by age) include a puzzle ball, soft stacking rings and more. See the following box for our top picks for toys for infants.

2 MOBILE FOR CRIB. Sure, a mobile sounds like the perfect accessory for any crib, but how do you choose one? Here's our best advice: look at it from underneath. It's surprising to see the number of flat two-dimensional mobiles out there—get underneath them and look from the baby's perspective and what do you see? Nothing—the objects seem to disappear! The best mobiles are more three-dimensional. Most mobiles are $40 to $60; two good, less-expansive brands for mobiles are *Dolly* (800) 758-7520 (www.dolly.com) and *Infantino* (800) 365-8182 (www.infantino. com). We've seen both online for $20 to $30. Under the "too cute to be legal" category, we should also mention the North American Bear "Flatso" mobiles (see the mention of the Flatso line later in this chapter).

3 ACTIVITY CENTER/BUSY BOX. Ah, the old stand-by. This venerable toy (about $15) features various spinning balls, bells, phone dialer, squeakers, etc.—all attached to molded plastic. One famous brand is the *Fisher-Price Activity Center* (web: www.fisher-price.com), which has been around since 1973. The center (like other toys) has a strap that enables you to attach it to the crib. We found two problems with this: first, it's hard to do, since the crib's bumper pads may be in the way. Also, such crib toys make it difficult to put the baby down to sleep—any time you touch the crib, the toy makes a sound, and the baby might wake up. Our advice: plan on using "noisy" toys outside the crib.

4 ACTIVITY GYM. Among our favorites is the Gymini by Tiny Love (for a dealer near you, call 800-843-6292; web: www.tinylove.com). The Gymini is a three-foot square blanket that has two criss-cross arches.

The Top 5 Best Toys for Infants

Here are our top picks for the Best Toys for Baby. Most of these are available in toy stores nationwide or online from sources like Amazon.com.

1 STRIDE TO RIDE WALKER *(Fisher Price, $25). For ages nine months and up.* Despite the name, this toy isn't a walker in the traditional sense of the world. Your child must be able to stand to use it. Once they are ready however, we love the clever design. First, it is a push toy. Then it converts to a ride-on. The Stride to Ride has music, lights and more—or can be used in a quiet mode. Web: www.fisher-price.com.

2 LAMAZE SOFT SORTER *(Learning Curve, $20). Six months and up.* Various fabric cubes and shapes have different textures and sounds. The "sorter" has special size openings for each shape, teaching baby how to sort.

3 BUFFOODLES. *(Mary Meyer, $10) Infant and up.* Cute, colorful puppets in soft velour. Web: www.marymeyer.com.

4 OCEAN WONDERS FISHBOWL *(Fisher Price, $15). Six months and up.* Babies love this mesmerizing toy, with music, lights and sound all set to an aquatic theme. Web: www.fisher-price.com.

5 PLAYABOUT KINGDOM *(Little Tikes, $25). Nine months and up.* A castle with all sorts of fun stuff (trap doors, stacking turrets and more). Web: www.little-tykes.com.

You clip rattles, mirrors and other toys onto the arches, providing endless fun for baby as she lies on her back and reaches for the fun items. The Gymini comes in three different versions: a basic version in black, white and red is $35 and the "deluxe" model (a Noah's Ark Design) is about $50. The more expensive versions have more toys, including ones that play music. Another plus for the Gymini: it folds up quickly and easily for trips to Grandma's.

5 **ACTIVITY SEAT/BOUNCER WITH TOY BAR.** An activity seat (also called a bouncer) provides a comfy place for baby while you eat dinner, and the toy bar adds some mild amusement. The latest twist to these products is a "Magic Fingers" vibration feature—the bouncer basically vibrates, simulating a car ride. Parents who have these bouncers tell us they'd rather have a kidney removed than give up their vibrating bouncer, as it appears the last line of defense in soothing a fussy baby short of checking into a mental institution.

What features should you look for in a bouncer? Readers say a carrying handle is a big plus. Also: get a neutral fabric pattern, says another parent, since you'll probably be taking lots of photos of baby and a garish pattern may grate on your nerves.

So, where can you get one of these wonder products? Fisher Price (www.fisher-price.com) makes the most popular one in the category; most are about $30 to $40, depending on the version. A good choice: the Kick 'n Play bouncer ($35, pictured) with an interactive toy bar.

Yes, other companies make similar products (Summer makes one for $40, Combi has some ranging in price from $38 to $75 version, etc.) but the feedback we get from parents is that Fisher-Price is the best.

One caveat: a reader complained that no one warned him about the auto shut off feature to Fisher Price Soothing Bouncer. "I must tell you how surprised and aggravated I was to find out from Fisher-Price that their Soothing Sounds Bouncer Seat (model 79598) is one of the few models on which the vibration feature automatically shuts off in ten minutes. This so-called 'feature' of automatic shut-off has caused my wife and me no small amount of frustration. The vibration calms our babies (we have twin boys - they're 8 weeks old now) and helps them to sleep, and when the vibration shuts off, our babies usually wake up. I shouldn't have to tell you that that is a big deal! Hence, one of us parents has to re-start the thing every ten minutes."

Kolcraft has two Tender Vibes bouncers for $20 to $30. The more expensive model has a music feature that is sound activated (hence, when your baby cries, strains of Led Zeppelin's "Stairway to Heaven" start to play. Just kidding. It's actually Bjork). They also have a Jeep branded bouncer with a car themed toy bar for about $45.

Here's another money-saving tip: turn your infant car seat into an activity center with an attachable toy bar. Tiny Love makes a toy bar with soft steering wheel, phone and airplane toys for $28. Infantino's car seat toy bar has detachable toys for $23. Lamaze also has a car seat toy that velcros to the seat. It includes crinkle and jingle toys, as well as a teether for $20. Another plus: your baby is safer in an infant car seat carrier than in other activity seats, thanks to that industrial-strength harness safety system. Safety warning: only use these toy bars when the car seat is NOT inside a vehicle (that is, at home, etc.). Toy bars are not safe in a vehicle as they can be a hazard/projectile in an accident.

6 **TAPE PLAYER.** Gotta have something to play those Raffi tapes on. Actually, there is quite a good selection of musical tapes for babies that are less irritating than you might think. Look for a tape player designed specifically for use with small children. Such products have child-safe battery compartments and simple controls. Most of the "general" baby catalogs mentioned in this book carry a tape player or two for about $20. If your baby shows a budding interest in music, check out the *Music Blocks* from Neurosmith (562-296-1100; web: www.neurosmith.com). This smart toy ($65) lets babies create complex musical compositions. By mixing and matching the blocks, it cranks out a variety of harmonies and music styles.

7 **SELECTION OF BOOKS.** As book authors, we'd be remiss if we didn't recommend that you buy lots of books for your baby. Visit your local bookstore, and you'll find stiff board books (easier for young hands to turn or, at least, not destroy) as well as squishy cloth books. There are even books made of vinyl to make bath-time more fun. Obviously, a bookstore that specializes in children's books is a best bet. Used bookstores are another excellent source as are book sales at libraries and other charity events. If your child will be in a day care center, check to see if the school participates in the Scholastic Book Club—prices are low and sales benefit your school.

Discovery Toys

When our son Jack was born, we received a box of Discovery Toys as a gift and were quite impressed. The line of developmental toys, books and games (sold through local representatives; call 800-426-4777 in the U.S. or 800-267-0477 in Canada for more information; web: www.discoverytoysinc.com) are featured in an 80+ page catalog that relates how toys develop certain skills. You'll find toys that teach "thinking/learning," "creativity," "senses and perception" and more—the catalog features little symbols to point out the skills each item promotes.

8 **FLATOBEARIUS.** Our hip California cousins Ken and Elizabeth Troy turned us on to this adorable line of small stuffed animal rattles. "Flatobearius" is a flat, squishy bear rattle, part of the "Flatso" series from North American Bear Co. (to find a dealer near you, call 800-682-3427 or 312-329-0020 web: www.nabear.com). Once you get hooked, you'll have to acquire the entire collection of animal rattles—Flatopup (pictured, Flatjack (a rabbit), and Squishy Fish to name a few. The small Flatso rattles are about $10 (not cheap, but a nice splurge), and they even have a couple of larger versions ($25 to $55) and mobiles.

Safe & Sound for Toys

Walk through any toy store and the sheer variety will boggle your mind. Buying toys for an infant requires more careful planning than for older children. Here are nine tips to keep your baby safe and sound:

1 **CHECK FOR AGE APPROPRIATE LABELS.** Yes, that sounds like a no-brainer, but you'd be surprised how many times grandparents try to give a six-month old infant a toy that is clearly marked "Ages 3 and up." One common misunderstanding about these labels: the age range has NOTHING to do with developmental ability at this stage; instead, the warning is intended to keep small parts out of the hands of infants because those parts can be a choking hazard. Be careful of toys bought at second-hand stores or hand-me-downs—a lack of packaging may mean you have to guess on the age-appropriate level. Another trouble area: "Kids Meal" toys from fast-food restaurants. Many are clearly labeled for kids three and up (although some fast food places do offer toys safe for the under 3 crowd). One smart tip: use a toilet paper tube to see if small parts pose a choking hazard . . . anything that can fit through the tube can be swallowed by baby.

2 **MAKE SURE STUFFED ANIMALS HAVE SEWN EYES.** A popular gift from friends and relatives, stuffed animals can be a hazard if you don't take a few precautions. Buttons or other materials for eyes that could be easily removed present a choking hazard—make sure you give a stuffed animal the once over before you give it to baby. Keep all plush animals out of the crib except maybe one special toy (and that only after baby is able to roll over). While it is acceptable to have one or two stuffed animals in the crib with babies over one year of age, resist the urge to pile on. Once baby starts pulling himself up to a standing position, such stuffed animals can be used as steps to escape a crib.

3 **BEWARE OF RIBBONS.** Another common decoration on stuffed animals, remove these before giving the toy to your baby.

4 **MAKE SURE TOYS HAVE NO STRINGS LONGER THAN 12 INCHES**—another easily avoided strangulation hazard.

5 **WOODEN TOYS SHOULD HAVE NON-TOXIC FINISHES.** If in doubt, don't give such toys to your baby. The toy's packaging should specify the type of finish.

6 **BATTERY COMPARTMENTS SHOULD HAVE A SCREW CLOSURE.** Tape players (and other battery-operated toys) should not give your baby easy access to batteries—a compartment that requires a screwdriver to open is a wise precaution.

7 **BE CAREFUL OF CRIB TOYS.** Some of these toys are designed to attach to the top or sides of the crib. The best advice: remove them after the baby is finished playing with them. Don't leave the baby to play with crib toys unsupervised, especially once she begins to pull or sit up.

Oppenheimer Toy Portfolio

A reader recommended a terrific book for selecting toys, books, videos, music and software: The Oppenheimer Toy Portfolio (web: www.toyportfolio.com). Here's what she had to say about the book and web site:

"I got tired of driving my sleep deprived self, my wonderful but heavy daughter and her heavy carrier to the local Toys R Us to return toys she hated or was scared of. Once I bought this book, I understood better what to look for in a toy and what was skill/age appropriate—not what the manufacturers listed on the boxes! We have made many fewer return-the-toy trips and I am a much happier person. The book also includes games to play with your infants and no toy was required!"

8 **BATH SEATS SHOULD NOT BE USED.** It looks innocuous—the baby bath seat—but it can be a disaster waiting to happen. These seats suction to the bottom of a tub, holding baby in place while she takes a bath. The problem? Parents get a false sense of security from such items and often leave the bathroom to answer the phone, etc. We've seen several tragic reports of babies who've drowned when they fell out of the seats (or the seats became un-suctioned from the tub). The best advice: AVOID these seats and NEVER leave baby alone in the tub, even for just a few seconds.

9 **DO NOT USE WALKERS.** And if you get one as a gift, take it back to the store and exchange it for something that isn't a death trap. Exactly what are these invitations to disaster? A walker suspends your baby above the floor, enabling him or her to "walk" by rolling around on wheels. The only problem: babies tend to "walk" right into walls, down staircases, and into other brain damage-causing obsta-cles. It's a scandal that walkers haven't been banned by the Consumer Products Safety Commission. How many injuries are caused by these things? Are you sitting down? 6200 a year.

To be fair, we should note the industry has tried to make walk-ers safer—with a large amount of prodding from the CPSC. While the government decided not to ban walkers outright in 1993, the CPSC did work to strengthen the industry's voluntary standards over the past few years. The result: redesigned walkers with safety features that stop them from falling down stairs. Some have special wheels or "gripping strips" that prevent such falls.

The result of these new safety features: walker injuries have dropped 70% since 1995. But we still think 6200 injured babies is 6200 too many. Our advice: don't put your baby into a walker, no matter how many new "safety" features are built-in.

What about walker alternatives? So-called "stationery" play cen-ters made a big splash on the baby market in recent years, led by Evenflo's Exersaucer. Most stationary play centers run $50 to $90 and are basically the same—you stick the baby into a seat in the mid-dle and there are a bunch of toys for them to play with. (The more money you spend, the better the toys, bells and whistles). While the unit rocks and swivels, it can't move. And that's a boon to parents who need a few minutes to make dinner or use the bathroom.

So, should you get one? Well, no. We're troubled by studies that have shown infants who use walkers and stationary play centers suf-fer from developmental delays when compared to babies who don't use them. According to a study in the October 1999 Journal of Developmental and Behavioral Pediatrics, researchers at Case Western Reserve University found "babies who were placed in walk-ers were slower to sit up, crawl and walk than those raised without walkers. The mental development of the children also appeared to be slowed," according to an Associated Press article on the study.

Researchers studied 109 infants, including 53 who did not use walkers. On average, babies who used the walkers were delayed at least a month on average in sitting up, crawling and walking. Non-walker using kids also scored 10% higher on mental development tests than walker users.

The researchers concluded that "restriction in a walker may exert its greatest influence on mental development during the 6- to 9-month age period, a time regarded as transformational in a child's intellectual development," according to the AP article. Noticeably, walker babies were able to catch up to non-walker children after they started crawling—and hence used the walker less often.

Why do walkers and stationary playcenters have such a dramatic effect on a child's development? Researchers speculate that "the opaque trays placed on the newer walkers as a safety device prevent the children from seeing their legs, blocking the feedback they get from moving a limb and seeing the leg actually move," the article stated.

While this study focused on walkers, we interpreted the results to also apply to stationary play centers. Why? Because both play centers and walkers use those "opaque trays" that keep baby from seeing their feet. As a result of this research, we don't recommend parents buy or use walkers or stationary play centers.

Another study from 2002 and conducted at the University of Dublin School of Physiotherapy in Ireland concurred with the results of the Case Western study. They concluded "this study provides additional evidence that baby walkers are associated with delay in achieving normal locomotor milestones . . .The use of baby walkers should be discouraged."

 Wastes of Money

1 **FANCY TOYS.** We interviewed one couple who bought a fancy set of expensive toys for their infant daughter, only to be dismayed that she didn't want to play with them. What did baby really like to play with? Their keys. The lesson: sometimes it's the simple, inexpensive things in life that are the most fun.

2 **FANCY BOOKS.** Walk through any children's section in your local bookstore and you'll see a zillion children's books, all lavishly illustrated and beautifully packaged. And do you know what most babies want to do with books? Eat them. We liked the suggestion that one mom discovered when it came to books: many popular hardcover children's books come in soft-cover or paperback versions, at substantially lower prices. That way if Junior decides his favorite book looks like lunch one day, you're not out as much money. Board books and even cloth books are good to chew on too.

Tummy Time Toys: A Waste of Money?

"People keep telling me that Tummy Time for my baby is a must. I've heard that my daughter might even be developmentally slower than other babies if I don't include tummy time in her day. What is it and why is it so important?"

Do babies spend too much time on their backs? That's one concern parents and child development specialists have brought up in recent years. Before the advent of the Back to Sleep campaign, the SIDS awareness program that encourages parents to put their babies to bed on their backs, babies were more likely to be placed in a variety of positions. Nowadays, however, babies spend an inordinate amount of time on their backs. And some folks wonder if that is causing a delay in creeping, crawling and walking.

The solution is a simple one: just put your baby on her tummy for a few minutes a day when she is awake. And there is research that shows that extra tummy time can help your child reach developmental milestones sooner. But keep in mind that normal babies who don't participate in increased periods of tummy time still meet developmental milestones within the normal time period. So there is no need to panic if your baby isn't getting "15 minutes of tummy time daily."

In fact, many parents have noted that their babies hate being on their stomachs. For those babies who object to being on their tummies, you simply don't have to force them. Of course, baby products manufacturers have jumped on this new craze to come up with more stuff you can buy to make Tummy Time more fun. For example, Camp Kazoo, the makers of Boppy pillows (www.boppy.com) make a Boppy Tummy time exercise mat for $25. This smaller version of the famous Boppy includes an attached mat and loops for favorite toys.

Don't think you need to buy extra stuff to make tummy time successful in your house, however. Save your money and just get down on the floor with your baby face to face. After all, you're the thing in her life she finds most fun, so get down there and spend some quality tummy time with her.

3 **FANCY BURP PADS.** Do you really need to spend $5 on a burp pad—a scientifically designed piece of cloth for you to put on your shoulder to keep spit-up off your clothes when Junior burps? No, just put a cloth diaper on your shoulder (average price 50¢ or less) and save the money.

4 **BLACK AND WHITE MOBILES.** Yes, they are all the rage today. True, your baby is attracted to high-contrast black and white images in the first four months, and such mobiles may be quite fascinating. But $20-$40 seems like a lot of money to be spent on an item that's used for just a few months (or weeks). We liked the money-saving suggestion from one dad we interviewed: he drew patterns with a black pen on white index cards and then attached the cards to a regular color mobile. The baby liked the improvised version just fine, and the parents saved $20 to $40. (One safety tip: make sure the cards are attached firmly to the mobile. And, as always, remove all mobiles from the crib after five months when your baby sits up). Another money-saving tip: forget the mobile altogether. Some parents we interviewed said their baby got along fine without one. If you get a mobile as a gift, consider re-hanging over a diaper changing area once you remove it from the crib. That gives you more use without the safety hazard of having it in the crib.

 Money-Saving Secrets

I **USE WEB COUPONS.** Yes, you've heard about all the hype on great deals folks get online. But where can YOU find such deals? One of the biggest bargains online is special electronic "coupons" you can use to save big. See the box on the next page for details.

2 **DON'T FORGET CONSIGNMENT STORES.** A great item to find at second-hand stores specializing in children's products: mobiles. Most aren't handled by babies so they're in excellent condition—at prices that are typically 50% or more off retail. We found quite a few in our local baby consignment store for $10 to $20; compare that to the $50 retail price these fetch at specialty stores. Since you tend to use a mobile for such a short period of time, you can then re-consign it at the shop and get some money back! Of course, these stores sell much more than mobiles—you can pick up toys, high chairs, and, of course, clothes at tremendous savings. Check your phone book under "Consignment" or "Thrift Stores"; many are also listed under "Clothes & Accessories—Infant & Child—

Retail." For a great online source to local second hand shops, check out www.narts.org. Another great source for bargains: garage sales. Refer back to Chapter 4 for more tips on shopping garage/yard sales.

3 **GO FOR REFILLABLE PACKAGES.** Take diaper wipes, for example. You can often buy refillable packages of wipes to fit into those plastic boxes. The savings: about 20% off the cost of buying a new box. And you save another plastic box from the landfill.

Coupon deals cut the cost of online shopping

How do baby product web sites generate traffic and sales? One tried and true method is the online coupon—a special discount, either in dollars or percentage off deals. Sites offer these as come-ons for new customers, returning customers . . . just about anyone. Coupons enable sites to give discounts without actually lowering the prices of merchandise. You enter the coupon code when you place the order and zap! You've saved big.

How big? Well, when the Internet gold rush was on in 1998 and 1999, some sites were going nuts with coupons—like $50 off a $60 purchase for first-time customers! Or 30% off and free shipping. Those steals are gone, but good deals are still out there. How do you find them? You don't have to spend hours surfing; instead just visit coupon web sites—these sites track deals on other sites.

A good example for baby products is DotDeals (www.dot-deals.com). Their special section on "Kids & Toys" lets you see all the current deals at a glance. A recent scan of the site revealed $10 off a $30 purchase at a big baby products web site, 30% off any purchase at another site and even 25% off a purchase at a toy web site if you use American Express. Some deals are for first-time customers; others are for anyone. Just note the coupon code (a series of letters and numbers) and the expiration date and you're on your way.

Other web sites that track coupons include Amazing Bargains (slow to load, ugly to look at but very comprehensive at www.amazing-bargains.com), the oddly named Flamingo World (www.flamingoworld.com), Just Wright Gifts (www.justwright-gifts.com), and It's Raining Bargains (www.itsrainingbargains.com).

But you say, Alan and Denise, please give us more coupon sites! Sure, here are some more. Readers have recommended Deal of the Day (www.DealOfDay.com), eDealFinder (www.eDealFinder.com), ImegaDeals (www.ImegaDeals.com), Big Big Savings (www.BigBigSavings.com), Fat Wallet (www.FatWallet.com), and Clever Moms (www.CleverMoms.com).

Now, go fire up the browser and start saving!

4 **REUSE THAT MOBILE.** Safety experts say crib mobiles should be removed when baby starts to sit up. Why? Those strings can be a strangulation hazard. But that doesn't mean the mobile is garage sale fodder. Instead, reuse it—we hung ours over the changing table to entertain baby during those zillion diaper changes.

5 **MAKE A BABY DRAWER IN THE KITCHEN.** Who needs fancy toys? Buy a $200 wagon at a toy store and chances are baby is more interested in the box. So, why fight it? Simple household items like wooden spoons, old boxes or Tupperware containers can provide hours of fun. In the kitchen, give baby a drawer of his own and fill it with some fun items.

6 **ORGANIZE A TOY EXCHANGE.** As one television network says, if you missed the original episode, the repeat is "new to you." The same goes for toys—pop over to a neighbor's house and you'll notice all those toys seem new and fascinating to your child. So, here's an idea: organize a toy swap with other parents in your neighborhood or playgroup. Label a dozen toys with your name and pop them in a box. Trade that box with another family for toys their children have grown bored with. Voila! Instant new toys for free. Every month, swap again, this time with another family.

7 **CONSIDER CREATIVE ALTERNATIVES TO TOY BOXES.** A wooden toy box can run $150 to $300. But there are ways to save. First, check out unfinished furniture stores, which have toy boxes for $100 or less. Another idea: use a rolling cart (about $18), wicker laundry baskets ($25) or other inexpensive storage ideas.

8 **ONE WORD: EBAY.** If you haven't discovered this fantastic bargain source, you should return your bargain shopper license— eBay is an amazing source for baby products. Samples: we clicked on "play pen" and whamo! 152 results, including a brand new Graco Pak N Play with bassinet. The bids for this item were just $60, compared to the $120 retail. Another reader found a $200 breast pump for $140, again brand new. And here's a little secret to getting the best deals: look for baby product makers, catalogs and stores who are selling overstock products quietly on eBay. Yes, you can often get brand new product (still in the box, with all directions, etc.) by just careful searching. Be sure to read product descriptions with a fine tooth comb to make sure an item is new, "in the box" or damaged/used. Most sellers honestly report the condition. Once you find a baby store/catalog that is selling online, you can view all their auctions by clicking on their name.

Do it By Mail

BACK TO BASICS TOYS

To Order Call: (800) 356-5360; Fax (800) 759-8477.
Web: www.backtobasicstoys.com (this catalog's fulfillment is now being done by Amazon.com)
Shopping Hours: 24 hours a day, seven days a week.
Or write to: 1 Memory Lane, Ridgely, MD 21685

In business since 1988, Back to Basics Toys catalog theme is "they DO make them like they used to." An excellent index lets you zero in on a certain age group of toys. The "early childhood" section featured such classics as "Rock A Stack" toy by Fisher Price for $4. Altogether, there are over 20 pages of toys for children up to five years, complete with color pictures, great descriptions and age specifications. Back to Basics Toys has a joint web site with Amazon's toy site. There you can find some pricey items like $500 wooden playhouses, but also plenty of affordable items as well. We like the retro toys (Lincoln Logs, Raggedy Ann and Andy, Radio Flyer trikes) best among the online offerings.

CONSTRUCTIVE PLAYTHINGS

To Order Call: (800) 832-0572 or (816) 761-5900; Fax (816) 761-9295.
Web: www.constplay.com
Shopping Hours: 24 hours a day, seven days a week.
Or write to: 13201 Arrington Rd., Grandview, MO 64030.
Retail Outlets: They have seven retail stores; call the phone number above for a location near you.

Yes, this catalog can seem cluttered, but we like the organization by age group. The "First Playthings" section, for example features infant stimulation toys, foam blocks and other affordably priced items. Heck, we didn't see much over $50 in this section, which is a contrast to other toy catalogs that seem weighted down with expensive offerings. We liked the "First Learning" section that featured a good selection of educational toys. Constructive Playthings has greatly improved their web site since our last visit— now the navigation is easy and the organization excellent. Check out the "sale products" section for the best deals.

KAPLANCO.COM

To Order Call: (800) 533-2166; Web: www.kaplanco.com

Kaplan Company bought out the Great Kids Company catalog a few years ago and discontinued the print version. But you can still shop their great selection of educational toys online at KaplanCo.com. We liked the well-designed web site, with special buttons that highlight toys by age, "exceptional children," "outdoor classroom" and more.

PLAYFAIR TOYS

To Order Call: (800) 824-7255; Fax: (303) 440-3393
Shopping Hours: 7am to 7pm Mountain time.
Or write to: PO Box 18210, Boulder, CO 80308
Web: www.playfairtoys.com; Retail store: 1690 28th St, Boulder, CO.

Yeah, the catalog's organization is a jumbled mish-mash of different age groups, but we liked Playfair's helpful product descriptions. No, this isn't a discount catalog (most of the prices are at full retail), but the large selection of arts and crafts supplies is unique. Playfair carries Ambi toys and kids' furniture (likes desks and sofa sets). The web site is pretty basic but functional—we wish they had more thumbnails of products instead of text listings.

SENSATIONAL BEGINNINGS

To Order Call: (800) 444-2147; Fax: (734) 242-8278.
Shopping Hours: 24 hours a day, seven days a week.
Or write to: 987 Stewart Rd., PO Box 2009, Monroe, MI 48162
Web: www.sensationalbeginnings.com

Characters like Madeline and Bob the Builder are the focus of Sensational Beginnings, a well-organized catalog that includes a nice selection of infant items (play centers, activity gyms and more). We saw lots of Brio and Thomas the Tank Engine items, as well as non-toy baby products like the Baby Bjorn carrier. While the catalog's prices are regular retail, Sensational Beginnings web site features specials at 20% to 30% off. That web site, by the way, is spectacular—you can shop by age, brand, category and more. Their "Wow! Gifts" are great splurges (hint to the grandmothers reading this book). You can even find a small selection of baby products like strollers, carriers and the like.

TOYS TO GROW ON

To Order Call: (800) 542-8338; Fax: (310) 537-5403.
Shopping Hours: 24 hours a day, seven days a week.
Or write to: 2695 E. Dominguez St., PO Box 17, Long Beach, CA 90801
Web: www.toystogrowon.com

As the name implies, Toys To Grow On specializes in education toys. We liked the selection of dress-up "imagine" toys, science projects and arts and crafts supplies. There isn't a big selection of items for children under 2, but they did have some tub toys, soft rattles and blocks. The best deal: Toys to Grow On sells a train table and board for Brio or Thomas that was HALF the cost of what we saw in retail toy stores. We ordered this table from Toys to Grow On and were impressed (it was well made and easy to assemble). As for Toys to Grow On's web site, we loved the "20 under $20" section as well as their "What's Hot" section. You can shop by category (examples: Pretend Play, Bath Toys, etc.) but there are no recommendations for toys by age, unfortunately.

♦ **More toy catalogs.** We have to issue a warning before we discuss the next catalog. Here's what we've learned from seven years of parenthood: Thomas the Tank Engine is like an addictive drug for toddlers. Once they get started playing with it, look out— you'll soon be searching toy stores and web sites for Thomas pajamas and lunch sacks . . . and that darn obscure "Mike" train.

So, you can imagine our son's delight when the ***Totally Thomas' Toy Depot*** catalog (800-30-THOMAS; www.totallythomas.com) showed up in our mailbox. This catalog carries Thomas clothing, backpacks, toys and, of course, trains—engines, track, accessories and more. It was all we could do to rip the catalog out of his little hands to write this review. (Hint: you can learn more about Thomas on their official web site at www.thomasthetankengine.com).

Hearth Song (800) 325-2502 (www.hearthsong.com) sells arts and crafts supplies, as well as an entire line of Peter Rabbit toys and games. The catalog also has a nice selection of seasonal items and musical instruments like guitars and lap harps.

Imagine the Challenge (888) 777-1493 (www.imaginetoys.com) boasts a section of education toys for kids under three, including a wooden workbench, a play-and-fold clubhouse, and a cute "My First Camera." Most of the items are under $50, which makes this one of the more affordable catalogs we reviewed.

Leaps & Bounds (800) 477-2189 (www.leapsandboundscatalog. com) focus on "dress up and pretend toys" as well as furniture options like desks, play tables and kid-size sofas. Leaps & Bounds is owned by the same parent company as the One Step Ahead catalog.

SmarterKids (web: www.smarterkids.com) is an excellent web site with educational toy recommendations by age and lots of bargains in their clearance section.

Monitors

For her first nine months, your baby is tethered to you via the umbilical cord. After that, it's the baby monitor that becomes your surrogate umbilical cord—enabling you to work in the garden, wander about the house, and do many things that other, childless human beings do, while still keeping tabs on a sleeping baby. Hence, this is a pretty important piece of equipment you'll use every day—a good one will make your life easier . . . and a bad one will be a neverending source of irritation.

 Smart Shopper Tips for Monitors

Smart Shopper Tip #1
Bugging your house

"My neighbor and I both have babies and baby monitors. No matter what we do, I can still pick up my neighbor's monitor on my receiver. Can they hear our conversations too?"

You better bet. Let's consider what a baby monitor really is: a radio transmitter. The base unit is the transmitter and the receiver is, well, a receiver. So anyone with another baby monitor can pick up your monitor—not just the sound of your baby crying, but also any conversations you have with your mate about diaper changing technique.

You'll notice that many monitors have two channels "to reduce interference," and some even have high and low range settings—do they help reduce eavesdropping? No, not in our opinion. In densely populated areas, you can still have problems.

We should note that you can also pick up baby monitors on many cordless phones—even police scanners can pick up signals as far as one or two miles away. The best advice: remember that your house (or at least, your baby's room) is bugged. If you want to protect your privacy, don't have any sensitive conversations within earshot of the baby monitor. You never know who might be listening.

Are there any monitors on the market that scramble their signal for privacy? Yes, Fisher-Price did make a model like this (called the Direct Link), but it is now discontinued. Despite that sounding like a no-brainer idea, other manufacturers do not offer this feature as of this writing. Why don't manufacturers offer digital spread spectrum monitors that would guarantee privacy, like what you see in cordless phones today? Who knows? It hasn't occurred to them yet.

What about higher frequency monitors—are they harder to

intercept? Well, yes and no. A 900 MHz monitor may be a bit harder to snoop on with a police scanner, but if your neighbor has the exact same model, guess what? They can probably hear everything in your house.

The best advice: only turn on your monitor when baby is napping. Leaving it on all day means others can listen in to every noise and sound.

Smart Shopper Tip #2
Battery woes

"Boy, we should have bought stock in Duracell when our baby was born! We go through dozens of batteries each month to feed our very hungry baby monitor."

Most baby monitors have the option of running on batteries or on regular current (by plugging it into a wall outlet). Our advice: use the wall outlet as often as possible. Batteries don't last long—as little as 8 to 10 hours with continual use. Another idea: you can buy another AC adapter from a source like Radio Shack for $10 or less— you can leave one AC adapter in your bedroom and have another one available in a different part of the house. (Warning: make sure you get the correct AC adapter for your monitor, in terms of voltage and polarity. Take your existing AC adapter to Radio Shack and ask for help to make sure you are getting the correct unit. If not, you can fry your monitor).

Another solution: several new baby monitors (reviewed later in this chapter) feature rechargeable receivers! You'll never buy a set of batteries for these units—you just plug them into an outlet to recharge the batteries.

Smart Shopper Tip #3
Cordless compatibility

"We have a cordless phone and a baby monitor. Boy, it took us two weeks to figure out how to use both without having a nervous breakdown."

If we could take a rocket launcher and zap one person in this world, it would have to be the idiot who decided that baby monitors and cordless phones should share the *same* radio frequency. What were they thinking? Gee, let's take two people who are already dangerously short of sleep and make them *real* frustrated!

After hours of experimentation, we have several tips. First, consider buying a newer cordless phone that works on the 2.4 or 5.8 GHz frequency. If you don't have this feature, you may find your phone and monitor are always in conflict, no matter how many times you flip that "Channel A or B" switch on the baby monitor.

Another tip: consider buying one of those new cordless phones that work on the 900 MHz frequency—this lessens the chance of interference. (For techno-heads out there, most cordless phones and baby monitors work on the 46 to 49 MHz radio frequency). The only disadvantage to this tip is that the new cordless phones can be pricey—as much as twice the cost of regular cordless phones.

Of course, just to confuse you, we should note there are new baby monitors that also work on the 900 MHz frequency. These are touted as having longer ranges (600 to 1000 feet), but those claims are hard to verify in real-world conditions. And of course, these can interfere with cordless (and cellular) phones that work on the same band.

Baby monitors have one of the biggest complaint rates of all products we review. We suspect all the electronic equipment in people's homes today (cell phones, computers, fax machines, large-screen TV's the size of a Sony Jumbotron), not to mention all the interference sources near your home (cell phone towers, etc.) must account for some of the problems folks have with baby monitors. Common complaints include static, lack of range, buzzing sounds and worse—and those problems can happen with a baby monitor in any price range.

The best advice: always keep the receipt for *any* baby monitor you buy—you may have to take it back and exchange it for another brand if problems develop. It sure would be nice if manufacturers of cordless phones and baby monitors would label their products with the radio frequency they use, so you could spot conflicts before they happen.

Smart Shopper Tip #4
The one-way dilemma
"Our baby monitor is nice, but it would be great to be able to

Shopping 'Bots

Okay, you know there are deals on the 'net. But where do you find them, short of searching for hours on baby product web sites? One idea: DealTime (www.dealtime.com). This free service (a shopping robot, or 'bot) has a special baby section. Click on this web site's "Babies & Kids" tab and do a search for monitors. Whamo! 30 prices for different baby monitors from a slew of different sites (see Figure 1 on the next page). Among the steals: a Fisher Price monitor that retails for $50 for just $27.92 on Overstock.com. DealTime lists sites that have free shipping with corresponding quick links.

buzz my husband so he could bring me something to drink while I'm feeding the baby. Are there any monitors out there that let you communicate two ways?"

Yep, Evenflo, Graco and Safety 1st have models that do just that (see reviews later in this chapter). Of course, there is another alternative: you can always go to Radio Shack and buy a basic intercom for about $40. Most also have a "lock" feature that you can leave on to listen to the baby when he's sleeping. Another advantage to intercoms: you can always deploy the unit to another part of your house after you're done monitoring the baby. Of course, the only disadvantage to intercoms is that they aren't portable—most must be plugged into a wall outlet.

Here are two other features to consider when shopping for monitors:

◆ *Out of range indicators.* If you plan to wander from the house and visit your garden, you may want to go for a monitor that warns you when you've strayed too far from its transmitter. Some models have a visual out of range indicator, while others beep at you. Of course, even if your monitor doesn't offer this feature, you'll probably realize when you're out of range—the background noise you hear in your home will disappear from the receiver.

◆ *Low battery indicator.* Considering how quickly monitors can eat batteries, you'd think this would be a standard feature for monitors. Nope—very few (if any) current models actually warn you when you're running out of juice. Most units will just die. At this writing, only the Phillips monitors (reviewed later) have this feature.

 ## More Money Buys You

Basic baby monitors are just that—an audio monitor and transmitter. No-frills monitors start at $20 or $25. More money buys you a sound/light display (helpful in noisy environments, since the lights indicate if your baby is crying) and rechargeable batteries (you can go through $50 a year in 9-volts with regular monitors). More expensive monitors even have transmitters that also work on batteries (so you could take it outside if you wish) or dual receivers (helpful if you want to leave the main unit inside the house and take the second one outside if you are gardening, etc.). Finally, the top-end monitors either have 900 MHz technology (which extends range) or intercom features, where you can use the receiver to talk to your baby as you walk back to the room. In the last year or so, the most expensive monitors have added features to soothe a fussy baby—a sound and light show displayed in the nursery ceiling or an intercom to hear mom's voice. At the top end of monitor market are units that monitor a baby's "movement" and sound an alarm if baby stops breathing.

The Name Game: Reviews of Selected Manufacturers

If you've ever looked at monitors, you might ask yourself, "what's the difference?" Most models have all the neat features that you want—belt clips, flexible antennas, two switchable channels. But, there are some differences as we mentioned above. We'll try to make some sense of these choices in the following reviews.

Use the phone numbers listed below to call to find a dealer near you (most manufacturers don't sell directly to the public). All these monitors can be found at stores like Babies R Us, Baby Depot and Toys R Us, as well as on the baby product web sites mentioned throughout this book (an example is BabyStyle.com).

The Ratings

A **EXCELLENT**—*our top pick!*
B **GOOD**— *above average quality, prices, and creativity.*
C **FAIR**—*could stand some improvement.*
D **POOR**—*yuck! Could stand some major improvement.*

Evenflo *For a dealer near you, call (800) 233-5921 or (937) 415-3300. Web: www.evenflo.com* When Evenflo bought out Gerry Baby Products in 1997, the company inherited Gerry's baby monitors. And that was a both an asset and a liability. While Gerry had a big monitor line, it also had a quality problem—there were several recalls of their products after the monitors allegedly sparked house fires. As a result, we've always been leery of Evenflo monitors, which were just repackaged Gerry models. In the past year, however, Evenflo tried to distance itself from that bad PR by re-christening their monitor line "Constant Care." The Constant Care 1500 is an entry level model with sound and light display for $25 while the 3000 offers rechargeable batteries, sound and light display, out of range indicator and an intercom feature for $50. In the past year, Evenflo debuted the Constant Care 4000 Parent Pager Monitor with a small-sized unit that is smaller than most other monitor's receivers. The 4000 uses 900 MHz technology, but doesn't have a rechargeable battery. The feedback on Evenflo's monitors has been positive, so we'll raise their rating this time out. Of the three models, we'd suggest the 3000 since it has the rechargeable batteries. FYI: we noticed that Evenflo's monitors aren't widely distributed in some stores, but you can find them online. ***Rating: B***

First Years *To find a dealer near you, call (800) 225-0382 or (508) 588-1220.* Sometimes, we goof. In a previous edition of this book, we recommended First Year's "Crisp & Clear Plus" monitor ($50) as a best bet. And it had some great features: rechargeable batteries, 900 MHz frequency for better reception and a sound/light display (a double receiver version of the Crisp & Clear is called the Peace of Mind—same features, just two receivers for $50). Best of all, the receiver had an all-but-non-existent antenna. The only problem? The unit buzzed, crackled and popped—and those were the unit's *better* days. Our readers carpet-bombed us with emails complaining about this monitor and we listened—First Years is NOT on our monitor recommended list this time out. We don't know if First Years had a bad production batch or what, but the problems seem to center around interference (especially cellular phones) that created nasty static or buzzing sounds. That was strange since our field test of the Crisp & Clear showed it to work fine, without any interference. Go figure. Anyway, First Years tried to redeem itself last year with a new model, the Safe & Sound Monitor with Finder Feature. Yep, this monitor has a pager button so you can find a misplaced parent's unit quickly. The unit also features sound and light display and rechargeable batteries. Not bad for $30, but it will work on the old 49 MHz frequency (an admission that their 900 MHz monitor is a bust? We're not sure). We don't have much feedback on that newer model, but given the barbequing we withstood for recommending this brand last time, we'll not take the chance. ***Rating: B-***

Fisher Price *To find a dealer near you, call (800) 828-4000 or (716) 687-3000. Web: www.fisher-price.com* Fisher Price is the market leader for baby monitors and for good reason—these are among the best-made monitors on the market. You want choice? Fisher Price offers an amazing array of FIVE models, ranging from $20 to $50 (see a chart on this page for comparison of models/features). Our recommendation: stay with the simple units like the Sounds 'N Lights—this monitor comes in single ($20) and double ($30) receiver versions and features a sound/light display. Nothing fancy, but it does the trick. Also good: the 900 MHz Long-Range monitor ($35), which the company claims has three times the range of its regular monitors (it also has a more compact design with no bulky antenna).

F-P's MONITORS	*An overview of Fisher Price's monitors*	2 Channels	Sound/Lights	900 MHz	Rechargeable batteries	Dual Receiver
SOUND & LIGHTS $20		✔	✔			
DUAL SOUND/LIGHTS $30		✔	✔			✔
900Mhz VIBRATING $35		✔	✔	✔	✔	
CALMING VIBRATIONS $40		✔	✔			
SOOTHING DREAMS $50		✔	✔			

Prices quoted are actual street prices seen online or in stores.

Unfortunately, we can't recommend Fisher-Price's most expensive monitor, the Soothing Dreams. More like the Annoying Nightmare Monitor from Hell, said our readers. This $50 unit was supposed to lets parents activate soothing music with a touch of a button on the parent's unit. The baby's unit then displays a light show on the ceiling above the crib (this turns off after a period of time). Nice idea, bad execution. The unit had a mind of its own, like something out of bad Stephen King made-for-TV movie. One mom said hers would come on in the middle of the night with the sound/light show . . . waking her sleeping baby. Others complained about static and popping noises from the receiver. All those complaints make us nervous about Fisher-Price's newest model, the Calming Vibrations. This unit has a "crib soother" unit that vibrates your child's mattress (or plays wave sounds) that can be activated by the parent's unit. While this unit is too new for us to get much of a gauge on parent feedback yet, we think it is a safer bet to stay with the three simpler models (Sound 'N Lights or 900 MHz Long Range). FYI: unfortunately, Fisher-Price has discontinued their previous models that had rechargeable batteries. Bummer. ***Rating (for the Sound 'N Lights or 900 MHz Long Range units only): A-***

Graco To find a dealer near you, call (800) 345-4109, (610) 286-5951. Web: www.gracobaby.com Yes, Graco is better known for its strollers and playpens, but the juvenile products giant launched its monitor line a couple of years ago. The result? Yawn, said our readers. Most of these monitors are just knock-offs of Fisher-Price's offerings, with few new or innovative features. Worse, parents say the quality on the units with walkie-talkie features is terrible. Example: the "Family Listen 'N Talk" unit ($70) with two receivers, 900 MHz technology and a walkie-talkie function. Parents we interviewed hated it . . . and that's putting it charitably. Readers were more favorable with Graco's simpler models—the UltraClear Monitor ($50) has a sound/light display and dual receivers. The quality of this monitor is good, although a few folks reported static problems. A similar version of this monitor, called the Sound Sleep, runs $30 at stores like K-Mart. All Graco's monitors offer dual receivers. That's nice, but no model has rechargeable batteries, which is a major omission. **Rating: B-**

Philips Web: *www.consumer.philips.com.* Here's a dark horse brand to consider if you don't mind buying a monitor site unseen. Yes, Phillips monitors are sold in a few stores (at times, Target carries them), but most likely you're going to have to buy it online, direct from Philips web site. We say take the chance—the feedback we get from readers on these units is very positive. The quality and clarity of these models is excellent. The entry-level Super Sensitive Monitor (SC763) is a 900 MHz monitor that features an in-range indicator, small antenna, low battery warning and rechargeable batteries for $46. Yes, that's $5 to $10 less than competing models with similar features. The Ultra Compact Monitor (SC765, $58) has basically the same features as the entry-level unit, but adds a small pager-size parent unit. That unit doesn't have a sounds/lights display, which might be a trade-off some will be willing to make for the smaller size. Phillips top-of-the-line monitor, The In-Touch Monitor & Intercom ($69) adds an intercom feature and baby's room temperature readout. We like the fact that all Philips monitors work on the 900 MHz frequency and feature rechargeable batteries. **Rating: A**

Safety 1st *To find a dealer near you, call (800) 962-7233 or (781) 364-3100. Web: www.safety1st.com* Safety 1st figures more is better with monitors—the company's monitor line at one point had TEN models, including several innovative combo video/audio monitors. In the last year, the company pared that back to five offerings, but you'll still their older models sold in stores and online. You can find everything from a bare bones model with no sound and light display (Crystal Clear, $20-$25) to elaborate models with rechargeable batteries and 900 MHz technology. So, which is best? We like the Super Clear Rechargeable Nursery Monitor (#49241, $30). Yes, it works on the old 49 MHz frequency, but it does have rechargeable batteries and sound and light display. At $30, it's about $10 to $20 less than similar monitors from Fisher Price and First Years. In the past

monitors

year, Safety 1st debuted the "Sound & Sight TV Monitor," the first combo audio/video monitor we've seen on the market. A wireless camera sends a picture to any television; a regular "audio" monitor can be used separately. Pretty cool for $90, but its probably overkill for most parents. All in all, Safety 1st's wide array of offerings looks impressive, but their quality has troubled us. In 1997, the company recalled 25,000 monitors whose rechargeable batteries ruptured in 76 reports to the CPSC. While that was a few years ago and the company hasn't had a monitor recall since, we still have qualms about recommending this company's offerings. **Rating: C**

◆ **Other Brands.** Like most gadgets that **Sony** sells, their "Baby Call" monitor is an attractive unit but grossly overpriced. We liked the rounded antenna (on both the transmitter and receiver), but it's missing a sound-activated light display. And the price ($70+) is too much for what it is. Nonetheless, it has its fans—parents tell us it works well.

Do you need a baby monitor that monitors your child's breathing? A small company called Angelcare debuted the first monitor for that purpose in the late 1990's . . . although the model was innovative, Angelcare found it didn't have the muscle to market it and sold the monitor to Safety 1st. Then Safety 1st gave up, eventually selling the product to **BeBe Sounds** (web: www.unisar.com) in the past year. There, the Angelcare has found new life. So how does it work? A special device that is slipped under the crib mattress to monitor baby's breathing. If the unit determines baby has stopped breathing for 20 seconds, the parent's unit sounds an audible alarm. There's also a function that sends an audible tick to the parent's unit with each breath baby takes (this can be turned off). The unit can also be used as a regular baby monitor (sound only) and features a sound/light display. The disadvantages to Angelcare? The unit does not use rechargeable batteries and features a rather skimpy 200-foot range; also some cribs require the placement of a board under the mattress for the AngelCare to work properly. Price: $99. So how well does it work? Quite well, say our readers. It does what it say. Now, who would really need this? Who would need this? If you have a preemie or a baby with health problems, AngelCare might be a plus. For most parents, however, it is overkill.

New to the monitor market this year is **Summer** (www.summer-infant.com), which introduced three models. Their basic Baby's Quiet Sounds Nursery monitor features a sound/light display, while the Movement & Sounds Monitor ($60) is similar to Angelcare (described above). Finally, Summer offers a video model, described below. Since these models were so new as of press time, we didn't have much feedback on their quality or reliability.

What about a baby surveillance camera? Yes, it sounds a bit

Orwellian, but you can buy a baby VIDEO monitor. This was a fad that peaked a couple years ago, when there were several models on the market. Yet the trend never caught on, due to the units' high prices (many were $150 to $300). **Safety 1st** is still trying to crack this market—their **Child View Monitor** is the first hand-held color video monitor that can also be used as a television. It's about $150. Also new: in the past year, Safety 1st introduced a combo audio/video monitor—see their review earlier in this section for details. Summer (see above) just debuted the Quiet Sounds Dual video monitor (yes with two cameras) for $150. A simple one-camera monitor from Summer runs $100. If you look around the internet, you might still see a video monitor from Fisher Price or Smart Choice.

All of them work the same way: a wireless camera sends a black and white picture (with sound) to a parent's 5" monitor in another room. We tested a **Smart Choice Baby Cam** and thought it worked OK. A low-light sensor lets you see grainy pictures at night (*Consumer Reports* says that Fisher Price's camera worked somewhat better in low-light situations than the Baby Cam, though). For most parents, however, a video monitor is probably overkill. We found we could tell whether our child really needed us based on his different cries—no picture was necessary. On the other hand, parents who have babies with medical problems that need constant monitoring might find video monitors helpful.

Our Picks: Brand Recommendations

Here are our picks for baby monitors, with one BIG caveat: how well a monitor will work in your house depends on interference sources (like cordless phones), the presence of other monitors in the neighborhood, etc. Since we get so many complaints about this category, it is imperative you buy a monitor from a place with a good return policy. Keep the receipts in case you have to do an exchange.

Good. Evenflo's Constant Care 3000 (pictured top) is the best pick if you want a monitor with rechargeable batteries—it also founds an out of range indicator and intercom feature. But it is rather pricey at $50 and works on the old 49 MHz frequency.  Another choice in this category would be the $46 Philips Super Sensitive Monitor (pictured bottom), which features both 900 MHz technology *and* rechargeable batteries for $4 less.

monitors

Better. Want a 900 MHz monitor to reduce the possibility of interference with a neighbor's monitor? We'd recommend the Fisher Price 900 MHz Long-Range monitor for its compact design and affordable price ($35). Unfortunately, this unit does not have rechargeable batteries, however. If that's important, consider the Philips unit mentioned above.

Best. Sometimes it is the simplest product that does the job best. The Fisher Price "Sounds 'N Lights" monitors are our top pick for baby monitors. The basic version is $20; if you need two receivers, go for the $30 model that offers that feature. No, you don't get rechargeable batteries or fancy features like an intercom, but you do get a quality baby monitor that does its job well. If you *have* to have a monitor with an intercom feature, go fro the Philips In-touch Monitor & Intercom with rechargeable batteries for $69.

BABY MONITORS	*A quick look at various features and brands*	
NAME	**MODEL**	**PRICE**
EVENFLO	CONSTANT CARE 1500	$25
	CONSTANT CARE 3000	$50
	CONSTANT CARE 4000	$40
FIRST YEARS	CRISP & CLEAR PLUS	$50
	SAFE & SOUND	$30
GRACO	ULTRACLEAR	$50
	SOUNDS SLEEP	$30
	FAMILY LISTEN N TALK	$70
PHILLIPS	SUPER SENSITIVE	$46
	ULTRA COMPACT	$58
	IN-TOUCH	$69
SAFETY 1ST	CRYSTAL CLEAR	$20-$25
	SUPER CLEAR	$30

KEY

✔= Yes

SOUND/LIGHT: indicates whether the monitor has a sound and lights display. This additional visual clue helps determine if baby is crying when the receiver is in a noisy environment

Swings

You can't talk to new parents without hearing the heated debate on swings, those battery-operated or wind-up surrogate parents. Some think they're a godsend, soothing a fussy baby when nothing else seems to work. Cynics refer to them as "neglect-o-matics," sinister devices that can become far too addictive for a society that thinks parenting is like microwave dinners—the quicker, the better.

Whatever side you come down on, we do have a few shopping tips. First, ALWAYS try it before you buy. Give it a whirl in the store or borrow one from a friend. Why? Some babies love swings. Others hate 'em. Don't spend $120 on a fancy swing only to discover your little one is a swing-hater.

Should you buy a manual (wind-up) or battery operated swing? We've been impressed in the past few years with the improvements of wind-up swings. These units now work effectively with only a little effort on part of a parent; so it's a toss-up whether you should get a manual or battery operated swing. You can save $20 with a wind-up instead of a battery-operated model, as well as the addi-

Continued on page 320

RECHARGE. BATT.	SOUND/LIGHT	900MHZ	INTERCOM
	✔		
✔	✔		✔
	✔	✔	
✔	✔	✔	
✔	✔		
	✔	✔*	
	✔		
	✔	✔	✔
✔	✔	✔	
✔		✔	
✔	✔	✔	✔
✔	✔		

900MHZ: Most monitors work on the 46-49mhz frequency; some work on the 900mhz frequency, which eliminates interference with cordless phones and extended a monitor's range.

INTERCOM: Does the monitor have a two-way intercom feature?

*One version of the Graco Ultra Clear has 900mhz technology.

Pet meets baby

If you already have a pet and are now expecting a baby, you're probably wondering how your "best friend" is going to react to the new family addition. Doubtless you've heard stories about how a pet became so jealous of its new "sibling" that he had to be given away. How can you avoid this situation? Here are 9 tips on smoothing the transition.

1 **IF YOUR DOG HASN'T BEEN OBEDIENCE TRAINED, DO IT NOW.** Even if you feel confident that your dog is well trained, a refresher course can't hurt.

2 **BEFORE YOU GET PREGNANT, HAVE YOUR CAT TESTED FOR TOXOPLAS-MOSIS,** a disease that is caused by a parasitic organism that is transmitted to humans from cat feces. Toxoplasmosis is dangerous and may cause the fetus to become seriously ill or die. If your cat is infected, have it boarded at a kennel or have someone take care of it for the period of infection (usually about six weeks). It's also best not to get pregnant during this time. You can avoid getting the infection yourself by having someone else clean out your cat's litter box. If you keep your cat indoors and he or she doesn't catch mice or birds outside, chances are the cat won't be infected (outdoor cats are more likely to be exposed to toxoplasmosis). Consult your doctor and your cat's veterinarian if you have any questions about this serious problem.

3 **DON'T OVERCOMPENSATE.** You may start feeling guilty while you're pregnant because you won't be able to spend as much time with your pet after the baby comes. So what mistake do expectant parents make? They overcompensate and give a pet extra attention before the baby arrives. Do this and then the animal really misses you and resents the new baby. While it might seem counter-intuitive, gradually give your best friend less attention so he or she can adjust before baby comes.

4 **IF YOUR PET HAS NEVER BEEN AROUND BABIES,** now is the time to introduce him—before your baby is born.

5 **CONSIDER BUYING A BABY DOLL.** Why? If you practice loving and attending to a baby doll for a few weeks prior to your baby's actual arrival, your pet can begin to get used to you paying attention to small bundles wrapped up in blankets. We did this, and our dog ZuZu got over her curiosity about it quickly. By the time the baby arrived, she didn't much care what we were carrying around (as long as it didn't smell like doggie biscuits!).

6 BEFORE THE BABY COMES HOME FROM THE HOSPITAL, have a friend or relative bring home a blanket or piece of clothing the new baby has slept on or worn in the hospital. This helps your pet get used to the smell of the new addition before you bring on the actual baby. We put a blanket the baby slept on in our dog's kennel, and we really think it helped smooth the transition. Another idea: one mom told us she had the nursery staff tape the cries of babies in the hospital nursery. She then put the tape inside the crib and let it "cry" for a while. "By the time my son came home, our pets were so used to hearing a baby's cry, it didn't bother them at all," she said.

7 STRATEGIES FOR BRINGING BABY HOME. Make sure your dog is under control (on a leash or under voice command) when you first come home with your new baby. Greet your four-legged friend first, without the baby. This allows your dog to release some of his excitement and jumping (remember he hasn't seen you for a few days), without you worrying about the dog harming a baby in your arms. Next, Dad should hold the dog by the collar or leash while Mom shows Fido the baby. Give your dog time to sniff a little, but don't let the dog turn the situation into a lick-fest. If everything looks OK, you can release the dog.

8 WHAT ABOUT USING A NET OVER YOUR BABY'S CRIB? While it's an old-wives tale that cats have an unnatural attraction to babies, cats DO love to sleep in warm places. And often a baby's room will the be warmest place in the house. While your cat probably won't want to sleep in the crib with the baby, you still might want to prevent them from visiting the crib and leaving pet hair/dander on the sheets. The Cozy Crib Tent ($60), manufactured by Tots in Mind (800) 626-0339 web: www.totsinmind.com is a mesh crib topper that attaches to the side railing. It completely encloses the crib. Some parents use a crib tent to keep older siblings from tossing toys into the crib. Another idea: train your cat where not to go by using double sided tape on such items as the crib, changing table, etc. One couple decided to install a screen door on the baby's room. They could see in and hear the baby, but the cat couldn't enter.

9 NEVER LEAVE YOUR PET ALONE WITH THE BABY—especially if it has shown any signs of jealousy toward your child. Don't allow your dog to sleep under the crib (there have been incidents of dogs standing up and pushing the mattress off its supports, causing the mattress to crash to the floor). Always supervise how your baby plays with the pet. For example, when our son was older, he found our Dalmatian very interesting. However, he tended to pull on her ears and tail whenever he got a hold of them. So, we constantly encouraged gentle petting.

tional savings in batteries. Wind-up swings start at $30 and go up to $50; battery operated swings run $50 to $100. Second-hand stores are great places to look for deals on swings; we've seen some in good condition for just $20 (check with the CPSC at www.cpsc.gov for recalls before you buy second hand).

Remember to observe safety warnings about swings, which are close to the top ten most dangerous products as far as injuries go. You must always stay with your baby, use the safety belt, and stop using the swing once your baby reaches the weight limit (about 25 pounds in most cases). Always remember that a swing is not a baby-sitter.

Babee Tenda's "safety" seminar: Anatomy of a Hard Sell

We got an interesting invitation in the mail during our second pregnancy—a company called "Babee Tenda" invited us to a free "safety seminar" at a local hotel. Our curiosity piqued, we joined a couple dozen other expectant parents on a Saturday afternoon to learn their expert safety tips.

What followed was a good lesson for all parents—beware of companies that want to exploit parents' fears of their children being injured in order to sell their expensive safety "solutions." Sure enough, there was safety information dispensed at the seminar. The speaker started his talk with horrific tales of how many children are injured and killed each year. The culprit? Cheap juvenile equipment products like high chairs and cribs, he claimed. It was quite a performance—the speaker entranced the crowd with endless statistics on kids getting hurt and then demonstrated hazards with sample products from major manufacturers.

The seminar then segued into a thinly veiled pitch for their products: the Babee Tenda high chair/feeding table and crib. The speaker (really a salesperson) spent what seemed like an eternity trying to establish the company's credibility, claiming Babee Tenda has been in business for 60 years and only sells its products to hospitals and other institutions. We can see why—these products are far too ugly and expensive to sell in retail stores.

How expensive? The pitchman claimed their crib retailed for $725—but is available for you today at the special price of $489! And what about the high chair/feeding table (which converts into a walker, swing, etc.)? It "regularly" sells for $450, but we'll give you a special deal at $298!

Our picks: Brand recommendations

What's the best brand? We'd give the award to **Graco**, whose "Open Top" swings (that is, no overhead bar) are best sellers—they start at $69 and have various do-dads that increase the price (more speeds, more tunes, etc). The top of the line **Graco "Gentle Choice"** swing ($100 to $120) features six speeds, 15

musical tunes, and (we're not making this up) "cruise control." That last feature adjusts the swing to your baby's weight to ensure consistent speed. There's even an auto shut-off timer. Yes, Graco still

We found Babee Tenda's sales pitch to be disgusting. They used misleading statistics and outright lies to scare parents into thinking they were putting their children in imminent danger if they used store-bought high chairs or cribs. Many of the statistics and "props" used to demonstrate hazards were as much as 20 years old and long since removed from the market! Even more reprehensible were claims that certain popular juvenile products were about to be recalled. Specifically, Babee Tenda claimed the Evenflo Exersaucer was "unsafe and will be off the market in six months," an accusation that clearly wasn't true.

The fact that Babee Tenda had to use such bogus assertions raised our suspicions about whether they were telling the truth about their own products. Sadly, the high-pressure sales tactics did win over some parents at the seminar we attended—they forked over nearly $800 for Babee Tenda's items. Since then, we've heard from other parents who've attended Babee Tenda's "safety seminars," purchased the products and then suffered a case of "buyer's remorse." Did they spend too much, they ask?

Yes, in our opinion. While we see nothing wrong per se with Babee Tenda's "feeding table" (besides the fact it's god-awful ugly), you should note it costs nearly four times as much as our top recommended high chair, the very well made Fisher Price Healthy Care. (At some seminars, the price for the feeding table is $400, but you get a free car seat with your purchase. Whoopee). There's nothing wrong with the crib either—and yes, Babee Tenda, throws in a mattress and two sheets. But you can find all this for much less than the $500 or so Babee Tenda asks.

So, we say watch out for Babee Tenda (and other similar companies like Babyhood, who pitches their "Baby Sitter" in hotel safety seminars). We found their "safety seminar" to be bogus, their high pressure sales tactics reprehensible and their products grossly overpriced.

sells the old-style swings with overhead bars, but we don't recommend them (you always seem to clunk baby's head on the bar when putting them in the swing).

A good second bet would be the **Ocean Wonders Aquarium cradle swing by Fisher Price** with its two different motions and integrated mobile for $99. (FYI: even though Fisher-Price calls this product a "cradle swing," it really is a misnomer. Baby sits in a seat, rather than lying flat in a cradle—we do not recommend swings that incorporate a  bassinet or cradle, as we believe it is not safe to have infant in a prone position in a swing).

How about a swing for Grandma's house? We like the Take-Along Swing, again by Fisher-Price. This cool swing folds up for portability, making them a good bet for $60.

Playpens

The portable playpen has been so popular in recent years that many parents consider it a necessity. Compared to the old wooden playpens of years past, today's playpens are made of metal and nylon mesh, fold compactly for portability and offer such handy features as bassinets, canopies, wheels and more. Some shopping tips:

◆ *Don't buy a second-hand playpen or use a hand-me-down.* Many playpen models have been the subject of recalls in recent years. Why? Those same features that make them convenient (the collapsibility to make the playpen "portable") worked too well in the past—some playpens collapsed with babies inside. Others had protruding rivets that caught some babies who wore pacifiers on a string (a BIG no-no, but that's another subject). A slew of injuries and deaths has prompted the recall of ten million playpens over the years. Yes, you can search government recall lists (www.cpsc.gov) to see if that hand-me-down is recalled, but we'd skip the hassle and just buy new.

◆ *Go for the bassinet feature.* Some playpens feature bassinet inserts which can be used for babies under three months of age (always check the weight guidelines). This is a handy feature that we recommend. Other worthwhile features: wheels for mobility, side-rail storage compartments and a canopy (if you plan to take the playpen outside or to the beach). If you want a playpen with canopy, look for those models that have "aluminized fabric" canopies—they reflect the sun's heat and UV rays to keep baby cooler.

◆ *Consider alternatives.* In Chapter 2, we reviewed the "Bed-side Co-Sleeper" by Arm's Reach, which is a combo playpen and co-sleeper (sort of a bassinet that attaches to your bed). Want something bigger than the standard playpen? Baby Trend makes an "extra large" playpen called the Nursery Care Center XL ($90) that is 38 x 38 and has a bassinet and changing station feature. Graco makes a similar model called the TotBlock ($90), but it omits the bassinet and changing station.

Our Picks: Brand recommendations

What are the best brands for playpens? Once again, we give it to Graco—their *Pack 'N Play* playpens are the best designed and least-recalled. Last we looked, they had 12 models that ranged from $59 to $139.

So, which model should you get? We like the basic Pack N Play with bassinet attachment for $100. If you plan to use the playpen outdoors, go for one with a canopy that is aluminized to cut down on the heat ($130).

What about the other playpen brands? Yes, you can find playpens by Baby Trend, Evenflo, Kolcraft and Fisher Price, but we don't think their quality or features measure up to Graco's offerings.

The Bottom Line:
A Wrap-Up of Our Best Buy Picks

In the nursery, we highly recommend the Diaper Champ as the best diaper pail . . . but the Diaper Dekor is a new option worth a look. No, we're not too wild about wipe warmers, which have safety concerns.

The best toys for infants include a basic set of stacking cups ($5), an activity center ($15), and a play center ($30). An activity/bouncer seat with a toy bar is a good idea, with prices ranging from $30 to $60—we like the Fisher Price bouncers best. An affordable alternative: adding a $10 toy bar to an infant seat.

As for bathtubs, we thought the EuroBath ($25) by Primo was the best bet, although it is a big. A better bet for Grandma's house might be the simple Fold-Up Tub by Safety 1st ($13).

With baby monitors, the simpler the better—a basic Fisher Price unit will do the trick; if you want a unit with rechargeable batteries, go for the Philips Super Sensitive Monitor.

For swings, we like Graco's Open Top swings ($70 to $100) best. And Graco also makes the best playpens (Pack 'N Plays, $59-$139).

playpens

CAR
SEATS

CHAPTER 8

Car Seats: Picking the right child safety seat

Inside this chapter

What's the best car seat for your baby? What is the difference between an infant and a convertible seat? How will new safety standards affect child safety seats? We'll discuss these issues and more in this chapter. You'll find complete reviews and ratings of the major car seat brands as well as informative charts that compare the best choices.

Here's a sobering figure: last year, motor vehicle crashes killed 1,135 children under age ten and injured another 182,000. While the majority of those injuries and deaths occurred to children who were not in safety seats, the toll from vehicle accidents in this country is still a statistic that can keep you awake all night.

Every state in the U.S. (and every province in Canada) requires infants and children to ride in child safety seats, so this is one of the few products that every parent must buy. In fact you may find yourself buying multiple car seats as your baby grows older—and for secondary cars, grandma's car, a caregiver's vehicle and more.

So, which seat is the safest? Easiest to use? One thing you'll learn in this chapter is that there is not one "safest" or "best" seat. Yes, we will review and rate the various car seat brands and examine their recall/safety history. BUT, remember the best seat for your child is the one that correctly fits your child's weight and size—and can be correctly installed in your vehicle.

And that's the rub: roadside safety checks by police reveal 80% to 90% of child safety seats are NOT installed or used properly. Although the exact figure isn't known, a large number of child fatalities and injuries from crashes are caused by improper use or installation of seats. Realizing that many of today's child safety seats are a failure due to complex installation and other hurdles, the federal government has rolled out a new safety standard (called LATCH) for child seats and vows to fix loopholes in current crash testing. We'll discuss these changes in-depth in this chapter.

Getting Started:
When Do You Need This Stuff?

You can't leave the hospital without a car seat. By law, all states require children to be restrained in a child safety seat. You'll want to get this item early (in your sixth to eighth month of pregnancy) so you can practice wedging it into the back seat. Also: some of the best deals on car seats are found online. You'll need to leave a few weeks in shipping time to insure the seat arrives before baby does.

Sources to Find Car Seats

1 **DISCOUNTERS.** Car seats have become a loss leader for many discount stores. Chains like Target and Wal-Mart sell these items at small mark-ups in hopes you'll spend money elsewhere in the store. The only caveat: most discounters only carry a limited selection of seats, typically of the no-frills brands.

2 **BABY SPECIALTY STORES.** Independent juvenile retailers have all but abandoned car seats to the chains. With the exception of premium brands like Britax, you'll only see a few scattered offerings here.

3 **THE SUPERSTORES.** Chains like Babies R Us, Toys R Us and Burlington Coat Factory's Baby Depot (reviewed in depth in Chapter 2) tend to carry a wider selection of car seats than discounters. And, sometimes, that includes the better brands. Prices can be a few dollars higher than the chains, but sales often bring better deals.

4 **MAIL ORDER/THE WEB.** Yes, you can buy a car seat through the mail or online. More on the 'net next. A run-down of other mail order sources appears later in the chapter. Prices are usually discounted, but watch out for shipping—the cost of shipping bulky items like car seats can outweigh the discount in some cases. Use an online coupon (see the previous chapter for coupon sites) to save and look for free shipping specials.

Parents in Cyberspace:
What's on the Web?

The web is teeming with both information and bargains on car seats. Here's the best of what's out there.

◆ **NHTSA.** The National Highway Traffic & Safety Administration site (www.nhtsa.dot.gov) is a treasure trove of car seat info—you can read about recalls, the latest news on changing standards and installation tips. The NHTSA's brochure "Buying a Safer Car For Child Passengers" is a must read for any parent. If you don't have web access, you can order it by calling (888) DASH2DOT. You can also contact the government's Auto Safety Hotline at 800-424-9393 to ask car seat related questions. As we went to press, we heard the NHTSA was gong to publish ratings on car seat ease of use in mid 2003 (see discussion later in this chapter). These ratings will appear on the NHTSA's web site.

◆ **The American Academy of Pediatrics** (www.aap.org, go to "You and Your Family") is an excellent resource for buying tips.

◆ **The National Safe Kids Campaign** (www.safekids.org) has a helpful interactive "car seat locator" that helps you determine which seat is right for the age and weight of the child.

◆ **Safety Belt Safe USA** (www.carseat.org) has a good site with tips on picking the best seat for your child, as well as the latest recalls and info on child safety seats.

◆ **Car Seat Data** (www.CarSeatData.org) has an "interactive compatibility database" that lets you search for which seats work in which vehicles. Very cool.

◆ **ParentsPlace** (www.parentsplace.com) has a car seat FAQ, buying guide and message board dedicated to car seats. BabyCenter.com is another good site to check out.

◆ **Our web site** has a message boards dedicated to car seats. Plus: we have a brochure called "Buying a Better Car Seat Restraint" produced by a Canadian auto insurance institute. This publication (downloadable as a PDF, portable document format) has excellent advice on buying a seat. The institute's web site (www.icbc.com) has rating charts that compare major brands of car seats—go to "Road Safety," then "Child Seats" and then finally to "Buying a Child Seat."

....

For a link to the brochure and the ratings web page, go to www.BabyBargainsBook.com and click on the "Bonus Material." section for a link to this car seat guide.

◆ **Where to buy online.** Many of the large baby product web sites (and catalogs) reviewed in Chapter 12 (Etc.) sell car seats at competitive prices. When you find an online coupon for these sites (see Chapter 7, Around the House, for a list of such sites), the deals can be even better. One great site: BabyCatalog.com has rock-bottom deals on car seats (and often have free shipping specials).

 More Money Buys You . . .

As you'll read later in this chapter, all child safety seats are regulated by the federal government to meet minimum safety standards. So whether you buy a $50 seat from K-Mart or a $240 brand from a specialty store, your baby is equally covered. When you pay extra money, however, there are some perks. First, on the safety front, the more expensive seats have shock-absorbing foam that protects a seat from side-impact collisions. The more expensive seats are also more comfortable for the child—they typically feature reclining seats, more padding, pillows and other comforts. For infant seats, when you spend more money, you get an adjustable base (which enables a better fit in vehicles), canopy to block the sun and plush padding.

 Smart Shopper Tips

Smart Shopper Tip #1
So many seats, so much confusion
"I'm so confused by all the car seat options out there. For example, are infant car seats a waste of money? Or should I go with a convertible seat? Or one of those models that is good from birth to college?

Children's car seats come in three flavors: "infant," "convertible" and "boosters." Let's break it down:

◆ **Infant** car seats are just that—these rear-facing seats are designed to be used with infants up to 20 lbs. or so (one model from Cosco can be used up to 35 lbs. but that is the exception) and 26" in height. On average, parents get about six months of use out of an infant seat (of course that varies with the size/height of the child). Infant car seats have an internal harness (usually five-point) that holds the infant to the carrier, which is then snapped into a base, which is secured to the car.

◆ **Convertible** car seats (see right) can be used for both infants *and* older children (up to 40 lbs.)—infants ride rear facing; older kids ride facing forward. Convertible seats have different harness options (more on this later); unlike infant seats, however, they do not have snap-in bases.

◆ **Booster** seats were once used exclusively to position the vehicle's safety belt to correctly fit a young child up to 80 pounds (hence, they are called belt-positioning boosters). In recent years, some boosters have added five-point harnesses (see picture) for use by younger children weighing less than 40 pounds (after that time, the five-point harness is removed and the seat is used with the vehicle's safety belt; see lower picture). These new seats are called "transitional boosters" or "combo seats."

Since this book focuses on products for babies up to two years of age, this chapter only reviews and rates infant and convertible seats. Please see our book *Toddler Bargains* (check the back of the book for more info) for reviews of booster seats.

Of course, just to make things more confusing for you first-time parents, these neat categories have blurred somewhat in recent years. One car seat maker, Cosco/Eddie Bauer, has introduced seats that morph from a convertible seat to a booster. One such model: the Cosco Alpha Omega (also called the Eddie Bauer Three in One), which can be used rear-facing from 5 to 30 pounds, then forward-facing to 40 lbs. From 40 lbs. to 80 lbs. the Alpha Omega converts to a booster seat that uses the auto safety belt to restrain an older child. We'll review this seat later in this chapter.

So does it make more sense to buy one car seat (that is a convertible car seat) and just skip the infant car seat? Nope. Safety experts say it's best for babies under 20 lbs. to be in an *infant* car seat—they're built to better accommodate a smaller body and baby travels in a semi-reclined position, which better supports an infant's head and neck. Yes, some convertible seats recline—but the degree of recline can be affected by the angle of your vehicle's seat back. And certain convertible seats (those with bar shields or t-shields instead of five-point restraints—more on this later) simply don't work well with infants. Furthermore, most babies don't reach the 20-pound mark until six months (and some as late as 12 months)—and that can be a very long period of time if you don't have an infant car seat.

Why? First, it's helpful to understand that an infant car seat is more than just a car seat—it's also an infant carrier when detached from its base. Big deal, you might say? Well, since infants spend much of their time sleeping (and often fall asleep in the car), this *is* a big deal. By detaching the carrier from the auto base, you don't have to wake the baby when you leave the car. Buy a convertible car seat, and you'll have to unbuckle the baby and move her into another type of carrier (and most likely wake her in the process). Take it from us: let sleeping babies lie and spend the additional $60 to $90 for an infant car seat, even if you use it for just six months. Remember: babies should be REAR-FACING until they reach one year of age, regardless of weight. If your child outgrows their infant car seat before one year of age, be sure to use a convertible seat that in rear-facing mode for as long as possible. Most convertible seats can be used rear-facing until 30 or 33 lbs.

Smart Shopper Tip #2
Infant seat versus convertible
"My friend thinks infant car seats with snap-in bases are danger-ous—she thinks in a crash, the seat will detach from the base. Is it safer to just skip the infant seat car seat and go to a convertible used rear-facing?"

This is a common debate in car seat circles—what is the safest for newborns, an infant or convertible seat? Fueling the debate was the recall of several defective infant car seats in the 1990's that did sep-arate from their bases in government crash tests. While those prob-lems are now fixed, fears about infant seats linger among some par-ents and car seat advocates. Among the concerns: infant car seats that are not correctly latched into their bases (you can hear a click) can come loose in a crash. And some safety advocates claim the gov-ernment doesn't crash test infant car seats with bases at high speeds.

We hear all these concerns, but still think the infant car seat is the way to go. First, they are designed to fit infants better than larg-er convertible seats (more on this in a moment). Yes, the snap-in base is really a *convenience* feature, not a safety feature—but that does not make the bases *unsafe*. Reports of seats detaching from bases during high-speed crashes are so rare, we don't think this is an issue either.

And let's take a look at the alternative to the infant seat for a newborn—a convertible seat. Many seat makers advertise their seats can work from 5 pounds and up . . . but the real factor in determining whether a newborn will fit in these larger seats is the height of the lowest harness slot. The reality: some seats have lower slots (and hence are more newborn compatible) than others. Parents have complained to us that some of the seats we recommend don't really fit their small newborns. The best convertible seats with the LOWEST slot heights are: Graco's ComfortSport (formally the Century Accel), Evenflo's Titan and Evenflo's Triumph. For example, the lowest slot of the Graco Comfort Sport is 8.5"—that's a full 1.5" under the Britax Roundabout (whose lowest slot is at 10").

Bottom line: your child is equally safe in an infant car seat with base as they are in a convertible seat, provided they fit the seat and the seat is correctly installed in your vehicle. If you decide to forgo the infant seat, be sure to get a convertible seat whose harness fits your newborn.

Smart Shopper Tip #3
New standards, new confusion?

"I hear the federal government has issued new car seat standards. Should I wait to purchase my baby's car seat? And what's wrong with the old seats anyway?"

Stop any ten cars on the road with child safety seats and we'll bet eight or nine are not installed or used correctly. That's what road-side checks by local law enforcement in many states have uncovered: a 1998 study by the National Highway Traffic and Safety Administration stopped 4000 drivers in four states and found a whopping 80% made mistakes in installing or securing a child safety seat.

What's causing all the problems?

Our view: current child safety seats have failed parents. Installation of a car seat can be an exercise in frustration—even parents who spend hours with the instructions can still make mistakes. The number one culprit: the auto seat belt—it is great at restraining adults, but not so good at child safety seats. And those seats simply won't work well if they aren't attached to a car correctly . . . that's the crux of the problem. Simply put, thanks to the quirkiness of auto safety belts (different auto makers have different systems), putting a child safety seat in a car is like trying to fit a square peg into a round hole.

The bottom line: some child safety seats simply DON'T FIT in some vehicles. Which cars? Which seats? It's hard to tell. There is one good web site with a car seat compatibility database (www.carseatdata.org), but it doesn't cover every seat and every vehicle. Often, parents find it's trial and error to see what works.

Finally, there is good news to report, however: The federal government has rolled out new, mandated "uniform" attachments (called LATCH or ISOFIX) required for all vehicles and safety seats made after September 2002. LATCH stands for "Lower Anchors and Tethers for Children." ISOFIX stands for International Standards Organization FIX, which is the international version of LATCH. (More on ISOFIX later in this section). Instead of using the auto's seat belt, car seats attach to two anchor bars installed in the lower seatback.

The result: no more confusing installations, locking clips or other apparatus needed to make sure the seat is correctly attached. (Another part of the new standard: tether straps, which are discussed later in this section). See picture of a LATCH installed car seat at right).

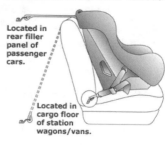

Located in rear filler panel of passenger cars.

Located in cargo floor of station wagons/vans.

As with the transition to any new standard, however, there is quite a bit of confusion about the new LATCH seats (judging from our reader email). Here is a sum up of frequent questions we get on the new LATCH seats:

◆ *Which manufacturers sell LATCH seats?* Answer: all. Every infant and convertible car seat sold now includes LATCH. Note: we have noticed that some web sites are still selling off old stock of previous models that do not have LATCH. Be sure to read the description carefully before you buy if you want a LATCH seat.

◆ *Will I have to junk my old car seat after 2002?* Of course not. If you have an older model vehicle and an older (non-LATCH) car seat, that is fine—the law just mandates you use an appropriate safety seat, it doesn't specify a LATCH seat.

◆ *I just bought a new car that has the new LATCH attachments* but I got a hand-me-down seat from my sister that does not have LATCH. Can I use an old seat in the new vehicle? Yes . . . but here is our advice: if you have a vehicle that has the new attachments, get a seat that takes advantage of the system. One solution: some car seat makers sell LATCH retrofit kits for their older models. At press time, Evenflo, Cosco and Graco/Century had LATCH retrofit kits available at retailers like Babies R Us for $25 or so.

CAR SEATS

Unfortunately, some seat makers (like Britax) have chosen NOT to produce a LATCH retrofit kit. Can you use a Graco LATCH retrofit kit on an Evenflo seat? NO—never use a LATCH retrofit kit for a car seat that it was not intended for.

◆ *I've seen two different LATCH systems, straps/clips and a rigid bar.* Which is best? We discuss this issue in depth in the following box.

◆ *My car does not have LATCH. What is the safest seat I can buy?* Remember the safest seat is the one that best fits your car *and* your child. There is no one "safest" seat. Get the best seat you can afford (we'll have recommendations later in this chapter) and use it with a tether strap. And get your car seat safety checked to make sure you have the best installation and fit.

◆ *I need to move my LATCH seat to a second car that doesn't*

Which flavor of LATCH is best?

The party line on LATCH from child passenger safety experts is that LATCH is supposed to be a more convenient option for installing a car seat—and this will curb the incorrect installation of non-LATCH seats that has been so prevalent. While we see that point, we're going to wade into the deep end of the controversy pool with some observations about test results of LATCH versus non-LATCH installed seats.

Fact: LATCH seats perform better in crash tests than seats just belted in the old way (with the auto safety belt and a locking clip), even when the latter uses a snug tether strap. We base that opinion on the results of crash tests by Ford Motor Company. What about government data showing little difference between LATCH and non-LATCH crash tests? The problem is that the government used car seats that were tightly installed with less than one-eighth of an inch of lateral movement—yes, that is possible in a lab, but most parents can't or don't install a seat that tight in the real world.

So, you're sold on the idea that LATCH is the safest option. Now, which type of LATCH seat should you get? LATCH seats now come in three flavors:

◆ *Single Flexible strap:* These seats have one strap that loops through the seat and attaches to the anchors. Examples of these seats include the Cosco and Eddie Bauer seats. Many LATCH retrofit kits sold for older seats also use this system.

---

have the new attachments. Will it work? Yes, you should be able to secure a LATCH seat in an older car using the auto's safety belt. But always check the car seat's instructions to make sure this installation is possible.

◆ *I know the safety place for a baby is in the middle of the back seat. But my car doesn't have LATCH anchors there, just in the outboard positions! Where should I put the seat?* Our advice: use the LATCH positions, even if they are just in the side of the car. Now, some car seat and vehicle makers say it is okay to use a LATCH seat in the middle of the back seat if you use the LATCH anchors in the outboard positions—check with your car seat and vehicle owner's manual if this is permissible.

Smart Shopper Tip #4
Strap Me In
   "What is a tether strap? Do I want one?"

◆ **Double flexible strap:** As the name implies, these seats have two separate belts that attach to LATCH anchors. Examples of these seats include the Britax Roundabout.

ISOFIX flexible (belt) mount system

◆ **Rigid ISOFIX:** These seats have rigid connectors (called ISOFIX) that snap to the LATCH anchors. Examples of these include the Britax Expressway ISOFIX and the Baby Trend Latch-Loc.
   So, which is best? According to crash tests (again,

ISOFIX rigid mount system

by Ford), the double flexible strap seats or rigid ISOFIX were the safest options. This was especially true for side-impact crashes. No, that does not mean a single flexible strap LATCH seat is *unsafe*—those seats still meet federal safety requirements. It just means the former seats have an extra measure of safety, as judged by performance in crash tests.

   We like the rigid ISOFIX seats better than the flexible strap LATCH seats for another reason—they are easier to install. There is no tightening of straps; just snap and go! The problem: there are few rigid ISOFIX seats on the market. The above two options are basically it as of this writing.

Back in 1999, the federal government mandated that all convertible child safety seats be sold with a tether strap—these prevent a car seat from moving forward in the event of a crash. How? One end of the tether strap attaches to top of the car seat; the other is hooked to an "anchor bolt" that is permanently installed on the back of the back seat or on the floor in your vehicle.

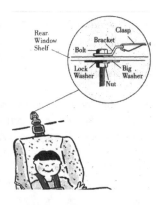

Most newer vehicles already have installed anchor bolts, making the use of a tether strap a snap. (Hint: check your owner's manual to find instructions on using tether straps). Older vehicles may have pre-drilled anchorage points—just ask your car dealer for the "anchor bolt installation kit" (a part number that's listed in your owner's manual in the section on installing child safety seats). You can install the bolt or have the dealer do it.

Of course, really old cars are trickier since they lack anchor bolts or even pre-drilled holes—to install the anchor bolt, you may need to drill through your car's sub floor (a job for the car dealer, as you can guess). And just finding out the part number for the anchor bolt can be a challenge; some car dealers are clueless about this issue.

(One tip: call a CANADIAN dealer to find out the part number of the anchor bolt for child safety seats. Why? Tether straps have been required for years in Canada. Hence, car dealers there are more familiar with this request. You can find a Canadian dealer's phone number on most automobile maker's web sites.)

A side note: most car seats can only use tether straps when they are FORWARD-FACING. Only two models (the Britax Roundabout and the Combi Avatar, reviewed later) have a tether which can be used in either the rear or forward-facing position. Note: tether straps are typically not used with infant seats or booster seats (but always consult your seat's directions for specific advice on this).

So, is the tether strap worth all the hassle? Yes—crash tests show car seats are SAFER when used with a tether strap. The strap keeps the car seat (and hence, your baby's head) from moving forward in a crash, lowering the chance of injury. So are seats used without tethers unsafe? No, the federal government requires seats to be safe even when a tether is not in use. Of course, the tether adds that extra measure of safety and is always preferable to a tether-less installation.

Smart Shopper Tip #5
One Size Does Not Fit All

"My friend has a car seat that just doesn't fit very well into her car. Does anyone put out a rating system that says which seats are most compatible? Safest?"

There is good news on this front. In 2000, Congress passed the "Transportation Recall Enhancement, Accountability and Documentation (TREAD) Act " that instructed the Department of Transportation to come up with a rating system for car seats. (What a concept!) After years of complaining from safety advocates, we have to give Congress a hand for passing this legislation (particular thanks to Senator John Fitzgerald R-Ill. and his aide, Evelyn Fortier, for seeing this to fruition).

The new ratings system will provide "practical, readily under-standable, and timely information to consumers for use in making informed decisions in the purchase of child restraints." As we went to press, we heard the NHTSA was planning to publish ratings on car seats (based on "ease of use") sometime in mid 2003. This will appear on the NHTSA's web site (www.nhtsa.dot.gov). Again, sub-scribe to the newsletter on our web page (BabyBargainsBook.com) for the latest details.

We should also point out the new car seat law requires the fed-eral government to develop new crash tests for car seats that sim-ulate rear-impact and side-impact crashes, a long overdue change.

Smart Shopper Tip #6
Recalls

"I saw in the paper that a particular car seat is being recalled. Should I be skeptical of other seats by that manufacturer?"

Here's a sobering fact of car seat shopping: EVERY major brand of car seats has had a recall over the past five years. We've seen recalls on cheap seats sold in Wal-Mart and $200 car seats sold in specialty stores, so recalls are a fact of life no matter what brand you consider. How can you make a smart decision?

First, realize that some recalls are more serious than others. Some car seats are recalled for minor problems, like incorrect labels. Other companies do voluntary recalls when their own testing reveals a problem. The key issue: look to see if there are any deaths or injuries associated with the defective product. Obviously, car seats that are so defective as to cause injury to babies are much more serious than minor labeling recalls.

Another issue: how does a company handle a recall? Do they fight the government, forcing regulators to order a recall? Or do they voluntarily recall the item and set up an efficient process (toll-free phone number) to get replacements or retrofit kits to consumers? In the past, we lowered the rating for one major car seat maker (Evenflo) for the abysmal way they handled a recall for their On My Way infant seat.

When a company announces a recall, the product is typically removed from store shelves (if the recall is for the current production run). If the recall is for a product's previous production run, you may still see it on store shelves (since the defect may have been corrected months before). That's why it is key to see WHEN the recalled

Registering a Complaint: Do Some Seat Makers Ignore Registered Users During Recalls?

As a new parent, you try to do everything you can to make sure your baby is safe. Besides researching which products are safe, many parents also diligently fill out warranty and registration cards with the expectation they will be contacted in case of a future safety recall.

Yet many parents are surprised to learn that baby product companies fail to mail out notices of defective products to registered users. Why? Companies complain that mailing costs are too high—instead they issue a press release to the media, hoping local newspapers, radio and TV will spread the word about a defective product.

Case in point: the March 2002 recall of the Graco Snug Ride infant seat. Graco discovered that over 900,000 units of the popular infant car seat were defective. The problem: a number of the bases had missing components that were used to attach the carrier to the base (Graco has subsequently fixed the problem and we still recommend that seat).

Registered users of the Snug Ride probably expected Graco to drop them a note about the problem. If so, they were sorely disappointed. Graco did send a press release to the media regarding the recall, but made no effort to contact registered users directly.

Hello? Is this insane or what? Parents take the time and effort to fill out and mail those registration cards that manufacturers include in product boxes, but for what? Instead of receiving a courtesy call or postcard that the car seat they are using might be a death trap, you are supposed to be watching the local news at exactly the right moment to hear your car seat is recalled? Or see page 16A of the local paper?

Companies like Graco should be ashamed. Let's do the math—assuming only one-third of all Snug Ride users actually registered their seats (and that is a conservative guess), Graco would have to send out notices to 300,000 parents. What does a postcard cost to mail these days? A whopping 23¢. So, Graco's total costs would be about $75,000 (assuming some printing costs). That seems a small price to pay for a company with $600 million in annual sales.

product was manufactured. Of course, different car seats in the same manufacturer's line may be totally unaffected by a recall.

Another tip: make sure to fill out the registration card that comes with any car seat you buy . . . and send it in! In most cases, this will get you expedited recall info and repair kits. Also: sign up for a recall list like the free e-newsletter on our web site (see the back of the book for details). Unfortunately, with some car seat makers, even if you fill out a registration card you may not get a recall notice. For more on this problem, see the following box.

And what about email? Last we looked, most of the world used the 'net to communicate. Yet Graco and nearly all other juvenile product makers do not allow parents to register online. Emailed recall notices? Forget about it.

Last year, the Consumer Products Safety Commission (CPSC) issued 341 recalls. That's nearly one per day! So, what can a parent do to keep up with what's safe and what's recalled? Here are our tips:

◆ *Track your purchases.* In order to know whether you have a recalled product, you first have to know what you got to begin with. One parent told us she kept a spreadsheet with the following info for all her baby products; manufacturer, model, serial #, date manufactured, company phone number/web site, where purchased and price paid. Okay, perhaps that's a bit overboard for most parents. But at least put all your receipts and product manuals into a file or shoebox. The goal: create ONE place you go to when a recall is announced.

◆ *Stay informed.* Register for free email alerts about recalls. Our web page (www.BabyBargainsBook.com) has a free newsletter that sends out email alerts to readers whenever a baby product is recalled. Other sites like SafetyAlerts.com will send out similar alerts, and they also do food allergy recalls and other safety warnings.

◆ *Consider buying products from web sites that will inform you of recalls.* Case in point: Amazon/Babies R Us does a good job of letting customers know of recalled products. One reader was amazed when Amazon sent her a recall notice (with detailed instructions on what to do) for a bassinet she bought over a year ago.

◆ *Be careful with eBay and other second-hand purchases.* Yes, eBay has great deals, but be sure you aren't buying a recalled product. Do a search of the CPSC's web site (www.cpsc.gov) to find whether that car seat deal is really a dud.

CAR
SEATS

Smart Shopper Tip #7
Watch the height limit

"My son isn't anywhere near the 20 lb. limit for his infant seat, but he's so tall I think it isn't safe anymore—he has to bend his legs when we put him in!"

Here's a little known fact to most infant seats: in addition to WEIGHT limits, all infant car seats also have HEIGHT limits. And like everything in the car seat world, each seat has different limits (check the sticker on the side of the carrier—by law, the manufacturer must list both height and weight limits). Once your baby exceeds EITHER the height or weight limit, you should move them to a convertible seat.

One note on this: while the weight limit is important, do one other test if your child is approaching the height limit—is the top of your child's shoulders ABOVE the top harness slot in the infant seat? Is there less than an inch of seat left above baby's head? If so, then move them to a convertible seat (facing the rear of the vehicle until they pass one year of age).

With the bigger babies everyone seems to be having these days (credit more breastfeeding? Genetically modified foods?), this isn't a moot point. A large infant might exceed the height limit BEFORE he or she passes the weight limit. Here's the scoop: height limits range from 26" for the Graco Snug Ride to 29" for the Eddie Bauer (Cosco) and one version of the Baby Trend Latch-Loc. Most infant seats have weight limits in the 20lb to 22lb range, although one Cosco model has a whopping 35 lbs limit. Later in this section, we'll have a chart that lists the height and weight limits of all major infant car seats. See the box on the next page for more on this topic.

Finally, remember WEIGHT limits are more reliable than height limits with seats. Why? Some babies have longer legs, while others have longer torsos. Babies that have longer legs may technically surpass the height limit, even though their shoulders are still below the top slot and you still have more than an inch of space above their head to the top of the seat. In that case, leave them in the infant seat until they outgrow it by weight.

Smart Shopper Tip #8
Do I have to buy THREE seats?

"My baby has outgrown their infant seat. Can I buy a combo seat that converts to a booster?"

The short answer: yes. Do we recommend it? No. Why? We think the safest place for an infant who has outgrown an infant seat is in a CONVERTIBLE seat in rear-facing mode. Leave them there until they are AT LEAST a year of age—longer if they still are under the weight limit. Note: all of the "combo" seats that have a five-point harness and then later convert to a belt-positioning booster are FORWARD-FACING only seats. Examples of combo seats include the Evenflo Comet, Safety 1st Vantage Point, Century Next Step and so on.

So, what is best? When your child outgrows their convertible seat, THEN we recommend a booster seat (combo or regular). Now, we realize what you are thinking: have we lost our minds? We are recommending you buy THREE seats for your child: infant, convertible, and then a booster. Wouldn't it be cheaper to get one of those all-in-one seats or at least one that combines the convertible/booster function? No, not in our opinion. The all-in-one-seats (like the Eddie Bauer Three-In-One or Cosco Alpha Omega) are a poor choice, see review later in this chapter. And while those combo boosters are good choice for a three or four year old child that has outgrown their convertible seat but not mature enough to sit in a belt-positioning booster, combo seats are NOT good for infants—they often don't recline and have less sleeping support than convertibles.

That's why you won't see reviews of combo seats in this book—they are best for children over two years of age. Yes, we review combo seats and regular boosters in our *Toddler Bargains* book.

Smart Shopper Tip #9
Holding Your Baby Back: Safety Harness Advice
"Which safety harness is best—the 5-point, bar-shield, or T-shield?

Car Seat Lesson 101: understanding the different harness systems available on the market. For INFANT seats, you have two choices: three point or five-point belts (although nearly all infant seats now have five-point harnesses). For CONVERTIBLE seats, you have three choices: five-point, bar-shield or t-shield.

Three (or five) point belts refer to the number of points in which the belt attaches to the car seat. A t-shield is a plastic shield that buckles in below baby's crotch. A bar shield lowers over the baby's head and snaps into a buckle.

Our recommendations: for INFANT seats, in past editions, we thought three-point systems were just fine, based on crash test data we reviewed. That said, we note that most new models of infant seats have five-points, which are of course OK . . . it's just easier to buckle a newborn with a three-point seat than a five-point. Hence, if you see a model with a three-point harness still on stores shelves, it is a perfectly acceptable alternative. (Note: some safety advocates say five-point harness infant seats are safer since they fit infants better—that's probably encouraging more companies to go this route).

For CONVERTIBLE seats, we recommend the five-point version. Why? Safety experts say it's the best choice because you can tighten the belts to securely hold your baby in her seat. T-shields are second in preference (but don't work well for small infants). And bar shields have another problem—some don't adjust well to growing children. Even those expensive models that feature *adjustable* shields only adjust so much—if your child grows quickly, they still might outgrow the car seat. The result? You'll have to move them into a booster seat (making an extra purchase) sooner than you want to.

Another major problem with bar shields: wiggling toddlers can get out of them way too easily. One mom told us she was horrified to look in her rear view mirror one day and find her 18 month-old child STANDING in his car seat while the vehicle was moving. We think five point harnesses are safer since it is very difficult for baby to wiggle out when the belts are tightened correctly.

Let's be honest, however: the five-point harness is the *least convenient* to use. You have to put each strap around baby's arms, find the lower buckle (which always seems to disappear under their rump) and then snap them in. Bar-shields and t-shields slip over the baby's head in one motion and are easier to buckle.

The fact that the five-point harness is inconvenient is just the way it goes. Simply put, it's the safest choice for your baby. And sometimes as a parent you have to do what's best for your child, even if that makes your life less convenient.

Are higher price seats better?

When you shell out $200 instead of $100 for a car seat, do you get a car seat that is twice as safe? Answer: no, price is not always an indicator of quality. For example, some expensive seats have leather covers. Yes, they cost $200, but often you are paying for a fancy pad or designer name, not the safety features of a seat.

Now, that said, we should note that in some cases you DO get better safety features when you spend more. Example: Britax seats are pricey ($200 or so), but they have extra EPS foam for crash protection, no-twist straps and a slew of other safety and convenience features. Plus you can tether these seats either forward OR rear facing, unlike most of the competition, which is just forward-facing. The tether has been shown to greatly reduce seat movement in a crash. Now, THAT is a safety feature. And if a seat is loaded with features that make it easier to use, you could argue that parents would be less likely to mis-use the seat—and that makes it safer.

Here are ten more shopping tips for car seats:

◆ *How easily does it recline?* All convertible seats are supposed to have a recline feature to make sure baby is at a proper angle. Of course, how easily the seat reclines varies from model to model. And up-front recline lever that is easy to use is best. Check it out in the store before you buy.

◆ *No-twist straps.* Better car seats have thicker straps that don't twist. The result: it is easier to get a child in and out of a seat. Cheaper seats have cheaper webbing that can be a nightware— "twisty straps" are a key reason why parents hate their car seats. Later in this chapter, we'll point out which seats have this problem.

◆ *Check the belt adjustments.* You don't merely adjust the car seat's belts just when your baby gets bigger—if you put Junior in a coat, you'll need to loosen the belts as well. As a result, it's important to check how easily they adjust. Of course, every car seat maker seems to have a different idea on how to do this. The best car seats let you adjust the belts from the *front*. Those models that require you to access the back of the seat to adjust the belts are more hassle. FYI: do not put your child in a bulky coat or snowsuit and the buckle in them in a child seat. In the case of an accident, the bulky coat might compress, compromising the safety of the seat. At most, only put a child in a thin coat (like a polar fleece) when they are riding in a child safety seat. (To keep an infant warm, consider a seat cover-up, which goes on the outside of the seat. We'll discuss examples of these products later in this chapter.

◆ *Change the harness height.* Some seats require you to re-thread the belts when you change harness heights. Try this in the store to see how easy/difficult it is. Note: the best seats have automatic harness height adjusters that require no re-threading.

◆ *Look at the chest clip.* The chest clip or harness tie holds the two belts in place. Lower-quality seats have a simple "slide-in" clip—you slip the belt under a tab. That's nice, but some older toddlers can slip out from this type of chest clip. A better bet: a chest clip that SNAPS the two belts together like a seat belt. This is more kid-proof.

◆ *Are the instructions in Greek?* Before you buy the car seat, take a minute to look at the set-up and use instructions. Make sure you can make sense of the seat's documentation. Another tip: if possible, ask the store for any installation tips and advice.

car seats

◆ *Is the pad cover machine-washable?* You'd think this would be a "no-brainer," but a surprising number of seats (both convertible and infant) have covers that aren't removable or machine washable. Considering how grimy these covers can get, it's smart to look for this feature. Also check to see if you can wash the harness.

◆ *Does the seat need to be installed with each use?* The best car seats are "permanently" installed in your car. When you put baby in, all you do is buckle them in the seat's harness system. Yet some infant car seats and even a few convertible models need to be installed with each use—that means you have to belt the thing into your car every time you use it. Suffice it to say, that's a major drawback.

◆ *Watch out for hot buckles.* Some inexpensive car seats have exposed metal buckles and hardware. In the hot sun, these buckles can get toasty and possibly burn a child. Yes, you can cover these buckles with a blanket when you leave the car, but that's a hassle. A better bet is to buy a seat with a buckle cover.

◆ *Is it shopping cart compatible?* Some infant car seats are better at this than others. One simple test: while you are in a store like Babies R Us, Target or Wal-Mart, take the infant carrier and try snapping it into shopping cart. You'll some fit better than others. Now, we should point out that many safety advocates cringe when they see infant seats snapped into the upper part of a shopping cart—they say this makes the cart top-heavy, which could cause it to tip over. Advocates say safest place for baby is in their infant seat in the *main* part of the basket or carried by mom or dad. Some stores now realize this problem and have shopping carts with integrated infant seats, eliminating the need for you to bring your own.

◆ *How heavy is it?* This is a critical factor for infant car seats, but still important for convertibles. Why? First, remember you are lugging that infant seat WITH a baby that will weigh 7 to 10 lbs *to start*. At the end of its life, your baby will weigh 20 to 22 lbs in addition to the seat. We list the weights for major infant car seat brands later in this chapter. What about convertible seats? If you buy one seat and plan to move it from car to car, realize weight may be a factor here as well.

◆ *Buying a new car?* Consider getting a built-in (also called integrated) child safety seat. The cost varies from car maker to maker, but is about $200 to $400. Remember that most built-in seats can only be used with children one year or older in a FORWARD-FAC-

ING position; you'll still need to buy an infant car seat for babies under one year of age. And if your child outgrows their infant seat before a year of age, you will need to use a convertible seat in rear-facing mode. That obviously eliminates some of the advantage of an integrated seat; that said, since the built-in seat is designed as part of the vehicle, you are getting a very safe seat. Note: the limits for integrated seats vary by vehicle maker, so check before purchasing.

Safe & Sound

1 **NEVER BUY A USED CAR SEAT.** If the seat has been in an accident, it may be damaged and no longer safe to use. Bottom line: used seats are a big risk unless you know their history. And the technology of car seats improves every year; a seat that is just five years old may lack important safety features compared to today's models. Another tip: make sure the seat has not been recalled (see the contact info below for the National Highway Traffic Safety Administration). Safety seats made before 1981 may not meet current safety standards (unfortunately, most seats aren't stamped with their year of manufacture, so this may be difficult to determine). The bottom line: risky hand-me-downs aren't worth it. Brand new car seats (which start at $50) aren't that huge of an investment to ensure your child's safety.

2 **GET YOUR SEAT SAFETY CHECKED.** No matter how hard you try to buy and install the best seat for you child, mistakes with installation can still occur. There's nothing like the added peace of mind in having your car seat safety checked by an expert. Such checks are free and widely available. The National Highway Traffic Safety Administration's web site (www.nhtsa.dot.gov) has a national listing of fitting/inspection stations. Another cool program: Daimler Chrysler has a FREE car seat inspection—just take your car to a Chrysler dealer and they'll check your seat to see if it is safely installed. No, you don't need to have an appointment, nor do you have to own a Chrysler. Call 877-FIT-4-A-KID or web: www.FitForAKid.org to find a local participating Chrysler, Jeep or Dodge near you.

3 **DON'T TRUST THE LEVEL INDICATOR.** Yes, many infant car seats come with "level indicators" and instructions to make sure the seat is installed so the indicator is in the "green" area. When in the green, the seat is supposedly at the correct angle to project your baby in case of a crash. Nice idea, but thanks to the myriad of back seat designs in dozens of cars, the seat may be incorrectly installed even

CAR SEATS

How big is normal?

A quick glance at the "average" growth charts for infants makes you realize why kids outgrow their infant seats so quickly. Most infant seats are only rated for babies up to 20 pounds and 26" in height (although a few go to 22 pounds and 29" height). The average male infant hits 20 pounds at about eight months (at the 50th percentile). But for boys at the top of the growth chart, that could happen at a mere four months! Girls are of course a bit behind that curve, hitting 20 pounds on average at ten months of age (at the 50th percentile). Girls at the top of the chart might hit 20 pounds as soon as six months.

When a child outgrows his infant seat, he must go into a convertible seat—and there is the rub. Safety advocates say babies should be rear facing to one year of age and AT LEAST 20 pounds. But some convertible seats (especially older models like the Century 1000STE) are only rear-facing to 20 pounds . . . odds are the average infant will hit that before one year of age. So, that's why we recommend convertible seats that are rear facing to at least 30 pounds.

What about height? Boys hit 26" at around 5 months (again the 50th percentile). But some really tall baby boys can hit 26" as soon as three months. For girls, the average age when most infants hit 26" is six months, but it can happen as soon as four months. You'll note that on average, babies hit the upper limit for height restrictions for infant seats three or four MONTHS before they outgrow the seat weight-wise. That's why we strongly recommend infant seats with 29" height limits—that milestone typically isn't reached until ten months for boys and 12 months for girls.

Bottom line: keep your child REAR-FACING as long as possible, given your seat's limits. It is the safest way for them to ride.

Source: National Center for Health Statistics, www.cdc. gov/growthcharts

if the indicator says it is fine. At car seat safety checks, many techs ignore the level indicator and instead use this test. They take a piece of paper and fold one corner to form a 45 degree angle. Then they place the side of the paper against the back of the infant car seat where the baby's back would lie. When the folded corner is level with the horizon, the seat is at the correct angle—even if the indicator says it ain't so. If you aren't sure your seat is installed to the correct angle, take it to a car seat safety check.

4 **HOW TALL IS TOO TALL?** You'll notice that most child safety seats utilize two types of limits: weight and height. It's the latter limit that creates some confusion among parents. Convertible seats have both a rear and forward facing height limit—this is required by federal law (for those inquiring minds, the standard is FMVSS 213). Most safety techs say the maximum height for a child is when their head is one inch below the top of the shell (the 1″ rule) or if your child's shoulders exceed the height of the top harness slot. The problem: some car seat makers have more strict height limits than the 1″rule. Kids often outgrow the seat height-wise before they reach that 1″ rule or their shoulders are taller than the top harness slot, leaving some to wonder if they should continue using the seat. The problem is one of interpretation: while the federal law requires every seat to have height limits, car seat makers are free to interpret this rule (and usage of the seat). Some seat makers just interpret the rules more strictly than other car seat makers. Bottom line: while we understand seat makers might have their own take on federal safety standards, it is generally safe to use a seat until your child's head is 1″ below the top of the seat or their shoulders exceed the top harness slot—even if their height is slightly above the stated limit for the seat.

5 **READ THE DIRECTIONS VERY CAREFULLY.** Many car accidents end in tragedy because a car seat was installed improperly. If you have any questions about the directions, call the company or return the car seat for a model that is easier to use. Another tip: read your vehicle's owner's manual for any special installation instructions. Consult with your auto dealer if you have any additional questions.

What's the number-one problem with car seat installation? In the past, figuring out what to do with that darn locking clip was perhaps the most misunderstood part of your child's car seat. Vehicles made before September 1, 1995 typically require the use of a locking clip, a small piece of metal that "locks" the safety belt, attaching right above the buckle. Newer vehicles made after that date may have safety-belt locking features that eliminate the need for locking clips—check your owner's manual for details. Without a locking clip in older cars, the seat could become a projectile, injuring or killing your child. Make sure the safety seat is held firmly against the back of the car seat and doesn't wobble from side to side (or front to back).

Thankfully, some child safety seat makers have woken up to the locking clip problem—two models we'll review later actually have built-in locking clips. Also, the new LATCH or ISO-FIX car seats eliminate the locking clip as well.

Finally, it's always good to put your knee on the seat and push down with your full weight while you tighten the seat belt. This eliminates belt slack and ensures a snug installation.

6 **USE YOUR CAR SEAT.** Don't make the mistake of being in a hurry and forgetting to (or just not wanting to) attach the restraints. Many parents merely put their child in the seat without hooking up the harness. It is more dangerous to leave your child in a car seat unrestrained by the safety harness than it is to put him or her in a regular seat belt. And always observe weight limits. As we mentioned earlier, children should ride REAR-FACING to one year of age, regardless of weight. Make sure your child's safety seat is able to accommodate her weight in that position.

7 **PUT THE CAR SEAT IN THE BACK SEAT.** Air bags and car seats don't mix—several reports of injuries and deaths have been attributed to passenger side air bags that deployed when a car seat was in the front seat. As a result, the safest place for kids is the back seat. In fact, whether the car has an air bag or not, the back is always safer—federal government statistics say putting a child in the back seat instead of the front reduces the risk of death by 27%. And where is the safest part of the back seat? Safety experts say it's the middle—it is the furthest away from side-impact risks. The only problem with that advice is that some cars have a raised hump in the middle of the back seat that makes it difficult/impossible to safely install a car seat. Another problem: safety seats are best held against the car's back seat by a three-point belt—and many middle seats just have a two-point belt. Finally, consider the LATCH problem we noted above (where many vehicles has no LATCH anchors in the middle of the back seat, only the sides). Bottom line: while the middle of the back seat is safest spot, sometimes you just can't install a seat there. The next best place is in an outboard position with a lap/shoulder belt.

What about side curtain air bags you see in the back seats of some cars? Most of these cars have a lap/should belt in the center position of the back seat—put your car seat there, out of the way of the airbags that might deploy in an accident.

8 **REGISTER YOUR SEAT.** Don't forget to send the registration card back to the manufacturer. As we mentioned earlier, that's one way you'll be notified of any recalls or problems that may be discovered in the future. Yes, earlier we discussed how some manufacturers ignore sending notice to registered users when a car seat is recalled (instead, relying on a media announcement), but others will send notice.

Baby's Away: Vacation Rentals

Just because you're a parent doesn't mean you'll never take a vacation again. Yet, how do you travel with baby . . . or more importantly, with all baby's stuff? Well, the good news is you don't have to lug all that baby equipment with you on the plane (or in the car). Baby's Away (800) 571-0077 (web: www. BabysAway. com) rents everything you need at many resort and vacation spots in the U.S. You can rent name-brand cribs, strollers, high chairs, safety gates, potty seats, toys and more at reasonable rates (either by the day or week).

9 **DON'T USE A SEAT OVER SIX YEARS OLD.** Car seats don't last forever—parts wear out, extreme heat and cold in a vehicle takes a toll on a seat's internal mechanics and more. And safety standards change and improve over time. That's why experts say don't use a seat that is over six years old. What about seats sold on eBay that might have been sitting in a wearhouse for several years? Again, don't take the risk. Finally, let's talk about those seats that promise you can use them for kids up to 65 or 80 pounds? Britax makes one (the Marathon) which can be used up to 65 pounds with a five point harness (or about six to seven years of age), while Eddie Bauer/Cosco claims their Three-in-One (or Alpha Omega) seat will last up to 80 pounds as a belt-positioning booster. 80 pounds is equivalent to an 8 to 10 year old child. Notice a problem here? If it is unsafe to use a seat up beyond six years, does it make sense to go for that Eddie Bauer seat? No, not in our opinion.

While we do recommend the Britax seat (as 65 pounds or six/seven years would be the outer limit of any seat use), remember the PRACTICAL limits of any seat. Car seats can get pretty gross after a few years of use. Even if you are diligent about keeping the cover clean, you still might have to replace it after three to four years of use (and not all car seat makers sell replacement covers as an accessory).

Recalls

The National Highway Traffic Safety Administration (NHTSA) has a toll-free hot line to check for recalls or to report a safety problem. For info, call (800) 424-9393 or (202) 366-0123 (web: www.nhtsa.dot. gov). You can have a list of recalled car seats automatically faxed to you at no charge. Note that this is a different governmental agency than the Consumer Product Safety Commission, which regulates and recalls other juvenile products. (For Canadian recalls and safety seat rules, see the special section at the end of this book for more info).

Money-Saving Secrets

1 **GET A FREE SEAT!** A reader emailed in this great tip—her health insurance carrier (Healthnet) provides free infant car seats to parents who complete a parenting class. No specific class is needed . . . you just provide proof of completion. And health insurance providers aren't the only ones with car seat deals—check with your auto insurance provider as well. One large insurer, USAA, offers a $25 rebate per car seat; you can use this up to SIX times per family. And grandparents can use it too. Use this tip six times and you just saved $150! Of course, it is insurance carriers best interest to hand out free seats or rebates—each child safety seat used today saves auto insurers $100, private health insurers $45 and the government $45 in costs that would otherwise be incurred from unrestrained kids in auto crashes. Insurers pay out a whopping $175 in claims annually resulting from crashes in which children age birth to four were traveling unrestrained in motor vehicles (source: "Child Safety Seats: How Large are the Benefits and Who Should Pay? by the Children's Safety Network).

2 **IF YOU HAVE TWO CARS, YOU DON'T NEED TO BUY TWO INFANT SEATS.** Instead, just buy one seat and then get an extra stay-in-the-car base. While it's not widely known, major infant seat makers like Graco and Evenflo sell their auto bases separately for $30 to $40. If you can't find them in stores likes Babies R Us, check out baby web sites that stock them.

3 **WEB SHOPPING 'BOTS AND COUPONS TO CUT PRICES.** Who has the lowest prices on car seats? It depends—stores like Babies R Us and Baby Depot are very competitive on car seat prices. But, the web can have even better deals, especially if you use an online coupon or find a free shipping offer. Again, using a shopping 'bot like DealTime.com (go to the Babies & Kids section) is a good way to compare prices for a model or brand across several sites at once. Look for the free shipping deals for the best bargains, since bulky car seats can be expensive to ship. Before you order, check which sites have coupons (see Chapter 6 for a list of such sites like DotDeals.com and FlamingoWorld.com).

4 **EXPENSIVE MODELS AREN'T NECESSARILY BETTER.** If you spend $100 on a car seat, are you getting one that's twice as safe as a seat that's $50? Not necessarily. Often, all you get for that additional money is plush padding and extras like pillows. Bottom line: the $50 seat may be just as safe and probably as comfortable for baby.

Outlet

Cosco has an outlet store in Indiana (812-526-0860) at the Prime Outlets at Edinburgh (I-65 at US 31, exit 76B). You can find car seats, play yards and strollers, all at 10% to 60% off retail prices. All the stock is first quality, including some discontinued colors. You can also find current items. We found the Alpha Omega car seat (current model and fabrics) for just $109 for the five-point version ($119 for either the bar shield version or Eddie Bauer five-point model). That's about $10 to $20 less than we found in other stores. Look for periodic clearance sales for even bigger deals.

The Name Game: Reviews of Selected Manufacturers

Here are our reviews of the major car seat makers sold in the U.S. and Canada. Many of the infant seats reviewed here are sold as part of stroller/car seat combo products; the strollers are reviewed separately in the next chapter. Of course, you don't have to buy a travel system—nearly all these seats are sold separately.

Special note: this section gives you an overview of each brand; we now review each model seat separately later in this chapter! All seats are LATCH-compatible, unless otherwise noted.

The Ratings

    A **EXCELLENT**—*our top pick!*

    B **GOOD**— *above average quality, prices, and creativity.*

    C **FAIR**—*could stand some improvement.*

    D **POOR**—*yuck! Could stand some major improvement.*

Baby Trend *For a dealer near you, call (800) 328-7363, (909) 902-5568, Web: www.babytrend.com.* Better known for their strollers and other baby products, Baby Trend entered the car seat market in 2002. Their single offering is the Latch-Loc infant seat (also called the Pegasus), which is the only infant seat at this writing that has a "rigid" ISOFIX-type LATCH attachment system. As you might expect, the Baby Trend infant seat fits into to their strollers and is sold as a travel system ($129, see stroller chapter for details).

Safety Track Record. Since Baby Trend is new to the car seat market, there is no track record here. So far, the seat has performed well in cars, according to parents we interviewed. The seat has not been crash-tested by *Consumer Reports*, however.

Baby Trend's infant seat is reviewed on page 356.

Britax *460 Greenway Industrial Dr., Ft. Mill SC 29715. For a dealer near you, call (888) 4-BRITAX or (803) 802-2022. Web: www. britax.com* European-based Britax came to the U.S. car seat market in 1996 and immediately made a big splash—their convertible seats (particularly the Roundabout) became best sellers thanks to their innovative features. Britax got its start providing child seats for Mercedes and Porsche and translated that Euro safety-know-how into innovative features not seen before in the U.S. and Canada. The Roundabout is the only car seat that can use a tether in either the front or rear-facing position (Britax calls this their Versa Tether feature). Britax seats also use a patented "lock-off" clamp (for use in non-LATCH cars) that securely attaches the seat to the car's belt. As a result, the seat doesn't require a locking clip, that often misunderstood and poorly installed piece of equipment every other car seat maker requires. And Britax does offer the rigid or ISOFIX system on its forward facing Expressway. Finally, we're impressed that Britax is the only child seat manufacturer with its own state-of-the-art crash test sleds that can certify seats to various government safety requirements.

That said, Britax did hit some speed bumps in the past few years. The biggest stumble: the Roundabout was recalled when crash tests showed some seats made in early 1999 failed to meet federal standards (Britax blamed the problem on a supplier that improperly molded the seat's shells). *Consumer Reports* knocked the Roundabout in a review for this reason. Yet, Britax handled the recall professionally, voluntarily recalling the seats and offering a free retrofit kit to affected owners. There were no injuries associated with the problem.

Britax has also struggled to keep up with demand for some of their popular seats; the result has been waits of several weeks for certain models. Another frustration: the company often announces new models (including plugging them on their web site), only to miss their targeted release dates by *months* (and, in one case, two years). Britax blames this on their extensive safety testing, which of course is understandable—but it is still frustrating. The company should stop promising new product until it is ready to deliver.

Safety track record: Well, no one's perfect. Besides the Roundabout recall (discussed above), Britax also had a minor recall on the Freeway seat back in 1997. So, is all this talk about Britax's safety just sales hype? No, we still think these are among the best seats on the market. And since these two recalls had no reported injuries associated with them, we'll still give Britax high marks.

Britax's infant seat is reviewed on page 357. Britax's convertible seat reviews begin on page 363.

Century. This brand, owned by Graco, was discontinued in 2002. See our web page BabyBargainsBook.com (click on bonus material) for our previous review of their offerings.

Combi *199 Easy St., Carol Stream, IL 60188. For a dealer near you, call (800) 752-6624, (800) 992-6624, (630) 871-0404; Web: www.combi-intl.com.* This company is better known for their strollers, but in recent years they've been expanding into other baby gear categories (like high chairs and now, car seats). By the time you read this, Combi will release an infant seat (Tyro), convertible seat (Avatar), and booster seat (Apogee). While we previewed prototype of the seats, we decided not to rate them until we have more parent feedback on how they perform in the real world.

Safety track record. These are Combi's first car seats, so we don't have any handle yet on how well they will perform. While Combi is a reputable company, it is always risky to buy a "version 1.0" of any product—especially a car seat.

Combi's infant seat is reviewed on page 359. Combi's convertible seat is reviewed on page 366.

Seat cover-ups provide warmth

Okay, you aren't supposed to put baby in a car seat with a bulky coat. But what if you live in, say Maine and its currently 10 degrees outside as you read this? Try a cover-up that fits OVER the car seat and hence doesn't compromise the  seat's safety. One of our favorites: **Kiddopotamus's "Great Baby Cover Up" Fleece Warmer** ($25), a multi-purpose cover-up that can be used as a front carrier warmer, stroller warmer . . . or for car seats. The same company also offers several other innovative travel products, including the Sun Shade (a cover-up for infant seats and strollers). For more details, call (800) 772-8339 or web: www.kiddopotamus.com.

What about other infant body pillows or warmers? If it does not come in the box with your infant or convertible car seat, we wouldn't use it. Add-on or after-market products that are not manufacturer-tested may compromise the seat safety. The same thing goes for car seat toy bars or special mirrors so you can see baby from the front seat. We say don't use them. They could come loose in an accident, becoming a dangerous projectile.

car seats

CAR
SEATS

Cosco *2525 State St., Columbus, IN 47201. Call (812) 372-0141 for a dealer near you (or 514-323-5701 for a dealer in Canada). Web: www.coscoinc.com* Owned by Canadian conglomerate Dorel Industries, Cosco has staged a comeback in the car seat market in recent years. Previously an also-ran in the car seat business, Cosco hit a home run with their Alpha Omega seat (described below) and Eddie Bauer-licensed products. Yet, we are still troubled by Cosco's poor safety track record, which we'll discuss at the end of this review.

Before we get to the models, let us point about that Cosco makes three versions of their car seats: one under their own name and versions under the "Eddie Bauer" and "NASCAR" names. Note that in all cases, the seats are just the same, only the colors/fabric patterns have changed. Of course, you will pay extra for the name.

FYI: Cosco imported car seats made by their European subsidiary, Maxi Cosi. These seats were discontinued these in 2002.

Safety track record: We are still quite troubled by Cosco's safety track record, which has been marred by recent recalls—11 at last count since 1990. Among the worst was a 1999 recall involving 670,000 Arriva and Turnabout infant car seats. The seats' handle unexpectedly released in some cases, causing the seat to flip forward and dump out the child. 29 children were injured due to this defect. And the problems for Cosco continued in 2002—the company was investigated by Transport Canada (the Canadian equivalent of the NHTSA) for "omitting" foam padding in several car seats. Sears of Canada then withdrew Cosco seats from their shelves

What is the lightest infant car seat carrier?

Here at BABY BARGAINS we have Ivy League-trained scientists who help us determine important stuff like which infant car seat weighs the least (and hence, is easiest to lug around). Oh, we're just kidding. Actually, we the authors just went to our local baby store and stood there in the aisles lifting each infant seat and saying things like "Yep, this one is lighter!" For this edition, we actually employed a scale to get accurate readings (and you thought only the folks in lab coats at *Consumer Reports* got to play with such toys). Our official results: the lightest seat is the Evenflo Discovery (5.5 lbs) followed by the Evenflo Portabout (6.5 lbs) and Graco Snug Ride (7 lbs). The heaviest seats? The crowns go to the Eddie Bauer (Cosco) seat, as well as the Baby Trend Latch-Loc—both weighed in at 9 lbs. We list the weights for infant seat carriers in a chart later in this chapter. Of course, the weight of an infant seat isn't the only factor we used to decide which was best, but it certainly is important.

pending the investigation. There was no formal recall, but Cosco quietly asked Canadian retailers to stop selling several models.

Reviews of Cosco's infant seats start on page 359, while Cosco's convertible seat reviews start at on page 367.

Eddie Bauer. These seats are made by Cosco; see the previous review for details.

Evenflo *1801 Commerce Dr., Piqua, OH 45356. For a dealer near you, call (800) 233-5921 or (937) 415-3300. In Canada, PO Box 1598, Brantford, Ontario, N3T 5V7. (905) 337-2229. Web: www. evenflo.com* Evenflo is like the Avis of car seats—they try harder because they are number two. In the last few years, the company has tried to put several disastrous recalls behind them and add innovative features to their car seats. The results? Mixed—some seats like their Portabout infant seat and Triumph convertible seat (both reviewed later in this chapter) are winners, with innovative features that make the seats easier to use than the competition. But Evenflo often seems outflanked in the car seat market; Britax trumps them on safety features and Graco outguns them in the lower-price points. Even lowly Cosco has a hotter license (Eddie Bauer) than Evenflo, whose OshKosh line seems dated fashion-wise. FYI: The OshKosh seats are exactly the same as Evenflo's offerings, just different fabric.

Safety track record: In March 1998, Evenflo was forced to recall 800,000 On My Way infant seats after 89 children were injured

Consumer Reports crash tests vs our ratings

Every time *Consumer Reports* comes out with a report on car seats, our phones and email light up—many readers want to know how we sometimes come to different conclusions as to which are the best car seats. It's quite simple: *Consumer Reports* actually crash tests car seats, something we don't have the budget to do here at *Baby Bargains*. When we rate a car seat, we look at the seat's overall features, ease of use and value based on parent feedback and our own hands-on inspections. We also look at the company's recall track record and (if they are available) any *Consumer Report's* crash test reports. Even though we might use different rating methodologies, most of the time we agree with *Consumer Reports*. In the case of a major discrepancy, we'll often comment on this on our web page at www.BabyBargainsBook.com. For more on this topic, see the discussion in Chapter 1.

when the seat's handle failed to lock and the seat tipped forward. What really bothered us was how Evenflo handled this situation—while we realize car seat recalls are an all-too-frequent fact of life, we were miffed that Evenflo first blamed parents for mis-using the product when reports of the problem first surfaced. Only after arm-twisting by the federal government did Evenflo reluctantly recall the seat and admit the production defect. A top safety regulator heav-

The NYC Taxi Dilemma

Here's a common email we get from parents in New York and other urban areas: are there any portable car seats that can be used in taxis? Something that is lightweight, easy to install and collapses to fit inside a small purse when not in use? Well, the answer is no—there's no perfect solution to this. Let's break out our advice for New Yorkers by age:

◆ *Infant* (birth to six months). The safest way to for an infant to ride in a taxi is in an infant car seat. Most (but not all) can be strapped into without the stay-in-the-car base. An exception: the Peg Perego Primo Viaggio, which CANNOT be strapped into a taxi just with the belt.

◆ *Older baby* (six months to four years). This is where it gets trickier. Our advice here would be the *Cosco Tote 'N Go* (formerly3 called the Travel Vest)—basically a small seat with a five-point harness for babies 25 to 40 pounds. It can only used forward facing. Best of all, it weighs just 4 pounds—we can hear those parents on the way to Zabar's cheering  right now. Is it safe? Yes, for that occasional taxi ride. Would we use it every day in a vehicle? No—while the Cosco Tote 'N Go meets federal safety standard, parent testers we've interviewed say it is hard to get a good, tight fit with it, no matter whether they installed it with just a lap belt or with a lap and shoulder belt.

What about belt-positioning devices? The jury is still out on these products (lightweight devices that simply adjust a vehicle's belts to better fit a child). Some safety advocates say they don't provide any protection and the government has no data on them—yet. The National Highway Traffic Safety Administration has pledged to study belt-positioners, but we're unsure when they'll announce the findings. Stay tuned.

ily criticized Evenflo's foot-dragging, calling the company one of "the most difficult to work with" in the industry. That kind of behavior is inexcusable; as a result, we gave Evenflo poor ratings in the last few editions of our book.

So, what's up with Evenflo now? The company has tried to mend its ways. The entire management team that was in charge in the 1998 infant seat fiasco is now gone, replaced by a new crew that seems to care more about safety. So, we are cautiously recommending a couple of their seats this time out, as you'll read shortly.

Reviews of Evenflo's infant seats start on page 360, while Evenflo's convertible seat reviews start at on page 368.

Fisher-Price Fisher Price withdrew from the car seat market in 2001. That's too bad, because the company had some great models with innovative features. See our web page BabyBargainsBook. com (click on bonus material) for our previous review of their offerings.

Graco *Rt. 23, Main St., Elverson, PA 19520. For a dealer near you, call (800) 345-4109, (610) 286-5951. Web: www.gracobaby.com.*

Graco makes it easy—they offer just one infant car seat (the Snug Ride) and one convertible seat (the Comfort Sport). The latter is an old Century seat (the Accel), just re-packaged under the name. No, these seats don't have a fancy license like Eddie Bauer, but they are excellent offerings with good features at decent prices.

Safety track record: While Graco is a relative newcomer to the car seat market, their sister company (Century) has a much longer track record for their convertible seats (which is what Graco is now selling as the Comfort Sport). Century did have several recalls in the mid 1990's, but has been clean since then.

Graco's infant seat is reviewed on page 361. Graco's convertible seat is reviewed on page 369.

Maxi Cosi. This is an imported line of European seats sold in the U.S. and Canada by Cosco prior to 2002. They are now discontinued.

OshKosh. These seats are made by Evenflo. See their review earlier for details.

Peg Perego *3625 Independence Dr., Ft. Wayne, IN 46808. For a dealer near you, call (219) 482-8191. Web: www.perego.com* After seeing their stroller sales eaten away by travel systems for years, Peg Perego has finally decided to address this long shortcoming with the debut of an infant seat (and travel system) in 2001.

Safety track record: Underscoring how difficult it is to crack the car seat market, Peg Perego had not one but TWO recalls during in the past year. While no children were injured by the recalls, the misfires made us question whether Perego's infant seat was really ready for prime time in our last edition. Since then, however, Perego has worked out the kinks in this seat.

Peg Perego's Primo Viaggio is reviewed on page 362.

Safety 1st. These seats are made by Cosco; see earlier review

Infant Car Seats (model by model reviews)

BABY TREND LATCH-LOC AND LATCH-LOC ADJUSTABLE BACK

Price: Latch-Loc: $80; Latch-Lock Adjustable Back: $90. Extra bases $40.

Type: Infant seat, five-point harness.

Limits: 20 lbs and 26" for the Latch-Loc; 22 lbs and 29" for the Adjustable Back.

Pros: Only infant seat on the market that uses the rigid or ISOFIX version of LATCH. Some versions go to 22 pounds.

Cons: Carrier is somewhat heavier than other models; level indicator can get stuck, giving false readings.

Comments: This is one of our two picks as the best infant seat on the market. No, it isn't perfect, but we love this seat's rigid or ISOFIX version of LATCH—the result is a rock-solid installation in cars that have LATCH. The seat itself has nice features—you get two harness slots, an adjustable crotch strap, EPS foam for head crash protection and a machine washable pad. The base is adjustable and uses an all-steel connection for the seat—all that steel provides great safety, but makes the BASE quite heavy (in fact, the carrier is also heavy, weighing nine lbs). You can buy a separate base for $40 for a second car or use the seat without the base in a car by strapping it in with the auto safety belt. All in all, this is a great seat—we like the fact you can use it in grocery shopping carts and the large canopy is great. The downsides? The somewhat cheesy level indicator can get stuck, giving false readings. And the strange triangle handle takes a bit of getting used to. Finally, we've noted there are two different versions of this seat on the market—the Latch-Loc (model 60xx) and the Latch-Loc Adjustable Back (model 61xx—the last two digits, xx, denote the color). As the name implies, the latter model features an adjustable headrest that allows you to move shoulder belts in one of seven positions. Even better: this version has a more generous 22 lbs. weight (and 29" height) limit and a boot to keep baby warm. Between the two, we'd go for the Adjustable Back version.

Rating: A

BRITAX COMPANION
Price: $150 (estimated)
Type: Infant seat, five-point harness.
Limits: 22 lbs.
Comments: As of press time, this seat was "coming soon"—Britax will only say it will be out "sometime in 2003." We did see a prototype of the new seat and thought it had some interesting features: an adjustable base, rear-facing stability bar, three harness height positions and special impact foam to protect baby. You will be able to use this seat with or without a base.
Rating: Not available yet. Given Britax's track record, however, we expect this seat to perform well.

BRITAX HANDLE WITH CARE
Price: $100
Type: Infant seat, five-point harness. No base. Not LATCH-compatible.
Limits: 20 lbs, 26".
Comments: As we went to press, Britax was phasing out this seat to make way for the new Companion model (see above). This expensive seat (which started out at $150 retail but since came down in price) lacked a stay-in-the-car base, which was a deal killer for most parents. You had to buckle it in with each use. Readers who have this seat, however, say its features outweigh any inconvenience. Parents say they get the hang of installing the seat after a few tries and the lack of a base means it's easier to move from car to car. The only gripe: the chest clip sometimes slides down during use. This seat had two harness heights, but only one crotch position. Like all Britax seats,

Leaving On a Jet Plane

Which car seats can be taken on an airplane? All of the seats reviewed in this section are certified for use in an airplane. But will they fit? That's a tougher question—each airline has different size seats. Hence, large seats like the Evenflo Triumph may not fit (especially if you're required to keep the armrests down for take-off). Check with the airline before you get to the airport if you have questions about car seat compatibility. A better bet: simple seats like the Graco Comfort Sport or Century 1000STE (both are narrow and light in weight) usually do the trick. We've used a 1000STE on several airplanes without a problem.

this one also had EPS foam around the head area for additional crash protection. Note: this seat was not LATCH-compatible. While it is discontinued, you may still see it sold online or in stores. The lack of a base lowers our rating on this seat.
Rating: B-

Mighty big controversy

In the past edition of this book, we recommended the Mighty-Tite car seat belt tightener, which removes slack and provides for a tight car seat installation. It's $20 at Babies R Us and other stores, call 888-336-7909 or web: www. mighty-tite.com. Similar belt-tighteners are made by other companies. However, since our last edition, we noticed belt-tighteners like the Mighty-Tite are a bit controversial among safety advocates.

Their biggest concern about the Mighty-Tite: it might mislead parents into thinking the add-on belt tightener will make any car seat fit in any vehicle. As you've read in this chapter, there are simply some seats that don't work in some vehicles. Yes, you can check a web site like Car Seat Data (www.CarSeatData.org) to see what might work in your vehicle, but sometimes you have to buy a seat on faith. The Mighty-Tite sort of promises to let you cheat car seat installation—enabling a tight fit even if you can't get the seat to work in a vehicle. Not true, say safety advocates—if a seat is incompatible with the back seat of a vehicle, no add-on product will fix it.

Safety advocates also blast the company's marketing tactics, which claim the Mighty-Tite passes federal crash standards. But those standard are written for seats, not add-on products say advocates. And even Mighty-Tite's instructions say you should install your car seat according to the manufacturer's guidelines . . ., which of course, should provide for a rock-solid fit, even without the Mighty-Tite. Car seat techs would rather parents learn how to correctly install a seat (or take it to a safety check) instead of using add-on products to shortcut the installation process.

So, what's the verdict on the Mighty-Tite? Well, we'd like to see some more testing on this product, preferably from a third-party to confirm add-on belt tighteners are truly safe. So, until that happens, we'll take a pass on recommending the Mighty-Tite.

FYI: The new LATCH system eliminates the need for any add-on belt tighteners like the Mighty-Tite—so if your vehicle is equipped with this system and you use a LATCH seat, this debate is moot for you!

COMBI TYRO

Price: $130

Type: Infant seat, five-point harness

Limits: 22 lbs., 29" height.

Comments: This seat should be available by the time you read this—while we saw a prototype of this model, we have yet to see the final version. As a result, we won't assign a rating yet. This will be Combi's first infant car seat. The Tyro will have a rubber handle grip, two-position adjustable base, one-pull harness adjustment and level-indicator. You will be able to buy additional bases. The Tyro will also have an adjustable canopy, infant body pillow and padded shoulder straps. The seat will work with a Combi Ultra Savvy, Savona or Tetra stroller as a travel system (although they will be sold separately).

Rating: Not yet.

COSCO DESIGNER 22. See the Eddie Bauer infant seat review later in this section. The Cosco Designer 22 is the same as this seat.

EDDIE BAUER INFANT CAR SEAT (AKA GRIDLOCK OR DESIGNER 22)

Price: $90

Type: Infant seat, five-point harness

Limits: 22 lbs, 29" height.

Pros: Adjustable base. Three crotch belt positions. Front belt adjuster. One of the few seats that can be used up to 29" in height.

Cons: No level indicator, heavy carrier.

Comments: This seat is basically a re-packaged version of the old Cosco Designer 22 car seat. Dressed in "Eddie Bauer" colors (read: charcoal grey and yellow trim), this infant seat's snazzy looks can't overcome its drawbacks—namely, it's darn heavy. Weighing in at a whopping nine lbs, it is a full two pounds heavier than our top pick (the Graco Snug Ridge) in this category. Yes, there are a few nice features (we like the three crotch belt positions and adjustable base), but you spend $90 and don't even get a level indicator? While we like the fact you can use this seat up to 29" in height, remember this one is really made by Cosco . . . whose safety record gives us pause. In fact, Cosco had to recall the Designer 22 in May 2002 when the handle on the seat released "unexpectedly" from the carry position.

Rating: C

EVENFLO COZY CARRY. See Evenflo PortAbout on the next page.

EVENFLO DISCOVERY
Price: $50
Type: Infant car seat, three-point harness.
Limits: 20 lbs, 26".
Pros: Lightweight carrier, canopy, low price. Z-shaped handle is easy to carry.
Cons: Non-adjustable base, no level indicator, must adjust belts from the back.

Comments: This bare-bones seat is sold in discount stores like Wal-Mart. The carrier (at 5.5 lbs) is among the lightest on the market. You don't get many features with this seat—the base doesn't adjust, there is just one crotch strap position and there is no level indicator. Want to adjust the straps? You'll have to do that from the back of the seat, a major pain. That said, it is only $50. Our advice: spend an extra $10 and get an Evenflo PortAbout if you want an Evenflo infant seat.
Rating: C+

EVENFLO PORTABOUT
Price: $60 to $90; extra base, $35.
Type: Infant car seat, three and five-point harness versions
Limits: 22 lbs, 26".
Pros: Level indicator, adjustable base, two crotch strap positions, lightweight carrier (6.5 lbs). Z-shaped handle is easy to carry.

80 pounds of confusion

You bought a seat that is good up to 80 pounds, so that means you can use that five-point harness until your child is child is in elementary school? No—not if the seat is the Eddie Bauer Three in One (also called the Cosco Alpha Omega). You can use the five-point harness for this seat only until your child hits 40 pounds . . . after that point, you must stop using the harness and instead use the seat as a belt-positioning booster with the auto's safety belt. Even though the instructions and box for that seat clearly state this fact, many parents who use this popular seat seem confused by the "to 80 pounds" marketing pitch. They erroneously believe they can use the five-point harness up to that weight, according to car seat safety techs who watch this issue at safety checks. So be sure to check the instructions for your seat. Yes, some seats like the Britax Marathon can use a five-point harness beyond the traditional 40 pounds limit (for the Marathon, it is up to 65 pounds), but that is the exception to the rule.

Cons: Some parents find handle hard to use.

Comments: This seat was previously known as the Cozy Carry, which itself replaced the On My Way. First, let us warn you the PortAbout comes in four different versions: a three-point harness ($60) version and three models that have a five-point harness ($70 to $90). The latter range from a simple model (PortAbout 5) to a plush version (PortAbout 5 Premier Comfort Touch, $90) that has a padded handle and boot/blanket to keep baby warm. All of the PortAbout's have Evenflo's "Press 'n' Go" handle that enables one-hand release of the handle. Cool, no? Well, it frustrates some parents we spoke with, who found it difficult to use. That said, this seat does have some other attractive features—lightweight (6.5 pounds), adjustable base and level indicator. This seat is our third choice in this category, behind the Baby Trend Latch-Loc and Graco Snug Ride.

Rating: A-

GRACO SNUG RIDE

Price: $60 to $100; extra base $35.

Type: Infant seat; comes in both three-point and five-point harness versions.

Limits: 20 lbs., 26" height.

Pros: Our top choice for infant seats. Lightweight carrier (7 lbs), level indicator, canopy, easy to use. Front belt adjuster on some models.

Cons: Only one crotch position. Watch out for older models with back adjustments for the harness.

Comments: Here it is folks—our top pick for infant seats. Now, before we rave about this seat, let us point out that Graco makes SEVEN versions of the Snug Ride. There is one version that has a three-point harness, while the rest feature a five-point. Most of the difference is fashion—there are fancier versions of this seat with a foot warmer (boot) and extra padding that can cost $100 (model 8448). A basic Snug Ride is $60. While we don't have a preference as to which version is best, we do suggest you get one with a front-belt adjuster. A few older models (called DX) had back adjusters, which are a pain to use. All in all, however, this is an excellent seat—you get a lightweight carrier (seven lbs), adjustable base, level indicator, nice canopy and straps that don't twist. Best of all, parents say the seat is easy to use. One caution: this seat can only be used up to 20 lbs or 26" in height. If you know you are going to give birth to a large baby, our other top picks for infant seats (the Baby Trend Latch-Loc Adjustable Back and the Evenflo PortAbout) may be better choices, as they have 22 lb limits. If Graco could make one improvement to this seat, it would be larger weight/height limits.

Rating: A

CAR SEATS

Chocolate donuts with sprinkles?

Here's a confusing thing about car seat shopping: most car seat makers offer their models in a plethora of versions. At one point a couple of years ago, one infant seat maker had FIVE different versions of the same seat: the Classic, Plus, Elite, Supreme and the Extra Crispy. Okay, there wasn't an Extra Crispy, but you get the point. The key thing to remember: the seat was basically the very same seat in each configuration, just with minor cosmetic variations (an extra bit of padding here, a pillow there, etc). Okay, sometimes there are more significant variations like a five-point harness (versus three-point) or an adjustable base. But often there isn't much difference. Think of it this way: car seat makers produce a chocolate donut and top it with different color sprinkles—the rainbow sprinkle version goes to Wal-Mart, the green sprinkle donut goes to Target, etc. That way the companies can offer "exclusives" on certain "models" to large customers, so they don't have to go head-to-head with other chains on price. Basically, it's the same donut. Bottom line: don't get caught up in all the version stuff. If the basic seat has the features you want, it doesn't really matter whether you buy the Plus or the Elite. Or the Extra Crispy.

PEG PEREGO PRIMO VIAGGIO
Price: $150; extra base: $50.
Limits: 20 lbs, 26" height.
Pros: Matches Perego's hot-selling strollers. Level indicator, adjustable base, front harness adjustment. Plush padding.
Cons: Carrier is heavy, low weight limit, can't use without base. Did we mention it is $150?

Comments: In the last edition of this book, we mentioned this seat wasn't ready for prime time—it was expensive and lacked features the competition long ago added. Well, Perego has been playing catch up and now the seat does have an adjustable base and level indicator. But it is still too expensive—$150! Yes, you do get those plush "Italian fabrics," but that is a high price to pay to look stylish. And this seat got off to a rocky start when it was recalled not once but TWICE during its first two years. Those problems have now been fixed, but it gives us pause. Most parents get this seat because they want to pair it with a Perego stroller. We understand that, but we have to dock this seat rating-wise for running $50 to $75 more than comparable seats. And the skimpy weight limit (20 lbs) means your expensive investment in this seat could be short-lived if you have a big baby. Another bummer: this seat CANNOT be used without a base, unlike most other models.
Rating: B

SAFETY 1ST DESIGNER 22. This is the same as the Eddie Bauer seat, reviewed later in this section.

◆ *Other infant car seats and car beds.* Cosco has two other infant seats that are a bit hard to find. Example: the bare bones *Arriva* infant seat (rating: C). This entry-level seat ($30 to $50; rear-facing to 22 pounds) is sold in versions with and without a stay-in-the-car base. The simplest Arriva has a three-point harness and no base. Next up, is a version that adds a canopy that wraps around the handle. We think this is a rather lousy design, since you then can't carry the carrier under your arm. Cosco also makes an Arriva version with an "adjustable canopy," which is better.

The *Cosco Designer 35* ($80 to $100, rating: C-) is the only infant car seat that is rated to a whopping 35 pounds. While that sounds good, we seriously wonder how any parent could carry a 35 pound infant in a carrier under their arm—heck even a 22-pounder would stress the average non-steroid using parent. Nonetheless, Cosco pulls out all the stops for this seat—you get plush padding, four-position headrest that adjusts the harness without rethreading, multi-position canopy and more. The Designer 35 comes in two versions: a basic model and a plusher LX. Parents we interviewed found this seat hard to use and overpriced; it is rather hard to find at retail, but you can still see it online.

The *Cosco Dream Ride* ($60, rating: A) is one of the few "travel beds" for premature infants and other babies that must tray lying down. A similar product: *Graco Cherish Car Bed* ($60, rating: A) is designed for preemies (up to nine pounds) that must ride lying down.

Finally, we should do a brief mention of the Evenflo *Tot Taxi* (rating: C-), which was a bare-bones infant seat without base that sold in discount stores. It is now discontinued.

Convertible and Forward Facing-Only Car Seats (model by model reviews)

BRITAX ROUNDABOUT

Price: $200 to $230.

Type: Convertible, five-point harness.

Limits: 5 to 33 lbs rear facing, 20 to 40 lbs forward facing.

Pros: Excellent features—EPS foam, no-twist straps, can be tethered rear- or forward-facing, easy to adjust harness, double-strap LATCH, nice colors.

Cons: Expensive. Only goes to 40 pounds. Harness slot a bit too high for smallest infants.

Comments: Here it is, folks—our pick once again as one of the best convertible seats (besides the Britax Marathon). Yes, it is expensive, but you get a boatload of extras (like the layer of comfort foam, a thick pad that is easy to remove to machine wash, etc). And the safety of this seat is also top-notch: the lock-off clips give a rock solid installation in case you don't have LATCH. If you do, the Roundabout features a double strap LATCH that we think is superior to the single-strap LATCH you see elsewhere. Minor quibbles: the lowest harness slot (10") is too tall for the smallest infants, even though this seat is rated for use from five pounds and up. Other seats like the Evenflo Triumph (8.0") and the Graco Comfort Sport (8.5") have lower harness slots and hence would be a better choice if you decide to forgo the infant seat and just buy one convertible. Another slight problem: the Roundabout is a bit wide—1" to 3" inches wider than other competing seats. Not a big deal . . . except if you try to take this seat on an airplane. While it is approved by the FAA for aircraft use, we think it is probably too wide to fit into some airline seats. (See our recommendation earlier for the best convertible seat for aircraft use). Another issue: in a previous testing article by *Consumer Reports*, the magazine said this seat performed poorly when used *without* a tether (with a tether, it was great). Therefore, if you have an older model car without a tether bolt anchor, skip this seat. Those problems aside, this is a great seat and a top recommendation.

Rating: A

BRITAX MARATHON
Price: $250.
Type: Convertible, five-point harness.
Limits: 5 to 33 lbs rear facing, 20 to 65 lbs forward facing, 48" tall.
Pros: Wow! Up to 65 pounds with a five-point harness! Plush pad, EPS foam, same pros as Roundabout.

Cons: Did we mention it is $250? Some parents don't like the HUGS harness system. Top harness slot (18") is too low, meaning some kids will outgrow this seat before they hit the weight limit. Taller, wider than the Roundabout.

Comments: Yes, this is the only seat on the market that can use a five-point harness up to 65 pounds! That's rather amazing, since most seats stop at 40 lbs and most parents realize the five-point harness is the safest option for larger, older babies. Before you drive down to the store and plunk down $250 for the Marathon, however, be aware of its limitations. First, the top harness slot height—at 18" it is only 2" higher than the Roundabout. So? Well, that means that larger children may outgrow this seat by height before they hit that 65-pound limit, which eliminates some of this seat's advantage. If you have a child who is at the top-end of the growth chart, this may not be the seat for you. And let's talk about the HUGS system. Britax says this harness system is designed to "better distribute webbing loads to reduce head movement and minimize the chance for webbing edge loading on the child's neck in the case of an impact. In addition, it is designed to reduce the chance of improper positioning of the chest clip." Parents complain that the first version of HUGS didn't fit larger children—the chest clip is above the armpits and cannot be adjusted down. Others gripe that the whole HUGS thing is confusing to use. Britax responded to this by coming out with a larger HUGS strap and attempting to clarify use of the seat. Most of the problems we heard about this seat were probably due to the "version 1.0" nature of any new model—since it debuted in 2002, Britax has made improvements to the Marathon, including the adding of an EPS foam insert to increase shoulder width room by another 1.5 inches. Finally, let us warn parents that the Marathon is bigger/wider (it's 19.5" wide and 28" tall) than the Roundabout and hence may not fit into some smaller cars (go to www.carseatdata.org to see what vehicles work and which ones don't). These concerns aside, we still give this seat our top rating, thanks to that 65-pound feature.

Rating: A

BRITAX EXPRESSWAY ISOFIX

Price: $190 to $220
Type: Forward-facing only.
Limits: 20 to 40 pounds.
Pros: Only convertible seat on market with rigid ISOFIX, which gives rock solid installation. Same pros as the Roundabout, see below.

Cons: Only can be used forward facing. Expensive.

Comments: Yes, crash tests results indicate that the rigid ISOFIX attachment performs better than other LATCH attachments (see discussion earlier in this chapter for more on what rigid ISOFIX is). And this is one of the very few seats on the market that has that feature. But why would you spend $220 on a seat that can only be used forward-facing to 40 pounds? Well, let's say you have a smaller infant that can stay in an infant seat until they are close to one year of age. At age one, you can switch to this seat and know you are getting all the advantages of the Roundabout (see that review below), yet will save $30 or so bucks.

Rating: A

◆ *More Britax models: Advantage, Wizard, Galaxy, Husky,*

Roadster, Starriser Comfy. Just to confuse you more, Britax has three more convertible seats (Advantage, Wizard, Galaxy), two boosters (Roadster and Starriser Comfy) plus a "special-needs" seat called the Husky. Since these seats are much less popular (and harder to find) than the Roundabout, Marathon and Expressway, we'll review then briefly here.

The **Britax Advantage** ($250, rating: B) is basically the same as the Roundabout but with one added feature: you get a height adjuster knob that lets you make finite adjustments to the harness heights (instead of being stuck with the three positions you see in the Roundabout). Hence, you don't have to re-thread the belts every time your child grows. Okay, that's nice, but whether it is worth an extra $50 is up to debate. We say the Roundabout is just fine.

The **Britax Wizard** ($250 estimate, rating: B) is a "ditto"—same features as the Marathon, just add the height adjuster knob. The Wizard isn't out as of this writing, but Britax says it is "coming soon" . . . sometime in 2003.

The **Britax Galaxy** ($240, rating: B-) is a convertible seat that is much like the Roundabout, but adds a six-point harness, a rear-stabilizing bar, and an improved recline feature that the company says ensures a better fit when in that mode. Okay, that's nice, but since this seat isn't as widely available as the Roundabout, you'll probably have to shell out another $30 to $40 for it. Again, the Roundabout is fine.

The **Britax Husky** ($240, rating: B+), which used to be called the Super Elite, is a forward-only facing seat that can use a five-point harness up to an amazing 80 pounds. Great, but this seat is a monster—21.5" wide and 28" tall! That means it won't fit into smaller vehicles (heck, even some mid-size ones). Yes, it does have an extra, fourth harness slot at 19", but the risk with this seat is the same as the Marathon—your child may outgrow it by height before weight. Along the lines of the Husky, Britax also makes a "special-needs" seat called "Traveller Plus" ($450, rating: B) that goes to 105 pounds with a five-point harness. This seat is designed for disabled children who need the protection of a five-point harness.

Britax's booster seats (**Roadster** and **Starriser Comfy**) are reviewed in our book, *Toddler Bargains*. See back of this book for details.

COMBI AVATAR
Price: $200
Type: Convertible, five-point harness.
Limits: 5 to 30 lbs rear-facing, 20 to 40 lbs front-facing.
Comments: This seat should be available by

the time you read this–while we saw a prototype of this model, we have yet to see the final version. As a result, we won't assign a rating yet. The Avatar is Combi's first convertible seat–it will feature a tether that will work forward and rear-facing, a pivoting two-position base height adjustment, one-pull harness adjustment as well as infant body pillow, and padded shoulder straps.

Rating: Not yet.

COSCO ALPHA OMEGA. See Eddie Bauer Three in One.

EDDIE BAUER THREE IN ONE
(a.k.a. Cosco Alpha Omega)
Price: $160.
Type: Convertible, five-point harness.
Limits: 5 to 33 lbs rear-facing, 20 to 40 lbs front-facing, 30 to 80 lbs as a booster.

Pros: It's an infant seat! It's a convertible! It's a booster! Wow, three uses in one!

Cons: *Consumer Reports* says don't use it as a booster. Twisty straps. Poor recline. And much more!

Comments: This best-selling seat began its life as the Cosco Alpha Omega. The big pitch: buy just one seat, as this one is good from infant through college (okay, just 80 pounds or eight years of age). The problem: it just doesn't live up to the hype. It is poorly designed, hard to use and expensive. Worst of all: *Consumer Reports* warned parents not to use this seat as a booster since the belt guide can introduce dangerous slack when used in booster mode (July 2001 report). So, that eliminates the key "cool" feature of this seat. Our reader feedback hasn't been kind to this seat: readers knock the instructions as "vague and confusing," the belts are hard to adjust in the rear-facing mode and the straps are so thin they constantly get twisted and snagged. Yet another problem: the highest harness slot in this seat (14.5") is a full inch lower than other seats like the Britax Roundabout. Why is this a problem? That low slot means some parents will be forced to convert this seat to booster mode too soon for larger children. And it just goes on and on. Eddie Bauer should be ashamed to put its name on this piece of junk. (FYI: This seat is also sold without the Eddie Bauer name for $10 to $20 less–we even saw it in Costco for $100).

Rating: D

◆ *Other Cosco models:* Besides the more famous Alpha Omega (aka Eddie Bauer Three in One), Cosco does make a handful of other less expensive seats. Example: the entry-level *Touriva* ($50 to $75, rating: C) comes in five-point and bar-shield (which is not

convertible seats

adjustable) versions and is sold in stores like K-Mart. It suffers from the same twisty straps as the Eddie Bauer/Alpha Omega. The plusher *Olympian* car seat ($60 to $100, rating: C) also comes in five-point and adjustable bar-shield versions. We were not impressed with these car seats, which lacked features and the ease-of-use you see in similarly priced seats. FYI: The Cosco *Summit* and Safety 1st *Vantage Point* are combo boosters that are reviewed in other our book, *Toddler Bargains* (see back of this book for details).

EVENFLO TRIUMPH

Price: $120 to $130.

Type: Convertible seat; five-point harness

Limits: 5 to 30 lbs rear-facing, 20 to 40 lbs. forward-facing.

Pros: Special harness "remembers" last setting, EPS foam, up-front five-position recline and harness adjustment (no re-threading). Good price.

Cons: Tension knob hard to adjust when seat is in rear-facing mode. Wide base may not fit in smaller cars.

Comments: Evenflo finally hit a home run with this seat—it is feature-packed, but costs almost $100 less than seats by Britax. This well-padded seat has several innovative features: among them, a cool "Memory Harness" that lets you "let out" the belts and then returns them to their original tension, so it is easier to move baby in and out of this seat. Also neat: the "HeightRight" harness system that lets you adjust the height of the harness without threading the belts. Yep, that is the same feature you see on the Britax Advantage . . . for over $100 less here. So, what's not to like? First, this is a BIG seat—19.5" in width. That's 2-3" bigger than most other car seats and as wide as the Britax Marathon (but that seat can be used up to 65 lbs; the Triumph stops at 40 lbs). As a result, you may not be able to fit it in smaller vehicles. Another problem: the neat-o adjustment knobs that are placed up front. When the seat is placed in rear-facing mode, these neat-o knobs are impossible to access (as you might guess). That said, this is a good seat overall and we do recommend it. If you don't want to shell out the big bucks for a Britax, this is a good alternative.

Rating: A

EVENFLO VANGUARD

Price: $80

Type: Convertible; comes in five-point and bar-shield versions.

Limits: 5 to 30 lbs rear-facing, 20 to 40 lbs. forward-facing.

Pros: Includes extra pad, two position recline,

four harness height positions (most seats have just three).

Cons: Hard to adjust/tighten straps. No crotch strap adjustment

Comments: Yes, Evenflo has loaded this seat with a cushy pad and some nice features (especially that fourth harness slot position). But parents we interviewed HATED the seat's belt adjustments . . . and those were the kind reviews. This seat was especially problematic when used in rear-facing mode. Lousy design.

Rating: D

◆ *Other Evenflo models:* The Evenflo *Victory* ($55 to $60, rating: D) is much like the Vanguard, except with a less-plush pad. Parents we interviewed had much the same complaints about the Victory as they did with the Vanguard—the straps are hard to adjust and poor design make the rear-facing mode difficult for parents to use. The Victory used to be called the *Odyssey*).

The Evenflo *Secure Advantage* ($80, rating: C-) is an overhead bar shield seat sold at Babies R Us. We don't recommend bar shields (they aren't as safe as five-point harnesses, in our opinion), so we won't recommend this seat. Ditto for the *Tribute* ($100, rating C-)—another bar shield seat.

The Evenflo *Titan* ($60 to $80, rating: C) comes in both five-point and bar shield versions. Again, difficult harness adjustments as well as twisty straps make this seat a poor choice.

GRACO COMFORTSPORT

(formerly the Century Accel)

Price: $70 to $100.

Type: Convertible, five-point harness. (Wal-Mart has a version with an overhead bar shield, which we don't recommend).

Limits: 30 lbs rear-facing, 20 to 40 lbs forward-facing.

Pros: Great low-end seat—nice features, good price. Front belt-adjuster, level adjuster, easy to use. Most expensive versions have more plush pads and cup holders.

Cons: Cheaper versions have skimpy padding.

Comments: This seat is our recommendation for a bare bones seat, a good choice if you are on a tight budget or need a seat for a second (or Grandma's) car. Be forewarned, however: the cheapest ComfortSports ($60) have very skimpy padding. Spend an extra $10 and you get plusher padding. If you want to spend $100, you get leather-like trim and cup holders (model 8431). All in all, Graco offers EIGHT versions of this seat, so you have lots of choice as to padding and colors. All the seats have five-point harnesses and feature front belt adjustments. Best of all, parent find the seat easy to use. No you don't get all the gee-whiz features of seats like the Britax Roundabout or Evenflo Triumph—but then again, you are spending $50 to $150 less. This is the seat for that second car or for airline travel—it's narrow width (17″) should make it work in most airline seats and light weight (16 pounds) make carrying it through an airport easier than seats that can weigh nearly 20+ pounds.

Rating: B+

◆ *More Graco models: Graco CarGo* is a combo booster seat line that is reviewed in our other book, Toddler Bargains. Ditto for the Century NextStep and Century Breverra models.

Other brands to consider: New to the U.S., *Safety Baby/ Nania* is a subsidiary of French-based Team Tex (web: www.team-tex.com). The company is owned by Yves Nania, who ran the Renolux car seat company back in the early 1990's. Safety Baby has infant car seats and convertible models, as well as boosters. The best known: the *Airway* ($100, rating: C), sold at Baby Depot. This seat is a combo booster—it can be used forward-facing from 20 to 50 pounds with a five-point harness and then as a belt-positioning booster to 80 pounds. Innovative yes, but this company has little distribution and no safety track record yet in North America, so we'll take a pass on recommending them.

The Sit N Stroll ($160) from Safeline Corporation (800) 829-1625, (303) 457-4440 (web: www.safelinecorp.com) has won a small but loyal fan base for its innovative car seat/stroller. With one flick of the hand, this convertible car seat morphs into a stroller. Like the Batmobile, a handle pops up from the back and wheels appear from the bottom. Presto! You've got a stroller without having to remove baby from the seat.

We've seen a few parents wheel this thing around, and though it looks somewhat strange, they told us they've been happy with its operation. We have some doubts, however. First, unlike the four-in-one car seat/stroller combos reviewed later in this chapter, the Sit N

Booster seats

As you read this section, you might wonder where are the reviews for booster seats, those seats for older children who've outgrown their convertible seats? Since these seats are designed for older children (most of whom are three or four years of age), we've included this topic as a large chapter in our book *Toddler Bargains*. See the back of this book for details.

Stroll's use as a stroller is quite limited—it doesn't have a full basket (only a small storage compartment) or a canopy (a "sunshade" is an option). We'd prefer a seat that reclines (it doesn't) and you've got to belt the seat in each time you use it in a car—even if you don't take it along as a stroller. Not only is installation a hassle, but the Sit N Stroll's wide base may also not fit some vehicles with short safety belts or contoured seats. Plus, lifting the 14-pound car seat with a full-size child out of a car to put on the ground is quite a workout. So, we're not sure we can wholeheartedly recommend this seat. On the other hand, we did hear from a flight attendant who loved her Sit N Stroll— it wheels down those narrow plane aisles and is a FAA-certified flight seat. So, it's a mixed bag for the Sit N Stroll. While we salute the maker for its innovation, the product's drawbacks may limit its appeal.

As you can imagine, the child safety seat world changes quickly—check out our web page (www.BabyBargainsBook.com) for the latest updates and changes.

Our Picks: Brand Recommendations

Here are our top picks for infant and convertible seats. Are these seats safer than others? No—all child safety seats sold in the U.S. and Canada must meet minimum safety standards. These seats are our top picks because they combine the best features, usability (including ease of installation) and value. Remember the safest and best seat for your baby is the one that best fits your child and vehicle. Finding the right car seat can be a bit of trial and error; you may find a seat CANNOT be installed safely in your vehicle because of the quirks of the seat or your vehicle's safety belt system. All seats do NOT fit all cars. Hence it is always wise to buy a seat from a store or web site with a good return policy.

Best Bets: Infant car seats

Good. Let's be honest: if you're on a super-tight budget, consider not buying an infant car seat at all. A good five-point, convertible car seat (see below for recommendations) will work for both infants and children.

Better. The *Evenflo PortAbout* ($60 to $90; extra bases $35) has a 22 lbs. limit, level indicator, adjustable base, two crotch strap positions and a z-shaped handle. This seat varies in plushness, from a basic model that is $60 to a loaded version for $90 (PortAbout 5 Premier Comfort Touch) with padded handle and foot warmer (boot).

car seats

Best. For $60 to $100, the **Graco Snug Ride** impressed us with its plush padding, level indicator, padded handle and more. The only downside: the 20 pound weight limit and 26″ height limit means big babies might outgrow this seat too soon. If you go for a Snug Ride, make sure you get a version that has up-front adjustments for the harness (a few older models had back adjusters). This is our top recommendation if you don't have a LATCH car. Yes, Graco Snug Ride is LATCH-compatible, but we like the following seat better for LATCH because it uses a rigid instead of flexible LATCH system (see earlier in this chapter for a discussion on this topic).

Best LATCH infant seat. The *Baby Trend Latch-Loc Adjustable Back* ($90) is the only infant seat on the market with a rigid LATCH system—we think this gives a more rock solid installation than flexible LATCH straps. This seat comes in two versions—go for the "Adjustable Back" model (61xx), as it will have a higher weight limit (22 lbs, 29″ height) and adjustable headrest that lets you position the harness height without re-threading. The only caveat to this seat: it is a heavy

INFANT SEATS			
	The following is a selection of the better infant car seats and how they compare on features:		

MAKER	**MODEL**	**PRICE**	**WEIGHT/HEIGHT LIMITS**
BABY TREND	LATCH-LOC	$80	20 LBS/26″
	LATCH-LOC ADJ. BACK	$90	22 LBS/29″
BRITAX	HANDLE W/CARE	$100	20 LBS/26″
COMBI	TYRO	$130	22 LBS/29″
EDDIE BAUER	GRIDLOCK/DESIGNER 35	$90	22 LBS/29″
EVENFLO	DISCOVERY	$50	20 LBS/26″
	PORTABOUT	$60-90	22 LBS/26″
GRACO	SNUG RIDE	$60-100	20 LBS/26″
PEG PEREGO	PRIMO VIAGGIO/TRAVELLER	$150	20 LBS/26″

KEY

AUTO BASE: Does the seat have a stay-in-the-car auto base?

HARNESS TYPE: Does the seat have a 3 or 5-point harness? "Both" means either type is available, depending on the model.

LEVEL IND.: Does the seat have a level indicator for easier installation?

nine pounds—that's about two pounds more than the competition. So, you'll get an upper-body work out using this seat. Other than that, it is a winner and our top choice if you have LATCH-compatible vehicle.

Best Bets: Convertible & Forward-Facing car seats

Good. For a decent, no-frills car seat, we recommend the *Graco ComfortSport.* This seat ranges from $70 to $100, depending on how plush the pad is. Nothing fancy, just a good five-point harness seat and up-front belt-adjustment. (FYI: Wal-Mart sells a version of this seat with a bar shield, which we don't recommend). The Graco ComfortSport is a great choice for that less-used second car, Grandma's Hummer or for airline travel.

Better. The *Evenflo Triumph* is a good bet if you want to spend $120 to $130 but not skimp on features—you get a "memory harness," EPS foam, up-front harness height adjustment that eliminates

Auto Base	Level Ind.	Harness Type	Harness Adjustable	Carrier Weight
Yes	Yes	5-Point	Yes	9 lbs
Yes	Yes	5 point	Yes	9 lbs
No	No	5 point	Yes	8 lbs
Yes	Yes	5 point	Yes	N/A ‡‡
Yes	No	5-point	Yes	9 lbs
Yes	No	3-Point	Yes	5.5 lbs
Yes	Yes	Both	Yes	6.5 lbs
Yes	Yes	Both	Yes	7 lbs
Yes	Yes	5-point	Yes	8 lbs

Harness Adjustable: Is the HEIGHT of the harness straps adjustable?

Carrier Weight: This is the weight of the carrier only (not the base).

Notes:

‡‡ *The weight on this seat was unavailable as of press time.*

re-threading and more. This seat is a good bet if you have the room in your car (it is rather wide at the base).

Best. So, what is our top recommendation for convertible car seats? For this edition, we have three picks and they are all Britax. Which model is best for you depends on your child and vehicle.

First, we highly recommend the **Britax Roundabout**. This excellent five-point harness seat has EPS foam, no-twist traps, easy-to-adjust harness and a "double strap" LATCH system. Best of all, you can tether this seat either rear OR forward facing, for an extra measure of safety. Yes, it is expensive ($200 to $230), but you are getting a top-notch seat that is well designed and easy to use.

The **Britax Marathon** is another good choice—the only seat on the market that works up to 65 pounds with a five-point harness. You also get a plush pad, EPS foam and many of the same advantages as the Roundabout. Okay, it is expensive at $250, but the

CONVERTIBLE SEATS

The following is a selection of the better convertible car seats and how they compare on features:

MAKER	MODEL	PRICE	WEIGHT LIMITS (IN POUNDS) REAR	FORWARD
BRITAX	ROUNDABOUT	$200-$230	33 LBS	40 LBS
	MARATHON	$250	33	65
	ADVANTAGE	$250	33	40
COMBI	AVATAR	$200	30	40
EDDIE BAUER*	3-IN-1	$160	33	80
EVENFLO	TRIUMPH	$120-130	30	40
	VANGUARD	$80	30	40
GRACO	COMFORTSPORT	$70-$100	30	40
SAFELINE	SIT N STROLL	$160	30	40

KEY

All of these seats have five-point restraining harnesses.

MODEL: These are the company's flagship models. For an overview of the company's entire offerings, refer to their review earlier in this chapter.

RECLINE: Most seats recline, but the reclines are not equal—some extra use out of this seat may make it worth the investment. One caveat: it is BIG, so make sure you have a vehicle that can accommodate its 19.5" base.

Do you only need a forward-facing seat? If you child is over one year of age and you have LATCH attachments in your car, we would recommend the *Britax Expressway ISOFIX*. This excellent seat ($190 to $220) is the only convertible seat on the market with a "rigid" LATCH attachment (called ISOFIX—see discussion earlier in this chapter). That means you get a rock-solid installation, plus all the advantages of the Roundabout (EPS foam, no-twist straps, etc).

Remember the Britax Roundabout and Marathon are CONVERTIBLE seats that can be used rear-facing to 33 pounds and then forward facing to 40 and 65 lbs, respectively. The Britax Expressway is only a forward-facing seat for children 20 to 40 pounds. As always, check our message boards at www.BabyBargainsBook.com to read parent reviews of any car seat

car seats

RECLINE	COMMENT
Yes	Built-in locking clip; Snap-together chest clip
Yes	Highest weight limit on market with 5 pt harness
Yes	Can adjust belts without rethreading
Yes	Pivoting 2 position base height adjustment
3-pos	Converts to booster seat for toddlers
Yes	Memory Harness; can adjust belts without rethread
Yes	Difficult belt adjustment
No	Best buy for bare-bones model; good for planes
No	Converts to stroller

recline more than others. Generally, the more positions, the more the recline. "3-pos" means a three position recline.

Notes:
The Eddie Bauer 3-in-1 is also known as the Cosco Alpha Omega.

CAR SEATS

Flying the unfriendly skies: Survival Tips & Advice

Most parents know the safest place for any child (newborn, infant, toddler) onboard a plane is buckled into an approved child safety seat. Reports of passengers injured during in-flight turbulence only serve to reinforce this recommendation.

Yet, have you actually tried to use a car seat on a plane? Get ready for a torture test, thanks to a myriad of FAA and airlines rules that are at best family-unfriendly . . . at worst, downright cruel.

First, consider the car seat itself—most are not designed to be carried through a long airport terminal. You aren't suppose to carry any seat by the harness straps, so that involves finding a place on the back of the seat to grip . . . plus your child, luggage, sanity and so on. Yes, infant seats are easier (since your newborn can obviously ride in the seat), but life gets more complicated when you move to a convertible seat.

Then, let's talk about boarding. Many airlines have eliminated the courtesy pre-board for families, forcing parents to struggle with car seat installation while corralling a wayward child . . . . this takes skill—and the ability to withstand the icy stares of fellow passengers waiting in line behind you. (Fortunately, a few airlines do allow families to pre-board—check with the airline ahead of time to determine their current policy. And you can always beg the gate agent to let you pre-board . . . if they are in a good mood, some will let you even if the official airline policy is no).

What about seats? FAA rules require child safety seats to be put next to the window. If you are traveling alone, that means you (the parent) gets stuck with a middle seat. And, inevitably, you'll have to use the restroom during the flight . . . requiring you to climb over the passenger in the aisle seat. Want the bulkhead for extra room? Tough luck, say some airlines. Example: United saves those seats for big-dollar business travelers (read: not you). Of course, when you get to the airport, you can again beg the gate agent for bulkhead if it isn't already taken.

Changing planes is another major hassle—requiring you to go through the hassle of boarding, securing a car seat and so on all over again.

So, how can you can travel by plane with baby without losing your sanity? We've taken dozens of trips with our kids, from newborn age through toddlerhood and beyond. Here's our advice:

◆ *Buy a seat for your baby.* Most airlines don't require parents with children under 2 to have a separate seat—you can carry them in your lap. Remember, there is the law and the law of physics—a child safety seat is the best and safest place in case you encounter turbulence or a rough landing. And given how full planes can be, you don't want to take a chance that the middle seat will be open.

◆ *Use that child safety seat.* Yes, we just discussed how much a hassle it is to use a car seat on a plane–but it is still the safest way to fly. Remember: while you can use an infant or convertible seat on a plane, booster seats that require use of a shoulder belt can NOT be used onboard (since airline seats don't have shoulder belts, of course). If possible, install a convertible seat REAR-FAC-ING. Yes, that is impossible on some airlines because of how tight the seats are packed together. But try anyway!

◆ *Which car seat is best for airline travel?* We like the Graco Comfort Sport (which used to be called the Century Accel DX). It is affordable ($70 to $100), lightweight (16 pounds) and relatively easy to install. Larger/wider seats like the Britax Roundabout may not fit certain narrow airline seats. Remember: the airline will require the arm rests to be down for take-off and landing–that's why super-wide seats don't work.

◆ *What about gadgets like Baby B'Air?* These "flight vests" ($35) tether a child to an adult's lap belt aboard a plane. The goal is to avoid injury to a child during turbulence. The problem: You can NOT use these flight vests during take-off, taxi or landing, per FAA regulations. Bottom line: the safest place your baby during a flight is IN an infant or convertible car seat, since you can use these seats during all phases of a flight.

◆ *Always get pre-assigned seats.* When you make a reservation, always request seat assignments right then and there. If the flight is getting full, the airlines may require you to wait until you get to the airport to get seats (the seats are "under airport control.") One trick: many airlines can assign seats on so-called full flights one or two days before flight. Call then to see if you can snag seats instead of gambling and seeing what is available at the airport. For airlines that don't pre-assign seats (Southwest), arrive early to get a low-number boarding card (which enables you to board earlier).

◆ *Go non-stop if possible.* Yes, the flight to hell probably includes a change of planes in O'Hare. If you have a choice of flights that range from non-stop to those with a stop/change of planes, always go non-stop. Yes, this can sometimes cost extra–but changing planes always raises the risk of a delay, missed connection or worse.

◆ *Rent a DVD player.* For toddlers, there is nothing better for

car seats

long flights than a DVD player and cartoon or Disney movie. InMotion Pictures (www.inmotionpictures.com) rents DVD players for just $12 a day—and that includes one DVD per day. They have locations on 18 airports or you can rent a player round-trip.

So, how can the FAA and the airlines improve air travel for families? (Attention all U.S. Representatives and Senators, and their staffs, reading this book—the following contains actual legislative action you could take to make families' lives easier). First, the FAA should require the airlines and aircraft makers to supply parents with a standard, rear-facing safety seat that should work for all children up to 40 pounds. Perhaps a joint effort between the airlines/aircraft makers and the government should include a car seat maker like Britax, tapping their experience in child passenger safety. Yes, parents should pay a nominal fee ($5?) for renting the seat for a flight to help defer the costs. This seat should attach to airline seats like LATCH car seats attach to LATCH-equipped cars—a rigid bar that makes snapping in the safety seat a, well, snap. Barring that bold action, the FAA should at least require airlines to let parents pre-board to secure a child safety seat. And the bulkhead should be reserved for traveling families.

 The Bottom Line

Now that you've got the car seat covered, let's move on to that next great mystery of baby transportation—the stroller. Close your eyes and click your heels three times. It's off to Stroller Land.

CHAPTER 9

Strollers, Diaper Bags, Carriers and Other Gear To Go

Inside this chapter

What are the best strollers? Which brands are the most durable AND affordable? We'll discuss that plus other tips on how to make your baby portable—from front carriers to diaper bags and more. And what do you put in that diaper bag anyway? We've got nine suggestions, plus advice on dining out with baby.

Getting Started: When Do You Need This Stuff?

While you don't need a stroller, diaper bag or carrier immediately after baby is born, most parents purchase them before baby arrives anyway. Another point to remember: some stroller models have to be special-ordered with at least two to four weeks lead time. And some of the best deals for strollers and other to-go gear are found online, which necessitates leaving a week or more lead-time for shipping.

Sources to Find Strollers, Carriers

Strollers and carriers are found at similar sources as we mentioned for car seats in the previous chapter. Once again, the discounters like Target and Wal-Mart tend to specialize in just a handful of models from the mass-market companies like Cosco, Kolcraft, Graco and so on. The baby superstores like Babies R Us and Baby Depot have a wider selection and (sometimes) better brands like Peg Perego and Combi. Meanwhile, juvenile specialty stores almost always carry the more exclusive brands like Maclaren, Zooper and other upscale brands.

Yet perhaps the best deals for strollers, carriers and diaper bags are found online—for some reason, this seems to be one area the web covers very well. Perhaps this is because strollers are relatively easy to ship (compared to other more bulky juvenile items). Of course, more competition often means lower prices, so you'll see many deals online. Another plus: the web may be the only way to find certain European-made strollers if you live in less-populous parts of the U.S. and Canada (most of their dealers are concentrated on the East and West coasts).

Beware of shipping costs when ordering online or from a catalog—many strollers may run 20 or 30 pounds, which can translate into hefty shipping fees. Use an online coupon (see Chapter 7 for coupon sites) to save and look for free shipping specials.

Parents in Cyberspace: What's on the Web?

Online info on strollers, diaper bags and carriers falls into two categories: manufacturer sites and discounters who sell online. Here's a brief overview:

◆ *Most manufacturers do not sell online, but you can find a wealth of info on their sites in some cases.* With stroller makers, you may find fabric swatches and other technical info about different models. This is helpful since most stores don't carry every available fabric, accessory or model. Among the better sites is Combi (www.combi-intl.com), which includes detailed info on their models and even comparison charts so you can analyze several models at once. Combi also has an outlet store on their site where they sell discontinued models, overstock and showroom samples—when we last visited, we saw last year's Savvy Z for $125 (it sold in stores for up to $200). Baby Jogger has a similar area on their site for overstocks and customer returns.

◆ *Discounters.* Besides previously mentioned web sites like BabyCatalog.com (which has excellent stroller deals), readers say they've had luck with smaller sites like TravelingTikes (www. travelingtikes.com). Another site to check out for stroller deals: BabyCenter (www. babycenter.com). This site's "clearance center" often has deals with up to 30% off and free shipping. Readers also praise Net Kids Wear (www.netkidswear.com) for their stroller deals as well.

Of course, any mention of online bargains for strollers wouldn't be complete without discussion of eBay (www.eBay.com), the massive bargain bazaar. Go to eBay's baby section and choose both

the "general" and "stroller" categories for deals (see Figure 1 on the next page). Sure, there are some dogs here (like Graco or Evenflo models that are virtually worthless at resale), but you'll also find new-in-the-box Perego models as well as jogging strollers by the score. Do your price research up front (know what things really sell for at retail) and you'll find many 50% off bargains.

Strollers

Baby stores offer a bewildering array of strollers for parents. Do you want the model that converts from a car seat to a stroller? What about a stroller that would work for a quick trip to the mall? Or do you want a stroller for jogging? Hiking trails? The urban jungle of New York City or beaches of LA?

And what about all the different brand names? Will a basic brand found at a discount store work? Or do you need a higher-quality brand from Europe? What about strollers with anti-lock brakes and air bags? (Just kidding on that last one).

The $180 million dollar stroller industry is not dominated by one or two players, like you might see in car seats or high chairs. Instead, you'll find a couple *dozen* stroller makers offering just about anything on wheels, ranging from $30 for a bare-bones model to $500 for a deluxe stroller from Europe. A recent trend: SUV-like strollers with air-filled wheels from makers like Zooper and Mountain Buggy, as well as a boom in joggers.

We hope this section takes some of the mystery out of the stroller buying process. First, we'll look at the six different types of strollers on the market today. Next, we'll zero in on features and help you decided what's important and what's not. Then, it's brand ratings and our picks as the best recommendations for different lifestyles. Finally, we'll go over several safety tips, money saving hints, wastes of money and a couple of mail order sources that sell strollers.

What Are You Buying?

There are six types of strollers you can buy:

◆ **Umbrella Strollers.** The name comes from the appearance of the stroller when it's folded, similar to an umbrella.

WHAT'S COOL: They're lightweight and generally cheap—that is, low in price (about $25 to $35). We should note that a handful of premium stroller makers (Maclaren and Peg Perego) also offer pricey umbrella strollers that sell for $150 to $250. Pictured here is a no-frills Kolcraft umbrella stroller.

WHAT'S NOT: They're cheap—that is, low in quality (well, with the exception of Maclaren and Peg Perego). You typically don't get any fancy features like canopies, storage baskets, reclining seats, and so on. Another problem: most umbrella strollers have hammock-style seats with little head support, so they won't work well for babies under six months of age.

◆ **Carriage/Strollers.** A carriage (also called a pram) is like a bed on wheels—most are similar in style to a bassinet. Since this feature is most useful when a baby is young (and less helpful when baby is older), most companies make carriages that convert to strollers. Pictured here is the Peg Perego Milano carriage stroller.

WHAT'S COOL: If your baby is sleepy, she can lie down. Most combo carriage/strollers have lots of high-end features like plush seats, quilted canopies and other features to keep the weather out. The best carriage strollers and prams have a dreamy ride, with amazing suspensions and big wheels.

WHAT'S NOT: Hefty weight (not easy to transport or set up) and hefty price tags. Another negative: most Euro-style "prams" have fixed front wheels, which make maneuvering difficult on quick trips. Some carriage/stroller models can top $300 and $400. These strollers once dominated the market but have lost favor as more parents opt for "travel systems" that combine an infant seat and stroller (see below).

◆ **Lightweight Strollers.** These strollers are our top recommendation: they're basically souped-up umbrella strollers with many convenience features.

WHAT'S COOL: Most offer easy set-up and fold-down; some even fold up similar to umbrella strollers. Many models have an amazing number of features (canopies, storage baskets, high-quality wheels) at amazingly light weights (as light as seven pounds). Combi's Savvy (see review later; pictured at right) is this category's leader, although many companies (namely Graco) have introduced low-priced, Savvy knock-offs in recent years.

WHAT'S NOT: Can be expensive—most high-quality brands run $200 to $300. The smaller wheels on lightweight strollers make maneuvering in the mall or stores easy . . . but those same wheels don't perform well on uneven surfaces or on gravel trails. Skimpy baskets are another trade-off.

◆ **Jogging (or Sport) Strollers.** These strollers feature three big bicycle-tire wheels and lightweight frames—perfect for jogging or walking on rough roads.

WHAT'S COOL: How many other strollers can do 15 mph on a jogging trail? Some have plush features like padded seats and canopies—and the best fold up quickly for easy storage in the trunk. This category has boomed in recent years; now it seems like every stroller maker is rolling out a jogger model.

WHAT'S NOT: They can be darn expensive, topping $200 or even $300. Jogging strollers are a single-purpose item—thanks to their sheer bulk and a lack of steering, you can't use one in a mall or other location. On the plus side, the flood of new models is helping lower prices. New, low-end jogging strollers run $100 to $150. The trade-offs to the new bargain price models: heavier steel frames and a lack of features.

◆ **All-terrain Strollers.** The baby equivalent of four-wheel drive sport-utility vehicles, these strollers are pitched to parents who

want to go on hikes or other outdoor adventures.

WHAT'S COOL: Big air-filled tires and high clearances work better on gravel trails/roads than standard strollers. These strollers are great for neighborhoods with broken or rough sidewalks. All-terrain strollers still have convenience features (baskets, canopies, etc.), yet don't cost as much jogging strollers (most are under $100). Besides, they look cool. Pictured here is the Zooper Buddy (reviewed later in this chapter).

WHAT'S NOT: A few models have fixed front wheels, making them a hassle to use—when you want to turn the stroller, you have to lift the entire front half off the ground. Even if the front wheels swivel, the larger wheels make the stroller less maneuverable in tight spaces. All-terrain strollers are wider than other strollers, which could make them troublesome in stores with narrow aisles. Another caveat: new models now boast "pneumatic" (inflated) wheels for a smoother ride. The only bummer—what if you get a flat? Look for brands that include a pump. While pneumatic-tire strollers seem to be the new hot trend, most folks who really want to go on a hike will opt for a jogging stroller instead of an all-terrain.

◆ **Travel systems.** It's the current rage among stroller makers—models that combine infant car seats and strollers (also called "travel systems"). Century kicked off this craze way back in 1994 with its "4-in-1" model that featured four uses (infant carrier, infant car seat, carriage and toddler stroller). Since then, just about every major  stroller maker has jumped into the travel system market. Travel systems have just about killed sales of carriage strollers; now even carriage stroller king Peg Perego has bowed to the travel system trend. Pictured here is the Graco MetroLite travel system.

WHAT'S COOL: Great convenience—you can take the infant car seat out of the car and then snap it into the stroller frame. Voila! Instant baby carriage, complete with canopy and basket. Later, you can use the stroller as, well, just a stroller.

WHAT'S NOT: The strollers are often junk—especially those by mass market makers Graco and Evenflo. Quality problems plague this category, as does something we call "feature bloat." Popular travel systems from Evenflo and Graco, for example, are so loaded with features that they tip the scales at nearly 30 pounds! The result: many parents abandon their travel system strollers for lighter weight models after baby outgrows his infant seat. And considering these puppies can cost $150 to $250 (some even more), that's a big investment for such short use. On the plus side, quality stroller makers Peg Perego, Maclaren and Combi have jumped into the travel system market, albeit with different solutions (see reviews later in this chapter).

Safe & Sound

Next to defective car seats, the most dangerous juvenile product on the market today is the stroller. That's according to the U.S. Consumer Product Safety Commission, which estimates that over 13,000 injuries a year occur from improper use or defects. The problems? Babies can slide out of the stroller (falling to the ground) and small parts can be a choking hazard. Seat belts have broken in some models, while other babies are injured when a stroller's brakes fail on a slope. Serious mishaps with strollers involved entanglements and entrapments (where an unrestrained baby slides down and gets caught in a leg opening). Here are some safety tips:

1 **NEVER HANG BAGS FROM THE STROLLER HANDLE**—it's a tipping hazard.

2 **DON'T LEAVE YOUR BABY ASLEEP UNATTENDED IN A STROLLER.** Many injuries happen when infants who are lying down in a stroller roll or creep and then manage to get their head stuck in the stroller's leg openings. Be safe: take a sleeping baby out of a stroller and move them to a crib or bassinet.

3 **THE BRAKES SHOULDN'T BE TRUSTED.** The best stroller models have brakes on two wheels; cheaper ones just have one wheel that brakes. Even with the best brakes, don't leave the stroller unattended on an incline.

4 **FOLLOW THE WEIGHT LIMITS.** Most strollers shouldn't be used for children over 35 pounds.

5 **CHECK FOR THE JPMA CERTIFICATION.** The JPMA (the Juvenile Products Manufacturers Association) has a pretty good safety certification program for strollers. They require that strollers must have a locking device to prevent accidental folding and meet other safety standards, such as those for brakes. You can contact the JPMA for a list of certified strollers at (856) 231-8500 or www.jpma.org.

6 **JOGGING STROLLERS ARE BEST FOR BABIES OVER ONE YEAR OF AGE.** Yes, some stroller makers tout their joggers for babies as young as six weeks (or six months) of age. But we think the neck muscles of such small infants can't take the shocks of jogging or walking on rough paths (or going over curbs). Ask your pediatrician if you need more advice on when it is safe to use a jogger.

Recalls: Where to Find Information

The U.S. Consumer Product Safety Commission has a toll-free hot-

Guaranteed Frustration:
Baby gear warranties can leave you fuming

It's a fact of life: sometimes you buy a product that breaks only days after purchase. So, you pick up the phone and call the manufacturer and ask about their warranty. "Sure, we'll help," says the customer service rep. In no time, you have a replacement product and a happy parent.

Fast forward to real life. Most parents find warranties only guarantee frustration—especially with baby products like strollers and other travel gear. Numerous hassles confront parents who find they have a defective product, from endless waits on hold to speak with a customer service rep (on a non-toll free line) to the actual process of returning a product.

First, consider the process of actually registering an item. Filling out a warranty card often requires information that you can only find on the product box or carton. Some parents find this out the hard way . . . after they've hauled all the boxes off to the trash. Even worse: some baby product makers like Peg Perego actually request a copy of the sales receipt for their warranty form. Hello? What about gifts?

Then, let's say something goes wrong. Your new stroller breaks a wheel. That brand new baby monitor goes on the fritz after one week. If it is a gift or you lost the receipt, the store you bought it from may say "tough luck"—call the manufacturer. With many warranties, you have to return the defective item to the manufacturer at your expense. And then you wait a few more weeks while they decide to fix or replace the item. Typically you have to pay for return shipping—and that can be expensive for a bulky item like a stroller. And then you must do without the product for weeks.

Dealing with the customer service departments at some baby product makers can add insult to injury. It seems like some companies can count their customer service staff with one hand—or one finger, in some cases. The result: long waits on hold. Or it takes days to get responses to emails. The U.S. offices of foreign baby product companies seem to be the worst at customer service staffing (Chicco, Perego), while giant firms such as Graco and Evenflo have better customer service. We have to give a special prize for inadequate customer service to Chicco—the Italian juvenile product maker's U.S. importer has exactly ONE person who staffs their customer service

line at (800) 638-2772 (web: www.cpsc.gov) for the latest recall information on strollers and other juvenile products. It's easy to use—the hotline is a series of recorded voice mail messages that you access by following the prompts. The same info is online. You can also report any potential hazard you've discovered or an injury to your child caused by a product. If you prefer, you can write to the US Consumer Products Safety Commission, Washington, D.C. 20207.

department. While we hear she's a very nice person, that explains why it can take DAYS to get a response to a call or email to Chicco.

And customer service can go from good to bad in a blink of an eye. Combi was known for its good customer service until a meltdown in 2001—then a large influx of calls from a recall and a staff shortage created long waits on hold, unreturned emails and frustrated consumers. Combi has since the fixed the problem, but other companies (notably Fisher Price, Chicco, Peg Perego) continue to struggle with providing decent customer service.

The bottom line: it's no wonder that when something goes wrong, consumers just consider pitching a product in the trash and buying a new one. And let's be realistic: paying $20 in shipping to send back a broken $39 stroller doesn't make much sense. Here's our advice:

◆ **Keep your receipts.** It doesn't have to be fancy—a shoebox will do. That way you can prove you bought that defective product. If the item was a gift, keep the product manual and serial number.

◆ **If something goes wrong, call the manufacturer.** We're always surprised at how frustrated consumers forget to first call the company—you might be surprised at how responsive some companies are at fixing an issue.

◆ **If the problem is a safety defect, immediately stop using the product and file a complaint with the Consumer Product Safety Commission** (www.cpsc.gov). Also contact the company.

◆ **Attack the problem multiple ways.** Don't just call; also send an email and perhaps a written letter. Be reasonable: allow the companies 1-2 business days to reply to a phone call or email.

◆ **Let other parents know about your experiences.** The best way to fix lousy customer service? Shame companies into doing it better. Post your experiences to the message boards on our site (BabyBargainsBook.com) and other parenting sites. Trust us, companies are sensitive to such criticism.

strollers

Smart Shopper Tips

Smart Shopper Tip #1
Give it a Test Drive

"My friend was thinking of buying a stroller online, sight unseen. Should you really buy a stroller without trying it first?"

It's best to try before you buy. Most stores have at least one stroller set up as a floor model. Give it a whirl, practice folding it up, and check the steering. Once you've tried it out, shop for price through 'net or mail order sources. Ask retailers if they will meet or beat prices quoted to you online (many quietly do so). What if you live in Kansas and the nearest dealer for a stroller you want is in, say, Texas? Then you may have no choice but to buy sight unseen—but just make sure the web site or catalog has a good return policy. Another tip: use message boards like those on our web site (www. BabyBargainsBook.com) to quiz other parents about stroller models.

Smart Shopper Tip #2
What Features Really Matter?

"Let's cut through the clutter here. Do I really need a stroller that has deluxe shock absorbers and four-wheel drive? What features are really important?"

Walk into any baby store and you'll encounter a blizzard of strollers. Do you want a stroller with a full recline? Boot and retractable canopy? What the heck is a boot, anyway? Here's a look at the features in the stroller market today:

Features for baby:
◆ *Reclining seat.* Since babies less than six months of age sleep most of the time and can't hold their heads up, strollers that have reclining seats are a plus. Yet, the *extent* of a stroller's seat recline varies by model. Some have full reclines, a few recline part of the way (120 degrees) and some don't recline at all.

◆ *Front (or napper) bar.* As a safety precaution, many strollers have a front bar (also called a napper bar) that keeps baby secure (though you should always use the stroller's safety harness). Better strollers have a bar that's padded and removable. Why removable? Later, when your baby gets to toddler hood, you may need to remove the bar to make it easier for the older child to access the stroller.

◆ *Seat padding.* You'll find every possible padding option out there, from bare bones models with a single piece of fabric to strollers with deluxe-quilted padding made from fine fabrics hand woven by monks in Luxembourg. (Okay, just kidding—the monks actually live in Switzerland). For seating, some strollers have cardboard platforms (these can be uncomfortable for long rides) and other models have fabric that isn't removable or machine washable (see below for more on this).

◆ **Shock absorbers or suspension systems.** Yes, a few strollers do have wheels equipped with shock absorbers for a smoother ride. We're unsure how effective this feature really is—it's not like you could wheel baby over potholes without waking her up. On the other hand, if you live in a neighborhood with uneven or rough sidewalks, they might be worth a look.

◆ **Wheels.** In reality, how smooth a stroller rides is more related to the type of wheels. The general rule: the more the better. Strollers with double wheels on each leg ride smoother than single wheels. Most strollers have plastic wheels. In recent years, some stroller makers have rolled out models with "pneumatic" or inflated wheels. These offer a smoother ride.

◆ **Weather protection.** Yes you can buy a stroller that's outfitted for battle with a winter in New England, for example. The options include retractable hoods/canopies and "boots" (which protect a child's feet) to block out wind, rain or cold. Fabrics play a role here too—some strollers feature quilted hoods to keep baby warm and others claim they are water repellent. While a boot is an option some may not need, hoods/canopies are rather important, even if just to keep the sun out of baby's eyes. Some strollers just have a canopy (or "sunshade") that partially covers baby, while other models have a full hood that can completely cover the stroller. Look for canopies that have lots of adjustments (to block a setting sun) and have "peak-a-boo" windows that let you see baby even when closed.

Features for parents:

◆ **Storage baskets.** Many strollers have deep, under-seat baskets for storage of coats, purses, bags, etc. Yet, the amount of storage can vary sharply from model to model. Inexpensive umbrella strollers may have no basket at all, while other models have tiny baskets. Mass-market strollers (Graco, etc.) typically have the most storage; other stroller makers have been playing catch-up in the basket game. Combi, for example, has added new models with bigger storage baskets. One tip: it's not just the size of the storage basket but the access to it that counts. Some strollers have big baskets but are practically inaccessible when the seat is reclined. Others are blocked by a support bar.

◆ **Removable seat cushion for washing.** Let's be honest: strollers can get icky real fast. Crushed-in cookies, spilt juice and the usual grime can make a stroller a mobile dirt-fest. Some strollers have removable seat cushions that are machine washable—other models let you remove *all* of the fabric for a washing. Watch out for those models with non-removable fabric/seat cushions—while you can clean these strollers in one of those manual car washes (with a high-pressure nozzle), it's definitely a hassle (especially in the winter).

◆ *Lockable wheels.* Some strollers have front wheels that can be locked in a forward position—this enables you to more quickly push the stroller in a straight line.

◆ *Wheel size.* You'll see just about every conceivable size wheel out there on strollers today. As you might guess, the smaller wheels are good for maneuverability in the mall, but larger wheels handle rough sidewalks (or gravel paths) much better.

◆ *Handle/Steering.* This is an important area to consider—most strollers have a single bar handle, which enables one-handed steering. Other strollers have two handles (example: Maclarens as well as Perego's Pliko line). Two handles enable a stroller to fold up compactly, like an umbrella. It's sort of a trade-off—steerability versus easier fold. There are other handle issues to consider as well. A handful of strollers feature a "reversible" handle. Why would you want that? By reversing the handle, you can push the stroller while the baby faces you (better for small infants). Later, you can reverse the handle so an older child can look out while being pushed from behind. (Note: models with reversible handles seem increasingly rare in recent years; we'll note which models still have this feature later in this chapter). Another important factor: consider the handle *height*. Some handles have adjustable heights to better accommodate taller parents (more on this later). A few stroller makers offer "one-touch fold" handles. Hit a button on the stroller and it can be folded up with one motion. Later in this chapter, we'll have a box that lists strollers with height-adjustable handles and one-touch folds.

◆ *Compact fold.* We call it the trunk factor—when a stroller is folded, will it in your trunk? Some strollers fold compactly and can fit in a narrow trunk or airline overhead cabin, which is great if you plan to do much traveling. Other strollers are still quite bulky when folded—think about your trunk space before buying. Unfortunately, we are not aware of any web site that lists the size/footprint of strollers when folded. You are own your own to size up model when folded in a store, compared to your trunk (hint: take measurements before you hit the baby store). Not only should you consider how compactly a stroller folds, but also how it folds in general. The best strollers fold with just one or two quick motions; others require you to hit 17 levers and latches.

◆ *Durability.* Should you go for a lower-price stroller or a fancier European brand? Let's be honest: the lower-priced strollers (say, under $100) have nowhere near the durability of the models that cost $200 to $400. Levers that break, reclining seats which stop reclining and other glitches can make you hate a cheap stroller mighty quick. Yet, some parents don't need a stroller that will make it through the next world war. If all you do is a couple of quick trips to the mall every week or so, then a less expensive stroller will probably be fine. Yet, if you plan to use the stroller for more than one child, live in a urban environment with rough sidewalks, or plan extensive outdoor adventures with baby, then invest in a better stroller. Later in this chapter, we'll go over specific models and give you brand recommendations for certain lifestyles.

♦ *Overall weight.* Yes, it's a dilemma: the more feature-laden the stroller, the more it weighs. Yet it doesn't take lugging a 30-pound stroller in and out of a car trunk more than a few times to justify the expense of a lighter-weight design. Carefully consider a stroller's weight before purchase. Some parents end up with two strollers— a lightweight/umbrella-type stroller for quick trips (or air travel) and then a more feature-intensive model for extensive outdoor outings.

One factor to consider with weight: steel vs. aluminum frames. Steel is heavier than aluminum, but some parents prefer steel because it gives the stroller a stiffer feel. Along the same lines, sometimes we get complaints from parents who own aluminum strollers because they feel the stroller is too "wobbly"—while it's lightweight, one of aluminum's disadvantages is its flexibility. One tip for dealing with a wobbly stroller: lock the front wheels so you can push the stroller in a straight line. That helps to smooth the ride.

Smart Shopper Tip #3
The Cadillac El Dorado or Ford Escort Dilemma

"This is nuts! I see cheap umbrella strollers that sell for $30 on one hand and then fancy designer brands for $300 on the other. Do I really need to spend a fortune on a stroller?"

Whether you drive a Cadillac El Dorado or Ford Escort, you'll still get to your destination. And that fact pretty much applies to strollers too—most function well enough to get you and baby from point A to point B, not matter what the price.

So, should you buy the cheapest stroller you can find? Well, no. There *is* a significant difference in quality between a cheap $30 umbrella stroller and a name brand that costs $100, $200 or more. Unless you want the endless headaches of a cheap stroller (wheels that break, parts that fall off), it's important to invest in a stroller that will make it through the long haul.

The real question is: do you need a fancy stroller loaded with features or will a simple model do? To answer that, you need to consider *how* you will use the stroller. Do you live in the suburbs and just need the stroller once a week for a quick spin at the mall?

strollers

Or do you live in an urban environment where a stroller is your primary vehicle, taking all the abuse that a big city can dish out? Climate plays another factor—in the Northeast, strollers have to be winterized to handle the cold and snow. Meanwhile, in Southern California, full canopies are helpful for shading baby's eyes from late afternoon sunshine.

Figuring out how different stroller options fit your lifestyle/climate is the key to stroller happiness. Later in this chapter, we'll recommend several specific strollers for certain lifestyles and climates.

One final note: quality, name-brand strollers actually have resale value. You can sell that $300 stroller on eBay, at a second-hand store, or via the classifieds and recoup some of your investment. The better the brand name (Peg Perego, Combi, Aprica, Maclaren, Zooper, Mountain Buggy), the more the resale value. Unfortunately, the cheap brands like Graco, Century, Evenflo and Kolcraft are worth little or nothing on the second-hand market. Take a quick look at eBay's stroller section to see what we mean.

What if you buy a stroller that is great, except for a simply canopy? You can fix that with a cool sunshade from Australia called the Pepeny (web: www.pepeny.com). This shade screens out the weather, sunlight and UV . . . and is all the rage in New York City. The Pepeny comes in several colors and fits most stroller models. It's about $35 to $40 and available in stores and on web sites like ForTheNewMom.com and Skin-Savers.com. This would also be a good idea for California parents to screen out low-angle sun.

Smart Shopper Tip #4
Too tall for their own good

"I love our stroller, but my husband hates it. He's six feet tall and has to stoop over to push it. Even worse, when he walks, he hits the back of the stroller with his feet."

Strollers are made for women of average height. What's that? About 5'6". If you (or your spouse) are taller than that, you'll find certain stroller models will be a pain to use.

This is probably one of the biggest complaints we get from parents about strollers. Unfortunately, just a few stroller models have height-adjustable handles that let a six-foot tall person comfortably push a stroller without stooping over or hitting the back of the stroller with his feet. (See box later in this section for such models). One smart shopping tip: if you have a tall spouse, make sure you take him or her stroller shopping with you. Checking out handle heights in person is the only way to avoid this problem.

Smart Shopper Tip #5
The Myth of the Magic Bullet Stroller

"I'd like to buy just one stroller—a model that works with an infant car seat and then converts to full-featured pram and then finally a jogger for kids up to age 4. And I want it to weigh less than 10 pounds. And sell for just under $50. What model do you suggest?"

Boy, that sounds like our email some days! We hear from parents all the time looking for that one model that will do it all. We call it the Myth of the Magic Bullet Stroller—an affordable product that morphs into seven different uses for children from birth to college. Sorry, we haven't found one yet.

The reality: most parents own more than one stroller. A typical set-up: one stroller that holds an infant car seat (or a stroller frame) and then a lightweight stroller that folds compactly for the mall/travel. Of course, we hear from parents who own four, five or six strollers, including specialty models like joggers, tandem units for two kids and more. One of our readers and frequent contributors to our message boards, StrollerQueen, takes the prize for owning the most strollers. First-time parents wonder if these folks have lost their minds, investing the equivalent of the gross national product of Aruba on baby transportation. Alas, most parents realize that as their baby grows and their needs change, so must their stroller. Far be it from us to suggest you buy multiple strollers, but at the same time, it is hard to recommend just one model that works for everyone. That's why the recommendations later in this chapter are organized by lifestyle and use.

Wastes of Money

1 **GIVE THE "BOOT" THE BOOT.** Some expensive strollers offer a "boot" or apron that fits over the baby's feet. This padded cover is supposed to keep the baby's feet dry and warm when it rains or snows. Sometimes you have to spend an extra $50 to $75 to get a stroller with this accessory. But how many parents walk their baby in the rain or snow anyway? We say save the extra cost and use a blanket instead. Or try a produce like the Cozy Rosie or Bundle Me (mentioned later in this chapter), which are made of fleece and provide more warmth than a typical stroller boot.

2 **SILLY ACCESSORIES.** Entrepreneurs have worked overtime to invent all kinds of silly accessories that you "must have" for

your stroller. We've seen stroller "snack trays" ($15) for babies who like to eat on the run. Another company made a clip-on bug repellent, which allegedly used sound waves to scare away insects. Yet another money-waster: extra seat cushions or head supports for infants made in your stroller's matching fabric. You can find these same items in solid colors at discount stores for 40% less.

So which stroller accessories are worth the money? One accessory we do recommend is a toy bar (about $10 to $20), which attaches to the stroller. Why is this a good buy? If toys are not attached, your baby will probably punt them out the stroller. Another affordable idea: Rinky Links ($9, in most chain stores) enable you to snap toys to plastic rings that attach to the stroller. We also like Kelgar's Stroll'r Hold'r cup holder ($7, call 972-250-3838 or web: www.kelgar.com).

What about stroller handle extensions? If you find yourself kicking the back of the stroller as you walk, you might want to invest in one of these $20 devices (sold in catalogs like One Step Ahead 800-274-8440). They add up to 8" in height to your stroller handle.

3 **"NEW" OLD STOCK.** A reader alerted us to this online scam—the problem of "new" old stock. She ordered from a small web site what was described as a "new Chicco stroller" in 2001. Turns out, the stroller she got was from 1994. Yes, technically it was "new," as in "not previously used" and still in its original box. Unfortunately, since it was sitting in a warehouse for seven years, it had a cracked canopy, torn fabric and other problems. Apparently, there must be warehouses full of "new" old baby products out there, perhaps left over from the dot-com bust. Our advice: if you see a great online deal, ask what MODEL YEAR the stroller or other product is from. While previous year models can be a great deal, we wouldn't buy anything over three years old. . . even if a web site says it is "new."

Money-Saving Tips

1 **CHECK OUT THE DISCOUNTERS.** As we discussed earlier, the web is a great source for stroller bargains. But don't forget stores like Babies R Us and Baby Depot. They sell quality brands (including Peg Perego) and have frequent specials.

2 **WHY NOT A BASIC UMBRELLA STROLLER?** If you only plan to use a stroller on infrequent trips to the mall, then a plain umbrella stroller for $30 to $40 will suffice. One caveat: make sure you get one that is JPMA certified (see the Safe & Sounds section earlier). Some cheap umbrella strollers have been involved in safety recalls.

3 **CONSIDER THE ALTERNATIVES TO BULKY (AND EXPENSIVE) TRAVEL SYSTEMS.** Among the best bets: the Kolcraft Universal Car Seat Carrier stroller frame ($50) or the Snap N Go (also called Kar Seat Karriage, $50 to $60) from Baby Trend (800) 328-7363 or (909) 902-5568 (web: www.babytrend.com). You pop just about any name-brand infant car seat carrier into these stroller and voila! Instant travel system at half the price. Another idea: consider a front carrier or backpack instead of a bulky stroller. Later in this section, we'll discuss our picks for carriers and backpacks.

4 **CHECK FOR SALES.** We're always amazed by the number of sales on strollers. We've seen frequent sales at the Burlington Coat Factory's Baby Depot, with good mark-downs on Aprica and Peg Perego strollers, to name a few. And just the other week we received a coupon booklet from Toys R Us that featured a $10 off coupon on any Graco stroller over $70. That's nearly a 15% savings. Another reason strollers go on sale: the manufacturers are constantly coming out with new models and have to clear out the old. Which leads us to the next tip.

5 **LOOK FOR LAST YEAR'S MODELS.** Every year, manufacturers roll out new models. In some cases, they add features; other times, they just change the fabric. What do they do with last year's stock? They discontinue it—and then it's sale time. You'll see these models on sale for as much as 50% off in stores and on the web. And it's not like stroller fabric fashion varies much from year to year—is there really much difference between "navy pin dot" and "navy with a raspberry diamond"? We say go for last year's fabric and save a bundle. See the Email from the Real World on the next page for a mom's story on her last year model deal.

6 **SCOPE OUT FACTORY SECONDS.** Believe it or not, some stroller manufacturers sell "factory seconds" at good discounts—these "cosmetically imperfect" models might have a few blemishes, but are otherwise fine. An example: one reader told us Combi occasionally has "showroom models" that are offered to the public at good discounts on their web site. She found a factory second for just $99—that's much less than the $250 retail price. Call Combi at (800) 992-6624 or (708) 350-0101 for more info (web: www.combi-intl.com). Another reader told us Baby Jogger sells factory seconds on their site, BabyJogger.com. This site sells re-conditioned Baby Joggers used in amusement parks. Sample price: a Baby Jogger Twinkle (12" wheel) for $79.

E-MAIL FROM THE REAL WORLD
Last year's fashion, 50% off

A reader emailed her tip on how she saved $100 on a stroller purchase:

"When looking for strollers you can often get last year's version for half the price. I purchased the 2001 Maclaren Vogue from dmartstores.com for $135 versus the Babies R Us price for the 2002 model of $250. As far as my research could tell, the models are identical except for the color patterns. I just typed in 2001 Maclaren Vogue into the Google search engine and found a number of sources that were selling them, colors are limited (dmartstores had the widest selection) but it is a great way to save $100 for a very nice stroller."

7 **DON'T FALL VICTIM TO STROLLER OVERKILL.** Seriously evaluate how you'll use the stroller and don't over buy. If a Toyota Camry will do, why buy a Lexus? You don't really need an all-terrain stroller or full-feature pram for mall trips. Flashy strollers can be status symbols for some parents—try to avoid "stroller envy" if at all possible.

8 **SELL YOUR STROLLER TO RECOUP YOUR INVESTMENT.** When you're done with the stroller, consign your stroller at a second-hand store or sell it in the classifieds or on eBay. You'd be surprised how much it can fetch. The best brands for resale are, not surprisingly, the better names we recommend in this chapter (Perego, Combi, Aprica, Maclaren).

9 **WAREHOUSE CLUB DEALS.** Yes, Sam's and Costco periodically sell strollers, including joggers. At point last year, Costco was selling Peg Perego strollers from their web site (Costco.com) at 40% under retail. Of course, these deals come and go—and like anything you see at the warehouse clubs, you have to snap it up quickly or it will be gone.

10 **EBAY.** It's highly addictive and for good reason—the site is more than just folks trying to unload a junky stroller they bought at K-Mart. Increasingly, baby stores and other retailers are using the web site to discreetly clear out overstock. Better to unload the stuff that isn't moving online than in the store, and risk the rather of local customers who bought the model for full price last week. An example: a reader scored a brand new Peg Perego

Milano XL for HALF the stroller's retail price through an Ebay auction. Other readers regularly report saving $100 to $200 through Ebay. Hint: many strollers sold online are last year's model or fashion. Be sure to confirm what you are buying (is it in an original box? No damage?) before bidding.

The Name Game: Reviews of Selected Manufacturers

Here's a wrap-up of many of the stroller brands on the market today. We evaluated strollers based on hands-on inspections, interviews with recent parents, and conversations with juvenile product retailers. For us, the most important attributes for strollers were safety, convenience and durability. Of course, price to value (as reflected in the number of features) was an important factor as well.

One key point to remember: the ratings in this section apply to the ENTIRE line of a company's strollers. No, we don't assign ratings to individual strollers, but we will comment on what we think are a company's best models. Following this section, we will give you several "lifestyle recommendations"—specific models of strollers to fit different parent lifestyles.

The prices quoted here are street prices—that is prices we saw in stores or on the 'net. In other cases, we used manufacturer's estimated retail prices. Yet, prices can fluctuate widely: in areas with heavy competition among stores (like the Northeast or West Coast), prices are lower. In more isolated communities, however, you may find prices in stores to be higher than what's quoted here.

The Ratings

   A **EXCELLENT**—*our top pick!*
   B **GOOD**— *above average quality, prices, and creativity.*
   C **FAIR**—*could stand some improvement.*
   D **POOR**—*yuck! Could stand some major improvement.*

Aprica 400 W. Artesia Blvd., Compton, CA 90004. For a dealer near you, call (310) 639-6387 or (201) 883-9800 (web: www.apricausa.com). Aprica (pronounced Ah-pree-cah) is one of two Japanese-made stroller brands sold in the U.S. (Combi is the other). Readers of the past edition of this book will probably notice our review of Aprica hasn't changed much (if at all) from last year . . . or the year before that—that's because Aprica's strollers haven't changed much either. Why the company seems stuck in neutral is a mystery; Aprica has only released a handful of new models in the last five years. And while Aprica strollers still have such neat-o features as height adjustable handles and "one-touch" open/close handles which fold (or unfold) the stroller, we're disappointed the prices are so high ($380 to $600). Here's an overview:

The models. Aprica divides its line into two categories: Prestige (pricey, lightweight aluminum frame strollers) and Royale (less expensive, heavier steel-frame strollers). In the Prestige line, you can get a G-Impact cushion (a five-layered air cushion that absorbs bumps and shocks) as an additional option. The top-of-the line "Windsor Prestige" model (also known as the Intreccio) features the one-touch open/close, plush padding, triple-padded head support, zip-off boot and pop-up head protection. This model (which is based on the old Prima stroller) also has a height adjustable handle and weighs just 13.5 pounds. Price: $400. Ouch! If you want an even lighter-weight stroller that folds compactly, consider the "Super Zap," which weighs a mere ten lbs ($450). Although it doesn't have as many features as the Windsor, the Super Zap does have a fully reclining seat, one-touch fold, and a height-adjustable handle. Also in the Prestige line: the Flash ($350 to $400, a seven-pound stroller with one-touch open/close). We should also point out that Aprica makes the only tandem stroller (Prestige Embrace) on the market with a reversible handle. It runs about $450.

Realizing those prices are hard to swallow, Aprica launched a few years ago a lower-price line (Royale) made with heavier steel frames. Of course, "heavy" is a relative term—many of these strollers are still much lighter than the competition. Basically, the Royale models are based on similar Prestige strollers—the Quantum Royale ($300, 16 lbs.) is similar to the Windsor, the Calais Royale ($279, 14 lbs.) is the same as the Super Zap (but no height-adjustable handle or boot), and the Sprint Royale ($240, 9 lbs.) is similar to the Flash.

In the past year, Aprica has rolled out several new models. Among the offerings: the Pram First ($460 to $520, 16 lbs), a full-size, full-recline carriage stroller with one-hand close. The Pram First has a reversible handle and G-impact cushion. Not expensive enough for you? Then try the Milano Slim stroller (12.1 lbs), another new model from Aprica. This one runs $550 to $750, which is hard to believe. Why the difference in price? One version of the Milano Slim (model 94917) has extra padding, hence the extra $200 in price.

Looking for something high fashion? Aprica offers the "A Mode Mistral" strollers (10.6 lbs, $500) in such fabrics as day-glo orange or purple. Again, you get a full-recline stroller with one-hand fold. Ditto for the A Mode Rebecca (10.6 lbs, $500)—it is basically the same as the Mistral, except the Rebecca strollers have fabric with bright check patterns. The A Mode Classic and Italian Sport Series are the same stroller with different fashions. Just to confuse you more, Aprica also has "B Mode" strollers. The B Mode Future Series (7.9 lbs, $480), which is much like the Flash but with fancy fabrics.

Our view. Let's be honest: these are feature-packed strollers, but the prices are way too high. $500 for a lightweight stroller? The Royale line is a step in the right direction, but Aprica remains a brand that few parents can afford. Yes, you can find these strollers discounted online, but even then you are talking $300 for most models. As for Aprica's quality and durability, we've received scattered complaints about the brand in recent years—folks complain about the skimpy baskets, shaky suspensions, somewhat complicated folding mechanism (and in one case), a hood that broke off a stroller. At this price level, you'd expect the stroller to be darn near perfect, so Aprica is a disappointment overall. **Rating: B**

Baby Trend *For a dealer near you, call (800) 328-7363, (909) 902-5568, Web: www.babytrend.com.* Baby Trend's biggest selling stroller isn't really a stroller at all—it's a stroller *frame*. Here's an overview of the line:

The models. The Snap N Go is such a simple concept it's amazing someone else didn't think of this years ago—basically it's a stroller frame that lets you snap in most major-brand infant car seats. Presto! Instant travel system at a fraction of the price. The original Snap N Go was just a frame and wheels for $30. In the last few years, Baby Trend has improved the line by adding new models: The Snap N Go Lite ($40) sits higher than the original model and

strollers

Who's who?

A big trend in recent years in strollers are licensed names—stroller makers try to add cache to their strollers by slapping a better-known company's name on it. Here's a run-down of the major licenses and who to look up in this chapter for a review of their parent company:

LICENSE	MADE BY
CARTER'S	KOLCRAFT
EDDIE BAUER	COSCO
JEEP	KOLCRAFT
MARTINELLI	PEG PEREGO
OSHKOSH	EVENFLO
SAFETY 1ST	COSCO
SWAN	BABY TREND

the Snap N Go LX or Sport ($50 to $60) adds a big basket. Also be aware that the Snap N Go's doesn't work with ALL infant car seats. Consult Baby Trend's web site (FAQ's) for a current list.

While the Snap N Go is innovative, Baby Trend now has competition in this category—Kolcraft's Universal Car Seat Carrier is a similar product. Which is best? Our readers like the Kolcraft version better.

The big news at Baby Trend this year is their roll out of travel systems, which combine their new infant car seat (see Chapter 8 for a review of that seat) with their strollers. A sample: the Santa Fe Trendsport Traveler system for $129 (car seat plus stroller). That's a great price, but the stroller (18 lbs) is nothing fancy—steel frame, three-point harness and two-position recline. You do get a decent canopy, one-hand fold and a big basket, but the recline is only to 145 degrees (not a full recline). Similar in design is the Symmetry stroller ($70, 20.5 lbs), which adds a full-recline seat and more plush padding.

Baby Trend's tandem strollers are innovative—the Sit N Stand LX ($159 to $179) is a concept imported from England. This "pushcart" is a regular stroller (with reclining seat, canopy and basket) that has a place for an older child to stand (or sit in a jump seat) in back. The latest model of this stroller (the LX3, $149 to $179) can also accommodate an infant car seat.

We were also impressed with the functionality of Baby Trend's tandem (front/back) double strollers. The Caravan Lite LX ($199-249) lets you attach one or two infant car seats and gets generally good marks from parents for its features and ease of use.

Baby Trend is a big player in the jogging stroller market (we'll discuss these models later in this chapter in the "Exercise This" section). New this year is a jogging stroller travel system (the Expedition LE, $189), which pairs the Baby Trend infant seat with a jogger. We should also note that Baby Trend markets their products under the name "Swan" for specialty stores. Basically, these are the same products/models as Baby Trend makes, albeit with a few cosmetic differences (fabric color, etc.).

Our view. We're not sure what to make of Baby Trend—parents seem to love some of their products (particularly the Snap N Go) and loathe others (basically, most of their other strollers). Yes, the jogging strollers get good marks but Baby Trend has been dogged by numerous quality problems when it comes to their tandems and more expensive models. Parents say parts break, wheels fall off and worse—"bad engineering" was how one parent put it when talking about her tandem stroller. And before you buy the Baby Trend travel system, be sure to read the caveats to their infant car seat in our last chapter. So, it's hard to assign a rating. If we were just looking at the Snap N Go or the joggers, we'd give them an A. Yet, the other models would barely earn a C. So, we'll compromise. **Rating: B-**

Different versions spark confusion

Here's a common question we get here at the home office: readers go into a chain store like Babies R Us and see a major brand stroller they like. Then, they visit a specialty store and see a similar model, but with some cosmetic differences . . . and a higher price tag. What's up with that? Big stroller makers like Graco have to serve two masters—chain stores and specialty retailers. Here's a little trick of the baby biz: stroller makers often take the same basic model of stroller and make various versions for different retailers. Hence, you'll see a Graco stroller with basic fabric in Babies R Us—and then the same model with the name "Graco Baby Classics" and fancier fabric in specialty stores. Peg Perego does the same thing with their Martinelli brand, a specialty store version of their Perego strollers. So is there any real difference besides the fabric color to justify the increase in price? No, not in our research. The strollers are almost exactly the same. Our advice: if you can live with the chain-store version, go for it.

strollers

Bébé Maison This new line of strollers is made by J. Mason (clever, eh?) for specialty stores. Basically, these are same as Mason's Chinese-made strollers, dressed up in fancy fabrics and loaded with special features like reflective material. We saw prototypes of these strollers at a trade show recently and weren't that impressed. Adding a French name and blue fabric to a mass-market stroller doesn't really change its quality. **Rating: C**

Bugaboo See the "Urban Jungle" recommendations later in this chapter for our comments on this brand.

Carter's These strollers are made by Kolcraft; see their review at the end of this section in "Other Brands."

Century *Web:* www.centuryproducts.com Century's owner, Graco, has phased out all Century strollers. See our web page at www.BabyBargainsBook.com (click on bonus material) to read an archived review of their older models.

Chicco *4E Easy Street, Bound Brook, NU 08805. For a store near you, call (877) 4-CHICCO or (732) 805-9200. Web: www.chiccousa.com* Chicco (pronounced Kee-ko) has a 50-year history as one of Europe's leading juvenile products makers. Along with Peg

Perego, Chicco is Europe's biggest producer of strollers and other baby products and toys. In the U.S. and Canada, however, Chicco was always an also-ran while Perego was a top-seller. Chicco has tried to turn that around in recent years by emphasizing their light-weight stroller models instead of full-featured carriage models. Here's an overview:

The models. Chicco has gone to an all-Chinese made line of strollers in the past year. Their entry-level Caddy ($50, 11 lbs) has a five-point harness, two-position recline and a rather skimpy sun-shade (but no basket). Parents love the included rain cover and bright colors—the quality is very good and the handle height is great for taller moms. You can find this stroller at Babies R Us.

A step-up in terms of features is the London model, which is new. The London ($70, 15 lbs) has a five-position recline, adjustable leg rest, padded handles, canopy, rain cover . . . and basket. No, it doesn't push as smoothly as a Maclaren—but it is half the price!

The Caddy and London are Chicco's main offerings this year, but you'll probably see several older Chicco models sold online. Among them is the Ponee, which is a 15 lb. aluminum stroller with one touch fold, child tray and semi-full recline for $120. The Fly (12 lbs) is an earlier version of the Caddy for about $60—it has a fancier canopy.

Our view. Chicco finally has two winners with the Caddy and London—we think they combine the best of both worlds, light-weight, decent features and great prices. These strollers are great alternatives to the massive travel system strollers you see out there that weigh in at 30 lbs. Quality is good, so we'll raise Chicco's rating this year. Two caveats: first, don't go to Chicco's web site to find additional information about their strollers. Their web site is a joke. And second, be aware that Chicco has among the worst customer service in the baby biz (see our comments on this earlier in the book). So, our rating is somewhat discounted to reflect those problems. *Rating: B+*

Combi *199 Easy St., Carol Stream, IL 60188. For a dealer near you, call (800) 752-6624, (800) 992-6624, (630) 871-0404; Web: www.combi-intl.com.* This year marks a strategic shift at Combi, the Japanese-stroller maker that is best know for their high-quality, lightweight strollers. After several years of offering both inexpensive and expensive models, Combi is throwing in the towel at the low-end. The company just couldn't compete with mass-market brands like Graco at the entry-level price points (below $80) and parents griped that Combi's cheaper strollers were, well, cheap. So the company will concentrate on doing more models at the moderate to high end of the market ($80 to $250).

Another major change: Combi will offer its first car seats this year, enabling parents to pair a Combi infant car seat with a Combi stroller to create a seamless "travel system" (although each will be sold separately—see a review of Combi's infant car seat in the last chapter). In years past, Combi offered a "Perfect Match" system that allowed parents to attach other maker's infant seats to Combi strollers. This was a good idea in theory, but only worked so-so in the real world—parents thought the infant seats didn't securely "lock" into their Combi strollers and others didn't like the lack of a coordinated look. To hedge its bets, however, Combi will still offer several "Perfect Match" strollers in addition to models that work with their own car seats. We'd bet that at some stroller point the Perfect Match system will be phased out down the road.

The models. Combi's most successful model must be the "Savvy," a terrific stroller that is among the lightest weight strollers on the market. The compact-folding Savvy comes in three versions: the Travel Savvy ($80, with a steel frame, 12 lbs), the Soho ($100 with aluminum frame and travel bag, 11 lbs) and the top-of-the-line Ultra Savvy ($260, 15 lbs). The Ultra Savvy is the only Savvy with a full-recline seat (hence it can be used with infants). FYI: The Ultra Savvy is the only Savvy that has Combi's "Perfect Match" system that lets you attach any major brand infant car seat. Or you can attach a Combi infant seat (Ultra Savvy TS).

So, which Combi strollers work with their new infant car seat to form a travel system (TS)? First, consider the new Savona TS (14 lbs, $160 for the stroller). It features a height adjustable handle, removable/washable seat cover and large basket. The Tetra TS is much the same, but adds an adjustable footrest and parent tray–it weighs 22 lbs ($140). Just to confuse you, you can also buy both the Savona and Tetra strollers in "Perfect Match" versions to work with other brand car seats (those models have "PM" as a suffix). Be sure which one you are buying by checking the box at the store or the model number online.

Got twins? The Combi Twin Savvy is a side-by-side model that weighs a mere 15 pounds and sports a removable napper bar, machine washable cushions, a 165-degree reclining seat, a separate canopy and a stroller pack with two insulated bottle holders. At 30" wide, this side by side should fit through most doors. The price is a bit steep, however: about $340.

Combi has discontinued their lower-price "Convenience" line, but you may still see them in stores. These strollers (6500, 6600 series) ran $80 to $120.

Our view. Combi is one of our favorite strollers; the Savvy is an all-time bestseller and for good reasons. The lightweight is a great plus for a suburban lifestyle (that is, hauling in and out of a trunk). Combi's quality and durability are excellent–even for their lower-price models. Yes, some models have skimpy baskets but overall we think this one of the best stroller brands out there for the dollar. And we have to give Combi kudos for an excellent web site that has detailed info on their models and even an outlet store with bargains on discontinued strollers. What about the Combi "travel systems"? Well, the jury is still out on Combi's infant car seat (see review in the last chapter), but we applaud the company for trying to address parent comments about the shortcomings of the Perfect Match system. ***Rating A***

Cosco *2525 State St., Columbus, IN 47201. Call (812) 372-0141 for a dealer near you (or 514-323-5701 for a dealer in Canada;. Web: www.coscoinc.com* Long an also-ran in the U.S. stroller market, Cosco (owned by Canadian conglomerate Dorel) is probably better known as its alter ego, Eddie Bauer (Cosco's parent Dorel has licensed the Eddie Bauer name and slapped it on just about everything they make). Cosco strollers are mostly found at discount stores like Wal-Mart. Here's an overview:

The models. Like most mass-market stroller makers, Cosco's emphasis in recent years has been their travel systems. A typical offering: the Eddie Bauer Aluminum Travel System ($200). Yes, the stroller has some attractive features, including a one-hand fold, five-point harness and large basket. But remember this is paired with a Cosco Designer 22 car seat (reviewed in the last chapter as the Eddie Bauer Infant seat)–we only gave that seat a C rating because of its heavy carrier weight.

So, that basically eliminates just about any Cosco/Eddie Bauer/Safety 1st travel system from consideration, as they are all paired with that rather inferior infant car seat.

Cosco is a big player in the double stroller market with their Two Ways Tandem. It has a reversible front seat, so the children can face one another. And the price is hard to beat at $120 to $140, making this one of the lowest price tandem strollers out there. And Cosco is a player in the low-end jogger market, making "sport" strollers with inflated wheels under the Safety 1st brand. Cosco's flagship jogging stroller (The Safety 1st Two Ways Jogger, $150) features a reversible seat (which is a first in the jogger market). The telescoping handle is quite cool, as is the infant seat attachment system (another first). The steel frame for this model is a bit heavy, but the five-point harness is nice as are the full size (16") rear wheels.

New this year: Cosco has knocked off Combi's Savvy stroller under the Eddie Bauer label—this one-hand fold model is sold for about $70.

Our view. Let's talk frankly about Cosco's strollers. Most parents are suckered into buying one of these models by the Eddie Bauer name, which they *think* indicates good quality. Then they see the cool Eddie Bauer colors—sold! Fast-forward three months. Suddenly, parents aren't so enamored. The reviews are rather harsh from parents who frequent our message boards. We hear about strollers that break after only a few months of use, canopies that snap off and other quality woes. And there are the safety concerns: Cosco has suffered through several safety recalls in recent years, including the Two Ways Tandem in 1999. That stroller's folding mechanism broke during use, causing the strollers to suddenly collapse. Cosco received 250 reports of the strollers collapsing, causing over 200 injuries. So, we just can't give a thumbs-up to this brand. ***Rating: C-***

Eddie Bauer These strollers and travel systems are made by Cosco. See the above review for more info.

Emmaljunga *Web: www.emmaljunga.com* This Swedish stroller brand withdrew from the U.S. market in 2001; as of this writing, they have no distribution in the U.S. or Canada. You might still see their strollers on eBay and at second-hand stores, but since they are no longer on the market we'll skip them for review in this section.

Evenflo *1801 Commerce Dr., Piqua, OH 45356. For a dealer near you, call (800) 233-5921 or (937) 415-3300. In Canada, PO Box 1598, Brantford, Ontario, N3T 5V7. (519) 756-0210; Web: www.evenflo.com* Evenflo's claim to fame, stroller-wise, is their one-handed steering. All of Evenflo's strollers and travel systems have this feature. Here is a breakdown:

The models. Evenflo offers travel systems for both their entry-level Discovery infant seat or the more deluxe PortAbout infant seat. Whatever version you get, the stroller is basically the same—one

---

Strollers with height-adjustable handles, one-touch folds

Which strollers have height adjustable handles that make life easier for tall folks (basically, anyone over 5'8"?) And which strollers have one-touch folds that make putting the stroller away easier? Here is a list of popular models with such features:

◆ **Aprica** models with height adjustable handles: Super Mini Prestige, Super Zap, Flash Prestige, Windsor Prestige, Embrace and Quantum Royale. Aprica models with one touch fold: Super Mini Prestige, Super Zap, Flash Prestige, Windsor Prestige, Sprint Royale, Quantum Royale, Calais Royale.

◆ **Combi's** Savona has a height adjustable handle.

◆ **Evenflo.** All travel systems have one touch fold feature. No height adjustable handles though.

◆ **Graco**. The CitiSport and MetroLite have one-touch fold. The MetroLite also has a height adjustable handle. Coach rider has one-touch fold, as does the Citi-Sport.

◆ **Maclaren.** All models work well for tall parents.

◆ **Mountain Buggy.** All models have height adjustable handles.

◆ **Perego.** The Venezia, Milano and Pliko families have height adjustable handles.

◆ **Simo.** The Bertini has a height adjustable handle.

◆ **Zooper.** The Kroozer has a height adjustable handle.

Bottom line: while the above models have height adjustable handles, tall parents tell us the best brand is Maclaren.

---

touch brake, one hand fold, large basket, parent "console" with cup holder and a reclining seat.

The Discovery Deluxe V Travel System runs $100, which is a good deal. Step up to the Comfort Dimensions travel system and you get the PortAbout infant seat and a plusher stroller for $150 to $229. In fact, Evenflo sells seven different versions of the Comfort Dimensions travel systems—all that changes is how plush the stroller is (extra padding, etc). There is also an OshKosh version of this system that runs $229.

New this year is the Journey Travel System. Evenflo has made small improvements to this model, including a feature that lets the stroller fold "up" to you (no bending over when folding the unit). You also get an oversized canopy and front/back wheel suspension for a smoother ride. The Journey comes in two flavors: a "premier" version $170 and a "ultra" ($190 to $220). The difference? The more expensive one has more (you guessed it) padding and storage pockets. You can buy the Journey stroller separately for $80 to $120.

Discontinued but still available, the FeatherLight Plus (12 lbs) was a decent model for $80 that featured one-handed steering, a large storage basket, parent console with cup holders and front wheel suspension (but the front wheels did not feature a locking option). The FeatherLight came in a travel system version for $120.

Evenflo for the time being has abandoned the super lightweight end of the stroller category. Their Light & Easy stroller (9.5 lbs) was a Combi Savvy knock-off that sold for $90—you still might see some in the clearance bin.

As with infant seats, Evenflo also makes Osh Kosh versions of their strollers and travel systems—these have the exact same features, just denim fabric and a different name. And the price is about $20 higher.

Our view. Can you say "feature bloat"? Evenflo is perhaps the worst offender when it comes to the weight game—these strollers often weigh in 25 pounds empty! Add an infant seat and you've got 40 to 45 pounds even before you've added a baby.

Evenflo's previous travel systems were hampered by quality problems according to complaints from our readers. We're happy to report Evenflo's more recent models seem to have fared better, quality-wise. As a result, we've upped Evenflo's rating this time out. We'd put them ahead of Cosco and about equal with Graco in terms of quality and durability. They still have a long way to go to equal the better brands in this category, but they are improving. And kudos to Evenflo's customer service department, which earns good marks from our readers for promptly taking care of problems. ***Rating: C+***

Fisher Price. *See J. Mason. Web: www.fisher-price.com* Fisher-Price is a bit player in the stroller market, but their offerings are sold at discounters like Wal-Mart so they have quite a bit of exposure. (All FP strollers are made by J. Mason). A typical offering: the Comfort-Lite LX ($80). This stroller has an adjustable leg rest, cup holders and large storage basket. Basically, it is similar to the Graco LiteRider. Fisher-Price also has one of the cheapest tandems on the market, the Comfort Lite Tandem LX (also known as the My Bear). For $80 (at Wal-Mart), you get a one-hand fold, large storage basket, parent tray and front swivel wheels that can lock in position. Yes, that is a quite a deal, considering most tandems are twice the amount. But what about the quality? These are very cheap, Chinese-made strollers that are short on padding and features. If don't have any high expectations for durability, you won't be disappointed. We'd put them on par with Cosco's offerings. **Rating: C-**

Graco *Rt. 23, Main St., Elverson, PA 19520. For a dealer near you, call (800) 345-4109, (610) 286-5951; Web: www.gracobaby.com* Graco is a great example of what's right (and wrong) with American-made strollers today. The company (a division of Rubbermaid) is probably the market-leader in strollers, with affordable models that are packed with features like oversized baskets. You'll find Graco everywhere: discount stores, baby superstores, specialty shops and more. But, as we'll discuss later in this review, those low prices often mean low quality. Graco's line is huge, so let's get to the highlights:

The models. Graco divides their stroller line into five areas: Jogging strollers, CoachRiders, LiteRiders, Quattro Tour (carriage strollers), UltraLite and tandem models.

Graco's jogging strollers are the LeisureSport models. These tri-wheel joggers have 12" wheels and all the features you'd expect from a Graco—parent tray, five-point harness, easy fold and front and rear suspension. You can buy this stroller separately ($100) or as part of a travel system ($200). FYI: All Graco travel systems include their excellent infant seat, the Snug Ride (see review in the last chapter).

Graco's top of the line carriage strollers are dubbed "CoachRiders." The CoachRider is sort of Graco's pram, with a reversible seat, one hand fold and a reclining seat to 180 degrees. This top of the line stroller features lots of padding and other goodies like a removable canopy. The stroller is $150 and available as a travel system with the Snug Ride infant (called the Chauffeur) for $225.

The best-selling stroller in Graco's line has to be the LiteRider. It is relatively lightweight for Graco (19lbs.), has a reclining seat, an easy fold and a huge storage basket. As you'd expect, Graco makes the LiteRider in a zillion versions, from $39 to $99. We've heard very good feedback on this stroller from parents, who like its convenience and low price.

Graco offers several travel system versions that pair the LiteRider with the Snug Ride infant seat—the Breeze ($120), Cirrus ($149), Glider ($169-$179) and Sterling ($199). As you might expect, the difference in price depends on the plushness of the car seat/stroller. Graco even offers a version of the LiteRider with pneumatic (air-filled) tires, boot and rain guard for $230. New this year is an Aspen LiteRider travel system (basically, the same stroller in Graco) and the EuroGraco travel system (imagine Graco goes to Germany).

Graco's most plush lightweight stroller is the Quattro Tour, again available separately for $100 or as part of a travel system for $200. You get an aluminum frame, four-position full recline seat, one hand "gravity fold," parent tray and three-point harness.

Perhaps Graco's most successful new stroller in recent years was their knock-offs of Combi's Savvy. The "UltraLite" strollers include the CitiLite and MetroLite models. The CitiLite ($89) is a 10.8-pound stroller with one-hand fold and removable, washable seat pads. The upgraded MetroLite features a larger basket, kid snack tray, adjustable handle and more. The MetroLite comes in both three-point ($99) and five-point versions ($129), the latter of which has larger wheels and a head support cushion. There will also be travel system versions of the MetroLite, again both in three-point ($150) and five-point ($200) models.

Finally, double strollers are Graco's other major forte—the DuoRider ($130) is Graco's side-by-side model, while the DuoGlider ($150) is a front/back tandem. Graco's claim to fame in the tandem market is their "stadium seating," where the rear seat is elevated. Of course, you get all the standard features: huge storage baskets, removable canopies, etc. Graco also offers the DuoGlider in a travel system that will now accept two infant car seats (note to parents of twins) for $240, but that price just includes one infant seat.

Our view. The adage "you get what you pay for" unfortunately applies to Graco. Sure, they're affordable and packed with goodies. That's the good news. The bad news: Graco strollers suffer from far too many quality problems. Yes, they are $100 or $200 less than similar European or Japanese brands, but these strollers just aren't as durable—levers break, reclining seats stop reclining, retractable canopies stop retracting, etc. That's probably why we see many parents who used a Graco for their first child buy a better brand for child #2. Another bummer: these strollers are far too heavy. Many full-feature Graco models tip the scales at over 30 lbs., which may have you cursing the thing in a parking lot. Yet, if all you need is a very light-duty stroller that doesn't have to survive more than one child, a Graco is not a bad choice. The LiteRider would

strollers

make a good budget stroller for quick trips to the mall. The MetroLite is OK—but parents complain (again) the quality is cheap and some of the design features make this stroller frustrating to use. Example: when MetroLite's seat is reclined, just try to get something out of the basket. Go ahead, we'll wait right here. **Rating: C**

Inglesina *(877) 486-5112 or (973) 746-5112; web: www.inglesina. com).* Inglesina has always played second fiddle to its Italian cousins Peg Perego and Chicco in the stroller market. While other Italian players have had significant success peddling their wares to North American parents, Inglesina always seemed stuck in low gear.

Not any more. Inglesina has a hot-seller with the Zippy, a cool one-hand fold model that has lit up our message boards with positive comments from parents. As a result, we've bumped Inglesina into the big leagues with an expanded review. Here's an overview of Inglesina's models:

The models. Okay, what's so cool about the Zippy? Check out the one-hand fold—you lift up on a lever on the back of the stroller and poof! Instant folded stroller. This 17 lbs. model has all the cool features most urban moms want—full recline, adjustable backrest, removable front bumper and storage basket. Best of all: the Zippy has a universal car seat adapter that lets you secure an infant car seat to the stroller. So what's not to love? First, the Zippy is darn expensive: $250 to $270, depending on the store. Second, it comes in two colors: dull and duller. Actually, there are four colors but many parents who spend this kind of money are a bit disappointed with the Zippy's lack of fashion, despite the Italian pedigree. Basically, the Zippy is much like the Peg Perego Pliko, but costs $50 more for that much easier fold.

Inglesina also has a version of the Zippy that includes a bassinet called the Zippy System, but that version was not in stores as we went to press (you have to special order it). In fact, most of Inglesina's other stroller models are also hard to find—the Swift and Easy Evo ($199-$229, 16 lbs.) are very similar to the Zippy, but they don't have the one-hand fold. All these models replaced the Ace and Planet, which were last year's models. Inglesina also has three traditional European-style pram models (Classic, Vittoria, Emma), but their high price ($500 to $700) and limited distribution mean few parents consider them.

Parents of twins and triplets may want to give Inglesina's double and triple strollers a look-see. Inglesina's side-by-side duo (Twin Jet $419) is a compact-folding model with four-position reclining seats and full boot. The Biposto and Trio carry two or three kids at once, at prices that range from $500 to $700.

Our view. The quality on Inglesina's strollers is high and we'll give them kudos for their innovative Zippy. The reviews from parents say this an excellent stroller. ***Rating: A***

J. Mason *(818-993-6800; web: www.jmason.com).* This company was best known for the cheap-o umbrellas that are sold for $20 or $30 in discount stores like Wal-Mart. But in recent years J. Mason has tried to move beyond that niche. First, the company has hired a slew of former Graco executives who were purged from that company during one of their many downsizings. Second, J Mason has signed license deals with companies like Sesame Street and Fisher Price to give their offerings more brand clout. Finally, the company has tried to expand its reach into specialty stores with a more upscale line called Bébé Maison (reviewed earlier in this section). So, what's the result of all these changes? Well, the company's line now looks a lot like Graco, with models in different segments from umbrella to joggers.

Among the more interesting models: the J Mason Freedom Trail jogger sold in the One Step Ahead catalog for $200. This model is the first jogger that includes a bassinet so it is safe (allegedly) for newborns, claims the catalog. Later the bassinet detaches and you can use the stroller as a regular jogger. We'll give J Mason bonus points for creativity with this one, but we still don't like the idea of a newborn in a jogging stroller—their neck muscles just aren't up to the jostling if you really plan to run with this model. Yes, it would be fine for occasional walks, but that's not how it is pitched. And we wouldn't recommend this stroller for serious exercise anyway, since the smallish 12" wheels won't really work for runners.

As for the rest of J Mason's strollers, these Chinese-made models are basically duplicates of what Graco and Baby Trend offer. Quality is only average. If J Mason wants to be a serious player in this market, it will need more innovative offerings like the Freedom Trail and less of the $20 throwaway umbrella models. ***Rating: C***

Kolcraft *3455 West 31st Pl., Chicago, IL 60623. For a dealer near you, call (773) 247-4494; Web: www.kolcraft.com.* Kolcraft has always been an also-ran in the stroller business, thanks to their lackluster travel systems. Kolcraft exited the car seat business in the last year as a result of slumping sales.

The models. Realizing their own questionable standing in the marketplace, Kolcraft has licensed different brand names to hawk their products: Carter's and Jeep. The Carter's strollers (and other products) are exactly the same as Kolcraft's models, albeit with nicer looking fabric. A more interesting license is Jeep—Kolcraft has an entire line of Jeep strollers, complete with SUV-like knobby wheels, beefed up suspension, and sporty fabrics at affordable prices ($30 to $109). The Jeep Wrangler stroller is $49 and is basically a souped-up umbrella stroller. This year, Kolcraft is rolling out the Jeep Wrangler Sport (12 lbs) for $30—it's a stripped down version of the Wrangler, but you still get a basket. The more deluxe Cherokee and Grand Cherokee ($89 to $109) have toy steering wheels, bigger seats and four-wheel independent suspension. These strollers look rather amazing (our favorite detail: simulated lug nuts on the wheels), but we're still leery about recommending the Jeep strollers given Kolcraft's past quality track record (which was poor). A better bet: Kolcraft has a knock-off of Baby Trend's Snap & Go called the Universal Car Seat Carrier (13 lbs) for $50. This stroller frame will accommodate most car seats and has a large basket and one-hand fold. Parents rave about this stroller frame and we agree—it is the better choice when compared to the Snap & Go.

This year, Kolcraft continues to expand the Jeep line with a tandem model called the Jeep Wagoneer ($140 to $190, depending on the version). This affordable tandem has won kudos for readers for its basket, which is the size of Montana. It also holds any brand infant car seat, which is another nice plus. Also new in the past year: the Liberty stroller, a three-wheel stroller with steer-able front wheel for $120.

Our view. These strollers appeal to suburbanites who just need an occasional stroller for the mall or county fair. We will give credit to Kolcraft for the good design—folks love all the storage pockets and dads seem to be drawn to the more beefy looks of these models. But Dad better be working out if he plans to haul these things in and out of a trunk—many of these models suffer from feature bloat that adds to their weight. Sample: the simple Jeep Cherokee is a whopping 25 lbs. Empty. What about quality? We'd put these strollers a notch or two ahead of Graco, but still far behind the Combi and Perego's of the stroller world. **Rating: B-**

Jeep These strollers are made by Kolcraft. See the previous review for details.

Maclaren *4 Testa Place, S. Norwalk, CT 06854. For a dealer near you, call (877) 504-8809 or (203) 354-4400; Web:www.maclaren-baby.com* Maclaren is a British brand that sells 500,000 strollers each year in 30 countries worldwide. Their specialty? High-quality umbrella strollers made from lightweight aluminum. Maclaren's distribution is limited to the East Coast and the brand has many fans in New York City and Boston. You might wonder whether these parents (who fork over $200 to $300 for a Maclaren) have lost their minds—can't they just go down to a discount store and buy an umbrella stroller for $30? Well, unlike the cheap-o umbrella strollers you find at Toys R Us, Maclaren strollers are packed with good features, are ultra lightweight and are built to last, withstanding all the abuse an urban jungle can dish out. Plus, they look cool which is important when you're in Central Park.

The models. Okay, let's take a deep breath. Maclaren offers TEN models, so there are lots to review. There will be quiz at the end of this review.

Maclaren's entry-level model, the Volo (8.2 lb., $100) is a super light stroller that is a stripped down version (no basket or hood) of their more full-featured offerings. You do get a five-point harness and a mesh seat but that's about it. For the same money, the Combi Savvy Soho is probably a better deal, or save $50 and get a Chicco Caddy.

A more full-featured model from Maclaren is their "Triumph," (formerly called the Daytripper, $150) which weighs 11 pounds and features a fully enclosed protective hood. This seat does have a two-position recline, which is a new feature for this price point.

Next up is the Quest (12.3 lbs), which adds more padding, a four-position seat recline, extendable footrest and one-hand fold. Price: $200. An upgraded version of the Quest is called the Vogue (13.2 lbs)—it adds even more padding and a fully reclining seat for $250. The Techno XT (14.3, $289) is the top of the line Maclaren—it features the most padding, a new flip-down sun visor and three-position adjusting handles that ca be extended to a height of 42 inches. The Techno also has upgraded wheels and reflective trim.

Want to use a Maclaren with an infant car set? Until recently, you were out of luck. Fortunately, Maclaren now has a model (the Global, 17.6 lbs, $260 to $300), which lets you attach any major brand infant car seat. The Global does have a fully reclining seat and is similar to the Vogue in terms of plushness.

The biggest news at Maclaren this year is their first sport stroller, the Mac3 (18.3 lbs, $300). This tri-wheel stroller has 12" quick release air-filled wheels, five-point harness, two-position reclining seat, large protective hood and adjustable height handle. Very cool and we're sure to see these in Central Park, but the $300 price tag is too high for a quality "sport" stroller. Serious runners probably need bigger wheels than this, but we doubt Maclaren had joggers in mind when designing this.

One important caveat to this line: all Maclaren strollers (with the exception of the Global) do NOT have napper or bumper bars on the front of the seat. Yes, these models all have five-point harnesses to keep baby securely inside the strollers, but the lack of a napper bar will turn off some parents.

Finally, we have to talk about Maclaren's top-selling side-by-side strollers, the Rally Twin (22 lbs, $300) and the Twin Traveller (25 lbs, $350). The basic difference between these models is the Twin

strollers

Traveller has fully reclining seats; the Rally Twin has a two-position partial recline. Parents of twins rave about these strollers, which are among the best made side-by-side models on the market. Maclaren's doubles are also good for older child/infant needs as well.

One non-stroller note: Maclaren has debuted a namesake baby carrier (made for them by Theodore Bean) for $70. See Theodore Bean's review later in this chapter for details.

Our view. While we still think Maclaren is one of the best quality stroller brands on the market, there are a couple of caveats. First, while this brand staked its reputation on its British heritage, Maclaren switched all its production to China in 2001. The result? Mac fans say they've noticed a small slippage in quality, from the finish on the fabrics to the durability of some features. Maclaren insists it uses the same quality specs in China as it did when it made the strollers in England, but we still are getting the occasional complaint about Mac quality when there were few to none before. Yes, the brand is light years ahead of Graco and Cosco in terms of quality, but when you shell out $200 or $300 for a stroller, you expect darn near perfection. Speaking of perfect, Maclaren's customer service is far from it. Parents use words like "terrible" and "atrocious" to describe their customer service—getting replacement parts seems especially troublesome. Yet, Maclaren could go a long way in making parents happy by just returning messages and putting nicer folks on the phone. Maclaren has shifted its customer service among three different companies in the last three years and we're sure that has contributed to the chaos. But if you sell pricey strollers, we expect the customer service to be stellar. And Maclaren has a way to go on that count. **Rating: B+**

Martinelli These strollers are made Peg Perego. See their review later in this section.

Mountain Buggy Web: www.mountainbuggy.com. This little company from New Zealand has a hot seller in its rugged, all-terrain strollers, which have won fans in both urban areas and the 'burbs. These tri-wheel strollers feature lightweight aluminum frames (17-19 lbs depending on the model), 12" air-filled wheels with polymer rims (great for use near the beach), full reclining seats, height adjustable handles, one step folds and large two-position sun canopies. The key model is their Urban Single, which has a front wheel that can swivel or be fixed. The result is great maneuverability, unlike other joggers with fixed wheels (which limits their appeal for more urban uses). If you don't need the swivel front wheel, Mountain Buggy also offers a model with a fixed front wheel (the Terrain Single). Mountain Buggy also sells two double models (the

Stroller overload?

Whoa! Finding yourself overwhelmed with all this stroller stuff? Take a break for a minute. We realize making a stroller choice can seem daunting. Here's our advice: first, read our specific recommendations by lifestyle later in this chapter. We boil down all the options to our top picks, whether you live in Suburbia or in downtown Giant Metropolis. Second, realize that you don't have to make all these stroller decisions BEFORE baby is born. Most parents will buy an infant car seat—pair this with an inexpensive stroller *frame* from Kolcraft or Baby Trend ($50) and you've got an affordable alternative to those pricey travel systems. This will last you for your baby's first six months . . . or longer. That will give you plenty of time to think about/research your next stroller, when baby outgrows their infant seat.

Urban Double with swivel front wheels and the Terrain Double with fixed wheels). So, how much is this going to cost you? Here's the bummer: Mountain Buggy's are darn expensive. The Urban Single is $339, the Terrain Single $289. The Urban Double is $500; the Terrain Double $419. That said, they do have a weight limit of 100 pounds, so you can use this stroller for a LONG time. And parents love the slew of optional accessories, including bug shield and full sun cover . . . AND a clip that lets you attach an infant car seat to their single stroller models. (Note: as we went to press, this clip only worked with Century car seats, but Mountain Buggy is working on a universal adapter that will be out later this year). Too tall for most strollers? Mountain Buggy also sells a "handlebar extender" that adds 3″ in of height for taller parents. So, we'll give this brand our top rating despite the stiff prices. The high quality, rave parent reviews and added flexibility from all those accessories make these strollers worth it. FYI: Mountain Buggy is so new to North America that these strollers are hard to see in person. Nonetheless, if you have a dealer near by, they are worth a look-see. **Rating: A**

Osh Kosh These strollers are made by Evenflo. See their review earlier in this chapter for more details.

Peg Perego *3625 Independence Dr., Ft. Wayne, IN 46808. For a dealer, call (219) 482-8191;. Web: www.perego.com* Perhaps the biggest frustration with buying a Peg Perego stroller is simply deciding what model to purchase—this hot-selling Italian brand offers a bewildering list of two dozen different models, from simple compact-folding strollers to prams to strollers for twins or triplets. Adding to the confusion: the company rapidly discontinues models, coming out with slightly different versions only months later. Perego goes through more models than Italy goes through governments.

Yet, why is Peg Perego so popular? In a word: quality. These are possibly the best-made strollers on the planet, loaded with features to please both parent and baby. Perego strollers are still made in Italy, while other European brands (namely, Maclaren and Chicco) have moved their production to China. While the Chinese have come a long way in making a quality stroller, many parents think the Europeans still have a slight advantage in quality when it comes to fabrics and finish.

Unlike other European brands, Perego is widely available (it is even sold in Babies R Us) with opening price points around $200, even less on sale. Peg Perego's durability has made it a favorite in urban areas, where strollers are parents' primary vehicle and take quite a beating. Here's an overview of the line.

The models. The biggest news at Perego in the past year was their new travel systems. Paired with their infant car seat (the Primo Viaggio), Perego now offers a slew of travel system options. For the record, we weren't wild about Perego's infant car seat (see review in last chapter), but it has improved enough to make Perego's travel systems worthy of consideration. We'll discuss which Perego strollers are available in a travel system at the end of this section.

The "Venezia" (21 lbs., $289-319) is Perego's entry-level carriage stroller. This stroller/carriage features fully reclining seat, reversible handle, and removable boot that snaps and folds back plus a height adjustable handle. Like all Perego's, the Venezia has a decent size storage basket and stylish fabrics. New this year, Perego added a "snack and go" tray for baby to the Venezia and dubbed it the Venezia SNG. If that doesn't excite you, Perego offers a more plush carriage stroller called the Milano XL ($370, 20 lbs.), which is larger and adds a boot that has a zip-out top portion. (Memo to Perego: for $300, how come you can't add a cup holder to these strollers?)

Now, we should note right here that both the Venezia and the Milano will hold Perego's infant car seat. Or, for $20, you can buy an adapter bar that will hold any other major brand infant seat. Unfortunately, this bar does NOT work with Perego's popular Pliko strollers, reviewed next. Yes, Perego USED to make an adapter bar for the Pliko, but discontinued it recently . . . to the consternation of parents everywhere. (We wonder if the Venezia and Milano adapter bar will be next on the chopping block).

In recent years, Perego has greatly expanded their lightweight, umbrella strollers (the Pliko family). The Pliko stroller line (16 lbs) features a five-point safety harness, storage basket, full reclining seat, adjustable leg rest, and adjustable height handle, removable/washable seat cushions. Perego makes the Pliko in several versions: the basic Plikomatic ($200) has smooth wheels, while the Pliko Sherpa ($229) and Trek ($249) feature knobby wheels (for rougher sidewalks). The Trek adds a rain cover that rolls into the canopy, while the Pliko Sherpa Bubble ($249) has a detachable rain cover. New this year is the Pliko Completo ($230), which is includes a boot, rain shield and (surprise) a cup holder for the parent.

Realizing the Pliko stroller is a bit heavy at 16 lbs, Perego decided to introduce an even lighter weight model a couple of years ago—the Aria CSR ($179, 10 lbs) features a seat that reclines to 150 degrees, decent size storage basket, canopy and a five-point restraint. What's missing? The Aria lacks an umbrella-style fold like the Combi Savvy or a one-hand fold like the Inglesina Zippy—but parents seem to love it anyway, thanks to that light weight. Yes, the Aria does hold the Perego infant car seat and there is also a twin (side-by-side) version of the Aria that is 32" wide and sells for $290. Parents of twins give the Aria twin high marks. Bargain alert: readers have spied Aria's (previous year models) on sale for as little as $50 to $100 at discounters like Value City and Big Lots.

Looking for a European-style pram? Perego has several offerings that combine a bassinet and stroller—the Giovane and Culla ($400 to $550). Because these prams aren't big sellers in the U.S., they are bit hard to find.

New this year, Perego is offering a stroller frame a la the Snap & Go—the Caravel Chasis ($150) holds a Perego infant car seat or $200 bassinet. Leave it to Perego to design a stroller frame that costs three times the competition!

For parents looking for double strollers, Perego offers the Tender XL tandem ($400 to $450) and the Duette ($500)—either model lets parents of twins to attach TWO infant car seats to the stroller, which is great. The big difference between the Tender XL and the Duette is the Duette has seats that can face each other, while the Tender XL doesn't. And yes, Perego even has a Triplette stroller for a whopping $680.

Whew! Now, what about those Perego travel systems? Perego offers travel systems for their Aria ($300), Pliko, ($350), Pliko Trek ($350), Pliko Completeo ($430) and Venezia ($450). Same strollers as described above, just add Perego's infant seat. Just to confuse you, there is one additional Perego travel system, the Atlantico ($430). The Atlantico stroller is much like the Venezia, except it includes parent and child trays, as well as a boot. Parents have given mixed reviews to the Atlantico, which is bulky and has an awkward fold that insures the seat fabric gets dirty when you put it in a trunk.

Is that it? Nope, Perego also markets an entire line of strollers called "Martinelli." These models will have limited distribution (just fancy specialty stores) and feature upgraded fabrics and leather trim. We previewed this line at a recent trade show and weren't impressed—Martinelli strollers are EXACTLY the same as Perego models, just different names. What's the point? We assume this line is only meant to give specialty stores a different brand name that would be hard to comparison shop.

Our view. Perego strollers are the best you can buy, quality-wise. We are consistently impressed with how durable and functional these models are. Yet, Peg Perego's popularity has been a double-edged sword—there are often shortages of popular Perego models. The company also seems perpetually behind in production and slow shipping from Italy doesn't help either. Each year, Perego promises juvenile retailers it's going to step up production and fix the shortage problem . . . and each year, nothing happens. We wonder if they don't intentionally short-ship the U.S., artificially creating shortages to give this brand cache. And speaking of bogus cache, the Martinelli line looks like an excuse for retailers to sell Perego strollers at steeper mark-ups.

And while Perego is still hot on the East Coast, we noticed that Maclaren and Chicco are quickly catching up to Perego in places like Manhattan. Perego's high prices (especially for their travel system) have curbed some of their appeal.

So, what's the best stroller in the Perego line? In our opinion, we'd go for the lightweight Aria or the Pliko line. The Venezia and Milano are overkill for most parents. Skip the travel systems. Finally, we have to put in a brief word about Perego's web site, which was recently redesigned. Awful. Enough said. ***Rating: A***

Safety 1st These strollers and travel systems are made by Cosco. See the above review for more info.

Swan This brand is made by Baby Trend. See their review earlier in this section.

Zooper *(503) 248-9469; Web: www.zooperstrollers.com* Zooper is one of the few stroller brands to break out in the last year. Our message boards and email have been lit up with Zooper kudos—parents love their smartly designed models, with combine rugged sport looks and high-quality features. An overview:

The models. The Buddy (31 lbs, $280) is Zooper's flagship tri-wheel stroller. No, it isn't cheap, but check the specs: it has as four-position full reclining plush seat that reverses so you can see baby when pushing it, full canopy, boot, rain cover, decent size basket and (drum roll) it holds an infant car seat. Note all the extras that usually are pricey extras with other brands—that is Zooper's secret sauce. The Walk-Air (29 lbs, $275) is much like the Buddy, except it has four knobby air tires.

At first glance, you might think the Zooper Sport (24 lbs, $230) was really a Maclaren. But this stroller offers a napper bar, ergonomic handle and air-filled tires—all things most Maclarens lack. And Zooper again throws in all the extras (full boot, rain cover, basket, infant carrier compatibility) that make it a much better deal than most Macs. The Zooper Sport has a compact fold and five-position, full seat recline.

If you want something lighter weight and don't care about air-filled wheels, the zStreet (17 lbs, $200) is much like the Sport but has regular plastic wheels and two separate handles (like the Perego Pliko; the Sport has one handle). Even more bare bones is the EZ ($130, 15 lbs), which omits the napper bar, boot and rain cover. You still get a four-position reclining seat (but no full recline), canopy and basket.

New this year, Zooper is rolling out a "CoolZone" option for its Buddy, Sport and zStreet models. The CoolZone versions are designed for parents in hot climates—as such, they have light-reflecting fabric and UV-filtering mesh vents but omit the boot and rain cover. You'll see the CoolZone versions at lower prices since they omit those extras (Buddy $259, Sport $199, zStreet $179). FYI: The CoolZone version of the Sport strollers has plastic (not air filled) wheels.

Finally, the icing on the cake at Zooper this year is their futuristic new model, the Kroozer ($349). Available in both three- and four-wheel versions, this funky stroller looks like one of those concept cars you see at auto shows. It has a "magnesium encased multi-direction suspension system," new reversible seat system and height adjustable handle.

Our view. Zooper combines the best of all worlds—great features, quality, fashion and value. Yes, we said value . . . even though most Zoopers are $200+, all the extras (rain cover, boot, etc) make these strollers standout when compared with competitors. Best of all, Zooper has great customer service. And the manly fabric choices mean Dad won't be embarrassed to push this stroller.

So, where would Zooper strollers work best? We've heard from quite a few New York City moms and dads who are raving about their Zoopers, which of course is the ultimate torture test for most strollers. For urban environs, we say the Zooper Sport with its steerable, yet air-filled wheels, boot and rain cover is a good bet. For the 'burbs, the tri-wheel Zoopers such as the Buddy would be a great stroller for brisk walks or hikes on gravel roads. No, Zooper's fixed wheel strollers really aren't designed for runners, but they would work for most folks who just want some exercise. Overall, this is an excellent brand we recommend highly. **Rating: A**

◆ ***Other brands to consider.*** *Regalo* (web: www.regalo-baby.com; rating: C-) is a small player in the stroller market that debuted in 1996 but has all but disappeared recently. You might see their Chinese-made strollers in the bargain bin at a discount store, but they were nothing to write home about.

Simo is another brand on the wane as we speak. Simo's U.S. distributor (800-SIMO4ME or 203-348-SIMO; web: www.simostrollers.com, rating: B+) announced as we were going to press that they were going to de-emphasize the Simo brand this year and instead concentrate on another import, Bertini (see below). Based in Norway, Simo came to the U.S. in the late 1990's but had little success selling their expensive prams to a North American market more obsessed with lightweight models. A sample model was the Nordic Cruiser ($370)—this 35 lb. steel frame model converts from a pram to a stroller and features a fully reclining seat and full boot (an optional bassinet is $150 more). Simo's distributor says they will still sell the line through this year in North America and offer customer service/parts to Simo buyers, but it is unclear what will happen after that.

Bertini (web: www.bertinitstrollers.com; rating: B) is an Australian-designed, Chinese manufactured pram stroller line with one claim to fame: most of their models have air-filled wheels that *turn* (most Euro prams have fixed wheels). Their flagship model is the M5 ($310), a stroller with 12" steerable wheels, boot, two-position full recline seat and height adjustable handle. Yes, it looks very sharp, but parents who've used it complain about its weight (27 lbs) and difficulty in steering. Plus the Bertini doesn't take an infant car seat.

Add ***Bebecar*** to the list of European stroller companies that have failed to crack the U.S market. While their innovative models did have a few fans (the Raider A/T Plus was a good one), the high prices ($400 for a stroller, anyone?) turned off most parents. We've seen the Raider discounted to $150 online, but that was for a previous year model that doesn't have steerable wheels. As we went to press, Bebecar was in flux. Their U.S. distributor (Kidco) had dropped them and they were hoping to launch a reentry into the U.S. with a Canadian distributor.

Speaking of ***Kidco*** (800-553-5529, 847-970-9100, www.kidco-inc.com; rating: B-), this Illinois-based juvenile products company won initial fame as Maclaren's U.S. distributor before Maclaren decided to go it alone. Since then, Kidco has cast about in the stroller market, looking for an identity. Their latest offerings are called the LifeStyle strollers, a handful of lightweight models made in China that are (no surprise) Maclaren knock-offs. Example: the Kidco Finale (14.8 lbs) with five-point harness, five-position seat recline, extendable leg rest and napper bar. The price ($200) was too much for most parents and we last saw this model for sale on eBay for a mere $100. There is also a double version of the Finale for $300. What's the quality of these Kidco models? We had little feedback from parents, but what we heard wasn't promising. One parent called her Kidco double stroller "a piece of junk." One bad review doesn't mean this entire line is trash, but we'd be wary of Kidco unless you great a deal on one.

Even though the list of European stroller companies that have washed out the U.S. and Canada is long, there is one new entrant that is trying to crack the market: *Teutonia*. This German-made stroller brand (rating: B) is a sister-company to Britax and hence you'll see their offerings on Britax's web site (www.britaxusa.com). As you might expect, these strollers are well engineered but very heavy and pricey. Example: the Teutonia Y2K weighs over 30 lbs and runs a whopping $469. Yes, it looks much like the Zooper Buddy (it has fixed front wheels), but costs about 70% more. The few parents who've purchased these strollers tell us they are wonderful (easy to push and steer), despite the weight. FYI: Heritage Baby, a store in La Jolla, CA (web: www.heritagebaby.net), is one of the few retailers that carries Teutonia in the U.S., but that might change as Britax tries to expand Teutonia's distribution. Readers have spied Teutonia sold on eBay from time to time.

Finally, let's briefly mention two discount brands you might see in Wal-Mart: *Spectrum* and *Babies Luv/Snoopy* (made by Delta, 718-385-1000). You can lump these brands in with Cosco—low-quality strollers that aren't even worth their dirt-cheap prices.

Our Picks: Brand Recommendations by Lifestyle

Unlike other chapters, we've broken up our stroller recommendations into several "lifestyle" categories. Since many parents end up with two strollers (one that's full-featured and another that's lighter for quick trips), we'll recommend a primary stroller and a secondary option. For more specifics on the models mentioned below, read each manufacturer's review earlier in this chapter. Let's break it down:

Mall Crawler

You live in the suburbs and drive just about everywhere you go. A stroller needs to be packed with features, yet convenient enough to haul in and out of a trunk. Mostly the stroller is used for the mall or for quick trips around the block for fresh air.

In the past, we recommended buying a travel system that combined an infant seat and stroller. This time we have one word of advice when it comes to travel systems: DON'T. Don't waste your money on those huge, bulky systems from mass-market brands like

Graco, Eddie Bauer/Cosco, or Evenflo. Why? Parents repeatedly tell us the stroller parts of these travel systems are aggravating to use, thanks to low quality and hefty weight. Many readers tell us they usually chuck the stroller when their baby outgrows the infant seat.

Instead, consider one of the great new alternatives to the massive travel system—first, look at stroller frames like **Kolcraft's Universal Car Seat Carrier** for $50 (we like it better than the similarly priced Baby Trend Snap & Go). Snap in any major brand car seat and you've got a "travel system" without the expense. Of course, if you go  this route, you'll have to buy a second stroller after baby outgrows the infant seat (we'll have some thoughts on this in just a second).

Another idea: go for a stroller that has a car seat attachment bar. Many of the top-rated stroller brands we reviewed earlier (Combi, Inglesina, Maclaren, Mountain Buggy, Zooper) have the ability to attach an infant car seat. Yes, sometimes you have to buy an optional accessory to make this work, but it is an alternative.

But, really Denise and Alan, which travel system do you like? No matter how much we editorialize against pre-packaged travel systems, we still get emails from parents who still want to go this route. Okay, if you want to ignore the above advice, we'd suggest one of Graco's more affordable offerings, such as the **Cirrus** or **MetroLite** travel systems (both about $150). At least then you are getting a decent infant seat (the Graco Snug Ride). Please don't email us, however, when you decide you hate the stroller after three months . . . or when the wheels fall off.

What about the Perego travel systems? Yes, we realize parents love that coordinated Perego look, but since their system prices *start* at $300, we simply can't recommend them. Yes, we like Perego strollers in general, but there are better choices for the infant seat.

Second stroller. If you buy a stroller with a car seat attachment bar, you won't need a second stroller. But if you decide to add a second stroller to your collection, go for something that is ultra lightweight and folds compactly. At the budget end, the **Graco LiteRider** ($39-$99) boasts a large number of features at an affordable price.

The best mid-price stroller for suburbanites is probably the **Combi Savvy Soho**—for $100, you get a lightweight (11 lb) stroller with five-point harness, napper bar and large canopy. Note: the Soho only has a partial recline (to 140 degrees) so it is best for infants over six months old (but we figure this is okay, as you will really start using it after your baby outgrows their infant seat).

Is Grandma paying for your second stroller? The best options at the top of the market for suburban parents are probably the *Inglesina Zippy* ($250 to $270), the *Maclaren Techno XT* ($289) or the *Perego Aria* ($180) or *Perego Pliko Completo* ($230). We also like the *Ultra Savvy* from Combi ($260) in this category as well. A stroller with air-filled tires is probably overkill for most mall trips, but you could also go with a model like the *Zooper Sport CoolZone* for $200 (which has regular wheels). We realize we didn't narrow down these options to just one or two choices, but we think you get the idea that there are now many quality options in the upper-end price category for this lifestyle—try out each with your baby to decide which one is best for you.

Urban Jungle

When you live in a city like New York, Boston or Washington D.C., your stroller is more than just baby transportation—it's your primary vehicle. You stroll to the market, on outings to a park or longer trips on weekend getaways. Since you're not lugging this thing in and out of a trunk as much as suburbanites, weight is not as much of a factor. (On the other hand, strollers can't weigh TOO much—lugging a 30-pound stroller up a flight of subway stairs ain't fun). This stroller better take all the abuse a big city can dish out—giant potholes, uneven sidewalks, the winter from Hell . . . you name it.

In the past, we liked Peg Perego's carriage strollers (Venezia and Milano XL) best in this category as the primary "urban jungle" stroller. But this year, we're going to give the crown to *Zooper's Sport* (24 lbs, $230) with its fully reclining seat and compact fold. Yes, it looks like a Maclaren, but offers much more—you get a napper bar, ergonomic handle and air-filled

tires . . . all things most Maclarens lack. And Zooper again throws in all the extras (full boot, rain cover, basket, infant carrier compatibility) that cost you much more with Perego or Maclaren.

How about a pram? These full-featured and weatherized strollers are made for the urban jungle, especially for lengthy walks. Sure, they weigh 30+ lbs, but you aren't likely to be hauling this thing in and out of a trunk. Which pram is best? Well, you could spend $500 or more on a Teutonia, Perego or Inglesina pram, but we think the *Bertini M5* is a better deal at $310. The M5 is a stroller with 12" steerable wheels, boot, two-position full recline seat and height adjustable handle. Note the words "steerable wheels"—that does *not* mean you can turn on a time like an umbrella stroller, but it does make it easier to maneuver than a pram with fixed wheels.

A dark horse for primary stroller for the Urban Jungle would have to be the *Mountain Buggy Urban Single* ($340), an all-terrain model with a steerable front wheel. The wide number of accessories for this model (rain shield, boot, fleece liner, sun cover) means you can equip the Mountain Buggy for just about any type of weather you see in urban areas—albeit, at an extra price.

Finally, we should also mention the **Bugaboo Frog** (web: www.bugaboo.nl) in this discussion—the first stroller made famous by sex. *Sex in the City,* that is. When Cynthia Nixon's character in the HBO series was spotted pushing her baby in a Frog, it caused quite a stir among urban fashionistas. Turns out Bugaboo is a small Dutch stroller maker and their Frog model, while a very cool all-terrain stroller, is only sold in a handful of stores and runs $700. Nope, not a typo—it is $700. For the curious, you can see it on TravellingTikes.com.

Second stroller. While full featured carriage strollers and prams are all nice, they do have one disadvantage. They're heavy (many are 20 to 40 pounds) and most don't fold compactly. Sometimes, all you need is a lightweight stroller that can withstand big-city abuse YET quickly folds like an umbrella so you can get in a taxi or down a set of subway stairs. (Just try lugging a Perego up the stairs at a T stop in Boston). The solution: Maclaren—their strollers weigh just ten to 14 pounds and fold compactly, yet offer top-quality construction and durability. The entry-level *Maclaren Triumph*

STROLLER ROUND-UP

Here's our round-up of some of the best stroller models by the following manufacturers.

MAKER	MODEL	WEIGHT	PRICE	RECLINE
APRICA	SUPER ZAP	10 LBS	$450	FULL
BERTINI	M5	27	$310	FULL
CHICCO	LONDON	15	$70	FULL
COMBI	SOHO	11	$100	PARTIAL
	SAVONA	14	$160	PARTIAL
GRACO	METROLITE	15	$100-130	PARTIAL
INGLESINA	ZIPPY	17	$250-270	FULL
JEEP/KOLCRAFT	CHEROKEE	21	$90	FULL
MACLAREN	TRIUMPH	11	$150	PARTIAL
PEG PEREGO	ARIA	10	$179	PARTIAL
	PLIKO MATIC	16	$200-250	FULL
ZOOPER	BUDDY	31	$280	FULL

*BEST FOR: See our lifestyle categories for more info on these classifications

($150; pictured top) has all the features you'd need (including a partially reclining seat) yet weighs a mere 11 lbs. If you want, you could spend a bit more and get a plusher seat and other upgrades with the Maclaren Quest, Vogue or Techno XT.

Another recommendation for a light-weight stroller for urban parents would be the *Chicco London* ($70, 15 lbs), which has a five-position recline, adjustable leg rest, padded handles, canopy, rain cover and basket. The *Savvy Soho* (discussed in the Mall Crawl section) is a good buy at $100 and weighs even less at 11 lbs. If a stroller with an one-hand fold is a must, the *Inglesina Zippy*

($250 to $270; pictured bottom) is pricey but very cool at 17 lbs.

While it's easy to spend less money than one of these recommendations, don't be penny-wise and pound-foolish. Less-expensive strollers lack the durability and weatherproofing that living in an East Coast city requires. And since baby spends more time in the stroller than tots in the suburbs, weatherized fabrics and padding are more of a necessity than a luxury.

strollers

FRAME	BEST FOR*	COMMENTS
ALUMINUM	MALL CRAWL	ONE-TOUCH FOLD
STEEL	GREEN ACRES	PRAM WITH STEERABLE WHEELS
ALUMINUM	MALL CRAWL	INCLUDES RAIN COVER
ALUMINUM	MALL CRAWL	INCLUDES TRAVEL BAG
ALUMINUM	MALL CRAWL	HEIGHT ADJUSTABLE HANDLE
ALUMINUM	MALL CRAWL	HAS 3PT OR 5 PT VERSIONS
ALUMINUM	URBAN JUNGLE	ONE-HAND FOLD
STEEL	MALL CRAWL	SUV STYLING, SUSPENSION
ALUMINUM	URBAN JUNGLE	FULLY ENCLOSED HOOD
ALUMINUM	URBAN JUNGLE	SWIVEL FRONT NAPPER BAR
STEEL	URBAN JUNGLE	5 PT HARNESS; ADJUSTABLE HANDLE
STEEL	GREEN ACRES	INCLUDES BOOT, RAIN COVER

Green Acres

If you live on a dirt or gravel road or in a neighborhood with no sidewalks, you need a stroller to do double duty. First, it must handle rough surfaces without bouncing baby all over the place. Second, it must be able to "go to town," folding easily to fit into a trunk for a trip to a mall or other store.

This is a tough category to recommend a stroller for—there are many so-called "all-terrain" strollers on the market. Yet, we found those made by the big guys (Graco, Evenflo, Jeep) were just pretenders. Yeah, the box says "all-terrain" and they have larger wheels and shock absorbing suspensions, but we just don't think most of them could really cut it in the real world. Like faux-SUV's that couldn't handle two inches of snow, these strollers are long on promise and short on delivery.

There is good news on the Green Acres front: in the past year, more "all terrain" models have debuted, providing parents more choice. Now, the best choices for this lifestyle would probably be the Zooper Buddy or Mountain Buggy Urban Single.

The **Zooper Buddy** (pictured on page 384) is a hybrid between a jogging stroller and an all-terrain—you still get the tri-wheel configuration and 12" air-filled wheels (as with joggers), but the Buddy has a real stroller seat (no sling or mesh seat) with nice padding and other features. Yes, the Buddy is pricey ($280), but you get a raft of included extras such as a rain canopy, boot, basket and (this is important) the ability to snap in an infant car seat. FYI: Zooper makes a version of the Buddy without the winter wear accessories like boot and rain cover called the "CoolZone Buddy" for $259.

Alright, the Buddy is great, but what if you want am all-terrain stroller with a swivel front wheel? Check out the **Mountain Buggy Urban Single** (pictured). Nope, it isn't cheap at $340 but it is built to last with quality features like polymer wheels that won't rust (memo to parents who live near an ocean). We describe the Mountain  Buggy in more detail earlier in this chapter, but suffice it to say, this is one great stroller.

Okay, let's say that all those strollers are overkill. If you want to go more on the budget end for Green Acres, we'd suggest an entry-level jogging stroller like those by **Baby Trend** or **InStep** (discussed in the next section). These run about $100. Or you could opt for the **Graco LeisureSport** travel system, which combines our top-rated infant seat and a semi-decent all-terrain stroller (the LeisureSport) for $200.

Exercise This: Jogging and Sport Strollers

How times have changed. When the first edition of this book appeared in 1994, there were just a handful of jogging or "sport" strollers on the market, most of which cost $200 or more. Today, the number of offerings in this category has exploded—over 30 jogging strollers are offered on the market at last count, with prices as low as $100. And it's not just the small companies . . . the big boys like Graco and Cosco are busy rolling out joggers and sport strollers as well.

So, what's all the fuss about? Most jogging or sport strollers have three wheels and are built like bicycles—they boast large rubber wheels with rugged tread that can handle any terrain, yet move smoothly along at a fast clip. Folks who like to jog or even walk for fitness favor joggers over regular strollers for that reason.

How young can you put a baby in a jogger? First, determine whether the seat reclines (not all models do). If it doesn't, wait until baby is at least six months old and can hold his or her head up. If you want to jog or run with the stroller, it might be best to wait until baby is at least a year old since all the jostling can be dangerous for a younger infant (their neck muscles can't handle the bumps).

The prime time to use a jogger is when your baby is a toddler (18 months or two years and up), as those children seem more suited to longer outings. Hence, we have decided to put an expanded discussion of joggers in our other book, *Toddler Bargains*. (We also have more room there, as the explosion of options is out-stripping the room we have here). In the *Toddler Bargains* book, you'll find in-depth analysis of jogging stroller brands and detailed model-by-model reviews. Meanwhile, in this book, we'll give you a brief overview of the major players and a sum-up of our top choices.

Before heading out to buy a jogging stroller, consider how you'll use it. Despite their name, few parents actually use a jogging stroller for jogging. If you just plan to use the stroller for walks in the neighborhood, a lower price model (we'll have specific recommendations below) with 12" wheels will do fine. If you really plan to run with a jogger, go for 20" wheels for a smoother glide and a higher-quality brand name for durability.

Another decision area: frame material. The cheapest strollers (under $120) have plastic frames. Steel frames are seen on mid-price models (under $200)—they're strong but also heavy (and that could be a drawback). The most expensive models ($200 to $350) have aluminum frames, which are the lightest in weight. Once again, if you plan casual walks, a plastic or steel frame is fine. Runners should go for aluminum.

Check the seat fabric carefully. The best strollers use Dupont Cordura, which is also used in backpacks for its durability and strength. As for other features, go for a model that has a hand brake on the handle (the cheapest models omit this). The brake is used to slow the stroller when you are going down a steep incline. And always check the folding feature: some are easier than others.

Finally, remember the Trunk Rule. A great jogger is a lousy choice if you can't get it easily in your trunk. Check the DEPTH of the jogger when it is folded–compared this to your vehicle's trunk. Many joggers are rather bulky even when folded. Yes, quick release wheels help reduce the bulk, so check for that option.

Here's an overview of the new players (in alphabetical order):

Dreamer Design (formerly Fitness First, 509-574-8085; web: www.dreamerdesign.net, rating: A-) is best known for their great bubble canopies that provide more coverage than most joggers. Most Dreamers have aluminum frames and run $200 to $300– that's about $100 less than competitors.

Gozo (415-388-1814; web: www.getgozo.com; rating A-) offers the only tandem jogging stroller on the market–their stroller frame can be configured to carry one or two seats. The strollers (21 lbs. with one seat, 26 pounds for two) feature quick-release 16" wheels, three-position reclining seats, sun canopies, five-point harness, removable/washable seat covers, a storage basket and aluminum chassis. The stroller itself is $335 to $350, while the second seat is $135. We were very impressed with these innovative strollers.

Kelty (303-530-7670, web: www.kelty.com, rating: B+) is best known for their backpacks, but jumped in the jogger market in 2001. Kelty have a single jogger (the Joy Rider, $300) that is available with either 12", 16" or 20" wheels and a double jogger (Deuce Coupe, $400) with 16" or 20" wheels. The Kelty strollers have five-point harnesses, a unique umbrella-style fold, quick release wheels, storage basket but no reclining seats. You'll either love or hate

SPORT STROLLERS

How top sport/jogging strollers compare:

MODEL	CAPACITY	PRICE	HARNESS
BABY JOGGER III	75 LBS.	$340-400	5-POINT
BABY TREND EXPEDITION	50 LBS.	$110	5-POINT
BOB SPORT UTILITY	70 LBS.	$280-325	5-POINT
GOZO 1x2	55 LBS.	$335	5-POINT
INSTEP 5K 16"	50 LBS.	$90	5-POINT
KELTY JOYRIDER 16"	75 LBS.	$300	5-POINT
KOOL STRIDE SR 16"	75 LBS.	$320	5-POINT
MOUNTAIN BUGGY URBAN	100 LBS.	$339	5-POINT

Kelty's funky two-handle system—great for taller parents, but no one-hand steering with this one. The Kelty joggers also have rather narrow seats, which don't work well for larger/taller toddlers.

Tike Tech (web: www.xtechoutdoors.com, rating: B+) by X-Tech Outdoors is the newest of the new guys. Their aluminum joggers are sold online at BabiesRUs.com. Early reviews are quite positive—parents like the quality and prices are affordable. Sample model: the Roadster (18.5 lbs, $180) features five-point harness, rain shield, 16" wheels and reclining seat. A double version is $300. These strollers appear to be a good compromise between the ultra-cheap models (see below) and the $300+ models by Baby Jogger.

Yakima (web: www.Yakima.com, rating: A-) is perhaps better known for their bike racks and trailers. Last year, they debuted their first jogging strollers. Sample model: the Beetle ($325), which has 16" wheels, aluminum frame, alloy, rims, adjustable height handle and more. Quality is great, but the canopy is too skimpy at this price.

Zooper (503-248-9469; web: www.zooperstrollers.com) is reviewed in depth earlier in this chapter. Their models are hybrids between true joggers and regular strollers.

Whew! And those were just the new guys. So, which jogging stroller do we recommend? Let's break that down into two categories: low-end and high-end.

At the affordable end, there are really just two choices. *InStep* and *Baby Trend*. InStep (800-242-6110; web: www.instep.net. rating: B-) offers models in just about every price range, from a $90 steel frame stroller (the 5K) to a $200 aluminum model (the Elite). Baby Trend's affordable joggers (see earlier review) are sold in Babies R Us and other chain stores. The entry-level Expedition ($109) has five-point harnesses, canopy and two-position seat

Suspension	Seat Recline	Sun Shade	Pin-free folding
	✔	✔	
	✔	✔	
✔	✔	✔	✔
	✔	✔	✔
	✔	✔	
		✔	✔
	✔	✔	
	✔	✔	✔

strollers

recline. These steel frame strollers will do fine for occasional walks and other light-duty use.

What if you really want to jog or run with a sport stroller? Or you plan to use it intensively for exercise (say more than two times a week)? Or go for hikes? Then go for the gold standard of baby joggers: Baby Jogger.

Baby Jogger (509-457-0925; web: www.babyjogger.com; rating: A-) is the company that pioneered this category back in the early 1980's. Their flagship stroller is now the Baby Jogger 3 ($340 for the 16" wheels, $370 for 20", $400 for 24"; pictured with 24" wheels). Yes, this stroller is actually available with 24" wheels, the biggest on the market. This new model has a wider seat than older Baby Joggers and offers a reclining seat. Cool new accessory form Baby Jogger: an infant car seat adapter ($35) that works with three of their models (including the 3). No, we don't recommend running with an infant but you can always go for walks.

Of course, Baby Jogger has a plethora of different models besides the 3—you can find models with all sorts of wheel sizes, down to 12". While that's nice, if you don't plan to really run or exercise with the Baby Jogger, it is probably overkill. Note: Baby Jogger makes double and triple versions of their strollers. If Baby Jogger's prices sound too high, remember Baby Jogger is often discounted online.

We are still impressed by **Kool Stop's** joggers (800-586-3332, 714-738-4973; www.koolstop.com; rating: A). Each Kool Stride has a five-point safety harness, reclining seat, and retractable hood. Another plus: Kool Stop's rear wheels are angled by five degrees for improved tracking. Quick release wheels and simple fold up make the stroller easy to transport. Like Baby Jogger, Kool Stop makes both single and double models. Their flagship mode is the "Senior" ($320) with an all-steel frame, reclining seat and quick release wheels. Yes, Kool Stop may be a bit harder to find, but we think it's worth the effort. New this year, Kool Stride has a new "Kool Fold" feature for their models—basically, this is an easier one-step fold process, which is indeed rather cool. Also new this year: the "Gad About" model with 16" rear wheels and a 12" front wheel for $200.

If you want to go whole hog, check out the **BOB** "Sport Utility Stroller" (pictured; 805-541-2554; web: www.bobtrailers.com; rating: A) It's got a fully padded reclining seat, pin-free folding mechanism and "multi-position coil spring shock absorbers." Yea, it's $280 to $325 but the quality is very

high. In the past year, Bob rolled out a double stroller for $400. New this year at BOB: a $35 accessory canopy that provides much more shade and a $40 Weather Shield with mylar windows that keeps the weather out, but baby can still see out.

So, what's best—Baby Jogger, Kool Stop or BOB? In Toddler Bargains, we divide our picks into two categories: high and low end. For high-end joggers for serious runners, we liked the Dreamer Design Deluxe 20 ($290) and the Baby Jogger III ($340 to $400). For low-end strollers, the Baby Trend Expedition ($109) is good for occasional walks/hikes. The same advice for brands applies to double joggers—the better brands for single joggers are

Three mistakes to avoid when buying a jogging stroller

With jogging strollers at every places from Target to high-end specialty stores, it is easy to get confused by all the options. Keep in mind these traps when shopping for a jogger:

◆ **Rust.** Warning: cheaper jogging strollers are made of steel—rust can turn your pricey jogging stroller into junk in short order. This is especially a problem on the coasts, but can happen anywhere. Hint: the best joggers have ALUMINUM frames. And make sure the wheels rims are alloy, not steel. All-terrain strollers like Mountain Buggy use polymer wheels to get around the rust problem.

◆ **Suspended animation.** The latest rage with joggers are those with cushiony suspensions, which smooth out bumps but can add to the price. But do you really need it? Most jogging strollers give a smooth ride by design, no added suspension is necessary. And some babies actually LIKE small bumps or jostling— it helps them fall asleep in the stroller.

◆ **Too narrow seats**. Unlike other baby products, a good jogging stroller could last you until your child is five years old—that is, if you pick one with a wide enough seat to accommodate an older child. The problem: some joggers (specifically, Baby Jogger and Kelty) have rather narrow seats. Great for infants, not good for older kids. We noticed this issue after our neighbors stopped using their Baby Jogger when their child hit age 3, but our son kept riding in his until five and beyond. Brands with bigger seats include Kool Stop, Dreamer Design and BOB. (As always, confirm seat dimensions before committing to a specific stroller; seats can vary in one brand from model to model).

strollers

the same as the ones for doubles.

Which joggers are easiest to fold? That would be the Kool Stop, BOB and Dreamer Design.

Plan to take your jogger out in the cold weather? Instead of bundling up baby, consider a stroller blanket. The *Cozy Rosie* by Sew Beautiful ($50-$55, 877-744-6367 or 914-244-6367; web: www.cozyrosie.com) fits over the stroller and is made of washable polar fleece with Velcro fasteners. A similar product is the *Bundle Me* (web: www.bundleme.com) for $40 to $50. We also like the Buggy Bagg—pricey at $70 to $80 (web: www.buggybagg.com) but readers love it. It really isn't for strollers but designed more for grocery store shopping carts and restaurant high chairs.

Double The Fun: Strollers for two

There are two types of strollers that can transport two tikes: tandem models and side-by-side styles. For the uninitiated, a tandem stroller has a "front-back" configuration, where the younger child rides in back while the older child gets the view. These strollers are best for parents with a toddler/older child and a new baby.

Side-by-side strollers, on the other hand, are best for parents of twins. In this case, there's never any competition for the view seat. The only downside: some of these strollers are so wide, they can't fit through narrow doorways or store aisles. (Hint: make sure the stroller is not wider than 30" to insure door capability). Another bummer: few have napper bars or fully reclining seats, making them impractical for infants.

So, what to buy—a tandem or side by side? Our reader feedback shows parents are much more happier with their side-by-side models than tandems. Why? The tandems can get darn near impossible to push when weighted down with two kids, due to their length-wise design. Yes, side by sides may not be able to fit through narrow shopping aisles, but they seem to be work better overall.

Double strollers can be frustrating—your basic choices are low-price (and low-quality) duos from Graco, Cosco or Baby Trend or high-price doubles like those from Perego, Maclaren or Combi. There doesn't seem to be much in between the low-price ones (at $150) and the high-end ($300 and up).

Given the choices on the low end for tandems, we like the *Graco DuoGlider* best (37 lbs, $150). Yes, this one accepts not one but TWO infant car seats, but probably most parents who buy this will have an older/younger child configuration. The DuoGlider has stadium seating (the rear seat is higher than the front)) and the rear seat fully reclines for infants. Plus, you get a giant basket.

Another good bet on the low end: the **Baby Trend Sit N Stand** ($150). It really isn't a tandem, but a pushcart—the younger child sits in front while an older child stands in back (there is also a jump seat for the older child to sit on).

If money is no object, then we'd recommend the **Peg Perego Duette** ($500), a superb tandem stroller that can also hold two infant car seats. Mountain Buggy's side-by-side all-terrain strollers are also excellent at $420 to $500.

What about side-by-side strollers? For parents of twins, we'd recommend the **Combi Twin Savvy** (pictured). This 15-pound stroller is pricey ($340) but feature-packed, including removable napper bars, reclining seats and more. The Maclaren side-by-side strollers are also excellent: the **Twin Traveller** (25 lbs) might break the bank at $350, but you are getting a stroller that has two FULL reclining seats and will last for years, not months. We would also recommend Perego twin **Aria** ($290) as a choice in this category as well.

The best budget side by side stroller is probably the **Kolcraft**— their bare bones umbrella double is a deal at $60; perfect for the airplane or if you just need an occasional double for the mall trip.

strollers

E-MAIL FROM THE REAL WORLD
Biting the bullet on a pricey twin stroller

Cheapo twin strollers sounds like a good deal for parents of twins, but listen to this mother of multiples:

"Twins tend to ride in their strollers more often and longer, and having an unreliable, bulky or inconvenient stroller is a big mistake. As you suggest, it's a false economy to buy an inexpensive Graco or other model, as these most likely will break down before you're done with the stroller. My husband and I couldn't believe that we'd have to spend $400 on a stroller, but after talking to parents of multiples we understand why it's best to just bite the bullet on this one. We've heard universally positive feedback about the Maclaren side-by-side for its maneuverability, durability and practicality. It fits through most doorways and the higher end model (Twin Traveler) also has seats that fully recline for infants. We've heard much less positive things about front-back tandems for twins. These often are less versatile, as only one seat reclines, so you can't use them when both babies are small (or tired). And when the babies get bigger, they're more likely to get into mischief by pulling each others' hair and stuff."

Do It By Mail

THE BABY CATALOG OF AMERICA.

To Order Call: (800) PLAYPEN or (203) 931-7760; Fax (203) 933-1147
Web: www.babycatalog.com
Or write to: 738 Washington Ave., West Haven, CT 06516.
Credit Cards Accepted: MC, VISA, AMEX, Discover.

This web site won't win any design awards (the main stroller section is just a list of models with no thumbnails), but what they lack in graphics is made up for in selection. Baby Catalog has it all—three-dozen models from such brand names as Peg Perego, Combi, Baby Jogger and more. Prices are rock bottom, about 20% to 30% below retail. Once you click to each stroller's page, you'll find detailed pictures and fabric swatches that make shopping easy.

Baby Catalog has been in business since 1992, first as a printed catalog and now primarily a web site (don't waste your time with the printed catalog as it is only produced sporadically and the web site has more up to date stuff). The company has a good (but not spotless) record when it comes to customer service—most folks are happy with their orders. The complaints we get focus on backordered items (one customer was charged for an item that was backordered for over a month) and mis-described items on the site (where an item ships in a different color/pattern than what's displayed online). And the baby gift registry also has a few kinks left to be ironed out (readers complain about mistakes with orders, etc.).

Fortunately, these complaints are few and far between—most of the time, Baby Catalog does a good job.

Of course, this site sells much more than strollers—they also discount Avent bottles, Dutailier gliders, designer bedding and more.

One tip: you can save an additional 10% off the site's prices by purchasing a membership, $25 for a year (or $49.95 for three years). With each membership, you also get three "associate" memberships for friends/relatives to purchase items for you at the same discount. Interestingly, this is a clever way to get a premium brand that is rarely discounted online—for some reason, manufacturers who don't allow sites to discount their products don't seem to mind when Baby Catalog offers their members that 10% discount.

Top 6 Tips for Traveling with Baby

1   **AIRLINE-PROOF YOUR STROLLER.** Even if you have a stroller that folds as compact as an umbrella, you may still find the airline will ask you to "gate check" it if the plane is full (read: 98% of

the time). That means before you board the plane, you leave it outside the aircraft door . . . and pray you'll see it again in one piece. It's the ugly part of traveling with baby–having an airline baggage handler manhandle your stroller. We've heard numerous stories of strollers that disappeared into cargo holds, only to reappear damaged, trashed and worse. Our advice: take an affordable umbrella-type stroller on the road (prices start at $30 to $50), not that $200 import. That way, if the airline trashes it, you don't take that big of a financial hit.

2 **PACK FOOD AND DIAPERS, TIMES THREE.** Ever try to buy diapers at a major airport? While airports are great at catering to business travelers, families stuck with a three-hour delay are often out of luck when it comes to finding baby necessities. A word to the wise: calculate how many diapers and formula/snacks you need for a trip and then triple it to deal with delays. Yes, if you are breastfeeding, you have that part covered, but other supplies can be hard to track down if you run out.

3 **ALWAYS GET THAT KID'S MEAL.** Airlines keep shrinking the meals they give all passengers (if they give any at all), so it is wise to always request a child's meal on a flight that still serves food. Yes, request that kid's meal even if your child is still breastfeeding. Why? You can always eat the meal if you are still hungry. And trust us, hauling all those diapers from tip #2 through the airport requires a significant amount of energy.

4 **THINK "SHERPA."** Those expert mountain guides in Nepal know how to pack smart and you should too. Always consider the WEIGHT of any item when you travel. Buy a lightweight, simple car seat like the Graco ComfortSport for the airplane and leave that heavy Britax at home. Ditto for the stroller.

5 **USE A CARRIER.** The best way to move through an airport is with a front carrier like the Baby Bjorn, reviewed in this chapter. That way, you have two hands free to carry everything else. Yes, we still recommend buying a baby a separate seat and using a child safety seat when actually in the air. But the rest of the time, use a carrier instead of a stroller.

6 **PACK YOUR OWN CRIB SHEETS.** Yes, most hotels have cribs, but some try to cheat when it comes to bedding–attempting to wrap a crib mattress with a twin sheet or worse. Be safe: pack your own crib sheets just in case.

Bike Trailers, Seats & Helmets

Bike Trailers. Yes, lots of companies make bike trailers, but the gold standard is **Burley** (866-248-5634; web: www.burley.com). Their trailers (sold in bicycle stores) are considered the best in the industry. A good exam-

ple is the **Burley "d'Lite."** It features a multi-point safety harness, built-in rear storage, 100 lb. carrying capacity and compact fold (to store in a trunk). Okay, it's expensive at $350 but check around for second-hand bargains. All Burley trailers have a conversion kit that enables you to turn a trailer into a jogging stroller (although we hear mixed reviews on the Burley as a jogging stroller for its wobbly steering).

Kool Stop's (the jogger company reviewed earlier in this chapter) new trailer, the Koolite, is a departure from the usual design. They have the towing bar in the center rather than to the right or left as with Burley (Burley then bends the bar so the trailer stays centered behind the bike). Kool Stop claims the center bar helps "enhance towing, tracking, turning and control." These new trailers sell for a whopping $415 on sites like Traveling Tikes (www.travelingtikes.com).

What about the "discount" bike trailers you see for $150 to $200? *InStep* makes a few of these models (Ride N Run—$124, the DuoCruiser—$144 and the Quick N EZ—$99). What do you give up for the price? First, the wheels are molded plastic. In the past, they did not offer bicycle tires, although they've added them to all their models this year. The low priced models have steel frames and hence are heavier then the Burleys or Schwinns (which are made of aluminum). And the cheaper bike trailers don't fold as easily or compactly as the Burleys, nor do they attach as easily to a bike. A plus: they've added five-point harnesses to all their models. To be fair, we should note InStep makes one aluminum frame bike trailer, the Turbo Trailer ($200). InStep also makes the Schwinn bike trailer, which is an upgraded version of their regular line. The Schwinn has 20" quick release alloy wheels, five-point restraints, extra storage and a carrying capacity of 100 lbs.

Lastly, if money truly is no object, take a look at the *Tanjor* bike trailer (www.lodrag. com). Built to be streamline and aerodynamic, this bullet-shaped trailer is quite unique. A single seat model is a mere $455 while a

double is $495. They even have a three-seat model. Five-point harnesses are standard along with cup holders and storage behind the seat. Disadvantages to the Tanjor (besides price): rather heavy (27 lbs. for the two-seater vs. Burley's 20 lb. two-seater) and it doesn't fold.

The key feature to look for with any bike trailer is the ease (or lack thereof) of attaching the stroller to a bike. Quick, compact fold is important as well. Look for the total carrying capacity and the quality of the nylon fabric.

So, should you spring for an expensive bike trailer or one of the $150 ones? Like jogging strollers, consider how much you'll use it. For an occasional (once a week?) bike trip, we'd recommend the cheaper models. Plan to do more serious cycling, say two or three times a week? Then go for a Burley, Schwinn or Kool Stop. Yes, they are expensive but worth it if you really plan to use the trailer extensively.

Hint: this might be a great item to buy second-hand on eBay. We saw several used Burley trailers for sale on eBay (www.eBay.com) for $50 to $200, or 30% to 60% off retail.

A few safety precautions about bike trailers: you should wait on using a bike trailer until your child is OVER one year of age. Why? Infants under age one don't have neck muscles to withstand the jolts and bumps they'll hit with bike trailers, which don't have shock absorbers. Remember you might hit a pothole at 15+ mph—that's not something that is safe for an infant to ride out. And no, there is no bike trailer on the market that safely holds an infant car seat, which might cushion the bumps.

Bike seats. When shopping for a bike seat, consider how well padded the seat is and what type of safety harness the unit has (the best are five-points with bar shields; less expensive seats just have three-point harnesses). The more expensive models have seats that recline and adjust to make a child more comfortable.

One good model is the **CoPilot Limo Child Seat** ($130) by CoPilot (formerly called Rhode Gear), which has a florescent orange safety bar, three-point harness and four-position reclining seat. A simpler version of this seat is called the CoPilot Taxi for $95, which lacks the reclining seat. REI (www.rei.com) sells this seat. We've not seen any safety problems with the cheaper bike seats sold in discount stores; they just tend to lack some of the fancier features (padding, reclining seats) that make riding more comfortable for a child.

Bike helmets. Many states are requiring all children to wear bike helmets when riding in a bike seat or trailer. That makes sense, but it is sometimes hard to find a helmet to fit a small baby. One tip: add in thick pads (sold with some bike helmets) to give a better fit. Don't glue pads on top of pads, however—and adding a thick hat isn't a safety solution either. If your child cannot wear a bike helmet safely, put off those bike adventures until they are older. Be sure your child wears the helmet well forward on his head. If a helmet is pushed back and your child hits the ground face first, he will have no protection for his forehead.

Consumer Reports tested kids bike helmets in 2002 and recommended options from both **Bell** (who makes **Giro**) and **PTI Sports.** CR noted that all toddler models were a bit lacking in ventilation, but these two brands did a very good job at impact absorption. An example is Giro's Me2 helmet, which retails for a whopping $30, although we found it online for about $25 (rated for "infants"). Under the Bell brand, we found Babies R Us sells a toddler helmet for only $20 that is recommended for two to five-year olds. PTI's helmets can also be found at Babies R Us in combo packs with helmets plus pads for about $20.

The Well-Stocked Diaper Bag

We consider ourselves experts at diaper bags—we got *five* of them as gifts. While you don't need five, this important piece of luggage may feel like an extra appendage after your baby's first year. And diaper bags are for more than just holding diapers—many include compartments for baby bottles, clothes, and changing pads. With that in mind, let's take a look at what separates great diaper bags from the rest of the pack. In addition, we'll give you our list of nine items for a well-stocked diaper bag.

 Smart Shopper Tips

Smart Shopper Tip #1
Diaper Bag Science

"I was in a store the other day, and they had about one zillion different diaper bags. Some had cute prints and others were more plain. Should I buy the cheapest one or invest a little more money?"

The best diaper bags are made of tear-resistant fabric and have all sorts of useful pockets, features and gizmos. Contrast that with low-quality brands that lack many pockets and are made of cheap, thin vinyl—after a couple of uses, they start to split and crack. Yes, high-quality diaper bags will cost more ($30 to $40 versus $15 to $20), but you'll be much happier in the long run.

Here's our best piece of advice: buy a diaper bag that doesn't *look* like a diaper bag. Sure those bags with dinosaurs and pastel animal prints look cute now, but what are you going to do with it when your baby gets older? A well-made diaper bag that doesn't look like a diaper bag will make a great piece of carry-on luggage later in life. The best bets: Lands' End's or Eddie Bauer's high-quality diaper bags (see reviews later).

What's the hip new fabric for diaper bags this year? Two words: micro fiber. You'll see more of this super-soft fabric appearing as diaper bags in the months to come.

Smart Shopper Tip #2
Make your own

"Who needs a fancy diaper bag? I just put all the necessary changing items into my favorite backpack."

That's a good point. Most folks have a favorite bag or backpack that can double as a diaper bag. Besides the obvious (wipes and diapers), put in a large zip-lock bag as a holder for dirty/wet items. Add a couple of receiving blankets (as changing pads) plus the key items listed below, and you have a complete diaper bag.

Another idea: check out the "Diaper Bag Essentials" from Mommy's Helper (call 800-371-3509 or 316-684-2229 for a dealer near you; web: www.mommyshelperinc.com). This $30 kit is basically everything for a diaper bag but the bag—you get an insulated bottle holder, changing pad, dirty duds bag, toiletry kit, etc. That way you can transform your favorite bag or backpack into a diaper bag.

Top 9 Items for a Well-Stocked Diaper Bag

After much scientific experimentation, we believe we have perfected the exact mix of ingredients for the best-equipped diaper bag. Here's our recipe:

1 **TWO DIAPER BAGS**—one that is a full-size, all-option big hummer for longer trips (or overnight stays) and the other that is a mini-bag for a short hop to dinner or the shopping mall. Here's what each should have:

The full-size bag: This needs a waterproof changing pad that folds up, waterproof pouch or pocket for wet clothes, a couple compartments for diapers, blankets/clothes, etc. Super-deluxe brands have bottle compartments with Thinsulate (a type of insulation) to keep bottles warm or cold. Another plus: outside pockets for books and small toys. A zippered outside pocket is good for change or your wallet.

diaper bags

The small bag: This has enough room for a couple diapers, travel wipe package, keys, wallet and/or checkbook. Some models have a bottle pocket and room for one change of clothes. If money is tight, just go for the small bag. To be honest, the full-size bag is often just a security blanket for first-time parents—they think they need to lug around every possible item in case of a diaper catastrophe. But, in the real world, you'll quickly discover schlepping that big full-size bag everywhere isn't practical. While a big bag is nice for overnight or long trips, we'll bet you will be using the small bag much more often.

2 EXTRA DIAPERS. Put a dozen in the big bag, two or three in the small one. Why so many? Babies can go through quite a few in a very short time. Of course, when baby gets older (say over a year), you can cut back on the number of diapers you need for a trip. Another wise tip: put whole packages of diapers and wipes in your car(s). We did this after we forgot our diaper bag one too many times and needed an emergency diaper. (The only bummer: here in Colorado, the wipes we keep in the car sometimes freeze in the winter!)

3 A TRAVEL-SIZE WIPE PACKAGE. A good idea: a plastic Tupperware container that holds a small stack of wipes. You can also use a Ziplock bag to hold wipes. Some wipe makers sell travel packs that are allegedly "re-sealable"; we found that they aren't. And they are expensive.

4 BLANKET AND CHANGE OF CLOTHES. Despite the reams of scientists who work on diapers, they still aren't leak-proof—plan for it. A change of clothes is most useful for babies under six months of age, when leaks are more common. After that point, this becomes less necessary.

5 A HAT OR CAP. We like the safari-type hats that have flaps to cover your baby's ears (about $10 to $20). Warmer caps are helpful to chase away a chill, since the head is where babies lose the most heat.

6 BABY TOILETRIES. Babies can't take much direct exposure to sunlight—sunscreen is a good bet for most infants. Besides sunscreen, other optional accessories include bottles of lotion and diaper rash cream. The best bet: buy these in small travel or trial sizes.

7 DON'T FORGET THE TOYS. We like compact rattles, board books, teethers, etc.

8 **SNACKS.** When your baby starts to eat solid foods, having a few snacks in the diaper bag (a bottle of water or milk, crackers, a small box of Cheerios®) is a smart move. But don't bring them in plastic bags. Instead bring reusable plastic containers. Plastic bags are a suffocation hazard and should be kept far away from babies and toddlers.

9 **YOUR OWN PERSONAL STUFF.** Be careful of putting your wallet or checkbook into the diaper bag—we advise against it. We've left our diaper bag behind one too many times before we learned this lesson. Put your name and phone number in the bag in case it gets lost.

Our Picks: Brand Recommendations

We've looked the world over and have come up with two top choices for diaper bags: Land's End and Eddie Bauer (plus a couple of other smaller brands worthy of consideration). They both meet our criteria for a great diaper bag—each offers both full-size and smaller bags, they don't look like diaper bags, each uses high-quality materials and, best of all, they are affordably priced. Let's take a look at each:

Land's End (800) 356-4444 (web: www.landsend.com) sells not one but five diaper bags: The Do-It-All Diaper bag ($30), the Deluxe ($49.50), the Backpack Diaper Bag ($40), the Messenger Diaper Bag ($30; pictured) and the Little Tripper ($20).

The Do-It-All features a large main compartment for diapers and wipes, a clip for your keys, and a detachable waterproof pouch for wet clothes. Then there's another zippered compartment for a blanket or change of clothes, a waterproof changing pad and an expandable outside pocket for books and small toys. Outside, you'll find a zippered pocket on the other side and a small pouch with a Velcro closure. And, if that weren't enough, the bag also has two large pockets for bottles on each end of the bag. You'll also find a parent pocket to stow your wallet and cell phone and a bigger water-resistant pouch for "when disaster strikes."

Whew! That's a lot of stuff. But how does it work in the real world? Wonderful, as a matter of fact. We've spoken to parents who've hauled this thing on cross-country airline trips, on major treks to the mountains, and more. At $30, it's a good buy considering the extra features and durability. (Don't forget to check Lands End's outlet stores for diaper bag bargains).

How about those quick trips to the store? We bought the Little Tripper for this purpose and have been quite happy. It has a changing pad and waterproof pouch. With just enough room for a few diapers, wipes and other personal items, it's perfect for short outings.

In case you need more room, the Deluxe is a bigger version of the Do-It-All (about 30% larger). It has a bigger changing pad, two zippered pouches for wet clothes and other items, a zippered compartment on the outside, built-in toiletry kit and larger bottle pockets lined with Thinsulate to keep food cool or warm.

This might be a good place to plug the "Overstocks" page on Lands End's web site (www.landsend.com). This regularly updated section has some fantastic bargains (up to 50% off) on all sorts of Lands End items, including their kids clothing, bedding, diaper bags and more. You can also sign up for their newsletter, which updates you on the site.

Not to be outdone, **Eddie Bauer** (800) 426-8020 (web: www. eddiebauer.com) offers four diaper bags—the Microfiber Diaper Tote ($48), Diaper Daypack (backpack, $48), Diaper Case Bag ($48) and Diaper Day Pouch ($32). Each is made of fabric that's easy to clean and contains a removable changing pad, two exterior bottle pockets, and a detachable pocket for damp items (except for the smaller day pouch). The *Wall Street Journal* called Bauer's offerings "the most manly diaper bag available" and we have to agree—the look does not scream baby.

Besides Lands End and Eddie Bauer, readers say they've had success with Baby Bjorn's Diaper Backpack ($56), but it looked a bit bulky and cumbersome to us.

E-MAIL FROM THE REAL WORLD
Diaper Bag Find

This reader found a great diaper bag from California Innovations (web: www.ca-innovations.com) for $25. FYI: These bags are sold from time to time in Costco warehouse clubs.

"I got a fantastic diaper bag by a company called California Innovations. They have several different types but they all seem to be made from black or navy blue microfibre with insulated bottle compartments, plastic lined interiors, and lots of special pockets. The one I purchased has a removable plastic liner (for easy cleaning), a portable padded changing station, plastic "dirty bag", one insulated bottle pocket that holds two bottles, one outside bottle pocket, a separate insulated section that attaches to the bottom of the bag, a side zipper pocket for a wallet/keys/other small stuff, and snap on cell phone and pacifier holders on the outside. The straps are set up so it can be carried with a small handle like a shopping bag, used as a single or double strap backpack. A great find!"

A dark horse contender in the diaper bag wars is **Combi**, the stroller maker mentioned earlier in this chapter. Their six offerings have been surprising hits—the Deluxe Backpack ($49), Traditional ($40), Show and Tell ($40), Deluxe Tote Bag ($40), the "Urban Sling Messenger" diaper bag for $48. We like the backpack model best—it features all the doo-dads you'd expect from a diaper bag, including two insulated bottle pockets, zipper side pocket for parents, diaper changing bad and more. They've added a new backpack model this year, the Explorer ($50), with an even more masculine appeal. Backpack diaper bags from Avent ($50) and Nicole Miller ($110) have received kudos from some readers as well.

Speaking of which, those oh-so-hip **Kenneth Cole** bags are our least favorite in this category. Running as much as $90 for vinyl or $200 for leather, these bags feature fancy styling but lack some of the functional accessories and storage space you see in Lands End and Eddie Bauer. Hence, it's more style than substance. And did we mention it is twice the price of Land's End's bags?

Seems that the most talked about diaper bags on our message boards are those from **Kate Spade.** Now, we know they're popular, but we just can't seem to bring ourselves to recommend them. When they *start* at $180 and go up over $300 we'd be tarred and feathered for recommending them. So we'll let you decide. And check our message boards. Our readers have debated these bags quite extensively—including discussing fake versions of these bags sold on Ebay.

What about all those other diaper bag brands out there? Yes, you'll see a myriad of bags out there from brands as diverse as Gerber to Nicole Miller. Bottom line: stick with Lands End, Eddie Bauer or Combi for the best combo of price and features.

Carriers

Got chores to do? Looking for a way to free yourself up from carrying your little one everywhere? Carriers seem to be the products that parents turn to. Carriers free up your hands, help you keep track of your baby, even get a little exercise for yourself. But what kind of carrier is best for you? Let's take a look.

 What Are You Buying?

Carriers come in several flavors: slings, hip carriers, front carriers and frame or backpack carriers. Let's take a look at each type:

◆ **Slings.** Slings allow you to hold your baby horizontally or upright. Made of soft fabric with an adjustable strap, slings drape your baby across your body (see picture). The most famous sling, made with input from Dr. Sears (the father of "baby wearing"), is made by NoJo (pictured), but many other manufacturers have jumped into the sling market. Whichever brand you choose, devoted sling user Darien Wilson from Austin, Texas has a great tip for new moms: "The trick for avoiding backache when using a sling is to have the bulk of the baby's weight at the parent's waist or above.

Weight Limit: 20 pounds. *(Note: weight limits may vary by manufacturer. This is only an approximate weight limit. Please check the directions for each item you purchase.)*

Recommendations: While NoJo was the first, we don't really think they're the best slings out there. Readers complain that they hang too low and hurt their backs. Instead, our readers recommend the *Maya Wrap Sling* ($35; www.mayawrap.com) citing its flexibility and comfort. Others praise the *Over the Shoulder Baby Holder* ($30 to $40; web: www.otsbh.net). If you're looking for unusual fabrics so you can be a "stylish" baby wearer, go no further than the *ZoLo* sling (www.zolowear.com). The silk version (it's machine washable) will set you back a hefty $150 but wow, is it beautiful! And they'll send you fabric swatches if you have trouble deciding from one of their 13 fabrics. Finally, we liked the *Sling Baby* from Walking Rock Farm (www.walkingrockfarm.com) the well-padded strap plus soft knit fabrics make this a great option for $59 to $67.

Where to buy: Kangaroo Korner (www.kangarookorner.com) is a web site recommended by readers for their selection. They carry several brands and will even custom design a sling for you. Best of all, they offer tips and advice for using a sling.

◆ **Hip Carriers.** Hip carriers like the *Cuddle Karrier* (pictured; www.cuddlekarrier.com) are a minimalist version of the sling. With less fabric to cradle baby, they generally work better for toddlers. Baby is in a more upright position all the time, rather than lying horizontally. And like a sling, the hip carrier fits across your body with baby resting on your hip.

Weight/Age Limit: Manufacturers claim hip carriers can be used up to three years of age. *(Note: weight/age limits may vary by manufacturer. This is only an approximate limit. Please check the directions for each item you purchase.)*

Recommendations: Hip Hammock ($48; web: www.hiphammock.com) was recommended by a reader who had back problems as the most comfortable carrier she used. And she noted they can be use for children up to three years of age.

The Cuddle Karrier mentioned earlier runs $60 and claims to do everything but make toast. It converts from a carrier to a shopping cart restraint, high chair restraint, even a car seat carrier.

◆ **Front Carriers.** The most famous of all carriers is the **Baby Bjorn** (pictured), that Scandinavian wonder worn by moms as famous as Cindy Crawford and Madonna and as pedestrian as yours truly. Yep, we used the Bjorn and we loved it. Front carriers like the Bjorn are basically a fabric bag worn on your chest. Your baby sort of dangles there either looking in at you (when they're very young) or out at the world (when they gain more head control).

Weight Limit: 25 to 30 pounds. *(Note: weight limits may vary by manufacturer. This is only an approximate weight limit. Please check the directions for each item you purchase.)*

Recommendations: So why is Baby Bjorn our top recommended front carrier? In a Bjorn, baby can face forward or backward and is positioned for easy carrying. Adjusting the straps is also easy, since everything is up front. And best of all, you can snap off the front of the Bjorn to put a sleeping baby down. Imported from Europe by Regal Lager (for a store near you, call 800-593-5522; web: www.babybjorn.com), the Baby Bjorn isn't cheap (about $75 to $80 retail) but it's vastly superior to other carriers on the market. There is also a "tall" version of the Bjorn for vertically-blessed parents.

New this year, Bjorn has slightly redesigned its carrier with an improved latch system. They replaced the old buttons and snaps from years past with these easier latches. They also offer a "washable leather" carrier for $180. Obviously, we don't recommend THAT version—besides being so expensive, we can't imagine how hot a leather carrier would be to use. Yes, Bjorn has added ventilation holes into the carrier but we can see a bunch of sweating moms in Beverly Hills trying to use this thing in summer . . . and that isn't pretty.

One note of caution on the Bjorn: a recall in 1999 fixed a design problem with the Bjorn's leg openings. Bjorns made between 1991 and October 1998 had leg openings that were too large; as a result, a small infant (under two months) could slip out of the carrier. The company fixed the problem with a redesign and offered a retrofit kit for parents with the older model. If you get a hand-me-down Bjorn, make sure you have this kit (call toll-free 877-242-5676

carriers

to get one).

Another great front carrier: **Theodore Bean** (877-68TBEAN; web: www.theodorebean.com). Their basic Sport Carrier is $55 (we saw it online at www.travelingtykes.com) and has a myriad of adjustments and comfort features. Theodore Bean makes leather and micro fiber versions of their carriers as well as **Maclaren's Baby Carrier,** which sells for $70.

Canadian parents write to us with kudos for the **Baby Trekker** (800-665-3957; web: www.babytrekker.com). This 100% washable cotton carrier has straps that wrap around the waist for support. Canucks like the fact a baby can be dressed in a snowsuit and still fit in the Baby Trekker. The carrier ($80 US, $102 Canada) is available in baby stores in Canada or via the company's web site for folks in the U.S. New this year, they've added the First Journey model with lots of extra padding.

One mom wrote to us extolling the virtues of the **MaxiMom** carrier. "It does everything short of making dinner. It can be used as a front carrier facing forward or backward, backpack facing forward or backward, emergency high chair, sling and can be used for a child up to approximately 30 pounds. Here's the great part: MaxiMom is designed to also be used with multiples!" The cost: $75 to $95 depending on how many children you'll be using it for.

Looking for a front carrier that can also be used as a soft back carrier? Walking Rock Farm's **Hip Baby** ($68 to $72; web: www.walkingrockfarm.com) can be worn in front, on your hip or in back.

Finally, we also recommend taking a look at the **Kelty Kangaroo** ($75; web: www.kelty.com). This soft carrier is high quality and well designed. Sort of like an outdoor version of the Baby Bjorn.

What about those low-end carriers like **Snugli** and **Kapoochi**? We don't recommend them. Readers tell us they are uncomfortable and not as easy to use.

Where to buy: Most of these carriers are only available on their manufacturers' web sites. Baby Bjorn, however is everywhere. One reader recommended Best Baby Store (www.bestbabystore.com) online. They offer last year's Bjorns at good discounts.

◆ **Frame (or backpack) Carriers.** Need to get some fresh air? Just because you have a baby doesn't mean you can never go hiking again. Backpack manufacturers have responded to parents' wish to find a way to take their small children with them on hikes and long walks. The good news is that most of these frame carriers are made with lightweight aluminum, high quality fabrics and well-positioned straps. Accessories abound with some models including sunshades, diaper packs that Velcro on, and adjustable seating so Junior gets a good view. *Weight Limit: 45 to 50 pounds.*

Recommendations: **Kelty** (800-423-2320, web: www.kelty.com) and **Madden** (303-442-5828, web: www.maddenusa.com) have come to the rescue of parents with full lines of high-quality backpack carriers. If you want a frame carrier, Kelty offers seven models, including the Summit ($260) that has all the bells and whistles. Kelty still offer its combo backpack stroller (basically a Base Camp pack with wheels) for $140 that weighs just seven lbs.

Madden offers frame carriers such as the Caravan (pictured above). This carrier ($250) has an aluminum frame and suspension system to take the strain off your back. What most impressed us with Kelty and Madden is their quality—these are real backpack makers who don't skimp on details. Backpack carriers made by juvenile product companies are wimpy by comparison.

If those prices are a bit hard to swallow, check out the **Tough Traveler Kid Carrier** ($157, call 800-GO-TOUGH, web: www. toughtraveler.com). Adjustable for just the right fit, the Tough Traveler features cushioned pads, tough nylon cloth, and two-shoulder harnesses for baby. A comfortable seat provides head and neck protection for smaller children—you even get a zippered pouch for storage. Tough Traveler has several other models that combine great quality and decent pricing. Check out their web site recommendations regarding the best pack for your height.

So, what's the best backpack among Kelty, Madden or Tough Traveler? That's a tough one—each has great features. Readers give the slight edge to the Tough Traveler for its quick and easy adjustments, light weight and great storage. Madden makes a great carrier, but it doesn't fit smaller moms as well.

Our readers also recommend a couple dark horse backpack carriers. The first is by **Outbound**, a Canadian manufacturer (www.outbound.ca) that offers three frame carriers, the Kiddie Carrier, the Toddler Tote and the Cub Carrier with prices ranging from $139 Canadian to $219 Canadian. With the exchange rate, that makes them quite a good deal. They also praise the **Tatonka Baby Carrier** ($136) from another Canadian manufacturer, Sherpa Mountain (www.sherpa-mtn.com).

Where to buy: A good source for outdoor baby gear is the **Campmor** catalog (800) 226-7667. You can also find this gear at outdoor retailers like REI. You can find discounts on Tough Traveler's web site if you don't mind last year's models or factory seconds. As for those Canadian packs we mentioned, check out **Path Finder Outdoors** (www.pathfinderoutdoors.com) for the Outbound models. The Tatonka was available on Great Escapes' web site at www.greatescapes.com.

So, how do you decide which carrier is best for you and your baby? The best advice is to borrow different models from your friends and give them a test drive. For most parents, a front carrier is all one really needs, although some parents like slings.

The Bottom Line:
A Wrap-Up of Our Best Buy Picks

Strollers are a world unto themselves, with prices ranging from $30 for a cheap umbrella style to $500 or more for a deluxe foreign model with all the bells and whistles. The key message here is to buy the right stroller for your lifestyle (see specific recommendations earlier in this chapter). No one model works best for all situations.

In general, the best stroller brands are Peg Perego, Combi and Maclaren. For jogging strollers, the Baby Jogger is our top pick while we liked Burley bike trailers best in that category.

Who's got the best deals on car strollers? We use web sites and online coupons for the best pricing. But we have to give it to stores like Babies R Us and Baby Depot—their prices are competitive and the sales can't be beat.

For diaper bags, we love Lands End and Eddie Bauer best, although Combi offers a decent alternative.

Baby Bjorn runs away with the crown for best front carrier; for outdoor enthusiasts, check out the offerings from Kelty, Tough Traveler and Madden.

CHAPTER 10

Affordable Baby Proofing

Inside this chapter

Inside this chapter, you'll discover how to baby proof your home on a shoe-string budget. We've got room-by-room advice and several money-saving tips that might surprise you. Which devices work best? We'll give you the answers and share four mail-order catalogs that will save you time and money. Finally, learn what items should be in your baby's first aid kit.

Getting Started: When Do You Need This Stuff?

Whatever you do, start early. It's never too soon to think about baby proofing your house. Everyone we talked to admitted they waited until their baby "almost did something" (like playing with extension cords or dipping into the dog's dish) before they panicked and began childproofing.

Remember Murphy's Law of Baby Proofing: your baby will be instantly attracted to any object that can cause permanent harm. The more harm it will cause, the more attractive it will be to him or her. A word to the wise: start baby proofing as soon as your child begins to roll over.

Parents in Cyberspace: What's on the Web?

Go Make It Safe
Web site: www.gomakeitsafe.com

What it is: The online version of a Boston child proofing company.
What's Cool: This site offers an incredible array of high quality baby proofing products as well as excellent advice for new parents. They have an unbelievably comprehensive safe home tour you can take online to help you assess your own home. And the products are equally impressive. From window guards to toilet locks, its all here. The site's design is cute and easy to use.
Needs work: You'll find everything on this site at regular retail. But many of these items are hard to find, so it may be worth it to have a resource like this.

Safe &Sound: Smart Baby Proofing Tips

The statistics are alarming—each year, 100 children die and millions more are injured in avoidable household accidents. Obviously, no parent wants their child to be injured by a preventable accident, yet many folks are not aware of common dangers. Others think if they load up their house with safety gadgets, their baby will be safe. Yet, there is one basic truth about child safety: safety devices are no substitute for adult supervision. While this chapter is packed with all kinds of gizmos and gadgets to keep baby out of harm's way, you still have to watch your baby at all times.

Where do you start? Get down on your hands and knees and look at the house from your baby's point of view. Be sure to go room by room throughout the entire house. As you take your tour, here are some points to keep in mind.

General Tips

◆ *Throw away plastic bags and wrappings*—these are a suffocation hazard. And there are more plastic bags and packing in your house than you might realize—dry cleaning bags, grocery bags and bubble pack are all prime suspects.

◆ *Sign up for emailed recall notices on SafetyAlerts.com* (www. safetyalerts.com). Although this isn't the easiest site to navigate, they offer some wonderful information on safety, recalls and more. You'll find categories like allergies, child car seats, clothing, drugs and medicine, infant and child and more. In the section on infant and child we found articles on baby food, cribs, bedding, even pacifiers. For example, they listed a recall of First Alert plastic safety gates which can break into small pieces. You can sign up for email alerts in specific categories so you don't have to check back with the site frequently. SafetyAlerts is diligent about sending out recall notices as fast as the government issues them.

◆ *Put window guards on any windows you plan to open.* In June of 2000, the Consumer Product Safety Commission issued new standards for window guards. Each year about 12 children die in falls from windows while another 4,700 require hospital visits. You have two options with windows. You can place a stopper on the window frame so the window can only be raised up to four inches or you can install a guard. Window guards screw into the win-

What are the most dangerous baby products?

The Consumer Product Safety Commission releases yearly figures for injuries and deaths for children under five years old related to juvenile products. The latest figures from the CPSC are for 2001 and show an increase overall in the number of injuries. The following chart details the statistics:

PRODUCT CATEGORY	INJURIES	DEATHS
WALKERS/JUMPERS	6,200	2
STROLLERS/CARRIAGES	13,070	2
INFANT CARRIES/CAR SEATS*	15,370	6
CRIBS, BASSINETS, CRADLES**	11,380	27
HIGH CHAIRS	7,430	2
BABY GATES/BARRIERS	1,670	1
PLAYPENS	1,590	8
CHANGING TABLES	1,990	1
BATH SEATS	660	6
OTHER 10,140	11	
TOTAL	**69,500**	**65**

Key:
Deaths: This figure is an annual average from 1997 to 1999, the latest figures available.
*excludes motor vehicle incidents
** including crib mattresses and pads

Our Comments: The large number of deaths associated with cribs almost exclusively occurs in cribs that are so old they don't meet current safety standards. We encourage parents to avoid hand-me-down, antique and second hand cribs.

dow frame and have bars no more than four inches apart. The guards come in two flavors: stationary or removable. If your windows are in a standard two-story house (up to the sixth floor of an apartment building), you'll need a barrier that can be opened by

Our Picks for Best Gates

When you look at the options available in baby gates, you can get easily overwhelmed. KidCo, Safety 1st, Evenflo, SuperGate and First Years are just a few of the brands available. And you'll see metal, plastic, fabric padded, tall, short, wide, permanent mount, pressure mount and more. So, what to get? The temptation of many parents (including us) is to buy what's cheapest. But after buying and using at least six gates, here are our picks and tips:

Your best option from the start is to stick with the metal or wooden gates. Plastic never seems to hold up that well and looks dirty in short order from all those sticky finger prints. Our favorite brand is *KidCo*. They make the Gateway, Safeway and Elongate models plus a variety of extensions and mounting kits. We used the permanent mount gate (the Safeway $55-$60) which expands from 24 3/4 inches to 43 1/2 inches. We thought it was fairly easy to install and simple to use. The Gateway ($60-$80) is the pressure mounted version. The Elongate ($80) fits spaces from 44 inches to 60 inches wide. All three gates can be expanded further with inexpensive extensions.

Another interesting option for a pressure gate is the *First Years' Hands Free Gate* ($50). This metal gate has a foot pedal that adults can step on to open. If you have your hands full, this is a great way to get in and out. Soft gates have recently entered the market including the *Soft n' Wide* from Evenflo ($35). It is a stationary gate (does not swing open) with nylon covered padding at the top and bottom to protect baby from the metal frame. This is useful if you don't want to move the gate often and don't need to open the gate for access. Otherwise swinging gates are a better bet.

Finally, check out the plastic *Supergate* from North State Industries ($37), a gate our readers have recommended. This gate expands up to 62 inches and slides together and swings out of the way so you can easily clear a path. It is a permanent-mounted gate so it can be used at the top of stairs. You may also notice a new gate, the *Kiddy Guard*, that opens and retracts like a window blind. At $110, however, it's a bit on the expensive side.

Most of these gates can be found at Babies R Us.

an adult or older child in case of a fire. If you live in an apartment above the sixth floor, you'll need a permanently mounted option. Most window guards sell for $50 to $100; go to WindowGuard.org to find a local retailer near you or mail order catalog that sells these items.

◆ *Mini-blind cords can be a strangulation hazard.* Put them high off the floor or buy cord shorteners (available from many of the catalogs and web sites we review later in this chapter). Another money-saver: inexpensive "cleats" from hardware stores let you wrap up the cords, keeping them far from baby's reach.

◆ *Always use gates at the TOP and BOTTOM of stairs.* Placing a gate two or three steps up from the bottom allows your child to practice climbing without the danger. Gates at the top of the stairs should be permanently mounted (instead of pressure gates). If you have wrought iron railings or other challenging railings, consider gates from KidCo (800-553-5529 for a dealer near you, www.kid-coinc.com). KidCo makes adapter kits to make any gate compatible with wood banisters, hollow walls and wrought iron railing.

◆ *Eliminate pool hazards.* Pools are among the most dangerous outdoor hazards for a toddler; about 350 children under five drown each year according to the Consumer Product Safety Commission (CPSC). The CPSC actually studied the effectiveness of pool alarms in a report released in 2000. They looked at three types of alarms: floating alarms that detect waves on the surface, underwater products that detect waves under the surface and a wristband alarm worn by children that activates when wet.

The CPSC found that, in general, underwater alarms performed most consistently with less likelihood of false alarms (one surface alarm also performed well). The CPSC points out that underwater alarms can also be used in conjunction with a pool cover—surface alarms cannot. The wristband alarm was most impractical of all the devices since it requires a care giver to remember to put it on a child. Here are the alarms they recommended—for underwater alarms, Poolguard (PBM Laboratories, www.poolguard.com) and Sentinel LINK (Lambo Products; we found it on www.babyproofingplus.com). A good surface alarm: PoolSOS by Allweather (www. allweather.ca) Here are additional tips from the CPSC for safety around your pool:

1. *Fences and walls should be at least four feet high* and installed completely around the pool. Fence gates should be self-closing and self-latching. The latch should be out of a small child's reach.

2. *If your house forms one side of the barrier to the pool,* then doors leading from the house to the pool should be protected with alarms that produce a sound when a door is unexpectedly opened.

3. *A power safety cover* (a motor-powered barrier that can be placed over the water area) can be used when the pool is not in use.

4. *For above-ground pools*, steps/ladders to the pool should be secured and locked, or removed when the pool is not in use.

5. *If a child is missing, always look in the pool first.* Seconds count in preventing death or disability. Keep rescue equipment by the pool, and be sure a phone is poolside with emergency numbers posted. You or someone in your household should know CPR.

◆ *Keep your child out of garages and basements.* There are too many items stored in these areas that can be dangerous (like pesticides and gardening equipment). If you don't want to install a

---

Kids in Danger

Nancy Cowles, executive director for Kids in Danger (www.kidsindanger.org) a non-profit advocacy group, offers some food for thought to parents about juvenile products and safety:

"Except for cribs, bunk beds, pacifiers, and small parts in toys meant for young children, there are NO requirements in the US that manufacturers meet standards or test their products for safety. While most parents believe that if it is on the store shelf and is a recognized brand name someone has made sure it is safe for their baby, that is not the case. Voluntary standards (like the JPMA) exist for many products, but companies are in no way required to test their products to these standards. Even the mandatory crib standard does not cover all known hazards.

"Don't forget to check the products your child uses outside your home which you have carefully baby proofed. Don't let Grandma pull the old crib down from the attic, use a recalled portable crib at childcare, or any other hazards."

Kids In Danger has a brochure (Is My Child Safe?), which gives parents three easy steps to check their products for recalls and stay up to date on product safety. It is available on their website.

keyed lock to basement stairs, consider a hook and eye closure at the top of the door. This allows adults to open the door easily.

◆ *Put the cat's litter box up off the floor.* Even better: install a cat-sized pet door in the laundry room, put the litter box in there, and keep the door closed.

◆ *Keep pet food dishes and water dishes out of baby's reach.* Besides eating dog or cat food (and maybe choking on it), some pets jealously guard their food and might snap at an eager toddler. Water dishes are a drowning hazard.

◆ *Fireplaces can be a major problem.* Never leave your child unattended around a fire. Even if there is no fire in the fireplace, the soot left behind is a toxic snack. Fireplace tools aren't good play toys either; put them away in a locked cabinet. Consider buying a bumper pad to go around the hearth to prevent injuries.

◆ *Cover outlets.* You have two choices: outlet PLUGS that stick directly into receptacles and outlet COVERS, which are an entire face plate that is mounted over each pair of outlets. You can buy outlet covers from hardware stores or safety catalogs. Safety experts caution that those cheap outlet plugs are a potential choking hazard. Consider moving heavy furniture in front of some of your outlets as well. If you have a computer and other peripherals, consider a kid-proof outlet strip. We've seen such strips with covers that slide over unused outlets, and other models that keep baby from unplugging any cords (see the safety catalogs later in this chapter for more info).

◆ *Fire escape ladder.* If you live in a two-story home, purchase a portable fire escape ladder. These ladders fold up compactly for under-bed or closet storage. They cost about $100 depending on the length. We actually saw the Kidde fire escape ladder in Costco warehouse stores for a mere $28. Just shows you you can find the weirdest stuff in the most surprising places if you keep your eyes open.

◆ *Keep top-loading freezers locked.* An enterprising toddler can get a chair and climb inside if it's not locked.

◆ *Going to the grocery store?* Consider this: according to the Consumer Product Safety Commission 16,000 children under age five were injured in falls from shopping carts in 1996 (latest years' data). Sixty-six percent of those injuries were head trauma. And don't think all those injuries were from the seat. In fact, 49% fell out of the basket. Makes you think twice before putting your baby in a cart. Another concern: babies who teeth on the cart handle. Who knows what kind of germs are all over those handles!

So, what are parents to do? You've got to go to the grocery store at some point wtih your child. One answer: the **Buggy Bagg** ($65; web: www.babybagsdirect.com). Made for children from four months to four years of age, the Buggy Bagg can also be used as a restaurant high chair cover and a diaper bag. It covers the entire shopping cart seat and the handle as well. It can be inserted into the cart with one hand and is machine washable. Other options include the **BuggyBudd**y ($20; web: www.buggybuddy.com), the **Clean Shopper** ($30; web: www.cleanshopper. com) and **Baby a la Cart** ($45; web: www.babyalacart.com).

Bathrooms

◆ **Toilets make a convenient stepping stool** and can be used to reach the bathroom countertop. Take hair dryers and curling irons off the counter and put them in a locked cabinet.

◆ **Secure tub spouts or nozzles with protective covers.**

◆ **Set your hot water heater to a lower setting.** The best temperature for baby-friendly bathrooms is 120 degrees or less. As an alternative, you can purchase an anti-scalding device that attaches to showers or sink faucets. The ScaldSafe line of faucet anti-scald devices is an excellent safeguard. The shower version sells for $22, the tub spout for $39 and the sink model for $9.50. It shuts the water off immediately when it reaches 114 degrees. We found them on Efficient Home's web site (www.efficienthome.com).

◆ **Hide medication** (including vitamins), mouthwash, perfume, and anything else containing alcohol in a cabinet with a latch. Don't think that a childproof cap is really childproof. Junior is much smarter than those rocket scientists at the drug companies think he is. Keeping all items that pose a hazard out of reach is your best defense. Each year, one million children accidentally ingest medicines or chemicals. Sadly, 50 of those cases are fatal.

◆ **Get a toilet lock for all the toilets** (about $10 from hardware stores and safety catalogs). Toddlers are fascinated with the water in the bowl. If they fall in head first, they won't be able to get themselves out. Also, don't use those colored deodorant products in the toilet. Not only are they toxic and therefore inherently dangerous, but they also make the toilet water a more enticing blue color.

Baby Proofing in a Box

Don't know where to start when baby proofing? Here's a great idea: buy the Baby Safe & Sound safety kit (www.babysafe-andsound.com). This $30 kit includes a home safety video, babysitter guide book, CPR refrigerator magnet, glass door stickers, sponge tape, tub stickers, door stops, drawer latches, VCR lock, cabinet flex lock, cabinet slide lock, appliance latches, corner covers, cord wind-ups, door finger guard, bath thermometer, outlet plugs, door knob grips, stove knob covers, outlet covers and instruction booklet. Whew! You might also consider this kit as a great shower gift for new parents.

◆ *Check bath rugs and mats.* Get non-skid versions or buy rubber backing to keep baby from slipping when she starts walking.

◆ *Never leave buckets of water around, in the bathroom or anywhere in the home.* If your baby should fall in head first, the weight of his head makes it impossible for him to leverage himself out. The result could be a tragic drowning, even in an inch or two of water.

◆ *Separate your medicine and vitamins from the baby's.* You don't want to make any mistakes in the middle of the night, when you're sleepy and trying to get your baby's medication.

◆ *Don't store non-medicines in the medicine cabinet.* You might grab a bottle of rubbing alcohol instead of cough syrup by accident.

◆ *Bath rings and seats can be dangerous.* Yes, these items (which are attached to a bath with suction cups) are pitched to parents as a safe way to bathe baby. But, they are not foolproof. *Never* leave any child under five years old alone in the bathtub or with an older sibling. Remember that a young infant can drown in less than an inch of water. Bottom line: we do not recommend use of any bath ring or seat.

Kitchen

◆ *Remember the dishwasher is a fun toyland,* filled with all kinds of interesting objects. The best advice: keep it locked at all times. Another tip: never put dishwasher detergent in the dishwasher until you're ready to use it (and clean up any left over blobs after it's done). Dishwasher detergents are highly toxic.

Lock the oven door as well. However, as one reader wrote us, you can get "burned" following this tip: "My husband fixes appliances and received a frantic call on Thanksgiving Day. A mother had her turkey in the oven and had locked it to ensure that her enterprising toddler didn't open the door. Unfortunately, when you lock an oven door during use it will not unlock until the oven temp drops below a certain degree. It thinks you're trying to do a high temp clean. The frantic mother had a house full of people and turkey burning in the oven." Sounds like something we'd do!

◆ *Put all cleaning supplies and poisons into an upper, locked cabinet.*

◆ *Use safety latches on drawers with sharp cutlery and utensils.*

◆ *Latch any cabinets containing glassware.*

◆ *Lock up garbage in a place that's out of sight.*

◆ *Unplug those small appliances*—you don't want Junior playing with the Cuisinart.

◆ *Protect your child from the stove.* The best bargain tip here is to simply remove the knobs and keep them in a drawer until you are ready to use the stove. Another alternative is to use knob covers, sold in most chain stores.

◆ *Keep stools/chairs away from countertops, stoves, and sinks.*

◆ T*ablecloths can be yanked off your table* by an overzealous toddler, bringing dishes crashing down on her head. Use placemats instead when you're eating at the table; otherwise, the table should be cleared.

◆ *Get a fire extinguisher rated ABC* (which can handle any type of fire). If you have a two-story house, a second fire extinguisher upstairs would be a good idea as well.

Living Rooms

◆ *Remove floor lamps*. Floor lamps are easy for older babies and toddlers to pull over on themselves. At this point we haven't come across a way to secure them to the floor or wall, so we recommend parents remove them entirely.

◆ *Forget using that coffee table for just about anything—* remove any small objects and potential missiles. If it's breakable, it should go up on a high shelf or in a locked cabinet. Pad that coffee table with bumpers—especially if it's made of glass. See our email from the real world for a great money saving suggestion for padding the coffee table.

◆ *Anchor bookcases to the wall with nails or brackets.* Shelves present a temptation to budding rock climbers who might pull them over on themselves.

◆ *Inspect your house plants and get rid of poisonous ones.* Consult your local nursery or agricultural extension office for a list of poisonous plants. Of course, even a "safe" plant should be placed out of reach. And don't forget to check silk plants and trees to make sure leaves cannot be detached and swallowed.

◆ *Extension cords are a notorious hazard.* Use as few cords as possible and hide them behind (or under) furniture.

E-MAIL FROM THE REAL WORLD
A solution for those coffee tables

Reader Jennifer Kinkle came up with this affordable solution to expensive coffee table bumpers.

"When our son started to walk we were very worried about his head crashing into the glass top tables in our living room. We checked into the safety catalogs and found those fitted bumpers for about $80 just for the coffee table. Well, I guess being the selfish person that I am, and already removing everything else dangerous from my living room. I just didn't want to give up my tables!! Where do we put the lamps, and where do I fold the laundry?

"My mother-in-law had the perfect solution. FOAM PIPE WRAPPING!!! We bought it at a home improvement store for $3. You can cut it to fit any table. It is already sliced down the middle and has adhesive, (the gummy kind that rolls right off the glass if you need to replace it). The only disadvantage that we've come across is that our son has learned to pull it off. But at $3 a bag we keep extras in the closet for 'touch-ups'.

"Now the novelty has worn off, so I've had the same bag in the closet for a couple of months. And I'm happy to report that we've had plenty of collisions, but not one stitch!"

◆ *Make sure any TV or stereo cart can't be pulled over.* Babies also love to play disc jockey, so your stereo equipment should be moved far out of reach.

◆ *Consider buying a VCR lock* to keep your little one from feeding the tape player her Cheerios.

Bedrooms

◆ *Don't leave small objects like coins, jewelry, cosmetics, or medications on dressers or bureaus.*

◆ *Storing items under the bed is a no-no.* These are easy pickings for a baby.

◆ *Check how easily drawers in dressers can be pulled out.* Once babies can open the drawers, they may try using them as stepladders.

◆ *If you're concerned about your cat climbing into baby's crib,* consider a crib tent. The Cozy Crib Tent ($90), manufactured by Tots in Mind (call 800-626-0339 for a dealer near you), is a mesh crib topper that attaches to the side railing. It completely encloses the crib, making it impossible for cats to climb into a crib.

 Money-Saving Secrets

1 **OUTLET COVERS ARE EXPENSIVE.** Only use them where you will be plugging in items. For unused outlets, buy cheap plate covers (these blank plates have no holes and are screwed into the wall over the plugs). Another option: put heavy furniture in front of unused outlets. What type of outlet cover should you buy? We like the Safe-Plate ($3 from www.babyguard.com), which requires you to slide a small plate over to access the receptacle. In contrast, those that require you to rotate a dial to access the outlet are more difficult to use.

2 **MANY DISCOUNTERS LIKE TARGET, K-MART, AND WAL-MART SELL A LIMITED SELECTION OF BABY SAFETY ITEMS.** We found products like gates, outlet plugs, and more at prices about 5% to 20% less than full-priced hardware stores. For example, outlet covers at Target were an affordable $2.50. And don't forget to check home improvement stores like Home Depot. They also carry safety items.

3 SOME OF THE MOST EFFECTIVE BABY PROOFING IS FREE. For example, moving items to top shelves, putting dangerous chemicals away, and other common sense ideas don't cost any money and are just as effective as high-tech gadgets.

Do It By Mail

ONE STEP AHEAD.

To Order Call: (800) 274-8440; Fax (847) 615-7236.
Web: www.onestepahead.com
Shopping Hours: 24 hours a day, seven days a week.
Or write to: One Step Ahead, PO Box 517, Lake Bluff, IL 60044.

One Step Ahead has a convenient index that lets you zero-in on any product. The catalog's four pages of babyproofing products include such items as gates, "Tot Lok" cabinet latches ($12.95 for two locks and a key), and Toddler Shield coffee table bumpers. They even offer TV/VCR guards, power strip covers and appliance safety latches. We especially like their child-safe medicine cabinet. Prices are basically retail, but they've beefed up the selection.

CHILD SAFETY STORE

To Order Call: (800) 282-3836
Web: www.childsafetystore.com
Or write to: 1085 SW 15 AVE. E-3, Delray Beach, FL 33444

This great web site is organized by room, product or brand. For example, you can search for just kitchen safety items or zero on Kidco's Gateway gates. We liked the section on pool alarms, as well as cabinet locks. Sample price: $10 for the Tubbly Bubbly spout cover by Kel-Gar. Their email newsletter includes promotions and coupons, as well as other helpful tips. Our only complaint: the site is slow to load and contains annoying banner ads.

RIGHT START CATALOG.

To Order Call: (800) 548-8531); Fax (800) 762-5501.
Web: www.rightstart.com
Shopping Hours: 24 hours a day, seven days a week.
Or write to: 5388 Sterling Center Dr., Unit C, Westlake Village, CA 91361.

The Right Start Catalog seems to have added substantially to their safety items in the past years. Beyond the usual (Tot-Loks cabinet locks, stove guards and fireplace bumpers) they sell heat sensitive bathtub mats ($5.50) and driveway warning signs (Kids at Play, $11). Prices are regular retail but be sure to check their web site for special deals. They also have quite a few stores (usually in major malls across the country). Sales seem more frequent although the stores usually have a more limited selection than the catalog.

NOTE: We no longer recommend the Perfectly Safe Catalog we mentioned in previous editions of this book. We have received an overwhelming number of complaints from our readers regarding customer service from this catalog. Please see our message boards on our web site at www.BabyBargainsBook.com for more feedback from readers on this company.

 Wastes of Money

Waste of Money #1
Outlet plugs
"My friend thought she'd save a bundle by just using outlet plugs instead of fancy plate covers. Unfortunately, her toddler figured out how to remove the plugs and she had to buy the plates anyway."

It doesn't take an astrophysicist to figure out how to remove those cheap plastic outlet plugs. While the sliding outlet covers are pricier, they may be well worth the investment. Another problem: outlet plugs can be a choking hazard. If baby removes one (or an adult removes one and forgets to put it back), it can end up in the mouth. If you want to try plugs anyway, do a test—check your outlets to see how tight the plugs will fit. In newer homes, plugs may have a tighter fit than older homes. While we generally think the outlet cover plates are superior to plugs, we do recommend the plugs for road trips to Grandma's house or a hotel room.

Waste of Money #2
Plastic corner guards
"The other day I was looking through a safety catalog and saw some corner guards. It occurred to me that they don't look a whole lot softer than the actual corner they cover. Are they worth buying?"

You've hit (so to speak) on a problem we've noticed as well. Our advice: the plastic corner guards are a waste of money. They aren't very soft—and they don't have air bags that pop out when you hit them either. So what's the solution? If you're worried about Junior

How safe is Safety 1st?

If you ran a company named "Safety 1st," you'd think it would turn out products that were, well, safe. Yet we were troubled to notice Safety 1st (which controls a whopping 70% of the baby proofing market) fared poorly in a test by *Consumer Reports*. Among the products CR evaluated in a 1997 test, the majority were only rated fair and a few were "not acceptable."

How could these safety products be so unsafe? Unfortunately, no government agency tests safety products to make sure they actually work. Only after a product causes an accident or injury will the government consider an investigation.

To be fair, these problems aren't unique to Safety 1st—many companies that make "low-cost" (read: cheap) safety products suffered poor ratings from *Consumer Reports*. Many of these items are made of flimsy plastic or other materials that simply don't work in the real world.

And not much has changed since then. Safety 1st was acquired by Dorel (Cosco's) parent in 2000 and besides slapping the Safety 1st brand on car seats and strollers, there hasn't been much of a change in the safety products line.

So, what's a parent to do? Use high-quality safety products like the ones featured in the mail-order catalogs listed in this chapter. Another idea: consider calling a professional baby-proofer who is a member of the International Association for Child Safety (to find a member near you, call 888-677-IACS; web: www.iafcs.com). These folks sell high-quality baby proofing items and offer installation, or you can do-it-yourself.

safety

hitting the corner of your coffee table, you can either store it for a while or look into getting a soft bumper pad (up to $80 in catalogs—see our reader email earlier in the chapter for a more affordable alternative). Similar bumpers are available for your fireplace as well. On the other hand, you may decide that blocking off certain rooms is a more affordable option.

Waste of Money #3
Appliance safety latches

"I can't imagine that my daughter is going to be able to open the refrigerator any time soon. So why do they sell those appliance latches in safety catalogs, anyway?"

There must be some super-strong kids out there who have enough torque to open a full-sized refrigerator. Most infants under a year of age don't seem to have the strength to open most refrigerators or appliances. However, toddlers will eventually acquire that skill. One point to remember: many appliances like stoves and dishwashers have locking mechanisms built in. And, keep all chairs and stools away from the laundry room to prevent your baby from opening the washing machine and dryer.

A Baby First Aid Kit

Wonder what should be in your baby first aid kit? As a childless couple, we were probably lucky to find a couple of plastic bandages and an ancient bottle of Bactine in our medicine cabinet. Now that you're Dr. Mom (or Nurse Dad) it's time to take a crash course on baby medicine etiquette. *By the way, do not administer any of the drugs mentioned here without first checking you're your doctor. He/She will know the safest dosage for your infant.* Here's a run-down of essentials.

◆ *Acetaminophen* (one brand name of this drug is Tylenol). For pain relief and fever reduction. If you suspect your child may have an allergy to flavorings, you can buy a version without all the additives. You may also want to keep acetaminophen infant suppositories in your medicine cabinet in case your infant persists in vomiting up his drops. Or refuses to take them at all. Do NOT keep baby aspirin in your house. Aspirin has been linked to Reyes Syndrome in children and is no longer recommended by the medical community. Warn grandparents about this issue, as some may still think baby aspirin is OK.

◆ *Children's Ibuprofen* (one brand name of this drug is Motrin). This is another great option for pain relief and fever reduction. Typically, Ibuprofen will be a bit longer lasting than Acetaminophen.

◆ *Children's Benadryl.* To relieve minor allergic reactions.

◆ *Antibiotic ointment* to help avoid bacterial infection from cuts.

◆ *Baking soda* is great for rashes.

◆ *Calamine lotion* to relieve external itching. Some versions include Benedryl so check the label carefully.

◆ *A cough and cold remedy recommended by your pediatrician.* DO NOT use adult cough syrups. A small amount given to a small child or infant has been know to cause illness and death.

◆ *A good lotion.* Unscented and non-medicated brands are best.

◆ *Measuring spoon or cup for liquid medicine.* For small infants, you may want a medicine dropper or syringe. Droppers often come in the box with some medications.

◆ *Petroleum jelly*, which is used to lubricate rectal thermometers.

◆ *Plastic bandages like Band-Aids.*

◆ *Saline nose drops* for stuffy noses.

◆ *Tweezers*. For all kinds of fun uses.

◆ *A card with the number for poison control.* You may want to call your local poison control center and ask them what poison remedies they recommend having on hand. It used to be that everyone recommended Syrup of Ipecac to induce vomiting. However, many poison experts and doctors think this may do more harm than good. Find out what your local center thinks of this issue (they may recommend activated charcoal instead) and always call the center if your child ingests a dangerous or unknown substance. DON'T try to remedy the situation by yourself. Here is the national number for poison control: 1-800-222-1222. You can also get your local poison control number from the web site of the American Association of Poison Control Centers (www.aapcc.org).

◆ *Thermometer*. There are four types of thermometers you can use to take baby's temperature. A rectal thermometer, the old stand-by, is the most accurate. On the other hand, an ear thermometer is certainly convenient. Yet ear thermometers can give inaccurate readings particularly with infants whose ear canals are too small. The third possibility, especially for infants, is an underarm thermometer—again easy to use, but not as accurate as rectal ones (you'll have to use a formula to adjust the temperature reading). Some underarm thermometers can also be used rectally. Finally, we've seen a new entrant to the thermometer category: forehead thermometers. These take a temperature by applying a sensor to your baby's forehead.

When it comes to ear thermometers, certainly the most famous brand is *Braun's Thermoscan* ($50 in stores like Target). They've really improved the accuracy in recent years (although infants still aren't the best candidates for ear thermometers) and added new features including memory storage, beeping when it's done and more.

Omron has a three way instant thermometer that sell for $35 (we found it on www.drugstore.com). It can take oral, underarm and rectal temps in four to six seconds. It recalls the last reading as well.

TemporalScanner ($60) from Exegen takes your child's temperature when you merely stroke their forehead. How's that for easy? They use infrared technology to take the temperature from your child's temporal artery. We've see claims that the temporal temperature is as accurate as a rectal temp, but we'd recommend checking with your doctor first for advice on which thermometer is best for your baby.

Top Ten Safety Must Haves

To sum up, here's our list of top safety items to have for your home (in no particular order).

◆ **Fire extinguishers**, rated "ABC," which means they are appropriate for any type of fire.

◆ **Outlet covers.**

◆ **Baby monitor**—unless your house or apartment is very small, and you don't think it will be useful.

◆ **Smoke alarms.** The best smoke alarms have two systems for detecting fires—a photoelectric sensor for early detection of smoldering fires and a dual chamber ionization sensor for early detection of flaming fires. An example of this is the First Alert "Dual Sensor" ($25 to $35). We'd recommend one smoke alarm for every bedroom, plus main hallways, basement and living rooms. And don't forget to replace the batteries twice a year. Both smoke alarms and carbon monoxide detectors can be found in warehouse clubs like Sam's and Costco at low prices.

◆ **Carbon monoxide detectors.** These special detectors sniff out dangerous carbon monoxide (CO) gas, which can result from a malfunctioning furnace. Put one CO detector in your baby's room and another in the main hallway of your home.

◆ **Cabinet and drawer locks.** For cabinets and drawers containing harmful cleaning supplies or utensils like knives, these are an essential investment. For fun, designate at least one unsecured cabinet or drawer as "safe" and stock it with pots and pans for baby.

◆ **Spout cover for tub.**

◆ **Bath thermometer or anti-scald device.**

◆ **Toilet locks**—so your baby doesn't visit the Tidy Bowl Man. One of the best we've seen in years is KidCo's toilet lock ($15), an award-winning gizmo that does the trick. Check their web site at www.kidcoinc.com for a store that carries it.

◆ **Baby gates.** See the box earlier for recommendations.

The Bottom Line:
A Wrap-Up of Our Best Buy Picks

Some of the most affordable baby-proofing tips are free—lowering the setting on your water heater to 120 degrees or less, moving heavy furniture in front of outlets, not leaving plastic bags lying around, etc. Instead of buying expensive outlet covers for EVERY outlet in your home, just buy blank plates (less than $1) for unused outlets.

Most of the brands of baby-proofing products were pretty similar. Safety 1st is probably the best known, although we have mixed feelings about their products. Mail-order catalogs and web sites are good places to shop, with ChildSafetyStore.com and GoMakeItSafe.com as two of the most comprehensive.

Chapter 11

Etcetera: Announcements, Catalogs, Child Care & More

Inside this chapter

W*ho offers the most creative and affordable options for announcing your new arrival? How can you be a savvy mail order shopper? What about cyberspace—how can you use the Internet to get expert parenting advice, browse discount catalogs or simply chat with other parents? We'll look at all this, plus discuss day care hints, tips and advice in this chapter*

Announcements

Getting Started: When Do You Need This Stuff?

Most printers take between five days and two weeks for delivery of standard baby announcements. (A good tip: most printers can provide the envelopes early so you can get a head start on the addressing). You'll want to begin shopping for your design in advance, preferably when you're six or seven months pregnant. If you know the sex of your baby ahead of time, you can pick just one design. If it's going to be a surprise, however, you may want to either select two designs or one that is suitable for both sexes. When the baby is born, you phone in the vital statistics (length, weight, date, and time), and it's off to the printing presses.

Parents in Cyberspace: What's on the Web?

Stationers abound on the web, but we've discovered a few that specialize in birth announcements.

Babies N Bells

Web site: www.babiesnbells.com

What it is: Low cost stationery site.

What's cool: Here's a site that offers online samples of all their birth announcements. You can search their designs by themes (Noah's Ark, Sports) or by sex (Baby Boy, Baby Girl). Online ordering is available, the company will send free samples and they offer free proofs of your order. A reader raved about their "wonderful customer service."

Needs work: Unfortunately, there is no listing of actual manufacturers' names. The designs are all coded—what's the secret? We also found the navigation somewhat cumbersome. The samples are sometimes fuzzy as well.

Celebrate Invitations

Web site: www.celebrateinvitations.com

What it is: A discount birth announcement source.

What's Cool: One of the few sites that specializes in discounting high quality printers like Encore, William Arthur, Checkerboard and many more. They offer a free price quote on brands and have added retail prices to their price sheets. Be sure to note that Celebrate offers a 5% discount on the prices you see if you order on the web or by fax. A search option is also available.

Needs work: Since our last edition they've added samples (thumbnails and expanded views) to their site making it easier to get an idea of what you want. They've also posted prices on line—a huge improvement in our opinion. The tough part is finding the one you want. We recommend shopping around before you use this site so you know which brands and styles you want. The quality of the on line samples is not as good as what you see in a store.

Stork Avenue

Web site: www.storkavenue.com, see Figure 1 on the next page.

What it is: Affordable designer quality announcements resource.

What's Cool: Cute and affordable announcement cards for a mere $1.14 to $1.40 each. For only 15¢ more per card they'll add return addresses to the envelopes. They also offer free priority mail on all on line orders and 24 to 48 hour turnaround. We saw 27 different options for announcements from bears with balloons to antique toys to a big yellow crescent moon.

Needs work: It's a bit confusing to use the graphics on the home page. The rollovers aren't as clear as we'd like (you don't even know that's what you're doing at first), but once you get into the site, it works well with clear and simple graphics.

Figure 1: Stork Avenue offers quantity discounts for their announcements—email the site for details.

◆ *Other sites to consider: EInvite.com* offers a unique baby announcement option. They have a limited assortment of print-at-home announcements. A box of 100 runs about $15 to $18. ***Announcements by Jeannette*** is online at www.announcingit.com and offers six collections of announcement stock. The categories range from "elegant" to "doo-dads." What makes this site cool is you can order the cards printed or blank.

Card Creations (www.cardcreations.com) offers some unique options for photo announcements. Prices are pretty reasonable: $75 for 50 cards incorporating one photo and including any touch ups you might need.

The Fairy Godmother (www.thefairygodmother.com) carries some impressive designs from such manufacturers as Blue Mug. Prices are a bit higher than other sites at about $2.50 each.

AlphaBit Soup (www.alphabitsoup.com) is another site with beautiful options, both photo and regular announcements. Look for pretty bows and even vintage backgrounds on these affordable (about $50 for 50) announcements.

Afrocentric announcements can be found on ***Celebrating Children's*** web site (www.CelebratingChildren.com). Both custom designs and fill-in-the-blank options are available as well as terrific articles on different holidays and special occasions like Kwanzaa, Christmas, baby showers and even Grandparent's Day.

Money Saving Secrets

1 **ORDER 10% TO 20% MORE THAN YOU NEED.** Odds are you will forget that long lost friend or relative. Going back for additional announcements will be very expensive—most companies have minimums of at least 25 pieces. Ordering 75 announcements at the outset will be about 50% cheaper than ordering 50, forgetting some relatives, and then going back for another 25.

2 **CHECK YOUR LOCAL NEWSPAPER FOR SALES.** Many stationers have periodic sales with 10% to 20% discounts.

3 **LOOK FOR DISCOUNT STATIONERS IN YOUR AREA.** Discount Bridal Service, a company we review in our wedding books, has 500 reps across the country. While their main business is selling bridal apparel, DBS reps often have a discount invitations and baby announcements business too. You can find discounts of 20% to 40% off name brand manufacturers like Elite, Encore, William Arthur, Chase and many others. Call (800) 874-8794 for a dealer near you.

4 **COMPARE MAIL-ORDER PRICES.** At the end of this section, we list a couple of catalogs that offer affordable options for baby announcements.

5 **LASER IT YOURSELF.** Consider ordering a box of 100 sheets of specialty laser paper, designing the announcement on a computer, and then printing it out on a desktop printer. Paper Direct catalog (800-272-7377; www.paperdirect.com) has a wonderful selection of appropriate stationery. We like the "Sweet Dreams" (order #DT3041) design, with its adorable bear and toy border. Price: $24 for a box of 100. Coordinating envelopes are $19 for 50. All in all, there are a half dozen designs that would be appropriate. This requires a little more effort than the standard baby announcement but might be a fun project if you're so inclined. Another source: Kinko's copy shops sells laser compatible papers you could use for birth announcements. The cost is 19¢ per sheet and each sheet has two or four post-card size announcements. Matching envelopes are 10¢ each. With a little effort, you could do all of your baby announcements for under $10.

6 **GET CREATIVE.** Check out that do-it-yourself maven, Martha Stewart for ideas. On a recent visit to her web site, www.marthastewart.com, we saw several cute birth announcement samples. For example, we thought the diaper pocket idea was great. Using a template (downloaded from the site), you take leftover wallpaper from baby's room (or wrapping paper) and create a diaper shaped pocket. Then you slip a card with the vital info into the diaper pocket.

Other ideas can be found on craft sites like Michaels (www.michaels.com) and Hobby Lobby (www.hobbylobby.com). Or check the articles archives on baby sites like Parent Soup (www.parentsoup.com).

7 **TRY SOMETHING SWEET YET SIMPLE.** How about sending your friends and relatives a chocolate bar announcement? You can order wrappers to fit a regular Hershey's candy bar that say "He" or "She" in blue ink. Moosie Wrappers offers 175 to 200 wrappers for 90¢ each. (check their web site at www.mooisewrapper.com). Another company, Carson Enterprises (800-995-2288; web: www.carsonenterprises.com), sell the candy bar and wrapper for $1 per full size bar with a minimum of 24 bars per order. Miniature bars are 45¢ each (minimum 70). Finally, Angel Bars (www.angelbars.com) sells wrappers as well.

The Name Game: Reviews of Selected Printers

While dozens of companies print baby announcements, we think the six companies reviewed in this section are the best of the best. We should note that these printers do not sell directly to the public—you must place your order through one of their dealers (usually a retail stationary store). Call the phone numbers below to find the name of a dealer near you.

Carlson Craft *For a dealer near you, call (800) 328-1782 (web: www.carlsoncraft.com).* Carlson Craft can deliver your baby announcements in as little as seven days (although expect a 10-day wait for most orders). They cost on average $49 to $89 for 50 announcements. Carlson Craft has wonderful designs; we saw die-cut bunnies and border designs with cartoon baby clothes scattered about. ***Rating: B+***

Chase *For a dealer near you, call (508) 478-9220.* Chase's baby announcements include cute cartoons, twin announcements, and more—at very reasonable prices. Prices range from $42 to $92 for 50 announcements. The only negative: Chase takes a whopping three weeks for delivery. ***Rating: B***

announcements

NRN Designs *For a dealer near you, call (714) 898-6363.* California-based NRN Designs offers a unique option for baby announcements. While the printer doesn't have fancy die-cut designs, embossing or ribbons and bows, they do offer wonderful graphic designs. We were especially impressed with their Noah's Ark announcement—a hard-to-find design. Some of the envelopes even have coordinating graphics, creating a complete look from start to finish. NRN's prices aren't cheap, but you can buy them in any increment so you don't have to waste money buying more than you need. You can purchase as few as 25 announcements with coordinating envelopes for $3 each. ***Rating: A-***

William Arthur *For a dealer near you, call (800) 985-6581, (207) 985-6581 (web: www.williamarthur.com).* No discussion of birth announcements would be complete without the classic look of William Arthur. These higher quality card stocks feature sophisticated type styles, linings, ink colors and bows. One particular standout: a Beatrix Potter design in the palest of colors, suitable for boy or girl. Although 50 of these were $98, prices start at $75. One note of caution: if you choose the pink parfait ink, select a heavier type style. This ink is a bit too pale for delicate type styles. ***Rating: A***

If I had a million dollars . . .

Looking for a unique announcement? Is money no object? Consider checking out **Elite** (800) 354-8321) and **Encore** (800) 526-0497 (web: www.encorestudios.com). These printers have fabulous designs with real ribbons and beautiful embossing—we even spotted a die-cut baby shoe with real laces.

Encore's prices start at $73 and range up to $435 for 50 announcements. They require a minimum 50-piece purchase. Elite's designs are priced from $74 to $389 for 50, with a minimum order of 25.

If you don't have a million dollars but want announcements that make you look like you do, consider a stationery discounter. Our recommendation: Marcy Slachman of **Invitation Hotline** (800-800-4355; web: www.invitationhotline.com). With discounts up to 25% on brand names like William Arthur, Encore, Elite and more, this is one cool place to shop.

Do it By Mail

HEART THOUGHTS

To Order Call: (800) 524-2229; Fax (800) 526-2846.
Web: www.heart-thoughts.com
Shopping Hours: 8am to 5pm Monday through Friday, Central .
Or write to: Heart Thoughts, 6200 E. Central #100, Wichita, KS 67208.
Credit Cards Accepted: MC, VISA, Discover, AMEX.

Heart Thoughts offers affordable baby announcements in over 100 different styles. Their recent catalog included "classic" birth announcements with black and white line drawings, formal cards with ribbon details, and the usual cutesy, cartooned designs. All are available with quick shipment—just two business days, depending on the design (add an extra day if you want ribbons tied onto the cards).

Heart Thoughts' announcements are very affordable. At the bottom of the price range are the "classic" designs ($35 for 50 announcements); at the top are the "Ribbons & Lace" cards ($90 per 50). Included in the price are colored inks and ribbons, as well as a choice of eight typefaces. Heart Thoughts will even address them for you, plus print your return address on the back flap for an additional cost. Ribbon tying is also available for as little as $9 for 50. Shipping prices are reasonable: for example, it costs just $10 for next day air delivery.

In addition to announcements, Heart Thoughts also carries parenting books, pregnancy exercise videos, and other gift items. Although they do have a web site, at the time of this writing they did not have their catalog on line.

Adoption Announcements

Sure, standard baby announcements are cute, but what if you adopt? Many sites and manufacturers we review above offer announcements appropriate for adoptions. Here are recommended web site specifically for adoption announcements:

◆ **Artitudes,** PO Box 12408 Cincinnati, OH 45212. (800) 741-0711 or (513) 351-5412 (web: www.miracleofadoption.com). We saw a few samples of these invitations and were pleased. The sentiments are sweet and the graphics attractive. Pricewise, they are an affordable $1.25 each. Look for other adoption related items like t-shirts and prints.
◆ Another site to check out is **Adoption World Specialties** at www.adoptionstuff.com. They have several fill-in-the-blank cards for $7.50 per eight invites.

Online and Mail Order Shopping

Tired of the mall? Think those sky-high prices at specialty stores are highway robbery? Sit back in your favorite chair and do all your shopping for your baby by phone or computer. With over 8000 mail-order catalogs (and more web sites) out there, you can buy everything from bedding to furniture, clothes to safety items.

Yet before you pick up the phone (or fire up the web browser), a word on being a smart catalog shopper. Ordering from a mail-order company or web site that's miles away from you can be a nerve-racking experience—we've all heard the stories of scamsters who bilk money from unsuspecting consumers. As a result, there are a few precautions any smart shopper should take:

1 **ALWAYS USE YOUR CREDIT CARD.** Federal consumer protection laws cover credit card purchases. Basically, the law says if you don't get what you were promised, you must get a refund. Technically known as Federal Regulation C, the rule says you have 60 days to dispute the charge with the company that issued your credit card—but first you must try to work out the problem with the merchant directly. Call your credit card company to determine the exact procedures for disputing a charge.

What if you pay with cash or a check? If the company goes out of business, you're out of luck. We've interviewed some consumers who feel squeamish about giving out their credit card number over the phone or online. While you always have to be careful, ordering from a reputable mail-order or web company (like the ones reviewed throughout the book) with a credit card is very safe, in our opinion. And the consumer protection benefits of using a credit card far outweigh any risks.

2 **IF YOU'RE BUYING A HIGH DOLLAR ITEM (ANYTHING OVER $200), IT PAYS TO BUY FROM A WELL-KNOWN VENDOR.** If you aren't familiar with a business, check with the Better Business Bureau or state attorney general's office in the state where they do business. Don't buy from a business located overseas unless you're very confident in their reputation.

One caveat: watch out for sales tax. Some catalogs and e-tailers will require you to pay sales tax if they have a bricks and mortar store in your state. An example: Lands End. Now that they are owned by Sears, you'll find yourself paying tax plus shipping I virtually every state. One plus, however, you can return Lands End goods to Sears now. In cases like this, look for free shipping deals to lessen the blow on the sales tax.

National Parenting Center

Looking for more consumer information on the latest baby products? The National Parenting Center is a California-based group that produces a "Seal of Approval" product report three times a year (spring, fall and holiday times). The 30-page book reviews the latest infant products like furniture, toys, music, computer software and educational items. A one-year membership for $19.95 ($17.95 for online users) gets you this report, a monthly subscription to the "Parent Talk" newsletter, and various discounts on child-rearing products. For more information, call (800) 753-6667 or (818) 225-8990 or write to The National Parenting Center, 22801 Ventura Blvd., Suite 110, Woodland Hills, CA 91367 (web: www.tnpc.com).

3 **READ A WEB SITE'S PRIVACY POLICY.** Check on whether a catalog sells its mailing list. If you don't want to find yourself on other emailing lists or catalog mailing lists, be sure to check the company's policy and inform the company you don't want your info sold to others. To protect your privacy, consider setting a free email account with a service like Hotmail. Then direct all the sale announcement and promotional email you'd get to this address instead of your personal or business email.

4 **WATCH OUT FOR SITES THAT ASK FOR MORE INFO THAN YOU'RE COMFORTABLE GIVING.** In most cases, your password, credit card number and shipping information are the only information a company should require to take your order.

5 **IF AN INTERNET COMPANY REQUIRES A PASSWORD TO BUY AN ITEM, DON'T USE THE SAME PASSWORD AS YOU USE TO LOG ON TO YOUR COMPUTER.** In fact, you should change passwords every time you register with a new site. Keep a list of passwords and corresponding sites handy so you don't have to re-register.

6 **ORDER ONLY ON A SECURE SERVER.** Buy only from web vendors that protect your financial information when you order online. To confirm that you're on a secure server, look for an unbroken key or padlock at the bottom of the browser window. These symbols mean that the information you are sending is encrypted for safety.

shopping tips

7 **MOST COMPANIES HAVE RETURN POLICIES THAT ENABLE YOU TO GET A REFUND OR CREDIT WITHIN A SPECIFIED PERIOD OF TIME.** Make sure to confirm this before you order. Also ask who pays for the shipping on a returned item—some companies pay, while others don't. One tip: NEVER refuse an item that you've ordered but decided you don't need or want. This always delays your refund. Accept the package and contact the company about return procedures.

When you place an order, the customer service rep or web site usually tells you when to expect delivery. Sellers are required by the Federal Trade Commission to ship items as promised, and no more than 30 days after the order date. If an item is back ordered and can't be shipped within either the stated deadline or the 30-day deadline, the company must notify you, give you a chance to cancel your order and send a full refund if you've chosen to cancel. The site can cancel your order unilaterally at that time and refund your money as well.

DOT-COM GOOD VS. EVIL	*What makes a great baby products web site? Here's our list of what's good and what's bad*
	GOOD DOT-COM
SHIPPING COSTS	UP FRONT DISCLOSURE—EASY TO USE CHART OR CHARGE IS IMMEDIATELY ADDED TO ORDI
STOCK STATUS	IMMEDIATE INFO ON THE SITE OF WHAT'S IN STOCK AND WHAT'S BACKORDERED. REMOVE OUT OF STOCK OR DISCONTINUED ITEMS PROMPTLY FROM THE WEB SITE.
PAYMENT	WAIT TO CHARGE YOUR CARD UNTIL THE ITEM(S) SHIPS. ONLY CHARGE FOR ITEMS SENT ON PARTIAL ORDERS.*
CONTACT INFORMATION	EASY TO FIND BUTTON LEADS YOU TO PHONE NUMBERS, EMAIL AND PHYSICAL ADDRESS.
REFUNDS	IMMEDIATE CREDITS WHEN ITEMS ARE RETURNED OR ORDERS ARE CANCELLED.
TRACKING	EASY TRACKING VIA WEB SITE USING A TRACKING NUMBER OR CODE. TRACKING IS ALWAYS AVAILABLE
EXCUSES	NONE. WHEN THEY SCREW UP THEY ADMIT IT, APOLOGIZE AND CORRECT THE PROBLEM.
CUSTOMER SERVICE	QUICK REPLIES TO EMAIL QUERIES, LIVE CHAT, AND LIVE HUMANS ANSWERING PHONES PROMPTLY

* Federal law does NOT prohibit mail order companies from charging a c

8 **ALWAYS KEEP ALL INVOICES, RECEIPTS, AND ORDER CONFIRMATIONS.** Inspect all packages thoroughly upon arrival and keep the original packing, just in case you decide to return the item. For equipment, keep all boxes, documentation and instructions for at least 30 days. When purchasing clothing, wash the items immediately following the care label instructions. That way you can confirm the item does not shrink, etc.

9 **KEEP A LOG OF WHOM YOU SPOKE TO AT THE COMPANY.** Get any names and order confirmation numbers and keep them in a safe place. If you order online, print out any order confirmations or email receipts. The key issue: record the DATE when you ordered the item and estimated shipping times. That way you can track down overdue items that might have been backordered.

10 **CONFIRM DELIVERY METHODS.** Some companies use United Parcel Service to deliver merchandise. The prob-

---

Or one you want to take a rocket launcher to?

BAD DOT-COM

NO MENTION OF COST UNTIL YOU STEP ALL THE WAY THROUGH OR GO THROUGH SEVERAL STEP REGISTRATION PROCESS.

NO INFORMATION. THEY LET YOU PLACE THE ORDER EVEN IF THEY ARE OUT OF STOCK THEN TAKE DAYS/WEEKS/NEVER TO TELL YOU THE ITEM IS BACK ORDERED. NEVER SEEM TO REMOVE OUT OF STOCK OR DISCONTINUED ITEMS FROM THE SITE.

CHARGE YOUR CARD IMMEDIATELY WHETHER THE ITEM SHIPS OR NOT. WORSE CASE SCENARIO: THE ITEM YOU WANT IS NEVER SHIPPED, FORCING YOU TO ARGUE WITH THE SITE OVER A REFUND.

WHERE IS IT? CAN'T FIND ANY BUTTON FOR CUSTOMER SERVICE THAT GIVES PHONE NUMBERS OR ADDRESSES. SOMETIMES THE ONLY WAY TO CONTACT ANYONE IS TO SEND AN EMAIL TO AN UNKNOWN HUMAN.

ALL YOU GET IS FOOT DRAGGING AND EXCUSES, THEN WEEKS OR MONTHS GO BY. CUSTOMER IS FORCED TO DISPUTE CHARGE WITH CREDIT CARD COMPANY.

NO TRACKING NUMBER OR THE NUMBER NEVER WORKS. TRACKING FUNCTION IS ALWAYS DOWN.

ANYTHING YOU CAN THINK OF: IT'S THE SUPPLIER'S FAULT, THE WAREHOUSE IS HAVING PROBLEMS, THEIR DOG ATE YOUR ORDER, ETC.

WHAT SERVICE? EMAILS GO UNANSWERED, PHONE CALLS TO CUSTOMER SERVICE REQUIRE ONE HOUR WAITS ON HOLD.

before shipping goods. The best dot-coms only charge when they ship.

lem? UPS can't deliver to post office boxes and may require you to be present when the package is delivered. If you're not at home, they leave a call slip, and you've got to go to the nearest UPS office (which could be a long drive) to pick up the item. A possible solution: give your work address and specify any floor, suite number, or building location for the delivery. Or you could request delivery by the U.S. Postal Service (USPS). The downside to the USPS: most packages that go via parcel post or first class mail do NOT have tracking numbers. If it's an expensive purchase (say, over $50), request shipping via a method that can be tracked. Remember, most catalogs and many web sites ship only to the U.S. and sometimes Canada. Folks outside North America may be out of luck.

11 **THE TIME REQUIRED FOR SHIPPING WILL VARY WIDELY.** Some companies offer two to three-day delivery, while others may take weeks. Customized items (like monogrammed bedding) take the longest. As for the cost, mail-order catalogs use a variety of methods to determine shipping charges. Some charge a flat fee, while others use a sliding scale based on the dollar amount of the order or the weight of the package. Please note that mail order prices we quote in this book do not include shipping.

12 **USE THAT 24-HOUR FAX NUMBER.** Not all catalogs have operators standing by around the clock. However, many have fax numbers that you can use to place an order at any time. When you fax, request the company call you back to confirm they received the order.

13 **NEARLY ALL MAIL-ORDER CATALOGS ARE FREE FOR THE ASKING.** Even though some have a price printed on the cover, we've never had to pay for one.

14 **BE PREPARED TO WAIT.** Some catalogs take weeks to arrive, so plan ahead. Don't wait until baby arrives to request catalogs that look interesting. While you're waiting, you can always check out the catalog's web site. Not all have online shopping, but you can usually browse through some items, learn about specials, etc.

15 **GET A COPY OF WHOLESALE BY MAIL.** If you're serious about mail order shopping, you need *Wholesale By Mail* (by the Gail Bradney, $20, HarperPerrenial). This thick book (available in bookstores nationwide) gives mail order sources for just about anything you need to buy.

General Baby Product Catalogs

ONE STEP AHEAD

To Order Call: (800) 274-8440. Web: www.onestepahead.com
Shopping Hours: 24 hours a day, seven days a week.
Or write to: P.O. Box 517, Lake Bluff, IL 60044
Credit Cards Accepted: MC, VISA, AMEX, Optima.
Outlet store: Deerfield, IL (847) 714-1940

Illinois-based One Step Ahead is a jack-of-all-trades catalog that covers everything from clothes to toys, car seats to organizational items. Similar to the Right Start catalog, One Step Ahead has a slightly heavier emphasis on around-the-house items, as well as clothing, shoes, and linens. We also saw baby monitors, nursery decor, carriers, and thermometers, including many of the brand names we review in this book. The catalog is easy to use and features large pictures and helpful graphics. The customer service and delivery from this catalog is above average.

RIGHT START CATALOG

To Order Call: (800) LITTLE-1 (800-548-8531); Web: www.rightstart.com
Shopping Hours: 24 hours a day, seven days a week.
Or write to: PO Box 1259, Camp Hill, PA, 17011.
Credit Cards Accepted: MC, VISA, AMEX, Discover.
Retail stores: The Right Start has 60+ retail stores in major malls; call the above number for a location near you.

Is it a store? A catalog? A website? Actually, all of the above—the Right Start has built an empire by selling high-quality baby products like Perego high chairs, Britax car seats and more. The only bummer: prices are typically full retail, although sometimes the stores do have sales. New this year, we see an increased emphasis on educational toys and car seats. What we like best about the Right Start is their emphasis on cutting-edge products—if it's hip and new, you'll probably see it in their stores or catalog first. Even if you don't buy anything at the stores, it's nice to see, touch and try-out products in person.

Top 5 Things You Didn't Know You Could Do with the Web as a Parent-To-Be

I **GET YOUR FREE BABY NAMES HERE.** Used to be, in the old days, expectant parents had to go to the library or a book

shopping tips

store and pick up a baby name book. If you were looking for something unusual, you probably had to make it up yourself because you didn't have access to a wide variety of names beyond the usual Michael and Jennifer. But today, forget those giant tomes. You can check out a myriad of free web sites with baby name suggestions.

One of the top sites to visit is **Babynames.com** (www.babynames.com). Here you can search alphabetically or by meaning, vote your opinion of different names and even make "name art" (whatever that means). The site is free, but for $19 the site will even pick names for you! That's right, you tell them what kinds of names you like and they'll develop a list of six for you. We're sure you can handle this on your own. Don't forget to check out their message boards, especially ones like "unusual names."

Sites like **Parent Soup** (www.parentsoup.com), **Parenthood Web** (www.parenthoodweb.com), **Baby Center** (www.babycenter.com), and **Baby Zone** (www.babyzone.com) have baby name sections as well. For unique names we found a site called **Alphabette Zoope** (www.zoope.com). And the Social Security Administration has several reports on most popular names from the 20th Century. To find these reports, go to the **Social Security Administration's** web site at www.ssa.gov. Once there, enter a search for Note 139 (the name of the reports). You'll get a list of 15 reports organized by date. No surprise, but when we looked up most popular names for 1900 to 1910 topping the list was John and Mary. But names like Mildred, Bessie, and Viola were interesting to see as well. Try finding a Mildred at a daycare center these days.

2 **RECALLS AS THEY HAPPEN.** Tired of hearing only a couple words on the nightly news about a serious recall of car seats, playpens or toys? Want the details and fast? Consider a couple options. The **Consumer Product Safety Commission** (cpsc.gov) has a great web site you can use to look up past recalls. But even better, you can sign up to have recall info immediately emailed to you as it is released to the public. Plus you get more details on the recall (was it life threatening, was anyone injured or killed as a result, was it voluntary or did the company have to be forced to recall the item, how many items were sold, what kinds of remedies are available like retrofit kits, how to contact the manufacturer and more).

A similar service is offered by **Safety Alerts** (www.safetyalerts.com). They add in other topics like food allergy recalls, drug and medicine recalls and more. Both web sites allow you to report a problem with a baby product as well. We highly recommend that if you have discovered a problem with a baby product you report it to the CPSC as soon as possible.

3 **MAKE NEW (PREGNANT) FRIENDS.** If you're looking for other parents in the same situation as you, then the Internet has the answer. Back in the early days of the Internet, there were mailing lists. You signed up to be on a mailing list with a group of other parents whose babies were due in the same month. The only disadvantage to the mailing lists: every single email anyone in the group sent came to your address. This means you could get quite a bit of email. Today, you can also join "expecting clubs" or visit message board. All these options are organized by due date and the plus is you can get involved when you want to without getting oodles of email. *Parents Place* (www.parentsplace.com), *Parent Soup* (www.parentsoup.com), *ePregnancy* (www.epregnancy.com) and many of the large baby sites we review later in this chapter have message boards as well. Although they aren't organized by due date, we have our own message boards at www.BabyBargainsBook.com. You can post questions or comments on a variety of topics.

4 **COUPONS FOR SPECIAL DEALS.** The Internet has quite an array of sites whose sole goal in life is to find coupons and special deals. *Amazing Bargains* (www.amazingbargains.com), *Bizrate* (www.bizrate.com) and *Total Deals* (www.totaldeals.com) are just a few of the options out there. Check Chapter 6 for details.

5 **COMPARE PRICES AT THE CLICK OF YOUR MOUSE.** Consider using shopping bots to help you find great deals. Shopping bots are merely search engines that compare prices on the same product from different sites. Plug in a stroller brand and model, for example, and the bot will find every appearance of that item on the web and the cost. You then click on the site with the best price to buy or research further. Some of the most common shopping bots include: *My Simon* (www.mysimon.com), *Shop Best* (www.shopbest.com), *Smart Bots* (www.smartbots.com), *Price Scan* (www.pricescan.com), and *Deal Time* (www.dealtime.com).

 Parents in Cyberspace

Baby Center
Web site: www.babycenter.com
What it is: Baby information and shopping site.
What's cool: Right off the bat when you pull up Babycenter.com, you'll be able to check on your baby's development (before or after birth). It's a neat idea to pull you into the site which emphasizes its articles and tips with general topic areas like "prepregnancy," "tod-

dler" and more. The "Shop at our store" area leads you off to an easy-to-navigate page with every product area imaginable. They also list weekly specials, clearances and membership info. We like the clear shipping button ($5 on most orders), the links to the gift registry and new items and the variety of the most popular products.

Needs work: No matter how hard we looked, we couldn't find much to complaint about on Baby Center's web site. They have a well organized, easy-to-use site with a wide selection of items. If there is one caveat to their online store, it would have to be selection. Compared to BabiesRUs.com, Baby Center simply doesn't stock the variety you see elsewhere.

Baby Style

Web site: www.babystyle.com

What it is: Estyle.com's baby oriented off shoot.

What's cool: Estyle has always tried to position themselves as a hip, upper end site catering to style conscious folks. And that carries through to their attractive baby products web site. You'll see high dollar designers and manufacturers like Wendy Belissimo (bedding), DKNY baby (clothing), and Emmaljunga (strollers) to name a few. Navigation on the site is simple and clear.

Needs work: In many categories, this web site has only a few items available. The ads from manufacturers can be a bit irritating although they've tried to make them discreet. Prices are regular retail meaning that some items are quite expensive but they have an extensive sales page for each category.

◆ *Other sites:* There are a myriad of web sites targeting new and expecting parents. One of the more promising entries into the market is *Baby Ant* (www.babyant.com), a whimsical site with items ranging from safety gates to humidifiers to clothing.

Baby Super Center (www.babysupercenter.com) offers more than 17,000 baby products. Their site has a newsletter, assembly tips and news articles on pregnancy, childbirth and children.

A less sophisticated site, *Baby Products Online* (www. babyproductsonline.com) offers extensive line listings of products by brand, age, price and category. They even sell all terrain vehicles (a mere $1789). They offer free shipping within the U.S. *Baby Bundle* (www.babybundle.com) on the other hand, has a more limited selection and a more upscale price range. We saw a bassinet set, for example, for almost $500!

Specializing in the more popular mass market brands like Graco strollers and Cosco car seats, *Baby Super Mall* (www.babysupermall.com) offers closeouts mixed in with regular priced merchandise. They also carry bedding, clothing and toys. *Just Babies* (www.justbabies.com) is another general site carrying everything from maternity clothes to breast pumps to crib bedding and more.

Baby Universe (www.babyuniverse.com) is a pleasing site with products for health, safety, diapering, feeding and much more. In fact, they cover over 15 different topics. Likewise, *Baby Age* (www.babyage.com) stocks an amazing assortment of products. Users can peruse baby bathtubs, playpens, even kid size rockers and potty seats. Check their specials for deals. We saw an On My Way Position Right infant seat on sale for $55 (regularly $70 to $80).

BabyPressConference.com broadcasts live, streaming Web video of your newborn right from the hospital. The webcast is free; BabyPressConference.com makes its money by selling copies of the webcast to family members or a digital picture of the newborn. The site also owns UrbanBaby (www.urbanbaby.com) which has resource guides and an online store.

◆ *All purpose sites with good baby sections:* Many web sites offer a few items to parents shopping for baby products, but one of the best is *Overstock.com* (www.overstock. com). They sell exactly what it sounds like: overstocks and clearance items. We saw accessories, clothing, and bedding from makers like NoJo. An Amy Coe duvet set was a mere $166. Recently, we noticed their stock of baby items was low, so check back frequently. How do they get such deals? You've probably heard about the flame-outs of so many baby e-tailers in recent months. These guys failed at trying to sell juvenile products at low prices. While that's bad news for consumers who enjoyed the low prices, in the short term, you can often find deals on liquidator's sites like Overstock and another site to watch, *Smart Bargains* (www.smartbargains.com).

◆ *Bricks and Clicks.* These are web sites that have both real stores and great cyber sites. Examples include Baby Depot, Babies R Us (part of Amazon.com), Walmart, Kmart, and Target. Many of these sites are reviewed in detail in Chapter 2. Each of the major discounters include a baby section on their general site. These sections are small and include mainly mass market brands. The best bets: *Baby Depot* (www.babydepot.com) and *Babies R Us* (www. babiesrus.com).

◆ *Feedback sites.* With the myriad of baby product web sites out there, how do you really know who's reputable? Which sites have high satisfaction ratings from consumers? Feedback sites are a great way to take a quick pulse on which e-tailers to trust. One example is *Planet Feedback* (www. planetfeedback.com) where you can look up company report cards for various sites in their

shopping tips

"news and ratings" section. You can also read "shared letters" from consumers that either complain about or praise companies. To test the site, we looked up the ratings on the notorious e-tailer BabyGear.com, a bankrupt baby products supplier. They earned a dismal D+ on the site. By contrast BabyStyle.com earned an A.

Childcare

"It's expensive, hard to find and your need for it is constantly changing. Welcome to the world of child care," said a recent *Wall Street Journal* article—and we agree. There's nothing more difficult than trying to find the best child care for your baby.

With 59% of moms with children under age one back in the workforce today, wrestling with the choices, costs and availability of childcare is a stark reality. Here's a brief overview of the different types of childcare available, questions to ask when hiring a provider and money-saving tips.

 What are you buying?

On average, parents pay 7.5% of their pre-tax income for child-care. And if you live in a high-cost city, expect to shell out even more. As you'll read below, some parents spend $20,000 or more per year. Whatever your budget, there are three basic types of child care:

◆ *Family Daycare.* In this setting, one adult takes care of a small number of children in her home. Sometimes the children are of mixed ages. Parents who like this option prefer the lower ratio of children to providers and the consistent caregiver. Of course, you'll want to make sure the facility is licensed and ask all the questions we outline later. One drawback to family daycare: if there is only one caregiver, you might have to scramble if that person becomes ill. How much does it cost? Family daycare typically runs $3000 to $10,000 per year—with bigger cities running closer to the top figure. For example, in New York City or San Francisco, family daycare can run $200 to $250 per week (that's $10,000 to $13,000 a year).

◆ *Center Care.* Most folks are familiar with this type of daycare—commercial facilities that offer a wide variety of childcare options. Convenience is one major factor for center care; you can often find a center that is near your (or your spouse's) place of work. Other parents like the fact that their children are grouped with and exposed to more kids their own age. Centers usually give you a written report each day which details your baby's day (naps, diaper changes, mood). On the downside, turnover can be a problem— some centers lose 40% or more of their employees each year. A lack of consistency can upset your child. Yet center care offers parents the most flexibility: unlike nannies or family care, the day care center doesn't take sick or vacation days. Many centers offer drop-off care, in case you need help in a pinch. The cost: $3000 to $13,000 per year, yet some pricey centers can cost over $20,000 in the biggest cities. As with family daycare, the cost varies depending on how many days a week your baby needs care. We pay about $4000 per year for 20 hours of daycare per week for one child in Boulder, CO.

◆ **Nanny Care.** No, you don't have to be super-rich to afford a nanny. Many "nanny-referral" services have popped up in most major cities, offering to refer you to a pre-screened nanny for $100 to $200 or so. Parents who prefer nannies like the one-to-one atten-tion, plus baby is taken care of in your own home. The cost varies depending on whether you provide the nanny with room and board. Generally, most nannies who don't live in run $8 to $15 per hour. Hence, the yearly cost would be $10,000 to $20,000. And the nanny's salary is just the beginning—you also must pay social securi-ty and Medicare taxes, federal unemployment insurance, plus any state-mandated taxes like disability insurance or employment-train-ing taxes. All this may increase the cost of your $20,000 nanny by another $3500 or more per year. And the paperwork hassle for all the tax reporting can be onerous. The other downside to nannies? You're dependent on one person for childcare. If she gets sick, needs time off or quits, you're on your own.

Money Saving Tips

1 **ASK YOUR EMPLOYER ABOUT DEPENDENT CARE ACCOUNTS.**
Many corporations offer this great benefit to employees. Basically, you can set aside pretax dollars to pay for child-care. The maximum set aside per child is $5000 and both parents can con-tribute to that amount. If you're in the 31% tax bracket, that means you'll save $1550 in taxes by paying for childcare with a dependent care account. Consult with your employer for the latest rules and limits to this option.

2 **SHARE A NANNY.** As we noted in the above example, a nanny can be expensive. But many parents find they can halve that cost by sharing a nanny with another family. While this

childcare

might require some juggling of schedules to make everyone happy, it can work out beautifully.

3 **GO FOR A CULTURAL EXCHANGE.** The U.S. government authorizes a foreign nanny exchange program. "Parents can hire a young European to provide as much as 45 hours of child care a week as part of a yearlong cultural exchange," said a recent *Wall Street Journal* article. The wages are fixed at $138 per week for a nanny arriving after 1996, although that amount may adjust with any change in the federal minimum wage. You also agree to pay for the nanny's room and board, but the fixed fee is good for any number of children. Eight "au pair" agencies are authorized by the federal government to place foreign nannies in homes (call Au Pair in America 800-727-2437 x6188 for more details). These agencies charge placement fees of $5600 which cover health insurance, training and other support services.

4 **TAKE A TAX CREDIT.** The current tax code gives parents a tax credit for childcare expenses. The amount, which varies based on your income, equals about 20% to 30% of childcare costs up to a certain limit. The credit equals about $500 to $1500, depending on your income. Another tax break: some states also give credits or deductions for child care expenses. Consult your tax preparer to make sure you're taking the maximum allowable credit/deduction. New in 2002, the federal government expanded the adoption credit up to $10,000 for "qualified" expenses related to adoption.

Questions to Ask

Here are questions to ask a daycare center:

1 **WHAT ARE THE CREDENTIALS OF THE PROVIDER(S)?** Obviously, a college degree in education and/or child development is preferred. Additional post-college training is also a plus.

2 **WHAT IS THE TURNOVER?** High turnover is a concern since consistency of care is one of the keys to successful childcare. Any turnover approaching 40% is cause for concern.

3 **WHAT IS THE RATIO OF CHILDREN TO CARE PROVIDERS?** The recommended national standard is one adult to three babies (age birth to 12 months). After that, the ratios vary depending on a child's age and state regulations. With some day care centers, there is one primary teacher and a couple of assistants (depending on the age of the children and size of class). Compare the ratio to that of other centers to gain an understanding of what's high and low.

4 **DO YOU HAVE A LICENSE?** All states (and many municipalities) require childcare providers to be licensed. Yet, that's no guarantee of quality–the standards vary so much from locale to locale that a license may be meaningless. Another point to remember: the standards for family daycare may be lower than those for center daycare. Educate yourself on the various rules and regulations by spending a few minutes on the phone with your state's child care regulatory body. Check on the center's file with the state to make sure there are no complaints or violations on record. Some states are putting this info on the web.

5 **MAY I VISIT YOU DURING BUSINESS HOURS?** The only way you can truly evaluate a childcare provider is an on-site visit. Try to time your visit during the late morning, typically the time when the most children are being cared for. Trust your instincts–if the facility seems chaotic, disorganized or poorly run, take the hint. One sign of a good child care center: facilities that allow unannounced drop-in visits.

6 **DISCUSS YOUR CARE PHILOSOPHY.** Sit down for a half-hour interview with the care provider and make sure they clearly define their attitudes on breast feeding, diapers, naps, feeding schedules, discipline and any other issues of importance to you. The center should have established, written procedures to deal with children who have certain allergies or other medical conditions. Let's be honest: child-rearing philosophies will vary from center to center. Make sure you see eye to eye on key issues.

7 **DO YOU HAVE LIABILITY INSURANCE?** Don't just take their word on it–have them provide written documentation or the phone number of an insurance provider for you to call to confirm coverage.

8 **DOES THE CENTER CONDUCT POLICE BACKGROUND CHECKS ON EMPLOYEES?** It's naive to assume that just because employees have good references, they've never been in trouble with the law.

9 **IS THE CENTER CLEAN, HOME-LIKE AND CHEERFUL?** While it's impossible to expect a child care facility to be spotless, it is important to check for basic cleanliness. Diaper changing stations shouldn't be overflowing with dirty diapers, play areas shouldn't be strewn with a zillion toys, etc. Another tip: check their diaper changing procedures. The best centers should use rubber gloves when changing diapers and wipe down the diapering area with a

childcare

Does your nanny have a past?

Yes, it sounds like the plot of a bad Hollywood thriller—the nanny WITH A PAST! Still, many parents want to feel secure that the person they trust to take care of their child hasn't had any run-ins with the police. In the past, this required laborious background checks with local police or numerous calls to past employers. Today, the web can help. Several web sites now let you screen a nanny's background with a simple point and click. Examples: MyBackgroundCheck.com offers a range of searches for $25 to $77. ChoiceTrust.com has a proprietary criminal records database and court records search for $58. And USSearch.com has a nanny screening service that starts at just $40. Wonder if the background checking service you found online is legit? Ask the International Nanny Association at 888-878-1477, a non-profit group which keeps tabs on such agencies. Of course, you can hire someone else to do the checking—most high-quality nanny employment agencies do those background checks, but of course you pay . . . about 10% of the nanny's first year salary as a fee. One note: while criminal background checks are relatively easy, drivers' records are another story. You may need to contact your state motor vehicle's bureau and have the nanny ask for a copy of their own report.

disinfectant after each change. Finally, ask how often toys are cleaned. Is there a regular schedule for washing children's hands?

10 **WHAT TYPE OF ADJUSTMENT PERIOD DOES THE CENTER OFFER?** Phasing in daycare isn't easy—your child may have to have time to adjust to the new situation. Experienced providers should have plans to ease the transition.

Sources For The Best Child Care Facilities. Which childcare centers have the highest standards? The National Association of Family ChildCare (800) 359-3817 (web: www.nafcc.org) and the National Association for the Education of Young Children (800) 424-2460 (www.naeyc.org) offers lists of such facilities to parents in every state.

Bottom Line

Whew! We're almost done. You've learned about cribs, pondered the car seat choice and now even read about baby announcements and childcare. But how much can you really save using our advice? The next chapter provides a summary of our budget versus the national averages.

CHAPTER 12 CONCLUSION

What Does it All Mean?

How much money can you save if you follow all the tips and suggestions in this book? Let's take a look at the average cost of having a baby from the introduction and compare it with our Baby Bargains budget.

Your Baby's First Year

ITEM	AVERAGE	BABY BARGAINS BUDGET
Crib, mattress, dresser, rocker	$1500	$1280
Bedding / Decor	$300	$200
Baby Clothes	$500	$340
Disposable Diapers	$600	$300
Maternity/Nursing Clothes	$1200	$540
Nursery items, high chair, toys	$400	$225
Baby Food/Formula	$900	$350
Stroller, Car Seat, Carrier	$300	$200
Miscellaneous	$500	$500
TOTAL	$6200	$3791
TOTAL SAVINGS:		**$2409**

WOW! YOU CAN SAVE OVER $2400! We hope the savings makes it worth the price of this book. We'd love to hear from you on how much you saved with our book—feel free to email, write or call us. See the "How to Reach Us" page at the back of this book.

What does it all mean?

At this point, we usually have something pithy to say as we end the book. But, as parents of two boys, we're just too tired. We're going to bed, so feel free to make up your own ending.

And thanks for reading *Baby Bargains*.

APPENDIX A
Canada

If you walk into a baby store in Canada, you'll see many of the same baby products that are for sale in the U.S. One reason for the overlap: Canada sees about 380,000 births a year, which is less than 10% the U.S. rate. As a result, Canada imports many baby products from Asia, Europe and the U.S.

Canada has been a leader on many safety issues. Example: car seats. Canada required the use of tether straps since the late 80's, while the U.S. just adopted this rule in 1999. Canada also tests their car seats with different weight standards. As a result, not all car seats sold in the U.S. are be available in Canada. For more information on this and other issues regarding child safety seats, contact Transport Canada's Road Safety Office at (613) 990-2309 or on the internet at *www.tc.gc.ca/*.

The Canadian Automobile Association (CAA) also works closely with Transport Canada to provide child safety seat info. Contact their headquarters at www.caa.ca for more details or check your phone book for the number of a local CAA office. We noticed the British Columbia Automobile Association (604-268-5000) operates a web site (www.bcaa.bc.ca) that provides basic safety tips plus recall notices.

FYI: but also that the seat be anchored with the tether strap. Although the US has caught up to Canada requiring all car seats be sold with tether straps, there is no mandate requiring parents to use it.

General Safety Info

If you have a question about a juvenile product or a safety concern, contact any of these regional branches of the Canada Consumer and Corporate Affairs Product Safety Office:

LOCATION	PHONE
Ottawa/Hull (headquarters)	(819) 953-8082
Halifax	(902) 426-6328
St. John's	(709) 772-4050
Moncton	(506) 851-6638
Montreal	(514) 283-2825
Quebec	(418) 648-4327
Toronto	(416) 973-4705
Hamilton	(416) 572-2845
Winnipeg	(204) 983-3293
Saskatoon	(306) 975-4028
Edmonton	(403) 495-7198
Calgary	(403) 292-5613
Vancouver	(604) 666-5006

Recap of Canadian Sources

Many of the sources mentioned earlier in this book sell or ship to Canada. Here's a recap of specific Canadian juvenile product manufacturers (all prices are in U.S. dollars):

Cribs

A.P. Industries *See review on page 48.*
Cara Mia *See review on page 57.*
EG Furniture *See review on page 65.*
Forever Mine *See review on page 68.*
Morigeau/Lepine *See review on page 75.*
Mother Hubbard's Cupboard *See review on page 75.*
Natart *See review on page 75.*
Ragazzi *See review on page 77.*
Status *See review on page 80.*
Stork Craft *See review on page 81.*

Rocker-Gliders

We're not talking about the rocking chair you've seen at grandma's house. No, we're referring to the high-tech modern-day rockers that are so fancy they aren't mere rockers—they're "glider-rock-

CANADA COSTS	What does it cost to raise a child in Canada? These figures are from Manitoba, but are a good general guide for most Canadian parents. Costs of raising a child to age two (total cost for two years):

FOOD	$2049
CLOTHING	2118
HEATH CARE	290
PERSONAL CARE	101
RECREATION	438
CHILD CARE	10,600
SHELTER	3971
TOTAL	**$19,567**

Figures are for 2002 in Canadian dollars. Source: Manitoba government web page (http://www.gov.mb.ca/agriculture/homeec/).

also has an excellent web site (www.outletbound.com) with the most up-to-date info on outlets in Canada.

A reader called in this outlet find: the **Snugabye** outlet in Toronto (188 Bentworth Ave., 416-783-0300), which sells infant clothing at prices way below those in department stores.

Layette Items and Diapers

If you're looking for great shoes for your little one, reader Teri Dunsworth recommends Canadian-made **Robeez** (800) 929-2623 or (604) 929-6818; web: www.robeez.com. "They are the most AWESOME shoes—I highly recommend them," she said in an email. Robeez are made of leather, have soft skid-resistant soles and are machine washable. They start at $22 for a basic pair. "My baby wears nothing else! They have infant and toddler sizes and oh-so-cute patterns." Another reader recommended New Zealand made **Bobux** shoes (www.bobuxusa.com). These cute leather soft soles "do the trick" by staying on extremely well according to our reader.

A Canadian clothing manufacturer to look for in stores near you is **Baby's Own** by St. Lawrence Textiles (613) 632-8565.

The Mercedes of the cloth diaper category is Canada-made **Mother-Ease** (www.mother-ease.com), a brand that has a fanatical following among cloth diaper devotees. Suffice it to say, they ain't cheap but the quality is excellent. Mother-Ease sells both fitted diapers and covers; the diapers run $9 to $10 a pop, while the covers are about $9.75. Before you invest $73 to $375 in one of Mother-Ease's special package deals, consider trying their "introductory offer" (see details below in our money-saving tips section).

Other parents like **Kushies** (800) 841-5330 (web: www.kushies. com), another Canadian product. This brand offers several models.

One note: both Kushies and Mother-Ease are sold via mail-order only. Yes, you can sometimes find these diapers at second-hand or thrift stores, but most parents buy them via a catalog or on the 'net. Kushies are trying to branch out into retail stores—check your local baby specialty shop.

One great catalog and web site for cloth diaper and breast-feeding products and information is **Born to Love** (416-499-8309; web: www. borntolove.com). They have won numerous fans for their low prices. You'll see page after page of cloth diaper systems (including such name brands as Mother-Ease and Nikki's). Heck, there are even NINE pages of accessories, plus selections of nursing bras, breast pumps, toys, safety products and more. Yes, the web site is a jumbled mess, but there's lots of useful info, articles and links when you sift through it all.

TC KidCo (888) 825-4326 is another Canadian catalog that sells ers." Thanks to a fancy ball-bearing system, these rockers "glide" with little or no effort. Here's an overview:

◆ **Shermag/Conant Ball** *In the U.S., call 800-363-2635 for dealer near you or 800-556-1515 or 819-566-1515 in Canada.* We saw this brand at chain stores and the prices can't be beat. Sample: Target.com sells a Shermag glider AND ottoman for just $199 to $299 total. Yes, you read that right—prices start at $199. A similar Shermag available from BabiesRUs.com is $199—again, including ottoman! Okay, what's the catch? First, these styles are a bit smaller in size than other glider-rockers—they fit most moms fine, but those six-foot dads may be uncomfortable. The color choices are also limited (just one or two, in most cases). And you should try to sit in these first to make sure you like the cushions (no, they aren't as super comfy as more expensive options but most parents think they're just fine).

Of course, Shermag offers many more styles and options than just those rock-bottom deals at Target and elsewhere. We noticed other Shermag gliders were $300 to $350 while ottomans were an extra $150 or so. What's Shermag's quality like compared to Dutailier? Frankly, we couldn't tell much of a difference—both are excellent.

◆ Quebec-based **Dutailier** (call 800-363-9817 or 450-772-2403; web: www.dutailier.com), is to glider-rockers what Microsoft is to software—basically, they own the market. Thanks to superior quality and quick delivery, Dutailier probably sells one out of every two glider rockers purchased in the U.S. and Canada each year.

Dutailier has an incredible selection of 45 models, seven finishes, and 80 different fabrics. The result: over 37,000 possible combinations. All wood is solid maple or oak and features non-toxic finishes. You have to try real hard to avoid seeing Dutailier—the company has 3500 retail dealers, from small specialty stores to major retail chains.

Prices for Dutailier start at about $350 for a basic model at Babies R Us (although you can find them for less online). Of course, the price can soar quickly from there—add a swivel base, plush cushions or leather fabric and you can spend $500. Or $1000.

Outlet Stores

A great source for outlet info is Outlet Bound magazine, which is published by Outlet Marketing Group ($9.95 plus $3.50 shipping, 800-336-8853). The magazine contains detailed maps noting outlet centers for all areas of the U.S. and Canada, as well as store listings for each outlet center. We liked the index that lists all the manufacturers, and they even have a few coupons in the back. Outlet Bound

"Indisposables" all-in-one cloth diapers and diaper covers. You can buy from the catalog or from their direct representative. The catalog also has nursing bras, blankets, bibs and more.

Feel guilty about using disposables? The **Diaper Club** offers to recycle disposable diapers for a small fee for parents in the Toronto area. Call 800-566-9278 for details and info.

Maternity

Canucks looking for the world's best maternity bras need to look no further than their own backyard. Toronto-based **Bravado Designs** (for a brochure, call 800-590-7802 or 416-466-8652; web: www.bravadodesigns.com) makes a maternity/nursing bra of the same name that's just incredible. "A godsend!" raved one reader. "It's built like a sports bra with no underwire and supports better than any other bra I've tried . . . and this is my third pregnancy!" raved another. The Bravado bra comes in three support levels, sizes up to 42-46 with an F-G cup and a couple of wonderful colors/patterns (you can also call them for custom sizing information). Another. Available via mail order, the bra costs $32 U.S. (or $33.50 Canadian). Another plus: the Bravado salespeople are knowledgeable and quite helpful with sizing questions. Some of our readers have criticized the Bravado for not providing enough support, especially in the largest sizes. If you have doubts, just try one at first and see if it works for you before investing in several.

A reader recommend Montreal-based **Thyme Maternity** (514-729-3333, web: www.maternity.ca) which offers "decent maternity clothes at very reasonable prices." Another reader chimed in with her kudos, saying their "Bootleg Ottoman Pants" with adjustable waistband were excellent. Thyme has stores throughout Canada and a web site with online ordering.

What about nursing fashions in Canada? The Toronto-based **Breast is Best** catalog sells a wide variety of nursing tops, blouses and dresses as well as maternity wear. For a free catalog and fabric swatches, call (877) 837-5439 toll free or check out their web site at www.breastisbest.com.

Looking for plus-size maternity or petites? Canadian maternity maker **Maternal Instinct** has a catalog and web site (www.maternal-instinct.com; 877-MATERNAL). The line is also sold in a dozen stores in Canada (and another dozen or so in the U.S.). "They don't have a huge catalog inventory," writes one Vancouver mom, "but it's a nice, simple selection of plus-size and petite work and casual maternity clothes with a few pieces of formalwear thrown in."

Baby Food Web Site

Heinz has a Canadian-based web site (www.heinzbaby.com) which contains extensive nutritional advice and other helpful info. What makes this site great for Canadians are the coupons and rebate offers.

Car Seats

On a recent trip to Toronto, we noticed many of the same car seat brands that are sold in the U.S. are offered in Canada as well. Hence, it will be helpful to review Chapter 8 to get a complete picture of the car seat market. The biggest car seat seller in Canada is probably Cosco, which is also reviewed in depth in Chapter 8.

Carriers

Mountain Equipment Co-operative (MEC; web: www.mac.ca) is a unique, not-for-profit member owned co-op that sells baby carriers (among other outdoor products). A reader in Ottawa emailed us a rave for their "excellent" backpack carriers that are "renown for their excellent quality." At C$159, the MEC backpack carrier "clearly beats Kelty Kids and other U.S.-made carriers" at a much lower price. MEC has stores in major cities in Canada; call 800-747-7704 for details.

Canadian parents also write to us with kudos for the *Baby Trekker* (800) 665-3957; web: www.babytrekker.com. This 100% washable cotton carrier has straps that around the waist for support. Canucks like the fact a baby can be dressed in a snowsuit and still fit in the Baby Trekker. The carrier ($80 US, $102 Canada) is available in baby stores in Canada.

Our readers also recommend Outbound, a Canadian manufacturer (www.outbound.ca) that offers three frame carriers, the Kiddie Carrier, the Toddler Tote and the Cub Carrier with prices ranging from $139 Canadian to $219 They also praise the Tatonka Baby Carrier ($136) from another Canadian manufacturer, Sherpa Mountain (www.sherpa-mtn.com).

Web Resources

Yes, we have a large list of web sites that sell baby products in Chapter 11 (Do it My Mail and Online). One caveat for Canucks, however: not all sites ship to Canada. And that info is usually buried somewhere on their site that requires some digging. And remember prices are almost always in the U.S. dollar, not Canadian dollars. Given recent exchange rates and shipping costs, cross-border shopping is a bit painful as you can understand.

Canadian Parents Online (www.canadianparents.com) is a great resource, with advice columns, chat/discussion areas and recall info for Canadian parents. We liked their "Ask an Expert" areas, which included advice on childbirth, lactation and even fitness.

The **Childcare Resources and Research Unit** (www.childcare-canada.org) has great info and statistics on childcare costs in Canada.

Sears may not have a catalog any more in the U.S., but the Canadian version of **Sears** (www.sears.ca) has both a web site and printed catalog with baby products and clothes. A reader said the catalog has a nice selection of products and is a great resource for Canadian parents who might live outside the major metro areas.

Baby gear shopping in Toronto

Toronto mom Rhonda Lewis emailed us her experiences shopping for baby gear in Canada. Here are her comments about various stores in Toronto:

◆ **Lil' Niblets and Baby Sprouts** (416-249-9881) offers knowledgeable staff and decent brands (cribs b y Morigeau Lepine, AP and EG). The store also sells strollers and car seats, even offering help with car seat installation.

◆ **Macklem's** (416-531-7188) is family-run baby store in downtown Toronto sells higher-end strollers by Zooper, Maclaren and Peg Perego. They also have a good selection of cribs and bedding.

◆ **Dearborn Baby Express** (905-881-3334). A large selection of glider-rockers is the specialty of this store, along with cribs (EG, AP, Lepine) and strollers. Brands include Peg Perego and Zooper. You can find Evenflo and Graco car seats here.

Of course, Toronto has quite a few discount stores that sell baby products. Wal-Mart sells crib mattresses and a smattering of strollers in Toronto, while Costco has Shermag glider-rockers and baby supplies like diapers.

Rhonda had one other recommendation for Toronto parents: the **BabySteps Children's Fund** (www.babysteps.com). This non-profit has a online gift shop with various baby gifts; all proceeds go to the Hospital for Sick Children in Toronto.

APPENDIX B
Sample registry

Here's the coolest thing about registering for baby products at Babies R Us–that neato bar code scanner gun. You're supposed to walk (waddle?) around the store and zap the bar codes of products you want to add to the registry. This is cool for about 15 seconds, until you realize you have to make DECISIONS about WHAT to zap.

What to do? Yes, you could page through this book as you do the registry, but that's a bit of a pain, no? To help speed the process, here's a list of what stuff you need and what to avoid. Consider it *Baby Bargains* in a nutshell:

The order of these recommendations follows the Babies R Us Registry form:

Car Seats/Strollers/Carriers/Accessories

◆ **Full Size Convertible Car Seat.** Basically, we urge waiting on this one–most babies don't need to go into a full-size convertible seat until they outgrow an infant seat (that could be in four to six months or as much as a year). In the meantime, new models are always coming out with better safety features. Hence, don't register for this and wait to buy it later.

If want to ignore this advice, go for the **Britax Roundabout** ($180-$200) or **Evenflo Triumph** ($120 to $130). If you have a LATCH-ready car (see Chapter 8 for details) and have a child over one year of age, go for the **Britax Expressway** ($160) as a forward-only facing seat.

◆ **Infant car seat.** Best bets: the **Graco "Snug Ride"** ($60 to $100; the LX is a good option) or the **Baby Trend Latch-Loc Adjustable Back** ($90).

◆ **Strollers.** There is no "one size fits all" recommendation in this section. Read the lifestyle recommendations in Chapter 8 to find a stroller that best fits your needs. In general, stay away from the pre-packaged "travel systems"–remember that many of the better stroller brands now can be used with infant seats.

◆ **Baby Carriers.** Baby Bjorn ($75 to $80). You really don't need another carrier (like a backpack) unless you plan to do serious outdoor hikes. If that is the case, check Chapter 8 for suggestions.

◆ **Misc.** Yes, your infant car seat should come with an infant head support pillow, so if you buy one of these separately, use it in your stroller. There really isn't a specific brand preference in this category (all basically do the same thing). Any other stroller accessories are purely optional.

Travel Yards/High Chairs/Exercisers/Accessories

◆ **Gates.** The best brand is *KidCo* (which makes the Gateway, Safeway and Elongate). But this is something you can do later—most babies aren't mobile until at least six months of age.

◆ **Travel Yard/Playard.** Graco's *Pack 'N Play* is the best bet. Go for one with a bassinet feature.

◆ **High Chair.** The best high chair is the Fisher Price Healthy Care ($70 to $90)—go for the Deluxe version.

◆ **Walker/Exerciser.** Skip this. See Chapter 7 for details.

◆ **Swing.** We like Graco's *Open Top* swings ($70 to $120) best.

◆ **Hook on high chair.** Not really necessary; if you want one, get it later. We review hook-on chairs in our other book, *Toddler Bargains*.

◆ **Infant jumper.** Too many injuries with this product category; pass on it.

◆ **Bed rail.** Don't need this either.

◆ **Bouncer.** Fisher Price (www.fisher-price.com) makes the most popular one in the category—their *"Kick 'n Play"* is about $35.

Cribs/Furniture

◆ **Crib.** For cribs, you've got two basic choices: a simple model that is, well, just a crib or a "convertible" model that eventually morphs into a twin or full size bed. In the simple category for best buys, *Child Craft's 10171* is a basic maple crib with single-drop side for just $200. In a similar vein, a basic *Simmons* model at Baby Depot ran $240. Other features that are nice (but not necessary) for cribs include a double drop side, a quiet rail release and hidden hardware. If you fancy an imported crib, there are few bargains but we found that *Sorelle/C&T* has reasonable prices ($250 to start) for above average quality.

◆ **Bassinet.** Skip it. See Chapter 2 for details. If you buy a playpen with bassinet feature, you don't need a separate bassinet.

◆ **Dressing/changing table.** Skip it. Just use the top of your dresser as a changing area. (See dresser recommendation below.)

◆ **Glider/rocker and ottoman.** In a word: *Dutailier*. Whatever style/fabric you chose, you can't go wrong with that brand. Hint: this is a great product to buy online at a discount, so you might want to skip registering for one. **Shermag** is another great brand.

♦ **Dresser.** Dressers and other case pieces by **Rumble Tuff** were great deals—they exactly match the finishes of Child Craft and Simmons, but at prices 10% to 25% less than the competition. We liked their three-drawer combo unit that combines a changing table and a dresser for $450 to $600. Unfortunately, Rumble Tuff isn't sold in chain stores like Babies R Us (see chapter 2 for details).

♦ **Misc.** Babies R Us recommends registering for all sorts of miscellaneous items like cradles, toy boxes and the like. Obviously, these are clearly optional.

Bedding/Room Décor/Crib Accessories

♦ **Crib set.** Don't—don't register for this waste of money. Instead, just get two or three good crib sheets and a nice cotton blanket or the Halo Sleep Sack. See Chapter 3 for brands.

♦ **Bumper pads, dust ruffle, diaper stacker.** Ditto—a waste.

♦ **Lamp, mobile.** These are optional, of course. We don't have any specific brand preferences.

♦ **Mattress.** We like the foam mattresses from **Colgate** ($90 for the Classica I). Or, for coil, go for a **Sealy** (Kolcraft) 150 coil mattress for $60 at Babies R Us. Unfortunately, Babies R Us and other chains don't sell foam mattresses but you can find them online.

♦ **Misc.** Babies R Us has lots of miscellaneous items in this area like rugs, wallpaper border, bassinet skirts and so on. We have ideas for décor on the cheap in Chapter 3.

Infant Toys, Care & Feeding

♦ **Toys:** All of this (crib toys, bath toys, blocks) is truly optional. We have ideas for this in Chapter 6.

♦ **Nursery monitor.** In general, the **Fisher Price** line is best but keep the receipt—many baby monitors don't work well because of electronic interference in the home.

♦ **Humidifier.** The **Holmes/Duracraft** line sold in Target is best. Avoid the "baby" humidifiers sold in baby stores, as they are overpriced.

♦ **Diaper pail.** The **Baby Trend Diaper Champ** is best.

◆ **Bathtub.** While not a necessity, a baby bath tub is a nice convenience—try to borrow one or buy it second hand to save. As a best bet, we suggest the *EuroBath by Primo*—it's a $25 bath tub that works well.

◆ **Bottles.** *Avent* is the best bet, according to our readers.

◆ **Bottle Warmer.** Alsoo optional. Avent's *Express Bottle and Baby Food Warmer* ($40) can heat a bottle in four minutes. *The First Years "Night & Day Bottle Warmer System"* ($30) is an alternative. It steam heats two 8 oz. bottles in under five minutes (one reader said its more like three minutes). For night-time feedings, it can keep two bottles cool for up to eight hours (so there's no need to run to the kitchen). Yes, it fits Avent bottles, but one reader said just the small 4 oz ones, not the 8 oz variety.

◆ **Sterilizer.** Also optional, *Avent's "Microwave Steam Sterilizer"* ($25-30) is a good choice. It holds four bottles of any type and is easy to use—just put in water and nuke for eight minutes.

◆ **Thermometer.** *First Years* has a new high speed digital thermometer ($10) that gives a rectal temp in 20 seconds and an underarm in 30 seconds. Ear thermometers are not recommended, as they are not accurate.

◆ **Breast pump.** There isn't a "one size fits all" recommendation here. Read Chapter 5 Maternity/Nursing for details.

◆ **Misc.** In this category, Babies R Us throws in items like bibs, hooded towels, washcloths, pacifiers and so on. See Chapter 4 "Reality Layette" for ideas in this category.

Diapers/Wipes

◆ **Diapers.** For disposables, the best deals are in warehouse clubs like *Sam's* and *Costco*. Generic diapers at *Wal-Mart* and *Target* are also good deals. We have a slew of deals on cloth diapers in Chapter 4.

◆ **Wipes.** Don't go generic here. Brands like *Pampers Baby Fresh* and *Huggies* are the better bets.

Clothing/Layette

◆ See the "Reality Layette" list (Ch. 4) for suggestions on quantities/brands.

APPENDIX C

Multiples advice

Yes, this year, one in 35 births in the US is to twins. As a parent-to-be of twins and that can mean double the fun when it comes to buying for baby. Here's our round-up of what products are best for parents of multiples:

Cribs

Since twins tend to be smaller than most infants, parents of multiples can use bassinets or cradles for an extended period of time. We discuss this category in depth in Chapter 2, but generally recommend looking at a portable playpen (Graco Pak N Play is one popular choice) with a bassinet feature as an alternative. A nice splurge if your budget allows it: the **Arm's Reach Co-Sleeper**.

Cool idea: a mom of twins emailed us about a crib divider for $25 that lets you use one crib for twins. Available on MoreThanOne.com.

Bedding

Take our advice here and save by just getting high quality sheets and a good cotton blanket. Skip those fancy bedding sets—the last thing you need is to waste money on quilts, diaper stackers and other frills in a $300 bedding set.

Nursing help

Check out **EZ-2-NURSE's pillow** (800-584-TWIN; we saw it on www.doubleblessings.com). A mom told us this was the "absolute best" for her twins, adding "I could not successfully nurse my girls together without this pillow. It was wonderful." This pillow comes in both foam and inflatable versions (including a pump). Cost: $40 to $48.

Wal-Mart has a breastfeeding collection with **Lansinoh** products (including their amazing nipple cream). Check the special displays in the store or on their web site at www.walmart.com.

Yes, nursing one baby can be a challenge, but two? You might need some help. To the rescue comes **Mothering Multiples: Breastfeeding & Caring for Twins and More** by Karen Kerkoff Gromada ($14.95; available on the La Leche League web site, www.lalecheleague.com). This book was recommend to us by more than one mother of twins for its clear and concise advice.

Car seats

Most multiples are born before their due date. The smallest infants may have to ride in special "car beds" that enable them to lie flat (instead of car seats that require an infant to be at least five or six pounds and ride in a sitting position). The car beds then rotate to become regular infant car seats so older infants can ride in a sitting position.

For years, the only choice in this category was **Cosco's Ultra Dream Ride** ($50-$55, www.coscoinc.com). Now, Graco has introduced the **Cherish Car Bed**, which can be used up to nine pounds (up to 20 inches). Unlike Cosco Ultra Dream Ride ($40), the Cherish Car Bed has a "fabric hook and loop harness for a soft, snug fit."

Bottom line: while the Cosco is $10 to $15 more expensive than the Graco unit, it is the better bet. The Graco bed does NOT convert into a regular infant seat, so you'll be out another $50 or more when your baby surpasses nine pounds. The Cosco bed can be used up to 20 pounds and 26 inches. The only criticism we heard of the Cosco bed: sometimes it is a bit difficult to put in a smaller car when in the car bed position.

Strollers

Our complete wrap-up of recommendations for double strollers is in Chapter 8 (see Double the Fun in the lifestyle recommendations). In brief, we should mention that the **Graco DuoGlider** accepts two infant seats ($229 for a travel system that includes one infant seat). We should also note Baby Trend's tandem (front/back) double strollers. The **Caravan Lite LX** ($199-249) lets you attach one or two infant car seats and gets generally good marks from parents for its features and ease of use.

If Grandma is paying for a stroller as a gift, Perego's **Duette** double stroller ($500) allows parents of twins to attach TWO infant car seats (included) to the G-matic frame. (And there is also a *"Triplette"* version of this stroller).

Those strollers are great since they can handle two infant car seats, but most parents of twins find that side-by-side strollers do better for them than tandem (front/back) models. Why? Tandem strollers typically only have one seat that fully reclines (when parents of twins find they need two reclining seats). And the front/back configuration seems to invite more trouble when the twins get older—the back passenger pulling the front passenger's hair, etc.

Unfortunately, the brand choices here are rather limited. The best choices (Maclaren or Combi) in the side-by-side category are rather pricey. **The Peg Perego Aria Twin** is a good choice as well.

Graco and Cosco offer side-by-side models in the under $200 price range, but they are much less reliable.

In the dark horse category, consider the **Double Decker Stroller** (941-543-1582; www.doubledeckerstroller.com), a jogging stroller than can accommodate two infant car seats. It runs $235. New this year is the "Triple Decker," a model that will hold three babies!

As for other jogging strollers, the side-by-side versions of **Baby Jogger** and **Kool Stop** are probably best if you really plan to exercise with a sport stroller. The new tandem jogger by **Gozo** (again, see Chapter 8) is an interesting alternative as well.

Carrier

A mom of twins emailed us to rave about the **MaxiMom** carrier. She found it easier to use and adjust. The best feature: you adjust it to be a sling and nurse a baby in it. We saw this carrier on TwinStuff (www.twinstuff.com) for $75 to $80; a triplet version is $109. Gemini (morethanone.com) has a front carrier that lets you carry two babies up to 28 lbs.

Deals/Freebies

◆ Chain stores like Babies R Us and Baby Depot offer a 10% discount if you buy multiples of identical items like cribs.

◆ Get a **$7 off coupon for the Diaper Genie from Playtex** when you send proof of multiple births to Playtex (800) 222-0453; www.playtex.com.

◆ **Kimberly Clark Twins Program:** Get a gift of "high-value coupons" for Huggies diapers by submitting birth certificates or published birth announcements. (800) 544-1847).

◆ **The First Years** offers free rattles for parents of multiples when you send in copies of birth certificates. Web: www.thefirstyears.com.

◆ **Heinz/Beechnut**: Get coupons for baby food by calling 800-872-2229 in the US or 800-565-2100 in Canada. Web: www.heinz.com.

◆ **The National Mothers of Twins Clubs** (www.nomotc.org) has fantastic yard/garage sales. Check their web page for a club near you.

Source: Twins Magazine is a bi-monthly, full-color magazine published by The Business Word (800) 328-3211 or (303) 290-8500

TWINS

(www.twinsmagazine.com). Remember that offers can change at any time. Check with the companies first before sending any info.

Miscellaneous

For clothes, make sure you get "preemie" sizes instead of the suggestions in our layette chapter—twins are smaller at birth than singleton babies.

BabyBeat is a fetal monitoring device that lets you listen to your babies' heartbeats as early as 10-12 weeks. Best of all, BabyBeat lets you rent the device instead of buying—$30 to $50 per month depending on the model. You can also buy the unit at $445 to $549. For details, call 888-758-8822 or www.babybeat.com. Unlike cheaper ultrasound monitors that are low-quality, BabyBeat is similar to the Doppler instruments found in doctor's offices.

APPENDIX D

Phone/Web Site Directory

Contract Name	Toll-Free	Phone	Web Site
General Baby Product Manufacturers			
Baby Trend	(800) 328-7363	(909) 773-0018	babytrend.com
Century		(330) 468-2000	centuryproducts.com
Chicco	(877) 4-CHICCO		chiccousa.com
Cosco	(800) 457-5276	(812) 372-0141	coscoinc.com
Evenflo	(800) 233-5921	(937) 415-3229	evenflo.com
First Years	(800) 225-0382	(508) 588-1220	thefirstyears.com
Fisher Price	(800) 828-4000	(716) 687-3000	fisher-price.com
Graco	(800) 345-4109	(610) 286-5951	gracobaby.com
Peg Perego		(219) 482-8191	perego.com
Safety 1st	(800) 962-7233	(781) 364-3100	safety1st.com
Introduction			
Alan & Denise Fields (authors)		(303) 442-8792	babybargainsbook.com
Chapter 2: Nursery Necessities			
JCPenney	(800) 222-6161		jcpenney.com
CPSC	(800) 638-2772		cpsc.gov
Baby Furniture Plus			babyfurnitureplus.com
Baby News			babynewsstores.com
NINFRA			ninfra.com
USA Baby			usababy.com
EcoBaby			ecobaby.com
Hoot Judkins			hootjudkins.com
Crib N Carriage			cribncarriage.com
Baby Furniture Outlet	(800) 613-9280	(519) 649-2590	babyfurnitureoutlet.com
Buy Buy Baby			buybuybaby.com
Babies R Us	(888) BABYRUS		babiesrus.com
Baby Depot	(800) 444-COAT		coat.com
Room & Board			roomandboard.com
Baby Furniture Warehouse			babyfurniturewarehouse.com
Fun Rugs			funrugs.com
Decorate Today			decoratetoday.com
Rugs USA			rugsusa.com
NetKidsWear			netkidswear.com
Baby Bunk			babybunk.com
Cosco (outlet)		(812) 526-0860	
Child Craft (outlet)		(812) 524-1999	
Kiddie Kastle (outlet)		(502) 499-9667	
Baby Boudoir (outlet)	(800) 272-2293	(508) 998-2166	
Pottery Barn (outlet)		(901) 763-1500	potterybarnkids.com
Baby Catalog America		(800) PLAY-PEN	babycatalog.com
Baby Style			babystyle.com
Pottery Barn Kids			PotteryBarnKids.com
Danny Foundation			dannyfoundation.org
Great Beginnings	(800) 886-9077	(301) 417-9702	childrensfurniture.com
Good Night Ben			goodnightben.com
Rocking Chair Outlet			rockingchairoutlet.com

web/phone directory

Crib manufacturers

Alta Baby	(888) 891-1489		altababyweb.com
Angel Line	(800) 889-8158	(856) 863-8009	angelline.com
AP Industries	(800) 463-0145	(418) 728-2145	apindustries.com
Baby's Dream	(800) TEL-CRIB	(912) 649-4404	babysdream.com
Bassett		(540) 629-6000	bassettfurniture.com
Bellini	(800) 332-BABY	(516) 234-7716	bellini.com
Berg		(908) 354-5252	bergfurniture.com
Bonavita	(888) 266-2848	(732) 346-5150	bonavita-cribs.com
Bratt Décor	(888) 24-BRATT	(410) 327-4600	brattedecor.com
Canalli		(973) 247-7222	canallifurniture.com
Cara Mia	(877) 728-0342	(705) 328-0342	caramiafurniture.com
Child Craft		(812) 883-3111	childcraftind.com
Corsican Kids	(800) 421-6247	(323) 587-3101	corsican.com
Generation 2	(800) 736-1140	(334) 792-1144	childdesigns.com
Delta		(718) 385-1000	deltaenterprise.com
Domusindo			domusindo.com
E G Furniture	(888) 422-5534	(418) 325-2050	egfurniture.com
Forever Mine	(800) 356-2742	(819) 297-2000	forevermine.com
Kinderkraft			kinderkraft.com
Little Miss Liberty	(800) RND-CRIB	(310) 281-5400	crib.com
Million Dollar Baby	(877) 600-6688	(323) 728-9988	milliondollarbaby.com
Morigeau/Lepine	(800) 326-2121	(724) 941-7475	morigeau.com
Mother Hubbard		(416) 661-8201	mhcfurniture.com
Natart		(819) 364-2052	natartfurniture.com
Pali	(877) 725-4772		paliltaly.com
Pottery Barn	(800) 430-7373		potterybarnkids.com
Ragazzi		(514) 324-7886	ragazzi.com
Relics		(612) 374-0861	relicsfurniture.com
Sauder			sauder.com
Simmons		(920) 982-2140	simmonsjp.com.
Sorelle	(888) 470-1260	(201) 461-9444	sorellefurniture.com
Status		(514) 631-0788	statusfurniture.com
Stork Craft		(604) 274-5121	storkcraft.com
Tracers		(914) 686-5725	
Vermont Precision		(802) 888-7974	vtprecision.com
Mondi		(630) 953-9519	mondibaby.com
Moosehead		(207) 997-3621	mooseheadfurniture.com
Stephanie Anne	(888) 885-6700		stephanieanne.

Babies Boutique			babiesboutique.com
IKEA		(610) 834-0180	ikea.com
JPMA		(856) 439-0500	jpma.org
Arm's Reach	(800) 954-9353		armsreach.com
Ethan Allen	(888) EAHELP-1		ethanallen.com
Colgate		(404) 681-2121	colgatekids.com
Halo Crib Mattress		(218) 525-5158	halosleep.com
SIDS Alliance			SidsAlliance.org
Jupiter Industries			bopeepnurseryproducts.com

Sleep Tight Soother	(800) NO-COLIC		colic.com
Burlington Basket Co.	(800) 553-2300	(319) 754-6508	
Container Store	(800) 733-3532		containerstore.com
Rumble Tuff	(800) 524-9607	(801) 226-2648	rumbletuff.com
Camelot Furniture		(714) 283-4194	
Dutailier	(800) 363-9817	(450) 772-2403	dutailier.com
Rocking Chairs 100%	(800) 4-ROCKER		rocking-chairs.com
Brooks	(800) 427-6657	(423) 626-1111	
Conant Ball	(800) 363-2635	(819) 566-1515	

Relax-R	(800) 850-2909		
Towne Square	(800) 356-1663		gliderrocker.com
American Health	(800) 327-4382		foryourbaby.com
Closet Maid	(800) 874-0008		closetmaid.com
Storage Pride	(800) 441-0337		
Lee Rowan	(800) 325-6150		leerowan.com
Hold Everything	(800) 421-2264		holdeverything.com
Closet Factory	(800) 692-5673		closetfactory.com
California Closets	(800) 274-6754		californiaclosets.com
Sassy		(616) 243-0767	sassybaby.com
Shades of Light	(800) 262-6612		shades-of-light.com

Chapter 3: Bedding & Décor

Baby Bedding Online			babybeddingonline.com
Baby's Best Buy			babiesbestbuy.com
Country Lane			countrylane.com
Basic Comfort	(800) 456-8687		basiccomfort.com
Kiddopotamus	(800) 772-8339		kiddopotamus.com
Clouds & Stars			cloudsandstars.com
Michaels Arts & Crafts	(800) MICHAELS		michaels.com
Bumpa Bed	(800) 241-1848	(509) 457-0925	babyjogger.com
Stay Put safety sheet			babysheets.com
Baby-Be-Safe			baby-be-safe.com
Wall Nutz			wallnutz.com
Creative Images artwork			crimages.com

Outlets

Garnet Hill	(802) 362-6198
House of Hatten	(512) 392-8161
The Interior Alternative	(413) 743-1986
Laura Ashley	(703) 494-3124
Nojo	(949) 858-9496
Quiltex	(718) 788-3158

Bedding Manufacturers

Amy Coe		(203) 221-3050	amycoe.com
Baby Guess	(714) 895-2250		crowncraftsinfantproducts.com
Bananafish	(800) 899-8689	(818) 727-1645	
Beautiful Baby		(903) 295-2229	bbaby.com
Blueberry Lane		(413) 528-9633	blueberrylanehome.com
Blue Moon Baby		(626) 455-0014	bluebaby.com
Brandee Danielle	(800) 720-5656	(714) 957-1240	brandeedanielle.com
California Kids	(800) 548-5214	(650) 637-9054	
Carters	(800) 845-3251	(803) 275-2541	caters.com
Celebrations		(310) 532-2499	baby-celebrations.com
Cotton Tale	(800) 628-2621	(714) 435-9558	
CoCaLo		(714) 434-7200	cocalo.com
Crown Crafts	(714) 895-9200		crowncraftsinfantproducts.com
Gerber	(800) 4-GERBER		gerber.com
Glenna Jean	(800) 446-6018	(804) 561-0687	
Hoohobbers		(773) 890-1466	hoohobbers.com
House of Hatten	(800) 542-8836	(512) 819-9600	houseofhatten.com
Infantino	(800) 365-8182	(858) 689-1221	infantino.com
KidsLine		(310) 660-0110	kidslineinc.com
Kimberly Grant		(714) 546-4411	kimberlygrant.com
Lambs & Ivy	(800) 345-2627	(310) 839-5155	lambsivy.com
Luv Stuff	(800) 825-BABY	(972) 278-BABY	luvstuffbedding.com
Martha Stewart			kmart.com
Nava's Design		(818) 988-9050	navasdesigns.com
Nojo	(800) 854-8760	(310) 763-8100	nojo.com
Patchkraft	(800) 866-2229	(973) 340-3300	patchkraft.com

web/phone directory

Pine Creek		(503) 266-6275	pinecreekbedding.com
Quiltex	(800) 237-3636	(212) 594-2205	quiltex
Red Calliope	(800) 421-0526	(310) 763-8100	redcalliope.com
Sumersault	(800) 232-3006	(201) 768-7890	sumersault.com
Sweet Pea		(626) 578-0866	
Wendy Bellissimo		(818) 348-3682	wendybellissimo.com
Uhula			uhula.com
Riegel	(800) 845-3251	(803) 275-2541	parentinformation.com
Springs		(212) 556-6300	springs.com
Bebe Chic		(201) 941-5414	bebechic.com
Creative Images	(800) 784-5415	(904) 825-6700	crimages.com
Eddie Bauer	(800) 426-8020		eddiebauer.com
The Company Store	(800) 323-8000		companykids.com
Garnet Hill	(800) 622-6216		garnethill.com
Graham Kracker	(800) 489-2820		grahamkracker.com
The Land of Nod	(800) 933-9904		landofnod.com
Lands' End	(800) 345-3696		landsend.com
Pottery Barn Kids	(800) 430-7373		potterybarnkids.com

Chapter 4: Reality Layette

Bella Kids			bellakids.com
One of a Kind Kids			oneofakindkids.com
Preemie.com			preemie.com
SuddenlyMommies			suddenlymommies.com
Kids Surplus			kidssurplus.com
Internet Resale Directory			secondhand.com
Nat'l Assoc. Resale & Thrift			narts.org
Ebay			ebay.com
Minnetonka Moccasins		(718) 365-7033	minnetonka-by-mail.com
Robeez shoes	(800) 929-2623	(604) 435-9074	robeez.com
Bobux shoes			bobuxusa.com
Scootees			scootees.com
Once Upon a Child		(614) 791-0000	onceuponachild.com

Outlets

Carter's	(888) 782-9548	(770) 961-8722	
Esprit		(415) 648-6900	
Flapdoodles		(970) 262-9351	
Florence Eiseman		(414) 272-3222	FlorenceEiseman.com
Hanna Andersson		(503) 697-1953	
Hartstrings		(610) 687-6900	
Health-Tex	(800) 772-8336	(914) 428-7551	vfc.com
JcPenney outlet	(800) 222-6161		jcpenney.com
Osh Kosh		(920) 231-8800	oshkoshbgosh.com
Talbot's Kids	(800) 543-7123	(781) 740-8888	talbots.com
Outlet Bound mag	(800) 336-8853		outletbound.com

Clothing Manufacturers

Alexis	(800) 253-9476		alexisusa.com
Baby Gap	(800) GAPSTYLE		babygap.com
Cotton Tale Originals	(800) 628-2621		cottontaledesigns.com
Flap Happy	(800) 234-3527		flaphappy.com
Flapdoodles		(302) 731-9793	flapdoodles.com
Florence Eisman		(414) 272-3222	florenceeiseman.com
Gymboree	(800) 990-5060		gymboree.com
Hartstrings		(610) 687-6900	hartstrings.com
Jake and Me		(970) 352-8802	jakeandme.com
Little Me			littleme.com
Mother-Maid		(770) 479-7558	jordanmarie.com
Mulberri Bush (Tumbleweed too)			mulberribush.com
OshKosh B'Gosh			oshkoshbgosh.com

Patsy Aiken		(919) 872-8789	patsyaiken.com
Pingorama			pingorama.com
Sarah's Prints	(888) 4-PRINTS		sarasprints.com
Skivvydoodles		(212) 967-2918	skivvydoodles.com
Sweet Potatoes and Spudz		(510) 527-7633	sweetpotatoesinc.com
Wes & Willy			wesandwilly.com
Carter's		(770) 961-8722	carters.com
Fisher Price	(800) 747-8697		fisher-price.com
Good Lad of Philadelphia		(215) 739-0200	
Le Top	(800) 333-2257		

Catalogs

Childrens Wear	(800) 242-5437		cwdkids.com
Hanna Andersson	(800) 222-0544		hannaandersson.com
Lands End	(800) 963-4816		landsend.com
LL Kids	(800) 552-5437		llbean.com
Patagonia Kids	(800) 638-6464		patagonia.com
Talbot's Kids	(800) 543-7123		talbots.com
Wooden Soldier	(800) 375-6002	(603) 356-7041	
Disney Catalog	(800) 237-5751		disneystore.com
Fitigues	(800) 235-9005		fitigues.com
Campmor	(800) 226-7667		campmor.com
Sierra Trading Post	(800) 713-4534		sierratradingpost.com

Diapers

BioKleen		biokleen.com
All Together Diaper Company		clothdiaper.com
Baby Lane		thebabylane.com
Diapers 4 Less		diapers4less.com
Drug Emporium		drugemporium.com
CVS Pharmacy		cvspharmacy.com
Baby's Heaven		babysheaven.com
Diaper Site		diapersite.com
Costco		costco.com
Weebees		weebees.com
Baby J		babyj.com
BarefootBaby		Barefootbaby.com
Kelly's Closet		kellyscloset.com
Jardine Diapers		jardinediapers.com
Baby Bunz	(800) 676-4559	babybunz.com
Organic Bebe		organicbebe.com
Huggies		huggies.com
Luvs		luvs.com
Diaper Wraps		diaperaps.com
Tushies		tushies.com
Nature Boy & Girl		natureboyandgirl.com

Cloth Diaper Resources

Diaper Changes book	(800) 572-1826	
homekeepers.com		
Mother-Ease		motherease.com
Kushies	(800) 841-5330	kushies.com
DiaperDance		diaperdance.com
Daisy Diapers		diasydiapers.com
All Together	(801) 566-7579	clothdiaper.com
Bumkins	(800) 338-7581	bumkins.com
Indisposables	(800) 663-1730	
Baby Town		eskimo.com/~babytown
Sams Club		samsclub.com
BJ's		bjswholesale.com
Baby Works	(800) 422-2910	babyworks.com

web/phone directory

	PHONE		WEBSITE
Born to Love		(905) 725-2559	borntolove.com
Nurtured Baby	(888) 564-BABY		nurturedbaby.com
TC Kidco	(888) 825-4326		

Chapter 5: Maternity/Nursing

	PHONE		WEBSITE
Expressiva			expressive.com
Playtex	(800) 537-9955		playtex.com
Motherwear	(800) 950-2500		motherwear.com
Anna Cris Maternity			annacris.com
Little Koala			littlekoala.com
Maternity 4 Less			maternity4less.com
Mom Shop			momshop.com
One Hot Mama			onehotmama.com
Fit Maternity			fitmaternity.com
Birth&Baby			birthandbaby.com
Mommy Gear			mommygear.com
From Here to Eternity			fromheretomaternity.com
Just Babies			justbabies.com
Lattesa			lattesa.com
Liz Lange Maternity			lizlange.com
Mothers In Motion			mothers-in-motion.com
Naissance Maternity			naissancematernity.com
Pumpkin Maternity			pumpkinmaternity.com
Style Maternity			stylematernity.com
Thyme Maternity			maternity.ca
Twinkle Little Star			twinklelittlestar.com

Plus maternity sources

	PHONE		WEBSITE
Baby Becoming			babybecoming.com
Expecting Style			expectingstyle.com
Imaternity			imaternity.com
JCPenney			jcpenney.com
Maternal Instinct			maternal-instinct.com
MomShop			momshop.com
Motherhood			maternitymall.com
One Hot Mama			onehotmama.com
Plus Maternity			plusmaternity.com
About Babies Inc			aboutbabiesinc.com
Plus Size Mommies			plussizemommies.com
Majamas			majamas.com
Bravado Designs	(800) 590-7802	(416) 466-8652	bravadodesigns.com
One Hanes Place	(800) 300-2600		onehanesplace.com
Decent Exposures	(800) 524-4949		decentexposures.com
Fit Maternity		(530) 938-4530	fitmaternity.com
Title 9 Sports		(510) 655-5999	titleninesports.com
Hue		(212) 947-3666	
Motherwear	(800) 950-2500		motherwear.com
Breast is Best	(877) 837-5439		breastisbest.com
Elizabeth Lee Designs		(435) 454-3350	elizabethlee.com
Danish Wool			danishwool.com
Breast Feeding Styles			breastfeedingstyles.com
Sierra Blue			sierrablue.com
Wears the Baby			wearsthebaby.com
Leading Lady			leadinglady.com
Raising a Racquet			raisingaracquet.com
BoeBabyBiz			boebabybiz.com

Outlets

	WEBSITE
No Nonsense	nononsense.com

Maternity Chains

	PHONE		WEBSITE
Japanese Weekend	(800) 808-0555	(415) 621-0555	japaneseweekend.com
Motherhood	(800) 4MOM2BE		maternitymall.com

Chapter 6: Feeding
Breastfeeding

La Leche League	(800) LALECHE		lalecheleague.org
Nursing Mothers' Council		(408) 272-1448	nursingmothers.org
Int'l Lactation Consultants Assoc		(703) 560-7330	iblce.org
Bosom Buddies	(888) 860-0041	(720) 482-0109	bosombuddies.com
Avent	(800) 542-8368		aventamerica.com
Medela	(800) 435-8316		medela.com
White River Concepts		(800) 824-6351	
Ameda Egnell	(800) 323-4060		hollister.com
My Brest Friend	(800) 555-5522		zenoffproducts.com
EZ-2-Nurse	(800) 584-TWIN		everythingmom.com
MedRino			breastpumps-breastfeeding.com
Nursing Mothers Supplies			nursingmotherssupplies.com
Baily Medical			bailymed.com
Affordable Medela Pumps			affordable-medela-pumps.com
Affordadble Breast Pumps			affordable-breast-pumps.com
Affordable Breast Pumps			affordablebreastpumps.com
Mother's Milk			mothersmilkbreastfeeding.com

Baby Formula

Baby's Only Organic		babyorganic.com
BabyMil	(800) 344-1358	storebrandformulas.com
Mothers Milk Mate	(800) 499-3506	mothersmilkmate.com
Bottle Burper	(800) 699-BURP	

Bottles

Dr Brown's			babyfree.com
Munchkin	(800) 344-2229	(818) 893-5000	munchkininc.com
BreastBottle			breastbottle.com

Baby Food

Beech-Nut	(800) BEECHNUT	beechnut.com
Earth's Best	(800) 442-4221	earthsbest.com
Gerber		gerber.com
Heinz		heinzbaby.com
Well Fed Baby	(888) 935-5333	wellfedbaby.com
Super Baby Food book		superbabyfood.com

Chapter 7: Around the House

Kel-Gar		(972) 250-3838	kelgar.com
EuroBath			primobaby.com
Pure White Noise			purewhitenoise.com
Ear Plug Store			earplugstore.com
Comfy Kids	(888) 529-4934		comfykids.com
BabySmart	(800) 756-5590	(908) 766-4900	baby-smart.com
Nature Company			naturecompany.com
Container Store	(800) 733-3532		containerstore.com
Diaper Genie	(800) 843-6430		playtexbaby.com
Duracraft humidifiers	(800) 5-HOLMES		holmesproducts.com
Learning Curve	(800) 704-8697		learningtoys.com
Dolly mobiles	(800) 758-7520		dolly.com
Toy Portfolio			toyportfolio.com
Buffoodles			marymeyer.com
Infantino	(800) 365-8182		infantino.com
Gymini	(800) 843-6292		tinylove.com
Children on the Go	(800) 345-4109		gracobaby.com
Neurosmith		(562) 296-1100	neurosmith.com
North American Bear	(800) 682-3427	(312) 329-0020	nabear.com
EZ Bather Deluxe	(800) 546-1996		dexproducts.com
Discovery Toys	(800) 426-4777		discoverytoysinc.com

Coupon sites

BabyDollar	babydollar.com

web/phone directory

Deal of the Day	dealoftheday.com	EDealFinde	eDealFinder.com
ImegaDeals	imegadeals.com	Big Big Savings	bigbigsavings.com
Fat Wallet	fatwallet.com	Clever Moms	clevermoms.com
Image Deals	imagedeals.com	DotDeals	dotdeals.com
It's Raining Bargains	itsrainingbargains.com		

Catalogs

Back to Basics Toys	(800) 356-5360		backtobasicstoys.com
Constructive Play.	(800) 832-0572	(816) 761-5900	constplay.com
Edutainment	(800) 338-3844		mattelinteractive.com
Kaplan Co	(800) 533-2166		kaplanco.com
Playfair Toys	(800) 824-7255		playfairtoys.com
Sensational Begin.	(800) 444-2147		sensationalkids.com
Toys to Grow On	(800) 542-8338		toystogrowon.com
Totally Thomas' Toy	(800) 30-THOMAS		totallythomas.com
Thomas The Tank Engine			thomasthetankengine.com
FAO Schwarz	(800) 426-8697		faoschwarz.com
Hearthsong	(800) 325-2502		heathsong.com
Imagine/Challenge	(888) 777-1493		imaginetoys.com
Leaps & Bounds	(800) 477-2189		leapsandboundscatalog.com
Smarter Kids			smarterkids.com
Earthwise Toys			naturaltoys.com
Cozy Crib Tent	(800) 626-0339		totsinmind.com
DealTime			dealtime.com
Overstock			overstock.com
Phillips Baby Monitors			consumer.Phillips.com
BeBe Sounds			unisar.com
Summer Infant Products			summerinfant.com

Chapter 8: Car Seats

NHTSA	(888) DASH2DOT	(202) 366-0123	nhtsa.dot.gov
American Academy of Pediatrics			aap.org
National Safe Kids Campaign			safekids.org
Safety Belt Safe USA			carseat.org
Car Seat Data			carseatdata.org
Fit for a Kid			fitforakid.org
Safety Alerts			safetyalerts.com
ParentsPlace			parentsplace.com
Auto Safety Hotline	(800) 424-9393		
Might Tite	(888) 336-7909		might-tite.com
Fit for a Kid	(877) FIT4AKID		fit4akid.org
Britax	(888) 4-BRITAX	(803) 802-2022	childseat.com
Kolcraft		(773) 247-4494	kolcraft.com
Safeline SitNStroll	(800) 829-1625	(303) 457-4440	safelinecorp.com
Baby's Away	(800) 571-0077		babysaway.com
Kiddopotamus	(800) 772-8339		kiddopotamus.com
InMotion Pictures			inmotionpictures.com
Safety Baby/Nania			team-tex.com

Chapter 9: Strollers & To-Go Gear

Traveling Tikes			travelingtikes.com
Lots4Tots			lots4tots.com
PePeny canopies			pepeny.com
Dmart Stores			dmartstores.com
Aprica		(310) 639-6387	apricausa.com
Baby Trend	(800) 328-7363		babytrend.com
Combi	(800) 752-6624	(630) 871-0404	combi-intl.com
Emmaljunga			emmaljunga.com
J Mason		(818) 993-6800	jmason.com
Ingelsina	(877) 486-5112	(973) 746-5112	ingelsina.com
Maclaren	(877) 504-8809	(203) 354-4400	maclarenbaby.com
Moutain Buggy			mountainbuggy.com

Regalo	(800) 521-2234		regalo-baby.com
Zooper		(503) 248-9469	zooperstrollers.com
Simo	(800) SIMO4ME	(203) 348-SIMO	simostrollers.com
Bertini			bertinistrollers.com
Teutonia			britaxusa.com
Kidco	(800) 553-5529	(847) 970-9100	kidcoinc.com
Safety 1st		(718) 385-1000	
Baby Jogger		(509) 457-0925	babyjogger.com
Kool Stop	(800) 586-3332	(714) 738-4973	koolstop.com
Dreamer Design		(509) 574-8085	dreamerdesign.net
Gozo		(415) 388-1814	getgozo.com
InStep	(800) 242-6110		instep.net
BOB		(805) 541-2554	bobtrailers.com
Tike Tech			xtechoutdoors.com
Yakima			Yakima.com
Cozy Rosie	(877) 744-6367	(914) 244-6367	CozyRosie.com
Bundle Me			bundleme.com
Buggy Bagg			buggybagg.com
Burley	(800) 311-5294		burley.com
Schwinn	(800) SCHWINN		schwinn.com
Tanjor			lodrag.com
Rhode Gear			rhodegear.com

Diaper Bags

| Mommy's Helper | (800) 371-3509 | (316) 684-2229 | mommyshelperinc.com |
| California Innovations | | | ca-innovations.com |

Carriers

Maya Wrap			mayawrap.com
Over the Shoulder Baby Holder			otsbh.net
ZoloWear			zolowear.com
Walking Rock Farm			walkingrockfarm.com
Kangeroo Korner			kangerookorner.com
Cuddle Karrier			cuddlekarrier.com
Hip Hammock			hiphammock.com
Baby Bjorn	(800) 593-5522		babybjorn.com
Theodore Bean	(877) 68-TBEAN		theodorebean.com
Baby Trekker	(800) 665-3957		babytrekker.com
Kelty		(303) 530-7670	kelty.com
Madden		(303) 442-5828	maddenusa.com
Tough Traveler	(800) GO-TOUGH	(518) 377-8526	toughtraveller.com
Sherpa Mountain			sherpa-mtn.com
Pathfinder Outdoors			pathfindersoutdoor.com
Great Escpaes			greatescapes.com

Chapter 10: Safety

Baby Safe & Sound	babysafeandsounce.com		
SafetyAlerts	safetyalerts.com	Go Make it Safe	gomakeitsafe.com
Child Recalls	childrecalls.com	PoolGuard	poolgaurd.com
PoolSOS	allweather.ca		
Baby Proofing Plus	babyproofingplus.com		
Buggy Buddy	buggybuddy.com	Baby A La Carte	babyalacarte.com
Clean Shopper	cleanshopper.com		
Efficient Home			effcienthome.com
Intl Assoc Child Safety	(888) 677-IACS		iafcs.com

Chapter 11: Etc

Announcement Sources

| Babies N Bells | | | babiesnbells.com |
| Celebrate Invitations | | | celebrateinvitations.com |

web/phone directory

Stork Avenue	storkavenue.com	E-Invite	evinte.com
Card Creations	cardcreations.com	AlphaBit Soup	alphabitsoup.com
FairyGodmother	thefairygodmother.com	Angel Bars	angelbars.com
Announcements by Jeannette			announcingit.com
Celebrating Children			celebratingchildren.com
Paper Direct	(800) 272-7377		paperdirect.com
Hershey's wrappers	(800) 544-1347		hersheys.com
Homestead wrappers	(800) 995-2288		carsonenterprises.com

Announcement Printers

Carlson Craft	(800) 328-1782		carlsoncraft.com
Chase		(508) 478-9220	
NRN Designs		(714) 898-6363	
William Arthur	(800) 985-6581	(207) 985-6581	williamarthur.com
Elite	(800) 354-8321		
Encore	(800) 526-0497		encorestudios.com
Invitations Hotline	(800) 800-4355		invitationhotline.com
Heart Thoughts	(800) 524-2229		heart-thoughts.com
Artitudes	(800) 741-0711		miracleofadoption.com
Adoption World			adoptionstuff.com

Catalogs

One Step Ahead	(800) 274-8440		onestepahead.com
Right Start Catalog	(800) LITTLE-1		rightstart.com

BabyNames

Babynames	babynames.com	Alphabette Zoope	zoope.com
Parentsoup	parentsoup.com	Baby Zone	babyzone.com

Shopping Bots

My Simon	mysimon.com	PriceScan	pricescan.com
Shop Best	shopbest.com		

Baby Products Web Sites

Babycenter	babycenter.com	Planet Feedback	planetfeedback.com
BabyStyle	babystyle.com	Baby Ant	babyant.com
Baby Super Center	babysupercenter.com	Smart Bargains	smartbargains.com
Baby Bundle	babybundle.com	Baby Super Mall	babysupermall
Just Babies	justbabies.com	Baby Universe	babyuniverse.com
Baby Age	babyage.com	UrbanBaby	urbanbaby.com
Baby P.C.	babypressconference.com		
Overstock	overstock.com		
Nat'l Parenting Ctr	(800) 753-6667	(818) 225-8990	tnpc.com
Au Pair in America	(800) 727-2437 x6188		
Nat'l Assoc Family Child Care	(800) 359-3817		nafcc.org
Nat'l Assoc Educ Young Child.	(800) 424-2460		naeyc.org
My Background Check			mybackgroundcheck.com
Choice Trust	choicetrust.com	US Search	ussearch.com

Appendix A: Canada

Transport Canada		(613) 990-2309	tc.gc.ca
Canadian Auto. Assoc			caa.ca
British Columbia AAA		(604) 268-5000	bcaa.bc.ca
Canadian Parents Online	(877) 325-8888		canadianparents.com
Maternal Instinct	(877) MATERNAL		maternal-instinct.com
Mountain Equip Coop			mac.ca
Child Resources			childcarecanada.org

Appendix C: Twins

Twins Magazine	(800) 328-3211	(303) 290-8500	twinsmagazine.com
Baby Beat	(888) 758-8822		babybeat.com
Kimberly Clark Twins	(800) 544-1847		
Double Decker Stroller		(941) 543-1582	doubledecker.com

INDEX

index

index

index

index

How to Reach the Authors

Have a question about

Baby Bargains?

Want to make a suggestion?

Discovered a great bargain
you'd like to share?

Contact the Authors, Denise & Alan Fields
in one of five flavorful ways:

1. By phone:
(303) 442-8792

2. By mail:
436 Pine Street, Suite 600,
Boulder, CO 80302

3. By fax:
(303) 442-3744

4. By email:
authors@BabyBargainsBook.com

5. On our web page:
www.BabyBargainsBook.com

If this address isn't active, try one of our other URL's:
www.DeniseAndAlan.com or www.WindsorPeak.com.
Or call our office at 1-800-888-0385
if you're having problems accessing the page.

What's on our web page?
◆ *Updates on this book between editions.*
◆ *NEW BARGAINS suggested by our readers.*
◆ *MESSAGE BOARDS with in-depth reader feedback.*
◆ *CORRECTIONS and clarifications.*
◆ *Sign up for a FREE E-NEWSLETTER!*

Our New Book!

Toddler Bargains

Secrets to saving 20% to 50% on toddler furniture, clothing, shoes, travel gear, toys and more!
$14.95 (1st Edition)

The long-awaited sequel to *Baby Bargains*, with reviews/ratings of booster car seats, toddler strollers, potty seats, booster seats for meal time and much more! For kids age 2 to 5.

More books by Denise & Alan Fields

Bridal Bargains
Secrets to throwing a fantastic wedding on a realistic budget
$14.95 (6th Edition)

Your New House
The alert conusmer's guide to buying and building a quality home
$15.95 (4th Edition)

our other books

Call toll-free to order!
1-800-888-0385

Additional information on all our books is available on our home page www.WindsorPeak.com
Mastercard, VISA, American Express and Discover Accepted!
Shipping to any U.S. address is $3 ($4 for Canada)